the cinema of STEVEN SPIELBERG

DIRECTORS' CUTS

the cinema of
STEVEN SPIELBERG

empire of light

nigel morris

 **WALLFLOWER PRESS** LONDON & NEW YORK

First published in Great Britain in 2007 by
Wallflower Press
6a Middleton Place, Langham Street, London, W1W 7TE
www.wallflowerpress.co.uk

A catalogue record for this book is available from the British Library.

ISBN 1-904764-88-6 (paperback)
      1-904764-89-4 (hardback)

Book design by Rob Bowden Design

Printed by Replika Press Pvt Ltd., India

CONTENTS

ACKNOWLEDGEMENTS

This project's gestation goes back almost as long as Steven Spielberg's career. Numerous friends and colleagues have contributed in various ways; those not mentioned here will know who they are and forgive their absence due to lack of space. In particular, though, for inspiration, aspiration, encouragement, assistance, criticism and opportunity I should like to thank the following (in roughly chronological order): Joan Morris; Nick Sorensen; David Lyon; Esther Weatherill; G. A. M. Wood, Graeme Smith and Rory Watson; Cathy Kuhnau; Garrett Stewart; Rob and John McCormack; Brian Smith; Nell Sinyard; Chris Dunton; Una MacDonald and other colleagues at New College, Swindon; Miles Booy; Ian Cameron; Bob Ferguson, Phillip Drummond and my fellow MA students at the Institute of Education, University of London; Katie Gramich, Paul Poplawski and other colleagues in the former Department of English, Trinity College, Carmarthen; Julie Mills; Diarmait Mac Giolla Chríost; Brian Winston and colleagues in the Department of Media Production, University of Lincoln, especially Ann Gray, Dave McCaig, Dean Lockwood, Diane Charlesworth, Mike Mason, Sylvia Harvey, Tom Nicholls and Tony Richards; Wiltshire County Council Library Service; the British Film Institute library; Trinity College library; the National Library of Scotland; University of Lincoln library; Yoram Allon and his editorial team at Wallflower Press.

Elliott and Bevan Morris have tolerated my repeated absence during evenings and weekends but have also become keen film viewers and astute critics with an enthusiastic interest in this book. Above all, special thanks are due to Janice Morris for taking on far more than her share of domestic chores and parenting responsibilities over an unconscionable period. Without her, the book would never have happened. While its shortcomings are my responsibility, any achievements are as much hers as mine, and I dedicate it to her with all my love.

...the bourgeoisie had the devilish idea of using this new plaything to distract the masses, or more exactly, to divert the attention of the working classes from their fundamental objective – the struggle against their masters. Sunk in *the electrical narcotics of the cinemas*, workers in various stages of hunger and the unemployed gradually unclenched their iron fists and unconsciously gave themselves up to the demoralising influence of the cinema of their masters.

– Dziga Vertov: Introduction to
'Provisional Instructions to Kino-Eye Groups' (1926)

Scene: a picnic during the Battle of Britain...

Celia Johnson:	What a perfectly lovely day it's been. Lovely for us, I mean. I suppose that's very selfish of me, isn't it?
Noel Coward:	Extremely.
Celia Johnson:	I can't believe it's so dreadfully wrong to forget the war now and again. When one can – just for a little.
Noel Coward:	I think it's very clever of you with all Hell breaking loose imme diately over our defenceless heads.
Celia Johnson:	I made the most tremendous effort and pretended it wasn't real at all. They were toys having a mock battle just to keep us amused.
Noel Coward:	That's the most shameful confession: sheer escapism.

– *In Which We Serve* (1942)

For Janice – '*What a long strange trip it's been…*'

The Critical Context

'The Cinema of Steven Spielberg' has several meanings, including the following:

– films directed by a bearded, bespectacled Jewish American with seven children who was born in Cincinnati in the late 1940s
– films involving that individual as writer, producer, executive producer or studio mogul as well as those he has directed
– what cinema means to that filmmaker; the influences and tastes that shape his work and the view of the world it expresses
– the contemporary popular cinema his extraordinary commercial success has helped spawn, including audience expectations and attitudes
– a body of work, more or less self-contained as a critical entity, recognisable as distinctive for its themes, style and vision and identified by the director's credit, 'Steven Spielberg', which consequently labels it irrespective of which individual – screenwriter, cinematographer, composer, editor, art director, performer, and so on – is responsible for any aspect or whether it is consciously intended

Although these definitions overlap and interact, it is helpful to separate them where possible. This book deals with the first, but is not greatly concerned that Spielberg's parents divorced when he was young or that he suffered bullying at school. There are biographies available for those who want them. Spielberg's energetic involvement in other filmmakers' work is considerable; as mentor, financier or, in one controversial instance, as 'puppeteer' director, allegedly on-set daily. While the results have been variable – although many of the movies, regardless of quality, intriguingly evince stylistic and thematic continuities with Spielberg's – the filmography is too vast and raises too many conceptual questions to examine alongside them here. Nevertheless, confusion between this and the other categories has muddied critical as well as popular understanding of Spielberg's directorial concerns, often leading to over-simple interpretations; this matters when his films engage with politically sensitive issues. The cinematic vision Spielberg's movies express, in terms of cinema's nature, function, relation to reality and other movies – too often overlooked at the expense of the director's critical reputation – is, I argue here, fundamental to understanding their meaning. The contemporary popular cinema, shaped partly by Spielberg's blockbusters, is an institution providing opportunities and imposing restrictions which criticism must not ignore as the conditions for production and reception of his work.

Primarily, however, this book examines a collection of films released under the same director's name which share common properties and concerns. The 'Steven Spielberg' responsible for them is, except when the context indicates otherwise, a critical construct, inferred from the texts. While philosophical and methodological problems accrue to this auteur-structuralist approach, these are long recognised and well rehearsed; if not already familiar to readers, they are easily available in standard textbooks or on the internet. The approach has the advantage of acknowledging the author-function as central in the movies' financing, production, marketing, reception and criticism (as confirmed by the series to which this book belongs), whether or not, as auteurism originally claimed, authorial integrity is a mark of artistic quality that separates certain directors' work from the mainstream.

People once again take Spielberg seriously. *Amistad* (1997), *Saving Private Ryan* (1998), *A.I. Artificial Intelligence* (2001), *Minority Report* (2002), *Catch Me If You Can* (2002) and *Munich* (2005) all embrace adult themes and this later stage of his work attracts much academic commentary. The shift came after *Schindler's List* (1993), promoted and received as marking a new maturity in Spielberg's vision, unexpectedly triumphed critically and commercially. Inevitably, given its subject, the film generated controversy, but it rapidly gained general respect. In the US *Schindler's List* swept the boards with seven Academy Awards; these included Best Director, which, pointedly, had previously eluded Spielberg. In Britain, film and media teachers voted it one of 'Ten Films Which Shook the World', elevating it alongside *Battleship Potemkin* (1925), *Citizen Kane* (1941), *Psycho* (1960) and *The Godfather* (1972).

To a cynic these accolades have as much to do with the events portrayed as the merits of the movie. Academy Awards generally endorse liberal views and worthy topics. Moreover, the Academy lives up to its pretentious name by disproportionately nominating literary adaptations; *Schindler's List* came from a winner of Britain's prestigious Booker Prize. This is not, however, to denigrate Hollywood's first direct representation of the Holocaust. Given one studio executive's warning that Spielberg's budget would be better spent donating to a memorial charity (Brode 1995: 230), it was an extraordinary achievement that audiences crowded into theatres for a black-

and-white movie that lacked major stars, presented such an ostensibly bleak subject and exceeded three hours.

Nevertheless, this book insists, Spielberg's movies have always demanded proper consideration, even if – and I approach my task with some trepidation as a result – it was self-evidently amusing when Malcolm Bradbury in a parody of critical theory included an index entry, 'Spielberg, Steven, Deconstructionist film of' (1987: 104). What made *Schindler's List* successful is not radically different from Spielberg's previous output. Because he worked mainly in the critically despised and, until recently, academically neglected genres of fantasy and adventure, his films received remarkably little analysis. It may be precisely because these films foreground childish, regressive elements inherent in the pleasures of Hollywood that the industry's own glitzy Academy (like film professors determined to project a 'grown-up' image of their emergent discipline) maintained its distance.

When Robin Wood began his seminal book, *Hitchcock's Films* (1965), with the then provocative question, 'Why should we take Hitchcock seriously?' it was to argue that Hollywood, despite the industrial mode of production, could occasionally present a complex, nuanced view of the world, that entertainment could in some cases become great art. That is not my primary consideration in writing about Spielberg, although I will be happy if my analyses convince some readers that many of the films at least are more interesting than they appear to a prejudiced eye. My starting point is their phenomenal popularity, and what this reveals about commercial cinema and audiences who derive pleasure from it.

Peter Nicholls once calculated that

> according to the figures published by *Variety*, Spielberg has directed four of the top twelve money-makers of all time. *E.T.* (first), *Jaws* (fourth), *Raiders of the Lost Ark* (fifth) and *Close Encounters of the Third Kind* (twelfth). These four films have made over one billion dollars worldwide. (1984: 10)

The Indiana Jones sequels subsequently enjoyed similar success. *Jurassic Park* (1993) displaced *E.T. The Extra-Terrestrial* (1982) from pole position. Domestic video compounded the profitability, with *E.T.* becoming the best-selling videocassette in history (Kent 1991: 64–5).

Spielberg has more than once been hailed as cinema's saviour. *Close Encounters of the Third Kind* (1977) rescued Columbia from almost certain liquidation (indeed, the company's stock had fallen alarmingly when *New York* magazine slated the film after gate-crashing a preview (Grenier 1991: 76)). One-eighth of the US population saw *Jaws* (1975) within six weeks (Auty 1982: 277). *E.T.*'s release coincided with the slowing down, then reversal, of a quarter-century admissions decline.

Detractors quickly point out shortcomings in how commercial success is measured. First-run and longer-term profits are not immediately comparable. Distributors, hyping their product, ignore inflation when making historical comparisons. Profits expressed as a multiple of production costs create different results from subtracting expenditure from income. Is a $500,000 film recouping $2 million more profitable than one costing $100 million and recouping $150 million? Merchandising, profits from which may or may not be included, and promotion and publicity further complicate the equation. (The $100 million movie needs to gross $250 million before breaking even (Branston 2000: 76), given the exhibitors' share, interest charges and prints and advertising costs).

Yet however profitability is measured, and notwithstanding any Spielberg film's precise position in an all-time hit parade, his international success is a major commercial and cultural phenomenon. Box office takings from just four films equalled Hollywood's entire domestic returns for the year Nicholls was writing. Spielberg is the one director with a household name – exploited in marketing not only his movies but others on which he is executive producer. In 1998 he was the only director everybody knew in a multiplex spot poll (Malcolm 1998: 11), a finding corroborated in small surveys when Spielberg's name led many more times than any other when filmgoers listed five directors (Roberts 2005). 'Steven Spielberg' offers a promise analogous to stardom and genre. This is arguably unprecedented except by 'Disney' and 'Hitchcock'.

To understand such popularity appears crucial for media theory and media education. How little serious debate has appeared is therefore astonishing. Equally striking is the polarisation of critical attitudes. Yet it was not always thus. Michael Pye and Lynda Myles' 1979 account of Spielberg's early career, like many critical responses before his success became entrenched, is both reasoned and generally positive. After about 1980 (and the critical and commercial failure of the profligate *1941* (1979)) many writers position themselves in response to Spielberg's success rather than the films themselves.

Broadly speaking, academics and left-wing journalists capitalise professionally by presupposing that anything so successful must be suspect; popular writers capitalise financially by exploiting public fascination. This reflects the 1980s' politics, split between disappointment at the failure of 1960s' and 1970s' experimentalism to prompt revolution (or nostalgia for activism that preceded America's withdrawal from Vietnam and achievements by the Civil Rights and the Women's Movements) and celebration of competition and financial gain. Most books on Spielberg are uncritical popular hagiographies or highly critical personal biographies, while the films prompt enthusiastic but banal celebrations in cultish science fiction magazines. On the other hand, especially left-wing reviewers often sniffily dismiss the films on such grounds as conservative ideology, cuteness, racism, triviality and escapism. The sheer intensity of responses, critical or celebratory, contributes to the phenomenon:

'Steven Spielberg's *E.T.* … is so mawkish that I can barely manage to write about it' (Grenier 1991: 62).

E.T. The Extra-Terrestrial, however polished and manipulative, boded ill. Much ado about Martian munchkins, it was moving in a sickly, slickly optimistic way, the creation of a man so out of touch with both the joys and unpleasantries of modern life that he feels the need to pummel us with a starry simpering version of a grotesquely distorted garden gnome. Drool, drool. One can't help feeling that a few decades ago, he'd have been happiest producing vehicles for Shirley Temple, Deanna Durbin and Lassie (Andrew 1984: 17).

Such rhetoric reveals extraordinary vindictiveness – especially as the latter appeared two years after the film, which was massively more profitable than any of the star vehicles cited. Filmgoers did not consider themselves 'pummelled', while it is hard to see how 'a man so out of touch' could hold such appeal, or why the writer seems so determined to personalise his negative reactions. Alliteration ('Much ado about Martian munchkins'; 'starry simpering'; 'grotesquely distorted garden gnome'); internal rhyme and sibilance, implying something insidious, in 'sickly, slickly optimistic'; the overall emotive tone and breakdown of critical discourse ('Drool, drool'); all point to Andrew's obsession: fetishisation of the experience his language seeks to dismiss while simultaneously it savours, lingers over and attempts to capture it. Confirmation occurs in another passage in which language similarly poeticises itself and soars beyond prosaic needs of description – this time by an enthusiastic critic enthralled by *Close Encounters'* opening:

> White on black on silence. The pared-down, spare titles of Steven Spielberg's science fiction epic grow tense with premonition as a high-strung, portentous chord masses behind them, swells to breaking point, and rends the darkness into a dust-drenched sunburst on the Sonora desert. (Stewart 1978: 167)

The paradox in Andrew's account is resolved in light of an astute response to Andrew Britton's (1986) commensurately negative Marxist commentary:

> Psychoanalysis is compelled to acknowledge that extreme revulsion is *always* the sign of an equal unconscious attraction. The energy needed to denigrate a film has to be expended in order to prevent oneself falling in love with it; or, rather, to deny that one has already fallen in love with it.
>
> In his description of a scene from the film Britton refers to 'E.T.'s drunken odyssey through the deserted family house' ending with his 'fumbling with the television'. The writing here has the delectation of accurate description – the precision of words ('odyssey', 'fumbling') carefully chosen uniquely to evoke the events, conveys an enjoyment his analysis suppresses. The film has, after all, caught his desire, his passion and his pen. (Benson 1989: 64)

Andrew's phrase 'it was moving' – a sublimation of 'I was moved' – exposes a need to project the critic's contradictions onto the text and other spectators. Critics sometimes appear less than honest about their responses and define themselves contemptuously against mainstream audiences characterised as passive dupes. Far from 'analytical invective as an antidote to the functionings of ideology' – advocated by Robert Ferguson (1984: 40) – they use blunt invective in a self-congratulatory appeal to assumed radical consensus.

Some reasoned criticism has developed ideological objections, yet not without succumbing to language best described as vitriolic: '*Close Encounters* is nothing less than a Disneyland version of *Triumph of the Will* [1935], runs one not untypical response (Williams 1983: 23). Such analyses presuppose a relationship between the films and audiences in terms of harmful effects. They allegedly constitute escape from reality assumed (quite apart from considerations of content and style) to be unquestionably reactionary, therefore dangerous. At another extreme, right-wing commentators have seen in Spielberg's films anti-Americanism, symptomatic of creeping takeover by the Left of the nation's cultural institutions (Grenier 1991).

Clearly the films touch a nerve politically with their harshest critics, while exercising powerful emotional appeal to mass audiences. That these mainstream entertainments, apparently simple and unambiguous, elicit such contradictory readings, suggests audiences do not necessarily respond monolithically, as confirmed by Jacqueline Bobo's account of black American female viewers' qualified enthusiasm for *The Color Purple* (1985) (1988a; 1988b; 1995). The range of meanings and pleasures available help explain how such large numbers are attracted and satisfied.

While Spielberg's representations of race and gender have caused real offence – with varying degrees of justification – in the Indiana Jones series, *The Color Purple*, *Schindler's List* and *Amistad*, much of the more general ideological criticism appears over-simplistic in light of psychoanalytic theory concerned with subjectivity and pleasure. Rejection by the Academy Awards committee, neo-McCarthyite or Marxist criticism precludes analysis and thereby understanding, as does adulation. Part of the inability of much criticism to deal with Spielberg is failure to ask fundamental questions. If escapism *is* a factor in popular appeal, what are audiences escaping *from*, and what *to*? Do audiences *really* 'escape' at all? Why does it matter? Does alleged escapism have lasting effects beyond the screening? *Do* audiences succumb unconsciously? And how do critics avoid implication?

Such questions demand long-term audience research, beyond the scope of this book and impossible retrospectively. (Bobo's work with African American women – part of an explosion of audience-oriented studies in the 1980s and 1990s, reacting against high-minded theory that treated subjects as little more than effects of the text – although suggestive, uses a sample of only 15 and has to take their comments at more or less face value.) There remains a need to examine the films closely – not only through textual analysis but also in terms of their historical context (including marketing, promotion and publicity) and of the pleasures they offer (and mechanisms by which these are achieved).

One of Spielberg's characteristics is extensive pastiche and quotation from other films, including Hollywood classics, European art cinema and his own oeuvre. Annoying to many serious critics – although such playfulness is celebrated as postmodernism in more highly respected cultural forms – it clearly pleases fans if pedantic tracing of these allusions in popular publications is a reliable guide. Yet pleasure derived from spotting references – reminders that a film is being watched – seems incompatible with simple notions of passivity and escapism. Conversely, audience members may enjoy the films without noticing these references, or be aware of them; again this suggests more than one kind of pleasure, and that the appeal is more complex than allegations of mass manipulation imply.

Another characteristic is Spielberg's distinctive lighting code: 'diffused images … strongly backlit and countered with a weak fill light' (Mott & Saunders 1986: 89). This, I argue later, is consistently associated with the desires and fantasies of characters with whom the spectator is encouraged to identify. Light shafts (created by burning oil in the studio (Fraker 1979: 121)), demonstrably resembling projector beams, inscribe the cinematic apparatus onto the films. Metaphors for cameras, screens, projectors, audiences and cinema as an institution inform many sequences. The typical Spielberg identification-figure is a spectator, often also a surrogate director.

Many of the films' emotional appeal involves a recurring narrative structure centred on a family splitting which leads eventually either to reunion or a spiritual substitute. Through this theme of wish-fulfilment, together with the cinematic allusions and symbolic lighting, the films reflect upon as much as demonstrate the alleged function of popular cinema as an escape.

My intention, then, is to examine both text and process. This requires analysis informed by a theory of subject positioning, provided (not without controversy or difficulty) by Christian Metz's 'The Imaginary Signifier' (1975). (For guidance on Lacanian principles and terminology underlying Metz's arguments, see Benvenuto & Kennedy (1986) or Kaplan (1983: 11–20).) This theory, developed during the formative stages of Spielberg's career, is adopted quite simply because the films suggested, and continue to suggest, Metz's imagery. Metz holds that

> the cinematic institution is not just the cinema industry ... it is also the mental machinery – another industry – which spectators 'accustomed to the cinema' have internalised historically and which has adapted them to the consumption of films. (The institution is outside us and inside us...) (1975: 18–19)

Within this understanding, the broken family's reconstitution represents, psycho-analytically, the Oedipal drama resolved through the subject's return to the Imaginary or acceptance of the Symbolic – desire associated with light in Spielberg's films, and a constituent of the pleasure of 'cinematic fiction as a semi-oneiric instance' (1975: 18). Such a reading, reciprocally implicating spectatorial desire in the meaning of the text, and textual mechanisms in constituting the spectator as subject, imbricates the text and its reception in ideology. Apart from my core contention that Spielberg's films figuratively embody the terms of Metz's argument, the world's most profitable director should logically provide examples and test cases for theory which seeks to explore pleasure.

The book begins with *Close Encounters of the Third Kind*, Spielberg's fourth theatrical release, as it is the earliest of his films that most graphically demonstrates recurrent concerns thereafter traced chronologically, film by film, starting with *Duel* (1971). There follows at the end a consideration of theoretical implications not resolved in individual analyses. Each chapter, therefore, is relatively self-contained, although there is inevitably cross-referencing between them, and earlier chapters introduce ideas pursued subsequently. I omit *Poltergeist* (1982), subject of debate as to whether Spielberg directed it, for reasons of space. This book should assist readers for whom this is an issue to decide for themselves, and it is hoped, therefore, that this study will serve to revisit the entire work of Steven Spielberg and provide a coherent critical appraisal.

CHAPTER ONE

Close Encounters of the Third Kind: tripping the light fantastic

Title credits fade in and out on black, followed by thirty seconds of darkness. Musical tones emerge individually, building through a crescendo, like an orchestra tuning. At the climax, light floods the screen. It diminishes, revealing headlamps through a sandstorm. A car, then human figures, materialise on the blank screen: the diegesis gradually solidifies, anchored spatially and temporally by a caption, while the music modulates into sounds of wind and sand. The mysteriously shrouded figures, wearing dark glasses, are drawn to something off-screen, windward. One requests explanation. Their leader Lacombe (François Truffaut), appearing from the blankness, leads them towards a distant light. The solution – reappearance in a desert, after 32 years, of a missing fighter squadron in perfect condition – is startlingly impossible.

This deceptively complex opening on one level epitomises classical Hollywood narration: withholding information, gradual revelation, interest engaged through suspense. The title is enigmatic, while the final credit, 'Directed by Steven Spielberg', evokes a narrative image from *Jaws* (enhanced by pre-publicity stressing the secrecy of the production and majestic special effects), making this already a similarly significant event.

'Event' movies involve cross-media tie-ins and pre-publicity to prepare the audience for saturation release (Izod 1988: 184). *Close Encounters of the Third Kind* drew upon the successful merchandising of *Jaws*. Press releases prompting widespread speculation about UFOs, a novelisation (ostensibly by Spielberg), Bob Balaban's production diary and comic-book versions stimulated interest. Consideration of the appeal of Spielberg's blockbusters cannot ignore merchandising, as well as advertising and marketing. Nevertheless, as *1941* demonstrates, these alone do not assure success.

Darkness teases at the start of *Close Encounters*, heightening anticipation of spectacular pleasure. Tension, enhanced by the music, finally releases in a climax of light. Once begun, the scene exemplifies classical syuzhet construction. Restriction to less knowledge than the characters possess prolongs suspense; identification is encouraged because they remain one shot ahead in the relay of the look, awe-struck gazes off-screen cueing conventional expectations that we are about to share their vision. The final revelation satisfies curiosity but raises bigger questions. This pattern, consistent through subsequent scenes, repeats on a smaller scale within the scene. Balaban (Truffaut's translator, off-screen as well as on) appears looking remarkably like Richard Dreyfuss in *Jaws*, fulfilling then confounding expectation, reinforced by the credits only moments before, of Dreyfuss as the star. Explanations open further mysteries, deferring promised mastery.

Commercial feature films inevitably begin self-consciously; style has to declare itself, cueing appropriate mental schemata, and information has to be narrated quickly (Bordwell *et al.* 1985: 25). *Close Encounters* accordingly begins with explanatory titles and identifies important characters through close-ups – particularly Truffaut, introduced individually and framed to solicit recognition – to prevent distraction from the central enigma.

Described thus, the film appears as manipulative as Spielberg's critics contend. They assume his techniques 'work over' audiences, enslaving them to a reactionary worldview. In context, however, the scene is amenable to a complementary, although not necessarily 'alternative', reading.

Close encounters with realism

Whatever other discourses they embody, Spielberg's films operate as commercial entertainments within classical realist parameters. A tenet of realism is that the die-

Close Encounters of the Third Kind – the director in his element: Truffaut surrounded by cameras, lights and an inscribed screen

gesis springs fully formed upon the screen as though pre-existent; the narrative appears to develop independently of the camera or spectator's look. The reading offered here runs counter to hostile criticism that ascribes ideological effects to deep structures yet ignores or accepts unquestioningly what is visibly evident – in other words, takes realism as given. Andrew Gordon, for example, deems *Close Encounters* 'silly', an example of 'narcissistic euphoria' by which Americans escape from 'debasement of the environment, depletion of natural resources, and overpopulation' (1980: 156), although why films should be judged against these issues remains unclear. He considers it inferior to 1950s predecessors that at least manifested healthy Cold War nuclear terror (1980: 157). Yet, the criticism runs,

> repeatedly, incidents in *Close Encounters* occur not with any dramatic logic, but simply because they give the director an excuse for striking visual or emotional effects empty of content. The opening in the desert (a quote from *Them* [1954] or *It Came from Outer Space* [1953]) provides a sense of ominous mystery, but there is no necessity for the aliens to dump the planes in a desert or for there to be a sandstorm when the UFO followers arrive. (1980: 159)

The sandstorm, which requires a desert setting, is unquestionably necessary to my reading. *Close Encounters* offers more than the single fixed subject position proposed by Colin MacCabe's (1981) classic realist text thesis. It foregrounds and sustains a self-reflexive discourse utilising imagery and themes traceable throughout Spielberg's career. Aspects of mise-en-scène and editing, exceeding their narrational function, link together to suggest significance beyond localised effects. Within familiar narrative conventions, style inaugurates strategies of associational form to create an internal logic that nevertheless reflects upon more obvious thematic concerns.

Self-reflexivity

Darkness at the start (and after the end credits), together with a display of pure light, inscribes onto the film its own materiality and the spectating situation. Gradual fading in on a blank screen dramatises mental projection that occurs in the darkness through spectatorial anticipation; facilitates narration by evoking mental schemata; enables films to be regarded as addressing deep-rooted needs and desires; and consequently initiates spectatorial (mis)recognition of the self as subject of the enunciation. In Metz's words,

> there are two cones in the auditorium: one ending on the screen and start-ing both in the projection box and in the spectator's vision insofar as it is projective, and one starting from the screen and 'deposited' in the spectator's perception insofar as it is introjective (on the retina, a second screen). When I say that 'I see' the film, I mean thereby a unique mixture of two contrary cur-rents: the film is what I receive, and it is also what I release, since it does not pre-exist my entering the auditorium and I only need close my eyes to suppress it. Releasing it, I am the projector, receiving it, I am the screen; in both these figures together, I am the camera, pointed yet recording. (1975: 53)

The headlamps, penetrating the blankness, mirror (with all the Lacanian implications of that word) the spectator's projective gaze and the projector beam, while Spielberg's characteristic use of wind to signify heightened perception echoes Metz's metaphorical 'currents' of vision. 'Orchestral' tones in the darkness – analogous to a stage overture before the curtain rises – underscore the film's status as performance. The fading in of the fiction, moreover, enacts visual physiology, the spectator's eyes adjusting to brightness at this moment.

Similarly self-reflexive openings include Ford's *The Searchers* (1956), in which the screen blackens after the credits, placing the spectator (retrospectively) in the dark domestic space of the first shot from which a character, whose optical point-of-view initially matches the spectator's, opens a doorway onto the western landscape. Brian Henderson notes that 'Spielberg says he has seen it a dozen times, including twice on location with *Close Encounters*' (1980–81: 9). Consider too the Hitchcock films beginning with actual or metaphorical stage curtains rising such as *Stage Fright* (1950) and *Rear Window* (1954). Lloyd Michaels, who relates Bergman's *Persona* (1966) to 'The Imaginary Signifier', notes that its credits end 'with a white screen of projected light – the absence of all images – which then becomes the hospital wall of the narrative's first scene' (1978: 74). Critics recognise self-reflexivity in anti-narrative films such as Bergman's, or in Hitchcock and Ford films that cross the low culture/high culture threshold thanks to auteur theory. Yet the lure of narrative and spectacular pleasure, together with realist expectations and prejudices about populist cinema, distract from the significance (as opposed to mere recognition) of this facet of Spielberg's work.

Close Encounters plays with disavowal, soliciting Imaginary identification while asserting its presence as Symbolic. Captions occur extensively, even when unnecessary. *So what* if young Barry inhabits 'Muncie, Indiana'? How is understanding enhanced by knowing that a receiving dish is the 'Goldstone Radio Telescope Station 14'? As Liz Brown notes of translation subtitles in documentaries, they 'alter the image, rendering it an image with captions, which has consequences for the way it is read' (1978: 91). Conferring authenticity on images, captions simultaneously compromise realism, distancing the spectator by drawing attention to narrative agency. Moreover, viewers aware that Muncie markets itself as the 'average' American town, 'Middletown' in a classic sociological study (Lynd & Lynd 1929, cited in Brian Winston 1995: 212), enter knowing complicity.

Perceived self-reflexivity sets in train shifting subject positions: the historical spectator defined by his or her discursive formation brought to the auditorium, the subject of *discours* when the film declares its materiality, and the identifying subject sutured into *histoire*. This shifting is pleasurably fascinating, requiring work by the spectator, as in figure/ground perception problems. To the extent the spectator suspends disbelief in the film's impossibilities, it foregrounds mechanisms central to all mainstream cinema but particularly important in genres dependent on special effects.

Smoke and mirrors

Spielberg describes movies as 'a technical illusion that people fall for. My job is to take that technique and hide it so well that never once are you reminded of where you are.

If the audience stands up, points to the screen and says, "Wow! What a special effect!" – I've failed' (quoted in Crawley 1983a: 31). This should be a salutary warning to distrust directors' explanations of their craft. While Spielberg's point remains valid for most realist practice employing effects routinely (matte shots or, more recently, computer generated imagery (CGI) to change backgrounds, or miniatures to avoid location shooting or expensive sets), fantasy movies depend heavily on admiration for special effects in their own right. *Jaws*, grounded in plausibility, would be diminished if we saw hydraulic pipes operating what we have to forget is a mechanical shark. But the rolling boulder in *Raiders of the Lost Ark* (1981) or the mothership landing in *Close Encounters* satisfy because admiration for audacity and skill counterpoise implausibility. Audiences often gasp and even cheer at special effects, and discuss them animatedly afterwards.

Insisting on the self-reflexivity of Spielberg's practice in the face of his own comments, my claims might seem extravagant. Certainly my reading of the opening of *Close Encounters* would be untenable were it not supported by examples throughout. These, in light of Spielberg's subsequent output, are evidently concerned less with UFOs or – as several critics contend – messianic saviours, than with cinema itself. Garrett Stewart (1978) suffered no embarrassment advancing such an argument before it became fashionable to denigrate Spielberg for his childish appeal and commercial success, while both Neil Sinyard and Richard Combs, neither of whom develop their comments, recognised cinematic imagery (as opposed to merely references) in the films. Sinyard explains that '*Close Encounters* celebrates cinema in the way it incorporates the film experience into the action proper' (1987: 50), while Combs' journalism frequently shows how 'in Spielberg's best films, all of cinema is somehow there (or at least a sizeable and satisfying portion of popular narrative cinema), an encapsulation of its history as well as a playful toying with its possibilities' (1988a: 29).

Casting Truffaut – director, critic (intermediary to spectacle), creator of the auteur – makes sense given his role as director of a project coordinating technicians to master communication through light and sound. Indeed, he despatches a film crew after an encounter in the Gobi Desert; they accompany him to India; and he stands amongst a bank of movie cameras in the spectacular finale.

Spielberg's 'solar wind' motif, rendering psychic projection palpable as light, creates a Hitchcockian false climax when gathered UFO followers mistake helicopter searchlights for their objects of desire. This demonstrates how quickly Spielberg's lighting code becomes an intrinsic norm, and exemplifies how spectatorial and characters' vision coincide as we share the error. A cheat as well as shot/reverse-shots encourage identification: the helicopters are unheard until overhead. This, although the first 'dishonest' manipulation, is at least the third time the spectator is tricked – car headlights behind the protagonist Roy Neary (Richard Dreyfuss) set up the unexpected flying saucer ascension over his truck; resemblance between Balaban and Dreyfuss was earlier noted. Spectators are thus implicitly invited to modify perceptions (Brode 1995: 67).

Visible beams function consistently within the cinematic metaphor as 'mysterious lighting' (Sinyard 1987: 4) but more besides. During Neary's first encounter, for example, the solar wind oscillates a crossing signal, making dazzle from the spaceship flicker like film projection. William A. Fraker, cinematographer on *1941*, explains that smoke permeated every scene of that film, hiding wires for special effects models and creating distance perspective on miniature sets, but also to make lights flare and provide 'texture' (1979: 1211). Similar reasons probably caused many light shafts in *Close Encounters*; nevertheless, having evolved this visual style, called 'God Lights' after childhood experience of similar emanations in a synagogue (Baxter 1996: 20), Spielberg continues using it in conjunction with protagonists' desire in scenes lacking any obvious dependence on effects, as in most of *The Color Purple*.

Characters repeatedly are attracted to light, awestruck, their faces illuminated by their projected vision: air traffic controllers gathered by their radar screen, UFO experts around their computer, followers assembled at the roadside, as well as the main characters, Neary, Jillian (Melinda Dillon), Barry (Cary Guffey) and Lacombe. Representing the audience, they 'spend most of the film watching and listening to the lovely sights and sounds' (Corliss, quoted in Crawley 1983a: 88). Scientists applaud the spacecraft's aerial ballet towards the end. Combs likens Neary's urge to encounter his vision to that 'which draws audiences into the film, inviting them to become Everyman ... So what the film is "about", in a way, is its own illusionism' (1978: 64). Spielberg has claimed elsewhere that 'light is a magnet' (quoted in Crawley 1983a: 123); while Pye and Myles record that in the production stills – important contributors to the narrative image –'the only spectacle was blinding white light' (1979: 241).

Those attracted to the landing, Lacombe says, are 'compelled' to find 'an answer'. They parallel the spectator, carried forward in pursuit of narrative closure. In view of mainstream narrative's conventionalism, it seems appropriate that Neary asks 'If I've never been here before, how come I know so much?'. Devices such as subjective point-of-view and sound when Neary wears a gas mask invite identification with him (assumed anyhow by foregrounding his story), although shot/reverse-shots establish looser identification with others – with the entire 'audience' at the touchdown, so that spectacle explicitly becomes communal experience.

Neary and Jillian's relationship somewhat perfunctorily provides heterosexual romance, characteristically intertwined with classical Hollywood cinema's goal-oriented quest, confirming them as identification figures: separately, then together, they cue audience responses. Their spectatorship at the landing, hidden behind a boulder, is literally voyeuristic. Their dialogue contains cinemagoers' remarks – 'You wanna see better?' 'I can see fine'– while exclamations such as 'We're the only ones to know!' liken such spectatorship, as psychoanalysis insists, to children excitedly fantasising the primal scene. Glance/object editing collapses the camera's look into theirs, in turn becoming ours as we share their point-of-view. As in Hitchcock films discussed by Laura Mulvey, 'the audience is absorbed into a voyeuristic situation within the screen scene and diegesis which parodies his [sic] own in the cinema' (1981: 212), although scopophilia in Spielberg is often arguably de-sexualised. The scientists' sunglasses also signify voyeurism by emphasising their looking yet masking their eyes: this confers disarming power on the wearers, analogous to illusory mastery experienced by film spectators.

'Laying bare the device' foregrounds self-reflexivity, an aspect of 'artistic motivation' (Bordwell *et al.* 1985: 21) that throughout Spielberg's films is also realistically motivated. A tracking shot of chanting crowds in India fixes a boom microphone centre frame, ostentatiously transgressing a primary rule of 'invisible' narration. Searchlights mark the landing site, the big attraction, from afar, like a film premiere. (Or rock concert: the site is codenamed 'The Dark Side of the Moon'. Among the first sounds at the landing site is an engineer testing the public address system, while communication with the aliens occurs through synthesised keyboards accompanied by a light show.) As David Bordwell, Kristin Thompson and Janet Staiger observe, 'laying bare the device' encourages connoisseurship: 'only a discerning minority of viewers might take notice' (1985: 22).

The entire cinematic apparatus is present. With its cameras, lights, sound engineers and tannoy voice ('Gentlemen, ladies, take your positions please'; 'Could we have the lights in the arena down fifty per cent please?') the site resembles what it ultimately *is*: a studio set. Even the obsessive secrecy that surrounded Spielberg's project is paralleled within the film. Screens within the diegesis foreground the screen we are watching. Barry, captivated by off-screen lights, is filmed through a fly-screen, making visible the plane of the 'mirror' constitutive of primary identification. Secondary identification also is strongly encouraged; his wondrous expression, combined with evidence from the light beams that something is there, fuels desire to share his view. Spectators 'project' both into his situation and, as that desire is immediately frustrated, into the narrative (classical realist expectations virtually guaranteeing eventual satisfaction).

Screens and blinds intersect intradiegetic 'currents' of vision. Barred shadows render light visible. At the finale, the blinding white rectangle opening into the mothership draws both Lacombe and Neary – 'director' and 'spectator' respectively, central identification figures in converging narratives. 'Perception and consciousness are a *light*, as Freud put it, in the double sense of an illumination and an opening, as in the arrangement of the cinema, which contains both' (Metz 1975: 52). (Paul Schrader, who wrote an early treatment for *Close Encounters*, is an astute and knowledgeable critic well-versed in theory. Although the Writers Guild of America arbitrated in favour of Spielberg's sole screenplay credit when Schrader subsequently sought recognition, it would be interesting, in view of these emphases on vision, mirrors and identification, to know whether the homophony between 'Lacombe' and 'Lacan' is coincidental.)

Neary dissolves into the blank screen, preceding the spectator, as he drifts like Alice through the looking-glass from unsatisfactory suburban existence (collapsed marriage, unemployment) into fantasy, his sustaining object of desire. This is explicitly likened to cinema. Regression into noble savagery – marked by his smeared face and intense expression as he obsessively models the landing site from dirt and garbage inside his house – alternates with point-of-view shots, showing neighbours' domestic activities; as they rake lawns and wash cars, camera placement and mise-en-scène underscore Neary's alienation, likening them to 'pod people' in *Invasion of the Body Snatchers* (1956). The spaceship interior, conversely, recalls an enormous picture-palace foyer, a glistening chandelier at its centre. Rectangular screens both project and receive light, reminiscent of Metz's mutual opposing currents. (Reciprocity of projection and introjection is indeed highlighted by Neary and Jillian's creative compulsions.) The screens and their beams are photographed side-on in shots resembling the transition to the projection room scene in *Citizen Kane*, by which Spielberg's lighting code is undoubtedly influenced. The ship's hub is a gargantuan turning reel.

Disney's 'When You Wish Upon a Star' accompanies Neary's transportation. Cinema is less sub-theme than substance in this film, with its allusions, ranging from obvious, well-documented examples – the crop-spraying and Mount Rushmore sequences of *North by Northwest* (1959) in the climb up Devil's Tower – to arcane quotations and in-jokes. The bass from the mothership replicates tuba notes played by Capra's Mr Deeds on inheriting $20 million – *Close Encounters'* final agreed budget. Fences foregrounded in the opening sandstorm and later the incongruous ship in the desert are borrowings from *Lawrence of Arabia* (1962). Spielberg habitually makes explicit what Roland Barthes, Julia Kristeva and others have argued, that all production and reading are intertextual: any text, insists Barthes (1975a), is a tissue of quotations interpreted by bringing to bear memories of other texts.

In view of charges of manipulation against Spielberg, it is worth insisting that spectatorial involvement in many cases depends less on conventional strategies of invisible narration (present, after all, in most commercial cinema) than this notion of productivity, which obliterates subject/object distinctions. The subject becomes a position where the spectator's discourses interact with the text's (Henderson 1980–81). Hence the spectator often has the sense of being the subject of enunciation. In Spielberg's films, where the potential work on offer is considerable, the spectator may become pleasurably involved in the text beyond mere narrative comprehension.

Close Encounters and postmodernism

This makes Spielberg's films 'writable' texts, as defined by Barthes. My intention is not to recuperate them into high culture, but to propose that their complexity is easily ignored by critics imposing inappropriate reading models. 'Re-reading,' argues Barthes, 'is an operation contrary to the commercial and ideological habits of our society which would have us "throw away" the story once it has been consumed ("devoured"), so that one can move on to another story, buy another book' (1974: 15). If so with books, accessible wherever and whenever time allows, how much truer of films, which lack concrete existence for the spectator, for whom they are 'imaginary signifiers', and were – prior to video – generally perceived, unlike literature, as transitory. Indeed, Britton notes, 'to present something as entertainment is to define it as a commodity to be consumed rather than as a text to be read' (1986: 4).

Yet many people *do* return to films repeatedly. Hit-movie producers Don Simpson and Jerry Bruckheimer observed: 'American teenage boy audiences go back four, five, six times. You can meet people who've seen *Beverly Hills Cop II* fifteen times' (*Naked Hollywood,* programme 3; see also Walkerdine (1990) for how some film viewers use video in ways that make redundant older assumptions about consumption). *Close Encounters,* appealing to such an audience, invites close reading. So dense is the aural and visual information that jokes and references are half-hidden: the anonymous tannoy voice, buried in ambient sound and marginalised in the spectator's consciousness by pressure of narrative and enthralling spectacle, instructs the scientists to 'Watch the skies!' (reference: *The Thing From Another World,* 1951), reports that spacecraft are heading from 'the north-north west', and pages 'George Kaplan' – the non-existent personage in *North by Northwest* whose identity Cary Grant's character unwittingly adopts by appearing to answer the call. Spielberg's decision to modify *Close Encounters* for a 'special edition', whatever the commercial calculation, seems to confirm its amenability to repeated watching.

Particularly noteworthy – especially given promotional hype (endlessly recycled biographically) about Spielberg's belief in UFOs – are the lengths the film goes to *not* to be taken seriously, certainly not to present itself as realist. After the alien crafts' first display, the tannoy intones, 'That's all, folks!' – the Looney Tunes slogan. If spectators, paradoxically, feel involved in a film that plays with its own conventions rather than addresses serious issues, this suggests play is central to cinematic pleasure. As Metz argues, 'any spectator will tell you that he [sic] "doesn't believe in it", but everything happens as if there were nonetheless someone to be deceived, someone who really will "believe in it"'(1975: 70). This 'someone' is associated with childhood: 'Cinema, like dreaming, is regressive in that it calls up the unconscious processes of the mind and favours what Freud calls the pleasure principle over the reality principle' (Turner 1993:). The children's adventure tone of *Close Encounters* exemplifies this, with its obligatory wacky car chase and deceitful authorities trying to thwart our heroes' desires.

The central characters who are transported, because of their wonder and trust, are the infant Barry and the explicitly childlike Neary. (Neary plays with model trains, becomes breathlessly excited when attempting to describe his UFO sighting, and is rejected as a 'cry baby' by his son when he cracks under the confusion induced by his vision.) Neary's childlike nature is linked to cinema spectatorship: he wants to go and see *Pinocchio* (1940), an option his children reject, and his wife mocks him as 'Jiminy Cricket'. Moreover, the extra-terrestrials announce themselves by animating Barry's toys (delighting him and, thanks to childlike point-of-view shots, us) and his mother's kitchen devices (which terrifies her and, by use of her adult optical point-of-view, discomforts us).

Imaginary or Symbolic?

Spectatorial regression is partly a function of the viewing situation (darkness, comfort and physical passivity satisfy archaic urges to lose a sense of self which Jean-Louis Baudry (1974–75) considers inherent in the psychical structure); partly also a closely related result of continuity editing, positioning the spectator so that he or she forgets physical presence and '*identifies with himself* [sic] ... as a pure act of perception (as wakefulness, alertness)' (Metz 1975: 51); and partly a result of narrative, typically involving pursuit of a lost object. Even complex narratives re-enact Freud's *fort-da* game in which the infant masters its mother's absence:

> the pattern of classical narrative is that an original settlement is disrupted and ultimately restored ... Narrative is a source of consolation: lost objects are a cause of anxiety ... In Lacanian theory, it is an original lost object – the mother's body – which drives forward the narrative of our lives, impelling us to pursue substitutes for this lost paradise in the endless metonymic movement of desire. (Eagleton 1983: 185)

The Imaginary is associated with pre-Symbolic infancy when Barry and his mother embrace in the 'projector beam' from the unseen spacecraft before he leaves, and finally when her quest results in reunion; simultaneously Neary, embraced by extra-terrestrials resembling human infants, is absorbed into the appropriately named 'mothership'. The spectator too enacts the *fort-da* game, starting from pre-cinematic perception of the narrative image (associated here with blank light and reports of breathtaking spectacle) that establishes desire for the absent experience, and continuing through the UFOs' tantalisingly repeated appearance/disappearance. Tricks played on spectatorial perception, described earlier, similarly lead – through a process of illusory mastery – to confusion, to mastery regained.

The mother's body, however, 'stands as a representation, no more than that, of what is ultimately unrepresentable, in that the object that could overcome the lack is non-existent' (Lapsley & Westlake 1988: 68): it is the unsignifiable, consequently unremembered, antecedent to the Mirror Phase. Rosemary Jackson identifies the goal of artistic fantasy as 'arrival at a point of absolute unity of self and other, subject and object, at a zero point of entropy' (1981: 77) where, in Jacques Lacan's words, 'identity is meaningless' (1968: 191). This precisely describes the absorption of Neary, representative of both spectator and filmmaker, into the blank screen. He remains where we have to return from: through the looking-glass. Jackson emphasises that Lewis Carroll's Alice visits 'a realm of non-signification, of non-sense'; that *Through the Looking-Glass* contains an epiphanal moment in 'a place without words'; that *The Hunting of the Snark* has a topography which is 'a perfect and absolute blank'; but that Carroll was always destined to return to 'the empty pleasures of signs and language games' (1981: 143–4) – just as Spielberg and the spectator are left with their 'tissue of quotations'. Nevertheless, the film's spectacular climax takes us part way, by means of escape from language into abstract sound and light, the 'raw materials' of cinematic signification.

Neary's transportation, the projection of spectatorial desire, reverses the three determining moments in Lacan's account of childhood development. He regresses through the Mirror Phase, subsuming his identity to transcendental unity; he fulfils desire symbolised by the *fort-da* game, escaping from positionality in language; and in breaking family ties and defying authority to get there, he overturns the Oedipus complex (submission to the Law).

Spectatorial regression to the Imaginary occurs through primary identification with the camera and, consequently, secondary identification with characters standing in as the spectator's double, the Mirror Phase's more complete specular counterpart. The double positions the perceiving subject, while satisfying need for mastery by providing an object for voyeurism. As Metz claims,

> at the cinema … I am *all-perceiving* … absent from the screen, but certainly present in the auditorium, a great eye and ear without which the perceived would have no one to perceive it, the *constitutive* instance, in other words, of the cinema signifier (it is I who make the film). (1975: 51)

Typical of the fantastic, *Close Encounters* (like most Spielberg films) incorporates character doublings that similarly define roles mutually. Neary's and Jillian's odysseys begin with mirror shots, while the couple are filmed identically before they have met, moonlight casting leaf shadows across their faces: later, each sustains the other's determination to pursue the quest. Cross-cutting connects Neary, struggling with a map, to Laughlan, the cartographer who dispatches him on his quest and whose name, in turn, echoes Lacombe's. Lacombe is linked by a cut from a conference where he demonstrates sign language symbolising synthesised sounds, to Barry playing the same tune on his xylophone. At the finale, an extra-terrestrial mirrors Lacombe's signing, while the musical duet and light show explicitly establish the visitors as projecting back the scientists' desires. Moreover, the mothership's underside – envisaged as a 'city of lights' (Spielberg, quoted in Sinyard 1987: 47) – reflects street patterns already seen in aerial shots.

Celebration

Implications of the films' spectator/text relationships are considered in later chapters. By way of provisional conclusion, we can note that as public event *Close Encounters* shares elements of an ancient literary genre, the *menippea*. This 'broke the demands of historical realism or probability' (Jackson 1981: 14) and was linked with carnival – a ritualised festival where 'everyone is an active participant, everyone communes … The carnival life is life drawn out of its usual rut, it is to a degree "life turned inside out", "life the wrong way round"' (Bakhtin 1973, quoted in Jackson 1981: 15–16).

The mirror metaphor is apparent. Communion is important too, not only because the film's finale inscribes it, equating light with aspirations, a convention of religious iconography as well as a distinctive Spielberg characteristic; but also because cinema essentially entails social expression and containment of potentially subversive desires, a technologically sanitised version of *menippea*, in which legal and moral transgressions had free rein during periods of licensed misrule. Like carnival, cinema is *potentially* subversive in that it proceeds by deconstructing 'the most cherished of all human unities: the unity of "character"' (Jackson 1981: 82).

Truffaut admired *Close Encounters* for succeeding even with 'no bad guys in it' (Sinyard 1987: 47). Conflict is not so much *re*solved as *dis*solved: conflict implies difference, which the Imaginary abnegates. Just as *Rocky II* (1979), according to Walkerdine, fulfils vicariously 'the terrifying desire to be somewhere else and someone else: the struggle to "make it"' (1990: 341), *Close Encounters* offers relief from the self and life's contradictions – while never pretending to be other than illusion.

Britton describes seeing a horror film with an audience for whom 'predictability was clearly the main source of pleasure', noting that 'art had shrunk to its first cause, and I had the incongruous sense … of having been invited to participate in communion' (1986: 3). Ironically, his auteurist preference for films that address universal moral dilemmas blinds him to a major component of cinematic pleasure that *Close Encounters* unashamedly, although less predictably, celebrates. Fantasy and science fiction have since Georges Méliès been spectacles of light, excesses of signification contained by generic conventions. Paul Virilio argues: 'The *matter* provided and received in collective, simultaneous fashion by cinemagoers is light … In cinema, it would be even more appropriate to speak of *public lighting* rather than public image' (1994: 21). Literary and dramatic models of criticism fail to recognise that the signifier is as important as narrative and diegesis. Pleasure involves the cinematic apparatus as much as its representations.

CHAPTER TWO

Duel: the descent of Mann

What makes a man to wander? What makes a man to roam?
What makes a man leave bed and barn, and turn his back on home?
Ride away, ride away, ride away...
                    – title song, *The Searchers*

Blackness. A door slams; an engine starts. A bicycle, dimly emerging, rapidly diminishes: the camera is retreating, through a rectangular, screen-shaped, screen-sized aperture. Daylight: a garage door, drive, suburban house, left behind as the camera pans then speedily tracks forward on squealing tyres.

A contemporary Phantom Ride thus begins. Those Victorian films from an advancing vehicle celebrated the exciting danger of mechanical motion. They featured at funfairs alongside rollercoasters and Ferris wheels, anticipating affinities between cinema and theme park rides later exploited with *Jaws* and *Jurassic Park*. They exhibited film as attraction, spectacle and technology. Their present absence fascinated, rendering strange the everyday and familiar.

Duel, a made-for-television movie, drew reasonable audiences and positive reviews; but its scope, ambition and style were evidently suited for theatres. Spielberg, wanting to tell the story visually, rather than use wordy televisual exposition, had conceded minimal dramatic monologue at nervous executives' insistence (Taylor 1992: 74). Spielberg subsequently directed dialogue scenes and voice-overs – largely superfluous, judged by some 'embarrassing' (Freer 2001: 26) – for an extended overseas edition. These were retained, against his protests, on distributors' instructions. Despite these compromises, *Duel* won numerous festival awards and critical recognition. It grossed $8 million (over ten times its budget, already recovered with profit on delivery to ABC) in theatres abroad. In America it was eventually released after *E.T.* but suffered from cinemagoers' reluctance to pay to watch a ten-year-old TV movie.

Spielberg's Movie of the Week began on the highway. The theatrical version self-reflexively takes the experience out of the house and both alludes to, and incorporates as spectacle, the difference between television and cinema. The start, one of four added scenes, is in effect a reverse angle of the beginning and end of *The Searchers*. Darkness, shared by the auditorium, represents domesticity from which a frame opens – spreading over the screen and encompassing the spectator – onto the panoramic West: a landscape of intense light where desperate men engage in one-to-one struggles.

Speeding, the unseen motorist ignores a 'STOP' sign. Ensuing events suggest he has become complacent, cocooned in his ordered existence, about venturing into a competitive and alienated society, particularly – as hinted retrospectively – while angry. This equally connotes rebellion, a will to push boundaries and behave lawlessly. *Duel* does not endorse his suburban frustrations, which it arguably satirises. Rather, in withholding information about precise motivations and frequently adopting the pursuing tanker's position, it sadistically delights in testing both the protagonist's reasonableness and his resolve. It also becomes an attack on the spectator who, knowing little, is unable to judge with certainty – yet who, because unawareness removes potential obstacles, is facilitated in projecting conflicts onto the scenario.

It is difficult to imagine a narrative that did not involve characters, just abstract forces. (Eisenstein's plan to adapt *Das Kapital* and Einstein's suggestion to *Popeye*'s creators, Dave and Max Fleischer, that they should animate his theory of relativity, came to naught.) Abstractions do not inherently interest audiences. Narratives nevertheless personify abstract ideas. They probe experience in hypothetical scenarios whose outcomes do not seriously affect the audience. A human aspect personifies hopes, fears, desires, contradictions, confusions or aspirations, so these can be recognised and – perhaps – viewers recognise themselves in them. Partly motivating *Duel*, and sustaining involvement, is precisely what it never delivers: an identity for, hence a reciprocal relationship to, the tanker. The threat, conventionally defeated, escapes total mastery. Excess meaning remains: doubt whether what it represents, unspecified, has been contained. Certainly the car driver's name – David Mann (Dennis Weaver) – encourages allegorical reading; but whether he slays Goliath for himself or the world's salvation, whether his surname denotes universalised humanity or just peeved masculinity, is unresolved. Apart from its taut construction, the film benefits from these uncertainties – resistance to schematic interpretation, statement rather than solution of problems – consequently appealing to a wide audience.

Identification

If, as Metz (1975) contends, cinema spectatorship identifies with the apparatus, in a realist film the camera becomes my eyes and the soundtrack my ears. I disavow who and where I am and regress through the Mirror Phase into Imaginary unity with the screen. However, my Imaginary position has to be somewhere in relation to the events, observing from some relatively consistent and coherent viewpoint. This need not be singular; narratives externalise psychic conflict onto opposing forces.

Moreover, narrative progresses from disruption to closure by meting out story information gradually, withholding important matters for dramatic effect. One way films delay pleasurable mastery is restricting knowledge to that of one or more characters. Rather than omniscience, the film offers positions in the diegesis by constructing secondary identification with characters. Philosophical, psychological and political debates question how, why, to what extent, or even whether, this happens (Neill 1996; Barker 2000). Nevertheless, formal mechanisms narrate by positioning the spectator's viewpoint in relation to that of characters. *Duel* closely aligns with the car driver. This point-of-view – the angle events are seen from – largely coincides with the metaphoric point-of-view, in the sense of opinion or judgement, implied by the invisible, absent narrator (an apparent agency, actually an effect – considered shortly).

The start implicitly presents Mann as generally law-abiding, peaceful and harmless. Unless contradicted, the 'primacy effect' prevails, establishing baseline characterisation against which subsequent information is judged (Sternberg 1978: 93–6). The tanker, if only by disrupting normality, although also through anonymity and embodying undesirable qualities such as dirt and pollution, is automatically – the moment it first overtakes – malevolent. There is no question of another side to the story, even though distaste of oil and heavy machinery arguably assume middle-class experience and accord with suburban neatness and consumerist ignorance of production. That there could be an alternative is, in fiction, illusory. Narration creates the allegiance, together with the story. The diegesis and its angle(s) of accessibility are inseparable: interdependent facets of the same construction. In fiction this does not matter inherently, although the extent to which the perspective implies a structure of sympathy, and naturalises it, is ideologically significant. For example, feminist readings concentrate on how mainstream films construct masculine versions of events, leaving feminine discourse marginalised, silent or absent.

As the journey continues through city streets, commercials and traffic reports align the spectator's hearing with the driver, while the camera provides a visually analogous perspective. These also underline the banality within which the upcoming struggle occurs. There may, furthermore, be a nod here to one of Spielberg's formative texts: Orson Welles' broadcast *The War of the Worlds* (1938) simulated ordinary radio scheduling before a newsflash provided narrative disruption. (Welles pioneered layered sound and overlapping dialogue, among techniques Spielberg utilises frequently. Spielberg later bought Welles' *The War of the Worlds* script, which, sealed with *Citizen Kane* and *Casablanca* (1942) in a glass coffee table, he displays alongside Kane's Rosebud sledge. As a teenager he rented 8mm prints of the 1953 *The War of the Worlds* movie (Baxter 1996: 31, 110, 313), which, in 2005, he remade.) At a series of freeway tunnels, credits appear initially only over the dark frames; cinematic artifice self-consciously contrasts with an alternating 'reality' of space and light. Awareness of any of these allusions or performances of textuality – whether as a 1970s viewer or subsequently in light of Spielberg's star persona – proposes 'tertiary' identification: with Spielberg, unknown 'implied author' or auteur known to stuff texts with quotations, in-jokes and references; in either case as a shared position of cinephilia, alongside the text and its ostensible address.

Point-of-view shots, forward motion and, soon, involvement in a narrative played out on a radio phone-in encourage primary identification with the camera position and secondary identification with the still-unseen driver. The continuing enigma of who is driving, and where to, simultaneously solicits active involvement. Restriction to diegetic sound – later, voiced-over internal monologues and incidental music occur – naturalistically establishes the narrative as plausible.

The first external shot of the car, behind barbed wire, introduces western imagery. Despite connoting the open road, it suggests entrapment and potential violence. On the radio a house husband complains about a census: married 25 years, he no longer feels 'head of the family'. Masculine anxieties accompany a pan to the driver's eyes in the mirror and a cut-in close-up of the radio – a subjective shot that sutures the spectator into the driver's position, immediately followed by a close-up on him through the inscribed screen of the windshield. This brief sequence, directly before the truck challenges any notion of secure identity, is replete with Lacanian implications. The mirror, recalling a cinema wide screen, redoubles spectatorial identification with the specular Other through regression to the Imaginary. Equally, the shot through the windscreen – finally revealing the spectator's surrogate – reflexively re-inscribes a surface between spectator and protagonist. This implies separateness, detachment, diminution (the audience can no more ease Mann's plight than help Grace Kelly in Hitchcock's 3-D *Dial M for Murder* (1954), when she reaches out into the auditorium); but distance also allows potential awareness of the film as text, part of the Symbolic order. This alternation, and associated tensions, remains a consistently central and distinctive element of Spielberg's cinema.

Mann overtakes the rig as the radio complains, 'She can be just so aggressive.' This juxtaposition thematically connects the highway antagonism with gender. The visuals here being unremarkable, the radio becomes more compelling, so the spectator shares Mann's surprise as the truck overtakes, cuts in and slows down. He overtakes it again. It hoots and flashes. The duel commences.

Vision

Pulling alongside Mann in a gas station the tanker dominates an oppressive two-shot. Mann cleans his glasses, inaugurating an ongoing Spielberg theme, clarity of vision. A zoom in on the trucker's hand approximates to Mann's perspective. Everything is viewed through screens, explicitly when suddenly the image, like the supposedly burning celluloid of Bergman's *Persona*, blurs and runs: a forecourt attendant, now entering the shot, is washing the windows, creating a barrier to identifying the trucker. Cowboy boots alone are visible. Preoccupied by the feet, Mann declines a new radiator hose, responding distractedly to the attendant's pleasantry 'You're the boss': 'Not in my house I'm not.' Critics dismissive of Spielberg for making dumb action movies or children's flicks might reflect that such emphasis on hands and feet, repeated in *E.T.*, is this most cine-literate of directors' borrowing from Bresson, whose creed equally summarises Spielberg's practice: 'Accustom the public to divining the whole of which they are given only a part' ('Notes on Cinematography', quoted in Kelly 1999: 137). What are comic-book framings to critics unsympathetic to Spielberg's efficiently storyboarded narration (Baxter 1996: 79), within a different interpretive agenda become aesthetic rigour, pure cinematography. Pared-down simplicity, characters isolated in metaphorical cells, voice-over soliloquies, existential struggle in ordinary locations: these are Bressonian in a movie five years predating *Taxi Driver* (Schrader and Scorsese's rightly celebrated 1976 homage to Bresson, Hitchcock and *The Searchers*, the financing and editing of which Spielberg assisted (Smith 2001: 25–6) and which he considered directing (Argent 2001: 50)).

The attendant's bell chimes repeatedly, almost subliminally, the truck having intruded aurally as well as visually by parking on the hose. A standard horror device – irritating, ominous, ongoing sound – this also recalls the bell when trains stop in westerns. The trucker's arm, now in the foreground in silhouette, emphasising proximity while maintaining anonymity, reaches to sound the horn, imposing the truck's presence and reinforcing 'its' impatience.

Mann, phoning home, adopts an exaggeratedly masculine posture, uncertainly raising one foot upon a table, but straightaway moving it for a woman to enter. Deep-focus, extended long-shots again diminish, and distance the spectator from, this character who, when behind the wheel, fills the screen and seemingly drives the narrative. An arm in the foreground – answering to that seen outside in the cab, actually the woman's – opens a tumble drier. The shot continues, now through the circular glass door filling the frame. Mann literally is viewed through a female lens, this film repeatedly associating women, at the height of second-wave feminism, with household labour. His wife, her side of the conversation intercut, dusts the living room in a polka-dot frock and apron that parody 1950s commercials, with two children playing on the floor. Near the climax of the chase – just before Mann lures the tanker away from civilisation onto a quarry road, the deserted landscape of a *Road Runner* (1949–66) cartoon featuring only cable poles and tumbleweed – a woman is glimpsed pegging out washing. For the moment, he apologises for an incident Mrs Mann, fearing an argument, is reluctant to discuss. Evidently their relationship is uneasy. Though he wheedles the conversation forward, it turns to his supposed weakness. He asks, rhetorically, whether she expects him to fight an acquaintance who, she says, 'practically tried to rape' her in company while Mann stood by. She then tries to extract an undertaking that he will return punctually – 'It's your mother; God knows, she's not coming to see me' – before ringing off without endearments or farewells. The drier continues to be emptied in the foreground, emphasising separate male and female worlds: open road and home; violence, competition and nurturing, care. The travelling salesman has inherited the hunter/protector role. The truck hoots threateningly.

Focalisation

Mann is not necessarily aware of mythic reverberations or social significance in this bad day at work. Characters are textual constructs, not people, even if in film actual people impersonate them. Characters are clusters of meaning accruing to constellations of signs; characterisation occurs through interaction of performance, mise-en-scène and editing, constituting narration. Narratives are events undergone by characters. Characters, reciprocally, as textual embodiments of conflicting forces, cause or respond to events. It follows that they have no psychology other than that which the text creates for them, for they have no existence until activated through decoding. They have no past, no memories beyond what the text provides. For that reason, while psychoanalysis is powerful for investigating narrative structures and identifying symbolism, also for suggesting why spectators experience involvement and textual pleasure, psychoanalysing characters makes no sense. An assemblage of signs lacks a consciousness, let alone an unconscious. While one can usefully seek a text's unconscious – its ideologically symptomatic repressions or denials – a character lacks inner life beyond what the text manifests. It makes little sense to speak of character psychology. To assume Mann is unconsciously motivated to restore his threatened masculinity, or that he is conscious his masculinity is challenged, is to project attributes, suggested by the narration, which would appear reasonable if he were real.

The narrator is the implicit agent relating or recounting events and, with them, attitudes. The narrator is not the author. If an auteurist reading distinguishes Spielberg as author, he nevertheless might have constructed any scene differently. The director is outside the text, however recognisable are traces of his presence. The narrator, however, is the imaginary selector and controller of the information – another product of narration, along with the characters and narrative, who would still be there if Spielberg were unknown. Whether Spielberg appreciated the allegorical or ideological import of his directing is immaterial. The narrator, however, as a consciousness embodied in, say, structuring parallels and oppositions that make allegorical reading tenable, is an imaginary personification of the narration; a seemingly coherent position, with which the spectator can engage, from which the narrative seems most comprehensible. Hence it is trusted.

This account of narration, defying the notion that spectatorship is passive, has been modified by theory and empirical audience research that question whether all spectators are interpellated into inscribed subject positions. Feminist criticism emphasises gender difference in media reception and, as will become apparent in relation to The Color Purple, factors including race, class and historical context also affect meanings that viewers construct. Texts do not position all readers in the same way or there would be little disagreement over their status or meaning.

Rather than attempt an overarching theory of narration and how it influences the spectator, more productive is concentration on specific textual practices. A useful concept is focalisation (Genette 1980). This explicitly concerns relationships between the narrator – 'who speaks' or, more accurately in film, 'who enunciates' – and characters, centres of consciousness – 'who see'. Focalisation implies metaphors of looking through a lens: consequently angle, distance, focal length, inclusion or exclusion, filtering, clarity or distortion.

Whether the precarious state of Mann's masculinity – deduced to be his personal weakness (a regressive reading) or symptomatic of social developments (a progressive reading) – is his or the film's judgement is a question of focalisation. The narrator does not look or gain knowledge 'with' a character during narration, which even in flashback is always present tense. The narrator is elsewhere, *recounting* the story, already known, rather than living it, from a perspective outside and at a different time from events narrated. Viewers, however, can look 'with' and gain knowledge 'with' the character if that suits the narration, but can also know more than the character, or less. Hitchcock famously postulated a scenario in which a bomb under a table kills a character (see Truffaut 1978: 79–80). If he knows the bomb is there and we know also we may share his anxiety. But if the story demands he does not know and it blows him up the narration can present the event in alternative ways. The narrator withholds knowledge of the bomb: we witness a normal episode before being suddenly shocked. The narrator draws attention to it: we feel anxious and helpless, in suspense, not knowing whether or when it will explode. This controlled filtering involves two levels of knowledge: the character's and the narrator's, perfectly aligned or totally separate; their relationship can shift. Focalisation can switch freely between characters, be rigorously restricted to one or a few, or remain more or less aloof. Point-of-view alone cannot account for this.

Subjective mirror shots confirm internal focalisation as the truck forces Mann into increasingly deadly situations, causing him almost to lose control of his car. His masculinity bruised by his wife, he takes up the gauntlet and outmanoeuvres the truck by overtaking in a lay-by. Relaxed country music marks an interlude of normality once he pulls ahead and turns the radio back on after passing a sign for 'Chuck's Café'. Before reaching this haven (named amusingly yet ominously for *Road Runner*'s creator) the truck again tails him closely, edging him to ever-higher speeds. Internal focalisation through this single character nevertheless permits shots from the truck – close to the ground or near wheels to enhance the sensation of speed – or away from the duellists. Edited seamlessly into Mann's experiences, they emphasise, and confirm the objectivity of, his terrifying pursuit.

Various state licences suggest the truck's provenance is everywhere and nowhere in particular, part of a bigger picture than Mann's circumscribed world of freeways and meetings. Diversion from his usual route has led him into a road movie, where truckers, personifications of Western individualism following their own rules, are redneck counterpoints to the countercultural anti-heroes of *Easy Rider* (1969), *Two Lane Black Top* (1971) and *Vanishing Point* (1971). As ninety miles per hour approaches, the non-diegetic sound intrudes – discordant, percussive jangling – before the tanker shunts the car, when squealing and strumming strings predominate. As an extreme telephoto shot renders the car and truck out of focus – so much for Mann's understanding and control – music resembling Bernard Herrmann's *Psycho* score (a film already evoked by the scenery and front-seat driving shots), frantically muddled, culminates in the car swerving into a truck-stop and demolishing a white fence: metonym for a tamed wilderness.

The wrong man

Politeness and concern prevail as an old-timer enquires, 'You all right, Mister?' Mann's glasses have been dislodged, their association with vision, figurative and literal, emphasised as he blurs in the foreground while the old man, framed through the window, approaches, before the lens pulls both characters into focus – a psychologically effective portrayal of Mann's coming-to after the collision as well as a return to normality. This is short-lived, however. Masculinity resurfaces in the contrast between Mann, crying, and the old man's curt diagnosis: 'Just a little whiplash is all.'

In the sanctuary of the café, a labyrinthine, hand-held, backward-tracking shot frames Mann in close-up, creating a very different mood from the fragmented editing of the chase. As he washes, mirrors affirm his identity. A voice-over soliloquy externalises his thoughts (previously spoken aloud). Essentially trite and redundant – taking over eighty words to reach the un-startling observation, 'it's like … back in the jungle again' and to convey Mann's belief he is safe – the device works less effectively than in *Psycho*. (Here Marion's speculation about responses to her crime complicates the situation, confirms her motivations and conflict, and convinces because it plays as psychodrama using the characters' own voices, jointly recollected with the spectator.) Nevertheless, Mann's inner speech does tighten the focalisation essential to the subsequent scene, where restricted vision conveys paranoia, generating dramatic tension and forcing a crisis from an objectively uneventful situation.

As Mann sits down, suppression of his voice, quieter than the cook's who inquires after his well-being (quieter than the entire dialogue track), enhances a distancing from reality, motivated by his condition. It intensifies visual impact as strangers, commenting inaudibly, appear to mock him. Their gaze, directly to camera, flouting classical continuity, stresses his vulnerability. Drawing attention to the camera, the spectator's voyeuristic gaze compromises realism, shattering Imaginary involvement and encouraging colder, critical scrutiny of Mann's fears. The gaze returns on the spectator, reversing normal power relations. Paradoxically the dislodged subject position more strongly keys with Mann's sense of separation while sharing his anxiety for confirmation.

When he sees the tanker outside, a non-diegetic animal roar expresses his primal response as he peers around for its driver and evidence of conspiracy. Hereafter the psychological facet of focalisation predominates, which conveys a character's knowledge and/or emotions (Rimmon-Kenan 1983). A rapid pan onto a pool game edgily emphasises visual distractions, the scene's normality, that anyone could be the trucker, and Mann's isolation in the background. It further disorientates by breaking continuity, not matching his look in the previous shot.

Mann becomes, as in Metz's model, both voyeur – scrutinising the diners from inside his separate booth, staring through his fingers – and creator of the scenario as he projects anxieties onto presumably innocent people. The projected shadow of the 'OPEN' sign from the window onto the wall beside him echoes the analogy. The spectator's surrogate, as curiosity and misgiving motivate a track past faces at the counter, blurred to emphasise anonymity, he remains sharply focused in the background. A beer-drinking 'Marlboro Man'-type snaps into focus, an icon of American masculinity. Tense music underscores anxiety during a crane in on a pair of boots, which conventional continuity suggests belongs to the same man. He is a different cowboy: further disorientation. Cut-in reactions of Mann recall Hitchcock's application of the Kuleshov effect in *Rear Window*. A pan to another pair of boots and a tilt up to the first man looking briefly back at him precede a zoom out to a second, then a third, looking over their shoulders and suddenly a disembodied nervous laugh – Mann's? The waitress's? – as cutlery drops onto his table from out of frame. After this Hitchcockian false alarm, he again is aware of men looking and whispering: understandable, given his unusual arrival and suspicious behaviour, creating a Hitchcockian 'wrong man' situation. One wears dark glasses, inscrutable like the traffic cop in *Psycho*; another is condensed into a single eye in close-up: vision, corollary of knowledge, equating to threat.

Mann's voice-over rationalises why the truck turned back; the camerawork, conversely, becomes more erratic. Then, in controlled, decisive, subjective shots, Mann twice strides across to tackle his tormentor, only to have smoke blown in his face. These turn out to be fantasies, his projected desire and fear, interspersed with close-ups of his eyes, whereas he is too diffident even to ask the waitress for ketchup. The first suspect departs. The camera frames his crotch, signalling the phallic implications of the struggle, before panning to rest on Mann, who sees the cowboy run his hand along the truck, proprietorially. He leaves in a pickup. Mann's napkin is in shreds.

Another drinker, previously unnoticed, wearing boots, is eating boorishly. Mann provokes a fight, and is ejected. The truck starts off-screen. Having placed himself outside civilisation, Mann is now the pursuer, on foot. But to no avail.

Mad north-northwest

Back on the road, Mann stops for a school bus needing a push. That its driver has not seen the truck reinforces doubts concerning Mann's sanity. Children crawling over his car will not get down for Mann, further undermining his status, but instantly obey the bus-driver. Mann fails to maintain his objection that pushing the bus will jam his car underneath – which happens. Children jeer, pull faces, cheer him on, through the screen-like murky bus windows – an inscribed audience, ordinary kids, enjoying the adventure; but as a mirroring Other, in his vulnerable state their disrespect hardly helps his masculine competence. As the bus-driver attempts to free Mann's car, bouncing on its front, Mann fusses, desperately grasping at bourgeois normality – irrationally, given it has been shunted at ninety, veered into a fence and voluntarily used in an unlikely attempt to shove a bus. After Mann's faux pas in the café, the spectator is less likely now to accept his judgement, which imbues the scene with comedic undertones. This temporary shift in mood and focalisation makes all the more chilling the truck's slow, deliberate reappearance, ominously silhouetted in a tunnel, unobserved by the characters. When Mann notices, its headlamps blaze: the eyes of a demonic predator. Genuine good intention, to move children to safety, results in him again appearing crazy. Jumping on the car, hanging from the bus, until he frees it, Mann visually reverts to ape.

Humiliation increases as the truck, during Mann's getaway, graciously pushes the bus. Mann stops at a railroad crossing. Only paranoia would detect echoes of the gas station that morning in the train's hooter and crossing bells. Certainly Mann does not seem to make this connection as cutaways to his surroundings convey ordinariness, boredom even, until suddenly the truck is ramming him towards the passing wagons.

After this encounter, Mann proceeds cautiously, permitting a van to overtake comfortably without incident. The truck, waiting, crawls out in front. Mann steers into a gas station and private zoo. A covered wagon emphasises the western dimension. Caged rattlesnakes enhance the menace. As Mann calls the police, bunting flickers in the wind, producing ominous rattlesnake sounds. The truck, stationary ahead, starts once more. Whereas surprise, as Hitchcock explained it, operated at the crossing, here the effect is suspense: the spectator knows more than Mann, who is occupied with bureaucratic niceties, while the truck snakes around towards him. In a splendid re-proportioning of the avian attack on a phone booth in *The Birds* (1963), the truck hurtles down on Mann, who escapes at the last second. It circles in pursuit, the shots ironically resembling the crop-duster attack in *North by Northwest*, which ends with the plane exploding into an almost identical truck. Accompanied by discordant Herrmann-style strings, rapid cutting – as in the *Psycho* shower murder – provides overwhelming detail yet disorients by obscuring the bigger picture as snakes, giant spiders and lizards escape, compounding Mann's danger. Spielberg follows the Master but, unlike pastiche Hitchcock thrillers, adapts the techniques to his own sensibility.

In his car, hidden in a breaker's yard, Mann sarcastically imagines his wife greeting him: 'Hello, dear. Did you have a nice trip?' Again the experience is measured against middle-class patriarchal expectations. Languid dissolves, concluding with Mann asleep, abruptly end with a loud horn – a train, not the truck – and his laughter merges with the clattering wagons: 'ha, ha – ha, ha – ha, ha'. Whether the train and truck unite in mockery or his identity is unravelling is immaterial. He is on the edge, even if laughter brings relief.

Revelation

Resuming his journey, Mann slews the car sideways to a halt, oblivious to the near-collision this causes with a following car, as the truck once more awaits. As he screeches away, smoke spurts from the truck's exhaust in the foreground, an excellent example of Spielberg's economical and efficient use of synecdoche. The revving engine recalls a snarling beast. The truck creeps into Mann's path, forcing a U-turn. Leaving the car, he strides towards the truck, low-angle close-ups emphasising western parallels as he adopts a gunslinger's stance. The cat-and-mouse game persists as the truck slouches away, then stops again. Mann flags down an elderly couple. They seem harmless, the husband initially friendly, but the woman – perhaps disturbed by Mann's wild-eyed unkemptness – refuses to become involved.

The truck reverses rapidly to scare the couple off, belatedly suggesting it is a metaphor for the need of Mann's masculinity to assert itself – rather like Hemingway's bulls – as much as it is his enemy. The old woman's dress is the same colour as Mrs Mann's, the laundrette woman's, another's in the roadhouse – and his car. Such similarities imply correspondence. Social incohesion, marital dissatisfaction, insularity of life experienced through a windscreen, are opposed to the Real represented by the truck, which now parks provocatively in front of Mann's car, then chugs forward before idling just up the road. Panic, indicated by *Psycho* violins and discordant cow bells, seems to be followed by revelation. Three successive jump cuts close in on Mann, looking; a punctuation device, imitated from Eisenstein (and repeated, for example, in *Jaws* and *E.T.*), to stress the moment's magnitude.

Duel – Mann and woman: the politics of gender

Instead of retreating, Mann strides purposefully to his car. A big close-up of his glasses on the dashboard relates his decisiveness to vision. Putting them on is presented in the mirror, almost an optical point-of-view. Bold contrasts between shots – now a big close-up of the glasses and the side of his face from a high angle outside the window – and coordinated, complex camera movements reinforce his deftness and confidence. The camera tilts along his seat belt and he buckles it: a sheriff strapping on his six-gun. He accepts the trucker's challenge as a hand beckons, and deliberately passes.

Keeping ahead of the impossibly advancing truck, Mann sees a parked patrol car – an error shared by the spectator (a much-repeated Spielberg trick). When he briefly stops, the vehicle is advertising a pest-control service named Grebleips: spelt backwards, the director's equivalent of Hitchcock's personal appearances. Spielberg rewards attention and spectatorial complicity.

Mann's folly almost finishes him when the radiator hose bursts. This he refused to change in an earlier attempt at control, over the forecourt attendant, by exerting supposed authority and masculine knowledge of cars and salesmen's tricks. However, literally at the end of the road, he uses his personalised briefcase to jam the throttle and send the car towards the truck, which rams it – the car, rather than the gasoline tanker, exploding, a gag that plays upon Hitchcock's distinction between suspense and surprise, and recalls his sense of humour – before both plunge in slow-motion over a cliff. Mann annihilates his nemesis and alter-ego – now almost revealed in shots from inside the cab, close-ups of hands and point-of-view shots of instruments, which mirror Mann's portrayal – by jettisoning the objects (car and briefcase) that define his identity. Such metonymic condensation of an entire life or complex of values into an object is a recurrent Spielberg device.

The vehicles plummet to the sound of a dying monster from an existing movie, simultaneously suggesting a primal sub-humanity, ascribed to the totally anonymous driver, and sentience, ascribed to his anthropomorphised truck. Close-ups show the cooling fan inside the cab still rotating, blood or hydraulic fluid dripping off the steering wheel (the uncertainty serving further to elide the truck with its driver), and one of the wheels spinning slowly to a stop, suggestive of a creature gradually expiring. Meanwhile Mann, reborn as a man, jumps and gibbers like Kubrick's apes in *2001: A Space Odyssey* (1968), having triumphed in the use of tools, in this case vehicles, as weapons.

Although focalisation and change of pace mean that 'an act that in real life could be construed as murder, is greeted with sighs of relief' (Perry 1998: 21), the end is low key. Mann collapses and cries, sits and stares, backlit against the sun. Light, repeatedly to become a metaphor for cinema in Spielberg's films, here suggests revelation after a journey that began in darkness. Yet the movie provides no explanations. These would be reductive and limiting. Clearly masculinity, in the feminist age, is an issue, and homosexual denial is another reading (Pye & Myles 1979: 225): ignore the voice-over, and the café scene resembles an attempted pick-up in a gay bar. So too is class (although Spielberg refused to be pinned down on this, prompting left-wing critics in Rome to leave a press conference in protest in 1972). *Duel* is a genre exercise, dexterously combining thriller, road movie and western. Certainly the commercial for haemorrhoids treatment at the start sets the new West – sedentary, pampered – against the old, traces of which *Duel* unearths. But equally interesting is the film's experimentation, as with sound (which deservedly won an Emmy). Eisenstein predicted film's subordination to theatricality with the arrival of talkies (see Donald *et al.* 1998) and, with a few exceptions, notably Hitchcock and Welles, was largely proven right in the Hollywood mainstream until Walter Murch's pioneering work on sound design in the 1970s.

Duel is remarkably sophisticated, given the constraints of a 16 day shoot and an imposed episodic structure to accommodate commercial breaks. European critics responded to its craft rather than its symbolism. One of Spielberg's strongest influences, David Lean, proclaimed this new talent; Dilys Powell's *Sunday Times* review described *Duel* as 'spun from the very stuff of cinema'; and François Truffaut praised it for achieving the 'grace, lightness, modesty, elegance, speed' the New Wave had dreamt of (quoted in Baxter 1996: 83, 84). Its allusiveness and playfulness, while permitting Spielberg to flex stylistic muscles and demonstrate versatility, are consistently purposeful, pertinent and never gratuitous.

Duel brought Spielberg – veteran of numerous amateur projects, a theatrical short and television productions – his opportunity to enter feature films. It also earned him, on his first trip abroad, lunch with Fellini (of whom, 32 years later, he was still to describe himself 'a devoted fan' in advertisements for a season devoted to *il maestro* at London's National Film Theatre). Although he directed two more television movies, producers Richard D. Zanuck and David Brown were seeking go-ahead for *The Sugarland Express* (1974). This relationship led in turn to Spielberg's breakthrough into the public consciousness with *Jaws*, the film that changed Hollywood – and Spielberg's critical reputation.

CHAPTER THREE

The Sugarland Express: a light comedy?

The Sugarland Express was Spielberg's project, which had stalled at Universal, sister company to MCA-TV where he was still contracted. Although offered features after *Duel*, he wanted to proceed with something original. Alongside pitching proposals, he directed two more TV movies; one, he claimed, was 'the first and last time the studio ordered me to do something' (quoted in Taylor 1992: 80). Meanwhile Universal had exclusively entrusted Zanuck-Brown to restore the studio's leading position. The independent producers knew Spielberg, having produced one of his scripts, but now found themselves recommending a proposal Universal had already rejected. They resubmitted it among more commercial projects including *The Sting* (1973). Lew Wasserman, MCA and Universal chairman, attested to Spielberg's talent but considered anarchic youth movies finished. He reluctantly advised: 'Make the film, fellows. But you may not be playing to full theatres' (quoted in Pye & Myles 1979: 228).

Self-conscious narration

After a caption announcing the film's basis in real events in 1969, a road sign incorporating a Texas map immediately confirms the setting and genre. Cluttered signs suggest numerous ways the protagonist, approaching by bus, could go. A man in a cowboy hat examining a wrecked car prefigures the ending. The protagonist follows this direction from the crossroads, a shot recalling Thornhill's near-miss appointment with death in *North by Northwest*. Deep focus, creating layers of action, links the woman obliviously to what is happening across the road, suggesting predestination – 'real events' after all are prescribed before dramatisation. She is silhouetted in the background, viewed through long grass. This separation enhances voyeurism, objectifying her rather than encouraging empathy. It recurs in the key scene when she instigates a patrolman's kidnapping after crashing a stolen car; again finally when the hijacked police car, driven by her dying husband, crashes at the Mexican border. Cold, wintry light and muddy roads suggest sombre realism, distinguishing this from the usual Hollywood caper. Telephoto compression emphasises receding poles, a harsh, blankly repetitive perspective that undercuts Goldie Hawn's familiar persona as she removes dark glasses and comes into focus.

From the start, *The Sugarland Express* implies a viewer, actively reading across the text or already familiar with it, who knows more than the character. Technique flaunts itself for cinephiles, offering formalist aesthetic appreciation while serving narration's primary functions. Depending on expectation or response, Imaginary involvement and Symbolic detachment – either or both – are available. Officer Slide (Michael Sacks), for example, is introduced by a rightward pan framing a distant police car, approached by the forwardly mobile camera at a crossroads, then a track alongside (all one shot) before a seamless transition to the car interior. Efficient, 'invisible' continuity from establishing shot to close-up, with camerawork sustaining appropriate chase movie energy, is also stunning choreography.

As in *Duel*, barbed wire frames a car in which Lou Jean and Clovis Poplin (Goldie Hawn and William Atherton) have cadged a ride, highlighting the road-movie's western ancestry and conveying the characters' entrapment, before Slide apprehends it. As its driver points, from the verge, to a windscreen sticker, the camera pedestals down, motivated by the officer's shifting attention, bringing the car into shot, the Poplins inside. Spatial contiguity, emphasised by mise-en-scène, reinforces narrative continuity, as the next causal link is Lou Jean stealing the car. A reverse track inside the police car – deploying a special camera never before used (see Lightman 1973) – from Slide's eyes in the mirror to accommodate his view through the windscreen, similarly links his destiny with the fugitive car, while encouraging investment in his point-of-view. After hijacking Slide and his car, the Poplins hide from an officer driving the opposite way. Relishing a challenge akin to Hitchcock's *Lifeboat* (1944), Spielberg not only restricts entire scenes to car interiors, but cuts between cars with identically uniformed drivers, without confusion. Here a cut to the other driver suspiciously looking back precedes a close-up of Slide's eyes in his mirror, implying a transfer or interchange of gazes, solidarity, as a zoom back from the mirror restores some authority, focalisation having temporarily transferred to Slide. Later, seeing the fuel gauge – again Slide's focalisation – and realising its significance, viewers require no explanation when the car appears over a hill, then rolls back; Clovis's calling Captain Tanner (Ben Johnson) over the external speaker precedes an ellipsis as the car trundles into view again, pushed by Tanner's. As a tributary convoy augments the Sugarland Express from a slip road, a pan within the same shot finds a family against the sunset, waving. Whether achieved in-camera or by optical printing, it contributes to a casually accreting narration, whereby the audience seems to have known all along of public interest in the incident. A sharpshooter removing ornaments from the windowsill in Baby Langston's (Harrison Zanuck) foster home anticipates subsequent violence. As he aims at the approaching car, a contra-zoom alongside the rifle warps the mise-en-scène, signalling imminent tragedy: Spielberg's first outing of a technique which in *Jaws* became famous, surpasses its prototype (which lacked a character in shot) in *Vertigo* (1958). Earlier, as the runaways enjoy domesticity in a camper van, they laugh hysterically – apparently, as in *Always* (1989), this signifies coupledom for Spielberg; also, as in *Always*, cold blue illuminates one, golden warmth the other, as the harmonica score turns plaintive and laughter ceases.

Characterisation

Such technical accomplishments are always subordinate to narrative. Two Louisiana patrolmen (played by Gregory Walcott and Steve Kanaly) are filmed from outside their cars, their conversation framed through windows in a single mobile shot. We overhear their voices on radios, from which lights illuminate their faces alternately to clarify who is speaking. This is not merely self-conscious style. Although few viewers probably register it consciously, the shot confirms the Louisiana cops as peripheral to the central event – progressive bonding between the fugitives, Slide, Tanner and the populace. External focalisation underlines their grotesqueness as arrogant, hotshot hicks. Foils for the compassionately vulnerable Tanner and Slide, they appear machine-like when collecting their cars, military drums underlining their synchronised movements.

Narration unobtrusively patterns the cast into 'them' and 'us': everybody working against the Poplins versus ordinary folks (the couple's surname evokes 'the people'). It also establishes correspondences. When Lou Jean snares Clovis into threatening Slide with his own gun, he announces 'I never shot a man', prefiguring Tanner's pride in never killing anyone in 18 years' service; each instinctively desires peaceful resolution. Slide and Tanner, alone among the authorities, accept Clovis's insistence, 'We ain't no mental subjects', whereas the scale and nature of responses to the crime question the entire culture's sanity. Opposition between hostage and abductors dissolves when Slide mediates a marital dispute. Inclusion comes with sharing a meal. Clovis and Slide's bickering over the latter's driving completes the transition.

Slide, handcuffed and alone, hears Lou Jean's father on the radio warn her, 'God will get you.' After she returns and kindly, maternally, checks his well-being and compliments his good looks, he asks her to turn off the radio and reassures her she is basically good. Next morning Clovis apologises for cursing at Slide, who tells him, 'You ain't no mental subject either', before Clovis expresses ambition to join the police (proof that he *is*!). The three cooperate to hotwire a camper-van, before facing equal danger when hunters attack. Along the road, they join in country songs, while Clovis drives, wearing Slide's hat and glasses, living his fantasy. Slide reclaims the hat so they can be distinguished in a television interview, where they trade wisecracks like a pop group or sports team. They are simple kids from similar backgrounds, equally trusting in Tanner, naïve about what has been unleashed, dismayed by unflattering newspaper mug-shots.

Increasingly Slide becomes Clovis's voice of reason against Lou Jean's dangerous scheme. Slide senses something wrong at the end and tries to dissuade Clovis from approaching the house, although tragically he loses out to Lou Jean's maternal urges that insist, loudly and wrongly, on Langston's proximity. From a surrogate family, in which they complement each other – Tom Milne suggests 'the staid young patrolman has never before encountered such freedom and fantasy, while the young couple have never experienced such stability as he represents' (1974: 158) – they become a composite character. Clovis's weak ego is torn between the wisdom of super-ego Slide (literally, the Law) and the urgent desires of Lou Jean's id: her sexual drive in the prison at the start; impatience about getting her baby; hankering for food and material goods and delight in recognition at any cost; complications caused by her need to urinate after Clovis has explicitly warned her. Clovis, perhaps fearing abandonment by his near-double, shoots to prevent Slide escaping during the hunters' attack, yet calls him by his first name.

The destructive hunters who target them wear identical jackets to Clovis and Lou Jean, implying that 'normality' mirrors, exceeds even, the fugitives' lawlessness. Tanner, who realises from their petty criminal records that the couple 'ain't nothin' but a coupla kids', like Slide operates empathetically and intuitively, becoming a father to those in the car. (Clovis is orphaned, Lou Jean's father repudiates her as no-good trash, and Tanner is Slide's captain.) He seeks to control the growing posse by insisting of each member, 'If I can't call him by his first name I don't want him out there.' Lou Jean declares him 'a good man' after he promises to exchange the infant for Slide. Immediately recognising he cannot fulfil this, Tanner vents frustration on 'them two ol' boys' who prompted the first gunfire exchange and set the Sugarland Express back in motion.

Self-reflexivity

As John Baxter states, 'Spielberg's films are "about" cinema before … anything else' (1996: 104). *The Sugarland Express*'s self-conscious narration incorporates typically self-reflexive aspects which are rarely gratuitous. Near the start occurs an initially documentary-style shot of a tractor approaching along a path down which Lou Jean walks. A reverse-zoom through a rectangular aperture in a wall, a gatepost for the prison farm holding Clovis, transforms it. Reframing effectuates a split screen: blue sky and fertile farmland, into which the tractor continues, alongside prison brickwork penetrated by a metaphorical cinema screen, into which she diminishes, solitarily, as in many films' melancholy closing shot. Realism and flamboyant style interact in complex ways. As subsequently revealed, Lou Jean is crossing a boundary from relative freedom to imprisonment by a destiny she voluntarily, although unwittingly, shapes. The Law circumscribes her escape fantasy, symbolised by the open road. The aperture, representing on one hand the way out of her problems, also accesses a caper movie of her making, at the end of which she will be alone.

The distant camera tracks alongside Lou Jean, penetrating the prison fence before interposing another chain-link mesh in the foreground, enclosing her behind a plane isomorphic with the screen. Spielberg protagonists inhabit movies, not merely a diegesis

The Sugarland Express – Lou Jean imprisoned in her movie

resembling reality. Lou Jean is subject to celluloid conventions such as Keystone Cops-style chases and spectacular gunfights that harm nobody. Realism and artifice interknit. This major preoccupation for Spielberg has dogged his critical reputation among those who demand naturalism, high seriousness or innocent entertainment. As considered below, it impacted negatively on *The Sugarland Express* as a commercial commodity.

Sustained imagery justifies such convoluted interpretation of relatively straight-forward, if artistic, camerawork. Lou Jean's first mistake precipitates her into an alter-native script: she unnecessarily solicits a ride from inmate Looby's parents, whose bad driving attracts Slide's attention, prompting her car theft, the narrative's inciting incident. Clovis and she observe the elderly couple and the officer through the car window, while silhouetted in the patrol car is another inscribed spectator, an appre-hended drunk, who provides a running commentary until Clovis dismisses him during the kidnap.

Constant reminders that this is a movie include shots of characters through car windows, often zooming back from a detail to interpose a surface with reflections, or featuring voices over radios, in either case inscribing mediation. As Tanner pushes the hijacked car, his eyes in close-up in the widescreen-shaped mirror and the fugitives looking through their rear window create another split-screen, incorporating specta-tor and object in one image, emphasising simultaneous intimacy and distance, as in film viewing. Projective involvement through scopophilia co-exists with detachment as camerawork frequently positions the spectator outside characters' immediate space. A TV crew joining the event, and radio and newspaper reports, further emphasise mediation (reinterpretation of a true story). Inscribed spectators abound, such as townspeople at the roadside, but more pointedly when officers line up with binoculars and telescopic sights. They (and we) see Lou Jean as she imagines herself, sunnily backlit, gleefully accepting ribbons of trading stamps from a child in his father's arms, an idealised advertising image of family security. Lowering their instruments, a typi-cal Spielberg reaction shot, they exchange glances wordlessly – aware that the couple present no serious threat.

A low-angle close-up of one of the Louisiana cops blowing bubblegum violates this shared circle of knowledge. Like the vigilante hunters later, their departure is filmed inside a garage so they drive through a bright rectangular 'screen' into their own separate movie. The scene in which a huge attentive audience watches Lou Jean going to pee in a portable toilet is a wry observation on stardom. As night falls, Clovis plays with a torch, shining it under his chin, replicating expressionist lighting that conveys the monstrous evil he is incapable of (seen only by the spectator). Other instances of self-reflexivity include shining a searchlight into the camera, whereby a helicopter heralds its own spectacularity before emerging from dazzling light and deafening sound; inscription of the cinematic apparatus as a vigilante blunders around in the dark while morning sun shines into the camera, reducing him to a flat shadow against the metaphorical screen of the garage doorframe; and – a typical Spielberg in-joke, unavailable to audiences at the time and still likely to be missed – casting a look-alike of Spielberg's younger self as a hunter's adolescent son, who peers voyeuristically from behind a fence during the car-lot shoot-out, fascinated and appalled by what he has let loose, before fleeing, traumatised. A more obvious joke, encouraging reading of the entire image rather than merely following the action, is the sign, 'SUGARLAND AUTO WRECKING', the helicopter flies over near the end. One bizarre effect, seemingly accidental were it not replicated in *Raiders of the Lost Ark* (1981) occurs when helicopter rotor blades in the background resemble flashes from Tanner's eyes in close-up; he projects understanding and desire onto the siege he seeks to control, his metaphorical direction of the action further underlined as these pulses are answered by red and blue emergency lights flashing in time from surrounding cars.

Intertextuality

Overt intertextuality underlines such figurative possibilities. 'Intertextuality' was Kristeva's term for Bakhtin's 'dialogism': 'the necessary relation of any utterance to other utterances' (quoted in Stam *et al.* 1992: 203). An 'utterance' is any 'complex of signs'. The 'necessary relation' describes the social character of signs, which refer not to reality but encodings within which perceptions are always already structured, encodings that consist in discourses encountered in prior texts. The concept unites several approaches to how meaning is made: Umberto Eco's 'intertextual frames', Norman Fairclough's 'members' resources', Barthes' five codes in *S/Z* (1974) and Bordwell's cognitivist model of schemata, cues and inferences.

Intertextuality in *The Sugarland Express* exceeds generic conventions such as the car jumping in the initial chase, as in action sequences in *Bullitt* (1968) (which employed the same stunt crew and camera cars), or hints of Spielberg's beloved British war movies when cars scramble like fighter planes. For example, allusions to Kubrick's films, where the idea of an unstoppable machine recurs, heighten similar imagery here. The domed courtroom where Tanner appears resembles the War Room in *Dr Strangelove or: How I Learned to Stop Worrying and Love the Bomb* (1964), another satire of excessive response to perceived threat, with its own wilfully irresponsible cowboy grotesques. The low-angle tracking shot, accompanied by drums, of Tanner leaving the courtroom recalls *Paths of Glory* (1957), where an officer similarly balances duty and desire to protect life. Spielberg's vehicular 'mechanical ballet' (Pye & Myles 1979: 231) is a terrestrial, undignified counterpart to the spacecraft in *2001*.

Spielberg does not utilise genre as communicative shorthand so much as flaunt it as textual material, whether celebrated or deployed satirically as part of the mythology underlying the represented mindset. Compare the cold deliberation of *The Sugarland Express*'s Texas Rangers to the iconographic, non-diegetic attachment to *The Great Train Robbery* (1903), sensational and wild when the outlaw fires his six-shooter at the audience. Consider, too, how the vigilantes wear hunting caps and jackets that resemble Elmer Fudd's; stalking their quarry, they appear cartoonish, caps and rifle muzzles alone visible over a fence.

Spielberg plunders cinema for stylish and efficient techniques but equally sheer enjoyment, such as the crane up from a multiple crash that imitates a battlefield aftermath from *Gone With the Wind* (1939). His self-conscious contribution to the American New Wave – quirky movies with attitude by hot young directors promoted as the industry's salvation – is closer than usually acknowledged to the French New Wave, through which Spielberg's cinematic consciousness filters. Clovis, cigarette dangling from his lip and toying with a gun – blowing smoke into it to replicate a movie effect – resembles Jean-Paul Belmondo in *À bout de souffle* (*Breathless*, 1960). Prominent during the shootout is a pump emblazoned with an Esso tiger, like one featured in *Weekend*, in which also random violence and a holiday mood juxtapose with tracking shots alongside countless stalled and wrecked cars.

Outlaws finding sanctuary in cinema are obligatory in early Godard and Truffaut. *The Sugarland Express* pays its dues. Watching *Road Runner* on a nearby drive-in screen, Lou Jean laments having no sound. Clovis improvises accordingly. This follows her refusal to listen when he broaches the possibility of not getting their baby back. Cinema, then, initially figures as escapism. The cartoon reflects over them in the window, then is shown from behind them so that they and the viewer form one audience. Laughter and relaxtion, and Clovis completing the text, figure Metz's spectatorship as Imaginary unity. Clovis falls silent. The manic violence, superimposed over his eyes, now in close-up, as if he is projecting it, resembles their own chase. 'Escapism' reflects their situation. The cartoon soundtrack, semi-diegetic as he imagines it, replaces his, uniting him and the spectator in a shared premonition of his dispensability that excludes Lou Jean. Fade to black.

Gender

Goldie Hawn's comedy persona, complementing Lou Jean's apparent dizziness, distracts from her character being 'the film's mainspring' (Pye & Myles 1979: 229). Clovis is almost superfluous from the start. Although Hawn's beauty and youth cannot be ignored, the camera never fetishises her in the way Laura Mulvey (1981) argues is typical of classical cinema. Lou Jean is objectified, but by external focalisation that precludes close engagement and helps balance her motivation against that of others. When she dolls herself up for the media and her newfound fans, she becomes faintly ridiculous. From the start, the camera moves to follow her activity. Her gaze off-screen precedes Clovis's first entrance. Reversing the usual structure of the look subordinates him to her desire, although not sexually – immediately apparent from her distaste as her husband embraces her. She states her intention of leaving him although, in light of what follows, this may be a ruse to implicate him in her preposterous plan. She exploits sexuality, challenging him to prove his manhood while threatening, with a hard facial expression, to make this their 'last time' if he does not abscond with her. This, together with her passionate declaration, 'Oh Clovis, I've missed you' – silencing him when he questions how she obtained $65 bus fare – contradicts her initial announcement. Lou Jean's plan may be more instinctive and less thought through than it appears, and doubts persist about her morality, possibly hinting why the authorities consider her an unsuitable mother.

Lou Jean steals the first car as Clovis is advocating surrender. After crashing it, while Clovis appears resigned to arrest she feigns injury to filch Slide's gun. Increasingly, her 'female' enthusiasms, such as for baby accessories in a gift catalogue, silence Clovis, perhaps also because he considers them futile. Her one lucid assessment – 'Clovis, honey, don't do no good running from a tornado' – apparently accepting he will have to face consequences, ensues after Tanner offers the possibility of reopening Lou Jean's case but insists Clovis's charges must stick.

Like many buddy movies, *The Sugarland Express* becomes 'the sentimental love-story of the all-male couple' (Elsaesser 1975: 17) as rapport develops between Clovis and Slide, to the point where Lou Jean considers herself excluded. Feminist empowerment (although her motives are purely selfish) is suggested by Lou Jean's narrative agency and her (ultimately successful) challenges to welfare officials, Clovis, the penal system, the police, and privileged middle-class interests represented by Langston's foster parents – the combined forces of patriarchy. She is nevertheless a femme fatale who personifies uncontrollable female instincts and operates according to a sexist view of destructive dumb-blonde illogicality, narcissism, spontaneity and manipulative sexuality. An innocent abroad, as long as she controls events, she blithely trails havoc behind her, such as miraculous near misses as several cars skid at crossroads. Clovis's unconditional devotion is his downfall. Such contradictions, unresolved by incomplete narrative closure, make *The Sugarland Express* fascinatingly symptomatic of social struggles around the period of its making. As Clovis, watching the drive-in, intuits, episodic comic chases that only temporarily restore narrative equilibrium, so the conflict can resume in a different scenario, are not necessarily comforting.

Failure

The Sugarland Express, if remembered, is considered a failure. Wasserman's prediction proved accurate. Spielberg later declared it his one totally unsatisfactory movie, and astutely analysed its structural problems (considered below) (Taylor 1992: 83). Commercially, however, it was only a letdown relative to his other films. Re-released to cash in on Spielberg's fame after *Jaws*, and sold to television, by some accounts it earned a modest profit (Pye & Myles 1979: 231), although Baxter maintains it flopped outright (1996: 270). By then, the director had found his niche, and moved on. Until reissued on DVD in 2004 it was rarely seen – if broadcast, usually in a pan-and-scan format that mutilated careful widescreen compositions and editing structures.

As a calling card by a first-time feature director, let loose with a 5,000-strong cast after the minimalism of *Duel*, *The Sugarland Express* is an ambitious road movie and scathing examination of contemporary America that prompted enthusiastic reviews. Dilys Powell, who had championed *Duel*'s cinematic release, expected disappointment from 'the second film of a promising young director, but for once, anxiety was unnecessary'; Pauline Kael in *The New Yorker* considered it 'one of the most phenomenal début films in the history of movies', its framings and movement worthy of Howard Hawks (quoted in Crawley 1983a: 35). Vilmos Zsigmond, Spielberg's cinematographer, in interviews likened him to the young Welles (Taylor 1992: 83). The film would be better remembered had it not been swamped in hype surrounding Spielberg's later output and tarnished by attendant hostility.

The *Sugarland Express*'s failure lies, oddly, in its richness, variation, restlessness and inventiveness that ultimately lead to contradiction, confusion and tonal shifts. These together, in terms of aesthetic criteria of moral seriousness and coherence, or of commercial appeal, equal less than the sum of its intriguing parts. Despite 'action, humour, international appeal', according to Zanuck and Brown (in Pye & Myles 1979: 231), it suffered from disastrous marketing. Spielberg, ever willing to please the audience, and no doubt with an eye on future prospects, was prepared to excise twenty minutes and change the ending to something less downbeat, until Zanuck dissuaded him. Having delivered his final print in time for a promised Thanksgiving release, Spielberg endured five months' delay, losing the impetus of strong previews, to prevent Universal competition against *The Sting*. (However galling this seemed, *The Sting* became the year's top earner. Restoring Zanuck-Brown's credit, this enhanced Spielberg's prestige by association; postponement put the newcomer in the right place at the right time for *Jaws*; Zanuck-Brown's buoyancy encouraged willingness to go heavily over budget with *Jaws* and to grant Spielberg directorial freedom a second time; and *The Sting*'s success enhanced the bankability of Robert Shaw – one of *Jaws*' leading players.)

Even with time available, encapsulating *The Sugarland Express*'s multifarious elements into a coherent narrative image proved impossible. Goldie Hawn's presence suggests light comedy or women's concerns rather than an epic chase with tragic overtones, and her fluffy persona contrasts with Lou Jean's tough determination. The title evokes a children's fantasy. Universal tried 28 different campaigns, including one shot by Spielberg, before returning the problem to Zanuck-Brown. Despite release in 250 US cinemas, and winning Spielberg the screenplay prize at Cannes with co-writers Hal Barwood and Matt Robbins, *The Sugarland Express* earned rentals of less than $3 million and in Europe attracted fewer viewers than *Duel*. The day Spielberg began shooting *Jaws* he heard it was being withdrawn (Crawley 1983a: 36–7). In Britain it lasted a week, before being re-released in a double bill, with several cuts, including the entire *Road Runner* scene. Strangely, it was paired with *The Front Page* (1974) directed by Billy Wilder, who had called Spielberg 'the greatest young talent to come along in years' (quoted in Baxter 1996: 115).

Conclusion

Without the prejudice that greeted later Spielberg releases, *The Sugarland Express*, as 'Godard-lite', might justly be claimed to embody potentially subversive Brechtian elements. In its original context, such a possibility arose under the influence of television. This powerful competitor not only transformed industry economics but also meant that remaining filmgoers, whom the industry had to identify, cultivate and satisfy by offering something different – such as road-movies with victimised anti-heroes – no longer broadly represented majority ideological attitudes (see Elsaesser 1975).

The Sugarland Express's postscript, although not dramatised, concludes the story. Mother/child reunion, representing the lost Imaginary, narrative's driving force, is deferred beyond the performance. It necessitates removing the actual father, Clovis, and defeating the symbolic father, the authorities – primarily Tanner, but also the castrating figures of the sharpshooters – initially by kidnapping Slide and, more decisively, through Lou Jean's successful appeal. Unlike later Spielberg movies, it does not directly present this blissful wish-fulfilment, so often criticised as sentimental. Hence the movie maintains detachment, emotionally unsatisfying as entertainment, while downplaying feminist implications of Lou Jean's successful challenge to patriarchy (which her characterisation could never sustain) that might make a more intriguingly cerebral work.

The classical cinema, Thomas Elsaesser has argued, assumes 'a fundamentally affirmative attitude to the world it depicts', embodied in narrative structure: 'Contradictions were resolved and obstacles overcome by having them played out in dramatic-dynamic terms or by personal initiative; whatever the problem, one can *do* something about it' (1975: 14). Compare Clovis's incredulous, tight-lipped reaction when Lou Jean declares that once they pick up Langston they will 'settle down just like real folks'. The plot confirms dominant specularity, which privileges the visual and unspoken over the verbal, and creates a hierarchy of discourses (see MacCabe 1981) that at the time would tend to privilege masculine over feminine, and buy into class and gender stereotypes. But ultimately Lou Jean's discourse frames it, legitimised by the postscript.

Rather than that hierarchy, however, *The Sugarland Express* foregrounds Bakhtin's central concept, heteroglossia, or multi-voiced quality. Implicit in both carnival (social occasion) and *menippea* (artwork), this is the struggle of discourses comprising any text. Clovis's death aside, the movie's conflict constitutes inversions, challenges and free play akin to carnivalesque. Disproportion and repetition create comedy. A collision is nothing; a multiple pile-up caused by a maverick's initiative is hilarious. Individualism, car culture and populism receive indiscriminate mockery. Children sit on the roof of Slide's patrol vehicle, small boys excitedly miscount the convoy passing and the chase becomes entangled in a parade. Much of the absurdity is throwaway, demanding close attention, as when Lou Jean and Slide exchange photographs: 'Who's that standin' next to you?' she asks. 'My bull. I was in the FFA [Future Farmers of America],' he replies. Children race alongside as Lou Jean becomes a media celebrity, while her husband gets police driving lessons in a patrol car. Eventually she resembles royalty as, made-up (in her estimation) like a princess and surrounded by riches (golden trading stamps, later bestowed on the crowd), she insists, 'I wanna see the people. I like the people.' The people, lavishing gifts, such as a piglet that pees on her, like her. Her final shot is beatific; surrounded by red roses, naturally backlit, blonde hair blowing free, she appears sanctified.

Some critics complain that *The Sugarland Express* lacks sympathy for its main characters (Mott & Saunders 1986: 27). In fact, contrary to Spielberg's later reputation, it is uniformly misanthropic. The last shot of Langston shows him screaming in a distinctly ape-like manner, while in the penultimate shot Slide, like Mann at the end of *Duel*, crouches in silhouette against the reflections on the river, again resembling Kubrick's *2001* Neanderthals.

That would be a powerful representation if the culture's shortcomings were viewed from some coherent position. Spielberg was more interested in technique than his characters' situation and offered little analysis of how the American Dream had soured. Later he regretted not having spent the first half exploring Tanner's motivation and the authorities' position, with the drama in the car restricted to voices from the radio and occasional shots of 'three heads in the distance through binoculars'; the second half would re-tell the story inside the car (Taylor 1992: 83–4). Such a modernist approach to focalisation might have dramatised more effectively many issues in play and involved the audience more intently in the dilemmas presented. The road movie structure adopted by Spielberg and other New Wave filmmakers is ultimately self-defeating. As Elsaesser notes, the genre takes rebel protagonists through an oppressively conservative society that pre-exists and survives them; the silent majority remain untouched by the satire directed against them, which consequently warps into self-pity. That Lou Jean gets her baby, and Tanner and Slide continue working on the force, mean that, apart from Clovis's death, nothing changes: in anticipation of postmodern values that characterise later Spielberg films, 'we are left with the impression that all endeavour is basically senseless, signifying nothing' (Hess & Hess 1974: 3).

CHAPTER FOUR

Jaws: searching the depths

That's entertainment

Jaws became the definitive modern blockbuster as both large-scale production and box office attraction, profiting from enormous promotion and publicity as well as ancillary benefits. A sociological and economic phenomenon, its reception revolutionised industry practice by demonstrating how marketing 'could precipitate a national pop cultural "event", and make millions upon millions of dollars for a single studio with but a single film' (Gomery 2003: 73). *Jaws* doubled the stock value of MCA, Universal Studios' owner, which had already risen following positive previewing.

Selling *Jaws* exploited synergy – 'strategic cross-promotion of products in more than one medium, with sales of each helping to spur on the other' (Hall 2002: 20). As well as the best-selling source novel and screenwriter Carl Gottlieb's book (itself a million-seller) chronicling the troubled production, a vast array of tie-in commodities stimulated and exploited the public imagination. Seaside ice cream vendors offered 'sharkalate', 'jawberry' and 'finilla' flavours. The studio placed 'public service' posters of 'shark facts'. Resultant '*Jaws*-consciousness', as executives called it, prompted chat-show hosts to liken politicians to sharks, encouraged false sightings and, importantly, put these on the news agenda. When a Great White attacked a swimmer, *Jaws* made the cover of *Time* (Salisbury & Nathan 1996: 88).

Advance publicity featured attempts to penetrate secrecy surrounding hydraulic model sharks on location. Even this was stage-managed. Universal financed junkets giving journalists two hundred interviews with production personnel – 'three times the normal', admitted the studio press chief (Daly 1980: 110). Setbacks provided a flow of ongoing stories. The budget, originally $8.5 million, variously reported as 10, 11 and 12 million (Griffin 1999; Gottlieb 2001; Hall 2002) – discrepancies may depend on whether publicity and advertising are included – increased when shooting stretched from 55 to 150 days. Each aquatic stint involved four hours filming among eight 'anchoring boats, fighting the ocean and trying to get the mechanical shark to work' (Falk in Pirie 1981: 174). These difficulties, exacerbated by commencing too early, to circumvent a national screen actors' strike, delayed the unit in Martha's Vineyard during the expensive summer season, when real holiday crowds interfered with background continuity, causing further hold-ups. Spielberg's 36:1 shooting ratio contrasts strikingly with his subsequent legendary efficiency. The first announced budget was $3.5 million; over-spending, too, earned valuable publicity – although, as Gottlieb points out, budgets (like receipts) are guarded secrets because of recriminations over profits (2001: 53, 198).

The novel sold 7.6 million copies before the movie's release (Pye & Myles 1979: 236), with paperbacks sharing the film's advertising design. Zanuck and Brown even toured with the book for Bantam. Three thousand people arrived in a hailstorm to a preview after advertisements featured just the graphics without the title (Harwood 1975). *Jaws'* North American release eventually coincided with the summer holidays: conveniently, the 'silly season', when news supply dwindles.

Jaws opened simultaneously on 464 screens, many at seaside resorts. Although small by later standards – *Jurassic Park* occupied almost 3000 – nationwide release and holiday weekend timing marked a new approach. This strategy followed the triumph of the low-budget independent *Billy Jack* (1971), re-released in 1973 with unprecedented intensive television advertising in regions where theatres had been block-booked ('four-walling'). Advertising for *Jaws* accordingly included $1 million for commercials during every prime-time show on all three national networks for three evenings prior to opening. 'Gone were the days of a glamorous New York City or Hollywood premiere, critical reaction, and then gradual release first across the US' (Gomery 2003: 74). 'Front-loading' creates a national event and, when necessary, mitigates negative reviews or word of mouth. Adopting strategies previously reserved for anticipated failures (*The Sugarland Express* had been four-walled), cinema thereafter worked with television, to their mutual benefit, rather than as an aloof competitor, even while asserting its difference.

Jaws' initial release achieved domestic rentals of $123.1 million, $36 million during the first 17 days. These figures – what theatres paid the studio – partly reflect the fact that exhibitors had blind bid on the strength of the novel and previews, committing themselves to forwarding ninety per cent of receipts for three months (Harwood 1975). Nevertheless, 25 million tickets sold in the first 38 days (Schatz 1993: 19). Recovering production costs in two weeks, *Jaws* eventually grossed around $500 million worldwide, $260 million in the US. Interest, and attendances, mounted as *Jaws* became the first film to take $100 million, having supplanted *The Godfather* as all-time box office success, and proceeded to win three Academy Awards (sound, John Williams's music and Verna Fields' editing; but not Best Director).

Impressive facts, but the point is not uncritically to admire them, to perpetuate hype that enters into the spectacle bought and sold. Rather it is to underline why *Jaws* is an industry watershed. Ever since, Hollywood studios repeatedly gamble on the one film that might turn around or consolidate their fortunes. When successful, escalating expenditure drives profits further. Production budgets constitute proportionately smaller parts of cross-media packages as movies become more the vehicle for promoting a franchise – products sharing a trademark – than the primary project itself, although in *Jaws'* case, with what now seems unbelievable naivety, synergy did not extend to charging entrepreneurs for using the brand (Baxter 1996: 147). With *Jaws*, the franchise promoted sequels, a tendency now common. Contemporary movies are 'always and simultaneously text and commodity, intertext and product line' (Meehan 1991: 62).

However, nobody predicted *Jaws* would be so lucrative. It remains 'axiomatic in the entertainment industry that no one can tell in advance with any degree of certainty what constitutes a hit' (Gottlieb 2001: 11). Besides, a film's attractions cannot be reduced solely to commercially driven publicity. As Thomas Schatz acknowledges, 'whatever the marketing efforts, only positive audience response and favourable word-of-mouth can propel a film to genuine hit status' (1993: 18). The proof: 'equally huge numbers of people stayed away from the massively promoted *Sgt Pepper's Lonely Hearts Club Band* (1976), as word spread that it was poor' (Pirie 1981: 60). As David Pirie notes, though, other 1970s hits in the (then) all-time box office top 50, *One Flew Over the Cuckoo's Nest* (1975), *Rocky* (1976), *American Graffiti* (1973) and *Animal House* (1978) 'are not blockbusters in any recognisable sense'; they were comparatively cheap and their popularity totally unexpected (1981: 204).

Jaws was 'high concept' before the industry, for whom it lacks pejorative connotations ascribed by critics, had coined the expression. Such movies replicate and combine previously successful narratives; dramatise an idea that can be 'summed up and sold in a single sentence' (true also of the other hits just mentioned); and utilise, in print and television advertisements as well as across the range of merchandising, graphics abstracted from a key visual image (Wyatt 1994: 13, 19).

The boy wonder

Jaws appeared as academic film studies was rejecting traditional notions of authorship and attempting, initially through genre, to understand cinema's industrial and economic aspects within wider workings of ideology. Stephen Heath, in an important article on the 'pleasure-meaning-commodity complex' exemplified by *Jaws*, explained that popular films' entertainment value derives from meaningful structuration involving a 'communicative system' – signs and codes – reproduced and circulated by an industry for profit. These constitute a 'specific signifying practice', a representational mode audiences willingly consent to and pay for (1976: 26). The term highlights *how* representations are constructed, for it is not simply 'that the film articulates the current concerns, fears and desires of the people who see it and recommend it to their friends'

(Rubey 1976: 20) – very many in the case of *Jaws* – but also that the articulation is deemed sufficiently affecting.

Jaws was Spielberg's breakthrough, securing his public image and winning industry influence. However much cultural codes and conventions overdetermined his creative judgement, he articulated them into the satisfying form on-screen. Moreover, while academic theory advanced, *Jaws* was not yet seen as changing everything. Tendencies emerge slowly. Highbrow reviewing and fan culture were still coming to terms with auteurism, a conception singularly suited to Hollywood in the 1970s. Newer directors, including film school graduates aware of broader intellectual trends, took themselves seriously as artists, encouraged to do so by studios recently freed from Production Code constraints and desperate for fresh ideas to nurture a young, educated audience with art-house tastes. Specific signifying practices, in other words, incorporated authorship, commoditised into the text and exchanged in subsidiary practices of promotion and reviewing. Yet Michael Pye and Lynda Myles, who both analysed and nurtured these developments, argue in relation to *Jaws*:

> Since the story outline was prepared by Spielberg, Zanuck and Brown in the comfort of their cabanas, the film serves as an object lesson in the essential unreality of assigning authorship to a film. In this case at least seven people made major contributions to the script alone. (1979: 236)

In the 'Anniversary Edition' DVD release (2000) Spielberg happily acknowledges that Williams' score was central to the movie's success. Moreover, although Spielberg supervised editing in collaboration with Fields, they test-screened and adjusted accordingly. This for many critics detracts from integrity and reduces movies to the lowest common denominator. For one recent critic (an admirer), *Jaws* hardly counts as Spielberg's movie:

> Under extraordinary pressure ... simply to get the film made at all, he is in a more important sense freer than he ever has been or will be again. This is an *assignment*, so he doesn't have to square it with his artistic conscience ... And everyone knows it's an assignment so he doesn't have to be judged by it. The film belongs to a mixture of low genres so he doesn't have to invent tones, only orchestrate them, and he has plenty to play with. He has nothing, particularly, to communicate ... His actors are making up their lines which will never happen again. He has no reputation to live up to, no voice he need find. And vitally, his sense of humour has bumped into its perfect vehicle – a latent comedy. All he has to do is be effective. (Quirke 2002: 7)

Yet to 'orchestrate' with such facility demands qualities the novel's author, Peter Benchley, recognised, describing Spielberg as 'an encyclopaedia of the film industry' (in Salisbury & Nathan 1996: 83). *Jaws*, a seemingly impersonal studio film – a cultural rather than individual expression that nevertheless depends on its director's passion for cinema – neatly encapsulates auteurism's contradictions. Spielberg in 1975 acknowledged that *Jaws*' profitability 'lets me make two movies that will fail before

I have to start all over again' (in Crawley 1983a: 52). It earned freedom to follow his whims provided he delivered a hit from time to time. Also, as will be seen, *Jaws*, despite being a routine production, has much in common stylistically and thematically with movies Spielberg actively instigated. As auteur theory in its unadulterated, unpopularised version insists, continuities are not necessarily conscious or intended.

Success triggered resentment. To some, the skill of *Jaws*, seemingly devoid of modernist complexities or individual vision characteristic of the most interesting 1970s cinema, appeared effortless and – while selected American films were becoming appropriated into high culture – made life easy for the audience. Spielberg's apparent regression in *Close Encounters* to the conservative values of the 1950s, in the same year that *Star Wars* (1977) overtook *Jaws*' box office by reverting to nostalgic and childish simplicities, confirmed this view. Journalists and senior academics still confuse Spielberg with George Lucas (Solomons 2004: 7; Gledhill & Williams 2000: 111). Spielberg, because of *Jaws*, is blamed for dumbing-down movies, and for the shortcomings of other directors' products, whether high-concept blockbusters or exploitative imitations.

The reality, however, is more complicated. Tax loopholes and write-offs that had encouraged investment in independent films ended in the mid-1970s. The effect was to curtail diversity and innovation, despite the existence of a healthy art cinema (Schatz 1993: 20–1). *Jaws* was symptomatic rather than causal of the wary high-stakes industry economics it epitomises. Studios, after *Easy Rider*'s runaway success, had financed innovative, European-flavoured movies. New Hollywood's much lamented early era was 'an incredibly rich period of American film history; in many ways, the years 1969–75 can be characterised as a period of extensive experimentation in industrial practice, film form and content' (Wyatt 1994: 72). Such experimentation, not the result of any visionary strategy, was permitted because studios were blundering, at a loss how to reverse dwindling fortunes.

Spielberg, afraid of typecasting as an action director – the coolly ma̶   ̶,̶ after all, replicates the truck in *Duel* – had tried three times to exch̶a̶   ̶ ̶ome̶thing personal and prestigious, but was stymied by *The Sugar̶   ̶commer̶cial failure. He remained contracted to Universal, and Z̶   ̶own assigned him *Jaws* before *The Sugarland Express*'s release. Spielberg̶   ̶keep progressing, needed another feature and the producers needed a hit a̶   ̶eral disappointments. Even so, as a hired hand, Spielberg oversaw something more complex than the money-making machine critics frequently disparage *Jaws* for being (see, for example, Monaco 1979: 50).

Publicity backfired in one particular instance, creating an image Spielberg has still not entirely shed. A reported dispute in the *Los Angeles Times* entertainment section between Spielberg and Benchley, who had drafted three unsuitable screenplays (Daly 1980: 107), had the first-time novelist saying

> Spielberg needs to work on character ... He knows, flatly, zero ... He is a 26-year-old who grew up with movies. He has no knowledge of reality but movies ... Wait and see, Spielberg will one day be known as the greatest second-unit director in America. (Gottlieb 2001: 138)

Although Benchley's hostility, Gottlieb insists, arose from misquotations of Spielberg elsewhere, and the issue was swiftly resolved (Benchley appears in the film, ironically as a reporter), these remarks, in Hollywood opinion formers' daily paper, shaped subsequent criticism. For the moment, however, 'Among critics, [*Jaws*] established [Spielberg] as an artist, with the public as a showman, but last, and most important for his career, convinced the industry he was a money-maker' (Baxter 1996: 142).

Politics: contextual

The little coverage *Duel* and *The Sugarland Express* attracted was mostly enthusiastic. Limited distribution, 'discovery' by European intellectuals, similarities between *The Sugarland Express*, Terrence Malick's *Badlands* (1973) and Robert Altman's *Thieves Like Us* (1974), albeit to the commercial detriment of all three, and the bleak, negative, yet clearly artistic vision, made Spielberg not merely an auteur, but a serious cult figure discussed alongside Pollack, Boorman, Rafelson, Hellman and Ashby (Elsaesser 1975). If *Jaws* turned critics, especially on the left, against Spielberg, this occurred mainly retrospectively. While blockbuster status made *Jaws* synonymous with Hollywood, early political analyses treated it not as a stick to beat the little-known director, but as symptomatic of the industry or of social contradictions. For all its expense, skilful manipulation of reactions (which was rather widely admired) and inescapable hype, dominant ideological tendencies implied by extreme popularity were taken for granted in exploration of more particular meanings, or demonstrated in explications that held neither the text nor mass audiences in contempt.

Independence Day preparations and star-spangled banners in *Jaws* made it easy to generalise Amity's fears about its younger generation (vandalised picket fences; drinking, dope smoking and skinny-dipping) to the whole USA. Youthful unrest was motivated – amidst wider change and discontent – over Vietnam, the draft and heavy authoritarian responses to protest. (Ambivalence towards redneck Texas as microcosm surely was one of *The Sugarland Express*'s problems.) *Jaws* coincided with America's withdrawal, its first military defeat. President Nixon look-alike Mayor Vaughn (Murray Hamilton) his red, white and blue tie matching the garlands behind him, personifies beleaguered authority while his accomplice, the coroner, recalls Secretary of State Kissinger, who had accepted the President's resignation after Watergate exposed corruption and cover-up at the top.

Vaughn dissuades Chief Brody (Roy Scheider) from closing the beach, for commercial reasons, constantly evoking 'the public interest' in the way Nixon cited 'national security' to justify excesses (Biskind 1975: 26). The ubiquitous flags thereby associate business and government with greed, shortly before the Bicentennial that this holiday, overshadowed by guilt, mistrust and tragedy, anticipates. Vaughn's striped jacket against a background of striped awnings and bathing huts identifies him with the economy, community and nation. Herman Melville's *Moby-Dick* and Henrik Ibsen's *Enemy of the People* subtexts respectively dramatise desire for escape to authenticity (the frontier) and duty – however difficult – to take responsibility. Despite appearing weak according to action-hero expectations, Brody does all that could reasonably be required of someone under political pressure. Martial drums playing as if to underline individualistic purpose as Brody marches from the office turn out to be diegetic – a band practice – relocating his resolve in the context of wider considerations (an aural counterpart to the visual shift in the celebrated contra-zoom when he witnesses Alex Kintner's (Jeffrey Voorhees) preventable death). Overcoming phobia, Brody manifests 'courage and cunning; he has a strong sense of civic duty and even accepts the responsibility for the death of the Kintner boy when publicly accused by Mrs Kintner [Lee Fierro]' (Bowles 1976: 205) – 'a resonance of Vietnam', as Gill Branston suggests (2000: 51).

Robert Torry reads *Jaws* as a sustained allegory, when divided public opinion precluded representing Vietnam directly. The fish – read Vietcong – prompts an 'obvious wish fulfilment narrative of the annihilation of a murderous, devious and implacable enemy', largely unseen but mercilessly efficient (1993: 27). Its three hunters – as in many war movies – overcome interpersonal differences to defeat the common foe. Quint's (Robert Shaw) rash determination to avenge his *USS Indianapolis* shipmates, lost to sharks, and his consequent death nevertheless subtly warn against 'obsessive reaction to the trauma of American defeat' (ibid.) – a significant consideration given the post-Gulf War timing of Torry's analysis and subsequent raising of this issue in criticism of *Saving Private Ryan*. Misidentifications (bounty hunters capture the wrong shark; armed guards over-react to mischievous boys with a hardboard fin) distil, 'and to some extent ameliorate' (1993: 33), My Lai and other extremes and atrocities. 'The ultimately successful mission', Torry claims, 'provide[s] its American audience with the satisfaction withheld … in Vietnam, that of the complete devastation of an elusive enemy' (ibid.).

Quint's *Indianapolis* monologue also implies guilt, his or the West's generally, over Hiroshima. The association is circumstantial, but details suggest connections between two wars against a generalised Asian dark Other, as if Vietnam were retribution for the former. *Jaws* climaxes in a spectacular explosion that 'will satisfy Quint's rage' as Brody destroys the shark with 'a bomb-shaped air tank' (Rushing & Frentz 1995: 87). The shark reflects human savagery in war. Rubey (1976) recalls that US fighter pilots painted teeth on engine cowlings (as in *1941*). By equating Quint and the shark with less civilised aspects of America, Dan Rubey argues, the culture abjects them.

Jaws' international success, even if stoked up by the US reception, and its continuing popularity suggest it must retain broader appeal than these specific resonances. The shark 'arise[s] from the scriptures and from Darwin [to] tap the deepest recesses of our consciousness: the demon and the brute within' (Bowles 1976: 200). Without lapsing into mysticism or reduction to a single meaning, demonstrably the shark embodies ideologically reviled human attributes, made radically Other, to be expunged.

When Vaughn's crony enters the sea during the holiday weekend, bathers follow in droves with the mayor's approval. The camera observes at water level. A grandmother's evident anxiety elicits dread; these camera positions, after previous attacks, signify imminent danger. They do not simply align with the bathers' experience, however. As a shifting viewpoint detached from any visible origin they yield imaginative projection equally as predator and as potential victims. This relates to the camera's look, explicitly in shots that breach the surface, emphasising the camera/screen plane that holds back the darker water, and those in which characters transgress classical realism by staring at the audience (actually the as-yet unrevealed hoax fin). Hence, in terms of investment, the spectator remains outside the community or outside the diegesis (or both). This facilitates judgement. Mass incursion into the waves suggests consumerist conformity, as these tourists abandon sensible fears simply because everyone else does. Intercutting with Vaughn's emollient interviews as a reminder of why the beaches remain open reinforces the point. Sheer stupidity manifests in the stampede into water where the audience knows danger lurks; in determination to have fun notwithstanding the unresolved tragedy; in believing that government, despite officials, helicopters and powerboats out in force, has jurisdiction over nature; in trusting Vaughn; in falling for a childish prank; in the SWAT team's apparent over-reaction, training weapons on two kids. All, together with dominant focalisation through Brody and these characters' anonymity, seems profoundly misanthropic and implies culpability. This comes on top of the feeding frenzy as hunters competing for Mrs Kintner's bounty descend from across the Eastern states to scatter bait, cast explosives and risk lives in boats chartered from fishermen willing to carry as many as will pay. (Camouflage jackets, forage caps, facial hair and familiarity with explosives identify these representatives of the American Way as comprising Vietnam veterans.) Effectively replaced by the spectator's, no longer is the shark's vision employed. As Molly Haskell observes, Vaughn 'is not an isolated figure of sleazy corruption so much as the representative of a populace rife with hatred, callousness and ignorance from whom the three shark hunters flee, justifiably, with relief' (1975). (Earlier, on the beach before young Kintner's death, Brody – and the spectator – mistake bathers for the threat.) Although few critics dwell on the fact – perhaps because it contradicts subsequent received opinion about Spielberg – the *Orca*'s New Age frontiersmen parallel Twain's Huck Finn escaping West from a grotesque 'sivilization' he is more instinctively disgusted by than he realises:

> As in *The Sugarland Express*, Spielberg delights in showing us humanity – a kind of lynch mob perennially in the making – at its worst: a group of men grabbing a boat against orders and setting out for personal gain; the mother of a shark victim returning to the island in order to slap Roy Scheider's face. (Haskell 1975)

Politics: textual

The forward tracking shot that opens *Jaws* immediately places the spectator in the rapacious monster's position. The music leaves no doubt about the threat in the movement but also, in signposting thrills promised in the narrative image, encourages an anticipatory frisson. The primacy effect naturalises this movement so that later it is repeatable, despite the audience's full knowledge of what it entails. Like *Psycho*, the text presents no alternative to allegiance with a destructive force. Until the later sequences on Quint's boat (the perspective shifting entirely from the shark's to the human protagonists') little is known about the characters threatened – most are one-dimensional shark bait – even if human sympathy means Chrissie's (Susan Backlinie) screams at the start are surrogates for the spectator's, who is both victim and aggressor.

Presentation of human characters repeatedly stresses similarities with the Other. The joint passed during the pan across the beach party, the couple kissing, the young man smoking and drinking while feasting his eyes on Chrissie all immediately link consumption and oral gratification to the shark's instinct. The spectator's voracious gaze, observing Chrissie as she sheds her clothes, segues into the shark's as she swims, her body – unknown to her – displayed below the surface, objectified, while her consciousness remains elsewhere. As in Hitchcock's shower scene, scopophilia – the edit structure, starting with the boy's off-screen gaze, positions the look as *at* Chrissie, rather than with her – results in both punishment, as a misdemeanour, when the object of desire is destroyed, but also, troublingly, excitement in observing the spectacle of excessive consumption. Importantly, too, in view of countercultural connotations of hippiedom, Chrissie's independence, freedom and sexuality seem to be punished – hypocritical and excessive restoration of patriarchal Law as normative.

During the crowded beach scene as the camera advances underwater towards dangling legs, the shark theme again plays, whetting *the spectator's* appetite. The shark – Hooper (Richard Dreyfuss) unequivocally calls it an 'eating machine' – follows primal instinct. It has no consciousness, no expectation. Despite the seemingly 'subjective' optical point-of-view, the camera adopts a purely physical position. Sadistic anticipation is entirely the spectator's, as subject of the enunciation, in concert with the narration. The musical acceleration as the camera approaches the boy's inflatable raft indulges the spectator's pleasure in his imminent death; it in no way dramatises the swimmers' apprehension – they are oblivious to the threat – any more than it does the shark's intention.

The *perceptual facet* of focalisation, according to Shlomith Rimmon-Kenan (1983), conveys a character's sensory experience. Unlike at Chrissie's killing, this is now restricted to the shark's view until the attack becomes visible from the beach. The *psychological facet* focuses on knowledge and/or emotions, both of which a fish lacks. The *ideological facet* concerns how a character's perspective relates to the text's general system of values. This usefully accounts for how Brody's commonsense decency and professionalism ultimately prevail over greed and corruption but also – while reinforcing his white, masculine, middle-class conformity and authority – how they displace the intolerant, inhumane judgements the movie opens with (these being, according to some critics, its ideological position). *External focalisation* concentrates on certain characters rather than others but restricts knowledge to their actions and words; a good description of how the film treats shark victims.

These alignments and separations establish equivalences and oppositions between characters, and between them and the shark, further deconstructing any facile notion, implicit in mythical resonances, of Good against Evil. Many entail appetite and ingestion. Brody smokes and drinks, lighting up whenever pressure mounts. His and Ellen's (Lorraine Gary) painful awakening, in his first scene, to morning sunlight, implies one too many the night before. Rather than a repressive authoritarian – Vaughn's role – Brody's pleasures and vices render him, without imputation of corruption or hypocrisy, and despite his bourgeois domesticity, similar to the kids on the beach. (Besides, his conversation with Chrissie's pursuer confirms, these are starched-headband weekend hippies vacating from venerable colleges.) Brody removes an officer's cigarette in the harbourmaster's shed, full of flammable liquids – then smokes it himself. His picture book of horrors includes a shark champing on a canister; a set-up for the killer's fate, this also parallels both Brody and Vaughn's ubiquitous cigarettes.

Ellen brings whisky for Brody's tension and suggests they 'get drunk and fool around'; they drink, she leaning against him, implying a marriage based on compassion and companionship as well as attraction. Other principal characters are, like the shark, loners, including Vaughn, who we do not learn had family on the beach until after the third attack. The imagery of consumption continues. Following Mrs Kintner's confrontation, Brody stops eating. Hooper – whose first enquiry on the island is after a good restaurant – arrives with wine; he ravenously attacks the unwanted meal while Brody pours himself a tumbler full. Out on Hooper's boat, Brody, nervous, is still drinking; Hooper offers him a pretzel.

Oral emphases define Quint also. The town meeting juxtaposes Quint, chewing hardtack, baring his teeth, with a drawing of a shark swallowing a human. His $10,000 demand immediately establishes greed. Following this introduction are the mortuary scene, where Hooper makes clear what the shark does; the anarchic gold rush for the killer; a close-up of bloody shark jaws being opened by fishermen on the quay; the resultant media frenzy; Brody's elation; Hooper threatened with violence for doubting whether this is the wanted shark; Mrs Kintner's anger – then cutaways to Quint gliding into harbour, laughing toothily. When Brodie and Hooper hire him, sets of jaws bedeck his boathouse; clearly obsessed, he also probably profits from tourism. A previous sequence foregrounds a souvenir stall, displaying the dead tiger shark picture taken earlier and selling both jaws and US flags. The interests Vaughn protects are not merely eking an honest living but cynically exploiting holidaymakers' deaths. Flags on the ferry ship, and the 4th July setting, associate this sharkish behaviour with patriotism. Quint's demands – expenses, two cases of apricot brandy, lunch, and only then jokingly for further luxuries – again equate voraciousness with capitalism. The shelf above the stove where he boils more jaws – his hands covered with blood – is laden with multinational branded food products.

At sea, Quint opens a beer like a recreational fisherman and downs it in one. He chews on a toothpick, corresponding to Brody's cigarette. He, Brody and Hooper drink together in the galley at night. Quint performs his party piece, removing his front tooth, overtly recalling the shark's tooth left in Ben Gardner's (Craig Kingsbury) boat.

Quint's nemesis incorporates him when he slides into the shark's gaping maw. Brody, by contrast, despite tending towards Quint's alcoholism, spits out the sailor's hooch, separating himself from, rather than identifying with Quint's obsessions, machismo and affinity with sharks and water. It is the town (to which Quint also, although local, is an outsider) that chews up Brody and spits him out. Ellen, told she needs to have been born there to become an islander, craves integration into this community. Mrs Kintner posting a reward instead of working through his office alienates Brody, in dark clothing following Alex's death – attempting to fit in. Outcry follows his closing the beaches and hiring experts. Vaughn, speaking for the voters, overrules his ban. Mrs Kintner slaps and berates him.

The cylinder Brody thrusts into the shark's mouth res   e cheroot chewed by Clint Eastwood's Man with No Name, emphasising s   imilarities between this climax and a western showdown (Quirke 2002: 89   qually it is a cartoon capitalist's fat cigar (or a prosperous attorney's: the r   rk, it was well publicised, was called 'Bruce', after Spielberg's lawyer). But   recalls Quint, Vaughn (whose grey jacket with anchors associates him with   shark and its element) and Brody, who through its defeat rejects the mo   asculinity represented by these two patriarchs and, by implication, returns to   re self-confident and assertive following their Oedipal defeat.

A regular criticism is that *Jaws* is conservative. Robert Phillip Kolker puts all Spielberg's work 'at the lead' of a 'complex of ideologically conservative' 1970s and 1980s films, which became 'a clear and brilliant mirror of the dominant ideology' and marked the end of the Hollywood auteur (1988: xii). Peter Biskind (1975) argues that the townspeople's behaviour, at the point the film seems ready to ask, 'Who are the real sharks?', and that of Brody, who has remained morally spineless in his conformity, becomes naturalised when he confronts the shark. The shark thus ceases to be a metaphor. In symbolising nothing other than its terrifying concrete presence, rather than everything its absence projected into its space, it displaces political concerns. 'Spielberg's representation of political and social threats by a monster spawned in nature is itself an act that removes any responsibility for the threat, reducing the world to helpless victims in need of salvation', argues Kolker (1988; 288). This involves a curious rhetorical shuffle, however, that heaps political connotations onto a creature feature – justifiably (they are never ideologically innocent) – only then to reverse the equation and treat the film as if it intended to allegorise political arguments but copped out midway.

Such an approach, moreover, contrary to the greater ambivalence and complexity attributed to visual parallels above, relies on imputing highly selective viewing. This, paradoxically, (a) responds unconsciously to ideological reinforcement exercised figuratively while (b) noting only what is present and somehow forgetting – shedding – meanings that elicited profound affects shortly before and (c) differs greatly from the critic's experience of the text. While sometimes a shark is just a shark, once it has accrued additional significance it is unclear why this should evaporate. Here several factors – the film's provenance in the heart of the culture industries, its budget, the huge promotional spend and its success, not just at the box office but in permeating the culture – supposedly justify one of the less nuanced Frankfurt School positions, uniting audiences as masses in 'a state of anaesthesia' (Marcuse 1955: 104) and reading off one-dimensional meanings. *Jaws*, like *Close Encounters* and *E.T.* subsequently, is, as Neil Sinyard puts it, 'dedicated to restoring communal confidence. It prefers not to analyse the problem, but to annihilate it' (1987: 41). Nevertheless, it mobilises important social discourses and contradictions, and if these are unresolved in any convincingly realistic way it seems odd to single out this film for particular blame. Few mainstream releases purport to offer viable political solutions. The criticism is redundant.

On the importance of Brody's family, Kolker notes that:

> A major thematic of films during the 1950s and from the mid-1970s on is that middle-class comfort and security is a frail thing. Not only must it be fought for, but continually tested. Two things have to happen: the family unit needs to be secured against external threat and the male member of that unit needs not only to protect (or in some instances avenge) the family, but in the process must prove himself. (1988: 284)

Observe though that vulnerability in Brody's family is stressed as much as its strength. Marriage is tense before Brody leaves. Preoccupied, he ignores Ellen's offer to 'fool around'. When Hooper asks, 'Is your husband home? I'd really like to talk to him', she replies, 'So would I.' Brody, cradling his younger child, asks Ellen in the hospital whether she wants to take him home, to which she responds, 'Back to New York?' before stomping out. Like onshore politics, domesticity is no longer addressed once Brody sets sail. Although Ellen calls on the radio, Quint contrives to prevent her speaking to him. Brody, triumphant, is not seen returning home. Granted the family is a normative institution, the only other one in the film – and it is hardly obvious – is Vaughn's, as it appears the elderly couple he urges into the sea with young children are his parents and his offspring. While Brody's children are uncomfortably close to the third attack, the victims – sexually liberated Chrissie; Alex, with a lone parent; the anonymous oarsman; and Quint, who gleefully recalls 'celebrating my third wife's demise' – are none of them associated with the nuclear family. If this common facet of their characterisation is ideologically significant, that Brody avenges them confirms again his liberal status as authority figure (especially as conservative forces conspire to stop him asserting it).

Stephen E. Bowles believes the film excludes Benchley's emphasis on class-consciousness (1976: 209; see also Jameson 1979: 143) although he sees Brody's eventual triumph as 'affirmation of the middle-class' (1976: 211). Yet details such as Hooper wearing glasses and a tie, unlike Brody (who usually wears the former) during their nocturnal investigation, signify status differences grounded in expertise, explicitly class-related. ('Yes', Hooper answers when Brody, marvelling at his boat, asks 'Are you rich?') Social stratification is apparent in shots showing backpackers and cyclists as well as Rolls-Royces among the summer visitors, the tripartite model completed by the army surplus-clad fishermen desperate for cash. Quint inspects Hooper's 'city hands': 'You've been counting money all your life.' Hooper rejects such 'working-class hero crap.'

Quint's demise parallels the shark's. Certainly a recurrent monstrous 'Other' in American movies is the proletariat, from the visual coding of Frankenstein's monster to Freddy in *A Nightmare on Elm Street* (1984). As Robin Wood argues, 'the relationship between normality and the Monster ... has one privileged form: the figure of the doppelgänger, alter-ego, or double, a figure that has recurred constantly in Western culture ... Few horror films have totally unsympathetic monsters' (1979: 14–15). But there is nothing sympathetic about the shark. Either *Jaws* is an aberration; or doubling, as 'alter-ego' implies, involves identity as well as otherness. Quint and Vaughn equally are monsters.

Whether Quint's class, as opposed to egoism or outmoded machismo, is abjected is a matter of interpretation. *Jaws*, a product of troubled times, embodies contradictions among its discourses, visible in oppositions and image-structures. These, rather than unreflecting conservatism, produce ambiguity and thus appeal to various audiences. Contradictions undergo partial containment by the conventional narrative of individualism, masculine competition, the antagonist's defeat and the hero's victory in overcoming personal weakness. Nevertheless *Jaws* is arguably more critical of America than defence of a privileged smalltown community immediately suggests, not least because it does not reduce to overarching oppositions.

Vaughn, one must conclude, is sincere – he had his kids on the beach. Brody's weakness is in going along with something against his better instincts – he kept his children in a supposedly safer 'pond'. The result is moral complexity.

Ambiguity

'None of men's fantasies of evil can compare with the reality of *Jaws*' – radio commercial (quoted in Pye & Myles 1979: 234)

But what is the horror the film dramatises? Essential to its commercial success is that, as the breadth of continuing critical debate underlines, it can be almost anything: Watergate; government cover-up more generally; Vietnam, which, other than *The Green Berets* (1968), had received virtually no direct representation during the war (Torry 1993: 27); 'an emerging sense of panic in a complacent society' (McArthur & Lowndes 1976). Pye and Myles suggest dawning 1970s awareness of consumer vulnerability under the alluring promises of rapacious capitalism unchecked by inadequate authorities: 'an ill-considered drug, a dangerous car, an airplane with a fateful flaw, a killing industrial process' (1979: 234). And more:

> Cartoonists seized gratefully on the shark and sw   r as an infinite source of political metaphor: Ronald Reagan bared h   placidly swimming Gerald Ford; oil profiteers menaced the Cor   nergy Crisis threatened Government Ineffectiveness; the CIA att   ie of Liberty; and inflation loomed below a worried-looking figur   e Consumer. (1979: 237)

'The shark, all too obviously, can onl   young man's sexual passion, a greatly enlarged, marauding penis. Later on in the film, a dead shark, slit open, exudes a white, sperm-like fluid' (Biskind 1975: 1). Fine, except the movie was also 'really important' for feminists as 'word went round that *Jaws* was a "vagina dentata" movie symbolising the psychological violence of the devouring vagina and the threatened male' (Pollock 1976: 41). The shark condensed phallic power appropriated by the women's movement *and* castration fears this perceived threat unconsciously posed to patriarchy (Frentz & Rushing 1993: 79). Certainly the shark attacks Quint's boat at night, 'when the three men are drunk and unguarded, that is, when their conscious, rational faculties have been suspended' (Biskind 1975:1). Importantly, though, as Biskind suggests, the fact that sharks are real and dangerous and the implied horrors become concrete – as Quint indeed suffers 'castration' and death – naturalises those mythic dangers. Brody's eventual triumph – the hero always slays the 'unconquerable' dragon as part of his initiation (Kahn 1976) – destroys the symbol of those fears as a ritual scapegoating, but the absence of the shark for the greater part of the movie suggests they will always exceed it. The exorcism is merely formal. By externalising social conflicts onto the shark, they can be staged, thereby articulating discourses brought to the cinema by spectators, and ideological closure achieved in an ending 'which denies any possibility of concerted social action' (Rubey 1976: 20). This would be more of a problem if it were clear what issue precisely the film closes off ideologically. The ambiguity, attractive to multiple audiences, exceeds any one meaning while offering complexity to audiences seeking more than thrills.

Ambiguity extends to the minutiae of narration within the film's apparently conventional style. In the sound mix the ferry, gulls and breaking waves half-bury dialogue. This enhances involvement as the spectator has to pay attention to follow events. But missed details increase uncertainty. Michel Chion contrasts sound with what he calls cinematographic 'chiaroscuro'. The camera isolates objects, loses them in shadows, off-screen, in overexposure, motion blur or soft focus, and then foregrounds them instantly with clarity, but 'we must always hear every word, from one end to the other, in order that no word be lost, that each word be understood one after the other' (1992: 104). Spielberg, however, like Welles, employs overlapping dialogue that is not only more tense and naturalistic but also encourages the spectator to listen harder, although the gist remains clear. *Jaws* pushes uncertainty further by controlling the sound-image relationship beyond the sound mix. Which viewer listens to the perfectly audible businessperson who, in over-the-shoulder shots, almost blocks out Brody anxiously and impatiently attempting to observe everyone in the water?

The threat remains faceless for much of the movie. Spielberg's Great White, like Melville's whale, is a blank sheet (blank screen, rather) for viewers to project meanings onto: 'a symbolic vehicle ... essentially polysemous [in] function' (Jameson 1979: 142). Sharks, unlike most monsters, cannot be anthropomorphised (Quirke 2002: 6). Hence, as already suggested, this is not merely the counterpart of human attributes but appears radically Other, an excessive, engulfing force that nevertheless, juxtaposed with human affairs, seems causally connected by virtue of the need for mastery through explanation. *Jaws'* look, its setting and most of its characters, are prosperous, perfect, enhancing the sense of some repressed malaise. Long before *Blue Velvet* (1986) and *Twin Peaks* (1990–1991), huge lighting rigs flattened the pastel clapboard buildings, white picket fences and blue sky of Amity into picture-book blocks of colour (Cribben 1975). That the early morning sun is overhead when Brody drives to work ('My, you're up awful early', the station clerk comments in a room full of horizontal shadows) seems less a continuity error than a decision to eliminate shadows, to present middle-class life as 'pastiche or simulacrum – a postmodern hyper-reality which contrasts with the darkness to come' (Hauke 2001: 157) – and with the firelight shadows and surrounding darkness the night before. In the postmodern culture of irony, 'Any image of life and leisure presented without comment has come, sarcastically to signify its exact opposite. But at the time of *Jaws* it was a fresh intuition.' (Quirke 2002: 23) Of course the shark attacks *are* the comment, and the difficulty is what they mean(t).

The surface of the sea metaphorically links to the bland shops, houses and people and eventually to the movie screen when the shark bursts through. It updates a figure stated by Ahab in *Moby-Dick*:

> All visible objects, man, are but as pasteboard masks. But in each event – in the living act, the undoubted deed – there, some unknown but still reasoning thing puts forth the mouldings of its features from behind the unreasoning mask. If man will strike, strike through the mask! How can the prisoner reach outside except by thrusting through the wall? To me, the white whale is that wall, shoved near to me. (Melville 1972: 262)

Spielberg uses narrative delay and cinematic form to create both suspense and shock, so that the shark's eventual appearance, when it breaches the surface, as if into the auditorium, or unexpectedly the edge of the frame when it attacks Hooper in his supposedly protective cage, becomes an attack on the spectator, displacing illusory mastery. As Rubey noted, no one in the audience screams when Chrissie is killed, despite the horror represented, but they did when the shark's head and jaws rose out of the water into human space (1976: 23).

Genre

Extremely high awareness of the title meant *Jaws* did not require major stars. Its director also was little known. The narrative image would therefore seem to come down to generic qualities – both in terms of what the film appeared to offer in advance and what satisfactions prompted audiences to recommend it. However, the genre remains unclear, an overlying ambiguity that resonates through the narrative ambiguities. Yet genre, empirical research now recognises, works negatively in cinema-going choices (Altman 1999: 113). Generic indeterminacy therefore avoided alienating potential viewers. Because *Jaws* shares attributes of several genres, it attracts several different audiences: Steve Neale quotes a 1927 industry guide that recommends reaching the widest audience by identifying elements within films to market to different groups (2000: 238). Hybridity also offers a potentially wider tonal range, possibly enriching the permutations of emotional, visceral or intellectual impact for any individual viewer – as the hugely varying range of critical interpretations seems to confirm – while ensuring different but compatible satisfactions, and hence a successful excursion, for couples or groups. Moreover, while drawing on familiar conventions to maximise intelligibility, *Jaws* seemed to evade easy classification, and the uncertainties maximise the plot's unpredictability within classical narrative parameters. Thus, in line with how major releases have always been promoted (Altman 1999), it would have appeared original and unique – part of its event status – and also to be supra-generic, a pure movie experience, 'the epitome of "cinema"', as Stephen Heath calls it (1976: 25).

Self-reflexivity: Jaws as a Spielberg movie

Part of the difficulty of pinning down the genre is that, as Richard Combs writes of *Close Encounters*, all cinema is in there (1988a: 29). At the time of *Jaws*, critics expected European films generally to contain 'hidden' and double meanings, whether allegorical or just self-consciously clever. Hollywood movies narrated transparently, albeit sometimes stylishly. *Jaws* makes audiences look more carefully and rewards that attention with a commensurately intense experience. It respects its audience as its equal, delighting them with deceit, as when the shark fin turns out to be a replica guided by two small boys; but note how in this scene the film does not cheat, as the *Jaws* theme remains silent except when the threatening shark is present.

According to Quirke, the indeterminable sounds at the start 'reflect us. Sea-babble to accompany audience babble' (2002: 9). They aurally inscribe the notion of the screen as a mirror, the surface in which both the ideal-ego and the abjected Other appear. The movie's ingestion imagery links with the dual trajectory of spectatorship. Eating, incorporation into the body from outside, relates to the voracious, possessive desire of voyeurism; being eaten, an external threat to bodily integrity. The first figures mastery, the second fear of castration. The screen in the movie experience substitutes for the body as barrier between self and other. The Imaginary, involvement in the film, equates to desire to heal the rift; the Symbolic recalls threatened violation (castration – of which Chrissie's death is a warning, the boy's death confirmation, the man's death reiteration and Quint's death the realisation). The screen is both security and source of the anxiety, a penetrable barrier like the sea's surface. The process of suture, alternating involvement in and separation from the diegesis and narrative, and possibly between comprehension and conscious reflection and interpretation, seeks and ensures mastery through labile and shifting identifications rather than total investment.

The opening credit, 'Directed by Steven Spielberg', superimposes over the young man just as the pan over the beach party stops. He is looking off-screen, the implied inscribed director immediately becoming a spectator. Obscured dialogue renders him and Chrissie other, rather than assisting identification, thereby increasing a sense of voyeurism inherent in the sexual implication as she removes her clothes and he pursues her. The sun behind Chrissie shines into camera as she emerges from underwater in close-up. A shark's point-of-view shot of her swimming features the moon through the surface, as if behind the screen, part of a series of above/below alternations.

A shot of the blank eventless sea after her violent death dissolves to a graphic match to the sunny morning, the back of Brody's head in silhouette filling a third of the screen like a spectator in a row in front, blocking our view, both a relay for and an obstacle to our look. (This composition recurs several times: Brody trying to observe from the beach; a young artist who spots the shark moving into the pond.) A cutaway to Ellen on the bed reveals he is looking out the bedroom window, an inscribed frame. In this juxtaposition of horror and normality, the spectator's voyeurism links both.

Extremely economical narration reveals in apparently incidental dialogue that the Brodys moved from New York in the fall and it is now summer. In the kitchen Brody picks up the wrong phone – clearly not used to having two lines, or receiving work calls at home. 'I haven't fixed them yet', he says, referring to the children's swings, reiterating that they are newcomers, and as he is answering the phone to learn of a washed-up body (we infer), domesticity and patriarchal/parental responsibility, as Ellen deals with their son's bleeding hand, again juxtaposes with horror, this time spatially rather than temporally. The spectator, incorporating all this information, knows more than the characters, yet reciprocally becomes swallowed into their drama.

Brody is in focus in close-up, with his wife and child in the background in soft focus. There are nevertheless two compositional points of interest, reinforced by overlapping dialogue and equal status in the sound mix. The effect is edgy and disorienting. Where should attention focus? The speed and amount of narrative information distract from the fact that this is an unusually long (32 seconds) static shot and demands effort – freely given – to follow its significance. As Warren Buckland explains, the son asks to go swimming:

> The spectator can put together both pieces of information in the shot, and realise that it is not a good idea for Michael to go swimming, especially with a blood-stained hand in shark-infested waters. But neither Brody nor Ellen can put together the two separate pieces of information. (2003a)

A later extended shot works expressionistically, although its comment on the character and his situation is purely between the narration and the spectator, not focalised through Brody's consciousness. Brody requisitions a ferry (because he is scared of smaller boats) to warn boy scouts practising for a mile swim: the background changes disorientingly behind the fixed foreground as Vaughn, having driven on board, changes the contours of Brody's reality by persuading him, against his better instincts, to keep the beaches open. Spielberg subsequently uses deep focus shots, lasting one minute ten seconds and three minutes 37 seconds respectively. These employ Wellesian blocking of characters (Brody, Hooper and Vaughn), low angles and very tight framing, yet seem effortless, every fluid character and camera movement dramatically motivated, despite the freedom to place the camera anywhere in the wide open space of a cliff top.

These homages and experiments with Bazinian realism, in a movie going heavily over budget, belie accusations that it is a streamlined money-making machine. They complicate the prevalent view that *Jaws* (whatever the knock-on effects of its marketing and commercial success) ended a creative, modernist period of formally interesting

Jaws – following the initial horror an inscribed spectator obstructs the audience's searching gaze

Hollywood filmmaking. Like Hitchcock, Spielberg synthesised with the low-cultural projects available to him high-cultural artistry and awareness of tradition (the musical score, for example, alludes to Stravinsky and Holst as well as 1930s swashbucklers), without judgement, compromise or condescension. Commercial imperatives may very well have tended towards *Star Wars* (and later *Raiders of the Lost Ark*) if *Jaws* had never been made. The mistake was to assume that art cinema, sometimes vacuous and boring, is more significant or valuable because it is not palatable to mass audiences, and that blockbusters, because commercially motivated (as if artists do not have to make a living) cannot accommodate interesting technique or intelligent ideas.

Equally accomplished is the editing, combined with carefully storyboarded camerawork, even if what critics chose to recall was background information that Fields and Spielberg tweaked one sequence to make it scarier following a preview. As with negative reactions to *E.T.*, it seems resentment at the scale of publicity often rationalised uncomfortably intense responses, dismissed as manipulation in an attempt to reassert mastery, at the expense of considering what was actually on-screen. Before the attack on Alex Kintner, the camera pans left with a fat woman, its restlessness enacting Brody's anxious point-of-view, while telephoto compression encourages identification with his position, distanced and helpless. Significantly, empathy is not encouraged with the swimmers (who lack Brody's, and our, knowledge), the focalisation making whatever happens Brody's responsibility.

Alongside Brody's concern, however, the spectator, one step removed in the relay of the look, can objectify these optically distanced holidaymakers. The woman's ampleness jokingly makes her a tasty morsel for an underwater predator: an example of voyeurism's sadistic identification with the apparatus, which at this point exists only (as audiences know before entering the cinema) to present the spectacle of someone's gruesome death. A man with a black dog appears and a young couple enter the sea in the background. Introducing them now solicits recognition later in the scene, and the primacy effect suggests they are dramatically significant. Immediately the camera pans right with Alex, its uneasy movements pausing while he asks his mother if he can return to the water; the single shot continues by panning right again with Alex to rest on Brody in profile. He is in the right of the shot looking left, but the composition and soundtrack emphasise a conversation in the background. Brody's fear of water keeps him helplessly separated from the action in the same way as James Stewart's character in *Rear Window*, underlining his surrogacy for the viewer in the audience and the metaphor of the sea as a screen-like barrier: '*Jaws* is reflexive with its play on the unseen and unforeseeable', argues Heath (1981: 204).

Brody's droopy eyelids suggest fatigue at having to concentrate on so many seemingly inconsequential details. The spectator, too, positioned to be half-aware of Brody's presence, half-aware of background details, is distracted by the unremitting normality of it all but nevertheless made voyeuristically alert by the eavesdropping on surrounding interactions. A cut to Brody's optical point-of-view introduces shots of the man throwing a stick for his dog, the young couple gambolling, Alex on his air mattress, the dog swimming with the stick, a black object gliding in from left of frame (no, it's just the head of the dog owner, now swimming), the woman in the water, Alex. Which of them will the shark attack? More shots of the man with the dog on the beach, temporal ellipses sealed over by busy seaside ambient sound. Interspersed are reverse-shots of Brody, the cuts seemingly hidden by a 'wipe' effect of foreground characters passing in front of camera. The result is both documentary realism and flaunting of technique, while increasing tension by blocking the spectator's view and, implicitly, Brody's. Intensity and urgency increase as the camera moves in, by half-concealed jump cuts (a technique adapted from Eisenstein), to closer proximity, contrasted with the bland ordinariness of the situation and lack of anything alarming on the sound-track. Separation occurs between the enunciation and enounced as Brody's edginess is conveyed – sensed and provisionally shared by the spectator – while the narration appears to know either more or less than Brody. Then he's proved right! A black snout breaks the surface behind the woman floating on her back, oblivious. Cut away to Brody sitting up anxiously. It's just a swimmer's black bathing cap. Brody relaxes slightly, still clearly agitated, looks away. One of the locals squats in front of him with some tediously inconsequential problem, almost buried in the sound mix, occupying fifty per cent of the screen and blocking Brody's view, then ours in the reverse-shot. A scream. Brody bolts upright, fixated. A girl rises, squealing, out of the water, like Chrissie at the start ... on her boyfriend's shoulders.

Brody is distant, detached, as others, including Ellen, attempt to make conversation, while droves of children rush into the water towards Alex on his raft. Here, Kolker, notes, 'whatever reactions he shows will be a signal to the viewer that something terrible (and wonderful) is happening' (1988: 274). In fact – crucially, though it contradicts Kolker's incessant charge against Spielberg of manipulation – the viewer sees the shark attack *before* Brody. His reaction serves as punctuation, while the momentary delay in his response, in terms of focalisation, underlines his impotence and subsequent guilt.

During a rapid montage of children splashing and playing, the cuts come too quickly to register everything consciously. A stick floating on the water is a metonym learnt from the masters of montage: the ship's doctor's glasses hanging from the rigging after the mutiny in *Battleship Potemkin* and Lean's homage to Eisenstein, the goggles on a branch after the motorcycle accident that starts *Lawrence of Arabia*. Alerted to the possibility something is wrong, the spectator hears the *Jaws* theme over an underwater tracking shot of dangling legs. Above the surface, an explosion of water as the raft goes over precedes a geyser of blood; below, bubbles and a red cloud as the boy descends. The famous 'trombone shot' modelled from *Vertigo* conveys Brody's dizzying shock and provides a visual correlative and confirmation for the spectator's.

Jaws may not share the sensibility of a film such as, say, *Death in Venice* (1971) that is, the kind of serious, profound cinema it is frequently accused of displacing. But nor is it dumb, mechanical or purely functional.

CHAPTER FIVE

1941: war on Hollywood

Reception

Jaws and *Close Encounters of the Third Kind*, while both exemplify the modern blockbuster, demonstrated very different marketing. In contrast to high-profile merchandising strategies of *Jaws*, the release that established the pattern for New Hollywood, *Close Encounters'* narrative image, in accordance with its plot, withheld information. In what Columbia announced as its 'most ambitious advertising campaign' ever, 27 newspapers across the US featured two-page 'introductory' notices six months before a staggered release. The campaign mounted slowly and press releases stressed secrecy shrouding the production. Newspapers carried daily countdown advertisements before each opening, while theatres showed 'a long, sophisticated and wholly unrevealing trailer' (Pym 1978: 99). Restricted release calculatedly gambled on reports from other cities; curiosity stimulated by such publicity, together with the enigmatic title, created widespread desire to experience the phenomenon.

As *Close Encounters* proceeded to match *Jaws*, Spielberg's success became commonly attributed to hype. However, promotion and publicity alone cannot explain why certain films succeed over others. Indeed, American audiences rejected *1941* 'despite saturation ads' (Pirie 1981: 60) and Spielberg's increasing fame. In fact, it would never have existed if Spielberg's involvement had not seduced Universal and Columbia into believing the package almost failsafe. Even so, neither had confidence to finance it solely.

Critics also widely – although not universally – reviled *1941*, for failure as comedy and for the failure's epic scale. This represents the turning point in Spielberg's reputation, for it was as a Spielberg movie they judged it. Authorship's centrality in contemporary film culture becomes apparent. Without Spielberg, *1941*, if financed at all, would not have commanded such a budget. Yet without Spielberg it would not have caused such disappointment or rancour. For some it provided opportunities to castigate Spielberg's previous success, identified with escalated budgets and extended schedules. Such criticism may have affected subsequent determination to limit spending on *Raiders of the Lost Ark* – the movie that consolidated his image as an 'escapist', 'children's' filmmaker but also, within the industry, restored his reputation for economy and efficiency.

Some critics read *1941*'s black farce as satirising Hollywood itself, 'American militarism, in a similar vein to the helicopter attack scene in *Apocalypse Now* [1979]' (also scripted by John Milius), and the idealised American family, whose perfect house is systematically wrecked before sliding over a cliff when Pa hammers a Christmas wreath to the door (Buscombe 1980). That climax surely bears comparison with the cliff-house explosion in Antonioni's calculatedly countercultural *Zabriskie Point* (1970). *1941*'s reception, however, involved another dimension. The $26.5 million budget, then 'astronomically high' (McGillivray in Pirie 1981: 313), attracted widespread condemnation for expenditure on sets wasted in an orgy of on-screen destruction. This response, Ed Buscombe argues, was irrational. Notwithstanding how rarely movie sets become old people's homes after use, applying puritanical morality to one product's costs as opposed to the entire system makes little sense in a capitalist industry: 'The budget, after all, is dictated by what the people making the film think they need to invest in order to maximise their return. If they spend too much, that's a bad commercial decision, not a sin.' (1980)

In this respect, *1941* emblematised an industry seen as floundering. On one hand, the imperative to appeal to a US movie-going population of whom 49 per cent were aged 12 to 20 (Laskos in Pirie 1981: 14) was interpreted as dumbing-down, and betrayal of the *auteur* principle New Hollywood appeared to valorise. In fact crass commercialism was as much a response to as the cause of declining older audiences. Conversely, that same *auteur* approach encouraged indulgent filmmaking beset by problems of nightmarish proportions, such as *Apocalypse Now* (budget: $12 million, final cost: $31 million) and the film that bankrupted United Artists, *Heaven's Gate* (1980; $7.5 million to $36 million). Meanwhile, *Kramer versus Kramer* became 1979's surprise hit: an unassuming project with little predictable appeal to the core audience, a reminder that nothing in the industry was certain. Given that directors' average age was the lowest in fifty years (Thomson in Pirie 1981: 125), no doubt resentment of Spielberg's 'Movie Brat' ascendancy tempered responses. He was ripe for comeuppance.

Spielberg mounted an offensive, assuring *Saturday Review* that *1941* would nudge into the black following television, video, cable and reissue agreements: 'Still, the critics bury their heads in the sand and say, "How could this film do $50–$60 million when I gave it the worst review I've ever written?" Believe me, Hollywood is not being crippled by $30 million movies.' Spielberg, in the same interview, insisted proven filmmakers 'earned the right to spend someone else's money' if they intended to make money (June 1981; quoted in John Baxter 1996: 198). Fourteen years later, he argued on TV that 'What did it cost?' is irrelevant. 'Is it worth seven dollars [admission price]?' is what matters (Baxter 1996: 198).

In one sense, coming at Buscombe's answer from a different direction, Spielberg was right. *1941*, which earned respectable revenues in Europe and Japan, failed only *comparatively*, judged against Spielberg's previous hits. Furthermore, as Buscombe opined, 'maybe critics are entitled to say that if it isn't as funny as *Jaws* was thrilling, then it's a flop' (Buscombe 1980). Spielberg's proclamation was, nevertheless, slightly disingenuous. One reason *1941* commanded its budget and mustered such an array of stars was the practice of auctioning anticipated blockbusters, requiring exhibitors to 'blind bid' before production finishes. In addition, exhibitors often have to guarantee minimum runs or advances against expected rentals. For screening the film, successful bidders keep only ten per cent of gross takings (after a negotiated allowance for expenses), this portion increasing during the run. However, agreements limit this 'fixed minimum floor' such that exhibitors may eventually cover losses on a flop they had no opportunity to preview (Franklin in Pirie 1981: 95). Thus *1941*'s American box office disappointment did not cost its makers, who broke even, as exhibitors honoured their contracts. No one's heart should bleed for the exhibitors. Large chains seek to monopolise hits. They, rather than independent theatres, wager for successful bids. Yet the affront to powerful leisure organisations of forcibly subsidising profligacy hardly enhanced Spielberg's trade reputation.

A difficulty in discussing *1941* is that common sense dictates examining it as comedy. Yet humour is highly subjective. Screenwriting tutor Robert McKee argues: 'Comedy is pure: if the audience laughs, it works; if it doesn't laugh, it doesn't work. End of discussion. That's why critics hate comedy; there's nothing to say' (1998: 359). While sophisticated theories describe comedy both formally and functionally, applying these to an experience widely considered unsatisfactory on both counts seems futile. Analysis does not necessarily kill its object stone dead (that presumption would deny serious consideration of popular culture). However, without specific reasons, it would be perverse to dissect something that never worked in the first place.

Nevertheless, *1941* requires consideration for the sake of completeness – not least as a resumé of Spielberg's previous output and dress rehearsal for much to come. I shall subordinate conclusive evaluation in exploring two aspects, intertextuality and carnivalesque, as illustrations of approaches that illuminate his other work.

Failed comedy

One problem with *1941* is that Universal's backing intended to continue a string of teenage successes. These included *Animal House* and features involving comedians Cheech and Chong, Steve Martin and the *Saturday Night Live* (1975–date) cast, several of whom – notably Dan Aykroyd, John Belushi and Tim Matheson – starred in Spielberg's film. However, that humour, both anarchic and childish, embodied an anti-authoritarian and hedonistic mood fuelled by post-1960s drug culture and rising disillusionment following Vietnam and Watergate. What possible attraction was there for youngsters in satirising events from 1941?

Satire exposes and mocks folly from a superior position. *1941* certainly ridicules mindless acceptance of authority. Aykroyd's tank commander, whose gung-ho speeches suggest brainwashing, is unstoppable when spouting operational drills and, after a head injury, turns into Hitchcock's machine-like Memory Man from *The 39 Steps* (1935). Ned Beatty's solid citizen destroys by stages the home that symbolises everything he considers his duty to defend. The tank crew demands leadership from a zoot-suiter they were brawling with earlier, simply because he has donned a military tunic. If, in reality, shock and paranoia followed Pearl Harbor, eliciting the events *1941* burlesques, that was because of the innocence of a culture that had never experienced defeat or had certainties challenged. For Spielberg, however, 1941 meant *Dumbo*, *Helzapoppin'*, *Citizen Kane* and the year *Casablanca* is set, while *Fantasia* and *Pinocchio* (both 1940) were still on release. It ended an era culminating with two movies by Victor Fleming, one of Spielberg's most revered directors: *Gone With the Wind* and *The Wizard of Oz* (1939). He viewed affectionately and nostalgically the era the script essentially derides.

That perhaps explains *1941*'s unevenness. Sporadic hilarity intersperses with a different overall tone. In particular, Belushi's Wild Bill Kelso is too big and gratuitously unmotivated for such close-up attention, especially against other players' understated acting. These contrasts suggest an uncontrolled performance in an out-of-control movie in an uncontrollable industry. Belushi's frat-house slobbishness and adolescent prurience, repeatedly fetishising women's garter belts, detract from – and distance the movie from – the period lovingly recreated. The conception, craft and technology predicated on the budget – though Spielberg employed only effects available in 1941 – again overwhelm both the subject matter and any recreation of 1940s style. The script is highly variable, as are gags added during shooting. A brilliant aside, 'We've got to figure out a way of making these things smaller', subtitled as a Japanese submariner struggles to cram a cabinet radio through a hatch, is juxtaposed with the tired contrivance of naming a character Hollis Wood only because to Japanese sailors it will sound like 'Hollywood'. The radio gag exploits disparity between the casual comment and the ruthless organisation by which Japanese businesses supposedly achieve dominance, and the absurdity of a multinational industry beginning on such an unlikely premise. The cliff house joke works similarly because the tiny act of nailing a wreath has disproportionate consequences; because Pa misses what everyone else, within and outside the diegesis, can clearly see; and because the causality both surprises – the house falls, not, as expected, the door – yet also corresponds, through its logical plausibility, to immutable physical laws. In other words, comedy requires shared understanding that it both challenges and confirms. Radical or conservative, it fosters audience unity. *1941* is indiscriminate and arbitrary, proffering no subject position for the spectator other than largely un-amused detachment.

Relentless pace – almost certainly exacerbated by drastic trimming after previews – obscures too much action, especially set-ups and slow burns of meticulously constructed gags appreciable only on repeat viewings the movie does not merit. Elaborate jokes – a tank charging through a paint factory, emerging rainbow-hued, before crashing into a turpentine factory and being restored to its former camouflage – are lost if the viewer blinks. Conversely, the principle that it is invariably funnier to ride through trashcans when it would be easier to ride around them demonstrates neither wit nor shared recognition.

Modes of intertextuality

Gerard Genette (1997) refines intertextuality with a further term, 'transtextuality', glossed by Graham Allen as 'intertextuality from the viewpoint of structural poetics' (2000: 98) – the theory of reading that investigates, rather than particular works, systems within which texts are constructed, with or without readers' or writers' awareness.

Genette proposes five variants. 'Intertextuality', redefined, is narrowed down to 'co-presence of two texts': quotation, allusion or plagiarism (Stam & Flitterman-Lewis 1992: 206). 'Quotation' in *1941* presents parts of *Dumbo*, screened within the diegesis. 'Allusion' is less direct evocation, 'hopefully as an expressive means of commenting on the fictional world of the alluding film' (ibid.). *1941*'s radio dance concert, interrupted by the riot occasioned by tensions arising from invasion fears, alludes to a device used to make Welles' radio piece *War of the Worlds* realistic. This caused panic in New Jersey, subsequently explained as resulting from anxieties caused by U-boat sightings. Spielberg's allusion, partly homage, partly a shortcut to establish the diegesis, is confirmed by the jitterbug prize being an RKO contract (the studio that signed Welles afterwards, enabling *Citizen Kane*); by Japanese sailors being in a U-boat with a Nazi; and by Santa Monica funfair, substituting for Atlantic City. Further allusions include *It's a Mad Mad Mad Mad World* (1963), referenced by 'Mad Man' Maddox's nickname, another slapstick all-star epic with which *1941* shares many qualities; *Star Wars*, as planes dogfight down Hollywood Boulevard, alluding to a sequence itself alluding to Second World War movies; *Battleship Potemkin*, evoked by Maddox's cracked glasses – though only the number of extras justifies comparison with Eisenstein's masterpiece; and *The Birds*, when Kelso transforms a gas station into a fireball, though so rapidly, contrasted with Hitchcock's carefully mounted suspense, that these allusions mostly are not merely gratuitous but reminders of *1941*'s ineptitude.

Robert Stam and Sandy Flitterman-Lewis (1992: 207) formulate other, sometimes overlapping, categories. 'Mendacious intertextuality' refers to 'pseudo-intertextual' references – in *1941* a broadcast mentioning 'war nerves', or John Williams' pastiche of Benny Goodman numbers. 'Auto-citation', a Spielberg characteristic greeted with some critical disapproval, includes the *Jaws* parody that opens *1941* and the gas station scene, which reruns elements of *Duel*. Both utilise 'celebrity intertextuality', with actors from the earlier movies in similar roles. More generally, this includes any evocation of genre or cultural milieu by a star presence, and allusions circuited through them to specific texts: Aykroyd and Belushi embody *Saturday Night Live* attitudes; Slim Pickens, listing the contents of his pockets, alludes to *Dr Strangelove*, a satire on militarist insanity; Robert Stack imbues Stilwell with the virtues of Elliot Ness, who he played in TV's *The Untouchables* (between 1959–62); Sam Fuller's cameo alludes to serious and critically praised *auteur* war movies he directed; motivation for casting the august Toshiro Mifune remains anybody's guess except that he was in *Hell in the Pacific* (1968). 'Intratextuality', when 'films refer to themselves through mirroring, microcosmic, and mise-en-abyme structures', is exemplified by formal similarity between the rolling drum in the dance, that starts a domino run of folded chairs, precipitating the riot onto the street, and the Ferris wheel trundling down the pier, finale of the extended cause-and-effect train. This contains an amusing variation on Hitchcock's personal cameos. A Spielberg look-alike, comedian Eddie Deezen, ends this epic Hollywood disaster in the sea, enthusing, 'Boy, that was fun. Can we do it again?' (a joke about Spielberg's *Jaws* experience?); he also has a ventriloquist's dummy, modelled on Spielberg/Deezen, that – like its macabre *Dead of Night* (1945) counterpart – knows more than its operator. The Japanese attack on what they think is Hollywood – a fairground described as an 'industrial structure' – is wryly intratextual, especially as they believe it will demoralise America; so, too, when a submariner looks up beatifically, accompanied by Williams' heavenly choir, at Susan Backlinnie, naked on the periscope, and gasps: 'Horrywood!'

Genette's next class of transtextuality, 'paratextuality', includes 'accessory messages and commentaries which come to surround the text and which at times become virtually indistinguishable from it' (Stam & Flitterman-Lewis 1992: 207). It further subdivides (Allen 2000: 103–6). 'Peritext' comprises attachments such as classification cards, distributors' cards, and title and credit sequences, including music that establishes genre or mood, where these are separate from narration. 'Epitext' typically includes promotion and publicity: posters and trailers; criticism, interviews and behind-the-scenes reports, all, in turn, influenced by press releases; and commissioned *Making of...* documentaries. (Epitext blurs into peritext when DVDs repackage such elements together). *1941*'s paratextuality includes budget information and Spielberg's virtual disowning of the movie, which undoubtedly affect responses; the longer, possibly more coherent version, toned down after previews deemed it 'too loud'; the 1996 'restored' laserdisc; and – intriguingly from the perspective of authorship, as detecting an *auteur* does not necessarily imply quality – how subsequent releases are easily 'read in' ('pre-auto-citation'?): Donna's hand raised to her hat in awe of the bomber (*E.T.*, *Jurassic Park*); the dance hall fight (restaged in *Indiana Jones and the Temple of Doom* (1984) and in *The Color Purple*'s juke-joint); the pointless food fight (*Hook* (1991)); the sinister Nazi whose silhouette dominates the screen (*Raiders of the Lost Ark*, *Indiana Jones and the Last Crusade* (1989) and *Schindler's List*; the dinosaur model looming from darkness (*Jurassic Park* and *The Lost World: Jurassic Park* (1997)); Kelso's respectful salute to the Japanese (*Empire of the Sun* (1987)); a submerged Ferris wheel (*A.I.*); fascination with old aircraft (the Indiana Jones films, *Empire of the Sun*, *Always*, *Saving Private Ryan* and, previously, *Close Encounters of the Third Kind*) and with World War Two generally; and stylistic tropes and themes such as searchlights shining into camera, inscribed spectatorship, self-reflexivity, lost characters and faulty vision hinted by Maddox's broken lens. Genette furthermore separates paratexts into 'autographic', author-originated, closely related to the discredited intentional fallacy, and 'allographic', externally imposed (Allen 2000: 106–7). Autographic features include flashbacks to characters screaming in *1941*'s end credits. Different aspect ratios in video or DVD versions, and commercial breaks during broadcasts, are allographic. Paratextuality, then, explores textual boundaries, with the author-function one means of determination.

Genette's third type of transtextuality, 'metatextuality', concerns 'the critical relation between one text and another, whether the commented text is explicitly cited or only slightly evoked' (Stam & Flitterman-Lewis 1992: 208). Recorded facts concerning the events that inspired *1941* occupy this underdeveloped category – although, crucially, not the events themselves, which although they precede textuality are nevertheless available to historians only through paratexts and competing accounts. Aykroyd's character quietly mocks John Wayne and Jimmy Stewart roles, without explicitly declaring as much; and official records, news accounts and sociohistorical explanations – of 'the Great Los Angeles Air Raid', responses to the Santa Barbara submarine attack, the zoot-suit riots and the *War of the Worlds* incident – are implicitly rejected by blaming collective madness.

'Architextuality', Genette links to 'reader's expectations, and thus their reception of a work' as established specifically by generic indicators such as titles (quoted in Allen 2000: 102). A major Hollywood movie inevitably creates anticipation of entertainment and involvement. *1941*'s stark, minimalist title, sombre white on black, followed by a serious, detailed historical prologue crawling up the screen to a slow military march, cedes to a grainy, desaturated look with docudrama-style subtitles indicating location and precise time and date. While these contradict the colourful, zany cartoon posters that advertised the movie, omission of all reference to Spielberg and the cast quickly establishes an enigma and sets the tone for a war movie rather than comedy – and thus heightens the opening gag. As well as aligning *1941* to war movies and comedies, involving generic expectations it unsatisfactorily flouts, architextuality also embraces the *auteurist* category 'Spielberg movies', the industrial/critical 'Movie Brat movies' and the scandalous 'wasteful movies': frameworks that overdetermine judgement.

'Hypertextuality', Genette's final category, describes how a 'hypertext' 'transforms, modifies, elaborates or extends' an existing 'hypotext' (Stam & Flitterman-Lewis 1992: 209), equivalent to what theorists more commonly call the 'inter-text'. It differs from metatextuality in not implying criticism (as some avant-garde work does, for example, in relation to mainstream cinema). Spielbergian examples include *Always*, reworking its hypotext, *A Guy Named Joe* (1943). *The Color Purple* and *Empire of the Sun* are hypertexts of novels, and *Schindler's List* and *Amistad* of non-fiction sources. *The Lost World: Jurassic Park* as a sequel is hypertext to its predecessor. The Indiana Jones series transpose entire genres and cycles, knowledge of which heightens enjoyment. Quotation and allusion, classified under intertextuality, function hypertextually, as do parody and pastiche. Thus recognising *Peter Pan* as hypotext(s) affects meaning in *E.T.* and *Hook*. Individual texts relate hypertextually to genres they expand and modify. So too *auteur* theory predicates a corpus, linked hypertextually by discernible threads each new addition confirms or challenges. *1941* – although less controversially than *Schindler's List* – relates hypertextually to history. While Genette concentrates on deliberately hypertextual literature – Joyce's *Ulysses*, say, in relation to Homer's *Odyssey* – one might consider psychoanalytic approaches as revealing unconscious hypertextuality. *1941* embodies competitive male rebellion, clearly linked to sexuality, against taste, order, law and morality, eventually curbed by Stilwell's quiet authority. The Oedipus story, then – comfortingly rewritten, as in most popular narratives, with a socially assimilative outcome – is a fundamental hypotext. The movie's preoccupation with women's undergarments relates to castration anxieties associated with awareness of difference in the hypothetical, hypotextual, family romance. Stilwell, the only character maintaining sanity and dignity (hence, apparently, the touchstone for normality), significantly chooses to watch *Dumbo*, a tale centred on Spielberg's archetypal mother/child separation and reunion theme.

Although, superficially, scattershot inconsistency complicates *1941*'s relationship to specific hypotexts, its generic travesties match Genette's definition. This, perhaps, explains its failure to amuse. Generic conventions – abstract, necessary, hypothetical interpretive paradigms – are intrinsically no more absurd than a poetical meter or rhyme scheme in isolation from an actual word succession. Only textual manifestations – such as the *Jaws* opening – can be parodied, pastiched or travestied. These are too few, or insufficiently known, in *1941* for the burlesque to succeed. As Genette argues, when the hypotext is lost the hypertext becomes autonomous (Allen 2000: 111) – or, in postmodernist terms, a simulacrum, a copy without an original, which in the case of *1941* haemorrhages a main reason for existing.

Carnivalesque and the grotesque body

1941 is carnivalesque. An ancient tradition, carnival, Mikhail Bakhtin (1984) argues, counters hegemony by pitting comedy and bodily pleasure against constraints. It reverses logic, challenges aesthetics, hierarchies and barriers, and waives prohibitions. 'Free and familiar contact' replaces formalities (Stam 2000: 18). High culture idealises decorum and beauty, in life as in art. Carnival emphasises physicality, celebrating bodily functions but also representing the powerful, in masks, costumes and effigies, as obese, deformed and corrupt. Carnival briefly serves a communal function akin to more elevated religious rituals. A social leveller, it reminded the powerful of shared humanity and the common folk of the cares of office and potential risks of disorder. Releasing tensions in gaiety and reconciliation, it is subversive but also a safety valve to preserve the status quo, in that the laughter is indiscriminate, aimed at everyone including the participant revellers. It is not directed to any particular ends from any fixed position, unlike satire. In this respect, carnivalesque equates with postmodern relativism, debilitating from an austere avant-garde perspective.

Bakhtin (1981) associates the *menippea*, as an artistic mode, with carnival. Examining 'oxymoronic characters, multiple styles, violation of the norms of etiquette, and the comic confrontation of philosophical points of view', *menippea* facilitates understanding directors such as Buñuel, Godard, Ruiz and Rocha in terms of cinema's 'protean vitality' rather than as aberrations from a tradition (all quoted in Stam 2000: 18). Popular manifestations include the *Monty Python* comedies and subsequent Terry Gilliam films. Such texts foreground heteroglossia, multiple discursiveness, effectively comparable to inter- or transtextuality. Gilliam's notorious logistical and/or marketing disasters are clashes between an idiosyncratic, anarchic and spectacular vision and realist conventions. *1941* and its reception were similarly imbricated in discursive conflict, tearing too many ways rather than promoting either productive heteroglossia (dialogism) or monologic containment of excess. If *1941* had abandoned realism and looked more like *Helzapoppin'* or even *The Wizard of Oz* it might have proven acceptable.

This might also have loosened restraints that render *1941* a pale, sanitised carnivalesque. Condescension that nowadays associates carnival with mild frivolity marks the triumph of reason and control. Medieval carnival, invoked by Bakhtin, was obscene, scatological and offensive. It was imbued with a genuinely subversive disturbing power, residues of which some commentators, notably John Fiske, claim to detect in contemporary low cultural forms such as professional wrestling (1987a: 243-50).

1941 incorporates Bakhtinian tropes, from the mock-serious prologue onwards. The jitterbug dance, fairground and festival setting inscribe carnival; as does the sexual energy driving several main characters and manifesting itself in numerous gags, starting with female nudity juxtaposed with an enormously phallic periscope. Inversions include warfare during a celebration of peace. Conflict, frustration and aggression invert the Norman Rockwell idealisation of suburban life. Stilwell, a general who might be expected to be, if not a warmonger, at least engaged in the conflict, is relaxed and sentimental, while other military strategists and heroic characters are driven by bodily appetites or are stark raving mad. Presence of a dog in a sailor suit mocks authority, as does the rebellious civilian Wally's commanding of a tank.

Childishness and boorishness confront the Law, including everyday duties of life during wartime, the family and rituals of heterosexual coupling. Active female sexuality reverses Hollywood gender expectations. Deezen's character, Herbie, entrusted with responsibility, plays the Fool, a stock carnivalesque figure; reduplicated inversion occurs when his dummy spots the U-boat before he does and Herbie demands the binoculars to check. Kelso is Lord of Misrule, here specifically parodying John Wayne's loose-limbed macho casualness. (Wayne, objecting to the script's anti-patriotic tone, refused a part.) Other inversions include instant metamorphosis, at the beginning, of a respectable matron – her hair bunched tight – into a nature-loving hippie chick; Ma Douglas's (Lorraine Gary) refusal to allow guns just as a tank barrel crashes through her door; and Stilwell insisting to reporters there will be no bombs, as one rolls past behind him, exploding spectacularly. Stretch (Treat Williams) dropping Betty into a pit from which he has retrieved her confounds expectations of chivalry. There is also unexplained 'racial' reversal, presumably from an excised subplot, as a black soldier, in whiteface, orders a horrified white soldier, in blackface, 'to the back of the tank'.

Literal inversions include the Japanese sailor looking up at the girl on the periscope, and another with his head down the toilet. A rig that enabled Fred Astaire to dance up walls and across a ceiling was adapted for when Birkhead seduces Donna (Nancy Allen), their pilotless plane performing victory rolls around them. Dancers running up walls and executing back flips, a stunt from *Singin' in the Rain* (1952), emphasise physical exhilaration. Close-ups on female bodies, upside down in the jitterbug, stress 'the bodily lower stratum', as in Rabelaisian excess (Bakhtin 1984: 368–436). The image recurs when Betty and Maxine land in a pit, legs akimbo, skirts above their waists, and when only Ma Douglas's bloomers, garter belt and stocking tops show after the door falls in on her. While such moments, at best, celebrate and, more truthfully, impersonally denigrate the female form (distinctions that carnival, anyway, would mock), the movie otherwise restrains its employment of 'carnivalesque' images of 'huge bodies, bloated stomachs, orifices, debauchery, drunkenness and promiscuity' (Allen 2000: 22), itself a fairly restrained description. Scatological humour nevertheless occurs, as when Hollis has to drink prune juice after swallowing a toy compass wanted by the Japanese, or the 'mimed metaphor' (Carroll 1991: 30–1) whereby he drops his boots into the toilet to simulate the laxative effect. Profane language (which bothered some 1979 critics), another carnivalesque feature, is particularly evident here: 'You sneaky little bastards ain't gettin' doodly-shit outa me!'

This scene emphasises Hollis's grotesque body, stripped to his underwear. The image of the huge body, evident in casting performers such as Belushi and John Candy, is emphasised when (another residual gag) a huge Santa Claus figure (itself a sanitised Bacchanalian grotesque) encloses the former, just his comparatively tiny head projecting from the collar. The plump Maxine, precursor of Sofia in *The Color Purple*, ambiguously subverts conventional representations of feminine sexuality. Kelso, incessantly spilling and spitting food and drink, both affronts manners and indicates the plenitude carnival celebrates; likewise Elisha Cook, clothes covered in stains, waving spaghetti on his fork. Through all this chaos, ruthless cause-and-effect relationships mock human efforts at control. (Looney Tunes animator Chuck Jones was a 'special consultant'). Infantile rather than unsettling, *1941* nevertheless displays popular culture's potential to embody 'interests of the subordinate rather than those of the dominant' (Fiske 1987: 240).

Lynda Myles refuses as ultimately untenable serious reading of *1941* as 'an extended insult to Hollywood', instead finding it simply embarrassing (Myles in Pirie 1981: 131). However, carnival does not function on the cerebral level such criticism implies. Nor, though, do social attitudes and emotions concerning identity and nationhood, generally more passionately expressed in the US than in countries where *1941* fared better. The yellow Hawaiian shirt, covered in star-spangled banners and with a Pearl Harbor decal on the back, sported by Wally the jitterbugger, may or may not be authentic pre-war apparel. The teeth painted on Kelso's fighter are both genuine air force livery and another allusion to *Jaws*. The heteroglossia these display – signifying casual fun yet realities of world politics, destruction and death – concretises the movie's ambiguity. This jarred with what many Americans wanted amid financial scandal in Hollywood, painful reconcilement to defeat in Vietnam, Cold War tensions, the Iran hostages crisis and concomitant build-up of right-wing fervour prior to President Reagan's election on the promise of monologic certainties.

Like many classic comedies, *1941* reveals links with ancient rituals associated with carnival by assembling its cast for the finale and suggesting continuity; indeed formation of heterosexual couples, Stilwell's arrival to restore authority, and the final shot's implication that Pa Douglas is already planning a new house, recall the endings in Shakespearean comedy. Pa evokes communal spirit by referring to his holly wreath as 'this symbol of Christmas, this symbol of Peace', to counter 'enemy killjoys'. However, the ensuing gag cynically mocks his gesture. Spielberg's movies create an illusion of eliminating difference, with inscribed directors and spectators mediating filmmakers and audience, eradicating separation between the world and the screen. In *1941*, screams and explosions over the credits, accompanied by an upbeat military march, reinforce the carnival sense by resembling a climactic fireworks display. Nevertheless *1941* exemplifies popular culture that *excludes* the masses by refusing entry through potential identification. It also, through low-cultural excesses and lack of narrative exposition or character complexity, offends bourgeois tastes. Bakhtin (1984) titled a chapter 'The Language of the Marketplace' to emphasise the performance areas of ordinary people, grounded in real life, opposed to set-aside spaces for art of high seriousness. Audiences exercised freedom by rejecting *1941* in the movie marketplace.

While Robert Stam justifiably observes, 'we badly need analytical categories, such as those of Bakhtin, which subvert Manichean evaluations by allowing for the fact that a given utterance or discourse can be progressive and regressive *at the same time*' (2000: 314), both possibilities presuppose a meaningful audience response. Other than fitfully interrupted indifference, discomfort about the budget, or offence on the grounds of patriotism or taste, *1941* elicited little noteworthy reaction. Stilwell, the inscribed spectator who mouths the words to *Dumbo* and is the character portrayed most sympathetically, attempts to remain, significantly, cocooned in the cinematic Imaginary, away from the surrounding anarchy.

CHAPTER SIX

Raiders of the Lost Ark: lights, camera, action

Raiders of the Lost Ark appeared during a recession while Hollywood experienced continuing crisis, exacerbated by perceived competition from new outlets. Celebrating old-fashioned moviegoing, accessible to a wide audience when entertainment markets were fragmenting, it functioned as an industry flagship and assertion of confidence after several expensive and high-profile failures. Spielberg himself needed a hit, to recoup his boy-wonder popular image and restore professional status following *1941*'s profligacy; *Jaws* and *Close Encounters*, although phenomenally successful, had also gone heavily over budget. The result secured New Hollywood dominance for himself and George Lucas (executive producer and, with Philip Kaufman, story originator) by immediately entering the all-time top five.

After *Indiana Jones and the Last Crusade*, their third collaboration, the two together would have eight of the ten highest-earning movies in history, each garnering over $100 million in rentals (Schatz 1993: 25). Instead of up-front payment, an unprecedented profits deal – insurance for backers against failure – worked to the filmmakers' advantage when the production came in at half the $40 million budgeted, not only in terms of personal fortune but by strengthening leverage in subsequent contracts. *Raiders of the Lost Ark* also consolidated Spielberg's reputation as a director of adolescent fantasy, setting the agenda for popular and critical reception of his work.

What cinched *Raiders of the Lost Ark*'s profitability? Some academics, aware of Lucas's interest in mythology – particularly Joseph Campbell's Jungian approach in

The Hero with a Thousand Faces, discernible in *Star Wars* – read Jones' quest anthropologically (Tomasulo 1982; Roth 1983; Gordon 1991a). I do not eschew analysing deep structures, as narrative explorations in the next chapter on *E. T.* as well as psychoanalytic assumptions pervading this book show. However, as mythological criticism is descriptive and inductive – patterns identified from numerous narratives are checked against further examples – why one myth should prove more satisfying than another is unclear. Nor is much revealed by merely unpacking what filmmakers consciously put in. Furthermore, though one might concede that Lucas's success suggests he could be onto something, it is uncertain how constructing narratives on a pre-existing template should produce results more involving than any other, without consideration of how, under what conditions, and by whom meanings are produced, negotiated, consumed and responded to. Therefore, without denigrating such descriptions of *Raiders of the Lost Ark* I analyse first how the hero is constructed – not as an empty cipher waiting to be filled by Harrison Ford's performance and filmed by Spielberg, but as a complex of signs anchored in cinematic and other cultural codes – and then consider the nature and context of reception. Finally, although less obviously relevant to the movie's commerciality, I examine the film as a characteristic Spielberg product even though it is generally regarded as routine directorial jobbing.

The Man in the Hat

Jones is, foremost, American. His hat, leather jacket, open-necked shirt, canvas trousers, stubble, holstered six-gun and lasso-like whip, together with the desert setting of much of *Raiders of the Lost Ark* and the chase in which he gallops a white stallion to cut his enemies off at the pass: these recall westerns. There are echoes, too, of jungle explorers – explicit in the opening – such as his archaeologist alter-ego: this connotes class, expertise, 'disinterested' pursuit of truth and officially-sanctioned authority, tempering his maverick tendencies and imbuing him with unquestioned right to control. Such qualities relate him to a British tradition, adopted by Hollywood in the 1920s and 1930s: adventure yarns from boys' magazines and Victorian and Edwardian popular novels.

This dual tradition, manifest in his name (a State named after wars against Native Americans hitched to a quintessentially British patronymic), mythologises colonial conquest by white English speakers. Billed as 'the ultimate hero', Jones triumphs not only through personal qualities but by power exercised socially over others. His heroism, seemingly innate, despite his apparent autonomy (the credits list him as 'Indy') necessitates defining others as inferior.

Rugged individualism recalls the pioneering spirit enshrined in the principle of Manifest Destiny to conquer the wilderness. Similar missionary zeal permeates US expansionism since abandoning the Monroe Doctrine. *Raiders of the Lost Ark* assumes America's divinely-appointed role as protector of the Ark (hence, by implication, Judaeo-Christian civilisation). US insignia do not burn off their packing case, unlike German swastikas. Jones' Old-World adventurism likewise evokes 'the White Man's Burden', a racialised and religiously-sanctioned justification for colonialism. His hat symbolises dynamic, active authority ('The Man with the Hat is Back' declared posters for *The Last Crusade*), as when silhouetted against the evening sky while Egyptians labour for him. At one point he disguises himself in spotless Arab robes – an allusion to *Lawrence of Arabia*, in which white heroism and individualism triumph over tribal superstition and British military conformity. Like Lawrence, Jones appears masterful and dignified in this costume. As Eileen Lewis observes – in a study to which I am indebted – Jones' Egyptian sidekick, Sallah (John Rhys-Davies), conversely becomes ludicrous in attempting to appear Westernised: his European suit too tight, his hat too small, his singing from Gilbert and Sullivan incongruous. Despite his organisational capabilities, Sallah is unashamedly cowardly, a buffoon (1991: 27–8). His absurdity naturalises the ease and spontaneity of Jones' spectacular movements.

Jones' professorial identity places him among fantasy adventurers including the Scarlet Pimpernel, Tarzan (son of a Scottish aristocrat), Zorro, Superman and Batman. All have a refined existence contrasting with their aggressive heroism. Masculinity consequently appears divided, toughness adopted as a defensive mask. Like Clark Kent, Dr Jones is bespectacled, signifying vulnerability and a different, passive kind of authority, and dresses unfashionably. According to *Halliwell's Filmgoer's Companion*, his boss, curator Marcus Brody, is played by an actor of 'well-mannered ineffectual types', which neatly summarises the insecure persona Denholm Elliott brought to many parts. By contrast with the sharp-shooting overseas adventurer, the domestic side is implicitly feminised. Interestingly, Jones' mild-mannered cerebral attributes are portrayed as attractive to women; he is subjected to the desiring female gaze in the lecture room – one student inks 'LOVE YOU' on her eyelids. Also, they seem acceptably paternalistic: a male student leaving class silently deposits an apple on Jones' desk.

Masculinity's recurrent dual coding in adolescent adventures is hardly coincidental. Psychoanalysis deems infant sexuality polymorphously perverse. Repression and channelling enable social development into pre-defined sexual and gender roles. Subjection to the Law of the Father involves the Oedipal threat. According to Freud, a girl accepts the fact of castration. Her sexuality and gender are assured, for she has nothing to lose. Jones' student can feel attraction to her like, his feminine qualities, without undermining her identity. To boys, however, femininity recalls castration. It requires expulsion if masculine power is to be asserted.

Homophobia derives unconsciously from the syllogism that if heterosexual femininity and homosexuality are both opposites of heterosexual masculinity, then homosexuality equates to femininity; it threatens masculinity by transgressing boundaries and comes uncomfortably close to exposing masculinity as socially constructed, against femininity (another part of the psyche), rather than inherent. Hence homosexual men are coded effeminately. Women are generally comfortable expressing affection to each other and can acknowledge attractiveness in others; femininity retains the infant's potential bisexuality in non-sexual gender relations. Masculinity denies it. Clark Kent and Dr Jones – gentle, caring, neatly-dressed – are rendered comic, nervous and socially awkward – insecure boys, under the influence of absent mothers, who transcend their limitations by donning powerful, aggressive roles that identify authority with male competitiveness, exercised away from home through potential and actual violence. The male look at the male hero, involving identificatory desire, is relayed by the hero's look onto the woman (who typically has little significant narrative function) so its erotic component reaches an acceptable destination (Neale 1982; 1983).

One way popular movies promote masculinity is by rendering women silent, absent or marginalised (Kaplan 1983: 5). *Raiders of the Lost Ark* is not untypical with one female lead among half a dozen significant males. More telling is how she is used. During Jones' reunion with Marion (Karen Allen) it transpires he broke her heart ten years previously. 'You knew what you were doing,' he insists, hard-boiled, evasively, insinuating some casual affair rather than romance. Given her unambiguous statement, 'I was a child. I was in love. It was wrong and you knew it,' the revelation casts not the first of several aspersions on Jones' character. At any rate, it emphasises that heroes are older than heroines. Psychoanalysis regards as normal for a woman to seek a father-figure in her partner, whereas a man disavows any resemblance to his mother, which would represent regression to the Imaginary and renew the fear of castration that originally prompted separation and acceptance into the Symbolic. Patriarchal masculinity, demanding control, accordingly infantilises womanhood.

Marion starts as Jones' equal. In trousers, shirt and a scarf resembling a loosened tie, she has masculinised appearance and behaviour. (Because a woman does not tread masculinity's precarious tightrope, her sexual allure is not compromised in the way that male cross-dressing is comical, grotesque or monstrous.) She drinks a huge Sherpa man under the table. She socks Jones on the jaw. She smokes, insists she and Jones are partners, refuses to be ordered around in her own bar and plays her part fearlessly in driving off the Nazis who follow him.

Thereafter the film endeavours to get this successful entrepreneur 'out of pants and into a dress' (Tomasulo 1982: 333–4). Her independence and confidence obscure the difference on which masculinity is predicated. Intriguingly, too, however, her pigtail (she later wears her hair loose) makes her resemble an Oriental male. I shall comment later on the equation of foreignness with femininity. For now, suffice to say, femininity has to be restored to defuse suggestion of homoerotic desire.

The process begins in Cairo, where she wears a white dress and later thin baggy pants (associated not with masculinity but subservient womanhood – the harem). Of a tame monkey she remarks ambiguously, 'What a cute, adorable creature,' in a scene that marks her as soft and maternal, surrounded by children. Her weapon against pursuing villains is a frying pan, metonym for domesticity. At the end of the bazaar chase she becomes a distressed damsel, abducted, screaming for Jones' help. She dies, as far as Jones and the spectator are aware, in an explosion when the narrative has no further immediate use for her. Women – substitutes for the lost mother, tokens in Oedipal rivalry, further substituted by lost arks, holy grails, Maltese falcons, Rosebud sleds – are dispensable in masculine narratives.

Later Marion reappears, captured by Jones' arch-enemy and ruthless rival, Belloq (Paul Freeman). Despite selling his soul to the Nazis, Belloq is so like a father to Jones (an older, more learned, smartly-dressed version, almost always dominant within the frame) that he can say, 'It would take only a nudge to make you like me.' Unaware of observation, Marion is glimpsed, naked, in a mirror as she dons a dress Belloq has bought her. She is sexually objectified by the spectator's voyeurism, which the camera aligns with Belloq's in a textbook example of Laura Mulvey's account of the gendered cinematic gaze. The white dress, with white high-heeled shoes, totally inappropriate at an archaeological site, symbolises Belloq's intent to make her his bride.

Although Marion uses her prodigious alcoholic capacity to escape Belloq's clutches, Nazis immediately recapture her. Refusing to divulge information gleaned from her archaeologist father – Jones' former mentor, until the affair with his daughter caused a rift – she is thrown into the Well of Souls. Still dressed in white (also signifying sacrificial victimhood), she is caught by Jones, resembling a groom carrying his bride over the threshold. Later, at sea, she wears a white gown in bed. She no longer wears it on awakening while Jones straps on his gun, a classically indirect Hollywood innuendo. Independence and equality turn to repeated victimisation. Although she remains strong and resourceful, eating and drinking heartily without daintiness, the narrative pursues her containment. Repeatedly Jones rescues her from other men, as when the German agent Toht (Ronald Lacey) prepares to torture her with a phallic hot poker. When Jones fortuitously finds her in Belloq's tent after locating the Ark, he replaces her gag and leaves her, continuing his quest. In the snake pit, she wears a flimsy dress, with bare legs and one shoe; he has canvas trousers, a leather jacket and boots. When gibbering corpses and skeletons 'attack', she screams like a typical female horror movie victim. In the struggle involving the flying wing she wields a machine gun effectively, but becomes trapped in the flaming cockpit and again requires rescue. She is once more captured on the ship. Finally, then, Jones wins the woman from various father figures: Marion's father who, she says, loved him 'like a son', the Nazis, and Belloq, his greyer rival and symbolic double. From an autonomous, competent individual, she becomes an object of exchange. 'Owning' the woman asserts masculinity in a constant replay of Oedipal conflict. Twice Belloq asserts: 'There is nothing you can possess which I cannot take away.' Even so, Sarah Harwood suggests, Jones' victory is contained within patriarchy by 'the consequent procession of gifts [archaeological finds] he must offer to propitiate his new father-surrogate: Brody, and the state' (represented by the Military Intelligence officer with his fatherly pipe) (1997: 80).

Belloq's corrupt European authority underscores Oedipal rivalry, paralleling young America's rebellion against the Old World for what was desired as simultaneously the Virgin Land and the domain of bountiful (Mother) Nature. Unlike Jones' – grubby, sweaty, unshaven – Belloq remains absurdly dapper, cool and fastidious despite the jungle and desert, an ability shared with the spotless Marion and other conventional heroines. Appearance at the finale in High Priest's robes confirms his feminisation. The Islamic Imam, although on Jones' side, has a high-pitched voice, feminising his otherness. So, too, Toht, in leather greatcoat and hat and steel-rimmed spectacles, is frightening because of incongruity between these symbols of masculine hardness and his soft, feminine, full lips and smooth pale skin.

The Ark's survivors are American. They are a couple, and Marion survives by accepting Jones' authority, inseparable from his nationality and gender. At the start, though he travels with native porters and guides, he leads and the camera frames him to dominate. His identity is withheld, making him and his motivation the enigmas that suture the spectator into the narrative. Unlike the South Americans, predictably treacherous and cowardly, he is cool, knowledgeable, skilful and self-reliant. Confronting shocks and horrors, the Peruvians scream and run. The scene with

Marion in the Well confirms that such responses are, in movies, feminine, just as Jones' silence and detachment are, in Western social behaviour also, masculine. Sallah screams at a frightening statue, then apologises to Jones, who remains impassive at the sight. Eventually when the Nazis, bent on world-domination, succumb to the symbolic castration of destruction by the all-powerful Holy Father, they too scream while Jones stays silent. Screen masculinity involves systematic denigration of other races, nationalities and women.

Reaganite entertainment?

Ought *Raiders of the Lost Ark* to be read, then, as anti-feminist and a reassertion of colonial attitudes under President Reagan's conservative agenda? The nub is when Jones encounters a posturing swordsman in tribal regalia and exasperatedly withdraws his revolver and shoots him – when cinematic convention demands a spectacular fight at close quarters to top his defeat of a gang of similarly-armed Bedouins. Is this an objectionable representation of a Third World citizen, not simply being killed but also having pride and cultural identity casually dismissed by an agent of imperialism (with the audience's delighted complicity) or astute acknowledgment of values informing adventures that once seemed innocent fun? Or is it neither – merely what it purports to be: innocent fun itself?

Robert Phillip Kolker notes that the film contains 'no discussion or exposition of nazism *per se*' (1988: 266). Attitudes to the movie divide on issues such as whether this is a reasonable complaint against a popular entertainment that employs Nazis as universally recognised ready-made villains. Nor does *Raiders of the Lost Ark* explore the Ark's religious significance beyond it being a force against darkness. The film presents itself as no more than a high-budget updating of Saturday serials, achieving the exciting pace and effects the originals could never approach because, being cheap, they were studio-bound and dialogue-based.

Always with Spielberg, metatextuality and realism are crucial. According to George Lucas's biographer, Dale Pollock, 'the audience had to laugh with the picture, not at it' (in Taylor 1992: 104). Production values associated with Hollywood realism create local verisimilitude and spectacle in tension with implausibilities such as the rolling boulder, appropriated from *Road Runner*. In a film that declares fictionality before the opening shot, as the Paramount logo dissolves into a diegetic mountain, that represents international flights archaically with a line advancing across a map, and has the hero answer a question about his plans with 'How should I know? I'm making this up as I go,' it would seem fair to say any engagement with reality is unintentional. This is a pastiche of adventure serials and comics, structured into six episodes and gaping with plot anomalies, as unconcerned with ideological implications of its own practice or of what it is postmodernising as it is with three-dimensional characters and motivation.

The values of 1930s entertainment are not necessarily transferred wholesale into the 1980s. Jones' ominous first shot, in which he looms out of darkness, sinisterly lit, accompanied by threatening music, introduces him as dangerous – Robert Mitchum in *Night of the Hunter* (1955). Far from flawless, he is repeatedly presented this way – himself a 'raider', he remains, unlike Sallah, silhouetted and shadowy while approaching and caressing the Ark's 'sarcophagus' – lighting otherwise reserved for Belloq and the Nazis.

There appears something puritanically humourless about taking seriously a movie as ironic, knowing and boisterous as *Raiders of the Lost Ark*. However, ideological analysis reveals oppression and containment that may be unconscious. Audiences, it is often argued, especially by those who conceive of spectatorship as passive, are susceptible to suggestion when their guards are down, and filmmakers may be most at risk of reproducing ideology when taking themselves least seriously. If ideology is what goes without saying, it is likely to be reproduced uncritically in texts not consciously conveying a message. Hence the film is not uniquely reprehensible. Many 1980s movies, from the Rambo movie *First Blood* (1982) to *Pretty Woman* (1990), embody questionable attitudes more overtly. *Raiders of the Lost Ark*'s problem is that, flirting with serious issues and expressing affection for texts less liberal than it purports itself to be (historical perspective and cinematic sophistication imply superiority to hypotexts), it invites suspicion and hostility.

The treatment of the Arab swordsman, threatening and mysterious in his black costume (even if intended as homage to Omar Sharif in *Lawrence of Arabia*), always received most laughs. The joke is the discrepancy between his exaggerated gesticulating and the feebleness yet effectiveness of Jones' response. But one cannot ignore that the film appeared after Arab oil embargoes and during immediate repercussions of the Iranian hostage crisis, when military intervention to free over a hundred Americans ended disastrously. During the film's production, Reagan was elected on an agenda of tough foreign policy (inaugurating renewed expansionism) and nostalgic appeal to a mythical past. The movie's hero adventures to South America, where the US government was embroiled in El Salvador and Nicaragua, and to Asia, where Marion's drinking contest, accompanied by frenzied gambling, evokes the Russian roulette scenes in *The Deer Hunter* (1978), recalling Vietnam. The other main location is Washington, D.C., significantly as shame over Watergate still tainted politics (Tomasulo 1982: 331).

Reagan later declared the Soviet Union 'the Evil Empire' and nicknamed the Strategic Defense Initiative 'Star Wars', appropriating the popular imagery and simple-mindedness of Lucas's film while taking the world uncomfortably close to war. As *Raiders*' Ark is metaphorically the Bomb – armies carrying it are invincible, Hitler wants it as an ultimate weapon, it vapourises baddies in dazzling radiation, producing a mushroom cloud, and ends up in American hands for examination by 'top people' (according to an agent with an Oppenheimer-style pipe) – this seemed to confirm the film's accordance with Reaganism, even if it was more likely a casual borrowing from *Kiss Me Deadly* (1955) than endorsement of defence policy.

Against this background, the movie's simplistic nostalgia, avoiding the present rather than recalling anything demonstrably valuable from the past, its enormous takings and cheering audiences become problematic. 'Reaganism had its first explicit filmic representation,' writes Kolker (1988: 267), a refrain of much 1980s Spielberg criticism (Britton 1986). Frank Tomasulo argues that Belloq justifies the view, 'if America can't or won't exploit native cultures, someone else will' (1982: 333), and even presents a still of Reagan in *Hong Kong* (1952) dressed identically to Jones. (The filmmakers stated Jones' attire imitated Humphrey Bogart's in *The Treasure of the Sierra Madre* (1948) and Errol Flynn's in *The Adventures of Don Juan* (1948) (Taylor 1992: 105)).

It is improbable that a film in development since 1977, apparently conceived even before *Star Wars* (Tuchman & Thompson 1981: 54), deliberately reinforced reactionary attitudes towards events still unfolding. Because of long production and delayed release times of most features, they rarely reflect immediate circumstances. Yet *Raiders of the Lost Ark* undeniably emerged from the same hegemony as Reaganism. Political regimes express perceived social needs: their origins predate election. Nevertheless, films are part of culture, and meanings and effects are beyond filmmakers' control. This contradicts Kolker's view, at times smacking of conspiracy theories, that 'when a Spielberg film works, the response of one viewer ought to be the same as every other' (1988: 267–8). Even so, reinforcement of certain positions *precisely because* a film is uncommitted and open to multiple interpretations as a commercial strategy, may inadvertently become indistinguishable from propaganda. Steve Neale suggests that this and other contemporaneous films offered 'imaginary memory of an imaginary past' in inflecting traditional genres to youngsters unfamiliar with authentic genre movies (1982: 38). This parallels Reagan's appeal to voters that sold a synthetic past. It suggests too that most of the film's literally hundreds of transtextual instances were lost on the bulk of the audience, although enough were recognisable to allow almost anyone to believe the film specifically addressed them.

Patricia Zimmermann notes how *Raiders of the Lost Ark*'s narrative image, constructed in press kits, behind-the-scenes information and interviews, encouraged preferred readings faithfully reproduced in reviews; these eradicated 'political reading of the film's jingoism, Third World exploitation and backlash against feminism' or conflation of nuclear weaponry with religious and moral power (1983: 34, 37). According to the Paramount Pictures press kit, Spielberg insisted, 'keep in mind … it is only a movie. *Raiders* is not a statement of its times': a comment that, curiously, precedes negative criticism. By 'construct[ing] the audience as imaginary creators and insiders,' the promotional machinery 'install[ed] an imaginary coherence and unity in the public sphere' (Zimmermann 1983: 34). An analogous process, I maintain throughout this book, occurs during viewing, the result of alignment with inscribed spectators and with the filmmakers through recognised intertextuality. The effect was to limit ideological objections other than in radical academic journals, in which context they were dismissable as cranky.

Zimmermann notes also Spielberg and Lucas's promotion 'not as imaginative directors with a message, but as entrepreneurial managers operating efficient and cost-effective productions' (1983: 36); attention diverted from the film's content to their heroic role as Hollywood's saviours by reviving traditional approaches to manufacturing entertainment. Of course, such a campaign might deliberately have been mounted to downplay elements which, inadvertently or humorously included, now threatened embarrassingly to backfire through recuperation into the newly-dominant ideology. An oft-repeated story explained the swordsman's shooting: because Ford had dysentery, his adversary's expedient dispatch, replacing a scripted fight, enabled the day's shooting to be wrapped quickly. Accounts differ over whether the idea was Ford's or Spielberg's, allowing suspicion that the incident was invented to deflect anticipated censure.

Raiders of the Lost Ark, then, consolidates polarisation of Spielberg criticism. Flawlessly executed, it was accused of elevating spectacle and action over other values. To Henry Sheehan, generally a Spielberg admirer, this film joins 'a series of glib, manipulative thrill rides that slyly used the cover of "entertainment" to downgrade the expressive possibilities of the cinema' and 'is one of the most un-human, inhuman, and anti-human movies of all time' (1992: 54, 59). Shot quickly under Lucas's supervision and with Lucas retaining final cut, it was, John Baxter considers, Spielberg's least personal effort (1996: 221). Richard Combs, who usually engages positively with Spielberg's films within an *auteur* understanding, associates it with Lucas's 'lowest common denominator' (1981: 160). Connecting Spielberg in the public imagination with theme-park entertainments (Brode 1995: 88), it included troubling representations, such as Third World citizenry as a backdrop to an American's exploits. The popular notion of 'escapism', always reprehensible to Marxist critics as diversion from pressing issues, aligned in politically-motivated criticism with harmful effects. To most popular reviewers, the 'escapist' label made seriously criticising Spielberg's films pointless; to committed cultural critics, their status as Hollywood's most profitable manifestations rendered them effectively indistinguishable from anything else, dismissable in general terms without detailed analysis.

Such responses express disappointment after application of *auteur* assumptions to American directors in the 1970s. This had detected maturity and intelligence, based on awareness of tradition and self-consciousness, embracement of serious themes, and experimentation and daring more associated with European cinema. Under the new dispensation, risk-taking and individuality, ironically facilitated by the lack of control that was crippling the majors, would be less easy.

But movies are, after all, *movies*: concerned with *action* as spectacle. That said, *Raiders of the Lost Ark* offers more than wall-to-wall frenzied motion filmed perfunctorily, if efficiently, under pressure. For all the utilitarianism implied in the much-vaunted fact that shooting finished two weeks early, Spielberg's signature is clearly visible in a way that complements the countless allusions to other films. The film is, for better or worse, readable as a solipsistic text, hermetically sealed from life in a cinematic dimension.

From the start, the apparatus is inscribed. Light shafts in the jungle are associated with the closeness of Jones' quest object. Light beaming into the lens precedes deadly arrows and cobwebbed corpses. The pit Jones swings across is seen from below, a bright rectangle revealing the action, viewed from within darkness. Inside the temple a giant medallion resembles both a sun and a movie reel. As Jones approaches the statue it illuminates his face, while his helper imitates his actions, not merely as an onlooker but embodying spectatorial identification. Jones' desire to escape the underground complex is thwarted by warriors who block the light. Outwitting Belloq, though losing the prize, Jones escapes in a seaplane directly into the sun.

At the University, stained-glass windows flare between Jones and Brody onto the Intelligence officers investigating the Ark. The headpiece Jones describes is a lens to focus light and reveal truth. An ancient illustration shows the Ark as a dazzling light

Raiders of the Lost Ark – projected light as revelation

source that *creates* the abjection and suffering around it, like a projector screening a
Biblical epic. The page seemingly casts light onto the researchers, echoing the air traffic
controllers in *Close Encounters*. As Jones fantasises himself into using the staff to locate
the ultimate archaeological find, his shadow projects over his chalkboard drawing.

Jones' gigantic projected outline precedes him at Marion's bar, literally foreshad-
owing monstrous revelations. She, eroticised object of his gaze, is caressed by flickering
light before she punches him. (Such details encourage carnivalesque interpretation.)
Disconcertingly, when Jones confronts Belloq in Egypt he is shaded in close-up, his
nearer eye glinting while the further one appears to project a flicker – caused by a
ceiling fan in the background – towards his adversary, as the latter insists he is Jones'
reflection and that it would take only a nudge 'to push you out of the light'.

In the map room before Jones employs the headpiece, a bar of light links him to
the model that locates the Ark. He looks upward to dazzling light pouring through
an opening in a focused beam. Romantic Hollywood-epic music plays as he watches,
enthralled as the spectator also is intended to be, while rays directed through the
headpiece spread into a heavenly aura. Throughout this movie, and Spielberg's films
generally, the most reverential music accompanies dazzling illumination.

Having located the Well, Jones peers through a theodolite, which closely resembles
a movie camera. We share his projective, desiring gaze as he adjusts focus, correcting
his vision and ours simultaneously, in point-of-view shots. The spectator, aligned with
a metaphorical director who is also the hero, dressed as another hero (Lawrence), is
sutured, as Zimmermann (1983) suggests, into a closed circle that is the film and
its provenance. The sunset as Jones dons his hat at his own dig is accompanied by
a breeze, suggesting the characteristic Spielberg 'solar wind' as he believes his goal is
nigh. Lightning flashes as the Well opens, increasing visual stimulation. Meanwhile,
light bisects the scene, joining Belloq to Marion as he, offering the dress, verbalises
his desiring gaze: 'I would very much like to see you in it.' When she re-emerges,
having changed, backlighting and romantic music fetishise her, echoing a moment in
Vertigo.

Lightning outside recreates the flickering reflected on movie theatre walls as Jones and Sallah lift the Ark; indeed, as they carry it, the scene is presented not directly but as a projected shadow. Later, the Ark's opening begins, after establishing shots, with a spotlight directly into camera, obscured at first by the Ark in the foreground, then flaring out as characters pass before it. Brightness saturates the scene, like the end of *Close Encounters*, evoked in a high-angle establishing shot. Nazi filmmakers record the ceremony. Jones and Marion, bound to a lamp standard, spectate from afar, 'solar wind' teasing their hair and clothes. Drifting mist enhances visual stimulation in otherwise static shots, increasing anticipation. Suddenly all equipment shorts out as weapons are discharged – except, apparently, the movie camera, as the operator continues filming. *Citizen Kane*'s Rosebud theme plays as Belloq looks into the Ark: a rectangular container of light, an inscribed screen, flickering and glowing into brightness. Assembled spectators watch, apprehensive but fascinated. 'We see death pour out of the Ark like a lethal dose of projector light' (Rosenbaum 1995: 220), as the wind increases and columns of flame penetrate the Nazis' hearts. The camera operator is struck through the eyes, before disappearing in a blinding whiteout, via the lens and eyepiece of the camera, which remains unaffected.

Brode notes that this climax, in which purifying light destroys evil, inverts *Close Encounters*' ending (1995: 98). There the cinematic metaphor was of transcendence through incorporation into the Imaginary, and the spectacle elicited applause. In *Raiders of the Lost Ark*, Jones tells Marion 'Don't look at this!' and they survive by closing their eyes. Jones' admonition applies equally to children or others of a nervous disposition watching the film. Whereas in *Close Encounters* 'When You Wish Upon a Star' soars over the spaceship's launch, here screeching violins, recalling *Psycho*, accompany the Ark's retribution. (The close-up on the camera operator matches Norman Bates spying on another Marion before the shower scene.)

Raiders of the Lost Ark is a celebration of film, not an invitation to look away while the Neutron Bomb is unleashed. Yet its cultural significance may be that sectors of its audience discovered correlatives to their confusions and anxieties. Ironically, that would redouble its self reflexivity, even as the film was appropriated into other discourses. Matthew Bouch relates the fact that the audience sees what Jones and Marion cannot – a representation of no less than the power of God – to 'the power of cinema to reify the fantastic', because the characters will be annihilated if they open their eyes (1996: 21). Diegetically, the power that protects and can destroy is light. As stains on celluloid, shadows on a screen, light is their origin, giving life and movement. The *Citizen Kane* reference on which *Raiders of the Lost Ark* ends is a reminder that in Welles' film only the omniscient narration – transcending six inconclusive embedded narratives – and the perceptive spectator know the key to Kane. Such musings might seem inconsequential against issues of freedom and survival raised by Reaganism. But they are consistently the substance of Spielberg's cinema.

CHAPTER SEVEN

E. T. The Extra-Terrestrial: turn on your love light

Anyone able to explain why *E.T. The Extra-Terrestrial* became the highest-grossing domestic release, then an unprecedented video success, selling 13 million worldwide, would probably stay mum and join Spielberg in millionairehood. (Anon. 1982; 1988a; 1988b)

Like *Close Encounters of the Third Kind*, which prevented Columbia's liquidation, *E.T.* was an industry watershed, helping reverse a quarter-century decline in attendances.

The director himself was reportedly surprised. He supposedly regarded *E.T.* as a personal project (a luxury permitted by unusual creative freedom resulting from his commercial power, underlined by percentage shares accruing from his *Raiders of the Lost Ark* contract). *E.T.* was comparatively low-budget – modest effects, no major stars – clearly a factor in the astounding profitability that had Spielberg personally earning a cool million daily during 1982–83, from his ten per cent contract, and provided his 1988 Christmas bonus of $40 million (Adair 1982/83: 63; Sanello 1996: 110). This does not, though, account for the scale of the box office.

Promotion and publicity

Emulating the *Jaws* campaign, but with rights licensed for a fee rather than given away, *E.T.* was extensively promoted with tie-in merchandising, which alone grossed

$1 billion, nearly half as much again as the film. However, while plastic figures in the breakfast bowl undoubtedly raised potential awareness, marketing cannot guarantee attendances. Indeed P&A budgets substantially exceeding a film's production cost are hardly uncommon. Sometimes they pay off: *The Full Monty* (1997) grossed over $200 million after Fox spent ten times above its $3.5 million production budget on marketing; meanwhile *Titanic* (1997) earned the first billion-dollar gross after the same company's spend on P&A almost equalled the record $200 million production cost (Glaister 1998). Nevertheless four flops counter each success, and failed campaigns are soon forgotten outside of the industry.

An attractive explanation is that *E.T.* was perceived as a children's film (they were the merchandising market) – a family event, timed for the holidays (Independence Day in the US, Christmas in Britain). Matters are, though, less simple. Children's tickets are cheaper so, in terms of raw numbers, less lucrative than adult admissions. Disney realised this years ago (leaving aside huge income from franchised products the films themselves advertise). Disney withdraws films within weeks of release. The video retail period is similarly limited. Thereafter, an aura of unavailability permits instant 'classic' status on later re-release, at which point serious profits kick in for relatively minimal additional cost.

Distributors working with Amblin, Spielberg's production company founded in 1981, emulated Disney's long-term strategy: *E.T.*, out of circulation after a year, had a successful cinematic re-release prior to the video launch in 1988. But this is quite separate from its initial theatrical rentals. Furthermore, indications are that children were not the primary makers of *E.T.*'s success. The *New York Times* on 30 December 1982 reported a 'significant increase' in over-25s attending movies. The headline was unequivocal: 'Adults Lured Back to Films by *E.T.*'

Effective promotion generates sufficient interest that a film becomes newsworthy in itself, attracting publicity independent of paid-for advertising. *E.T.* fuelled extensive speculation about the meaning of its success (it took $300 million in six months), which not only aroused curiosity among American adults but also filtered abroad before overseas releases. Distributors UIP calculated that over $30 million worth of free coverage was obtained for $6 million spent (Harwood 1995: 150).

Occasionally a movie engages fortuitously with existing cultural discourses. *E.T.*'s New York audiences queuing around the block comprised not families on weekend outings but heterosexual childless couples in their late 20s and 30s. Many belonged to the emergent Yuppie class, wealthy manifestations of enterprise culture, identified by power dressing, expensive eating tastes and designer accessories. Why were such people, who had apparently lost or never acquired the moviegoing habit, attending this film in droves?

Much was made of *E.T.* being a regressive fantasy. 'We were crying for our lost selves,' claimed novelist Martin Amis (in Baxter 1996: 245). Yuppies were supposedly escaping from stress into childlike spontaneity and freedom, a soft-centred alternative to the aggressive goal-orientation of their work and competitive leisure. More intriguing were suggestions that couples were deferring child rearing to advance their careers: the film's emotionality gratified repressed parental instincts. A rumour alleged that Spielberg and Carlo Rambaldi, designer of the extra-terrestrial, visited maternity wards to take facial measurements from infants that nurses considered especially cute, and analysed data to produce the ultimate vulnerable baby. Whether or not this was true, E.T.'s cries at the start – which encourages empathy with the visitor through optical point-of-view shots and by portraying humans as shadowy, alien and frightening – resemble a newborn child's. The wrinkled pinkish-grey creature, wired to monitors as he lies dying alongside Elliott (Henry Thomas) in what resembles an incubator, tended by masked medics, recalls a premature baby in intensive care. (The film elsewhere engages pre-conscious instincts. In the forest, for example, a fierce animal roar accompanies the irruption of scientists' off-road vehicles.)

Reports of such an unlikely audience contributed to the narrative image – in which I am including expectations not consciously intended by publicists. Speculation reinforced word-of-mouth and reviewers' recommendations about the alien's uncanny credibility. (Four hundred and fifty preview screenings in the US confirm, nevertheless, that word-of-mouth was deliberately promoted.) Marketers ensured no clips showed E.T. in motion (Burgess 1983). Even the poster designers had not seen the film (Baxter 1996: 243). While dolls, puzzle books, candy wrappers and countless other epitexts, many unauthorised, made E.T.'s appearance familiar, trailers showed only his hand moving a branch (an optical point-of-view that inscribes his presence while keeping him off-screen) and his silhouette against the spaceship's illuminated portal. Audiences had to pay to discover if the puppetry was really convincing. Meanwhile, fantasy filled the gap between desire and fulfilment. E.T. answered to spectators' personal meanings even before they confronted him.

Other discourses sustained publicity, strengthening *E.T.*'s status as cultural event. The UK release coincided with telecommunications privatisation. To raise awareness of British Telecom's shares flotation, billboards, similar in size and shape to cinema screens, displayed a starry sky and the slogan, 'Give us time, E.T., give us time,' a reference to the creature's determination to 'phone home'. Universal sued for copyright, generating millions of pounds' worth of free publicity for both campaigns. (Sonia Burgess remarks that customers and potential shareholders were interpellated in the guise of E.T., suggesting an assumed identification (1983: 50).)

The 1980s saw domestic video become widely available, prompting predictable moral panic about imputed effects of any new medium. Debates concerning regulation spawned the phrase 'pirate videos' – a receptacle for lurid fantasies combining technological fears and images of vicious cut-throats (with xenophobic connotations of the South China Seas: for which read Asia, where the equipment originated). The paranoia, overlooking that most 'pirates' would be consumers copying illegally, was especially suggestive before anyone had seen one of these abominations. One of the first widely pirated products was *E.T.*

Poor copies, recorded from amateur equipment in a movie theatre, circulated widely in Britain. Students of mine remembered large gatherings in front rooms (video-cassette recorders were expensive, so few households owned one) and recalled the mystique of ghostly monochrome images – the American NTSC coding being incompatible with Europe's PAL. Apart from further publicity as a news item, this presumably contributed to cinema attendances as frustrated video watchers turned to the intended medium to complete the narrative image with colour, spectacle and high fidelity sound.

Reagan's administration and Margaret Thatcher's government in Britain were right-wing forces elected on a promised return to tradition. Reagan reasserted military confidence by invading Grenada, while Thatcher reversed opinion poll ratings from least to most popular prime minister by defeating Argentina in the Falklands. Given Cold War anxieties exacerbated by Soviet instability and Reagan's 'Star Wars' Initiative, there may be justification for arguing that *E.T.*'s message of love and acceptance of difference fulfilled a compensatory function. This would be the reverse of 1950s science fiction, often now interpreted as projecting repressed fears of Communism and/or the Bomb. Such compensation – although it counters the sanctioning of foreign policy alleged against *Raiders of the Lost Ark* – confounds criticism that considers Hollywood fantasy automatically complicit with oppressive discourses.

Hysteria surrounding video regulation partly meshed with a perceived crisis in family values that Reagan and Thatcher exploited. Psychoanalysis suggests *E.T.* might have formed part of, and benefited from this. Typically of mainstream narratives, it re-enacts an Oedipal scenario for the spectator regressed through the Mirror Phase by the cinematic apparatus. Portraying children's rebellion, from their perspective, against adult authority, *E.T.* ends with painless re-integration into the Symbolic Order.

The film begins with E.T. toddling childlike between trees, their size emphasised by music connoting religious awe. This idyllic scene (rabbits gambol unconcerned as aliens tenderly gather botanical specimens) represents unity, as the landing party's hearts glow in mutual empathy, underscored by literal harmony, wine glasses reverberating to represent their warnings to each other. This is the lost Imaginary: the alien 'family' remain secure while close to what critics significantly call 'the mothership' (never so-named in the film).

Enter human scientists who wreck this paradise, led by a mysterious figure with keys jangling from his belt. They stand for all adults who, until E.T.'s apparent death, when the medics remove their masks and contamination suits, are presented similarly (apart from Elliott's mother (Dee Wallace)): faceless, un-individuated, mostly male authority figures, shown in silhouette, from behind, or from shoulders to knees, from a child's level. The keys' association with phallic authority is unmistakable: repeated close-ups of them swinging at crotch level are the nearest a kid's film could approach to representing male genitalia. The credits explicitly call the man Keys (played by Peter Coyote) (the name of Walter Neff's older nemesis in that overtly Oedipal classic, *Double Indemnity* (1944)).

Elliott defiantly upsets his mother by referring to his father in Mexico with a girl-friend, prompting his brother Michael (Robert Macnaughton) to ask when Elliott will 'think about how other people feel for a change'. The mother's difficulty disciplining her children is linked to the father's absence, suggesting mild family dysfunction. Nostalgia replaces Elliott's aggression when aftershave on 'Dad's shirt' evokes happy memories. As made clear when a scientist asks, 'Elliott thinks its thoughts?' and Michael replies, 'No, Elliott feels his feelings' – both terms echoing Michael's earlier rebuke – the alien becomes Elliott's surrogate father, socialising him by teaching consideration and setting responsibilities. Sarah Harwood describes E.T. as a parodic father who 'uses the house for entertainment and servicing', gets drunk, throws beer cans at the television, wears Elliott's father's clothes, and employs his tools (1995: 159; see also Heung 1983).

When E.T. goes 'home', however, another father intervenes. As E.T. lies dying, Keys taps Elliott's oxygen tent to attract his attention, a close-up emphasising a two-fingered gesture already associated with E.T. looking through the branches. (Michael, who has repeatedly claimed the paternal role, as in the comment quoted, echoes this gesture when he awakens just before E.T.'s death.) Keys, now revealed as humane (the first close-up, minutes earlier, lit his face ominously from below), confides he once resembled Elliott and has dreamed of extra-terrestrials since childhood. Keys' visor reflects Elliott, merging them in one image, counterpart to E.T.'s earlier mirroring of Elliott's movements. Thus cyclical continuity overlays identity between Elliott and the creature, suggesting Keys can inherit E.T.'s role, freeing the latter to return to *his* 'family'. Keys accompanies Elliott's mother in the finale, completing the circle of children and pet dog. Meanwhile, the alien has escaped without serious conflict – agents pull guns (digitally transformed into radios in the 2002 re-release) but no violence occurs – and Elliott, having acquired a super-ego ('I'll be right here,' insists E.T., pointing at Elliott's forehead) is assimilated into the reconstituted Symbolic. The earlier scenes' castrating father is a kindly patriarch.

Reagan's construction of the family, American as Mom and apple pie, was mythic. (Attempts to recuperate Yuppies – another manifestation of Reaganism yet almost, by definition, opposed to the family – by reference to 'natural' parenting impulses towards E.T., emphasises the myth's flexibility and pervasiveness.) By the 1980s, a child living with both biological parents in their first marriage was exceptional. Narrative, however, generally seeks to restore the world to how a culture would like it to be rather than how it necessarily is. To blame the fantasy, typically unconscious, for complicity with party politics is misplaced, however. Concern should focus on grown-up leaders peddling fantasies as policy.

Self-reflexivity versus identification

At least the cinematic fantasy respects its recipients sufficiently not to expect them to take it seriously. From the opening – featuring a *Wizard of Oz* talking tree among the collected specimens – to the final shot of E.T. silhouetted within a closing circular portal like an iris shot ending a cartoon, accompanied by projector-like whirring, the film foregrounds fictionality. This facilitates the Imaginary/Symbolic alternation which informs the pleasure in Spielberg films. For the fantasy to satisfy requires belief that cycling children can fly across the moon. Yet nobody is 'taken in' (Metz 1975: 70), not even children. Here I disagree with Kolker who insists that Spielberg's 'self-conscious gestures' are 'never distancing' (1988: 272). Using the term 'manipulative' and its synonyms with obsessive frequency, Kolker presents a passive subject position(ing) – unshared, significantly, by him – as the *only* one available, which audiences have no choice in occupying.

E.T. as fantasy is emphasised by mother reading *Peter Pan* to Gertie (Drew Barrymore); we hear that Tinker Bell 'would get well again if children believed in fair-

E.T.: The Extra-Terrestrial – 'That's All, Folks!': the closing iris shot

ies' – redundant, unmotivated, but also virtually unnoticeable detail if the film really demanded unconditional subjection. Likewise, E.T.'s resurrection, though logically occasioned by the spaceship's return, appears contingent upon Elliott's and our belief. Yet eventually the part of the psyche engaged in the Imaginary is conflicted, between desire for E.T. to remain and for his reunion with his 'family'. This contradiction, together with simultaneous belief and disbelief, helps elicit the oft-cited emotional responses to the film; irresolvable oppositions provoke laughter or tears, sometimes difficult to distinguish.

The spacecraft's climactic reappearance, emanating light shafts and a 'solar wind' that ruffles hair and clothing of characters looking up, awe-struck and expectant – stand-ins for absent spectators, elsewhere, in movie theatres – symbolises the cinematic apparatus. As spectacle it engages the scopic drive, and as narrative function promises imminent closure. But other satisfactions require detachment. A serrated grill causes the spaceship to resemble the shark from *Jaws* – a self-referential indulgence that flatters Spielberg fans who notice it, and rewards close, active reading. Spherical, lit through portals that form a face, the spaceship is also a jack-o'-lantern, in accordance with the Halloween setting. (In *Close Encounters* Jillian describes mistaken helicopter lights in a similarly staged spectacle as 'Halloween for grown ups'.) This in turn constitutes a further allusion, to the *Peanuts* newspaper strip which, like *E.T.*, represents children's experience, with adults relegated to speech bubbles originating out of frame: specifically, every Halloween one character awaits 'The Great Pumpkin in the Sky'.

Central to *E.T.*'s popularity is not merely openness to multiple readings – true of any text – but differential audience address: to adults and children, cineastes and casual moviegoers. Narrative and spectacle provide armatures for various experiences exceeding any individual's interpretive competence. Consequently, as Umberto Eco (1987) points out, any but the most naïve response is a cult reading. The film addresses me and others 'in the know', as I recognise *Fantasia* when the scientists chase through the woods with flashlights, or as I revel in E.T.'s misrecognition of a trick-or-treat costume representing Yoda, a fellow Rambaldi creation, from *The Empire Strikes Back* (1980). Yet this awareness implies discourses I may be overlooking, threatening my mastery, and so encouraging further attention which, in turn, intensifies potential Imaginary identification and recognition of signs as Symbolic.

Constant repositioning occurs against the security of conventional narrative – an important difference between Spielberg's and less mainstream texts that, similarly disrupting spectatorship, are lauded as progressive (Stam 1985). Repositioning occurs also *within* the narrative. The E(lliot)T identity, whereby one becomes drunk as the other drinks, or acts out fantasies the other observes on television, figures the spectator's Imaginary relationship to the Other on-screen. Spectators are encouraged to identify with Elliott in his telempathic identification with E.T., partly because the viewpoint offered parallels E.T.'s as much as because E.T. is experienced through Elliott's focalisation. Optical point-of-view shots align with E.T. even before Elliott encounters him. We share E.T.'s vision as he leaves the house under a sheet. Elliott's descriptions of Earth ('This is a peanut: we put money in it') amuse precisely because we view our culture as an alien might. In a self-conscious 'mis-en-abime [sic] structure – while the mother reads the "clap your hands if you believe" passage to her daughter, the son and E.T. sit transfixed in the dark, listening unobserved in the closet just as the theatre full of parents and children listen unobserved in the dark' (Collins 1993: 260).

So far as spectators accept proffered identification, they suffer three abandonments (Harwood 1995: 153): when E.T. separates from Elliott (who falls asleep) in the forest, when he parts from Elliott by dying, and when he leaves at the end. Counterpointing each loss, necessary for Elliott's resignation to, and acceptance into, the Symbolic, is spectatorial awareness of transtextuality or obvious artifice such as the final rainbow in the sky (a 'boundary ritual', marking transition between states (Fiske & Hartley 1978: 166–9)). Unlike Neary, absorbed into his (cinematic) Imaginary, Elliott remains, alone in the shot, tears running down his cheeks like many in the audience, looking up at something which, declaring itself as Symbolic, is unreal, unattainable, exactly while the spectator too breaks from primary identification with the film. The adults' unmasking minutes earlier recalls masquerades that in many cultures ritualise passage from childhood into Symbolic knowledge (Metz 1975: 71) – fear of the mask resides in belief in its magic, which turns out to conceal benignly-presented patriarchy.

Harwood parallels the withholding of shots of E.T. (in the narrative image and early in the film) with the concealment of the nature of adult men, which results in both becoming objects of spectatorial desire (1995: 157–8). This reinforces patriarchy further to the film's marginalisation of female characters. Elliott's mother's authority, the Imaginary that must be outgrown, is repeatedly undermined. Gertie – who teaches E.T. to speak, suggests 'he' might be female, and repeatedly sees the truth of situations that her brothers deny – is equally 'ignored or derided' (1995: 156).

The narrative of E.T.

Intriguing connections therefore exist between *E.T.*'s representation of adults, guising practised at Halloween, and so-called 'primitive' belief systems. Examining *E.T.* in relation to some models of narrative, all of which involve negotiation of loss, offers further clues to its popularity.

Halloween relates to narrative's origins and function. A pagan ritual appropriated by Christianity, it was when evil had free reign. That this preceded All Saint's Day (All Hallows), one of the holiest in the Church calendar, was uncoincidental. The juxtaposition represented good triumphing over evil, light over dark: a basic narrative. Although literal belief in spirits declined, their symbolisation by disguises continues playfully. Nor is the season arbitrary. Winter's onset, heightening risks of starvation, cold, disease or attack, provoked fear and uncertainty. Halloween, then, gives vent to anxieties on a bigger scale: victorious light promises renewal next spring, sustaining hope, just as the *fort-da* game in Freud's account empowered the child to master separation.

Narratives function analogously, confronting substitutes for individual and communal anxieties and desires. 'Nowhere is nor has been a people without narrative ... Narrative is international, transhistorical, transcultural: it is simply there, like life itself' (Barthes 1975a: 79). This universality leads anthropologists as well as literary theorists to explore its function and workings. A recurrent finding is that narratives, despite surface differences, share similar structures. Linguistics shows how potentially infinite verbal utterances follow regular patterns internalised unknowingly; similarly, narratives follow underlying rules.

Tzvetan Todorov (1977) proposes a simple model. Narratives begin with equilibrium or plenitude. This is disrupted. An opposing force emerges to counter the disruption. Resultant conflict, precondition for any drama, is followed by triumph of either the disruptive or the opposing force, inaugurating new equilibrium or plenitude. The end differs from the start – the process is linear, not circular – but pleasure depends on closure to restore the fictional world to acceptable normality. Episodes in which first one then the other force dominates typically extend conflict, increasing involvement by means of suspense and exploring themes or testing character. The model is representable diagrammatically:

E.T.'s equilibrium (fig. 1) is the forest harmony; disruption the scientists' arrival, forcing the spaceship's departure, leaving E.T. stranded. Lack replaces plenitude

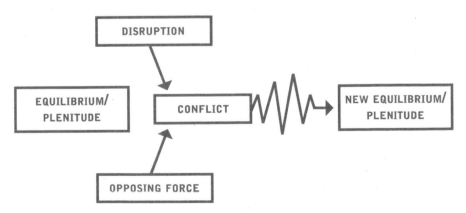

Fig. 1: Todorov's narrative model

E.T. loses the support and security of companionship and has no means of contacting his fellow voyagers. (All conventional narratives are driven by lack, often symbolised as a lost object: the Princess in fairy tales, self-confidence in deodorant commercials, Guy's lighter in *Strangers on a Train* (1951), the Lost Ark, Private Ryan, the Lost Boys in *Hook,* John Milton's *Paradise Lost* (1667), *The Lost World: Jurassic Park.*) E.T., aided by Elliott and friends, is the opposing force working for self-preservation and to restore communication. These needs create conflict with adults, represented by the scientists, committed to capturing and, Elliott believes, destroying the alien. Eventually, new equilibrium and plenitude occur as E.T. returns home. Simultaneously, Elliott's narrative has been disrupted by his father's departure – representing an untrustworthy adult world – so that E.T., fulfilling that role, becomes the opposing force that keeps Elliott in conflict with patriarchy until reconciliation with Keys compensates for the lack.

As that second application of the model indicates, story does not necessarily coincide with plot, the story's presentation in a text: Elliott's father leaves before the film begins. Story is the chronological, cause-and-effect order of events, whereas plot often respects neither causality nor chronology and omits events for dramatic purposes, such as enigma and suspense. Plot (syuzhet) can therefore be conceptualised as the textual ordering of events, the narrative signifier, while story (fabula) is a mental construct, the signified. Models of narrative structure apply most readily to story.

Mythology

Claude Lévi-Strauss (1955; 1966) examines ancient and contemporary myths and legends from cultures worldwide to investigate how narratives mediate reality. He concludes that narratives structure meaning as the human mind does: in binary oppositions. These are an immensely powerful system of describing and defining experience in relation to the user. That any disturbance to the system is either an abomination or fantastic illustrates their importance in maintaining mastery. Consider horror films: Frankenstein's monster is alive yet made from corpses, sensitive yet brutally strong, human yet a technological product; Dracula is neither alive nor dead, both human and animal. Horror is associated with the full moon, a phenomenon that elides polarities between day and night, light and dark, by transposing expected qualities. More controversially, women in films who challenge the binary structure man-senior-active-sexual versus woman-younger-passive-virginal, such as Alex in *Fatal Attraction* (1987), the *femme fatale* in film noir, or Thelma and Louise, are aberrations the narrative must destroy. Narrative is conservative.

Lévi-Strauss concludes that the overarching opposition is nature versus culture. In the above chart, qualities on the left are broadly aligned with nature, those on the right with culture. Furthermore, in this text nature is positive and culture negative, although this is not always so.

Binary oppositions split the world. Narrative, seeking Imaginary unity, heals the rift that remains open in actual experience. Horror and science fiction, conversely, often reassert distinctions that have blurred: vampires and zombies require expulsion from the realm of the living; *Jurassic Park*'s dinosaurs monstrously combine nature and

Space	—	Earth
Forest	—	Suburbia
Children	—	Adults
E.T.	—	Keys (1st half)
Flowers	—	Pollution
Fantasy	—	Science
Freedom	—	Law
Health	—	Sickness
Life	—	Death
Healing	—	Dissection
Feeling	—	Thinking
Wisdom	—	Knowledge
Keys (2nd half)	—	'The authorities'
Mother (present)	—	Father (absent)
Family	—	Separation
Wonder	—	Cynicism
Caring	—	Violence
Faith	—	Mistrust

Fig. 2: Binary oppositions in *E.T.*

technology, an affront resolved when nature evolves to re-establish conflict between those principles. Heroes, who often straddle nature and culture, accordingly eliminate or restore oppositions. Indiana Jones uses academic learning combined with survival instincts: intellect alongside physicality. Oskar Schindler recognises common humanity (nature) to overcome his alliance to Nazism (depraved culture) and exploits familiarity with the world of debased appetites (nature) to assert more civilised values of responsibility (culture) towards 'his' Jews. Both Keys, in switching sides, and E.T., who uses technology to build his transmitter, cross the divide – as does Elliott, in psychoanalytic terms moving from the Imaginary (nature) to the Symbolic (culture).

Conclusion

E.T. conforms to these and other narratological models, including Edward Branigan's (1992) and that proposed by Vladimir Propp's (1975) morphology of Russian folk tales (1975). That may help explain its ability to evoke widespread pleasure. Such a claim is not, however, an instance of the derogatory dismissal of Hollywood entertainment as 'formulaic', which implies prescribed schemes narratives conform to at the expense of integrity. *E.T.*'s typicality is not apparent during normal viewing, yet it links the film to unconscious processes. This alone cannot account for commercial success – after all, it stresses what *E.T.* shares with other narratives, rather than uniqueness (indeed narrative models ignore the specificity of how the story is told) – but in combination with factors discussed earlier it is highly significant. There is no escaping that such models presuppose a single meaning, a narrative inherent within the text, irrespective of readings constructed by spectators. Even so, recognition that verbal language is systematic and rule-governed does not preclude acceptance that it is ambiguous and polysemic; there appears no reason why analysis of audiovisual texts should not proceed under similar assumptions.

Finally, as critics immediately realised, *E.T.* contains striking parallels with the Gospel, observable in both mise-en-scène and narrative. Elliott (whose mother is called Mary) first encounters E.T. in a radiant outhouse which he approaches, carrying a tray like a Magus bearing a gift, by following lights ahead of him in the frame (Spielberg's characteristic signifier of desire); these include a crescent moon that hangs overhead, recalling the Bethlehem star, as Elliott kneels before the shed. Later, representatives of the persecuting authorities wear helmets like those of Roman centurions'. E.T. arrives from the sky, suffers little children to come unto him, and performs miracles: levitation, healing, reviving dead flowers. He dies and undergoes resurrection before returning to the heavens with the reverberating message, 'Be Good,' having reunited the spectator's textual surrogate with a father. He escapes from a sealed 'tomb' – an episode replete with rebirth symbols, such as the oval window on the storage vessel, the umbilicus to the van that breaks from the placenta-like bubble around the house, and the medical imagery mentioned earlier – then, shrouded in a white cloak, his heart glowing red, he extends two fingers in benediction. As paternal figure himself, as infant requiring nurturing and protection, and as inspirer of positive telempathic feelings that negate individual difference, he is at once Father, Son and Holy Spirit.

What to make of this is unclear. Spielberg, at that time a lapsed Jew, has never discussed in interviews whether these parallels were conscious. I do not claim that cinema fulfils functions hitherto attributed to religion – although its ritual aspects, the temple-like architecture of picture palaces, the overwhelming nature of the spectacle, stardom (whereby posters adorn walls which once might have displayed religious icons), its reinforcement of ideologies and its association with holidays present a powerful case. Nor am I reductively asserting that religion is merely another form of narrative. Nevertheless, one of the Western world's most profitable entertainments, and the most successful religion instituted there, display remarkable similarities.

I reject the Messianic readings many ideological critics make of Spielberg's films. Fantasies purportedly offering facile solutions are as likely to heighten dissatisfaction as to lull the masses to passive compliance with their own subjection. This is not to deny, though, that popular movies appeal to widespread psychological needs that express themselves recurrently as archetypes. Narrative models discussed above, as well as psychoanalysis, in their own terms presuppose this. Without succumbing to obfuscating mysticism, it seems reasonable to agree with Peter M. Lowentrout that E.T.'s is 'the mythically necessary death of the too pure and incorruptible in a corrupt world' (1988: 350). E.T.'s telempathic relationship with fellow aliens, with Elliott and with nature, and ability to perform miracles, posit a community amongst all things that radically contradicts individualism. Rather than complicity with essentialist conceptions of 'natural' order and identity, *E.T.* manifests a carnivalesque attitude with emphasis on Elliott and E.T.'s drunkenness, mistrust of authority, loss of selfhood through telepathy and disguises, E.T.'s grotesque body and his ambiguity in terms of age and gender. Carnivalesque is especially pronounced in the extended reissue, which presents Halloween trick-or-treating in disturbing imagery reminiscent of an urban riot.

CHAPTER EIGHT

Twilight Zone: The Movie: magic lantern man overshadowed

This chapter strategically adopts a biographical perspective, elsewhere marginalised in the book. The abysmal quality and peculiar circumstances of *Twilight Zone: The Movie* complicate this study's auteurist rationale and crucially relate it to industry practices.

Raiders of the Lost Ark and *E.T.*'s commercial strength facilitated Spielberg's first project with Warner Bros. The studio owned an idea by the late Rod Serling for a feature based on his TV series, *The Twilight Zone* (1959–64), uncanny stories bundled into anthology episodes. A portmanteau movie similarly would comprise sections by four directors. A Spielberg connection already existed. Apart from enthusiasm for the programmes, many scripted by Richard Matheson who wrote *Duel*, Spielberg had directed two episodes (1969 and 1971) of Serling's similar *Night Gallery*, including the pilot – Spielberg's first TV project. Science fiction/fantasy was resurgent, following *Star Wars*, *Alien* (1979), *Mad Max* (1979) and Spielberg's *Close Encounters* and *E.T.*, while *Star Trek: The Motion Picture* (1979) demonstrated the mileage in old television properties.

Spielberg, with executive producer Frank Marshall, recruited key personnel. Once Spielberg and his friend and rival John Landis signed as co-producers, George Miller (*Mad Max*), already with Warner Bros., and Joe Dante (*Piranha* (1978), an effective *Jaws* spoof) completed the quartet. Warner Bros., delighted at wooing him from Universal/MCA, proposed releasing the project as *Steven Spielberg Presents The Twilight Zone*.

The movie was effectively an independent production bankrolled by Warner Bros. Spielberg and Landis, retaining their Universal offices, enjoyed freedom from everyday interference. Remembering the excesses of *1941* and Landis's *The Blues Brothers* (1980), they determined to make this unorthodox arrangement work, apparently shooting 'fast and cheap' (Kilday 1988: 72). John Baxter records that Landis produced his segment and the prologue autonomously; 'communications between the Landis and Spielberg offices were kept tenuous' (1996: 254).

The best of times, the worst of times

With four massive hits and studios jostling for projects, Spielberg was riding high. On 23 July 1982, six weeks after release, *E.T.* became the fifth most successful film ever. But during the night catastrophe had struck.

Landis's segment transports a bigot into situations where his racism rebounds: he becomes a Holocaust Jew, narrowly avoids a Ku Klux Klan lynching and comes under American fire in Vietnam. As filming concluded, special-effects explosions crashed a helicopter onto actor Vic Morrow and two Vietnamese extras, a girl and boy aged 6 and 7, crushing one and decapitating the others. Landis and four associates immediately faced manslaughter charges.

Investigations uncovered negligence and employment irregularities. Minors could work until 6.30pm, with extensions to 8.00pm granted only exceptionally. The disaster occurred at 2.20am. No work permits existed, nor teachers or welfare supervision. The children lacked Screen Actors' Guild registration and nobody briefed their parents about potential danger. Within days Landis, his associate producer, a production manager and Warner Bros. were each fined $5,000 maximum penalty for 'allegedly "flagrant" violations' (Crawley 1983a: 146). Subsequently Landis and various others appealed against fines for 36 offences.

Reports that his first reaction was to ask whether Landis had a press agent besmirched Spielberg's reputation (Kilday 1988: 72), although how any third party knew this is unclear. A witness further implicated Spielberg, claiming he was at the location at the fateful time, but later retracted. Spielberg – who authorities never interviewed concerning the incident – faced criticism for distancing himself from the repercussions. This is hardly surprising: he was co-producer and the event became cloaked in scandal as Landis faced possibly six years' imprisonment. Studio lawyers mounted a coordinated defence campaign, while prosecutors threw the book at the accused. State and federal agencies, Hollywood craft unions, and aviation and film industry safety boards investigated individuals and companies involved in what the State Labor Commissioner termed an 'obscene tragedy'. The cases dragged on, fuelling rumours and speculation, as each inquiry awaited the others' conclusions (Crawley 1983a: 144). After unsuccessful plea-bargaining, whereby they would have admitted employment violations, Landis and co-defendants were acquitted of manslaughter nearly five years later following a highly publicised ten-month trial.

Meanwhile civil lawsuits cleared Spielberg, but the Directors' Guild of America quickly reprimanded Landis for unprofessional conduct. The case became inextricable from general Hollywood debauchery, as allegations emerged on and off the record. A technician told newspapers of a similar incident wherein a camera crew perished only three months previously. John Belushi's fatal cocaine and heroin overdose earlier in the year cast its shadow, amid allegations of stunt artists' drug abuse on set, live ammunition discharged during filming at Landis's location the night before the crash, and beer cans in the wreckage. Rumoured widespread cocaine use on *Poltergeist* reinforced such contentions. Against a backdrop of Reaganite morality and hugely inflated budgets that seemed extravagant when profits did not ensue, all this accompanied bankruptcy at Francis Coppola's Zoetrope studios. Public-relations departments continued to struggle with Columbia production chief David Begelman's embezzlement five years earlier of relatively minor sums (given his income) and consequent revelations (Laskos in Pirie 1981: 29). Highly public, chemically induced career burnouts included *Close Encounters'* producer Julia Phillips and star Richard Dreyfuss, who during the *Twilight Zone* investigations was committed for treatment (Baxter 1996: 250). Mere association implicated Spielberg, who eschewed even coffee and alcohol: *1941* starred Belushi, as did *The Blues Brothers*, in which Spielberg appeared, both movies notorious for decadent self-indulgence. These connections, along with Spielberg's extraordinary success and attendant wealth and power, arguably contributed to his failure at the Academy Awards as well as his subsequent move towards respectable adaptations.

Nonetheless Warner Bros. dissuaded Spielberg from ditching *Twilight Zone* as this could be construed as accepting guilt. The Landis episode, already filmed, survived largely intact but with no trace of the helicopter scene. This, by a grotesque irony, had been added, following the sole intervention by Warner Bros. executives, against Landis's original intention. It was meant to soften his segment (the only one not based on a Serling episode), in line with the lighter tone overall, by redeeming his misanthropic protagonist with humanity, demonstrated by saving Vietnamese children from American attack. The trade-off was a budget increase for the helicopter and explosions. Spielberg abandoned his section, a macabre tale that would have involved children in night-time filming. Instead he quickly commissioned Matheson, who scripted the Dante and Miller segments, to rewrite a 1962 tale in which nursing home residents rediscover their childhood and abscond. The original's writer and director, George Clayton Johnson, suggested changing the end. The characters, transformed mentally but restored to elderly bodies, resolve to remain and embrace ageing positively, instead of disappearing as children into the night, which after what had happened might have produced uncomfortable resonances. Warner Bros. stage-managed visits by top stars on Spielberg's last day of shooting to demonstrate solidarity.

'It's in the can'

Spielberg's segment, while technically adept, is a half-hearted, lacklustre affair, shot in six days (Crawley 1983b). In contrast to his customary involvement in many departments, the director avoided pre-production conferences, left the script supervisor to stage scenes and entrusted *E.T.*'s scriptwriter Melissa Mathison, hired pseudonymously for the final rewrite, with dialogue rehearsals (Freer 2001: 129).

Ostensibly illustrating the homily, 'where there is no hope, there is no life', 'Kick the Can' is fundamentally flawed. Stating the moral immediately, the voice-over

renders the remainder largely redundant, leaving little to discover. The tale actually shows sparse interest in hope but concerns itself with make-believe and play.
Generalisation to real life from this heavy-handed fantasy seems unlikely, although
camera positioning aligns the spectator with the residents. Further problems include
an overpowering score, which leaves little room for nuance or the audience's own
response, and the overstated dichotomy between the central premise and one character's scepticism – embarrassing, as his objection to the preposterous avowals is fully
justified.

There are nice incidental touches. Sunnyvale's arched gateway suggests the
entrance to Dante's Hell ('Abandon hope, all ye who enter here'). During a dull and
patronising lecture on 'calcium for good strong bones and teeth' one resident manu-
ally adjusts his dentures and another mashes his gums. Mottled light and leaf shadows
play expressionistically over a character emotionally conflicted. Self-reflexivity occurs,
albeit somewhat schematically. The rest-home lounge, sepia-toned and coldly lit, with
dark polished surfaces and stained-glass windows providing the only colour, initially
resembles a funeral parlour until the light turns gold under its newest resident's influence, whom the narrator calls 'an elderly optimist who carries his magic in a shiny
tin can'. Cans of magic for Spielberg mean one thing: film – a metaphor repeated in
The Terminal (2004) – and here the narrative again enacts regression, although its ris-
ible claims, whimsicality and perfunctory direction preclude Imaginary involvement.
Spielberg's 'twilight zone' is where darkened auditorium meets illuminated diegesis,
self encounters scopic other, reality confronts dream, projection reflects image. Light
restores life. The residents, rediscovering themselves and contemplating hitherto unre-
alised advantages of dotage, replace television quiz shows with gardening and picnics
in the Technicolor outdoors. One even forsakes adulthood and literally flies away to
the swashbuckling glamour of stage and screen, uttering pantomime speeches – and
irritatingly misquoting *Hamlet* (indicative of the production's coexistent carelessness
and portentousness). The others remain, staring towards camera through diaphanous
curtains. These inscribe the 'solar wind', metonym of his journey, and the figurative
screen through which they – and the actual screen through which the audience – spectate; simultaneously surface and aperture to fantasy. This character and the inscribed
director who motivates them earlier look out from the darkened interior, through a
rectangular window, to the shining world of children's play, while the latter draws up
a seat to watch, and applaud, his projected scenario.

These qualities and continuities with other Spielberg films are marginally interesting. Carnivalesque abounds: inversions – pensioners emulating children, children
garbed as adults, assertions that 'We'll break the rules', overturned attitudes towards
ageing – and bodily emphases: toothlessness, old people's underwear, and childlike sniggering and embarrassment when the lecturer informs residents they should
enjoy sex 'well into your eighties'. Lighting and sound so stylised that 'atmosphere
drips' (Combs 1983: 282) and the life-transformation theme, with allusions to *Peter
Pan*, recall *E.T.* and anticipate *Hook*. So also do intense performances from children,
although directorial straining after charm in the guise of innocence mawkishly play
into the hands of Spielberg's most negative critics. Many reviewers noted the segment's unintended closeness to self-parody.

'If you believe, I can make you all promise to feel like children again', is the central assertion; in this instance a Catch 22 that, frankly, insults. Light flashes off the can as it begins its magic. Discussion about how much better it is to see Halley's Comet at eighty than at eight recalls Spielberg's recurrent image of shooting stars. Highlights on the sceptic's eyes as he wakens surrounded by children emphasise vision, recalling other moral tales with similar revelations (*It's a Wonderful Life* (1946) or *A Christmas Carol* (1951)).

Foregrounded intertextuality occurs, obviously, in a television show remake. An on-screen TV highlights New Hollywood's assumption of cinema's intrinsic superiority. Here Spielberg scores an own goal. Many quiz shows are more satisfying and engaging than this 23-minute exercise, and considerably cheaper. While the original medium possibly sustained the story's slightness, a movie's disproportionate event status and production values cannot.

Casting a black protagonist anticipates *The Color Purple*, *The Lost World: Jurassic Park* and *Amistad*. While celebrity intertextuality draws on Scatman Crothers' supernatural role in *The Shining* (1980), this magic-lantern man comes across as a representation verging on racist. Ironically, given the unsubtle message of Landis's segment, blackness connotes magic; irrepressible optimism and dispensation of wisdom to white children regrettably recall an Uncle Tom (Combs 1983: 282).

Implications for authorship

Variety judged Spielberg's contribution a 'pencil sketch' rather than 'fully-painted picture' (Perry 1998: 118). The movie's triviality overall is anything but worth dying for. The screen romance pursued by Spielberg's Lost Boy contrasts shockingly, even discounting the outcome, with barely school-age children's subjection, after midnight, to blinding lights, a helicopter hovering 24 feet overhead, amid explosions and fireballs.

Although nothing linked Spielberg directly to the deaths, his reported behaviour, in the face of legal and media questioning, appeared 'weak, evasive, almost infantile' according to one biographer (Baxter 1996: 265). This undoubtedly solidified the emergent critical consensus that Spielberg's work was childish and solipsistic. Journalists hardly helped, having to report something when met with non-cooperation, recounting how luxury cocooned him among acolytes and sycophants. He had, in fact, left for London immediately after shooting his section, to work on *Indiana Jones and the Temple of Doom*. In Paris he visited the Cinémathèque Française with Truffaut, who shared his encyclopaedic knowledge and passion for film. However, the decision to distance himself from scandal and misdemeanour is understandable given his phenomenal commercial value; he had previously missed Belushi's funeral during *E.T.*'s post-production. Every Spielberg film since *Jaws*, apart from *1941*, was subject to ongoing legal action from claimants to profits, to the extent he could no longer even glance at unsolicited screenplays, and secrecy shrouded his productions.

Liability for the accident has implications for authorship. Landis laid claim in court to 'aesthetic or creative aspects' of filmmaking but insisted that specialists make final decisions about matters such as camera and actor positioning and helicopter movements (Farber & Green 1988: 196). Yet, Kilday (1988) argues, Warner Bros. executives had no active function in the production; Frank Marshall permitted Landis to go his own way; and the line producer was appointed by, and answerable to, Landis, while the assistant director, the camera operator and the pilot, among others, had expressed concern about the explosives. The point here is not to reopen a case settled judicially, but to note the control a successful director assumes and is granted. Crucial is the line between creative and 'final' responsibility. Despite Landis's disclaimer, Spielberg composes most shots and often operates the camera.

After *Rolling Stone* condemned Landis's role in the calamity (Sullivan 1984), 16 top directors signed a letter endorsing the distinction he drew. Equally eminent directors argued otherwise. William Friedkin averred, 'If you take the credit "A John Doe Film", you're saying to the world, "I am responsible for everything you see"' (Farber & Green 1988: 225). While, as Charles Tashiro argues, *Twilight Zone*'s particular circumstances demonstrate the difficulty of generalising about 'a system that seems to be a collection of exceptions' (2002: 28), the case provides empirical evidence concerning authorship, which, far from conclusively, illuminates an abstract and widely misunderstood question.

If nobody was responsible, Tashiro suggests – a logical conclusion from the acquittals and subsequent reduction of Health and Safety penalties to $1,350, just $450 per victim – the deaths must have resulted from Divine Will; a convenient legal fiction but not an answer materialist critics can accept (2002: 35–6). Hence, he argues, blame lies not with individuals but structurally, in the industry's political economy. The Dream Factory has ceded to a prevalent belief, persistent even among studio workers, that film permits individual expression.

Market forces and agents' and producers' strategies impose constraints, restricting which projects filmmakers hear about let alone which are packaged, then green-lighted. Auteurism, understood in the industry, and popularly, in terms of choice and individualism, underpins and provides an ideological rationale for how money circulates and where it ends up: 'Had *The Twilight Zone Movie* [sic] been a hit, it would have enhanced John Landis's position in the industry and raised his critical reputation' (Tashiro 2002: 28). Spielberg, moving on, further accrued power through ongoing commercial success that secured future employment and critical attention. One reward, only for those at the apex, but significant in validating the free expression ideology, was continuing ability to choose projects – provided they were potential blockbusters or did not compromise the blockbusters he had to make to counterbalance potential failure. Financially, however, such failure became increasingly unlikely. While reviewers and critics could be hostile, repeating a famous name 'eventually becomes self-confirming'; according to this view, 'It is, finally, not achievement that creates authorship but advertising' (Tashiro 2002: 29). Ease with which fingers pointed at individuals in the *Twilight Zone* case confirms the ideology, while its evaporation under forensic scrutiny suggests it is illusory.

The reality, Tashiro suggests, is a system whereby executives cultivate the myth of the artist to distract from their own activities and provide scapegoats for error: someone else's creative temperament to blame if productions over-run or audiences do not materialise. Executives pay themselves enormous salaries from distribution, exhibition and copyright ownership, while blaming labour costs for escalating budgets. They make excessive demands on staff flexibility and loyalty, while hiring and firing at whim, often contravening employment laws, knowing that thousands are queuing to do the job for even less in hope of a lucky break. The influence of craft guilds, representing technicians, support staff and performers, is limited to threatened or actual disruption during disputes and does not extend to production decisions. The talent and their agents lack budgetary control and have limited say over whom they work with. Tashiro summarises:

> If a film is a success, all share in the rewards, including the otherwise ghostly executives poised to consume the fruits of productive labour. If a film is a failure, or if a fatal accident occurs on the set, only the artists are blamed. Their careers are put at risk, while the executives move to another studio. (ibid.)

Successful players therefore start their own production companies to claim control. As Spielberg had at Universal, they may contract for several projects, mutually advantageous in that they gain artistic freedom on some while the studio keeps top talent from its rivals and trades on anticipated income. Power players also negotiate upfront payments because, as Tashiro bluntly puts it, 'they expect the studios to cheat them out of their fair share of any profits' (2002: 32). Janet Wasko notes, however, that 'incredibly complex definitions for the point at which a film begins making a profit' (2003. 98) and 'extremely wide variation in terms' when participations are calculated 'can become unbelievably confusing' (2003: 97). Spielberg and some of his associates nevertheless derive extraordinary riches from such arrangements because their profitability has raised them onto a par with executives whose careers they have saved. The studios need them more than they need any particular studio, so they move around, searching for the best deal – and indeed become executives on their own projects, a process that for Spielberg culminated in co-founding a new studio, DreamWorks SKG, in 1994. That being the case, unlike their employees or their studio-era predecessors, they enjoy freedom within the parameters of blockbuster filmmaking – which is to say total creative freedom, in that their incomes, their abilities, their contacts and their bankable names would enable them intermittent pursuit of any projects they wished.

As *Twilight Zone* demonstrates, however, auteurism implies more than creative freedom. Most people, free to do what they want with pen and paper, cannot equal a Shakespeare sonnet or a da Vinci sketch. Nor is quality dependent on individual vision, as many studio-era classic movies show. Nevertheless, 'Kick the Can' by most measures disappointing, clearly possesses stylistic and thematic qualities that mark it unmistakably as Spielberg's piece.

CHAPTER NINE

Indiana Jones and the Temple of Doom: anything goes

If *Raiders of the Lost Ark*'s promotion attempted strategic distancing from Reaganism, the blatant racism, sexism and xenophobia of *Indiana Jones and the Temple of Doom* suggest the filmmakers were either ignorant of or unrepentant concerning its alleged ideological import.

Cole Porter's 'Anything Goes' at the start suggests the latter. Establishing period and milieu (it is performed mainly in Chinese before an Oriental dragon and a girlie chorus of stylised coolies), the song, which could double as postmodernism's mantra, signals the movie's carnivalesque disdain for boundaries, freely and lavishly mixing genres and cycles. A rollercoaster of sensation (literally in the climactic mine wagon chase) – each thrill or gag immediately topped by another – the film's structure and design recall pre-1950s Republic Saturday matinee serials (Scapperotti 1985). Aimed at families and older children, *Temple of Doom* fell foul of censorship because of its violent depictions. Uncut in the US, it prompted so many complaints that a new category (PG-13) ensued. The British cut excluded 25 images, over a minute, to qualify as PG (Baxter 1996: 286).

How one feels about that excess, and the critical stance to adopt, depends on how one conceives of audiences and their responses. In that connection, modality needs consideration.

Modality

Modality refers 'to status, authority and reliability of a message, to its ontological status, or to its value as truth or fact' (Hodge & Kress 1988: 124) – its perceived fit with an ostensible reality (Hodge & Tripp 1986: 43). An utterance claiming and eliciting certainty has strong modality. Qualifications ('I believe', 'it seems to me', 'possibly', 'perhaps') weaken modality, as does excessive assertion. Linguistic credibility involves matching modal auxiliaries to context, whether intended ('Sources close to the White House suggest' in the news) or unconscious ('I really am very fond of you indeed, darling, honestly'). Nonverbal modality is less formally marked. Nevertheless, a gamut of possibilities – from Godard's anti-illusionism to replicated newsreel – enables moviemakers, like novelists, to 'express their degree of commitment to the truth of the propositions they utter, and their views on the desirability or otherwise of the states of affairs referred to' (Fowler 1986: 130).

This is complex and dialogic, involving viewers' prior subjectivity as well as montage effects of textual juxtaposition. Consider different intentions of and reactions to the device just mentioned – fabricated news footage – in *Citizen Kane* (1941), *Casablanca* (1942), *Zelig* (1983), *The Unbearable Lightness of Being* (1988), *JFK* (1991) and *Forrest Gump* (1994). This mendacious intertextuality enhances realism by evoking and appropriating non-fictional evidence (strong modality); alternatively it accentuates technical skill and audacity, eliciting pleasure from modal contradiction (strong enough formally to convince, weakened by whichever discrepancies signify falsification and hence foreground textuality).

Despite these difficulties, Robert Hodge and David Tripp's statements about modality apply to films. The receiver judges modality. Therefore the stronger the modality, 'the more it will be responded to both emotionally and cognitively as though it were reality', and the closer any behavioural or learning effect will be to those of similar situations in actuality (1986: 116). Arguably this has ideological implications. Conversely, the weaker the modality, the weaker the response, and the less learning occurs. Very poor modal fit reverses emotional values. Cartoon-style violence, for example, instead of conveying pain elicits pleasure. Nevertheless, such inverse modality maintains a literal content coexistent with the opposite meaning; such representations still satisfy real impulses. Recognising conventions weakens modality but, being learnt, these have different modality for receivers unequally familiar with their form. Hence *Temple of Doom* – indeed all Spielberg's films – may have lower modality for cineastes than general moviegoers, and lower yet for Spielberg fans. Finally – important for *Schindler's List* – modality varies according to external factors and 'can be affected simply by telling viewers that a film was either real or not' (1986: 118).

Modality and fantasy

'Fantasy', Robert Hodge and David Tripp argue, 'is weak modality: it is a kind of negative. To call something "fantastic" is to recognise that it is probably untrue, that the world really is not like that' (1986: 105). Yet psychoanalysis and ideological criticism predicate that fantasies express, and partially satisfy, real personal and social needs, and I have just stated that inverse modality incorporates its opposite at a literal level. Like a double negative, weak modality, asserting something is not the case, leaves traces of its positive. Acknowledging a representation's unreality is perhaps necessary for disavowal, making repressed material bearable in textual manifestation.

This presents enormous difficulties. Hodge and Tripp's 'fantasy' opposes conventional notions of realism. Realism, by definition, implies strong modality. Yet Hollywood realism is a specific signifying practice that materialises Western patriarchal capitalism's defining fantasies. On a less generalised level, how do nightmarish fantasies in *Temple of Doom* operate? Common phobias – flying, bats, snakes, eels, insects, incarceration, invasive surgery, heights – outdo the tarantulas and snake pit from *Raiders of the Lost Ark*. To phobics, the crawling mat of giant bugs must seem sufficiently real, matching expectations of verisimilitude, as precondition for the perverse pleasure of subjecting oneself to them; *A Bug's Life* (1998), in which anthropomorphised insects manifest weaker modality, presumably affects them less. Yet the context – *Temple of Doom*, which has weak modality compared to most serious drama, and as a sequel attracts audiences *expecting* fantasy – apparently does not diminish the modality of the local image. This is despite social elements of ritualised play-acting that enter into horrified responses during shared viewing.

In one minute, three characters bail out of an aeroplane without parachutes, inflate and get into a life raft, land unharmed on a Himalayan peak, glissade down a snowfield and into a canyon, land right side up in rapids and continue downriver. Nonetheless, a reviewer comments, 'these stunningly engineered adventures could have done with Spielberg's tongue being a little more often in his cheek' (Barkley 1984: 22). Perhaps multimodality better describes texts, in accord with Mikhail Bakhtin's heteroglossia (1981: 263) – co-presence of multiple discourses – compatible with my assertion that alternating Imaginary involvement and awareness of Symbolic address characterises Spielberg's brand of cinematic pleasure.

Modality and ideology

Modality is not exclusively textual; 'not merely reproduced, it is individually constructed', an attribute of the response (Hodge & Tripp 1986: 106). Films do not have modalities; readings do. Ascribing ideological effects is thus highly problematic.

Take *Temple of Doom's* opening. The first shot, dissolving from the Paramount logo to the same mountain in relief upon a gong, declares the film's discursive strategy. The transition obviously alludes to *Raiders of the Lost Ark*. But the gong's striking, imitative of a shot from *Gunga Din* (1939), a precursor to Jones' adventures, resembles another logo: for Rank, distributor of many British films Spielberg affectionately regards. Instead of cutting to the action, the camera pans (unusually in Spielberg), confirming that this doubly overlaid logo, an essential prop later, shares the nightclub's space before Willie's (Kate Capshaw) performance. The diegesis links metonymically, via the logos, to cinematic institutions rather than a referential real world.

Willie's act confirms this supposition: 'a bizarre but breathtaking stylistic marriage between Busby Berkeley and Josef von Sternberg' (Sinyard 1987: 91), in a club named after a *Star Wars* character. Its middle section, tap dancers in short skirts and bowlers, desaturated almost to monochrome against a sequined backdrop evoking scratched film as much as visual allure, occupies purely cinematic space. As in backstage musicals like *42nd Street* (1933), the staging is exclusively for the camera. Sweeping back and forth between the women, it visibly constructs the spectacle when a dolly-shot, choreographed to frame each successive dancer doing the splits, rewinds so they defy gravity, soaring back to their feet.

Willie's performance in a sparkling red sheath dress isolates her as object of the gaze. Her superimposition over the credits foregrounds the screen plane. Accompanied by a heavenly choir, she emerges from a cloud of smoke and adopts a static, *femme fatale* pose. The sequence recalls moments, described by Laura Mulvey, when classical Hollywood narratives congeal to contemplate the fetishised female form. As pure spectacle, Mulvey maintains, such moments have enormous ideological significance. They fix and naturalise the female as passive object of the gaze, propagating unequal power relations between gendered subjects. The camera disavows inherent voyeurism by adopting the hero's intra-diegetic look and the spectator identifies with his control within the narrative (consequently over the heroine). Mulvey's account accords with *Temple of Doom*:

> In *Only Angels Have Wings* [1939] and in *To Have and Have Not* [1944], the film opens with the woman as object of the combined gaze of the spectator and all the male protagonists... She is isolated, glamorous, on display, sexualised. But as the narrative progresses she falls in love with the male protagonist and becomes his property, losing her outward glamorous characteristics, her generalised sexuality, her show-girl connotations; her eroticism is subjected to the male star alone. By means of identification with him, through participation in his power, the spectator can indirectly possess her too. (1981: 211)

This parallels Willie's transformation from distant, unattainable fantasy into the image of a compliant 1980s wife and mother with a frizzed perm, white blouse and (ironically reversing Marion's treatment in *Raiders of the Lost Ark*) practical trousers (compare, for example, Anne Archer in *Fatal Attraction*). There are, however, differences. Significantly, given Spielberg's propensity for inscribed spectators during heightened spectacle, nobody within the film observes Willie's performance, directed to camera. She makes eye contact and winks at the spectator, and only at the end, when she delivers the final 'Anything Goes!' with a look off-screen, does classical continuity editing begin, retrospectively showing a diegetic audience. Furthermore, Jones does not view her act. This prefigures his indifference to looking at her throughout most of the film. Although she insists he is unable to take his eyes off her, she suffers indignities and denigrations in his presence while his attention is elsewhere.

Willie's otherwise flawless act includes skipping onto a step and tottering on her heels. Deliberate imperfection in an extravagant Hollywood homage shifts the modality of even such stylised fantasy. The moment could have been perfect. This crack in its production joins the wink and cinematic allusions to open a space between pastiche and parody. Awareness of either the gloss masking the labour of Kate Capshaw's performance or of the film's deliberately appearing cheaper and less professional than it

Indiana Jones and the Temple of Doom – complicity with the viewer: Willie's wink

actually is – or both – vacillates between these modes, neither of which, because they foreground textuality, has much to do with realism.

For all but the most naïve – children possibly upset by the graphic ritual sacrifice (although, Hodge and Tripp demonstrate, children's distinct modality judgements differ from those of adults' (1986: 100–31)) – this knowingly ridiculous film, formally enunciated as *histoire*, functions as *discours*. Spielberg and Lucas's movies, Allen Malmquist observes, are packed with 'out-jokes', rather than 'in-jokes' only their makers would understand. He suggests this 'breaks the fantasy *Temple of Doom* … seeks to create' (1985: 42). If fantasy, defined as weak modality, is breakable – suggesting it is potentially very involving while acknowledged to be unreal – models of spectatorship that assume unilateral subject positioning in relation to ideology would appear inadequate in discussing this film.

How can one assess, for example, the validity of psychoanalysis – integral to many radical accounts of spectatorship and narrative – to a film that appears to be ahead of the game? In view of the Lacanian account of narrative, repeatedly confirmed by Spielberg's fictional quests, one cannot overlook Willie's comment on meeting Jones: 'I always thought archaeologists were funny little men searching for their mommies.' 'Mummies!' Jones corrects her. Mulvey's thesis premises that regression through the Mirror Phase revives Oedipal anxieties so the female has to be fetishised, 'concealing … castration fear' in the implicitly male spectator (1981: 214). Body-shaping dresses and high heels help masculinity control what it dreads. If, then, the showgirl is a phallus substitute, how can one ignore that Jones in the nightclub deprives an older, powerful, explicitly fatherly adversary (his son appears, already injured by Jones), of his 'Willie'? When the obligatory final kiss closes the family romance involving Jones, Willie and the child, Shorty (Ke Huy Quan), it requires zealous and humourless application of feminism to assume the film condones Jones' extension of his phallic whip to prevent Willie's departure. This ludicrous display of patriarchal aggression gets results, in line with the ruthless dimension of Jones' personality glimpsed intermittently, but is hardly a credible model for courtship behaviour.

Psychoanalysis inextricably links racism and sexism, both charged against the film (French 1984; Hobermann 1984; Britton 1986). Moishe Postone and Elizabeth Traube (1985) demonstrate connections between imperialist and patriarchal discourses through the intertwined adventure and romance plots. As in *Raiders of the Lost Ark*, non-Europeans – every significant character apart from Jones, Willie and a British officer – are feminised. Archaic forces of evil, destruction and death taint femininity itself in this boys' adventure.

Shorty, as much as Jones, is the spectator's surrogate. At moments, as in *Raiders of the Lost Ark* and *E.T.*, a projective relay links the spectator to the action; in the village Shorty echoes Jones' gestures and expressions and his fight with the young Maharajah parallels Jones' with a Thuggee heavy. Shorty initially treats Willie as a rival for Jones, his unofficial and venerated father, and ultimately receives recognition after a life-restoring affirmation of love when the two males ritualistically restore their hats to each other. I disagree with Henry Sheehan that here 'it almost seems that Spielberg is introducing a homoerotic element' (1992: 60); the hats, as phallic symbols, respectively communicate Shorty's regard for Jones' reinstated authority and Jones' momentary acceptance of Shorty as equal. Nevertheless he quickly reverts to addressing him as a child – 'Quit fooling around with that kid', 'Shorty – quit stalling!' – the joke being Shorty's consistent heroism while Jones, an undependable father, loses control. The spectator shares Shorty's rather than Jones' knowledge here. Focalisation is with the boy. Juvenile male bonding leaves no place, outside narrative convention, for the woman, consequently ignored, punished and the butt of humour.

There is a darker side, however. Willie as sexual Other aligns with the Thuggees' racial and adversarial Otherness. Jones' quest, Postone and Traube observe, is to hell and back, from light to darkness and back into light: 'the energetic, action-packed pace and playful humour of the framing sequences contrast sharply with the increasingly oppressive, constricted atmosphere and total absence of comic relief that characterise the film's central sequence' – where, for many reviewers (and complainants also), it 'goes wrong' (1985: 12).

The beautiful aristocratic court masks evil and corruption. When Willie wears Indian costume and jewellery, Jones admits her loveliness for the first time. Significantly, Shorty runs away screaming from graceful dancing girls, as if with a premonition of the ensuing banquet's revelation: 'not so much ... the depravity *behind* exotic sensuality as ... the *identity* of sensuality and depravity', suggested by 'the lascivious pleasure with which the Indians consume the loathsome food' (Postone & Traube 1985: 13).

The unrelieved horror at the movie's heart involves worship of a Mother Goddess, intent on world domination, demanding human sacrifice. The threat to patriarchy, represented by abducting children to slave in mines, is symbolised by prostration of the village's phallic stone before Kali, the Earth Mother with a devouring furnace between her legs. As often in Spielberg, the hero reunites broken families, this time returning the village children and restoring power to patriarchal elders.

Equation between femininity and the Thuggees' wickedness occurs initially through the dancing girls, the young Maharajah's effeminacy, and – as with Belloq in

Raiders of the Lost Ark – contrast between the dapper Prime Minister and the unshaven Jones (who mislays his razor, the film establishes; thus he can maintain the appropriate tough-guy image when the action resumes).

The temple's horrors follow – result from – Jones' failed lovemaking with Willie. Structurally, his attraction to her remains in tension with fear of castration. Near the start she secures the antidote to Lao Che's (Roy Chiao) poison in her bosom, from where Jones desperately seizes it by force while both she and Shorty assume he is getting fresh with her. Confusion of sexuality with adventure survival recurs, along with the mammary motif, when Jones and Willie's mutual seduction fails over competition for control. While a death struggle with an assassin sublimates and displaces Jones' energy, Willie eagerly awaits his return and is annoyed when he attends more to a statue's breasts than her own. Expert caressing of these – they contain a hidden switch – opens a dark, moist, secret passageway to the inner chamber where Kali, the female principle, abides: a place of heat and intense thrills, suffused with crimson light, where captive men become entranced or lose their hearts and their lives. As Postone and Traube note, the symbolism incorporates disgust. Teeming creepy-crawlies displace healthy fecundity. Jones and Shorty almost perish in a chamber that closes on them with impaling spikes, a vagina dentata; as if to confirm the castration imagery, Jones reaches in to recover his hat – a moment that delighted audiences – a split-second before the jaws close. Furthermore the imagery associates Willie, initially 'born' in a red dress from a dragon's mouth, with the cavern's red interior. Only Shorty's intervention, with a phallic torch and affirmation of male bonding, frees himself and his surrogate parents from this primal scene's spell. The process repeats itself light-heartedly when, in the closing shots – Kali's followers defeated and the phallus returned to its shrine – Shorty's elephant sprays water over the kissing couple. Children's laughter supplants adult sexuality.

A plot lacuna assists this happy conclusion. Contrary to expectation established by the sacrifice, neither Jones nor the priest attempts to rip out Willie's heart before she descends into the pit, even though the priest tries to claw out Jones' during the climactic cliffhanger. Postone and Traube argue that, because a hero cannot cause irrevocable harm, we assume Jones' release will come through Willie as he reaches towards her. This untaken route, however – breaking the evil spell by touching the woman's breast –

> would have meant overcoming the dominion of Kali by separating the erotic, life-bringing woman from the consuming, death-bringing one, separating desire from death ... This in turn could have been the basis for a radically new masculinity, a masculinity no longer compelled to ally with little boys, to flee from women in adventures, or to perceive sensuality as depraved. (1985: 14)

The fantasy reproduces ideology by positing white masculinity as civilisation's basis.

Ideology or fantasy?

Postone and Traube consider *Temple of Doom* 'a light-hearted reaffirmation of old-fashioned sexism and racism ... as the necessary alternative to the forces of darkness'

(1985: 12). Compelling though their thesis is, nowhere do they consider modality: that these values are blatantly satirised, as cinemagoers may recognise.

The relationship between overt fantasy and ideological reinforcement is problematic. Fantasies symbolise, through unconscious processes analogous to dream-work, solutions and satisfactions to unresolved anxieties and desires. That films, collaboratively produced, relate similarly to *societal* values, seems a reasonable assumption. Representations with strong modality, concordant with dominant discourses, might naturalise certain understandings of the world. Less apparent is how or why weak modality, even if structurally congruent with recurrent fantasies (the Oedipal scenario, for example), could be re-encoded into repressed, necessarily unconscious, material. This would have to occur if sublimations of unresolved needs functioned as agents, rather than symptoms, of ideology. It would be a precondition of response, if one assumes consent occurs through unconsciously recognising structures concordant with one's own discursive formation. Hence the danger of oversimplification in rhetorically ascribing transitivity to texts, as when Postone and Traube charge that *Temple of Doom*: 'seeks to represent imperialism as a civilising, socially progressive force and so to legitimise Western domination of others' (1985: 12).

If, as Postone and Traube rightly claim, *Temple of Doom* ignores contemporary problems and overlooks everyday heroism in struggles against inequity and injustice, that does not in itself make it Reaganite. Most fiction films have always manifested those tendencies. Yet criticism often relates films to their political context, while psychoanalysis reveals repressed and contradictory material. If *Temple of Doom* really reasserts traditional attitudes against Third World and Eastern bloc challenges to America's self-image (Robinson 1984), why does it not go the whole hog and demand to be taken seriously (as *Rambo* and *Rocky IV* (1985), dealing solemnly – and childishly – with contemporaneous military and political crises, did a year later)?

That a movie relates to social discourses does not automatically mean it condones or reproduces one particular stance. Perhaps serious criticism, embracing Althusserian theory in the 1980s (and feeling threatened by the rise of the right), failed to distinguish sufficiently between *presence* and *promotion* of discourses. In the US, for example, *The Right Stuff* (1983) may have flopped precisely *because* it was discussed and dismissed as a gung-ho account of actual Cold War events (lacking the allegorical distancing and opportunities for clever critical exposition more overtly fantastic texts evidently offer). Britons received it as satirical, without in the least diminishing admiration for the individual heroism and collective vision of the space project. In different contexts the same text evinced different modalities.

Postone and Traube contend that the film, dividing Indians into two classes, identifies oppression with indigenous rule. This, then, justifies imperialism, figured both in the American hero's authority but also in a British colonial force's last-minute intervention. Outsiders' presence is implicitly desirable for the peasants, while imposing dependence on foreign involvement. Contemporary problems such as forced child labour consequently result not from multinational capitalism but local culture. Similarly, Andrew Britton argues, the film projects its own violence onto the Other (1986: 41).

Texts, however, do not unilaterally impose ideology. To understand better its reproduction the concept of hegemony needs consideration.

Hegemony, the ongoing struggle which makes ideology common sense rather than coercive, masks, displaces and naturalises social problems in popular texts. *Temple of Doom*, foregrounding gender conflict, apparently naturalises it as a consequence of Willie's seemingly essential silliness. Racial difference figures in the hero's superiority as the villagers' saviour and eradicator of villainy. Class conflict disappears to the far side of the world without any explicit political underpinning.

Yet texts, multi-discursive, are relatively open and contradictory. This is not to imply any meaning is available, rather to reassert, following Stuart Hall (1977), David Morley (1980) and others, that various constrained readings are possible. Interestingly, in this instance the dominant or preferred meaning – generally taken to be closely aligned with dominant ideology – is not necessarily what the filmmakers intended. It may be that children in particular, reading the movie literally, undergo exposure to unchallenged sexist and racist attitudes, in which case, unequivocally, it is *potentially* harmful. Postone and Traube's analysis typifies oppositional readings, which reinterpret texts within an alternative – in their case Marxist – framework. Negotiated readings are available also, including recognising racism and sexism as archaic discourses mocked from a position of enlightened superiority. There are, however, issues that sometimes you do not joke about. These included gender and race in the reactionary, repressive 1980s.

The modality of fantasy is, Hodge and Tripp suggest, both a problem and a solution in considering media effects (1986: 100). That *Temple of Doom* is obviously fantasy attracts condemnation for distracting audiences, even as it allegedly distorts reality. Such contradictions, resulting from 'forms of thought which simply "read off" a particular situation from certain pre-established general principles' (Eagleton 1991: 4), are, however, as much in the text as in its framing discourses.

Willie, for example, is opposed to Indian culture on arrival in the village when she is squeamish about unfamiliar food. Strong modality – flies buzz around and Jones reminds her that this represents a feast to poor villagers – makes it possible to liken Willie to tourists in exotic places seeking out McDonalds. Jones respects local customs, observing, 'You're insulting them and embarrassing me.' This is no simple distinction between 'positive' Americans and 'negative' Asians. Indeed for American teenage junk food consumers, inured to wastefulness and ignorant of other cultures, it is, given the hero's authority, progressively pedagogical.

Willie, however, is not *fixed* against Indian culture. In the palace, wearing Indian finery, she is willing to marry a maharajah, although the weak-modality 'gross-out' banquet punishes her for mercenary intent as much as fussiness over food. As a gold-digger, her dependent role as 'a brainless, whining ... dumb blonde' is not simply 'sexist portrayal' (Postone & Traube 1985: 13) but can be construed as an assumed construction by a tougher, scheming character (see, for example, Doane 1982). By the relatively strong-modality return to the village at the end she respects indigenous practices by adopting traditional greetings.

Moreover, contrary to Postone and Traube's insistence, the film does not overlook 'the darker side of imperialist domination' (1985: 13), although informed historical analysis is far from its project. In the palace – where now Jones insults his hosts – the Prime Minister complains, in Colonel Blumburtt's presence, that 'the British find it amusing to inspect us at their convenience' and 'worry so about their Empire – it makes us all feel like well-cared-for children': precisely the charge critics make about the film's attitude to the racial Other. Indeed Jones comments, in the three-way conversation including the uniformed colonel, 'It seems the British never forget the Mutiny of 1857': far from ignoring colonialism, the film foregrounds it even if the effect is mystificatory. In response to Jones insistently discussing Thuggee lore, the Prime Minister calls him 'a grave robber rather than an archaeologist', referring to an incident Jones maintains newspapers 'greatly exaggerated'. Jones is hardly unconditionally admirable. Conversely, Willie, asking for soup, addresses the waiter deferentially – 'Excuse me, sir' – the manner of an anxious visitor, not a confident oppressor.

Postone and Traube argue that the humour of the disgusting feast distracts from 'the content of ... a conversation that provided at least shreds of material for a historical understanding of the present conflict in a history of struggle' (1985: 13). Yet *they*, and I, paid attention, so what is one to make of their assumption about other audience members' responses? It is not my brief to defend this film, but I am bothered that imposing ideological models of criticism can distort textual evidence to demonstrate a predetermined case. This threatens to hinder understanding of the film and to invalidate what should be a productive critical approach. Without clearer understanding of how ideology is negotiated, there is danger of orienting critical insights towards the unremarkable conclusion that mainstream films reproduce mainstream attitudes.

One could contend that *Temple of Doom* presents a more nuanced version of race than reflex responses to stereotypes suggest. Both Shorty and Jones' Chinese waiter sidekick contradict what might otherwise seem xenophobic about Lao Che's characterisation. Dignified village elders contrast with brutal Thuggees. The Prime Minister's superficial urbanity proves not all Indians are as abject as the cowardly elephant drivers. Dress codes blur cultural boundaries: Lao Che's tuxedo, Shorty's baseball cap, Willie's Indian garb, the Prime Minister's European suit. If comparatively wealthy foreign visitors ride elephants while natives walk, that is real-world economics. Jones treats different cultures and nationalities respectfully unless reasons dictate otherwise. The Maharajah's innate goodness, enabling the heroes' escape, cancels previous treachery while under the same spell that entranced Jones. Willie's gold-digger mentality and Jones' scandalous past and lust for 'fortune and glory' compromise their moral superiority. Indeed, the villagers insist that Jones' arrival and destiny fulfil tribal prophecies: rather than a controlling hero, he is in thrall to their belief system. One might argue, if not for prejudices about Hollywood heroism, that their mythology is the metanarrative 'containing' his adventure.

As for the sexism, it is so patently exaggerated that it is hard to believe any adult does not read it ironically. How dumb would a blonde have to be to mount an elephant back-to-front? Where did her male companions gain their bareback elephant riding abilities? Is a construction of femininity that worries more about broken manicured nails and the smell of an elephant in the midst of life-and-death situations not one that *ought* to be ridiculed? When Jones and Shorty argue over a card game, completely ignoring Willie while she encounters all kinds of unfamiliar jungle life, including a giant snake, only for Jones to opine that her trouble is that she makes too much noise, which character is in the worse light?

To assert this kind of 'balance' assumes that the film operates as a unified structure rather than progression of isolated representations. Indeed, active spectatorship, if accepted, presupposes such synchronicity. Every moment creates meaning through association and juxtaposition; context qualifies everything. This, though, does not alter strong modality in localised representations, sufficiently authoritative to cause offence by neutralising humour and irony, just as scenes soliciting phobic responses demand credibility even within a weak-modality context. In fact it appears uncertain whether modality is, in complex audiovisual structures, adequately determinable from textual characteristics. People do, after all, cry at Bambi's mother's death, despite patently artificial animation.

Conclusion

Modality leaves ideological questions unresolved. It is a persistent problem underlying criticism of Spielberg films, whether as fantasies or, when dealing specifically with race – *The Color Purple, Schindler's List, Amistad* and *Munich* – as mediations of real-life inhumanity. More than recurrent, it is cumulative; Spielberg's fame ensures that untheorised auteurism determines critical responses. Objections to earlier films permeate reactions to later ones.

Outrage over *Temple of Doom*'s violence may have focused general unease over unreconciled contradictions. The palace scenes, constructed to resemble the faded Technicolor splendour of *The Thief of Bagdad* (1940), *Black Narcissus* (1946) and Bollywood musicals, clearly present themselves as fantasy. Yet there is disturbing realism about the Thugees' thin child victims: partly because the village exterior appears authentic but also because Third World residents feature so rarely in Western media – except as anti-Western fanatics, victims requiring aid or leadership (*Gandhi* (1982)), or relatively privileged but childlike, mysterious or incompetent, social or professional contacts for colonialists (*The Jewel in the Crown* (1982), *A Passage to India* (1984)). Here, perhaps, is where irony failed. *Temple of Doom* coincided with the Ethiopian famine, permitting easy alignment between its downtrodden farmers and those in Africa as a universal victimised Other. This probably did little to enhance real-life political understanding, but the modal clash uncomfortably ruffled the movie's tone. Faced with ideological contradiction, popular criticism focuses unease on what is more easily fulminated against: language, sex or, in this case, violence.

Much academic film writing, dissatisfied with the limitations of text-based and theoretical approaches to Hollywood ideology, turned in the 1980s towards empirical audience research. Instead of asserting or speculating about how films affect spectators, emphasis shifted to how filmgoers use and make sense of cinematic experiences, a useful corrective that presents new problems and limitations.

CHAPTER TEN

The Color Purple: sisters and brothers

Critics who saw Spielberg as a children's director, or routinely accused him of infantilising Hollywood, were sceptical when he acquired rights to three of the most illustrious and challenging books of the 1980s: Thomas Keneally's Booker Prize-winning *Schindler's Ark*, J. G. Ballard's Booker-nominated *Empire of the Sun* and Alice Walker's Pulitzer Prize and American Book Award winner, *The Color Purple*. His treatment of adult themes would either signal a turning point or confirm worst fears.

The Color Purple enters difficult areas including child sexual abuse, domestic violence, lesbianism, pantheistic religion and race against a background of colonialism and the legacy of slavery. Admirers hoped Walker's work would find a wider audience through Spielberg and that screening black female experience, feminism and alternative sexualities would air marginalised issues productively. Inevitably these aspirations provoked anxieties about any heterosexual white male's adequacy to handle them.

Hesitancy greeted the film among wider, inflammatory, social, political and economic controversies, re-election having reinforced Reagan's agenda. Given the sexism, racism and excessive violence charged against *Indiana Jones and the Temple of Doom*, the climate was hostile. Cynics saw Spielberg embracing literature to gain respectability and his elusive Academy Award. (*The Color Purple* was unsuccessfully nominated for 11 categories – excluding, unprecedentedly, Best Director, which normally accompanies Best Film.) Objections to Walker's representation of gender relations complicated matters. Some African-American men refused to see the film, opposing it in principle

(Milloy 1985, who later retracted: 1986; Brown 1986). The Coalition Against Black Exploitation complained in advance to the producers, picketed openings and berated Danny Glover, the best-known performer, for aiding oppression. Intellectuals invoked theorists such as Lorraine Hansberry on America's self-definition against the negatively portrayed 'exotic Negro' (1969: 93), to explain African-Americans' 'schizophrenic reaction' to the film's progressive elements while being made to 'wince' at 'some of the caricatures and representations' (Bobo 1988: 49). Yet, as Jacqueline Bobo's ethnographic research later confirmed, 'many black women had ... an overwhelmingly positive reaction' (1995: 97). Seemingly incompatible discourses of race, gender, class, sexuality, entertainment and didacticism overdetermined responses. The release 'marked', in one analyst's memorable phrase, 'a moment of verbal clutter, not clarity' (Butler 1991: 64).

These controversies, reported and waged within mainstream as well as specialist media, were a publicist's dream. Fuelling the limelight, they helped the $15 million movie gross $200 million (Walker 1996: 266), while complicating Spielberg's image in ways that determined later publicity. They launched Oprah Winfrey and Whoopi Goldberg as international stars. John Fiske argues a media event develops 'not at the whim of the media alone but ... gives presence to abstract cultural currents that long precede and will long outlast it' (1994: xxi). *The Color Purple* aired discourses hither-to ignored or repressed, making it a major event, whatever its faults or merits. As Bobo observes, 'Whether this was beneficial to black people or harmful in the long run remains to be seen. But the issues affecting the condition of black women in [American] society were debated nationally as they had not been before' (1995: 87).

Because 'only Spielberg could have obtained the financing to mount the kind of production that he did' (ibid.), examining *The Color Purple* as a Spielberg movie is particularly relevant in considering its impact. Rather than breaking with earlier work, it concords with the rest of his output, but this is on balance a strength rather than indicative of failure. Familiar elements include reconstitution of broken familial relationships; intertextuality, such as a comical barroom brawl straight out of a Ford movie and a reconstruction of shots from *The Searchers* as characters on a porch stare off-screen into the landscape at returning travellers; and allegiance with the central character Celie's (Whoopi Goldberg) experience underlined by explicitly reflexive cinematic images. The latter include an inscribed projection beam linking her desire to vision as she and her husband's mistress Shug (Margaret Avery) uncover letters to her from Nettie (Akosua Busia) – the sister he has banished – that he has hidden; and false shot/reverse-shot continuity edits that vividly 'project' her into situations she reads about, traversed by visible light beams, in the letters. Such details, crucially, align the narration closely with Celie, so that it becomes Nettie's voiced and, implicitly, Celie's unvoiced enunciation.

In no way does this chapter attempt a complete overview of enormously complex and impassioned controversies, nor do I intend to close down what has been, despite acrimony, healthy and productive argument. As a white heterosexual man observing from across the Atlantic and a rift of two decades, my position is essentially voyeuristic. My aim is not lofty pronouncement from a state of academic security on issues

The Color Purple – Celie's lost Imaginary: projected shadows

involving injustice, suffering and fear for millions, especially as nuances of felt experience – expressed in the heat of real political activism – will inevitably elude me. There is no position of 'truth' or 'balance' from which contradictions in that reality are reconcilable. Conflicts require working through: in debate, or 'by any means necessary', in Malcolm X's slogan. Any ideological position is riven with contradiction. This remains true of discourses of race and racism, texts in which they are inscribed and formations within which they are interpreted (Ferguson 1998: 54).

Robert Ferguson advocates 'internal arguing' as a step away from 'understanding representations of "race" as either acceptable or unacceptable and audience behaviour as either enlightened or blinkered and constrained'; it recognises that social life requires 'constant negotiation of dilemmas and contradiction' (ibid.). Individuals comprising contradictory formations make meaning from texts embodying contradictory discourses. 'Productive unease', Ferguson suggests, is an advance in hindering naturalisation of discourses by insisting on relations of power and subordination within which they occur (1998: 6).

Naturalisation operates partly through binary impositions as fixed categories rather than linguistic constructions. Although 'black', 'white', 'lesbian', 'straight', 'intellectual', 'ordinary', 'middle class', 'working class', 'progressive' and 'conservative' – all factors in discussing *The Color Purple* – have real currency and effect, they describe social rather than natural facts. This is not to postmodernise language into mystifying relativism – those terms have repercussions including lifetimes of disadvantage, assassinations and bombings – but to search through 'verbal clutter' towards what Ferguson calls 'dynamic contradiction' (1998: 66). Binaries express power relations that are explorable and, with sufficient will, changeable; they are not ahistorical structures neutrally shaping texts and other social situations from which they can be read off and simply described.

'Black' and 'white' were a crude classification for categorising people economically during slavery and colonisation, and for rationalising doing so. That they are internalised into individual and group identities is a fact of domination, hegemony and resistance; but these are ideological positions rather than reflections of significant essential differences (Dyer 1997: 1). Hansberry (1969) said the same from within oppositional consciousness when noting that white culture required the negative Other in order to define itself (see also Saïd 1978 and Morrison 1992). Ferguson puts inverted commas around 'race' to stress its lack of scientific status and ward off 'intellectual complacency' in examining 'a field which, though primarily discursive, has ... material consequences and correlates' (1998: 1). Similarly 'lesbian' and 'straight' remain simple defining categories whereas queer theory asserts the polymorphous nature of sexuality and considers social and political implications of its regulation. Other contradictions in the controversy surrounding *The Color Purple* likewise require problematisation.

Adaptation

The Color Purple's relationship, as a literary adaptation, to a serious and controversial source raises issues of the filmmaker's responsibility in mediating discourses already in the public domain.

Adaptation *by definition* involves change. Film and literature are distinct signifying practices. Cinema, lacking sound for a third of its history, developed 'highly elaborated visual rhetoric' in which words are often superfluous (Caughie 1981b: 3). Literature is nothing but words. *The Color Purple*, an epistolary novel, is an extreme case: it comprises not the illusory transparency of conventional realism but letters which accentuate their material presence through contrasts between Celie's untutored oral form of language and Nettie's Standard English. Consequently, however, because the character using vernacular is herself writing, little of Walker's authorial persona ostensibly intervenes between Celie and the reader (Stepto 1987: 102). This novel lacks the satirical irony that creates the characteristically American narrational duplicity stretching back to *The Adventures of Huckleberry Finn* (1885), which potentially questions the narrator's reliability and encourages complicity with, and admiration for, the implied author's mimicry and superior knowledge. *The Color Purple* aims to elicit respect, empathy and credibility for Celie's voice, rather than undermine it in the readerly American manner: 'The writerly voice of an under-educated rural black woman ... proves to be more powerful than that of her more educated and more worldly sister, and quite capable of telling a tale without the aid of an editor, amanuensis, etc' (Stepto 1987: 102). Spielberg's film, precisely because it is recognisably such, interposes a distinctive enunciation, despite the imputed transparency of Hollywood practice. Nevertheless, because Walker's novel lacks an explicit framing discourse outside Celie and Nettie's subjectivity, ambiguity remains.

Adaptation is never neutral transposition, for elements such as theme, character, plot and symbolism, activated only in decoding, lack objective existence. The reader's discursive formation, including knowledge of codes, negotiates meaning from interplay of signs. Each interpretative instance is unique. If we concede that story at least is transposable (Chatman 1978: 20), even a naïve reading requires application of schemata (culturally assimilated discursive patterns cued by textual conventions) to the frequently nonchronological, noncausal and invariably elliptical plot, from which story, a mental construct, emerges. If the reader produces narrative, it lacks objective existence beyond the extent to which reading is intersubjective, culturally determined. Which elements become foregrounded differ between readers. That *The Color Purple* – novel and adaptation – speak to and against highly disparate interpretive communities is important in understanding the heat they have generated.

Sometimes adaptors aim for, or receive praise for, 'fidelity' to the original; others accept alteration is inevitable but strive to preserve the source's 'spirit' or 'essence'. These metaphors, widespread in adaptation studies, idealistically posit meaning's origin somewhere beyond textual reception. In fact, even reverential versions cannot but seek objective correlatives in the new medium's conventions for meanings the adaptors construct. Meanings from verbal narration require cinematic expression in film: camerawork, casting, lighting, music, sound and the rest. Decisions often lack guidance from the original. A novel might mention a car, but a production designer orders a particular model, age and colour, filmed in a particular way in a specific time and place. Such literalness anchors connotations: cameras cannot present nouns devoid of adjectives, verbs without adverbs. Unavoidably, any film's visualisation of a novel differs from yours and mine. Lamenting this is futile. However, as Joan Digby (1993) demonstrates, such constraints can be exploited creatively. In Spielberg's adaptation, Shug's yellow car brings Celie joy and its departure marks her escape. It not only functions metonymically in Shug's characterisation – flamboyant, expensive, luxurious, racy – but links also to sunflowers, associated with Nettie, to Shug's tour bus that left Celie behind previously, and to Shug's dress when reconciled with her father. The film appropriates the novel's colour symbolism into its transtextuality.

Adaptation involves no inherent diminution of quality. Good films, after all, come from mediocre books. If a film travesties what is valued, criticism should identify and trace the fault if it is worth pursuing. Any study, and there are many, that treats adaptation as though direct replication is a criterion, will not get far. What is certain is that each relationship between texts is unique; few worthwhile generalisations are possible. Comparing novel with film is fairly pointless unless, as in the present instance, contested representations are involved. This can be worthwhile because 'film works on entirely different levels of perception, appealing through the senses to the emotions and spirit, and only then to the intellect' (Halprin 1986: 1) – leaving plenty of scope for misunderstanding.

Cinema and prose fiction operate within different, although overlapping and increasingly connected, cultural and economic contexts. A novelist enjoys relative freedom of expression at the expense of having to find time and means of support to write; if successful enough to command an advance, offset against royalties, this will normally be small. Feature films, by contrast hugely expensive, involve tremendous financial risk. Only one fifth are profitable, so investment represents a major gamble.

One way to maximise chances of profit is to market a story that has previously appealed to an audience. Its popular attraction already known, it also has a ready-made potential audience among people who have read, or at least heard of, the original (Izod 1993: 96). Retaining the title appeals to cultural memory, creating an immediately recognisable narrative image. This clearly helped *The Color Purple*, already a best-seller. Nevertheless, without commercial success almost guaranteed by Spielberg's involvement, the film could not have commanded a budget for anything near the scale and production values required to attract the non-literary audience Walker wanted it to reach (Dworkin 1985: 175; Halprin 1986: 1).

Adaptations target different audiences, employing three distinct approaches. Nearly a third of Hollywood films are based on existing or recently commissioned popular fiction, aimed widely (Ellis 1982: 3); *Jaws* is one, together with examples not generally recognised as adaptations. (The category expands into high-budget, star-studded versions of classics, such as *The Great Gatsby* (1974).) As a cross-over movie, using Spielberg's reputation and genre conventions of the traditional epic and women's film to draw a mainstream audience not necessarily aware of the book, *The Color Purple* qualifies for inclusion. A second category is classics sold on the strength of the author, for a smaller, more literary 'art-house' market, such as early Merchant/Ivory productions. Associated with 'heritage' in prestigious, often subsidised, national cinemas explicitly opposed to Hollywood, and descended from a tradition that intentionally cultivated snobbery to attract wealthier audiences (Izod 1993: 96), this appeals to older, more educated, irregular filmgoers; typical titles include *Jean de Florette* (1986), *Babette's Feast* (1987) and *Little Dorrit* (1988). Doubtless many who had hitherto not consciously seen a Spielberg movie attended through loyalty to Walker's novel. Third, classics interpreted as personal projects by auteur directors – Kubrick's *Barry Lyndon* (1975), say – embrace literary and cineaste audiences. Spielberg, rebranding his image with *The Color Purple*, courted respectability. Filmed novels receive the most Academy Award nominations. While *The Color Purple* failed to move the Academy, its audience diversity points to why potentially unpromising material succeeded commercially. It also partly explains the critical intensity and range, as few films seek interest beyond fairly specific groups and hence run less risk of disappointment or offence.

Differences between Walker's book and the film exceed alternatives to the unfilmable epistolary technique. The novel's Celie and Sofia achieve sisterhood through quilting after Celie incenses Sofia by misadvising Harpo to beat her. This reconciliation the film does not dramatise. Mister in the novel seeks Celie's forgiveness and they share evenings on the porch sewing; the film treats him less generously. Sofia reunites with Harpo, running the juke joint, but in the novel finds refuge with her extended family of Amazon-like sisters. The film's climax links to Shug's reconciliation with her father, not in the book. Such changes, however, need consideration alongside other aspects of the controversy, for it is not their occurrence that matters but their ideological import. For example, without pre-empting discussion, Mister's transformation in the novel – an aspect of Walker's message of healing – is arguably too far-fetched to dramatise convincingly given the film's accelerating pace towards its climax. Partly undoing consequences of his earlier villainy but remaining marginal, though present, at the concluding reunion, the cinematic Mister shows both remorse and potential for further improvement, thereby maintaining male dignity and earning a grain of sympathy. This is instead of yielding to the novel's 'new, female-centred order', which might be taking feminism too far for mainstream audiences (Dole 1996: 14).

Responses to *The Color Purple* conflate at least three senses of 'representation' which require unravelling to avoid propagating painful confusions surrounding discussion of the book and film. One involves a statistical sense. The film challenged media under-representation of non-white ethnic groups, particularly low-income African-American women, compared to actual numbers in society. Similarly, one could criticise the disproportion of non-judgemental images of homoeroticism. *The Color Purple* is arguably progressive on either count.

'Representation' also embraces the political sense of an individual embodying a particular constituency's interests, as in the US House of Representatives. When Celie asserts, 'I may be poor, black and, Dear God, I may be ugly, but I'm here', she voices bitterness and defiance for all who identify with her oppression through dependency, race, sex or lack of glamour, within patriarchy. This relates to the first definition in that black women are more likely to feature in media if conventionally sexy – which usually implies expensive clothing and grooming – and/or able to play a respected role, such as a judge, lawyer, professor or police officer, images with which ordinary women may not align themselves. This particular concept of representation caused enormous difficulties with masculine images in *The Color Purple*: suffice to say for now that so many films lacked black characters that rare exceptions became for some critics representative of *all* African-Americans.

Another academic use of 'representation' concerns how signs elicit meanings. Media do not reproduce reality through miraculous technology, though realist con-ventions encourage that illusion, but deliver re-presentations: ideologically mediated (because signs are social) versions of reality, a selection, processing and construction according to other people's largely unconscious interpretation. Unquestioned images express common beliefs and simultaneously reinforce those beliefs by proffering evidence to sustain them. Carefully studying representations normally experienced as unpatterned, fragmented and ephemeral assists in understanding social values by revealing recurrent structures. Underemphasis on black women's experience system-atically manifests abstract workings of racism and sexism. Affirmative action, such as increasing the number of black women on-screen, is of little use if it means filling talk shows with victims rather than offering positive role models, although this might use-fully articulate discourses otherwise hidden.

The contradiction is that if media represented reality statistically, more African-American women would play menial roles, which regressively might naturalise their position. Alternatively, increasing positive images could be seen either as progressive, putting media ahead of social attitudes, or as propaganda, Hollywood 'feelgood', denying inequality. This reveals a weakness of content analysis: only the most easily measurable categories are relatively value-free. The moment one tries to count positive or negative representations one is already imposing subjective, contestable attitudes.

Investigation is inseparable from semiotic and narrative analysis. Complex sign-clusters called representations have meaning only according to paradigmatic and syntagmatic positioning. For example, well-intentioned 1970s tokenism saw black performers increasingly in roles in which race seemed irrelevant: paradigmatically a positive development. But how a representation functions syntagmatically is as important as mere occurrence. Typically in police thrillers the black was the lower-ranking sidekick, often killed early on to justify the lone (white) hero's quest for justice. Content analysis proves what researchers already know, that misrepresentation occurs, not why and how it systematically disadvantages some groups.

Sometimes representations become so conflicting a category seems to split. This highlights the selective and constructed nature of all representations and usually marks a crisis within society. A salient example pertaining to *The Color Purple* was moral panic in mid-1980s America over so-called 'welfare mothers'. After years of civil rights campaigning a 'large and confident black middle class' had emerged and won respect (Hitchens 1986: 12). African-Americans occupied senior professional positions on a scale previously unthinkable. It appeared discrimination was finally waning. Prosperous black families featured in corporate advertising and mainstream entertainments such as *The Cosby Show* (1984–1992), personifying American values. Despite such advances, black males were seven times more likely to be murdered than whites. Their attackers were mostly black. Racist explanations were untenable, for these figures had risen rapidly. One reason gained media currency: the cycle of dependency, mooted by Senator Daniel Patrick Moynihan in a 1965 report, which conservatives insisted liberals played down although black and civil rights leaders considered it seriously. The thesis claimed that poorly qualified mothers could not survive on welfare with one child, whereas if they had more their state benefits rose disproportionately. This allegedly encouraged indigent mothers to have children without forming long-term partnerships. Results apparently included destruction of traditional family and associated authority structures, undermining of communal identity, loss of the work ethic, law and order breakdown and lack of mutual respect between the sexes – complex issues explained away by blaming the weakest members of society.

This rationalisation, highlighted in a CBS documentary, 'The Vanishing Family: Crisis in Black America' (January 1986), shortly after *The Color Purple* premiered, appealed to the 'moral majority' opposed in principle to taxation and welfare assistance. But it also highlighted class, 'a notion which has a disreputable recent history in America', according to an unlikely source, influential Reaganite commentator Charles Murray (in Hitchens ibid.). The Land of Opportunity had always de-emphasised class, tainted with Marxist connotations. Upwardly-mobile aspiration and success among African-Americans demonstrated a classless society. They were 'us', according to mainstream opinion. Nifty ideological footwork posited a new 'them' in the service of social cohesion: an 'underclass', positioned outside America – literally, being deemed to have rejected American values while living parasitically off the host, and geographically, inhabiting no-go areas in ghettoes. This frightening scenario painted the divide as wilful. That ethnicity was implicated in cumulative disadvantage – the 'underclass' happened, of course, to be mostly people of colour – was consequently no longer the fault of honest citizens, who had done their best.

New folk devils emerged. Commercial media commoditised discontent in rap music and concomitant imagery of 'gangstas' terrorising the 'hood'. This purveyed illusory glamour and power within the circumscribed experience of young men with few realistic aspirations, but unfortunately resurrected racist images of sexually voracious and promiscuous black men, shiftless, violent and criminal, which now were appropriated with pride. An alternative was dignified formality in the (significantly named) Nation of Islam's dress and behavioural codes; this also disturbed mass society by declaring a separatist brotherhood, indifference to mainstream approval, and attitudes towards women that defied liberal opinion. Meanwhile the imputed underlying cause, motherhood, no longer American as apple pie, was rescued by distinguishing 'bad' (single, welfare claiming, irresponsible) from 'good' mothers.

Christopher P. Campbell later discovered in American newscasts a consistent 'racial mythology': African-Americans as sporting heroes and musicians on one hand, and criminals, negligent mothers and various antisocial types on the other. Particularly damaging, Campbell concluded, was how positive imagery sustained the American Dream of equality, with the implication that others *chose* 'savagery and/or destitution' (1995: 133).

For conservatives, reassertion of the family was interpretable within backlashes against feminism and permissiveness. This was while harrowing evidence was emerging, anecdotally in talk shows and officially, of how widespread within that institution were domestic violence and sexual abuse.

Enter *The Color Purple*.

Race

A striking aspect of the outcry surrounding the film's representations, particularly of black masculinity, is that Alice Walker set her story 75 to 40 years in the past, apparently distancing it from immediate concerns. Anyone offended must have imputed contemporary parallels – presumably Walker's intention. Many objected to stereotyping – a problematic concept, I shall argue, that retains great force in ideological criticism. Jacqueline Bobo has clustered these objections into three issues: (a) 'black people as a whole are depicted as perverse, sexually wanton, and irresponsible' (this against 'massive cutbacks in federal support to social agencies'); (b) 'black men are portrayed unnecessarily as harsh and brutal', in a way that further damages gender relations; and (c) 'the film does not examine class' (1988a: 43).

While these points deserve careful consideration, discussion often became mired in name-calling. Novelist Ishmael Reed raised a familiar spectre in Spielberg criticism by dubbing the novel and film 'a Nazi conspiracy' (in ibid.). Courtland Milloy, a columnist who initially refused to see the film, reasoned that he 'got tired, a long time ago, of white men publishing books by black women about how screwed up black men are' (in Aufderheide 1986: 15); understandable, but this was not a response to a text, rather a protest against what he considered its conditions of existence. Such reactions demonstrate strong feeling; however, to understand the film's impact requires going beyond rhetoric to the substance of considered judgements.

The problem partly was a concern that recurs with *Schindler's List* and *Amistad*: 'ownership' of representation. This presented an insoluble paradox. For Walker's progressive discourse to reach audiences who did not read novels the film would have to be a commercial production backed by a major distributor; otherwise it would not play neighbourhood theatres. Although *The Color Purple*'s commercial success demonstrated demand for black-centred movies and helped some African-American filmmakers gain backing, at the time there was not a sufficiently bankable black director. Some critics were offended that a film portraying some black characters less than favourably, and dealing with problems between African-Americans, should have been made at all; it was betrayal, a public airing of issues that should only be addressed 'within the veil' because of the danger of fuelling racism (Bobo 1995: 62). Others were concerned by the patronising assumption that a white director, on whose name the movie was marketed, could articulate their experience and interests. (In fairness, one should note that the producer, Quincy Jones, a film composer, record producer and major Hollywood player, was black; Walker, who consistently refers to *The Color Purple* as 'our' movie, exercised a contractual right to ensure half the production personnel were women, people of colour, or of Third World origin (Walker 1996: 29, 42, 154, 176); and screenwriter Menno Meyjes, a white Dutchman who took over after Walker abandoned her own screenplay, collaborated with her on dialogue rewrites, as she was on set – as a credited project consultant – as far as health permitted, about half the time (Walker 1996: 30, 178).) Yet others defended the film's right to exist and welcomed its airing of problems not unique to African-Americans: the 'first true racial crossover movie' (White 1986: 113). Goldberg, who had asked Walker for a part, voiced a different racial discourse from many critics, that of universalism: having adopted a Jewish stage name, in her nightclub comedy she had addressed human suffering in a monologue about a junkie at Anne Frank's house. Its agenda already established, much debate was not really over the film at all but clashes between what Robert Ferguson calls 'discursive reserves' (1998: 130), unspoken assumptions about race and gender that it forced to the surface.

Spielberg typically included allusions to earlier Southern epics, *Gone With the Wind* ((1939) which he rather insensitively told Walker, given its portrayal of black house slaves, was 'the greatest movie ever made' (in Walker 1996: 150)) and the unashamedly racist *The Birth of a Nation* (1915). Was his version of that troubled history laudable, knowingly revisionist, decentring into black enunciation? Or did it perpetuate white ignorance? Expressed in those stark terms, the film *had* to be controversial.

Bobo identifies aspects of characterisation as 'stereotypically racist'. These include Harpo's proclivity for falling through roofs, discussed later, and 'subtle shifts' in his speech that 'recall caricatures of black people from past racist works' (1995: 79; Walker herself had qualms about these points (1996: 35, 161)). Bobo objects to the way Harpo, incurring impatience as he fumblingly saddles Mister's horse, says, 'Yessah, Pa, yessah. I's gitting to it. I's gitting to it.' She expresses puzzlement about how this sits with evident efforts elsewhere to avoid demeaning dialogue (1995: 80). However, representations are context-dependent. Such speech is characteristic of servants and slaves addressing whites in literature and films portraying the old South (and, indeed, of poor whites addressing those with power: see how the old Texan car-theft victim speaks to cops in the contemporary setting of *The Sugarland Express*). It indicates fearful deference, Mister's hegemony over his son, a relationship from which Harpo eventually extricates himself, although not before attempting to exercise it over Sofia. It dramatises a point explicit in the novel, that Old Mister, who similarly lords it over Mister, learnt attitudes to women and youngsters from his own white father. This transference of oppression, which Harpo overcomes and Mister ultimately regrets, blames undesirable black masculine behaviour firmly on white society, constantly present in the form of the mail deliverer and churchgoers at the periphery of Celie's narrative. In no way is brutality suggested to be culturally indigenous or genetic. In light of Harpo's speech, note how Corrine speaks to Celie in an educated form close to Standard English until a white store clerk contemptuously addresses her, when she reverts to a subservient 'Negro' form. (Having defended the film, I must acknowledge its reception would have been affected by the following, excruciating, full-page announcement in the *Hollywood Reporter*, which bears no relation to speech conventions in the film or the novel, nor the actor's voice:

> Dear God, My Name is Margaret Avery. I knows dat I been blessed by Alice Walker, Steven Spielberg, and Quincy Jones who gave me the part of 'Shug' Avery in *The Color Purple*. Now I is up fo' one of the nominations fo' Best Supporting Actresses that I is proud to be in the company of. Well, God, I guess the time has come fo' the Academy voters to decide whether I is one of the Best Supporting Actresses this year or not. (Quoted in Jaehne 1986: 60))

Bobo notes that early cinema established black women (a) 'as sexually deviant', the legacy of which in *The Color Purple* accords (in Hollywood terms) with Celie's sexuality and Shug's multiple relationships and dominant role; (b) 'as the dominating matriarchal figure', a fair description of Sofia before the mayor breaks her; (c) 'as strident, eternally ill-tempered wenches' – Squeak (Rae Dawn Chong) in the film; and (d) 'as wretched victims', true of every female character, even Shug in relation to her father's rejection. The last category, Bobo notes, continues, from maids to 'welfare' mothers (1995: 33). What stereotype criticism overlooks, however, is that *The Color Purple*'s women, independently and by mutual support, transcend these roles. Melodrama sugars didactic feminism to suggest confidence and sisterhood can empower, women can free themselves from restrictive subject positions internalised through socialisation.

Bobo considers whether the mayor's wife's mental derangement renders her exceptional, individualising her treatment of Sofia and thereby clearing other whites of racism (1995: 112). The untenability of this thinking, produced by the obfuscating, catchall currency of stereotypes, becomes apparent in Andrea Stuart's inconsistent declaration, in an otherwise illuminating essay, that the mayor's wife is 'an insulting sexist stereotype' (1988: 69). This subsumes the individual into a general category (on five dimensions, implicitly linked: class, race, gender, age and mental health), as also happens in the numerous objections to the film's black men as representing their entire race. Yet, by a breathtaking double standard, maintaining that the mayor's wife 'individualises the socio-political reality of racism' and thus renders Sofia's suffering random, rather than part of institutionalised oppression, she becomes *un*representative of society (1988: 70). In fact, as an overprotected neurotic, fearful of black men and sentimental towards black children, she conforms to an almost sacred, white Southern stereotype the film demonstrably condemns: she is sister to Blanche DuBois, decadent Southern belle, the 'pure' fragile woman defined by white supremacist patriarchy against the sexualised darkness and physicality of slave women.

Yet to trade stereotype for stereotype, as if they have fixed, self-evident meaning, rather than engage with the discourses characterisation helps activate, is sterile and self-defeating. Stereotypes have no objective textual existence – if you recognise one, it is already within your discourse. More useful would be to examine stereotyped responses, unproblematised attitudes towards recurrent representations. This would reflect back onto 'member's resources' critics bring to interpretations and reveal more of the power relations in play (Fairclough 1989: 11, 14). Media-wise commentators can spot a stereotype at a hundred paces. That becomes the end point of some criticism, with unexamined assumption about positive or negative 'effects' left implicit in a way that would not be tolerated in other aspects of media analysis.

As shown by the store clerks' routine attitude and, more extremely, the mob savagery after Sofia hits back against the mayor and the violence and severity of injustice meted out to her, the film does not downplay racism's pervasiveness. Like the novel, though, concentrating on blacks' relationships, it does not make racism its primary concern. Rather it addresses racism as one dimension of inhumanity. Nettie's letters include an explicit analogy between Olinka attitudes toward educating girls and arguments mounted by 'white people at home who don't want black people to learn'. Her description, visualised on-screen, of road builders, protected by soldiers, pushing through the village, starkly demonstrates colonial racism. The cut to an all-black rail gang singing an African-derived work song, seemingly still in Africa until Celie walks by, pointedly comments on American labour relations.

This universalising tendency explains why the film, although using Blues and Gospel in its narrative, employs traditional Hollywood extradiegetic music to cue spectators' emotions: the more remarkable as Quincy Jones wrote it, rather than John Williams, Spielberg's composer on almost everything since *The Sugarland Express*. Ed Guerrero complains: 'one ideology contains and dominates another as ... the Eurocentric soundtrack contains or packages Afro-American music for popular consumption' (1988: 56). Guerrero's verbs, where 'incorporates' would carry very different assumptions, oversimplify. They deny possibilities of discourse and dialogue, which, after all, Guerrero notes disapprovingly, is the function of the movie's reconciliation of church and juke joint. He posits binarily opposed, monolithic, essentialist and unequally matched categories, even though his article rightly asserts difference in discussing 'Hollywood' and 'Third Cinema', institutions that are mutually defining. Shug singing 'Sister' and the choir belting out their spiritual are arguably memorable long after the bland orchestral score.

The flaw in this 'containment' thesis becomes clear if it is inverted to imply black experience is not worthy of Hollywood treatment. Walker, Andrea Stuart suggests, diverts a tradition of 'classic black male authors' depicting racism in Standard English partly as 'an appeal for justice' to white readers (1988: 62). Instead, like earlier novels by Zora Neale Hurston, *The Color Purple* takes black female experience as given and presents it in an orally inflected form as an act of cultural self-definition (Stuart 1988: 65). That is reason enough to mistrust a Spielberg makeover. However, in the absence of a firm legacy of popular black filmmaking, Hollywood's further popularisation of such a text could be celebrated as evidence of respect and acceptance, provided imposition and knee-jerk condemnation of stereotypes is avoided, or at least deferred for deliberation. To condemn the film for not being more consciously political is to prejudge it for failing at something never attempted.

Nevertheless, Guerrero validly observes that Shug's reconciliation with her father, minister of what the book presents as 'white, hegemonic, patriarchal religion', reverses Walker's preaching through Shug of a liberatory, healing pantheism (1988: 56). While this falsifies the novel, it is debatable whether, in the context of the film alone, it constitutes racism.

Black masculinity (1): spectatorship

The Color Purple, instead of portraying one family, was often seen as typifying African-American existence. Much criticism assumed the male characters represent all black men. Perceptions of how the film treated them were even more contentious than its treatment of race generally. Nevertheless, Oprah Winfrey insisted, 'this movie is not trying to represent the history of black people in this country any more than *The Godfather* was trying to represent the history of Italian-Americans ... it's one woman's story' (in Butler 1991: 64). Stars' comments require caution as they are usually semi-scripted by publicists who, especially when handling controversy, attempt to impose preferred readings. It could be construed – though it sounds patronising – that powerful white interests ventriloquised Winfrey's discourse, together with, as was often implied, Walker's book and the actors' images and performances (Bobo 1995: 126).

Conspiracies notwithstanding, a commonsense white perspective tends to claim and assume authority, because of existing cultural relations. Knowledge cannot exist independently of actual people knowing, but white people often make universal pronouncements, 'not admitting, indeed not realising, that for much of the time they speak only for whiteness' (Dyer 1997: xiv). Therefore, while disagreeing with John Simon that 'all black men in the film were constructed to resemble animals' (in Butler 1991: 64), I have to respect that *The Color Purple* from another social position may look very different. Manthia Diawara (1988), for example, uses the film to explore whether a distinctly black mode of spectatorship exists. Respecting a point of view, though, entails willingness to question it. *The Color Purple* raises enormous and grave issues. It is important to escape journalistic sound-bite posturing and attempt, with goodwill and rigour, considered interpretation.

Assumptions that Walker criticises certain masculine behaviours because she 'hates black men with a passion' unite white conservatives such as Richard Grenier (1991: 245), mainstream media such as *Time* magazine – which glossed 'Walker's message: Sisterhood is beautiful, and Men stink' (in Walker 1996: 224) – and black spokesmen such as Simon, who averred that the film glares with bitter hostility towards black males (in Butler 1991: 64) . Because such views are widely advanced with often little evidence, it seems reasonable to indicate the debate's mood and cross-purposeness by quoting Walker on the song 'Sister', written for the film by Jones, Rod Temperton and Lionel Ritchie to substitute for the book's more explicitly physical love between Shug and Celie:

'Sister' ... which I immediately imagined as a signal of affirmation that women could hum to each other coast to coast, is an immeasurable gift to the bonding of women. And, because men of a certain kind wrote it, it includes them, necessarily, in that bonding ... I did not have to fear, as I sometimes did, that there were no black men who were healed enough to value the truth of my work. Or publicly affirm it. (1996: 31)

African film theorist Diawara writes of the movie's 'Manichean figuration of Mister as evil (with its implicit judgement of black males in general)' and 'simplistic portrayal of the black man as quintessentially evil' – (1988: 75) ignoring sympathetic characters like Harpo, Grady, Swain and Adam. This strikes me as simplistic. Cheryl B. Butler describes how such reactions occur, starting at the first scene, Celie's baby being taken:

The spectacle inspires disdain and contempt, and the black spectator, unconscious of the film's manipulation at first, casts a chastising gaze toward the image of Celie's fiend-like father. But the black male spectator, recognising the self in the black male image upon the screen, rejects that self as unrealistic, evil, and resists the film's discourse completely. The black female spectator, on the other hand, recognises herself in the sympathetic black female upon the screen and accepts the self. Because her history as an empowered subject upon the Hollywood screen is a dim one, she accepts the film's discourse completely and, in self-defence of this new empowered position, casts a 'blind eye' at the film's brutal depiction of the black man. (1991: 65)

In challenging theories of spectator positioning this assumes essentialist and unmediated racial and gendered identification. Do spectators simply recognise their socially positioned selves on-screen, irrespective of how and in what context the representation is constructed, narrativised and enunciated? Does secondary identification, activated by suture – whereby psychic conflict is dramatised through engagement with various characters (Ellis 1992: 85–6) – change because the representation is unusual? Perhaps so, in the way that I become more conscious of white male characters in Spike Lee's films. This is alertness triggered by wariness or expectation rather than direct response to the text. Yet it is not racism that makes it easy for me, a white, middle-class European male, to empathise with Celie and find Mister's behaviour monstrous. I can become intensely drawn into problems experienced by Spike Lee's Malcolm X or soldiers in *Glory* (1981), while remaining indifferent to most of the racial others in *Raiders of the Lost Ark*. Likewise *Psycho* depends on spectatorial positions Hitchcock artfully constructs, including filmgoers of either sex virtually becoming Marion.

Diawara probes theory's 'inadequacies', whereby positioning occurs through narcissistic identification with the apparatus, in turn entailing regression through the Mirror Phase to Imaginary unity: 'Since spectators are socially and historically as well as psychically constituted, it is not clear whether the experiences of black spectators are included in this analysis' – especially as examples like *The Color Purple* problematise it (1988: 66). As I have just suggested, and argue throughout this book, all spectators engage their discursive formations with a film. Every reading is more or less negoti-ated. Diawara conflates audience member, as real person, with spectator as textually positioned construct and separates social, historical and psychic constitution as if entry into the Symbolic were timeless, asocial and ahistorical for non-blacks. He also assumes white spectators undergo passive interpellation, unlike blacks. There seems no reason to assume black spectatorship is intrinsically different. However, the social and historical conjuncture in which it occurs, including certain texts, may – not necessarily through conscious resistance – elicit oppositional reading.

While not immune from stereotype hunting, Diawara makes the interesting and important suggestion that Hollywood treats black male characters analogously to how it treats women, according to Mulvey (1981): their figurative castration provides pleasure through mastery to the implicitly white, male spectator (1988: 70–1). Again, this is problematic. For example, in *48 Hours* (1982)

> the black character is only good at subverting order, while the white charac-ter restores narrative order … For the Afro-American audience, however, this racial tension and balance pre-empts any sense of direct 'identification' with [Eddie] Murphy's character because ultimately his 'transgressions' are subject to the same process of discipline and punishment – he is not the hero of the story, although he may be the star of the show. (1988: 72)

Psycho, again, undermines the principle delineated here. Marion, played by the star, undergoes punishment for transgression, yet 'direct' identification must occur for the film to make straightforward sense. Another assertion – 'the narrative pattern of blacks playing by hegemonic rules and *losing* also denies the pleasure afforded by spectatorial identification' (ibid.) – does not apply to a film Diawara himself analyses, as audiences do engage powerfully with Celie although she is a loser throughout most of the film. It is not as if identification is forged retrospectively after she finds her voice and triumphs.

Diawara draws powerful parallels between Mister pursuing Nettie and the notori-ous 'Gus chase' from *The Birth of a Nation*, in which a black character (played as an atavism by a made-up white actor) follows a white girl, proposes to her and further harasses her until she jumps off a cliff. Gus unmistakably embodies 'evil, inferiority and Otherness', so his desire, challenging white patriarchal law, demands symbolic cas-tration (1988: 68–9). He is lynched. 'The black spectator', Diawara argues (although I think most whites nowadays could be included, in accordance with his thesis that positioning is neither unilateral nor irresistible), 'is placed in an impossible position – drawn by the narrative to identify with the white woman, yet resisting the racist reading of the black man as a dangerous threat' (1988: 74). Structural similarities between the scenes are apparent, but the contexts are different. Miscegenation threat-ens in *The Birth of a Nation*. In *The Color Purple* aggressive sexuality is condemned, not Mister's race – unless one buys into stereotyping. Also, if Diawara is right in point-ing to similar textual devices that encourage identification with the intended victims, it is excessive to claim that the spectator is encouraged 'to desire lynching for Gus and punishment by death for Mister' (1988: 75). Only a hardened fanatic would desire lynching, while the extent of hatred for Mister in the two shaving scenes depends largely on the strength of identification with Celie. Why Mister is an 'implicit judgement of black males in general' rather than specifically of domestic abusers remains unexplored (ibid.).

There is no doubting Diawara's anger, grounded in institutionalised racism that white people, most of the time, are oblivious to. However to insist on unchanged attitudes over seventy years overstates the case so far as to distort what is potentially progressive in *The Color Purple*. As Judith Mayne (1993: 99) and Annette Kuhn (1994: 221) both point out, the dichotomous tendency of 1970s and 1980s film studies to divide movies into oppressive 'dominant' product and liberating 'alternative' and 'oppositional' works has yielded to pressure from new technologies and forms. Music video, variously self-conscious modalities in relation to classical realism, new theorisations of spectatorship and higher media literacy among consumers, for example, posit a continuum between contemporary Hollywood as one textual and institutional pole and overtly political and avant-garde experimentation as the other. Spielberg references D.W. Griffith's film both to pay homage to its landmark innovations and to comment on what his is not – pre-emptively to get it out in the open, as it were. Everyone knows *The Birth of a Nation* is racist.

Through crosscutting between the second razor scene and Adam and Tashi's ritual scarification, *The Color Purple*'s 'message is unmistakable', Diawara claims: 'The black man's place of origin, Africa, it is implied, is the source of his essential evil and cruelty' (1988: 75). In fact, Nettie's letters state an implicitly universal parallel – individuals are subjected to oppressive patriarchy everywhere – not teleology. Furthermore, Diawara's word 'essential' misrepresents the case. Mister's punishment is by no means on behalf of white masculinity, as Diawara wants to believe. Something more radical and interesting happens. Celie's wielding the razor explicitly, through crosscutting with the African priest, symbolises her castrating power: this is the moment she rejects Mister's domination. Prevented by Shug from murdering him, she contains her fury until it explodes verbally during the Easter dinner. Mister's punishment – far greater than in the novel – consists in being outcast from the final reunions' harmony and happiness. The patriarch, lynchpin of the community, finishes outside a community that thrives without him. This is progressive, not regressive justice, in that his expediting of Nettie's return demonstrates capacity to learn from his errors.

Black masculinity (2): social and historical context

Many black men's responses to the film were, to say the least, defensive: 'They have a hard enough time without this. Unemployment, declining educational opportunity, bad housing – and anyway, how many times do you see an attractive black man as role model on the screen?' (Hitchens 1986: 12). 'But let's not confuse racism with outraged male pride', warned Kathy Maio (1988: 38). Masculinity, closely related in patriarchy to fatherhood, was 'a site of fierce contestation' in debates around the films of the 1980s (Harwood 1997: 45), as many studies of film and media confirm (Cook 1982; Neale 1983; Easthope 1990; Tasker 1993). One of Bobo's discussion members concluded protest at the film was 'a sexist thing, and that upsets me because black people in general are oppressed. We worked in the same fields together; we walked in the same chain coffle together' (1995: 126). Bobo observes that negative reviews by mainstream critics and ongoing coverage of some black men's opposition led to both book and film being labelled 'controversial'. This affected expectations and responses by predetermining 'that the content ... was incendiary rather than that a particular reading of them was negative', and also, given the power discourses in conflict, seldom acknowledged women's feelings, which were broadly positive (1995: 52). It would be mistakenly reductive and essentialist, though, to characterise all African-American men as reacting identically.

Just as reductive, unfortunately, are some readings of the film. Robert Phillip Kolker claims it stereotypes Mister (1988: 106) in that his 'nasty picture postcards', as the novel describes them (Walker 1983: 106), portray white women. Kolker does not question whether, as seems unlikely, black pornography was equally available. A metonymic aspect of characterisation becomes a synecdoche for a ready-made stereotype of black masculinity to embody white sexual anxiety. This is externally imposed by the critic upon a character, absent from the scene, who has minimal interaction with white characters. Yet it forms the basis of a negative judgement.

Simon describes Harpo as 'a bumbling fool who falls through roofs' and Mister as 'an "unmitigated villain" who towers over his miniature victims as in a cartoon' (in Butler 1991: 64). Maio avers that 'Spielberg's ... racism shows less in the violence of Mister and Harpo, than in their oafishness', both of which qualities she delineates without explaining how they relate to race (1988: 38–9). These representations are in fact structurally connected, not independent distortions of referential black masculinity. Harpo's mishaps, certainly, aim at comic relief. But there is little justification for attributing his goofiness to filmmakers' attitude towards his ethnicity, for no other African-Americans become butts of humour apart from Mister, as when he loses his head over Shug's arrival and shows himself incapable of cooking or dressing himself formally. (This, incidentally, is less demeaning than some critics suggest, as he has always depended on women's domestic labour, a point made humorously rather than with bitterness; it also, to echo Simon, mitigates his villainy by suggesting vulnerability.) The point about Harpo, though, is his victimisation by Mister's teachings. Incompetent at traditional masculine tasks, such as building, he is happier – as the novel has space to make explicit – in the nurturing role Sofia imagines for him, but which contradicts patriarchal expectations. Eventually, with hard-earned wisdom, he attains respect and dignity by following his instincts, a journey to self-knowledge that parallels Celie's. As for Mister's cartoon villainy, less dismissive criticism might mention the film's consistent expressionism. Extreme low angles, deep focus and wide-angle lenses, clearly imitating *Citizen Kane*, convey relationships and abstract ideas through proximity to the camera and composition. Short lenses exaggerate the size of Mister's house and enable filming with little light, to suggest the scale of Celie's labours and the gloom felt during her early years there; when she obtains Nettie's letters, more light and a more neutral perspective prevail. When young Nettie arrives and passes mail to Mister, prefiguring his later interception, his hand in the foreground occupies more screen space than her entire body. Like Kane, the higher Mister towers the further he falls.

Walker rues being 'called a liar for showing that black men sometimes perpetuate domestic violence', while compassion for the women and children's suffering portrayed was rarely expressed (1996: 38–9). The film encouraged discussion of incest and family violence when their prevalence, certainly not exclusively within black households, was only beginning to receive recognition and often met denial. As Carl Dix wrote in *The Revolutionary Worker*, not a title one would automatically expect to support a Spielberg film:

> Some have been silly enough to say that the kind of brutalisation that the film depicts never happened among black people, or perhaps used to happen but doesn't anymore. Some have even amplified this foolishness with comments like, 'My father never beat my mother', or 'I never beat my wife.' Or even, 'My husband never beats me.' Setting aside the liars among these people for the moment, such people should be awarded a frog-in-the-well medallion for their additions to this debate. (Quoted in Walker 1996: 191)

Many women, not just African-Americans, testified to the film's truthfulness. The outrage provoked should be set against the fact that in Britain father/daughter incest was legal until 1908, just one year before Celie bears her second baby by her supposed father, and that children were commonly 'sold as objects of commodified exchange', as Celie is (Harwood 1997: 50). In view of how attitudes persist, as racism exemplifies, it appears reasonable to assume the family, supposedly protection from the world's evils, is for many a sham that protects their perpetrators.

These are sensitive matters, given the ideological centrality of the family, and involve horrible accusations. Bitterness and fury over False Memory Syndrome confirm general unease over relationships between individuals, families, society, the state and an economically-driven legal system. Alleged abusers have defended themselves by accusing psychiatrists of planting suggestions in supposed victims' minds. Such accusations, like those they counter, are largely neither provable nor defensible, but open to charges, against government agency therapists and personal defence lawyers, of political motivation or profit seeking. Outside the particular cases they resolve nothing either way, but raise the temperature of debate without supplying evidence. Social contradictions tend to become manifest in popular texts, as in *The Color Purple*, when they are not expressed adequately elsewhere.

Stuart situates Walker's novel complexly against white male culture, white feminism and black male writing (1988: 61). Black men's exploitation of black women had become taboo because acknowledging such abuse would betray 'racial solidarity', feeding negative images to racists (ibid.). Walker, for example, concerned that *The Color Purple* might be appropriated, wrote to Michele Wallace about how the latter's *Black Macho and the Myth of Superwoman* (1979) was '"used" by the Media, and the White Feminist Movement' … 'to validate, for whites, the negative and stereotypic views of black men held by whites' (Wallace 1993: 124). The conjunction of power, race and sex in slavery, and subsequent accusations of interracial rape that prompted lynchings, made sexual abuse within black families particularly sensitive (Stuart 1988: 62). Yet denigration of women in some black male writing remained unremarked, certainly not denounced, and so risked naturalising oppression. Moreover, degradation and brutality in the physical forms of rape and battery, in the psychological climate of 'a multi-billion-dollar pornography industry trading in violence against women', and in the economic disadvantage perpetuated by child-rearing, concern women everywhere, although impacting cumulatively more on the poor, who are disproportionately black (Dix in Walker 1996: 192). Walker's novel, challenging the 'context of silence', elicited shock and embarrassment in some quarters, but elsewhere relief that the secret was out (Stuart 1988: 61).

Celie – like others in her position – is silent not out of solidarity, however, but because her father and her husband, into whose protection she was born according to patriarchy, are her abusers and have power to silence her with threats. To maintain that silence in an attempt, however well intentioned, to pretend that African-American relationships are uniquely free of abuse, would be complicity in their perpetuation. Besides, no exclusive forum exists for black men and women to thrash out these difficulties without the attention and contribution of others, equally concerned, throughout society. To speak the taboo destroys it, opening the way to confront the problems it conceals.

As stated, I consider Stuart wrong in claiming that Spielberg 'almost entirely removes white society from the film's frame of reference'. This is crucial, as she continues that without racism as a context the black men resemble 'monsters acting out individual ego problems, rather than ... victims themselves, taking refuge in notions of masculinity which involve visiting their oppression on those weaker than themselves' (1988: 69). I have already accepted transference of oppression as an explanation, but it is only one factor. As Dix puts it,

> women's oppression is reinforced by the whole superstructure of politics, of culture and ideology generally ... The man acting as the lord and master in relation to his wife and children is put forward as the way things are and should be. Oppressed men buy into this too. (Quoted in Walker 1996: 193)

Characters' 'ego problems', far from 'individual', are structural, part of patriarchy's self-perpetuation. Although many black men's relative powerlessness intensifies these problems, their cause is not genetic. Indeed, as Sarah Harwood notes, across English-speaking culture at the time of *The Color Purple* 'the paternal role was most clearly repositioned ... in the relationship between father and child, effacing the male/female relationship scrutinised in the wife-battering discourses of the 1970s' (1997: 45).

The film is unequivocal in generalising Mister's brutality from the individual into patriarchy: 'You can't talk to my boy that way!' Old Mister interjects when Celie speaks out. '*Your* boy?' she replies. 'Seems like if he hadn't been *your* boy he might've made somebody a halfway decent man.' Mister's redemption begins when he ejects his interfering father after the latter advises him to find a young woman to tidy up and take care of the place, in other words to begin the cycle of dominance again. (Earlier, the Oedipal nature of their relationship emerges when they ritualistically circle each other until Mister submits by sitting down, only to have Old Mister's foot thrust between his legs.) The subsequent scene also differs from the novel. Mister is drunk, alone in the juke joint, after which the novel's Harpo takes him home and cares for him. In the film, with Harpo and Sofia reconciled and working in partnership, Harpo repudiates him, despite Sofia's explicit advice to take him home. Departing, Mister says, 'It sure is good to see you two together again', a reunion that obviously would not have happened, after Sofia's suffering, if Harpo was still attempting to beat her. The turning point, implicitly, occurred at the meal – Easter symbolising Celie's rebirth and Sofia's, who regains her voice, and Squeak's, who insists on being addressed by her proper name – when Celie squared up to Mister and articulated her feelings. The juke joint scene links by an appropriate sound bridge, a record of Shug singing 'Sister', to the transformed Celie – who, because of her poise, confidence and sophisticated dress, is initially mistakable for Shug – attending the funeral of the man she thought was her father, ending masculine dominance over her. Harpo and Sofia become equals – trying on the same trousers in 'Miss Celie's Folk Pants' store ('One Size Fits All'), Harpo having attained dignity and normality lacking under Mister's authority, a point overlooked if he is dismissed as an inflexible stereotype.

One reason broaching abuse met condemnation was that it necessarily gave a voice to those, like Celie, previously silenced. It irrevocably shifted, however slightly, gendered power. This was a feminist rather than a racial concern that many white women related to also. It was possible for white men, if uncomfortable with feminism, to dismiss the film as women's melodrama, or restore distance by treating it as a curio, set in a different era, another community. My surmise is that some African-American men, unused to black central characters, assumed – not through textual mechanisms of identification or positioning, but according to expectation of how one relates to screen representations – that the men in this white-directed film were intentional mirrors of themselves. The protests suggest many felt threatened, not necessarily out of guilt – which would imply identification – but because they felt unfairly implicated by female responses in the power relations culminating in the excesses of Mister and his like. Having lived under the burden of racism, this new attack on their identity, which – I repeat – was not racialised, proved intolerable. Mister's position at the end of the film, neither forgiven nor sufficiently redeemed, denies the mastery and knowledge that culminate narrative pleasure to spectators who, for whatever extratextual reason, cannot or will not identify with Celie. In watching films, if 'anxiety produced in the expectation of its satisfaction is not dissipated it returns as a kind of aggression' (Ellis 1992: 87).

Both novel and film recognise parallels between Pa's and Mister's abuses of Celie and the behaviour of slave owners. The connection between Olinka attitudes toward educating women and white American attitudes toward educating blacks reverberates with accounts, like that of escaped slave Frederick Douglass (1845), that stress the role of illiteracy in maintaining ignorance and lack of self-consciousness. Nettie teaching Celie to read is important not only because the logic of the texts' epistolary premise depends on it, but also because Mister is an obstacle. The copy of *Oliver Twist* Celie continues to read is not just a sentimental reminder of Nettie but a powerful symbol of Celie's potential independence and connectedness to a wider world. It appears in close-up, fallen to the ground with Celie's reading glasses – metonymic of her vision – when Mister strikes her at the culmination of the letter-reading sequence, the moment that precipitates rebellion.

Ed Guerrero identifies slavery motifs: Mister's house has a columned facade, relating it to plantation mansions; Pa rapes Celie and sells the resulting children; he and Mister bargain over Celie, subjected to examination as at a slave auction; Mister discourages her reading. Unfortunately, because he has predetermined that Hollywood 'depicts a world that is complete, where no social change is possible or necessary' (1988: 55), Guerrero is contorted into arguing that Mister 'keeps Shug, his concubine in the same house as his wife' (1988: 57) – wording that reverses the actual power relations. This sustains claims that the film deems 'blacks, and black men in particular … somehow responsible for slavery', and 'privileges sexism over racism, scapegoats black men, and … fragments the Afro-American impulse for political, economic and human rights' (ibid.). In fact, in portraying the cruel irony that a version of slavery persists by other means the film does not condemn African-American men alone, as the vicious racism perpetrated on Sofia confirms. The parallel is a consciousness-raising ploy rather than apportioning of guilt. This supposedly sugary film indicts an entire society deformed by its history, irrespective of colour. It portrays inhumanity common to societies with different histories, and projects hope that those with power to heal, who also have power to harm, will begin by healing themselves. As Mister finally does.

Sofia and Harpo's reconciliation and, more controversially, Shug's with her father – neither is in the novel – parallel the reunion of Celie's patriarch-free family. They underline the oneness and harmony that is Walker's healing project – from which, in the film, Mister disqualifies himself. Many feminist critics felt betrayed by Shug's determination to win her father's acceptance, particularly as she capitulates by going to the church singing a religious song, in contrast with her pantheistic rejection of a white male God in the book, which the film dilutes to perfunctory references to God as 'It' and everything's need for love. Whether Shug actually bows to patriarchy – certainly her father's vocation encourages a symbolic reading – or is initiating love and forgiveness, Spielberg's typical final reconstitution of family does apparently override other considerations.

This does not mean, though, as Maio claims, that men 'despite their violence … are still in control' (1988: 40). This implies no change, or capacity for change, which I have shown is not the case. Both Maio and Bobo (1995: 65) insist that Mister's presence at the happy finale reinforces his part in facilitating it. They may have taken their cue from a production interview with Alice Walker during which she worried whether, because Mister appeared so much, the film risked becoming his narrative (Walker 1996: 176). Certainly, remorse leads him to do right by Celie, but the closing shots leave him as a pariah. It is odd that these critics do not celebrate his attitude change as the triumph of Walker's faith in ultimate goodness, especially as the film refuses him forgiveness.

The film, like the book, is a feminist fantasy, which is why neither its ideology nor logic quite matches its magical ending's emotional satisfaction. References to *Oliver Twist*, and the enchanted moment of liberation when Celie throws golden (chocolate) coins from the back of a train, acknowledge improbabilities – Celie's wealth, independence, recovery of her children and sister, revelation that her incestuous father was not her real father – as Dickens' novels of self discovery are similarly suspect when scrutinised according to strictly realist criteria. Mister and Harpo's characterisations, especially the extreme villainy and the humour based on repetition, accord with both Dickens and fairy tales. As Stuart suggests, *The Color Purple* maintains the African-American oral tradition in which the protagonist achieves reward against overwhelming odds (1988: 66). That Celie escapes oppression for a new life and empowers herself by establishing a small business is not just a feminist parable or African morality tale in the Brer Rabbit mould: it ringingly endorses the American Dream.

Expressing sorrow for the actual and feared violence experienced daily in many African-American communities, Walker wonders whether life would have been better if older black men had been able to teach their youngers what I suggest Harpo discovers in the film: 'it is not black men we want out of our lives, but violence' (1996: 44). As Anita Jones wrote, '*The Color Purple* is not a story against black men: it is a story about black women. The fact that the men in the story are not all good guys needs no justification, for it is not the obligation of any work of fiction to present every possible angle of every possible situation' (Dix in Walker 1996: 226). Whoopi Goldberg put it succinctly: 'Sometimes black men in the movie abuse black women. Now people see lots of movies where white men abuse white women, and they never think "This movie stereotypes whites"' (in Taylor 1992: 118). But as Tony Brown maintained, 'because so few films are produced with black themes, it becomes the only statement on black men' (in Walker 1996: 224). Hopefully that is no longer true, with the emergence of A-list black stars, often in non-racially-specific roles, since 1985. As a coda, it is worth recalling that the worst single act of violence in the film is the calculated blow to Sofia from the butt of the deputy's gun, perpetrated on a black woman by a white figure of legal authority.

CHAPTER ELEVEN

Empire of the Sun: shanghai showmanship

Empire of the Sun is evidently another typical Spielberg film: its lighting, incessant camera movements, overwhelming music, separation/reunion plot and focalisation through a child are unmistakable. It differs significantly from J. G. Ballard's auto-biographical novel, but no more than most adaptations. Overall it retains Ballard's imagery and themes while deviating in detail. While the novel is wide-ranging and chaotic in representing mental confusion within a confused situation, the film conglomerates, re-orders, elides and renames characters and incidents for narrative expediency. Exploitation of cinematic possibilities achieves a complementary, self-contained work.

The novel's limited third-person narration offers trustworthy explanations ('The Chinese enjoyed the spectacle of death, Jim had decided, as a way of reminding themselves of how precariously they were alive' (Ballard 1985: 57)); the film leaves audiences to draw inferences from parallels and contrasts *shown* rather than explained. Nevertheless, Spielberg conveys his protagonist's subjectivity through largely internal focalisation. The film furthermore constructs an associational level of discourse around its showmanship and spectacle, in contrast to received notions of 'invisible' Hollywood narration and in line with Ballard's surrealist take on grim history.

Ballard's protagonist resembles the movie-obsessed boy that Spielberg projects as his own persona. The novel recounts as Jim's experiences localised details of characterisation and setting in imagery associated with light, more specifically of cinema.

Spielberg adapts this drastically into a sustained theme. My reading recognises divergences from the book that constitute a broader, cumulative discourse.

The opening presents a Japanese flag: a rising sun, Japan's self-image as ascendant power in the east. Moving out of frame, this reveals Shanghai, where imperialist aspirations will be realised. Eleven-year-old James Graham (Christian Bale) sings in the Cathedral choir, beneath a huge stained-glass window: pure sound (for most spectators, the language, Welsh, is unfamiliar) and pre-cinematic visual narrative, communication through light and colour, and in this alien setting fragments of remote British identity. The film interconnects culture, identity, vision and desire entirely cinematically, dramatising issues around subject positioning and spectatorship central to much theoretical debate about film.

If Spielberg's mode of expression was other than Hollywood blockbusters critics might laud his self-reflexive postmodernism. This constitutes more than 'pure narcissistic signals of an "intellectual" work of "art"', to quote Colin MacCabe (1981: 234) on bourgeois recuperation of Brechtian techniques: not least because Spielberg's self-reflexivity, identifiable mostly through juxtaposition rather than obvious distanciation, informs conventional narration. Despite its literary antecedent the film foregrounds cinematic qualities: precise and primarily visual echoes and patterns. These, however, exceed its 'entertainment' categorisation. Indeed, the relationship between Jamie's vision and events he becomes involved in posits questions about wish-fulfilment, the relationship between 'escapism' and 'the rest of life', that underlie much ideological criticism. In *Empire of the Sun* particularly, but also elsewhere, Spielberg achieves 'the transformation of representation into subjective extension and materialisation of an inner world [that] has given rise to the theme of the vision itself as the subject of the "discourse", notably in the films of Lang and Hitchcock' (Elsaesser 1981: 278).

Flights of fancy

Despite occupying a neo-Georgian mansion in suburbs resembling stockbroker-belt Surrey (a location used) and wearing traditional uniform to the Cathedral school, Jamie has never visited Britain. His reality is the Orient: street vendors and rickshaws; Chinese posters and banners; coffins in the harbour bobbing between junks; and thieves and beggars, including an old man always rapping a tin on the sidewalk outside the Grahams' gate; all introduced through Jamie's staring eyes, behind the protective glass of a limousine, in ever-changing tracking shots. Pinwheels explode like miniature suns throughout this sequence, underlining visual exhilaration. Jamie's focal position within his reality (almost congruent with the spectator's in point-of-view shots) becomes explicit as the chauffeur's reciprocal glances in the driving mirror, the beggar's imploring look, and the smiling nod of a European nun acknowledge his presence. The procession of close images, enhanced by off-key ethereal music, is disturbingly hallucinatory – an alluring disarray of colour and detail – yet curtails the field of vision. Jamie's focalisation thus mimics cinema spectatorship's privileged immobility. A sign for 'Alice's Club' recalls the *Close Encounters* looking-glass metaphor and hints at ensuing surrealism with Jamie's immersion into a world currently his scopic Other.

Emphatic detail, visual heightening induced by music distancing the diegetic sound, and Jamie's awe-struck expression imply 'concentration of psychic activity into a state of hyper-receptivity' – John Ellis's description of the 'particular kind of mental state in the commercial cinema viewer' (1982: 40) and an apt summary of Jamie's consciousness throughout both film and novel.

Cinematic spectatorship can be trance-like, close to dreaming – a state Jamie succumbs to through fatigue, malnutrition and disease. Initially, wealth and nationality distance him, transforming reality into spectacle. Voyeurism requires this gap between looker and object. (The film explicitly indicates the nature of Jamie's activity when he later observes Mr and Mrs Victor (Peter Gale and Miranda Richardson) making love, and has his look returned: vulnerable, he averts his gaze to a bombing raid, restoring distance between himself and the viewed object, reclaiming illusory invisibility.) Nevertheless, violence that later engulfs Jamie is presaged by a Chinese boy's taunts and a trussed chicken crashing against the window, smearing blood on the glass – rendering visible the protective cultural barrier, a metaphorical screen, while intimating its fragility. Reverse-shots from the crowd emphasise his limited perspective, revealing him as an isolated oddity.

Perhaps to escape this discomforting position, Jamie inhabits an imaginary world as a fighter pilot among model aeroplanes. He daydreams during his singing; he reads a war comic featuring an all-American aviator during the untroubled drive home at the start, the world scrolling by like an ignored movie in the Packard's rectangular rear window (Combs 1988b: 96). Once home, he is director, protagonist and spectator within his battle adventure, cycling around the garden, holding aloft a flaming model fighter before crashing it to earth.

Jamie's aircraft fascination explicitly equates light and aspiration, a convention within religious iconography as well as a distinct Spielberg characteristic, as his models spring alive in the projector-like beam of his flashlight. Christian Metz (1975) follows others in expounding the ideology of vision, prevalent since Quattro Centro painting, whereby monocular perspective resembles an illuminating and defining beam projected from the eyes, positioning the spectator in relation to the vanishing point and creating an illusion of control that is constituent of voyeurism. The spectator sutures into *Empire of the Sun*, encouraged to align with Jamie, not least because Jamie inhabits the screen most of the time (aurally as well as visually, for his singing fills the soundtrack at several emotional climaxes). Reverse-shots from his perspective restrict focalisation (such as the Chinese servant's reprimand when he stops singing during choir practice). Absence of major stars, whose image would compete for attention, precludes distracting narrative expectations. Most decisively, we share Jamie's imagination. This occurs unobtrusively, starting with not simply an optical point-of-view shot of the 'animated' models, but also an overlapping match cut on the soundtrack, as the scratch and spurt of Jamie's mother lighting a cigarette provides a rocket sound accompanying what, momentarily, seem like real aircraft during a raid. It is a textbook example of what Thomas Elsaesser terms 'the double "aspect" of the image as representation of an action and emanation of a participating consciousness ... undoubtedly one of the fundamental ways in which the narrative as story transforms itself into discourse' (1981: 278).

Jamie, flying a model, encounters a crashed fighter. Staring from afar, awestruck (ethereal music again), he approaches hesitantly in shots reminiscent of other Spielberg dreams-come-true: Neary and the scientists with their aviators' sunglasses meeting the *Close Encounters* mothership; Elliott first encountering E.T.; Celie and house-guests reuniting with her sister and children in *The Color Purple*. John Williams' music soars, the model flies across the sun, Jamie lowers himself into the pilot's seat, dons sunglasses, uncovers the firing button. Cut, from his view of the model approaching, to an exhilarating crane movement from the model's point-of- view, positioning the spectator in both Jamie's actual and projected experiences of the imaginary dogfight. Cinematic dissection of space informs Jamie's dreams, themselves movie-derived. (Jamie 'had begun to dream of wars', the novel explains. 'At night the same silent films seemed to flicker against the wall of his bedroom … and transformed his sleeping mind into a deserted newsreel theatre' (Ballard 1985: 11)). Editing splits Jamie's subjectivity, along with the spectator's. Fantasy and spectatorship become explicitly analogous: both stage intrapersonal conflicts. From here to the triumphal hallucination of a waving American pilot, or the surge of empathy that turns the dead Japanese boy into Jamie's younger self towards the end, Spielberg unreels a solipsistic *vision* of war, involving projection into different positions, rather than any attempt at objective realism. (It is an amoral and challenging vision in which the Japanese are not conventionally and unequivocally Evil, the Allied prisoners not simply oppressed representatives of Good – a factor in the film's relative commercial failure.) Primary identification with the camera underlies controlled engagement with Jamie, whose reciprocally cinematic vision distances him from threatening reality by emulating movie spectatorship: 'a place "down here" out-side, from which one can watch unobserved' (Brewster 1982: 5).

Jamie's archetypal Spielberg quest - family reunion - lacks patriotic motivation. Stoical British internees hold little appeal for him, and many find his energy and enter-prise insufferable. His ambiguity shows early when he calls the Sino-Japanese War, not the European conflict, 'our war', announcing his ambition to join the Japanese air force. In the dogfight sequence, during which he stumbles across a Japanese army unit, he is dressed for a party as Sinbad: a Middle Eastern voyager poised between Oriental cultures and a West he has never known. Far from establishing 'a cosy conspiracy of self-congratulation and spurious familiarity' with those of us 'in the know' (Britton 1986: 5), Spielberg declines the opportunity provided by the book to dress Jamie in 'an embroidered silk shirt and blue velvet trousers in which he resembled a film extra from *The Thief of Bagdad* [1943]' (Ballard 1985: 15). He chooses instead (stressing Jamie's uncertain cultural identity) Chinese imperial orange.

Jamie's primary motivation is to recover domestic security and parental love. Hence his desperate conjugation of Latin passive verbs – 'I was loved, I have been loved, I shall be loved' – when he breaks down during an air raid, blurting out to Dr Rawlins (Nigel Havers): 'I can't remember what my parents look like!' A treasured possession, carried between lodgings within the camp, is the Norman Rockwell *Saturday Evening Post* painting of a child's bedtime, mother crouching to kiss him while father looks on. This tableau is recreated in Jamie's bedroom near the start, identical mise-en-scène giving concrete form to Jamie's loss in a way not possible had Spielberg adhered to the novel's more specific but less suggestive photograph of a couple.

Psychoanalysis relates narrative to nostalgia for a lost Imaginary. The Rockwell allusion makes one significant addition to the image, namely model aircraft and a kite painted with bird's wings, thereby associating Jamie's parents with flight. His continuing obsession with aircraft suggests that the *fort-da* game again informs the narrative: separation from his mother occurs when he lets go of her hand to recover a toy plane that he cherishes for the rest of the War. Jamie, enacting the spectator's psychic activity, simultaneously seeks reunion (while trapped into helplessness) and denies loss by pursuing substitute relationships.

Wings of desire

Vision, identity, flight and desire for Imaginary oblivion interconnect, albeit cryptically for most spectators, in the Welsh lullaby 'Suo-Gan' that Jamie sings in the Cathedral and years later as Japanese pilots embark on a suicide mission. Sir F. Edwards' translation:

Sleep, my baby, on my bosom
Warm and cosy will it prove;
Round thee mother's arms are folding,
In her heart a mother's love;
There shall no one come to harm thee,
Naught shall ever break thy rest.
Sleep, my darling babe, in quiet,
Sleep on mother's gentle breast.

Sleep serenely, baby, slumber
Thing of beauty, gently sleep;
Tell me wherefore thou art smiling,
Smiling sweetly in thy sleep?
Do the angels smile in heaven
When thy happy smile they see?
Dost thou on them smile while slumb'ring
On my bosom peacefully?

Fear not, baby, 'tis a roseleaf
Beating, beating, on the door;
Fear not, baby, wavelets lonely
Whisper, whisper on the shore.
Sleep, my baby, there is nothing
Shall, my darling, make thee cry;
On my bosom smile so gently
At the angels in the sky.

External threat, represented by the plant scratching the door, enhances the domestic Imaginary, a trope familiar from *Wuthering Heights* (1939) and *Gone With the Wind* where branches tap on bedroom windows, but also *Close Encounters*, *Poltergeist* and *Hook*. Aircraft replace 'angels in the sky', metonyms for maternal protection, described as 'white' in a different translation and thereby associated in turn with Dr Rawlins' white coat, the Hiroshima blast, and the cinema screen (Stiller 1996).

Images of light typically establish Jamie's idyllic home life. These range from the glow from the refrigerator, packed with luxuries soon to be denied, to firelight projecting his father's shadow onto the door through which Jamie, unseen, observes, just as shadows through a doorway predicate Celie and Nettie's childhood relationship in *The Color Purple*. Later in the labour camp, a headboard shaped like a *broken* sun adorns the marital bed of the Victors, Jamie's unwilling surrogate parents, hinting at how their exasperation travesties the domesticity Jamie craves.

On Jamie's return home, before he admits the enormity of losing his parents, freedom from supervision is a schoolboy's dream. He bicycles indoors, enjoys forbidden pleasures such as chocolate liqueurs and catapults his spoon into his glass while dining at the formal table. This scene is the first to be suffused with shafts of light. The clock stops, underlining the end of childhood playfulness (and colonial privilege which the expensive imported timepiece, ringing the Westminster Chimes, epitomises), inaugurating need to go out and survive. This brief escapism suppresses a truth already known: his parents have returned and been violently captured. Footprints and handprints, tracks left by fingertips drawn across the bedroom floor, are 'photographic' traces in the spilled talc covering everything. Spectator and character alike project violent scenarios onto the flat white surface. Realisation leads him to open the window, dispersing these traces. He departs with a half crown his father lost earlier – a small, silver sun, token of the privileged British – and his sunglasses. Leaves blow past the camera craning low over the ground. The shot, imitated from Bertolucci's *The Conformist* (1970), echoes an almost identical tribute to the Italian director in *Mishima: A Life in Four Chapters* (1985) by Paul Schrader, Spielberg's former collaborator, whose equally self-reflexive movies enjoy higher critical regard, being less immediately pleasurable and quoting Michael Powell rather than Disney. Homage apart, this shot signifies, like the talc, how everything held dear has gone with the wind.

A giant billboard advertising *Gone With the Wind* in Chinese, reappears, dwarfing Jamie as he tries to surrender to the Japanese. Its inclusion is partly a humorous but pertinent aside, an ironic exclamation that in the world's furthest corners people were clamouring to see a Hollywood film about a mythologised American war as diversion from a world war exploding around them. (Several cinemas with Western names are observable.) Partly it recognises how Spielberg's project, echoing compositions and camera movements from the earlier movie, relates to a genre of war epics with gigantic casts. Partly it alludes to Bertolucci's *The Spider's Stratagem*, (1970) which itself alludes to (among others) *Gone With the Wind* by naming the setting Tara, and contains a scene inside a cinema. Partly also it comments doubly on Jamie's situation. As he passes a newsreel camera, Spielberg's camera tracks with him until the poster obliterates the actual war, foregrounding the notion that Jamie inhabits a subjective movie (Brode 1995: 171). Fleming's film is nostalgic for the Old South – a privileged, aristocratic society, based on slavery, gone for ever – just as the complacent international community (earlier characterised by fancy dress as pirates, clowns and Marie-

Antoinettes), privileged also, thanks to racial subjugation ('You have to do as I say', Jamie tells his minder), is similarly swept away by winds of change.

Searchlights excite Jamie as much as any American movie. One overhead shot, of crowds milling around Europeans' limousines amid sweeping searchlights, resembles nothing so much as newsreel footage of a film premiere. (*The Making of a Legend: 'Gone With the Wind'* contains shots Jamie could conceivably have seen). A beam pans directly into camera precisely as a barricade shuts across the foreground; the coordination positions the spectator behind Jamie's Imaginary screen, as though the searchlight projects the image. Given our eyes follow the movement, the shot concords with Metz's theorising:

> All of us have experienced our own look ... as a kind of searchlight turning on our own necks (like a pan) and shifting when we shift (a tracking shot now): as a cone of light...
> All vision consists of a double movement: projective (the 'sweeping' searchlight) and introjective: consciousness as a sensitive recording surface (as a screen). (1975: 52–3)

We thus fleetingly cross the screen/film plane itself, interface between historical reality and Ballard's/Spielberg's/Jamie's fiction, our subject position literally mirroring Jamie's. Spielberg's trope extends Welles' backlit projection room in *Citizen Kane*, another accessible narrative playing with relationships between cinematic vision and reality. Assuming recognition of such allusions, the spectator shares further privileged identification – with the director (both, according to Metz's metaphor, 'project' the screen image; literally, in the event of recognised quotation) – and again becomes conscious of the text. Such convolutions are unsurprising given the adaptation's screenwriter, Tom Stoppard; remarkable is their unobtrusive embedding in a mainstream film.

Leaving the house, Jamie fails to join British captives in transit. Physical separation underscores cultural distance from them. The gulf widens when Japanese soldiers remain indifferent as he proclaims, 'I'm British! I surrender!' The film poster appears seconds after he passes before a Japanese film crew. The war is *their* movie, with no role for him. (In the novel too 'even a few steps across a small room generated a separate war' (Ballard 1985: 301).) He tries unsuccessfully to join them in what to him is still a local war; his dream of interpellation – of being ascribed a role and positioned within a Symbolic order, a comforting replacement for the Imaginary – is momentarily projected as his shadow appears on the side of a tank.

As hostilities begin, Jamie occupies a hotel room (with a sun-shaped clock and a sunray headboard) where he projects his toy fighter's shadow across the walls. He signals back with his flashlight – projects a beam – to Japanese warships, another fantasy analogous to spectatorial mirror identification. (In the novel Jamie uses arm signals in daylight (Ballard 1985: 42).) When shells fly he believes he has started the war. Blasted to the floor, his reflection splits three ways in a dressing-table mirror. Violently intruding reality destroys Jamie's old movie, shattering the Imaginary unity preceding his Mirror Phase. The reflections connote alternative subject positions imposed after the imminent family separation and close encounters with death: as a Chinese, a Japanese and an American.

First, he learns to live like a Chinese. At the house he discovers his former servant, over whom he previously domineered, stealing furniture (although carrying it down from upstairs, rather than taking more accessible items, maintains the possibility that this is a racist assumption and she is recovering her property). Before long he too becomes adept at stealing, petty trading and self-abasement. Meanwhile she introduces him to the egalitarian order – smacking his face.

Returning to the city he is pursued by the Chinese orphan who abused him earlier, whose vagrancy he now mirrors. He too denies Jamie's identity by mistaking him for an American, and after Jamie's failed escape by surrendering he forcibly steals his shoes. Later in captivity Jamie replaces them with a pair scavenged from a corpse – a harsh survival lesson – and eventually earns long-coveted golf shoes after saving the hospital. Similarity to the Chinese youth is explicit in the labour camp: Jamie looks identical in a flying jacket (albeit with a sun stencilled on it), dishevelled hair matted, filmed from the same angle. He looks out over barbed wire at a small figure against an enormous sun, flying a model plane, which we have taken to be himself but who is a Japanese cadet. He contemplates his ideal self-image – the second alternative identity – and his privileged past, from behind a barrier that parallels the poverty formerly dividing the Chinese youth from him. Even reaching the camp taxes his newfound cunning: almost left behind at the internment centre, he persuades guards to take him as navigator. Other prisoners surrender their ration pails, but he retains his, hammering it frantically on the lorry's cab – recalling the beggar's tin. He throws it triumphantly into the air, joyful at leaving recent experiences behind; within moments he reasserts supremacism, ordering the Japanese driver: 'to do what I say!'

Jamie is arrested with two American freebooters. Frank (Joe Pantoliano) has rescued him from the Chinese vagabond and taken him to Basie (John Malkovich), sensing, from Jamie's uniform, rich pickings. Hungry and exhausted, the boy sees in their domestic arrangements aboard an abandoned freighter a semblance of the parental care he craves. Spielberg indicates this visually, using the motif already established: Basie, framed from the chest down, dressed in skirted Chinese clothing, is cooking, while behind him light from a porthole shines into the cabin in a focused beam. Basie searches Jamie's pockets, and removing the half-crown for himself – taking his identity – renames him Jim: 'A new name for a new life.' All we see is his cigarette below his cap as he checks Jim for gold teeth; then he puts Jim's sunglasses on, suddenly becoming the glamorous character from the comic. Jim acquires a third, American, potential identity.

This is purely Jim's projection – an instance of the unsatisfying substitution for the 'lost object' that impels narrative – but also of course the spectator's. That Basie represents for Jim heroic salvation is apparent when he lifts the exhausted boy into his arms, their postures echoing exactly Clark Gable and Vivien Leigh in the poster. Subsequently, it is shocking to see Basie without cap and glasses and to realise he is haggard and bald. The revelation comes as Basie returns the sunglasses before being beaten by Japanese officers occupying the Grahams' house. This recognition, and

Basie's that Jim is trustworthy, happens, Richard Combs reminds us, 'in the glare of a truck's headlamps [in fact, appropriately, a single headlamp] – another projector beam' (1988b: 96). Basie has been about to release Jim (after failing to sell him), having even returned the half-crown, when Jim mentions abandoned houses containing 'opulence': Basie reclaims the coin. His house illuminated like E.T.'s spaceship, Jim thinks he is home as his mother, in dressing gown, approaches from the brightness, and he hears a Chopin record she used to play: he misapprehends through his emotion a Japanese officer in traditional robes. Spielberg again uses light to portray desire and reinforce identification – audiences share the mistake – yet backlighting and conventional soft focus are realistically motivated.

Jim awakens, feverish, in the internment centre under Basie's care. This kindness reinforces Jim's admiration. It becomes clear – as when Basie sends Jim pheasant hunting to establish whether the labour camp boundaries have landmines – that the motive is self-interest: Jim is useful in black market enterprises. Here Basie insists on Jim obtaining shoes from a corpse. The body – an English mother – lies behind a canvas screen onto which, as Jim approaches, his shadow and Basie's are back-projected. (The shot echoes *The Color Purple* when the sunshine projects Celie and Nettie onto sheets on the washing line, seconds before the overbearing Mister destroys the image of their unity, interposing himself before the light.) The blank screen and dead mother emphasise Jim's mother's absence from his movie, while the two shadows suggest Jim's casting of Basie as substitute parent. The shot explains, and is underlined by, what would otherwise be a surprising change from Ballard's novel, where the setting is an open-air cinema. Spielberg instead uses a hangar, an enormous darkened space, penetrated by shafts of light; square windows high in a wall exactly resemble projection apertures behind an auditorium. While every afternoon in Ballard's novel the sun, to Jim's delight, projects onto the screen a 'spectacular solar film' (1985: 108) (shadows of a hotel sign and a patrolling sentry), such an image would confuse Spielberg's consistent use of light to signify desire.

At the camp, Jim follows Basie's co-operation with the Japanese, whereas the British appeal unsuccessfully to reason, protesting against forced labour. His immediate reward, a quintessentially Spielberg image, is finding himself facing a flight of Zero fighters. The novel, congruent with the film's Welsh lullaby, has him run 'towards the shelter of the aircraft, eager to enfold himself in their wings' (Ballard 1985: 160) – impossible to realise visually. Instead sparks from a welding torch confer awesome beauty as Jim reaches to touch one of these objects of desire while strains of 'When You Wish Upon a Star' merge with his non-diegetic singing. (Similarity between this and moments in Bergman's *Persona* (1966) when the boy reaches towards his mother's projected image reinforces Spielberg's concern with cinematic vision and the lost Imaginary.) He turns towards three Japanese pilots, shadowed against the sunset, whose puzzlement turns to pride and respect as they return his salute.

Visions

In the camp, this 'difficult boy' – Sgt Nagata's (Masatô Ibu) words – turns his energy to his (and Basie's) advantage, contracting for goods and services, bridging

Empire of the Sun – mother substitute: Jamie's lost Imaginary

various communities. He accesses the Japanese quarter, through a circular (eye-shaped) entrance; he learns their language, sees from their perspective, understands their psychology sufficiently to pre-empt reprisals following an air raid. He also frequents the American block, Basie's domain, graced by circular windows – both eyes and suns: Basie's power explicitly entails ability to *see*. (On the truck, Basie held a magnifying glass and wore a scarf covered in white hoops, resembling eyes.) Jim's cultural mobility links to vision, his confidence depending on detached willingness to project himself into these zones. He befriends his double, the Japanese cadet, whose dreams he shares and whose age and stature resemble his. Openness and mutual trust, recalling Elliott and E.T., prompt the boy to save Jim's life – already jeopardised by Basie deceiving him into crossing the potential minefield – by distracting the Sergeant. There is neither a figurative eye nor a close relationship with Jim among the British: dreary familiarity is not voyeuristically desired.

Jim becomes an honorary American after crossing the boundary with Basie's traps. 'Take me – I'm your friend', he has pleaded, unaware of the betrayal. The American Symbolic order is to Jim a new Imaginary; he stares into the light above his bed on occupying his position in this further dream-come-true. He mirrors Basie (already a projection of his own comic-book alter-ego, 'Ace', a name both Basie and his mother have called him) as he marches across the camp wearing flying jacket, American cap and dark glasses, chewing a cigar and joking about Hershey bars.

Basie's depravity (conveyed in his name), to which Jim is blind, subtly counterpoints Jim's triumphant entry as Basie draws back the curtain before his round window. Supplying backlighting to sustain the metaphor of Jim's desire, this also resembles an eye opening. Basie's expression conveys bemused respect for Jim's loyalty, alien to his own cynicism. So too the spectator's eyes are opened to Basie if the possibility is recognised of the boundary being mined, as appears from Chinese scavengers being blown up in the confusion of the previous night's bombing. Furthermore, Basie's emergence from behind the curtain recalls another all-seeing manipulator and deceiver of children, the Wizard of Oz, also rather less than his image suggested. The novel likens Basie to 'a white-faced rat teasing the brains from a mouse' (Ballard 1985: 98) and refers to 'his devious voice' (1985: 99), leaving no question about his character but remaining ambiguous as to whether the third-person narration reflects Jim's consciousness. The film focalises the business with the curtain through Jim, yet suggests doubts Jim presumably does not share. An analogous shot shows a close-up of Jim's feet in his new two-toned shoes; conveying Jim's pride in the long-coveted footwear, it also quotes *Strangers on a Train* – a reference unavailable to the character – thereby alluding to instability of both identity and moral certainties. Neither attempting manipulation through striving for total empathy, nor resorting to the crude distanciation of much polemical cinema, *Empire of the Sun* makes full use of ambiguities inherent in focalisation.

Basie retains trust in Jim – leaving possessions with him while recovering from a beating – and offers pragmatic fatherly advice. He shares practical wisdom, such as drinking only boiled water, leading Dr Rawlins to comment he is good for Jim to know: 'He's a survivor.' If Basie is Jim's false father – intending to become a pirate on the Yangtze River after the war; Jim's father was a fancy-dress pirate – Dr Rawlins, who shares Mr Graham's habit of stroking his lip, eventually fills the positive role. Having repudiated the British, and been turfed out of the American section after Basie's goods were plundered, Jim spends a night in the circular opening to the Japanese quarters – the closest he dare go. At daybreak pilots undergoing a solemn ritual before the enormous rising sun for a suicide mission, allure him – the 'divine wind' (*kamikaze*) of their aspirations, to subsume identity to their vision, made palpable by wind from the light source rippling their clothing and hair. While the suicidal implications presumably escape Jim, the glory does not: he stands to attention, saluting and singing his Cathedral lullaby in the golden sunlight, his voice soaring above the Japanese chanting, silencing the camp. His dream is realised: a plane roars skywards across the sun, echoing his model's flight. It explodes. American fighters bomb the runway. Jim exultantly clambers onto a roof to see better, endangering himself. He experiences his comic-book vision of the waving pilot (a subsequent shot shows the cockpit is closed) then becomes hysterical – the pilot is unattainable, the Japanese are defeated, he has nowhere to go, no identification figure.

Rawlins restrains Jim, as grief over his parents, the truth his dreams and activities have displaced, finally strikes him. The doctor, scooping him into his arms, tells him not to think so much. His white coat, their postures, the surrounding conflagration, constitute a second, exact, reproduction of the *Gone With the Wind* poster. As the war ends, this first gesture of genuine compassion inaugurates recovery of Jim's old identity ('I shall be loved'). Again, the reflexive cinematic imagery requires simultaneous detachment and involvement, willingness to read synchronically while attending to the moment. The poster parallel succinctly indicates Jim's hero-worship of Dr Rawlins and the sense of salvation, yet breaks identification: the poster recalled at this point was not significant to Jim when trying to surrender, nor is there any likelihood of his perceiving the visual similarity – it depends on camera positioning, in other words spectatorial point-of-view.

Trekking from the camp – following a prisoner wearing a rucksack decked out with lamps and mirrors – Jim throws his suitcase, containing possessions acquired in captivity, into the river; it reappears in the final shot, bobbing among coffins. He now wears four glinting identity tags – one for each former subject position. Illusions destroyed, his journey in this afterlife takes him through a heavenly gate: an ornamental archway comprising hundreds of doves, wings splitting sunlight into myriad beams, symbolically uniting his yearning for peace with his sustaining dream of flight – a contrast with the novel's concrete tunnel (1985: 258). The gateway presages a bizarre paradisiacal vision: a stadium containing impounded property, familiar from Jim's childhood. The spectacle – furniture, paintings, statues; crystal chandeliers and a white piano Jim had promised a disbelieving Basie; even the Packard with its winged mascot – resembles *Citizen Kane*'s Xanadu and surreal descriptions of studio lots in Hollywood novels such as *The Day of the Locust* (1939; film release 1975) and *The Last Tycoon* (1941; film release 1976). We see through Jim's eyes, tinged by desire and years of deprivation: everything appears sparkling new.

Here Jim is isolated, remaining to nurse the dying Mrs Victor. An intense flash, followed by waves radiating skywards, he believes is her soul ascending; only later does he learn that 'my light' is the atom bomb. Pervasive light signals another comforting image and another desire – the end of the war he thought he had started. Andrew Gordon (1991b: 215) notes that this scene, and his earlier mistaking of a Japanese officer for his mother, ends with a 'burn to white' that – like the opening of *Close Encounters* – literally illuminates the screen so we look *at* it rather than *through* it to the diegesis. The soundtrack here, as Gordon also observes, contains an 'eerie tinkling' (1991b: 218) heard earlier as Jamie looked up at his model aircraft from his bed. Realistically motivated by swaying chandeliers, it is another, gentle evocation of 'solar wind' accompanying desire – here, presumably, unconscious desire for death after losing all his parental substitutes: Basie, the doctor, the Japanese, his aircraft, now Mrs Victor.

Returning to the camp, Jim confronts his Japanese alter-ego, similarly alone and disabused of ambitions, lacking courage to commit *seppuku* after failing to take off on a *kamikaze* mission, his nation beaten. The two, freed from historical ties that divided them, prepare to share a mango when Basie and his 'Hell Drivers' crash their car – an emblematic sun painted on the door – through a flaming wall, free now to live their cinema-inspired fantasy. One shoots the Japanese boy: another act of faulty vision, he has assumed the sword held aloft was to decapitate Jim rather than halve the fruit. Jim furiously attacks him, then hunches like a foetus. Suddenly exclaiming that the bomb was 'Like God taking a photograph!' the former atheist perceives a universal vindication of his subjective visions: divine omniscience provides the totalising viewpoint within which all makes sense. Recalling the hospital when he applied coronary massage to a dead patient, until a blood surge stimulated eye movement, he now claims power to give life (like the director, and the spectator, without whom no film would exist). He looks in wonder at his hands, outspread fingers scintillating before the reflected sun. Backlighting and a wide-angle close-up, enlarging his head in relation to the hands, evoke the unborn child from *2001: A Space Odyssey*. 'I can bring everyone back', he declares, repeatedly, pummelling the boy's chest. At the climax of Jim's self-delusion, Spielberg links this belief in the efficacy of light to cinema – the dream machine that requires only belief for desire's fulfilment – by shooting from below, into the sun. Jim alternately obscures and reveals dazzling rays, increasing the rhythm until the sun originates a flickering, projector-like beam. He sees his younger self, substituted for the corpse he is trying to resurrect – this is a desperate attempt at narrative closure, returning everything to the original status quo! – before Basie grabs him and they tumble into a waterlogged ditch.

Rebirth, symbolically, does occur. Basie embraces Jim in the water, ironically suggestive of baptism after Jim's failed miracle. Unburdened from delusion as both he and Basie realise the war is over, he becomes Jamie again. Responsibilities lifted, he tears off his identity tags and regresses to grateful childhood, accepting a Hershey bar from an American (food rations have been dropping from the sky); in his earlier avatar as an honorary American *he* jokingly offered them to British children. He cycles indoors again through the deserted camp, his younger voice singing 'Hallelujah!' on the music track as food drops like manna through the roof, the canister exploding downwards in a shower of light. (Basie's reference to 'Frigidaires falling from the sky' explicitly recalls the security symbolised earlier.) Finally he runs up against a square-jawed American general – and surrenders. Even here, the imagery continues as Jim hands him a can of milk – metonymic token of Oedipal submission – which reflects onto the soldier's face as he drinks. Surrender to patriarchy ironically facilitates return to his mother.

The family reunion, a typical Spielberg ending in which the character returns to his true spiritual or emotional home, occurs in a large greenhouse: bounded entirely by light. This odd choice is explicable in that the whitewashed panes suggest an early film studio (Baxter 1975); specifically, the architecture resembles that of Georges Méliès' at Montreuil. Jim's first instinct, to check his mother's nails, teeth and hair, reflects his experiences in the slave market and disbelief at her well-groomed appearance and tangibility. Having ascertained her suitability for the role he wants to cast her in, that she is, indeed, real, he accepts her embrace, closes his eyes for the first time, regresses to the Imaginary – and the film ends.

The boy who craved war as excitement purveyed by movies has experienced the reality from four perspectives, learning that real participants tend to be powerless in the face of indifference, unlike screen heroes. Nevertheless, as long as he maintained a spectatorial position, kept reality distant, he experienced the illusion of control that characterises cinematic voyeurism.

Spielberg parallels actions and characters, linking them through cinematic allusions and imagery of light, in ways the novel does not. My explication depends on how the director presents his material rather than on overt content or dialogue, and in no way detracts from it as conventional – even simple – linear narrative.

Umberto Eco argues, rightly, that 'it would be semiotically uninteresting to look for quotations of archetypes in *Raiders of the Lost Ark* or in *Indiana Jones*: … what the semiotician can find in them is exactly what the directors put there' (1987: 210). *Empire of the Sun* is somewhat different. While Spielberg allows occasional Movie Brat indulgences such as a humorous reference to *Jaws* when the tail fin of a crashed bomber is towed across the background of a crowd shot, most allusions are not gratuitous. Spielberg's recognition that spectator and director forge a compact, that the screen projects shared dreams and beliefs, offers a coherent demonstration of the cinematic apparatus. I am not in the least claiming Spielberg is conscious of the arcane theorising of Metz and others. However, if that theorising is valid, it should come as no surprise that a film concerned with cinematic vision should coincide with it so closely. Reciprocally, engagement with these issues – demonstrably intentional and rigorously controlled, as otherwise inexplicable changes from the novel suggest – ought to recuperate Spielberg's work from charges of self-indulgence and frivolity that so often casually damn it.

The 'empire of the sun' is imbued with and created by light, the space bounded by the film frame and human imagination: cinema itself.

CHAPTER TWELVE

Indiana Jones and the Last Crusade: cut to the chase

After *The Color Purple*'s critical drubbing, *Empire of the Sun*'s indifferent commercial performance, and the American network television cancellation of Spielberg's *Amazing Stories*, *Indiana Jones and the Last Crusade* returned to the crowd-pleasing action cinema with which its director was synonymous. The $36 million movie attracted an unprecedented $40 million from exhibitors in non-refundable bids – virtually guaranteeing profit even before release (Taylor 1992: 112). Spielberg and Lucas's reputations and a cast including three of the hottest stars of their generations (Sean Connery, Harrison Ford and River Phoenix) were only part of the winning combination. The movie reintroduced *Raiders of the Lost Ark* elements including the characters Brody and Sallah, the latter now unequivocally competent and heroic. Further political caution included reversion to Nazis, rather than non-Europeans, as villains, and a strong and capable, if ultimately treacherous, female lead. First weekend takings, $46.9 million, touted as the highest ever, encouraged other moviegoers. Less was made of the fact that 2,327 prints screened simultaneously and ticket prices had been hiked 50 cents (Baxter 1996: 348).

Spielberg reportedly wanted to compensate for *Temple of Doom* – 'not ... one of my prouder moments' – which, he insisted, contained 'not an ounce of my personal feeling' (Taylor 1992: 110). Not entirely financially motivated – 'I could make a whole bunch of pitiful movies, and I'd still be bankable for a while' – he supposedly directed *The Last Crusade* to honour an agreement with Lucas to make a trilogy if

Raiders of the Lost Ark succeeded (Taylor 1992: 111). If *Temple of Doom* was expertly crafted but cynical and hollow beyond its sensational, carelessly offensive surface, *The Last Crusade* was more individual. Along with *Always, Hook* and *Schindler's List*, long-standing ambitions in development at the time, Spielberg made it from choice, not commercial necessity.

The result, though disarmingly facile, sustains the wit, versatility and humour that distinguished *Temple of Doom*'s opening but gleamed only intermittently thereafter. It develops more complex characterisation and relationships than its predecessors, creating a dramatic foil for comedy and action. If the final ride into the sunset is history's longest, it is an affectionate farewell, closing not only a chapter in the director's career but also a film that, for all its blockbuster values, respects its audience and its materials.

Hooray for Hollywood

The Paramount logo this time dissolves into Monument Valley, iconographic setting of John Ford westerns. Non-diegetic chanting, drumming and jungle sounds, utterly gratuitous evocations of *Raiders of the Lost Ark*'s opening, together with inordinate vegetation matted into the location shots, parody the looseness of Ford's geography (*Stagecoach* (1939) traverses Monument Valley repeatedly) and establish an exclusively cinematic milieu – something *Temple of Doom*, associated by critics with the real India, failed at. A file of horses ridden by figures wearing rangers' hats again evokes a western, even as the music and fantastic rock formations recall *Lawrence of Arabia*. The first obvious joke comes with realisation that these are old-fashioned Boy Scouts, while for adults potential pleasure lies in recognising allusions to *Picnic at Hanging Rock* (1975) and *A Passage to India* (the boys are warned, 'Some of the passageways in here can run for miles').

Light-hearted and endowed with typical Spielberg traits, the movie cuts to a scene of inscribed spectatorship and continues to flaunt textuality and intertextual relations. The western elements – alluding to the most enduring of genres, yet one that evolved as a specifically American variation of the chase picture – emphasise Jones' cinematic provenance. Two boys, unobserved, watch an off-screen event casting light onto their faces. Secondary identification occurs as the camera cranes towards the object of their gaze: a man in leather jacket and fedora directing labourers unearthing treasure. As his hirelings, shady as those accompanying Jones at the start of *Raiders of the Lost Ark*, whoop delightedly at becoming rich, the camera reveals him to be played not by Harrison Ford but an actor resembling Spielberg, Jones' creative progenitor. Fatherhood resonates thematically throughout this movie and retrospectively reinflects its predecessors. The point, of course, whether he resembles Spielberg or Jones, is that he is a mercenary.

'Indy, Indy', softly calls one of the boys – not to the man below but to his companion, revealed as the young Jones, precociously expert archaeologist, as a caption anchors the setting: 'UTAH 1912'. Jones, insisting the artefact belongs in a museum, demonstrates the selfless determination characteristic of the portion of his personality not later corrupted by 'fortune and glory'. A natural leader, he gives orders to his companion. Contrary to the Scouts' motto, 'Be Prepared', he already manifests improvisational flair; asked his intentions, he replies: 'I dunno – I'll think of something.' Having neither yet lost innocence in this Edenic cinematic Imaginary, nor acquired his single weakness, he grabs a rattler in his bare hands: 'It's only a snake.'

Jones whistles, in Saturday serial tradition, for his trusty steed – which he misses when attempting to jump onto it from an outcrop. His adversary more successfully echoes this action, summoning a truck and a car, highlighting similarities between young Jones and this more competent second self. The ensuing chase mimics silent westerns and comedies. Jones' companion – credited as 'Roscoe' – whom he has sent for help, resembles 'Fatty' (Roscoe) Arbuckle, whose involvement in a 1920s sex scandal popularly marked the end of Hollywood's innocence and precipitated the Production Code. His Scout uniform is particularly ironic, given the movement's phobia concerning sexuality (early manuals famously recommended cold showers).

Jones finds himself on an implausible circus train, recalling *The Greatest Show on Earth* (1952) – which in interviews Spielberg had celebrated as his first cinematic experience (Taylor 1992: 46–7) – and, in appearance, *Dumbo*. During a breathless pursuit along wagons containing alligators, rhinos and countless snakes, an overtly phallic python rears up between Jones' legs, precipitating his fall into the slithering mass below, screaming and panicking. Shortly thereafter, in one-to-one combat, Jones is pinned down on a canvas roof that is penetrated between his thighs by the horn of an enraged rhino. His adult fear of snakes inextricably, if jokingly and knowingly, relates to castration anxieties consequent upon rebellion against a threatening father figure. Attempting escape, he falls into a lion's cage and grabs a nearby whip to subdue the masculine beast. The moment recalls Willie's comparison of his appearance with that of a lion tamer in *Temple of Doom*. He suddenly notices a facial wound where Harrison Ford (hence the adult Jones) is scarred. The physical marking emphasises the incident's formative nature as, succumbing to patriarchy, he accepts assistance from his enemies, who haul him to safety using the whip.

Fleeing again, Jones, cornered, hides in a trunk. This collapses as the villain enters the luggage car, revealing itself as a magician's prop: Jones has disappeared. Apparently

Indiana Jones and the Last Crusade – the Great Train Robbery meets the Dumbo circus train

filmed in a single take – presumably the camera was stopped and restarted – this simple and purely cinematic illusion pays homage to Méliès, fantasy/special-effects pioneer, of whom Spielberg is the best-known heir.

A close-up reveals his adversary's admiration as Jones escapes. Shouting 'Dad! Dad!' in a plea for protection, the boy returns home only for his father, loath to be disturbed, to halt him with an imperiously raised hand. Jones' adventurous fieldwork contrasts with his father's cerebral composure. This scene emphasises the latter's remoteness by showing only his hands (and pragmatically avoids the difficulty of making Connery look thirty years younger). He calms, but also fobs off, his son by ordering him: 'Count to twenty. In Greek.'

Accordingly, when a corrupt sheriff (another negative patriarch) leads in the villain and parts Jones from the cross he fought to protect, permitting its sale to a middle-aged man in a white suit – reminiscent of Belloq – the baddies have considerably more presence than the hero's off-screen father. 'You lost today, kid', observes his adult alter-ego. 'But that doesn't mean to say you have to like it', he adds, placing his hat on the young man's head to the strains of the Indiana Jones theme. He thus confers a raider's identity, contrasted with the tweedy, bespectacled academic image inherited – we later infer – along with scholarship and independence, from Jones Senior.

Why are there two (three, four …) fathers?

Slavoj Zizek argues that the *femme fatale* in film noir is a male fantasy embodying universal corruption. Her attraction typically brings the hero into conflict with what Zizek calls 'the obscene father', an 'excessively *present* father', all-powerful, cruel and knowing (1992: 158). This contrasts with the traditional father who asserts authority, not literally through open display of power but symbolically, from a position of absence, through 'the threat of potential power', so that the Law is unquestioningly accepted (1992: 158–9).

Last Crusade's multiple hybridity contains noir elements consistent with Zizek's thesis. Cutting to a nighttime storm on a floundering ship years later, during which Jones' chin again bleeds as he is beaten while rescuing for the museum the same cross from the same white-suited man, the narrative emphasises continuity in his idealistic rebellion against patriarchal corruption. As the ship sinks, the defeated collector's hat floats in the foreground, underlining symbolic castration. A comic interlude at the university reintroduces the ineffectual symbolic father, Brody. It also reveals Jones' unreadiness to accept patriarchal responsibility himself: after an authoritative lecture to smitten co-eds, he exchanges amorous looks with one student before escaping through the window of his tiny office-cum-boiler room (he clearly holds a junior position), to evade hordes of students whose assignments he has not graded. Outside, in the sunshine, shadowy figures observe, beckon and surround him.

Apparently kidnapped, he is collected by agents of a wealthy antiquarian and museum benefactor, the suave Mr Donovan (Julian Glover). Urbane respectability conceals sinister activities. Like James Mason in *North by Northwest* and Godfrey Tearle in *The 39 Steps*, Donovan conducts business with the hero with exaggerated courtesy during a party in an adjoining room, prompting his wife to intervene, complaining he is neglecting his guests. Apart from heightening the normality that masks corruption, the wife's presence inscribes familial relationships into the text, thus rendering Donovan's relationship to Jones implicitly patriarchal.

The narrative takes a film noir twist when Donovan hires Jones like a gumshoe to investigate another researcher's disappearance while working for him to locate the Holy Grail. This, it transpires, is Professor Jones Senior. Jones blenches at his father's name. Tensing like the parricidal Bruno in *Strangers on a Train*, he describes him as 'a teacher of medieval literature. The one the students hope they don't get.' Nevertheless, on accepting the case he picks up his hat which has been resting in the foreground during the scene, and on arrival back at his father's house his shadow stretches before him onto the door, suggesting their relationship of both identity and difference, the super-ego that urges him to duty.

Jones' estranged biological father, now physically as well as emotionally absent – lost object of the narrative instigated by a powerful, present father – equates to the archetypal Grail. Ultimately the journey leads Jones to paternal reconciliation and incorporation into the Symbolic, represented in exclusively male bonding with Jones Senior, Brody and Sallah in the closing shot. It leads initially, though, to the *femme fatale*, Dr Elsa Schneider (Alison Doody). Her ensnarement lures him to the ultimate obscene father: his face-to-face (uncomfortably present) encounter with Hitler. It precipitates also another obscene father's symbolic defeat, Donovan's punishment for betraying both Jones and his country when the Grail – metonym of the Holy Father – destroys him for selfishly pursuing immortality: unnatural prolongation and assertion of presence.

Although Elsa – the only central female – is a betrayer, punished for her treachery, this misogyny operates structurally, as in film noir, rather than in her characterisation. At their initial meeting and during their lovemaking her repartee equals Jones'. Elsa takes the initiative in preceding Jones into the Venice catacombs. She remains cool, and is neither more nor less victimised than Jones, when confronted by thousands of rats and a conflagration. She actively and skilfully pilots a speedboat, eventually rescuing Jones, during a high-speed chase through canals and docks. Her *femme fatale* role is nevertheless stressed: Jones observes, 'Since I've met you I've nearly been incinerated, drowned and chopped into fish bait.' The library scene, when Jones distracts attention while using a metal post to smash through marble slabs by synchronising his blows with a librarian stamping books, alludes with comic hyperbole to another modern retro-noir, *Chinatown* (1974), in which the protagonist coughs to cover the ripping of a column from a library newspaper. Polanski's narrative leads to an excessively present obscene father, as well as sexual entanglements beyond the protagonist's imagination – as also, in lighter vein, does Jones'.

'Don't call me that, please'

Arriving at a Salzburg castle (an exaggeratedly phoney matte shot), Jones is dressed, like a Scout or dutiful son, in his adventurer's outfit plus an incongruous tie. True to form, when Elsa enquires about his plans he responds: 'I'll think of something.' His solution – significantly, given the as-yet-unrevealed sexual politics of the situation – is to exchange hats with her and enter the castle pretending to be a fussy Scotsman in a beret and mackintosh. The character unconsciously parodies his father (while the film may well be consciously parodying Connery's impersonation of an American). As Jones, frequently doubled by his shadow, explores, lightning and thunder prefigure with Gothic dread the paternal encounter, more disturbing than being in a Nazi stronghold. After daringly entering through a closed window by swinging on his whip over and back across the courtyard – 'kiddie stuff', he nonchalantly tells Elsa – he is hit over the head with a vase. Then his father, emerging into shot in a low-angle close-up, rhyming with Jones' introduction in *Raiders of the Lost Ark*, cuts him down to size with a single word:

> 'Junior?'
> 'Yes, sir!'
> 'Junior!'
> 'Don't call me that, please.'

The professor fusses over the broken antique, not Jones' head. However, the latter rallies, Oedipal rivalry aroused. Asserting archaeological knowledge over his father's authority, he declares the vase a fake.

Realising Jones can only have located him thanks to his Grail diary, the father thrusts his furled umbrella into the top of his briefcase – unmistakeably Freudian symbolism! – and reconciliation begins as light pours from the window behind Jones onto his father. Mutually proud, rivalry replaced by respect, they exchange compliments – 'Junior, you did it.' 'No, Dad, you did. Forty years.' Jones continues, like a boy recounting an adventure, but boasting of bravery in the face of the other's phobia, 'There were rats, Dad! *Big* ones!'

Connery's casting is richly suggestive. As James Bond, he was as much Jones' precursor as any cowboy, in both his 'lechery and ironic off-handedness under pressure, the sense of "making it up as he goes along"' (Baxter 1996: 194–5). (Spielberg wanted to make a Bond movie with Connery but was thwarted; only British directors were employed (Brode 1995: 173).) Certainly *The Last Crusade*'s powerboat chase resembles a Bond sequence above all. Less widely acknowledged in this context is Connery's role as an amoral adventurer, living by his own code and in pursuit of what Jones calls 'fortune and glory', in *The Man Who Would Be King* (1975). This epic, based on a Kipling colonial tale and employing spectacular Himalayan settings (actually filmed in Morocco and France), is a clear *Indiana Jones* prototype. It features, for example, a vertiginous rope bridge which is cut, as in *Temple of Doom*, crowded Indian market scenes with snake charmers, conjurors and dervishes, and Third World peoples clamouring for leadership from the white protagonists. Priceless treasures abound. The plot involves occult powers and knowledge as its two anti-heroes discover Masonic connections between themselves, Kipling (who appears as a character), and Himalayan priests who recognise their ceremonial seal as that of Alexander the Great before drawing them into their own mythology to fulfil ancient destiny. Clearly the villagers' anticipation of Jones' arrival in *Temple of Doom* parallels this, as does *The Last Crusade*'s Grail legend.

Harmony shatters after a Nazi enters, calling for Dr Jones. Father and son simultaneously respond. While reflected light flares off Professor Jones' glasses, metaphorically inscribing the sense of mirroring each other's desire, they bicker over Jones having brought the diary, the father remarking he 'should have mailed it to the Marx Brothers'.

Easthope analyses a poster for the film that declares 'The Man in the Hat is Back – and This Time He's Bringing his Dad!', noting how assonance between 'hat' and 'dad' underlines the headgear's phallic connotation. The poster also indicates, through Jones' cocky gaze at the viewer, and his father's expression (combining pride and suspicion as he watches his son over his shoulder), generational rivalry implicit in 'Jones' claim to take over the role of prime popular hero from James Bond' (1990: 90). The last straw comes when Jones' father again calls him 'Junior', denying the patriarchal status and autonomy of his own name, at which Jones grabs a guard's machine gun and kills three Nazis in a rage of phallic potency: '*Don't ever call me Junior!*'

The Oedipal theme complicates when Jones must choose between the woman and his father as a Nazi holds a gun to her head and Jones Senior insists she too is a Nazi. Relinquishing his weapon in unwitting acceptance of castration by the false woman, the obscene father's proxy, Jones allows Elsa the diary, token of the Symbolic order that epitomised sacred trust between the reconciled true father and son. Asked how he knew Elsa's real nature, Jones Senior replies, 'She talks in her sleep.' Her substitution for the emphatically absent biological mother heightens incestuous undertones; son and father have shared her while she remains the obscene father's 'possession'. Both duped, they become equal without the father suffering defeat by the rebellious son or the son succumbing to the Law of the Father. The shared challenge of defeating the obscene father and serving the Holy Father sublimates Oedipal conflict, which manifests instead as more like sibling rivalry. Later, when Jones objects, 'It's disgraceful – you're old enough to be her f... her *grandfather*', inability to express his initial thought suggests denial of its implications. The continuing exchange – 'I'm as human as the next man.' 'I *was* the next man.' – reasserts equality.

Hereafter, woman having been eliminated as a term between men, the movie treats paternal relationships light-heartedly. Father and son accept mutual dependence. After Jones eloquently praises Brody's chameleon-like qualities and multilingualism, a crosscut reveals Jones' surrogate father wandering in a white suit and panama through a Middle Eastern crowd, pleading to all and sundry, 'Does anyone speak English?' until Sallah spirits him away from obvious Nazis dressed in black with dark glasses and German accents. It transpires that Jones lies about Brody to deceive his captors: 'He once got lost in his own museum.' Jones Senior is similarly incompetent, removing any sense of hostile threat to the hero. Roped back-to-back to his son, he drops the lighter while burning through their bonds and torches the room; when he tries to inform Jones – 'I want to tell you something' – the latter replies, emphasising the paternal dimension, 'Don't get sentimental now, Dad. Save it for later', just as the film gears into slapstick. Much of the humour derives from Jones clinging to his briefcase and umbrella, signs of stern paternal authority, while fulfilling the innocently mischief-making role previously taken by Short Round.

Unimpressed by Jones' derring-do, he is oblivious of the havoc he himself causes. As Jones' biplane gunner he is warned of fighters at 11 o'clock, only to check his watch in an almost wilful misunderstanding typical of their relationship. When he finally gets the message he shoots off their own tail. Yet his scholarship prevails when he remembers Charlemagne and downs a fighter by using his umbrella to frighten gulls into its path. The incident is followed by a slow, dignified rendition of the Indiana Jones theme, and a reaction shot of Jones, choked with emotion, impressed.

Later, Jones loses his hat just as a runaway tank he is riding plunges over a cliff. The father tells Brody of his remorse concerning filial estrangement: 'I never told him anything. I just wasn't ready, Marcus. Five minutes would have been enough.' Sarah Harwood characterises the 1980s as a decade of failed fathers generally in Hollywood movies. Jones Senior fits her categories of 'negligent' and 'authoritarian' as well as 'absent' fathers (1997: 77). After Jones hauls himself back over the cliff, the two reveal their true emotions: 'I thought I'd lost you, son.' 'I thought so too, sir.' Again, acceptance supplants rivalry as the two embrace. However, habit intervenes and the father quickly regains his stiff upper lip, brusquely intoning, 'Righto, well done' before reasserting authority over his exhausted and battered offspring: 'Why are you sitting there resting …?' As Jones is left alone, his hat blows back into frame towards him and the Indiana Jones theme plays in minor key. Paternal acceptance and entry into the Symbolic are a qualified victory.

Nevertheless, as Harwood suggests, this film contrasts with the earlier two, which ended on the Final Romance with the heroine. With Elsa's punishment,

> the confirmed father/son bonding is entirely self-sufficient; all women having been lost along the way. The entire series thus constructs a quest for the father, awakened in *Raiders of the Lost Ark* but not satisfied until *The Last Crusade*, in which the sole solution to the absent father is his full restitution which, in turn, denies other familial possibilities. (1997: 81)

Reaganite family values produced a cinema of frequently absent mothers. During a scene when Jones Senior removes his hat, father and son refer cryptically to Jones' mother. The son angrily takes her side, implying the father's 'obsession' hastened her premature death. The father, however, before replacing his hat, insists she always understood it; and the narrative, in which his learning deprives the Nazis of world-conquering power, vindicates him. The scene's real significance, though, is return of the repressed. Inscribing the absent mother exceeds narrative necessity. The final, endless ride into the sunset is a masculine fantasy of regression into an Imaginary which denies desire for the mother, an eternally irresponsible freedom disguised as achievement of adulthood. 'After you, Junior', says the professor. 'Yes, sir!' replies his son, friction between them eliminated. Woman removed from the equation, male competition is purged.

Illumination

The final chase frames shots through observation slits in the tanks, interposing a widescreen view on the action. These internal frames again highlight textuality at the climax of a film that makes preposterous demands on suspended disbelief. After Jones wedges a rock into a tank cannon the barrel explodes when the gun is fired, splitting into a surreal flower as in a cartoon. Yet the explosion kills the gunner using the sight, similarly to the demise of the camera operator penetrated ocularly in *Raiders of the Lost Ark*. Vision entails power, even as the film deprecates itself as little more than a high-budget Chuck Jones animation. Such alternation – or paradoxical simultaneity – of Imaginary involvement and Symbolic separation is so recurrent it cannot be discounted in considering the popularity of Spielberg's work.

This passage of *The Last Crusade*, a hybrid pastiche of the epic, western and war genres, pays homage to the 1950s cinema that nurtured Spielberg. Matthew Bouch explains that 'widescreen publicity ... emphasised realism, technological advance, luxury, and especially participation in the dramatic action, or at least a heightened state of co-presence' (1996: 9). The trailer for *How the West Was Won* (1956), he notes, promises audiences will 'ride with the Indians', and that 'the extra-dimensional magic of Cinerama puts you in the picture' (ibid.). (Note that the mine chase in *Temple of Doom* incorporates overt allusions to the roller-coaster phantom ride emphasised in trailers for *This is Cinerama*. Spielberg protagonists such as Neary and Jim put themselves 'in the picture'.) Bouch quotes *The Ten Commandments* (1956), which claims, 'Those who see this motion picture ... will make a pilgrimage over the very ground that Moses trod.' He continues: 'In this publicity, cinema traversed a liminal nexus and created virtual reality. ... fantastical or Biblical subject matter emphasised this extraordinary power, by itself being outside the realm of actuality experienced by the audience' (ibid.).

The unity of the Imaginary Signifier, then, was offered. Yet the promised pleasure implied spectacle, awareness of illusory immersion and astonishment at the effects; in other words, re-emphasis, in the face of competing leisure activities, of central cinematic properties. Tensions between belief and disbelief, recognised in such early comedies as *The Countryman's First Sight of the Animated Pictures* (1901) and *Uncle Josh at the Moving Picture Show* (1902), have always characterised the medium.

Bouch comments pertinently on Jones, close to reaching the Grail, encountering an abyss. Recalling sacred translations in his father's diary, Jones moans despairingly, 'A Leap of Faith!' Knowing the Grail is the only hope of saving his father, whom Donovan has mortally injured, he instinctively steps onto an impossibly camouflaged bridge:

> Belief enables him to perceive the bridge. He must renounce a certain ideological notion of reality and substitute a belief in the act of mimesis: the architect's [sic] ability to construct a bridge that looks exactly like a bottomless chasm. He must believe in the 'magical' goodness of the Grail in order to perceive the representation of the chasm as a bridge. The bridge is then shown as a reality: the representation in its 'true' (real) nature. Thus, Indiana Jones becomes one of the audience: he experiences the same process of reification. (1996: 22–3)

Belief, enabling Jones to choose the true Grail, is necessary to resolve the narrative. Meanwhile Jones is again positioned as a child, echoing the credulous spectator's psychic regression, through crosscutting with the father he strives to save. Doubling and apparent telepathy between the two who now, reconciled, speak in unison although out of earshot, reinforce this notion. Like other similar Spielberg relationships – Elliott and E.T., Jim and the cadet – it intensifies spectatorial involvement by inscribing its like into the intradiegetic relay of the look. Asked by Jones what he discovered in his quest, the professor, contrasting himself with Elsa who 'never really believed' and thus dies, replies: 'Illumination.' That describes not only the seeker's eventual spiritual state but also cinema's material basis, foregrounded in Spielberg's themes and mise-en-scène.

CHAPTER THIRTEEN

Always: light my fire

Prompting mostly lukewarm, but some 'vicious' reviews (Taylor 1992: 16), *Always* proved modestly successful, with grosses of $43 million domestic and $77.1 million worldwide against a $29.5 million budget (Freer 2001: 181, 189). The first of Spielberg's five-movie package for Universal under new president Tom Pollock, who as Lucas's lawyer had brokered the *Raiders of the Lost Ark* profits agreement, *Always* gained coverage for being apparently disowned by its director and cast. (Most snubbed its London Royal Command Performance, although this may have been more Hollywood politics than commentary on the film.) Perhaps the frenetic cartoonish elements, along with fetishised old military aircraft, prompted strategic distance from a comparative failure that superficially recalled *1941* as well as *Empire of the Sun*'s disappointing performance and uncomfortable reception. Unlike the notorious earlier comedy, *Always* is generally written off as Spielberg's forgotten film (Freer 2001: 190).

Reviewers repeatedly caricatured Spielberg as Peter Pan, inept at dramatising adult themes or emotions. 'Most critics cringed at fey whimsy', and at least three British broadsheets likened *Always* to a marshmallow (Skimpole 1990: 9). Others succumbed to temptation, prompted by a scene in a sun-drenched wheat field, to proffer puns typified by the *Sunday Telegraph* headline: 'Hepburn Up to Her Knees in Corn' (Tookey 1990: 28; Baxter 1996: 351).

Undoubtedly this loose remake of *A Guy Named Joe* which had preoccupied Spielberg for years (Fleming's 1943 original appears on TV in *Poltergeist*), presented inherent difficulties both artistic and commercial. The central problem of 'letting go' after a lover's sudden death and the theme of inheriting responsibility and living up to another's heroic sacrifice (later *Saving Private Ryan*'s premise), while integral to the collective experience of wartime, lack contemporary resonance. As Ralph Novak in *People* expressed it,

> *A Guy Named Joe* responded to a most particular need. Coming in WWII, when young loves were so palpably precarious and the need for comforting illusion so great, it had a ready audience. These were Americans who, if not more naïve than we, were at least more willing to suspend their cynicism. (Quoted in Brode 1995: 190)

Pauline Kael, in the *New Yorker*, noted an embarrassing sexual awkwardness: 'Now that Spielberg is no longer twelve hasn't he realised there is a queasiness in the idea of playing Cupid to the girl you loved and lost, and fixing her up with the next guy?' (quoted in Freer 2001: 189). More is at stake, however. John Baxter diverges momentarily from pop psychoanalysis of *Always* as reworking Spielberg's marital problems and relationship with Holly Hunter, to quote pertinently from James Agee's reviews of *A Guy Named Joe*. The issue is what the Hays Code in the 1940s prohibited and what Spielberg, in a more permissive era, glossed over: 'Pete and the audience are spared what might have happened if [Dorinda] had really got either frozen or tender with [Ted], while Pete looked on.' Agee compares Fleming's movie with James Joyce's 'The Dead': for as

> the jealousy of a living lover for a dead man made one of Joyce's finest stories, the emotions a ghost might feel who watched a living man woo and cajole his former mistress seem just as promising to me ... but to make such a film – above all at such a time as this – would require extraordinary taste, honesty and courage. (Quoted in Baxter 1996: 353)

Restraint attributed to Spielberg is integral to the narrative. This, I argue below, inadvertently skirts subject matter that psychoanalysis considers latent in all story-telling but which in this instance manifests uncomfortably near the surface.

Unconsciously and for its impressive technique, *Always* – a typical Spielberg movie in terms of perceived weaknesses as well as pervasive style and themes – is more interesting, complex and sophisticated, but also problematic, than most reviews suggest.

Postmodern pastiche or marketing mongrel

Described by Thomas Elsaesser and Warren Buckland as 'a thoroughly classical contemporary filmmaker' (2002: 17), Spielberg in this instance, as elsewhere, throws such terminology into question. On one hand, *Variety* considered *Always* 'the kind of film he would have made if he had been a studio contract director during Hollywood's golden era' (Anon. 1989: 22). On the other, in characteristic postmodern fashion, *Always'* polysemic signifiers connect across the text, forming transient, synaptic webs of meaning, only some directly supporting the causality, continuity, invisibility and imputed realism of classical conventions. When the *New York Times'* Janet Maslin complains, '*Always* is filled with big sentimental moments [but] it lacks the intimacy to make any of this very moving', she judges according to melodrama expectations while ignoring action-adventure, special effects, fantasy and slapstick. To argue, as Maslin does, that '*Always* is overloaded. There is barely a scene that wouldn't have worked better with less fanfare' (quoted in Freer 2001: 189) is, irrespective of whether the movie succeeds, to monologise a multi-accented text.

A Jeep speeding towards a bomber recalls 'scrambles' from World War Two movies – except this is not a war movie. It is, however, in part romantic drama, as Maslin recognises. Yet that genre, Steve Neale observes, lacks specific iconography (2000: 16). If, as Neale also writes, 'genres do not consist solely of films. They consist also of specific systems of expectation and hypothesis which spectators bring with them to the cinema and which interact with films themselves during the course of the viewing' to 'provide … recognition and understanding' (2000: 31), it follows that expectations and hypotheses originate elsewhere.

They inform the narrative image in epitexts such as posters and press packs. The production notes' first sentence tagged *Always* 'both a love story and an adventure'. The title logo, uniting posters, press materials and opening credits, comprised elegant calligraphy associated with female genres. The posters, of a couple embracing against a distant conflagration, recalled *Gone With the Wind*. This interpretive framework compensates for the romance's lack of iconography, while targeting women and couples and downplaying comedy and aerial adventure. Yet the gentle love story promised by advertising copy – 'They couldn't hear him. They couldn't see him. But he was there when they needed him. Even after he was gone' – may have caused confusion like Maslin's and consequent poor word of mouth. For all its bittersweet complications, emotional restraint and tightly controlled direction, *Always* is excessive, a cineaste's ebullient celebration of entertainment.

That the production notes sought to specify a genre hybrid indicates perceived difficulties, possibly confirmed by test screenings, in marketing a diverse product. Usually two of three potential attractions – genre, stars and, in some cases, a well-known director – are sufficient and necessary to secure go-ahead. Spielberg's profile and Hunter, Dreyfuss and John Goodman's commercial stature, not to mention Audrey Hepburn's presence, would preclude consideration of genre – unless Spielberg's reputation had ebbed. Furthermore, Rick Altman (1999) shows, it is small independent companies that conceive and promote movies generically because they have to identify them to distributors; formerly to fit ready-made slots, such as double bills, nowadays presumably to find niche audiences. Big studios, however, hardly used generic terminology: marketing unique, prestigious pictures, they highlighted differences from films of their competitors. The reason simply was major studios owned theatres and could guarantee exhibition. In the post-studio era, the close relationship between industry sectors has changed little. Just as, when double features became common in the 1930s, majors ascribed their own B movies genre labels but refused to apply them to prestige films, so in the New Hollywood it is imitations – consider straight-to-video movies – that are strongly identified generically. Consequently, genre often has been (and is) utilised pejoratively. (Critics dismiss Spielberg as a 'science fiction', 'children's', or indeed 'genre' filmmaker.) If prestige pictures were ascribed special qualities, genre films represented lower production values and lack of originality. Contrary to received wisdom – that genres help audiences select – it was prestige films, *not* generically labelled, that attracted audiences. Empirical research in 1997 confirmed that filmgoers continued to use genre negatively: to avoid the kinds of films they dislike (Altman 1999: 113).

Altman compares film with other commodities to show that genre is less significant than often assumed (1999: 113–21). Anybody can compete by meeting demand for products similar to those that already exist. However, challenging brand leaders proves difficult. There are plenty of vacuum flasks, only one Thermos; many vacuum cleaners, only one Hoover. Successful products have exclusive brand names. Some, such as Nescafé, Tampax, Kit-Kat and Coca-Cola are worth more than the entire stocks of the products they denote.

Similarly, any film company can produce a thriller or a musical. But only one enjoys a special relationship with Nicole Kidman's agent, or has created a popular character such as Freddy Kruger, or owns the rights to a Steven King novel, or knows how to carry out particular processes, such as Industrial Light and Magic, or has a repeatable title such as *The Godfather* or *The Blair Witch Project* (1999), or an established studio image, such as Disney, or a product franchise, such as Harry Potter. Or has a contract with Spielberg. These are valuable because nobody else can offer them. They are brands that label subsequent and subsidiary products. Genre becomes important only for imitators trying to cash in. The original texts' producers avoid emphasising genre because it both narrows the potential audience and eases the way for competition. Thus genrification of *Always* is anomalous, again suggesting the Spielberg brand temporarily lost favour.

As well as generic affiliations, *Always* evokes specific 1940s intertexts. *A Matter of Life and Death* (1946) featured another doomed pilot's romance with a radio operator, glimpses into the afterworld and ghostly visitations. Pete's friend Al likens the setting to 'The war in Europe … It's *England*, man. Everything but Glenn Miller.' He continues with an explicit reference to movies: 'There ain't no war here. This is why they don't make movies called *Night Raid to Boise, Idaho* or *Firemen Strike at Dawn*.' Dialogue remains from *A Guy Named Joe*, unchanged. Other films from the period involving ghostly intervention include *It's a Wonderful Life* (Pete tells Dorinda, 'You're gonna have a wonderful life' after Al observes Ted has 'got wings') and *Blithe Spirit* (1945) (which contains the song 'Always').

Part of the excess of *Always* is the shift from comedy-adventure, when we see Pete's engine burning after he has extinguished Al's, to horror as his plane explodes. Ironic excess defines the banality of the Hereafter, comprising Hap, in white cable stitch sweater, in a golden-tinged oasis of grass, leaves and daisies, reminiscent of a knitting-pattern cover. Self-conscious dialogue narration in the same scene betrays Stoppard's uncredited contribution:

Hap:	Where was I?
Pete:	Time is funny stuff.
Hap:	It is. Space has its points too. Anyway, in the five months since you crashed –
Pete:	I thought you said it was six months.
Hap:	Yes, but that was then. You see, I'm telling you everything in the wrong order.

Also beyond love story and adventure narrational requirements are anti-realist, cartoon-style touches: the business with oily marks on Al's face after Pete's first landing; Looney Tunes voices produced by helium inhalation; a sideways track over Al's radio, his laden icebox, then up his four-foot drinking straw to bring him into frame; the absurd causal chain from the faulty 'Follow Me' truck to Al's cigar bursting into flame and the would-be fire-fighter, Ted, failing to extinguish with coffee the garbage can he also ignites; the extraordinary detail of trainee pilots bursting into song and dance, complete with red, white and blue umbrellas for the line: 'You must have showers.'

Red, white and blue dominate throughout, contrasting flames with clear Western skies, connoting life's warmth and deathly chill. This macro structure repeats fractally in countless details of art direction. Other artistically motivated devices, exceeding narrational or generic requirements, include elliptical cuts bridged by dialogue, imitated from *Citizen Kane*. An effect is reconstructed from Hitchcock's *Foreign Correspondent* (1940) when, inside Dorinda's crashing plane, water irrupts through the windshield in one continuous take. Characters, played by film stars, do impressions of film stars – one very badly, yet sufficiently recognisable that the audience shares both Pete and Ted's incredulity at Dorinda's inability to identify John Wayne.

Doubly-voiced discourse, such as Dorinda's advice to Ted over a chicken dinner – 'Anything that flies it's OK to pick up. Even in a good restaurant' – in which she inadvertently corroborates Pete's account of how he first met her, underlines the movie's insistence on textuality and rewards looking beyond realism. Allusions to other Spielberg films include the *Close Encounters* theme as Dorinda throttles up before flying to rescue the smokejumpers (having missed Pete's declaration of love before his fatal mission), repeated at the end as she leaves Pete for a future with Ted. The same scene features the Sugarland Express – airfield emergency vehicles, lights flashing – before Pete's ghost (played by the same actor as Neary) disappears down the runway towards distant light. This finale recalls the *Close Encounters* poster and – in Pete renouncing Dorinda for a higher purpose – *Casablanca*.

Fred Pfeil identifies as postmodern in mainstream movies the chronotope, in Bakhtin's phrase (1981), of two distinctive settings within the same diegetic timeframe. In *Always*, Pete occupies space inhabited by living characters, without their knowledge; in other words, the film coincides 'spaces whose distances from one another are not mappable as distances so much as … measurable in differences of attitude and intensity' (1993: 124). To stretch the conceit: Spielberg's typical chronotope, exemplified in *Always*, consists also of overlapping diegeses invoked by multiple allusions.

Promotion involving genre – and the dual structure of goal-oriented and romance plots, epitomising Hollywood classicism – hardly encourages viewing habits implicit in this reading. Nor, however, beyond formal conventions, does *Always* relate to realism, even while, like *The Color Purple* and *Empire of the Sun*, it exceeds family action-movie expectations accrued to Spielberg's name. 'That the film eschews even a nod towards reality in favour of movie patois and emotions may have accounted for its failure to find a really big audience' (Freer 2001: 191).

The medium is the message

Always begins by announcing, through auto-citation, a mode of address and preferred reception. An almost self-contained gag that conveys little narrative information, it seeks architextually to align expectations with 'the peculiar in-joke self-reference (or deconstructive logic) of the "New Hollywood"' (Elsaesser & Buckland 2002: 132); specifically, those appropriate to auteurist reading of a Spielberg movie.

Two anglers relax on a mountain lake. A seaplane descends towards their dinghy. Foreshortening renders the huge plane uncomfortably close. Extreme perspective compresses its propellers alongside the nose. The effect: a face. The engines resemble eyes – fanciful, if such a visage did not grace a robot in *Short Circuit* (1986) and an alien in **Batteries Not Included* (1987): poor *E.T.* imitations, but Spielberg-produced. Just as *Duel*'s truck appeared sentient, the menacing plane, prow raised as it takes off again, re-enacts *Jaws*. Indeed, one of the fishermen, abandoning their boat in panic, is Ted Grossman, whose oarsman in *Jaws* lost all but his leg to the shark (Freer 2001: 188).

Convoluted allusion and celebrity intertextuality, combined with spectacle and humour (not serious on any level, it contains Chinese boxes of in-jokes from the obvious to the obsessively arcane) forge a postmodern moment that justifies the epithet 'post-classical' but at the same time adheres to classical principles. *Always* exemplifies the point that post-classical Hollywood is better understood not as spectacle's triumph over narrative (a frequent assertion), but as '"excessive classicism", rather than as a rejection or absence of classicism, or as moments in a classical film when our own theory or methods appear in the film itself, looking us in the face' (Elsaesser & Buckland 2002: 18). This is particularly true of self-reflexivity. Indistinguishable from narration in that it occupies the same semiotic material, yet identifiable in that its potential effects are describable (from any other camera position the seaplane would be merely a seaplane), style reinforces narrative but in this instance also provides simultaneous commentary.

Immediate transition from clear water and blue sky to a forest fire continues the red, white and blue colour scheme inaugurated by the seaplane's intrusion. Maintained throughout, until Dorinda clears a path to the river to rescue smokejumpers from flames and Pete relinquishes her in a cool, blue underwater scene, colour imagery underscores Al's speech to Pete about love: 'There's flash fire that flames and burns itself out and leaves nothing. Then there's the long burning. That's nature's burn. When you think it's out, the forest floor's still warm to the touch. That's the kind you and Dorinda got.'

An establishing close-up on a 'Fire Eaters' decal motivates camera positions outside the aircraft; an archaic touch (from *Only Angels Have Wings* (1939), for example) that underlines artificiality but institutes an internal norm that becomes important by inscribing a transparent screen between character and spectator. Pete's bravery as he denies seeing obscuring smoke contrasts with what is patently visible; an ambivalent positioning and focalisation in which the image's intermittent obliteration sporadically illuminates the blank screen. Crosscutting to a flaming forest implies co-presence of another World War Two movie, *Bambi*, just as the airfield resembles a war movie, with Dorinda, off-screen, announcing 'Cavalry coming up inside four minutes.' A helicopter takes off and we see Dorinda anxiously holding her desk microphone, the counterpart of June in *A Matter of Life and Death* as she swivels on her chair into the foreground, an entrance inspired by *Citizen Kane*.

The entire opening, from birdsong metamorphosing into a fishing reel to a helium-enhanced rendition of 'The Woody Woodpecker Song' is unremittingly busy, allusive and jocular. Pete and Dorinda's wisecracking squabbles, recalling *His Girl Friday* (1940) and Hepburn/Tracy comedies, accompanied by Al's cartoon-style boxing commentary, set the pace for the visuals. In the bar, showing Dorinda a stylish time, Pete magically pulls a tablecloth from a laden table. Lanterns backlight the fluttering cloth momentarily, while a minor character projects a shadow figure with his hand: seemingly incidental, yet highly choreographed, detail, reminiscent of *Citizen Kane* when Susan calls the protagonist/director a magician. A lamp behind Dorinda fixes the metaphor of projected desire as Pete produces his birthday gift.

Projector beams realise Pete's desire and Dorinda's fantasy during their endless role-playing, symptomatic of Pete's inability to express love directly, as when Dorinda orders beer in a champagne glass. They are emphatically evident as she feigns self-mockery, imploring: 'Tell me you love me. Please, please, please' – a fact he has acknowledged to Al. The romance's artifice and fantasy coincide with those of the diegesis, reconfirming Spielberg's style as focalisation expressing characters' solipsism. The couple dance silently. Pete observes: 'It's too bad we don't have a song. You know how couples say: "Honey, they're playing our song"? Why don't we try that bit, that signalling to the band bit? Hey, it works in the movies. Guys –' The camera tracks in on the band, who play 'Smoke Gets in Your Eyes'. There could hardly be clearer indication not that life resembles movies but that these characters inhabit one. The trope continues: Al addresses Southern-accented Dorinda as 'Scarlett' before literally sweeping her off her feet. Pete, holding towels so that fire-fighters can wash before dancing with Dorinda in her new dress, performs an Italian comedian routine straight out of 1930s musicals. Al gets on down to a hot and funky dance solo. Cut to Pete, white towels thoroughly blackened. A non-diegetic cartoon sound signifying stretching accompanies Dorinda bent backwards in an over-enthusiastic tango. Several of her partners still, comically, wear hard hats and goggles. Such implausibilities construct a montage illustrating Pete's immature disengagement from social and emotional reality as he looks down from a balcony with a light before him, as though directing or projecting the entire scene. When eventually, for the first time and unheard, Pete shouts his last words on earth, 'Dorinda, I love you!', he is seen through a spinning propeller, imposing both a flicker and a whirring projector-like sound.

After Pete's death, Al joins Dorinda looking out from the control tower. The camera remains outside, emphasising the screen as separation, looking in voyeuristically, as Pete does later. Here there is no visible light beam, although Dorinda's hair moves, conforming to Spielberg's solar wind motif, and wind is heard during dissolves to a smoke cloud and a smouldering forest that recalls Al's comment on her and Pete's relationship. Pete saunters along, whistling, then sees a stag, reinforcing the *Bambi* allusion.

Hap produces a sheet to cut Pete's hair; bizarre, were it not related to Dorinda muttering 'Haircut!' in her dreams. Pete's presence henceforth enunciates not *his* experience but *Dorinda's* fantasy, at once comforting and nightmarish as *Bambi's* loss and separation are to a child. Pete, remaining as she remembers him, in her fantasy relinquishes her to Ted, a rationalisation to mitigate guilt about transferring her affections. This explains Hepburn's casting, whose radiant, backlit image reinforces already heavily marked self-reflexivity that identifies the movie's textuality with characters' subjectivity. The moment Hap pulls off the sheet, Pete's shadow, rear-projected onto it, covers the cut to the cornfield. She, through condensation and transference, partial substitution for another Hepburn ('Hap/burn'?), personifies cinema, no less – transporting the narratee (Pete and Dorinda interdiegetically, and the spectator) instantly between locations; another cut takes us to the centre of the airfield for the narrative's continuation. 'When you get the hang of it [communing with the living] they hear you inside their heads', Hap tells Pete, 'as if it were their own thoughts': apposite description of suture in the classical system.

Cinematic motifs proliferate. Pete continues playing director, sadistically manipulating a happy sweeper into looking into a mirror and occasioning emotional change by suggesting, 'I think you're a pretty silly-looking guy.' The sweeper parallels the spectator's narcissistic identification with the on-screen image. Just as Dorinda was filmed from *outside* the control tower, although interior sound continued, so that glass reflections inscribed a screen – a trope reinforced by other characters peering through binoculars at Pete's hazardous landing, emphasising vision in Spielberg's trademark composition from *The Searchers* – and just as Pete removed his glasses to watch Dorinda's dreadful landing, so too the flying school class is behind a window as Ted enters: this screen is followed by another as Pete visits Al's office, also fully glazed. Pete conflates spectator and director, observing externally yet transcending the screen barrier to enter the scene. Intervening for his own amusement, he (disembodiedly) embodies spectatorship's fantasised mastery, while an inscribed audience multiplies our position, reinforcing the community on which comedy depends, as students spectate through the screen from the classroom.

Bravura shots, possibly utilising invisible special effects, emphasise textuality for those not trapped in a realist mindset. One sequence begins with a pan from distant planes flying left to right. This continues with a close-up of a boom box carried by a man climbing a mound, whom the camera cranes up to follow. It then meets Al under his parasol as the planes pass behind, in a seemingly unbroken shot. This is a complex variant on Spielberg's signature crane shot that peers over a ridge to reveal low land beyond. Here Al, with cigar, shades and baseball cap, instructing and correcting the planes by radio from his canvas chair, is explicitly coded as a director. Spielberg must have given identical orders to achieve the shot. But also, continuing to comment on the action while *not* communicating with the pilots ('That's it. Beautiful. Bring that fat bomber in here'), Al parallels an engaged spectator or indeed embodies the director's expectation of audience reaction. Combined pans and curved tracks coordinate background action and foregrounded reaction, framing spectacle and spectator together. A cut to Pete and Ted in the air, where the windshield frame inscribes an internal screen, emphasises Pete too as director – recall *Taxi Driver* when Scorsese participates from the back seat – a role Pete alternates with spectatorship, here controlling Ted's slapstick mayhem. The gag culminates in a characteristic Spielberg metonym, a narrational indirectness learnt from Sergei Eisenstein and David Lean, as we see the boom box and ice box swept over, the parasol and chair abandoned on the horizon.

Light beams penetrating the bar from outside reinforce Rachel's desiring gaze at Ted as he voices his love. Pete, as director, comments, 'I think you're overdoing this', unaware that Ted is speaking about Dorinda. As Ted looks up, off-screen, his eye-line matches a shot of a flying plane as the sun flares directly into the lens. Al exchanges information with an air traffic controller who turns out to be Dorinda, intently watching a screen in the dark. The next scene, as Al laughs exaggeratedly to encourage her as she impassively watches TV, contrasts the different intensities of cinematic vision and the televisual glance associated with Dorinda's depression.

A later shot of Dorinda through her plane's cockpit canopy, the reverse of a crane in on Pete, again inscribes a screen as Pete and Ted fly away. When Ted makes a forced landing, a searchlight's circular glass, from which the camera tracks out and around, artistically frames his plane. Ted follows a light as hanging objects swing in the foreground, signifying, as in *Close Encounters* and *E.T.*, a strange presence, associated with 'solar wind'. As he edges into a darkened hangar, the light flickers, accompanied by a projector-like sound and what resembles a turning reel (actually a wind-powered vent). Light beams illuminate a Howard Hughes-like eccentric. (Resemblance to a visionary associated with film and aviation, about whom Spielberg had long been developing a screenplay, eventually Scorsese's *The Aviator* (2004), hardly seems accidental.) This shaman – or indeed, *medium* – can hear Pete's words. These he echoes as Pete speaks out loud to Hap and then, consciously through the old man, to Ted. This instances a recurrent Spielberg motif, interpretation. The medium, however, repeats selectively so that Pete inadvertently persuades Ted to return for Dorinda. The situation recalls an editing exercise demonstrated in *Lianna* (1983), in which writer-director John Sayles played a film professor who illustrates, using words, how selection and reordering can reverse meaning.

Cinema from the outset carried supernatural connotations. It mysteriously captured appearance, creating a perfect double yet eerily lacking the vitality of sound and colour, and in darkness summoned forth images luminescent and translucent. A reviewer at the Lumières' first screening was impressed less by motion or realism than the thought that 'death will cease to be absolute; it will be possible to see our nearest alive again long after they have gone' (in Christie 1994: 111). This is not unlike the comforting function of 1940s ghost movies alluded to in *Always*. It is also the reverse of Pete's situation: he sees Dorinda, and expresses through actions love he never communicated in words, after *he* has gone. Yet ability to impart 'a kind of presence and immediacy to the world unparalleled elsewhere, and undreamt of before the cinema was "invented"' (Elsaesser & Buckland 2002: 1), is, like Pete's comforting presence as guarantor of Dorinda's ultimate happiness, predicated upon absence, central paradox of 'The Imaginary Signifier'.

On Ted's return, initially represented by Rachel looking off-screen yearningly – Spielberg's recurrent *Searchers* allusion – Pete approaches Dorinda's door, filmed from inside; the shot refocuses, causing a hitherto invisible fly screen to break the image into pixels, bridging the cut to the interior (now filmed from outside) so that Pete penetrates both the diegetic screen and the metaphorically signified movie screen. Voyeuristically watching, Pete directs Dorinda, making her brush her hair from her eyes. Seated in the background, reacting to and laughing along with their dialogue, he remains as a spectator throughout her meeting with Ted.

When Ted impresses Dorinda by resuscitating the school bus driver (a confla-tion of scenes in *Duel* and *Empire of the Sun*) the swerving bus first appears through the wide-screen windshield of their land cruiser. The driver joins Pete, spectator from outside, continuing the trope of death as a screen separating a diegetic from an extradiegetic state. At dinner, Dorinda notes how Ted plucks his eyebrow as Pete used to. Pete, internally framed as if through a screen, does the same, emphasising character/specta-tor empathy. Light from behind Dorinda bathes Ted as she falls for his charms.

As smokejumpers seek rescue helmet-lights represent inscribed projectors. Ted's illuminated plane on the runway later becomes Dorinda's object of desire as she pur-posefully approaches, with light behind her. Pete, light behind him, watches. Separate windshields frame them as Pete enters the cockpit, trying to convince her of her inade-quacy. She repeatedly pushes her hair back – signifier of better vision – as he instructed earlier. Pete (like Spielberg on *Duel*) now directs from the back seat. Helmet-lights probe up towards the plane. After crashing into the lake Dorinda decides to drown, but Pete takes her hand, reminiscent of the *E.T.* poster and anticipating that for *Schindler's List*, returning her upwards along a light beam, to life.

'Girl clothes!'

The 'Fire Eaters' emblem makes the anachronism of *Always* immediately apparent: a sexist 1940s comic-book vision of a scantily-clad, leggy redhead. Gender becomes an issue from the outset. Dorinda begins as typically female: grounded, subservient, worrying and complaining while her man enjoys daring adventures. She one-handedly knots a spoon, indicating unreleased frustration – but also enormous strength. *Always* dramatises Dorinda's struggle to negotiate competing feminine discourses. Its seem-ingly old-fashioned qualities belie her journey from definition in relation to Pete to fulfilment of autonomous desire.

Pete responds patronisingly and dismissively to her concern for his safety: 'I love you in the kitchen, baby. You know that.' While she is determined to 'show him' by putting him through similar anxieties – action contingent upon confidence that he loves her – his reaction, while confirming that love, remains self-centred, ignorantly or wilfully indifferent to her. He relishes directorial control in extravagantly hiring Ted to deliver a birthday message, yet mistakes the date.

Camerawork several times effects a somewhat odd (and technically elaborate) trans-ference from aircraft to Dorinda as object of visual desire, as in the opening sequence when a pan with a plane on the runway continues, following Dorinda inside the con-trol tower. Later, after Pete's emergency landing, she strides purposefully towards him in a lateral tracking shot past several aircraft. This transference, embodying adolescent ambivalence that parallels Pete's attitudes and vision, recalls similar obsessions in *Empire of the Sun*. The dialogue emphasises it when the airfield commander warns Pete against irresponsibility:

Pete: C'mon, Nils. You know women.
Nils: I meant your plane.

Dorinda rejects Pete's birthday present and both emit raucous cartoon laughter as she mocks his unreconstructed sexism. Yet after he jettisons the box across the room, where the white garments tumble out, glittering in the projection beam of his desire, she looks over her shoulder and gasps, before advancing along the light beam to embrace them. Pete watches adoringly, though a low-angle shot imparts menacing power to his gaze, and as part of an inscribed audience. To his triumphant observation, 'So you *do* like dresses', she replies: 'It's not the dress, it's the way you see me.' She is flattered to be more than a pal. Yet he offers a pre-existent image, independent of any personal identity, that she can don to fulfil his desire. 'Nobody dances with this dress', she says later, effectively subsuming herself in the masquerade, 'until they've washed their hands', and is almost knocked over in the bathroom stampede. In a slower, less manic movie, this subjugation of female identity to projected masculine desire might more evidently recall dark undercurrents in Hitchcock's *Vertigo*.

In a shot/reverse-shot series that constructs Pete's point-of-view, the camera follows Dorinda upstairs, only for Al to enter the frame in close-up and displace the emphasis back to boyish matters with World War Two quips. Heavily underlined by camera movement, no fewer than seven reaction shots of an astounded Pete, Al and assorted fire-fighters herald Dorinda's return. She remains off-screen or fragmented into close-ups of her extremities, before the crowd parts like theatrical curtains, revealing her alluring splendour in a skin-tight, diaphanous, sequined dress, with one bare and one long-sleeved arm and shoulder. This cinematic fetishism, as theorised by Laura Mulvey (1981), compounds at least five looks: the camera's, the spectator's, the inscribed audience's, Pete's and Dorinda's, who has internalised his gaze. Although Dorinda complains, '*You* never laugh at my jokes' (unlike Karl the barman), stressing the sadism in Pete's attitude, she returns his gaze and his banter as they begin dancing. The intense visual pleasure expresses genuine desire, but is redefined quickly as another game in their protracted courtship.

In her cottage, Dorinda, wearing a pyjama top that recalls the dress, broaches becoming a tanker pilot like Pete. When he paternalistically denies permission, she delivers her ultimatum: retire to run a flying school or they are finished. Her mythical woman's intuition insists, 'Pete, your number's up', just as her later observation of her cat's uncharacteristic acceptance of Ted aligns her with instinct and superstition. Pete's response expresses arrogant, patriarchal assumptions in an intensely performed and finely balanced scene that articulates female discourse:

Pete: I think you should be at the funeral. Y'know, crying and looking terrific. Before you enter the nunnery.

> *Dorinda*: I've got better things to do and better men to do them with.
>
> *Pete*: Why don't you forget about those other men, Dorinda? You're never gonna be with another man
>
> *Dorinda*: I will too and he'll be tall.
>
> *Pete*: No, no, Dorinda.
>
> *Dorinda*: What makes you think so?
>
> *Pete*: Because you won't get over me.
>
> *Dorinda*: I love you, Pete, but I'm not enjoying it.

After explaining her feelings, Dorinda wins the argument, effecting reconciliation. Subsequent events provide a metadiscourse to confirm her version, even though Pete's agency plays some part.

Superficially, Pete's patriarchal control continues from beyond the grave, paralleling other female-oriented movies made around the same time: *Ghost* (1990), *Truly, Madly, Deeply* (1991) and *Titanic*. He tells the grieving Dorinda, as if granting consent: 'You're gonna go to bed happy, you're gonna wake up laughing, meet people, have fun. You're gonna have everything. Including love.' But the film's gender relations are ambivalent, not least in linking consummation of desire and acceptance of an adult relationship to Pete's death. As this immediately follows Dorinda's acceptance of his idealised image of her, one might recall Mulvey's observation that 'the look, pleasurable in form, can be threatening in content, and it is woman as representation/image that crystallises this paradox' (1981: 209).

When Ted inadvertently plays 'Smoke Gets in Your Eyes' after kissing Dorinda (not having heard Pete's jealous warning), Dorinda dismisses him gently. She dons the dress to dance alone to 'their' song. Unknown to her, Pete joins in. There can be no physical contact while, desiring a former state of unity, he subjects her to his gaze. Intriguingly, in the earlier dance, the chief smokejumper tells Dorinda, 'Hey, you look like an angel.' In this context – an overwhelmingly male private flying operation distanced from mainstream American society – the reference to *Only Angels Have Wings* is unmistakable, and pertinent to the Mulvey passage on the female protagonist's subjugation (1981: 211), quoted earlier in discussing *Temple of Doom*.

Although that process is broadly pastiched over their last evening, Pete now, like Metz's spectator condemned to watch from elsewhere, cannot possess Dorinda. Pete might be watching a film, 'a hermetically-sealed world which unwinds magically, indifferent to the presence of the audience, producing for them a sense of separation and playing on their voyeuristic phantasy' (Mulvey 1981: 207). He is invisible in the next shot; this, while restoring the scene to Dorinda, simultaneously – as Mulvey describes – sutures the spectator into the absent position and makes Dorinda the fetishised object (1981: 214). At the end of the song, however, she blows out her candle – exorcising him (a notion supported by her cat being called Linda Blair!). When, later, Pete confesses, 'I [unlike Ted] never laughed at your jokes but you were always very funny', a dissolve returns Pete to Hap's oasis, where it emerges that Hap had sent him back to say goodbye to Dorinda, thus freeing him. That Dorinda, although sleeping, finally hears the words she awaited, strengthens the impression that Dorinda is enunciating.

This possibility surely redeems Brad Johnson's widely criticised performance as Ted, who, according to *Variety*, 'comes off as the male equivalent of a dumb blond with a great figure' (1989: 22). Dorinda, after all, describes him as 'all twisted steel and sex appeal' – hardly a rejection, more in fact a comparison with Pete, even if it denies immediate attraction. While reversing the gaze is limited in progressive terms, because it leaves the structure intact, it does contain the earlier patriarchal discourse within Dorinda's.

Towards the end Dorinda occupies a conventionally masculine role, taking Ted's plane to effect a heroic, potentially suicidal rescue, even if, along the way, Pete – now perhaps little more than a guilty conscience ready for release – tries to convince her she is 'not good enough'. Eventually she hears him say: 'There's the rest of your life, Dorinda. I want you to go to them. I'm releasing you.' If this is Dorinda's enunciation, reliving the trauma of Pete's accident completes exorcism of his defining discourse from her construction of self. If it is Pete's enunciation, remember that, while he has guided her, it is through her skill and determination she survives – unlike him, whose masculine adventure proved fatal.

Harvey Roy Greenberg employs statistical content analysis to contrast Spielberg's alleged sexism with real fire-fighting, in which over a quarter of smokejumpers were female (1991: 170, fn.7). This bias, despite detailed advice from official agencies during the movie's production, is explicable, however, in narrative rather than personal terms. As Mulvey observes, some masculine texts, especially westerns, eschew marriage to the 'princess' – assimilation into the Symbolic – for 'nostalgic celebration of phallic, narcissistic omnipotence' (1990: 28). *Always* resolves its romance strand, centred on female experience and therefore requiring only one female protagonist, by forming Dorinda and Ted as a couple. Yet the action strand, characterised by masculine 'play and phantasy', denies the 'Oedipal trajectory' of narrative (ibid.) that would require a female object of desire. Hence the symptomatic displacements between woman and aircraft and critical and popular dissatisfaction with a film that avoids the two strands' usual interdependence.

Always subverts Hollywood's 'Oedipal trajectory' by transposing Pete as 'father' (older man, Dorinda's first 'possessor' and, as ghost, Ted's mentor) and Ted as the bigger, stronger male who, 'possessing' Dorinda, makes Pete jealous. Pete's acceptance of castration assimilates him into the Symbolic, expressed as binary oppositions: his eventual relegation to the realm of the dead restores equilibrium. Ted as John Wayne – underlined by physical stature, slow, loping movement and social awkwardness – recalls films such as *The Man Who Shot Liberty Valance* (1962), which similarly, as Mulvey discusses, tears the heroine between two men. In another of Mulvey's examples, *Duel in the Sun* (1946), the men represent not a divided hero function but personification of a split heroine, who has to choose between regressive tomboy freedom and a socially viable masquerade as a sexually passive, respectable lady (1990: 32–3). Dorinda, by contrast, remains tomboyish but also plays at domestication (throwing flour around to deceive Ted she has cooked a ready prepared meal) *and* retains both possibilities in her union with Ted. While this perhaps precludes 'having fun' – an expression characterising her relationship with Pete, although Mulvey quotes it in relation to the *Stella Dallas* (1937) itching-powder scene (1990: 33) – Dorinda is neither, unlike Stella, melodramatically excluded from society nor, unlike Pearl in *Duel in the Sun*, melodramatically destroyed by an impossible dilemma.

The Montana base's 'frontier' setting, with individualist heroes riding airborne steeds, masculine behavioural codes and canteen as saloon, contrasts with Dorinda's feminised cottage, surrounded by a tended garden, and the stultifying 'civilisation' of a flying school or air traffic control. The masculine Oedipal narrative evoked is thwarted, yet fulfilled vicariously by Dorinda. So too in *Always*, as in double-hero films Mulvey examines, identification with the heroine dramatises contradictions within 'the female spectator's phantasy of masculinisation at cross-purposes with itself, restless in its transvestite clothes' (1990: 35). *Always*, from a director popularly associated with the masculine genres of action and science fiction, is Dorinda's movie.

Psychoanalysis

In his production notes, Spielberg 'wanted the story to be somewhat timeless … like it's set in the 1940s, but, in fact, is set today'. This leaves *Always* exposed as postmodern whimsy – a re-run *Twilight Zone*, as Douglas Brode suggests (1995: 189), 'resolutely ignorant or uncaring about actual history' (Greenberg 1991: 166). But timelessness also implies archetypal qualities. These condense in the phallic joke of the collapsing windsock as Pete comes in 'dead stick', tanks empty. Al blows towards the limp cylinder while Dorinda mutters, 'Please': inscribed spectators, wholly involved yet helpless. Ted, incompetently crossing Pete's flight path, creates turbulence, providing lift, enabling Pete to glide to a perfect touchdown. The sequence invites psychoanalysis of spectator/text relations and narrative conflict centred on Dorinda.

A central light beam illuminates the canteen as Ted's entry transforms Pete and Dorinda's relationship into an Oedipal triangle. Along with this narrative trajectory, however, the hermeneutic pulls the spectator into a series of shifting subject positions, involving several perspectives and potential identifications. Pete discovers it is not Dorinda's birthday. Dorinda realises Pete has remembered it wrongly. Ted looks on, crestfallen, as they kiss and slow dance. Al watches, amused, dunking a chicken leg in his beer.

These perspectives motivate differing tones and emotions. At Pete's death, it is Al, comic sidekick and detached bystander, whose reaction we see in close-up, his breath occluding the cockpit window, inscribing a screen that is both vision and barrier. At what is thought to be Ted's farewell shindig, light beams from outside concretise Rachel's desiring gaze. Light shines from behind Ted as he melancholically reviews his options. Pete laughs manically as he realises he cannot break through to tell Ted about Rachel's attraction. As Pete recalls first meeting Dorinda, beams project from behind his head. Ted and Pete's affinity, like secondary identification between spectators and characters, is clear when Pete acknowledges separation from the world by ironically pretending to order a martini while Ted orders root beer, and they simultaneously request an olive. Then Ted looks up, demonstrating this imputed identification through focalisation as he, and we, see Dorinda dancing in a light shaft before a window. As Philip M. Taylor argues, 'By pointing light directly into his camera lens … Spielberg forces audiences to scrutinise his images more closely and … thereby

Always – Al as inscribed director and spectator

pull[s] them into the story' (1992: 29). The camera tracks forward, aligning itself with, and underlining, the characters' gaze, as both Ted and Pete sit enthralled, lights behind them. As the woman approaches, she turns out to be someone else – a trick accomplished previously in *Duel, Jaws, Close Encounters* and *Empire of the Sun*, but no less effective for that, such is the power of identification.

Pete and Dorinda, alone, appear mutually aware, although in Dorinda's case this may be projection of Pete's (and consequently our) desire. However, until Pete demonstrates the love he could never express, by respecting her abilities and finally freeing her – in other words *identifying* with her – she remains unreachable. Again the rift recalls film's characteristics as a *medium* predicated on 'loss, absence and desire' (Ellis 2002: 23–4).

This includes loss of self. The spectator accepts an Imaginary subject position: 'film is like the mirror', claims Metz. 'But … there is one thing … never reflected in it: the spectator's own body' (1975: 48). Pete, although we see him, is never there when observing Dorinda. 'The spectator is absent from the screen: … he cannot identify with himself as an object, but only with some objects which are there without him' (1975: 50): the music on Dorinda's stereo, the empty space Pete occupies as she dances, actions he believes other characters perform at his bidding (illusory mastery), finally Dorinda herself.

Pete, *in* the diegesis yet not *of* it, inhabits 'a primordial *elsewhere*, infinitely desirable (=never possible), on another scene which is that of absence and which nonetheless represents the absent in detail, thus making it very present' (Metz 1975: 62). Moreover, he possesses an ideal ego in Ted, the bigger, younger, handsome suitor whose experience he shares vicariously. As he does exactly what Pete wishes but is unable to do, in returning for Dorinda, light shafts radiate onto Ted; now confident, he wears a baseball cap and aviator sunglasses, the image of Jim's fictional hero, Ace, in *Empire of the Sun*. Ted's extinguishing practice fires with complete accuracy accomplishes Pete's identification with him.

'Deprived', unlike theatre, 'of a real or supposed consensus with the other', according to Metz, 'cinematic voyeurism, *unauthorised* scopophilia, is from the outset ... in direct line from the primal scene' (1975: 64). Here Metz invokes Freud's notion of the child fantasising its origins by imagining parental copulation. If Dorinda is Pete's lost object, substitute for the Imaginary mother, his vision of her with Ted is a regression through the mirror phase. Metz explores further similarities between spectatorship and voyeurism, in terms accordant with Pete's position. Spectatorship is typically solitary, in contrast to community in legitimate theatre. The object is unaware of observation. Screen space and auditorium are irreducibly segregated. Like the primal scene – formative fantasy rather than literal memory – 'film unfolds in [a] simultaneously quite close and definitively inaccessible "elsewhere"' (ibid.).

Ted successfully challenging Pete follows the Oedipal scenario of Hollywood narratives. Yet Pete's and, possibly, I have suggested, Dorinda's, focalisation accesses it, not Ted's. Moreover, as also suggested, the main characters' relative size (Pete's smallness emphasised against Al as well as Ted) and Pete's jealousy and powerlessness when spying on Dorinda with Ted, counter Pete's seniority and Ted's gaucheness. This arguably produces confusion at an unconscious level, compromising the movie's pleasurability, combined with conscious distaste of the kind Pauline Kael articulated. Multiple identifications enable various interpretations. Yet a film that dramatises Dorinda's narrative is misrecognised by Pete, and probably actual spectators, as his. Eventually he releases Dorinda and merges with the Imaginary, personified by Hap – but not before, at the height of Dorinda's exhilaration with Ted, Pete, in close-up, interjects, 'Don't forget – you're still my girl'; a chilling moment, even if he exists only in her thoughts. When, finally, he bestows his blessing – 'That's my girl. And that's my boy' – he asserts patriarchal authority that the narrative simply contradicts.

Air/craft

Confused and confusing though it may appear structurally, *Always* remains a technical *tour de force*. So busy and smoothly accomplished are its details that surface brilliance is easily overlooked. Metz writes, 'To adopt the outward marks of theoretical discourse is to occupy a strip of territory *around* the adored film, all that really counts, in order to bar all the roads by which it might be attacked' (1975: 23). However, my aim here is not necessarily to defend *Always* but to describe the kind of artefact it is, to understand better how Spielberg's output fits together.

When Pete opens Dorinda's fridge, icy blue light saturates him, which, when she wakes, concerned, expresses her dread in a point-of-view shot while she remains lit by her fire's golden glow – symbolism motivated purely naturalistically. Equally unobtrusive is an earlier transition from the dance sequence that sees Pete and Dorinda walking together between bushes in a scene modelled from *It's a Wonderful Life*. Pete moves into the ghostly blue floodlighting that, behind Dorinda in the reverse shot, reinforces the image as her focalisation, her projection, before the film's first dissolve. This superimposes crackling flames, reminiscent of forest fires already shown, over her close-up: intellectual montage, expressing her premonition, and a simple temporal ellipsis to logs burning in her grate to inaugurate cosy domesticity in which the couple negotiate their future.

Other shots involve astonishing coordination or disguised edits, such as the rapid pan to show Dorinda's plane landing, which stops on Pete and Al perfectly framed in the foreground. Even more impressive is the extended camera movement in Dorinda's rented house under the flight path. This follows Al, pacing decisively down the hall to the phone, then stops panning to frame an approaching plane through the window, before tilting upwards and over, combined with a 180-degree roll, to follow the plane passing overhead through a skylight and then catch Al again in a continuation of the same shot, finally resuming its leftward pan to Dorinda in the doorway, more or less where it began. There are, too, extraordinary incidental details. Ted bangs his head on a hatch as he first enters the canteen from the food counter, emphasising both his dumbness and his stature, while Al's hand enters from behind to steal a drumstick from his plate. A graphic match links Dorinda's bike wheels to the propellers of Pete's plane. Dorinda and Ted's dinner begins with Ted and Pete outside, then leaves Pete as the camera tracks and pans from the door to the kitchen to disclose Pete already standing there.

Whatever its faults or merits as entertainment or ideological mechanism, *Always* confirms Spielberg as a directors' director. Its significance lies in claims it makes for itself as a purely cinematic exercise. While remaining mindful of Metz's warning that 'discourse about the cinema is too often part of the institution, whereas it should be studying it [and] writings on film become another form of cinema advertising' (1975: 25), Metz, nevertheless, can provide the last word on the audience the film proposes yet appears to have missed:

> As for the fetish itself, in its cinematic manifestations, who could fail to see that it consists fundamentally of the equipment of the cinema (= its 'technique'), or of the cinema as a whole as equipment and as technique? The cinema fetishist … is enchanted at what the machine is capable of, at the *theatre of shadows* as such. For the establishment of his full potency for cinematic enjoyment (*jouissance*) he must think at every moment (and above all *simultaneously*) of the force of presence the film has and of the absence on which this force is constructed. He must constantly compare the result with the means set to work (and hence pay attention to the technique), for his pleasure lodges in the gap between the two. Of course, this attitude appears most clearly in the 'connoisseur', the cinephile, but it also occurs, as a partial component of cinematic pleasure, in those who just go to the cinema. (1975: 72)

CHAPTER FOURTEEN

Hook: an awfully big Pan(a)vision adventure

Hook is Spielberg's most and least typical film. From a crudely biographical perspective, it articulates interests and themes consciously discussed over years in interviews, and embodies concerns easily mapped in Spielberg's 'private' life. Studio publicity actively encouraged such readings, setting the agenda for reviewers. On the other hand, a massive calculated money-spinner – the kind Spielberg is widely associated with – *Hook* is arguably a project over which he had less creative control. It thus offers an interesting test for auteurism.

Hook was at the time reputedly the second most expensive production ever (the higher budget of *Terminator 2: Judgment Day* (1991) included Arnold Schwarzenegger's private jet). *Hook* was, to repeat a much over-used pun, severely panned by critics for excessive blockbuster values. These reconfirmed Spielberg's filmmaking as effects-driven and child-oriented. The $79 million budget and – unusually for Spielberg – A-list star cast, point to the project's economic importance for the industry.

Hook's economic importance

The Japanese conglomerates, having competed worldwide over domestic video, were vying over high definition television. This multi-billion-dollar prospect embraced not only broadcasting but digital home entertainment, electronic filmmaking and eventually digital distribution and exhibition. As well as providing all-important American consumer markets, the acquisitions included extensive film and television libraries and production facilities to supply the expected proliferation of channels.

Both deals consolidated Hollywood agents' and brokers' centrality. Before enforced studio divestiture in 1948, filmmaking resembled a production line operated by salaried staff. Since then, most new features were one-offs requiring temporary hiring of talent, labour, studios and equipment. Attracting investment by packaging creative personnel with a saleable concept and stars, targeted at a particular audience, was an increasingly sophisticated art.

The significance of this is clear in Sony's spending not only $3.5 billion on Columbia but another estimated $750 million to acquire two producers from Warner Bros. Among Peter Guber and Jon Peters' successes was *Rain Man* (1988), Dustin Hoffman's pet project which had involved Spielberg, offered it by their shared agent, Michael Ovitz – co-founder and head of CAA, the most influential agency. Reluctant to work for major stars, especially one as notoriously temperamental as Hoffman, Spielberg conceded the project to Barry Levinson and concentrated on *Indiana Jones and the Last Crusade*. Ovitz, while packaging *Rain Man*, was also consultant to the Sony-Columbia negotiations: he recommended the Guber-Peters contract. He then spent a year mediating between Matsushita and MCA, before personally closing that deal.

Ovitz established such leverage by attracting strong clients and, as their mutual agent, combining them in viable packages with minimal third-party interference. Most important in this success, Thomas Schatz argues, are 'the increasingly hit-driven nature of the entertainment industry, and in turn ... the star-driven nature of top industry products' (1993: 31).

While the most overt indication of Sony's involvement in *Hook* is product placement of a camcorder, the entire film in fact advertised Sony's presence in tinseltown. Sony boss Akio Morita wanted to launch the new studio with a prestigious Christmas hit. *Peter Pan*, purchased from Paramount who had been developing it for years until it became mired in turnaround costs, was an obvious choice. The widely known story had Christmas associations after decades of stage productions, Disney's cartoon and the novel, a perennial bestselling gift. Particularly advantageous was that the copyright, bequeathed by J. M. Barrie to London's Great Ormond Street Children's Hospital, appeared to have lapsed.

Hoffman, more recently involved, quickly returned and had the script rewritten to enhance his Captain Hook role. Ovitz offered the project, with the chance to pick his cast from CAA's catalogue, to Spielberg, apparently at Hoffman's suggestion. Spielberg had already spent so much on it in the early 1980s, after Paramount had bought it from Francis Ford Coppola, that Columbia under David Puttnam had axed it after Spielberg withdrew. Now Spielberg suited Sony's requirements perfectly. His name connoted family-oriented holiday releases and – importantly – could attract peak-time television audiences and hence gave enormous value to subsequent broadcasting rights. No expense would be spared. Soon Robin Williams too was signed.

Using stars to attract audiences is, however, as *Terminator 2* illustrates, a problem that recurrently jeopardises the industry. Stars encourage investment by supplying trademark value to sell the eventual product to exhibitors and audiences, thus reducing perceived risk of failure. Nevertheless, when stars' exorbitant fees inflate budgets, box office returns have to be so high before the movie becomes profitable that risk is again exacerbated. Furthermore, stars were not, as Spielberg's career testifies, particularly significant in post-*Jaws* New Hollywood blockbusters, though many actors from such films *became* stars as producers paid to repeat successful ingredients. Stars do not guarantee success. Yet they drive up costs, not only through their fees but also by increasing other production values and the scale of P&A consequent upon employing them.

Hoffman, Williams and Spielberg accepted minimal fees, freeing the budget for gargantuan elaborate sets, crowd scenes, stunts and special effects. (Julia Roberts, the top-billing female attraction following *Pretty Woman*, was originally hired for $2.5 million. Although she missed her studio deadlines, suffering highly-publicised personal problems, most of her performance as a minuscule fairy necessitated separate footage later incorporated into scenes featuring the rest of the cast. Her contribution was thus relatively easily rescheduled while insurers wrangled over her payment.) In return for deferments, however, CAA contracted Spielberg, Hoffman and Williams to share an unprecedented 40 per cent of the gross box office. While their takings would depend on the film's popularity, this effectively guaranteed huge personal gains: their slice, reserved before interest payments, taxes, distributors' and exhibitors' shares were calculated, was irrespective of profit. This meant *Hook* needed to gross $250 million simply to break even.

However, the package's strength attracted advance video and broadcast sales, merchandising tie-ins, foreign distribution and exhibition guarantees, taking *Hook* into the black before the camera started rolling. Insured against non-completion, Columbia could not lose and so permitted budgetary escalation as scenes were rewritten and set designs increasingly elaborated (Baxter 1996: 366, 368).

Insufficient constraints – the payroll even included a make-up artist to keep Roberts's feet clean – meant the production, as Spielberg admitted, often seemed out of control (Baxter 1996: 369). The Neverland set alone cost $8 million. Certainly many reviewers considered the finished movie profligate and undisciplined, criticism that touched a raw nerve in the recessionary climate and following financial scandals that rocked Wall Street and other international markets. Although *Hook* made respectable profits after a worrying start, it became synonymous with Hollywood's shortcomings. Industry analysts, and studio heads trying to scale down projects, willed its failure as a cautionary lesson.

Yet succeed it did. Later mega-budget productions, such as *Last Action Hero* (1993), which lost Sony $124 million and threatened their continuation with filmmaking, and the disastrous *Waterworld* (1995), vindicated the pundits. However, Spielberg's next film, *Jurassic Park* at $65 million, and later James Cameron's *Titanic* at $200 million made massive fortunes, while *The Full Monty* and *The Blair Witch Project* conversely demonstrate the commercial viability of much smaller projects. As ever, moviemaking remains a gamble.

Hook as a Spielberg movie (1): Hook and Peter Pan

Spielberg was, in the 1980s, saddled with a Peter Pan image, locked in Neverland. Partly this was due to self-promotion, referring to both his enthusiasm for adolescent playthings and his desire to film Barrie's classic. Biographical auteurism uncritically accepted such comments as a key to his work. By the time *Hook* arrived it was supposedly 'Spielberg's ultimate autobiographical project' (Taylor 1992: 136).

Such readings gained credibility from the *Peter Pan* passage in *E. T.*, a parallel story that similarly requires playful suspension of disbelief and tells of a 'lost boy' with an imaginary friend to take him on nocturnal flights, in the process embracing maturity. Authorial intention is, however, a dubious critical tool. Literal biographical interpretations of *Hook* ignore, contrary to their premises, that Spielberg at forty and father of a young son, had publicly abandoned plans to film *Peter Pan*: 'I've had it up to here with "I don't want to grow up"' (quoted in Brode 1995: 198). If this was conscious image management – Spielberg accompanied the announcement with a $1 million donation to Great Ormond Street – it nevertheless declared emphatic lack of interest in making the movie.

That *Peter Pan* returned to Spielberg within three years does not necessarily make it a personal project. It had undergone numerous rewrites and complicated bickering over credits and ownership. Formerly a Michael Jackson vehicle, it had mutated into a story about fathers who jeopardise childish playfulness rather than a boy who rejects ageing. That others considered Spielberg the obvious director, and he presumably accepted because the task retained some personal meaning, does not detract from the fact this was one of the most calculated blockbusters he had worked on. The compromise involved in such productions would seem to leave little scope for personal vision. Remarkable, then, given the egos and commercial interests concerned, and the enterprise's sheer mechanical excess, is how much *Hook* does resemble other Spielberg movies, stylistically and in the narrative.

Barrie's *Peter Pan* has been called 'a minefield of psychosexual obsessions' (Baxter 1996: 364). Nevertheless, it rapidly transcended individual expression, becoming a cross-media cultural phenomenon, a valuable commodity outside his control (Rose 1992: 67, 75). Though Barrie produced numerous theatrical and prose versions over thirty years, he never finalised a definitive text. Yet he created an immediate classic that acquired folkloric status, eclipsing personal authorship. This may be because of appeals to generalised regressive desires intrinsic to most narratives; those that, I contend, Spielberg's films intensify and foreground, helping explain their profitability.

It is hardly surprising that *Peter Pan* initially attracted Spielberg, nor that his version proved sufficiently popular, despite narrational flaws and lapses in taste condemned by many critics. Overlong, sentimental, 'often profoundly shame-making' and 'embarrassing' (Baxter 1996: 368) – at least for some adults – the movie contained something family audiences responded to. This, as much as anything original to Spielberg or Barrie, was its reinflection of wider 'psychosexual obsessions'.

Peter Pan dramatises escape from the Symbolic, and *Hook* its restitution. 'It is strange to think that Peter did not alight in the church [at Wendy's wedding] and forbid the banns', observes the novel (Barrie 1993: 145), and Spielberg's Wendy comments similarly. Indeed the film's Peter (Robin Williams) – an adult lawyer who demands of his ten-year-old son, 'When are you gonna stop acting like a child?' – is surnamed Banning. Adulthood is dull and mechanical, whether for workers in Barrie's novel, 'any day going to the office, each carrying a little bag and umbrella' (ibid.), or for Banning (like the novel's Mr Darling, 'one of those deep ones who know about stocks and shares' (1993: 5)) enslaved by his mobile phone. The wistful impossibility of the Imaginary – adventure, irrationality, spontaneity and anarchy within the security of Wendy's quasi-maternal nurturing – determines its diegetic name: Neverland.

This intangible projective desire and Oedipal conflict connect in Barrie's description of Mrs Darling, 'who would pirouette so wildly that all you could see of her was the kiss, and then if you had dashed at her you might have got it' (1993: 8). As Jacqueline Rose observes, 'it is too easy to give an Oedipal reading of *Peter Pan*' (1992: 35). Neverland, of course, is where the boy (traditionally played by an actress, subverting patriarchal gender ascription) repeatedly defeats the threatening Father, Captain Hook (usually the same actor as Mr Darling), whose missing hand and its steel replacement conflate both the fact and the threat of castration. Hook, for example, wants to defeat Pan, whom the Lost Boys call 'the Great White Father' (Barrie 1993: 87), to have Wendy as 'our mother' (1993: 77); Hook, nearly displaying 'Bad Form', 'was as impotent as he was damp, and ... fell forward like a cut flower' (1993: 117). Peter's most irritating quality, making Hook's 'iron claw twitch', is 'cockiness' (1993: 104). Banning's negative qualities as obscene father are displaced onto Hook, destroyed so Banning can be redeemed as the good father. Neverland evidently recalls the unconscious: Barrie describes dreamwork as 'repacking into their proper places the many articles that have wandered during the day' (1993: 8) and likens his fantasy world to 'a map of a person's mind' (1993: 9).

Parallels between Barrie's verbal and Spielberg's visual imagery further emphasise *Peter Pan*'s easy translation into a Spielberg text. Consider Spielberg's repeated figure of an inscribed screen bordering the Symbolic and the Imaginary – an actual diegetic plane or suggested rectangular space frequently penetrated in either direction. Barrie's Peter, in Mrs Darling's dream, 'had rent the film that obscures the Neverland', and his arrival 'was accompanied by a strange light' (1993: 12–13). In *Hook*, this light – Tinker Bell (Julia Roberts), the mechanism that carries Banning into the Imaginary, despite disbelief – occasions self-reflexivity. Her beating wings whir like a projector, cause the light to flicker, and produce the familiar solar wind as she insists that together they could do or be anything. Like Hap in *Always*, she personifies cinematic fantasy. 'I'm dying, I'm heading towards white light, I've left my body', Banning sarcastically responds, resistant, nevertheless suggesting loss of self entailed in Imaginary identification. That this requires willing regression, to recover innocence in vision, the movie's opening asserts. Infants gaze raptly off-screen, aligning the spectator with their look, at a school production of *Peter Pan* which engrosses the entire audience until Banning's mobile rings. A solo piano, recalling silent cinema, continues its accompaniment until curtailed by his phone ringing again at the point Banning excludes himself by despatching an employee to video his son's baseball game. Authentic vision, heightened by light rays on the Lost Boys onstage in the first scene, once more equates with film.

Self-reflexivity recurs also in *Peter Pan*. Again, affinities between its pleasures and those of Spielberg's texts hint at its attraction. Tension between involvement and textual awareness, Imaginary and Symbolic, comes into play, reinforcing the possibility that satisfaction arises not from narrative structures alone but shifting positionings in relation to them, which replicate and master formative experiences of loss. Examples include the play's moment when Peter steps out of the stage to invite theatregoers to clap if they believe in fairies, or when the novel's narrator breaks off to ask, just as Mr and Mrs Darling are about to discover Peter:

> Will they reach the nursery in time? If so, how delightful for them, and we shall all breathe a sigh of relief, but there will be no story. On the other hand, if they are not in time, I solemnly promise that it will all come right in the end. (Barrie 1993: 35)

At Hook's death in the novel a modal repositioning virtually anticipates the climax of many Spielberg films: 'All knew that what was about to happen concerned him alone, and that from being actors they were suddenly become spectators' (Barrie 1993: 120). The novel also employs intertextuality that would enhance self-awareness as consumers of fiction among readers heedful of it. When Hook is introduced – 'it is said he was the only man the Sea-Cook feared' (1993: 48) – the allusion to *Treasure Island*'s Long John Silver is sufficiently oblique to require conscious recall. It will go unremarked by many readers even as it asserts a place in the adventure canon. Furthermore, 'the same Bill Jukes who got six dozen on the Walrus' (1993: 47) refers to another character that, like Hook, does *not* feature in Stevenson's novel. Neverland's elusiveness tantalises even while affirming familiar territory. *Hook* too employs intertextuality beyond evident links to Barrie's and Disney's versions. Playfully transgressing boundaries between fiction and actuality, fantasy and belief, it refers to Barrie himself as the story's recorder, rather than originator, and incorporates the Great Ormond Street connection. It alludes also to Williams' star performances in *Good Morning, Vietnam* (1987) (Smee (Bob Hoskins) addresses the crowd through his megaphone: 'Good Morning, Neverland!') and *Dead Poets Society* (1989) ('Seize the day!' yells Tootles (Arthur Malet)). If shifting awareness features in certain textual pleasures – hard to prove empirically – it unlocks the impasse between screen theory, which assumes passive audience positioning, and ethnographic approaches that venerate viewers' accounts of media experiences without always considering wider structures of domination.

Hook as a Spielberg movie (2): self-reflexivity and subject positioning

Self-reflexivity layers in humour for adults in *Hook*'s targeted family audience. It also reinforces characterisation by expressing Banning's subjectivity. Furthermore, depending on whether viewers notice individual self-reflexive devices, it increases the available spectator positions and pleasures, offering modality shifts and identifications not necessarily accepted. What one spectator considers gratuitously excessive cinematography, a formal manoeuvre drawing attention to technique, might to another intensify emotion and identification, and to a third simply provide inherently enjoyable visual stimulation. Actual viewings may alternate modalities. Spectatorship involves ambiguity as well as pleasure in constant repositioning. Rather than uniformly imposed passive consumption, the movie elicits heterogeneous responses within and between spectators. This assertion does not intend value judgement – that *Hook* is superior because of its specific qualities – but recognition that such processes may occur is prerequisite to understanding the popularity and cultural significance of Spielberg's output.

Banning's Pan Am flight to London stresses that this film is a trans-Atlantic reworking, not a reverential attempt at replicating earlier versions. (That assumption, tinged by *Peter Pan*'s traditional ascription to high culture – even performed by the Royal Shakespeare Company in 1982 – against pantomime's vulgarity (Rose 1992: 94–6), caused several critics disappointment (for example, Heal 1992; Millar 1992). However, the film pre-empts such objections by having Wendy express ignorance of baseball, and Banning propose calling 'the American police' when Scotland Yard cannot explain his children's disappearance.) Rather than strengthening modality, naming an actual airline here renders textuality opaque for those who spot the joke. The captain's voice on the intercom during turbulence is evidently Hook's – an incongruously British accent for an American airline – intimating that the other Captain is precisely that: Banning's Other, his externalised fears, in this case flying. (Hook's later knowledge that Banning missed the most important game in his son Jack's (Charlie Korsmo) life proves, if logic applies in Neverland, that he embodies Banning's guilt.) Having quipped, 'Gotta fly!' on leaving his office – meaning it literally, sardonically confronting his phobia – the former Pan who has to regain flight by first recovering childhood spontaneity finds himself transported to a place named, ominously, 'Never … land.'

England is Neverland indeed. Christmas-card snow falls on Westminster Bridge yet windows sit conveniently open. The modality suggests this film expects to be received as warm-hearted allegory rather than presenting stark contrasts between historical reality and fantasy. Moira (Caroline Goodall) implores Peter: 'have fun … London's a magical place for children.' As the family approach Wendy's (Maggie Smith) house a forward track follows them, intersecting their taxi's headlamp beams. These streak across the lens, uniting the characters in a bright flare.

The house interior is rosily illuminated. However, cold blue light from the window initially silhouettes Wendy, framed from an intimidating low angle. Disturbing power over Banning, evident in her quizzical unwavering gaze, is quickly confirmed. To Jack's boast that Banning, as a mergers and acquisitions lawyer, 'blows' opponents 'out of the water', she makes the belittling judgement: 'So, Peter. You've become a pirate.' Similarly, a cold, ghostly 'solar wind', reminiscent of *Poltergeist*, although it turns out to be realistically motivated by an open window, ruffles Peter as he revisits the nursery. By contrast, the immaculate beds glow in a rosy hue. Warm light later represents maternal values – the Imaginary – when, echoing the novel, Wendy murmurs: 'Dear night lights, protect my babes.' Evidently Banning is disquieted by, alienated from, reminders of childhood security. Once Wendy steps into the warm light permeating this festive household, Banning seems to have excluded himself.

'Projector beams' entering the window illuminate point-of-view shots of nursery pictures: a pirate ship – accompanied by non-diegetic tropical bird noises, evoking the rekindling of Banning's imagination (which experiences identical sounds and images to the movie we are watching) – and Captain Hook, at which he shudders and fastens the window with a stylised hook. Another phone call interrupts his regression, a jolt back into adulthood.

Preoccupied with business, Banning fails to compliment Wendy on her dress, even though escorting her to an honorific function is central to his visit. His children, playing, irritate him, their shadows projected like a movie onto the wall, looming larger until he angrily demands silence. A close-up inscribes Wendy as a spectator, cueing the viewer's shared concern at Banning's patriarchal (indeed piratical) aggression, contrasted with the figurative Imaginary's unity and warmth behind him.

The Imaginary, within which the viewer is positioned (assuming concern *is* felt), reaches out to embrace Banning. As Jack stands alone, staring out the window, forlornly holding his baseball mitt – standard metonym for American father/son bonding – a tilted and awkwardly hand-held shot accelerates across empty space and into the nursery at rooftop level, implying a point-of-view, an unseen presence retrospectively identifiable as Tink – who, I argue, personifies cinema. This occurs as Wendy sits reading *Peter Pan* with Maggie (Amber Scott), who knows it by heart, inside a tent of bedding. Wendy points out her younger self in an illustration; the object of their concentration, the book, illuminates their faces. A shot of Jack rhymes with another illustration, as he looks out and upward into starlight. 'That is the same window and this is the same room where we made up bedtime stories about Peter and Neverland and scary old Captain Hook', explains Wendy. Cut to Wendy and Maggie's shadows projected onto the screen created by the bedclothes, figuratively inscribing the cinematic apparatus. Although the light source is an unseen reading lamp, it seems to come from the book. Jack is spectator and participant as he looks out yearningly, Maggie and Wendy recite the tale in unison. Imaginary plenitude, associated with projective desire, links Jack and the two females in shared experience, connects past with present, involves the viewer's cultural knowledge and desire, and blurs reality with fantasy. Once more imagination, flight, cinematic vision and motherhood correlate. Banning, the anxious father, destroys this reverie, rushing in to ask, 'Now, do we have open windows at home?' Jack's reply underlines his patronymic: 'No, they've all got bars on them.'

Banning, sensible embodiment of patriarchal rationality, dismisses the flower Maggie offers him at bedtime: 'It's paper, honey.' He lends Jack his watch, to 'keep track of the time' while the adults are out: time, Symbolic imposition on nature, opposite of the Imaginary's eternal plenitude; time, that Peter rejects in refusing to grow up, and that plagues Hook – a clock ticks inside the crocodile – before destroying him.

Banning's awkward incongruity continues during his speech to Great Ormond Street's trustees. Starting with a self-deprecating joke against lawyers, he then stumbles over the word 'effortlessly'. A master-shot includes over thirty bright lamps, conveying a warmth and unity that at first intimidate him. Banning establishes community, however, as his speech prompts other 'lost children' like himself – orphans, now middle-aged or elderly, whom Wendy had sponsored – to rise spontaneously to honour her, while his wife Moira, an inscribed spectator, looks on, sobbing.

Back at the house, a branch taps the window – Spielberg's recurrent omen, referred to also in Jim's song in *Empire of the Sun* – as Tootles, an original Lost Boy, barks in his sleep. Dreaming and cinematic fantasy commingle when he wakens, aware of Hook's proximity. Tootles looks in, through a glass surface, an inscribed 'screen', at a model of Hook's ship in a bottle. A cut to a stained-glass window of a ship, followed by a tilt down to the hook window latch, links his unease to the children's as Jack's eyes open in big close-up. Point-of-view shots, such as the window clasp, alternate with the children's reactions, encouraging spectatorial identification.

Intrusion into the children's Imaginary by the castrating father – abstract, intangible as yet, befitting psychoanalytic principles – crosscuts with an implied threat to Banning's newfound community, as a window at the hospital function inexplicably blows inward. Tootles simultaneously opens a window onto brightness outside; a zoom in on the back of his head surrounds him with an eerie glow as a powerful solar wind – emanating from the source of fascination, repressed unresolved conflict rather than positive desire – stands his hair on end. A tilt up, revealing the chandelier revolving, cuts to an overhead shot of Jack's bed as a nursery mobile spins and the boy hides under the covers. Compositionally, this recalls E.T.'s animated demonstration of his solar system; thematically, it similarly announces another surrogate for an absent father. Windows blast open, Wendy and Maggie's tent crumples, quilts fly up and off-screen, leaving the children unprotected; at the dinner Wendy almost collapses – buffeted from the window or overwhelmed by applause is unclear. As in *Close Encounters*, storms evoke primeval anxieties; malignancy, metonymically indicated, encourages viewers to project their unease.

Indirect narration continues as Banning returns to find the front door open, the glass cracked, the electricity off and deep gouges across the woodwork, along the walls and up the stairs. The mise-en-scène is subjective and objective, interiorised and external commentary: point-of-view shots invite identification with Banning – now victim rather than primary villain – yet most viewers know more than he, that the culprit is Hook. In one reaction shot, upward illumination casts shadows from Banning's spectacles, projecting pixie eyebrows: realistically motivated lighting functions expressionistically, confirming something he does not suspect: he is Peter.

Lisa, the housekeeper, reprises *Close Encounters*' old Mexican ('The sun sang to me') as she describes how the wind – already associated with light – entered the door and closed in on her before taking the children. Hook's summons, pinned to a door by his dagger, and Tootles' speech outlining Banning's task – the repeated Spielberg quest to rescue lost children and reconstitute the family – suggest that the wind, rather than malignant, represents Banning's repressed desires for both adventure and Imaginary regression. (Cinema offers both.) Told Hook is back, the adult Peter asks, 'Who?'

Hook acknowledges psychoanalytic implications. As well as joking about 'Peter Pan Syndrome', Banning's first address to Tink is replete with awareness: 'You're a complex Freudian hallucination, having something to do with my mother, and I don't know why you have wings – but you have very lovely legs and – What am I saying? I don't know who my mother was. I'm an orphan.' Structurally, Wendy's belief that Peter would forbid her marriage entails Oedipal connotations, and Banning has no memory prior to his adoption – subjection to patriarchal Law. His wedding photograph, confirming acceptance of the Symbolic order, is visible as Wendy explains how he stopped returning to Neverland and matured only after falling for the teenage Moira: that is, with awareness of sexual difference. Low angles present the sceptical Banning as big and grown-up, while high-angle reverse shots make Wendy, the believer, although many years senior, childlike. Denying his selfhood, he nevertheless adopts Peter's familiar stance, hands on hips, from the book Wendy shows him: a Mirror Phase, conferring an identity that, for now, he rejects, dropping his hands.

The notion of regression continues into the scene that equates Tink with cinema. Whisky being poured juxtaposes with Banning's shadow, another self, on the ceiling. A cradle with rising-sun headboards metonymically recalls his disappeared children, and thus in this context also associates light with the Imaginary and desire. Drunk, Banning opens the nursery window, looking out off-screen at something temporarily withheld. The answering shot sutures the spectator into his vision. The approaching 'firefly from Hell', reminiscent of the Good Witch's bubble in *The Wizard of Oz* and the lights heralding spaceships in *Close Encounters*, forces him into the cradle.

Banning puts on spectacles to see Tinker Bell. That he wears them upside down comically underlines the recurrent Spielberg theme of adequate vision. This Tink, masculinised by cropped hair, tomboy gestures and costume, is a miniature, winged Peter, a figure of childhood playfulness unsullied by gender. (Later, though, as well as her romantic interest in Peter that puts her in an evening gown, she takes a passive, observational role while Peter romps with the Lost Boys.) After sneezing out magic dust she has sprinkled, the determinedly sceptical Banning crawls, infant-like, toward the doll's house he has blown her into. When finally she subjugates Banning (forced to clap to revive her, all the while insisting he does not believe) and transports him to Neverland in a sling improvised from Maggie and Wendy's tent, physical currents again blast the spectating Tootles, now smiling, as they fly into the sunset. The next shot, introducing Neverland, shows Banning peeping through a hole in the tent, followed by a close-up on his eye – the very image of voyeuristic separation. The reverse shot, a clock with hands whirring in opposite directions, reinforces the subjectivity and anarchy of his about-to-be-recovered way of seeing.

Banning in Neverland

Displaced, unwilling to embrace fantasy, Banning asks for the nearest payphone as he strides along an enormous baroque quayside, one of the most expensive film sets ever. Among much crude slapstick – that adults find it embarrassing perhaps emphasises the difficulty of regression – Tink literally directs Banning as a pirate, so he blends in. Like *Empire of the Sun*'s 'maternal' quest objects, the aircraft, the eponymous hook – metonym and synecdoche for the still-unseen bad father, dreaded yet desired – emits sparks while being sharpened. Its terrible castrating force, later evidently phallic when Hook's moll gasps admiringly as she unscrews it for him, here manifests in displaced form as Smee carries it on a cushion past the skeleton figurehead of Hook's ship and as a close-up on it fades to black before recurring in nightmarish lightning flashes, then further darkness.

An iris shot punctures the darkness – actually Smee's mouth framed through his megaphone as he addresses the assembled low life. That Smee's more sophisticated rhetoric fails to move them but they laugh heartily at his simple puns, then receive Hook's polysyllabic sarcasms in awed appreciation, creates a mise-en-abyme as comprehending viewers respond differently from children in the audience. This continues

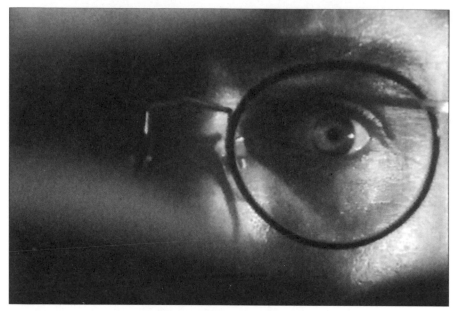

Hook – Banning peers through the screen at the Imaginary

throughout – part of the 'kidult' orientation (Turner 1988: 18) – not least when Hook attempts to re-educate Banning's children by explaining why they have bedtime stories. This account must make even the most lovingly conscientious parent squirm as Maggie defends her alternative conviction:

Maggie: Mummy reads to us every night because she loves us very much …
Hook: No, child. I think your mother reads to you every night in order to stupefy you to sleep – so that she and Daddy can sit down for three measly minutes without you and your mindless, inexhaustible, unstoppable, repetitive and nagging demands … They tell you stories to shut you up!
Smee: And conk you out.
Maggie: That's not true … You're a liar.
Hook: Lie? Me? Never! The truth is far too much fun. Oh, my child. Before you were born your parents would stay up all night together just to see the sun rise … Maggie, before you were born your parents were happier. They were free.
Maggie: You're a very bad man.

The parallel here with Banning dismissing Maggie's paper flower in favour of 'the truth' confirms Hook to be Banning's worst traits projected, even as Hook articulates sentiments every parent experiences when the going gets tough. The difference between Maggie's and Hook's discourses is precisely that between the Imaginary and the Symbolic. The scene's force lies in differential positioning, of children innocently dismissing Hook as the baddy and adult spectators uncomfortably confronting mixed feelings in contradiction to the childish discourse parenthood desires to preserve. As Jacqueline Rose observes of Barrie's play, 'as likely as not, there will be an adult with the child in the audience, watching the child at least as much as what is going on' (1992: 32–3).

At the end of Hook's first speech, when he addresses the ensnared Jack and Maggie – 'Hello children. Comfy? Cosy?' – the low angle embraces the audience, an effect calculated to terrify children while their elders enjoy Hoffman's hamming. Hook dons glasses to descry that Banning is 'not even a shadow of Peter Pan' – the villain sees correctly – while Tink, the spectator's stand-in, observes through the protective yet transparent barrier of a bottle, a screen metaphor accentuated by the size discrepancy between her and the figures performing.

She views a drama of disappointment as father Banning fails to match expectations established by businessman Banning. Unable to obey Jack's plea, 'Blow him out of the water, Dad!' or meet Hook's challenge to fly up and free the children, Banning, who confesses to a 'problem with heights', heroically climbs the rigging towards where they dangle. Inability to reach them prompts cries anticipatory of themes in subsequent Spielberg films: 'Please, don't ever give up!' and 'Dad, I want to go home!' Inscribed spectators – pirates and Tink – are visibly disillusioned.

Tink negotiates a delay before Banning's showdown with Hook. Mermaids rescue him from drowning. He sees Neverland's fantastic panorama. He endures further slapstick mishaps, then finally admits, 'I believe!' The Lost Boys immediately come out to play. Initially they reject this 'old fat grandpa man', while he expresses adult anxieties as Rufio (Dante Basco), 'The Pan', performs acrobatics. 'Kidult' dual address humorously emphasises the psychic gulf separating them: Banning repudiates 'this Lord of the Flies pre-school' and denies being a pirate – their mortal enemy – insisting he is a lawyer, for which they chase him anyway. Light beams visibly 'project' these harmless Neverland adventures as Rufio and others shoot Banning with toffee-apple arrows and pursue him on skateboards, *demanding* his participation. Radiant light that joins Banning to the small child who reaches out to touch him (shades of E.T. and Elliott, Jim and his mother), removing his spectacles ('scepticals'?), strongly suggests cinematic regression. All now touch him, closing with Imaginary unity the gap inherent in voyeuristic desire as this inscribed audience recognise Banning as the authentic Pan. Their function as relayers of the look, cueing intended audience reactions, now transfers to Tink.

Competition between Banning and Rufio, who announces, 'I got Pan's sword. I'm the Pan now', dramatises the Oedipal struggle for authority, here compounded with the search for a worthy father. Wrangling over this phallus, parallel with Hook's scheming for paternity of Jack, displaces Jack and Banning's conflict into two other relationships (pseudo-father and pseudo-son); these nevertheless are equated by costume design and the swordplay Banning enters into with both, rendering Rufio as Hook's carnivalesque inversion. The stratagem achieves resolution symbolically, asserting patriarchal continuity without dramatising the struggle directly.

Meanwhile, Hook, deprived of his defining Other by Banning's denial that he is Pan, unconvincingly attempts suicide. His lament, 'Death is the only adventure left to me', inverts Pan's famous line, 'To die would be an awfully big adventure', emphasising his function as half a duality. When he asks, 'Indeed, what *would* the world be like without Captain Hook?' his reflection splits between three mirrors, disintegrating illusory unity imposed by positioning in relation to Pan. Multiple reflections feature again when he envisions a new position as children's friend and nurturer – another Mirror Phase.

A pre-determined role positions Banning also. According to binary logic whereby the Lost Boys lay out cutlery 'so we don't have to use 'em', Banning remains alienated, unable to join their feast of invisible food, until he can enter make-believe. He regresses again, trading childish insults with Rufio; the lawyer's verbal dexterity triumphs. Defeating the clan's symbolic big daddy, suddenly he sees their sumptuous, garish banquet. Immediately he joins their Imaginary, the meal projects a warm glow onto their faces.

The ensuing food fight – further embarrassment for adults excluded by the movie's mode of address – could not have occurred in Barrie's novel because of genteel table manners imposed by Wendy, whether meals are make-believe or real (1993: 88). Yet it shares the spirit of unrestrained childishness that turns pretend meals into substantial nourishment. If sophisticated adults are interpellated minutes later -- I suspect few actually are – in shots of the infant Pan's separation from his mother that invoke *The Battleship Potemkin*'s (1925) Odessa steps sequence, it is churlish in a family movie to deny children some mindless fun. Lack of decorum and overall unity, manifest in unevenness of tone, offends critics who decry Spielberg's work as failed art in relation to cinema classics, even while it enhances its commercial appeal as entertainment. (According to Thomas Schatz, New Hollywood blockbusters are typically 'intertextual and purposefully incoherent … "open" to multiple readings and multimedia reiteration' (1993: 34).)

The fight finishes with Rufio maliciously aiming a coconut at Banning's head. Instinctively, Banning grabs a sword and bisects the projectile. Looking up, awestruck, the boys see him standing, sword aloft – a gesture repeated when Cinqué accepts leadership in *Amistad* – and acknowledge him as the Pan. This explicitly Oedipal moment (Rufio later bows, proffering his sword in allegiance) connects the patriarchal fantasy with loss of the Imaginary: as a Lost Boy entrusts the restored Pan with Tootles' marbles and happy thoughts, he discloses that his own happy thought is his mother and asks whether Peter remembers his. The scene crosscuts to pirates captivated by Maggie – separated from her mother by Hook's patriarchal authority – singing 'I'm never alone', prompting Banning/Pan to recall his mother's singing.

Next morning, surrounded by broken clocks indicative of Hook's chronophobia, analogous to Pan's deferred growing up, the Captain tempts Jack to smash Banning's watch with a mallet. Jack's reflections in clock faces constitute another regression through a Mirror Phase as he shatters them and, implicitly, his patrilineal identity, in retaliation against 'bannings'. He hides shamefully under his peaked cap while repudiating Banning; Hook raises the peak, disclosing his face again, before bestowing a baseball as token of his fatherhood.

The allusion to Disney's *Snow White and the Seven Dwarfs* (1937) as the Lost Boys disguise themselves as adults, one upon another's shoulders inside long overcoats, to sneak into the game, and use of fairground music and facial disguises align their Imaginary with Bakhtin's carnivalesque. The game proceeds without rules until Hook draws the line at shooting opponents as 'bad form'. The cheerleading pirates' transposition, 'Run Home' instead of 'Home Run', at Jack's innings, underlines his conflicting desires: to return to his family or achieve recognition, denied by Banning's parenting, for prowess. As he hits the ball clear of the park, Hook acknowledges him proudly as 'My Jack!', leaving Banning to echo the words disbelievingly, feebly asserting paternity.

As he attempts vainly to fly to Jack, Banning's hair is notably longer and untidier as his transition to Pan – someone who will play with his kids – continues. The baseball striking his head completes the process: reaching into a pool to recover this paternal token, he sees the child Pan's reflection, a Mirror Phase that flickers light onto his face. Now separated from his beckoning shadow, he becomes spectator and follower of his more powerful, more complete self, identifying with a projected form.

In Pan's tree-trunk home, penetrated by light beams in which memory of his mother finally materialises in flashback, he recalls the act of will that drove him from her as she voiced hopes for his adult future. Tipped from his runaway pram in the park, the infant Pan lies centred in a crazy paving circle: a spiral, otherwise resembling the face of Big Ben, hence signifying escape from time. Taken to Neverland and taught by Tink to fly, the older child Pan returns, looking through the nursery window at his parents with a new baby – a barrier and a screen, separating him from, and projecting his desire into, a lost Imaginary. He would return and chase his shadow in the nursery – again a separate character, a specular other – until finally merging with the shadow as if entering the screen, achieving Imaginary unity (as did Neary), at which point sixty years on he falls for Moira and gives her a real kiss, light flaring across the screen.

This recollection reminds Banning he chose fatherhood. His happy thought: 'I'm a daddy.' Empowered, he soars skywards, across the sun like E.T. across the moon. To protect his children he thinks and behaves childishly. Thus the narrative occupies the boundary between Symbolic (duty, positioning) and Imaginary (freedom, inconsequentiality) – alternating, as does entertainment film spectatorship. Watched by the Lost Boys and the cinema audience, Pan chases his shadow through clouds, whips off Rufio's trousers, and mounts bravura flying displays: back flips, victory rolls, basketball goals – flashy tricks exaggerating the kind adoring children might expect of their father. When Rufio approaches, sword upraised, framing through Pan's legs emphasises the castration metaphor before Rufio genuflects, proffering it to its rightful owner. Rufio alone remains in a light beam as the Lost Boys ally themselves with Pan, then joins them, extolling Pan's virtues and singing praises. Full and crescent moons shine simultaneously, illuminating this state of being and becoming, this Neverland outside time in which Banning's deadline nevertheless approaches.

Hook's defeat

Pan has forgotten his mission. Tink inhabits a clock full of dazzling light, that suddenly explodes, leaving her human-sized and backlit by projection beams, wearing a glamorous dress. In accordance with Laura Mulvey on visual pleasure, this sexualised spectacle reminds Pan of his masculinity and hence adult responsibilities. Light projected directly into the camera almost obliterates their kiss, as though viewed from behind the screen, within the Imaginary. Reawakened sexual difference and identity reminds Banning of Moira and the children, at which the image regains substance. Tink, hitherto jealous of Moira, having now worked her magic and returned Banning to his quest, renounces him for a higher goal and reverts to fairydom.

Spielberg's recurrent permeable screen, underpinning my argument concerning constant spectatorial repositioning, features twice as Hook prepares to pierce Jack's ear, a symbolic castration. As the Lost Boys plan battle against Hook, they walk through bamboo screens, emerging coated in samurai armour. The moment Hook approaches Jack's ear with his hook, Banning's sword penetrates a white sail – the blank screen. Pan's shadow, cut from the canvas, flutters down, combining his magical ability to separate from it with a prosaic, adult explanation.

The Lost Boys repel pirates with reflected light. While the fight involves excessively rich mise-en-scène and rapid editing that may have contributed to the critical drubbing, it alludes doubly to 1930s swashbuckling features as Banning's Pan costume and performance suggest Errol Flynn's Robin Hood transposed to a pirate adventure. Hook's murder of Rufio, who dies wishing for a father like Banning, might also have proved too much for critics wanting to preserve an illusion of innocence around *Peter Pan* that its latent psychosexual content cannot sustain. At any rate, Hook's wickedness prompts Jack to acknowledge his father and demand to go home.

The men's duel is projected, an enormous shadow on a wall, watched by the Lost Boys. As Hook prepares to dispatch Banning, whom he has pinned down, the latter asserts that he is dreaming – he really is Peter Banning – 'a cold, selfish man who drinks too much, is obsessed with success and runs and hides from his wife and children'. This self-appraisal from the super-ego is dialogised with the children and Tink insisting they believe in him. Identity, the movie maintains, is not either/or but requires self-recognition and empathy with others' needs.

With Banning and Jack acknowledging their relationship comes confirmation of Hook's fraudulence. Like Basie without his cap, this glamorous father surrogate, minus wig, turns out to be a seedy, balding old man. Concerned throughout with avoiding 'Bad Form', he nevertheless murders Rufio and fails to reciprocate Banning's chivalry as they fight. Panicked by multiple ticking clocks, he becomes impaled on the crocodile clock which, as he pulls it over while freeing himself, appears to devour him: a pre-echo of the lawyer's demise in *Jurassic Park*, the more interesting given Banning's profession and Hook's role as alter-ego.

Exhilarated by Hook's defeat, Banning reverts briefly to Peter, until Tink – positioned between his children – provides the light signifying his objects of desire and adulthood returns. Conferring his sword to leave in charge an obese black child – Neverland authority carnivalises status patterns in American society – Banning flies home with his children, leaving one Lost Boy to state what serious adult critics miss: 'That was a great game.'

Cinema as Imaginary Signifier re-materialises as the sky Banning flies into dissolves to the painted nursery ceiling and leaves blow in, indexical of the solar wind presaging the light beam on which the children travel; a heavenly choir accompanies their arrival as they observe how their sleeping mother resembles an angel. Banning has ended up under the Pan statue in Kensington Gardens where he converses with Tink, his connection with Neverland, before her image dissolves into the morning sun, symbolising his rejuvination. Despite painful pratfalls where previously he soared with grace, he pursues his restored instincts by shinning up the drainpipe to look in, as did Peter, on a family scene of Imaginary unity that excludes him. Rapping on the window, he is however welcomed in as the now benign patriarch, concluding that 'To live would be an awfully big adventure.'

Patriarchy and family values prevail. However, to argue that this is entirely conservative and occurs unproblematically would ignore the family's subterranean conflicts, that Banning abandons the 1980s work ethic for personally-defined, fulfilling goals, and that successful parenting – if one insists on taking this children's fantasy seriously – appears more difficult than corporate law. Moreover, unlike movies such as *Field of Dreams* (1989) and *Dances with Wolves* (1990), with which Collins aligns *Hook* as asserting 'sincerity that avoids any sort of irony or eclecticism' in seeking 'recoverable purity in an impossible past' (1993: 257), *Hook* resolves difficulties not in idealised American history but a place acknowledged to be Neverland. Innocence is not an essence but structurally opposed by adults against complicated experience, as *Hook* demonstrates by making Neverland a projection of Banning's needs rather than the children's desires, satiable here and now if Banning organised priorities. That the movie initially looked set for failure has less to do with its treatment of these aspects than the prosaic marketing problem that it contained little to interest Hollywood's primary audience, 16–24-year-olds.

CHAPTER FIFTEEN

Jurassic Park: another monster hit

The *Making of Jurassic Park* documentary – re-released with the movie on DVD, presumably under Spielberg's supervision – commences with a clip of Grant (Sam Neill) removing sunglasses to gawp at a dinosaur. This definitive, self-reflexive Spielberg moment, comprising vision, simultaneous belief, disbelief and projective desire, cuts immediately to Grant asking, 'How did you do this?' Hammond (Richard Attenborough) replies: 'I'll show you how.'

Creating dinosaurs through advanced biotechnology, as – like movies – larger-than-life spectacles, parallels their rendition through advanced special effects: each utilises complex codes and virtual reality imaging. A respected director plays Hammond, visionary and impresario (likened, in the source novel, overtly to Disney), who as a former flea circus entertainer founded his career on special effects. (Spielberg asked Attenborough, whose *Gandhi* (1982) pipped *E.T.* at the Academy Awards, to supervise *Schindler's List* temporarily so he could complete *Jurassic Park*'s post-production – eventually entrusted to George Lucas (Baxter 1996: 387)). Hammond's primary interest is audience reactions; Spielberg's bearded, bespectacled alter-ego, creator of a monster attraction, scrutinises his guests' awe-struck horror as a velociraptor lunches on a cow. *Jurassic Park*, 'a neat parable about Hollywood itself' (Black 1993: 8), was, Spielberg said, 'the story of any studio head having a bad year who needs a hit' (in Kennedy 2001: 94).

'Welcome to Jurassic Park'

Hammond's greeting to his guests, interpellating the spectator also, embraces his fictional project and the film, epitomising double-voiced discourse that reverberates throughout. The visitors, enthralled, observe cloned dinosaurs; we, enthralled, observe computer-animated dinosaurs. Hammond's gift shop contains identical souvenirs to movie theatre foyers and the stores outside – including, centre-screen, the *Making of Jurassic Park* book – all sharing a distinctive logo. The movie, advertising profitable merchandise that itself promotes the movie, asserts – yet toys with – its showmanship and the proto-cinematic dream of realism.

Equating illusion with reality motivated *fin de siècle* novelties such as simulators, Phantom Rides and Hale's Tours (films of tourist destinations viewed from mocked-up railroad cars). As attractions these existed for their own sake – sensations, celeb-rations of technology – as much as their ostensible content. Cinematic pioneers commonly filmed local sights and screened the footage publicly the same day; it was not the actual street scene, free of charge outside, which punters queued for. Parallels with Hammond's Visitor Centre presentation (in which the lawyer, Gennaro (Martin Ferrero), mistakes working scientists for animatronics) and the rail-guided Jeep tours, are striking. These emphasise in microcosm *Jurassic Park*'s delivery of cinema as spectacle and visceral experience. They also anticipate Universal Studios' *Jurassic Park* rides, utilising effects developed for the movie: 'a theme-park ride based on the movie *about* a theme park, a ride that delivers the visitor conveniently to its retail outlet' (King 2000: 42). Unprecedented synergies within MCA/Matsushita meant projected income from these rides underwrote Spielberg's production budget, along with in-house tie-in merchandise (Bennett 1993: 10; Balides 2000: 145).

Reproducing life from different times and places – literally and metaphorically, through fictional cloning and actual computer-generated imaging – blurs artifice and reality. Dinosaurs and cars steered by electric tracks were, after all, popular toys *before* the film logo graced their packaging. In a postmodern conflation, logo and title signify intra- *and* extra-diegetically, playfully *and* with ruthless commercial logic, in and around a text that ironises its own values and conditions of existence. Spectators enjoy the ride or appreciate the craft, humour and paradoxes available; or both – concurrently or serially enthralled, decentred, pleasurably alienated, or pulled in and out of Imaginary subject positions and Symbolic awareness. Any movie theoretically procures such alternatives; few combine them so variably as *Jurassic Park*, which appeals widely by offering not a lowest common denominator but multiple potential pleasures. It sustains and extends inherent contradictions in special effects, between belief when they are convincing and wonder at their achievement.

The spectacle of the first dinosaur seen in entirety emphasises this. Grant then looks off-screen, cueing expectations, answered by a long shot of wading brachiosaurs and gallimimuses, accompanied by majestic music. The composition, divided by perspective lines into a separate background and a foreground containing dwarfed humans, stand-in observers, creates a mise-en-abyme of spectatorship.

Jurassic Park invites self-reflexive reading throughout. Original audiences, primed by months of hype, hearing ominous music and animal noises accompanying the black-screen title credits, confronted in the first shot something mysterious rustling through close-up vegetation. Promised convincing monsters – much was made of potential psychological damage to children and consequent debates over classification – audiences were tantalised by initial non-appearance of a creature metonymically (that is, inferentially) present. Cut to a worker looking up, anxiously, off-screen: an inscribed spectator wearing a *Jurassic Park* hat as though he had already bought the merchandise. Light beams through branches. An inscribed audience, all in hats with logos, backlit, look intently upwards, the central figure chewing as if devouring popcorn. Smoke or steam motivates a shot included *only* to feature the light beam. A big-game hunter, heavily armed, underlines danger. Not only are these characters intensely backlit, reflected front-lighting emanates from the suspended crate before them. Contractors' lamps, rectangular, figure simultaneously as surrogate movie lighting, projectors and screens.

A point-of-view shot inside the crate confirms, yet defers the dinosaur's presence: an inscribed widescreen frame. This aperture contains the frightened workers' reaction shot, as if looking back out through the screen. To the extent secondary identification occurs, spectators feel, or imagine being, threatened. The unseen animal apparently sees them: the power of the gaze resides in the most powerful diegetic object – not where it is commonly supposed, in the spectating subject.

Light shafts improbably emanating from within the crate as well as projected onto it, reminiscent of Jean-Louis Baudry's diagrammatic cinematic apparatus (1974/75: 41), compound this notion of enfolded spectatorship. Another point-of-view shot through a widescreen aperture, a worker atop the crate, presages imminent release of the spectator's psychically 'projected', still unseen, dinosaur; in other words fulfilling desire implicated in the narrative image surrounding the film's long-anticipated release. The game warden directs his crew, shouting conceivably the same orders at the same moments – 'Step away! Gatekeeper! Raise the gate!' – as Spielberg during shooting. Light beams move with the gate, seemingly projecting its movements. Horror unleashed coincides with projection, discharge of spectatorial desire. As the unseen dinosaur moves, an invisible force seemingly sucks in the gatekeeper, literally along a light shaft. His violent demise occasions rapid montage that disturbs by disorientation rather than explicitness: close-ups on the game warden's and the dinosaur's eyes, the victim's hand and the warden's mouth court comparison with *Psycho*'s shower scene as he screams, 'Shoot her!' – another cinematographic pun.

The power of light, associated with death as electric stun guns attack the creature, refracts through the next sequence, in an amber mine, which associates it with creation. If the Park is excessively fecund – luxuriant vegetation, water and initially female dinosaurs abound – mining, like the applied science it here supports, is masculine, acquisitive. Malcolm (Jeff Goldblum) later calls discovery 'a violent, penetrative act ... the rape of the natural world'. While nature reincorporates the violently devoured gatekeeper, disappearing through slick, wet foliage in a reverse birth image, the miners seek the genetic origins of new life. Their helmet lamps probe the darkness for fossilised insects, while Gennaro, in the entrance, casts radiating shadows reminiscent of the projection theatre in *Citizen Kane*. Polishing the amber inevitably showers sparks, echoing Jim's encounter with his quest objects in *Empire of the Sun*. When Gennaro and several miners group to examine a specimen, converging helmet lamps elicit a glow as from within. Flamboyant reframing, wide-angle to macro, accompanied by John Williams' heavenly choir, reveals a preserved mosquito. Juxtapositions between scenes – horror/beauty, obscurity/clarity, darkness/light, nature/technology, fear/optimism, instinct/rationality, mass/diminutiveness, strength/delicateness, in the context of primal forces and religious connotations – recall dualities in William Blake's poem, 'The Tyger', itself epitomising ambivalence concerning both natural and scientific creation.

Cut from the insect to a palaeontologist's brush unearthing fossil bones matching the Jurassic Park logo: montage renders the film's diegetic content congruent with the framing text and institutional context, all correlated with the might of evolution. Again, Spielberg's director-figure presumes divine power, this time heading for a Promethean or, appropriately, Frankenstein-like downfall.

Grant on his dig is another character presented through filmmaking analogies. His palaeontologists – based, like a location crew, in trailers – literally take a 'shot' to image a buried fossil (firing a shell into the ground to generate seismic waves) and crowd around a monitor. 'I hate computers', Grant complains, as a degraded image slowly scans onto the screen, whereas his technician insists: 'This new programme's incredible. A few more years and we won't even have to dig any more.' Grant's reply, 'Where's the fun in that?' underscores similarities with the movie's transitional status between traditional methods and computer animation. While Grant talks excitedly of velociraptors – a forceful contrast with Nedry (Wayne Knight), cynical designer of Jurassic Park's computer control systems, greedy rather than visionary – the lens flares and wind agitates his hair.

Hammond's ambivalence and hubris, as filmmaking metaphor as well as in terms of scientific ethics, register when his helicopter blows sand over the excavations on arrival to recruit Grant and Sattler (Laura Dern). A line of laundry buffeting violently – Spielberg's solar wind – marks his presence metonymically as he carelessly destroys their painstaking efforts yet fulfils their professional dreams, initially by guaranteeing funding. Light shafts through a window behind them as they meet their benefactor, who glows in white clothing like a projection. This encounter, as he promises 'attractions' to 'drive kids out of their minds', pre-echoes his later presentation introducing 'the most advanced amusement park in the world, incorporating all the latest technologies' – effectively the movie and its spin-offs, even alluding to global marketing as he promises dinosaurs 'so astounding that they'll capture the imagination of the entire planet'. Grant's comment, 'We're out of a job', and Malcolm's reply, 'Don't you mean extinct?' were, according to the *Making of Jurassic Park* DVD extra, based on stop-frame animator Phil Tippet's comments on seeing computer rushes.

The flight to the island, its landscape framed in 'widescreen' windows, resembles a Cinerama, IMAX or Dolby demonstration. The waterfall, down which the helicopter descends and before which Hammond steps out, resembles a light beam, reinforcing cinematic/religious parallels and establishing Edenic connotations. Following dinosaur sightings, in which the lawyer differentiates himself by commercial speculation rather than spontaneous awe, the party enters the Visitor Centre through sunburst-carved portals. They occupy a part theme park simulator, part movie theatre, its screen brandishing the logo within a proscenium containing receding frames: a mise-en-abyme. Hammond, wearing white, approaches his on-screen double, in black, in virtual perspective. When the on-screen figure greets them, Hammond urges his guests, 'Say hello'; they do, affirming the need for active audience participation: a carnivalesque throwback to his flea circus. Like an actor leaving space for a special effect (as Attenborough, pro-filmically, is) Hammond forgets his lines and misses his cue. When he 'pricks' his double's finger for blood, the latter becomes much larger, clearly a movie image. Beams project over the inscribed audience as Hammond's virtual Other is repeatedly cloned, an overt association of genetic with cinematographic copying. (This splitting, moreover, into half-real, half-image, black and white, renders Hammond literally a 'projection character', an expression of authorial contradictions (Hawthorn 1994: 161).)

Hammond's movie explaining computer-assisted cloning now fills *our* screen, positioning us identically to the diegetic audience. Drawn animation, based on an early cartoon, *Gertie the Dinosaur* (1914), underlines the analogy – Gertie's creator, Winsor McCay, incorporated live-action footage so he could step behind the screen into the film – as do Hammond's comments that 'This score is temporary. We ought to have dramatic music of course', as though we are viewing rushes. Stressing the creative process likens *Jurassic Park*'s exponential developments to innovative early cinema.

Science fiction is inextricable from the display of effects technology (Stern 1990; Pierson 1999). Garrett Stewart notes, 'The genre's typical mise-en-scène is replete with viewing screens that function not only as tools in the narrative but as icons of continuity with the present-day science of communication or surveillance' (1998: 100): certainly true of the Park's control centre monitors, via which action elsewhere appears on closed-circuit television or is inferred. 'Alternatively in the genre', Stewart continues, 'a given film's present visual achievement may be measured against its screen predecessors, as when DeMille's parting of the Red Sea on the hero's TV establishes a baseline for the one-upmanship to come in *Close Encounters*' (ibid.). This applies with Gertie, and also with snippets of a 1950s flying saucer movie and *Tom and Jerry* watched by E.T.

Safety bars close down on the seats as what Hammond calls 'the tour' continues; this theme park adventure, as the auditorium rotates, reveals a laboratory, framed *as though* filmed, a postmodern conversion of reality into perceived simulacrum. The observers' reflections inscribe a screen and indeed the Lacanian film theory metaphor of screen as mirror. For knowing audiences, even the robot hand that turns incubating eggs and delicately takes shell from Grant's hand is an assertion of cutting-edge mechanical effects, which comprise a substantial part of the dinosaur footage.

Lunch occurs explicitly among banked projectors, shining over the diners' shoulders, displaying slides on the walls. Light beams figure characters' desires: 'We can charge anything' encapsulates Gennaro's limited vision, expressed as the pun 'Projected

Revenues' flashes beside him; whereas for Hammond, like a populist moviemaker, 'Everyone in the world will have the right to enjoy these animals.' Gloomy prognostications from Malcolm, the philosopher – spoken against sunny images of flowers and children – warn against meddling with nature, according the movie a moral, educational dimension. Malcolm's words avow entertainment's idealised serious potential, always part of the Disney theme park ethos. Dialogically, they embody – though their inclusion refutes – criticism of Spielberg's alleged superficiality and banality; some are particularly apposite in the knowledge that *Jurassic Park* secured *Schindler's List*'s go-ahead:

> I'll tell you the problem with the scientific power that you're using here. It didn't require any discipline to attain it. You read what others had done, and you took the next step. You didn't learn the knowledge for yourselves. You don't take any responsibility for it. You stood on the shoulders of geniuses to accomplish something as fast as you could and you patented it and packeted it and slapped it on a plastic lunch box and now you're selling it.

Hammond introduces his grandchildren, Lex (Ariana Richards) and Tim (Joseph Mazzello), as 'our target audience'. From here on, following the visit to the control centre that uses computers indistinguishable from those that made the movie possible, much narration occurs on monitors. A computer warns, for example, of stormy weather, the chance occurrence that triggers ensuing disasters.

'Tour initiated'

'Hang onto your butts!' exclaims Arnold (Samuel L. Jackson), monitoring events from his desk like *Close Encounters*' air-traffic controllers as 'Tour initiated' flashes on-screen: his advice is equally *histoire*, observed by the spectator, and *discours*, addressed to the spectator, as are the words 'Welcome to Jurassic Park' enunciated by the computerised guide. Reciprocally, the pan to a TV monitor, which shows automated cars moving, narrates what happens elsewhere but also establishes the control centre's relationship to physically absent events. A dual chronotope emerges: increasingly enforced passivity, associated with directing and spectatorship, where Hammond follows events on-screen, using a keyboard and wearing a headset as if in an editing suite; and Jurassic Park's fantastic 'interior' diegesis, associated with monster movies by dialogue explicitly likening the gates to those in *King Kong* (1933) as they resoundingly crash shut behind the tourists.

In the dilophosaurus paddock the party press against the Jeep windows, rather like Jim in Shanghai, excited by prospective close encounters. As the species spits poison, signs warn to keep windows closed, stressing the screen as both barrier and access to fulfilled desire as light flares off the glass. The characters' anticipation cues the spectator to crane to see, equally unsuccessfully. Shared frustration functions realistically to convey an actual safari's uncertainties, but also generates suspense, withholding fierce dinosaurs as well as setting up Nedry's later shocking death by motivating his killer's behaviour but deferring the creature's recognition.

Light shines in front of the game warden Muldoon (Bob Peck) in the control centre as he announces the anticipated moment: the tyrannosaur paddock. The party stare raptly at a live goat left as bait, with off-screen space reflected in the Jeep windows, superimposing viewer and object, what would conventionally be shot/reverse-shot, as if this enriched Bazinian deep focus denies nothing. Intra- and extradiegetic audiences again share disappointment. The creature fails to show. In another shot integrating two scenes of action, Hammond voices dismay as Malcolm ridicules this letdown, looming grotesquely into the monitor, tapping the lens and then breathing on it in close-up. This reinstates awareness of the screen, the separating apparatus, and invokes *The Big Swallow* (1901) in which a character devours the camera and hence the audience, alluding perhaps to cinema's capacity to incorporate viewers into its illusion.

Cameras feeding Nedry's surveillance monitor obliquely relay important narrative information, such as the embryo storage banks and the quay where he intends to hand over genetic contraband. In contrast to these mediations Malcolm flirts with Sattler, his object of desire, by constantly touching her, as when explaining chaos theory by trickling water over her hand. Grant and Sattler jump out of their moving Jeep to touch a sick triceratops; Grant lays his body full-length against it and Sattler delves elbow-deep into its excrement. Lex takes advantage of stumbling to hold Grant's hand. Physical contact abnegates distance inherent in spectatorship.

Graphic matches stress narrative causality and the moviemaking metaphor, including the amber tip of Hammond's cane rotated before the light, like a piece of film edited against the revolving warning lamp at the T-Rex compound, and the intellectual montage from Nedry clicking on 'Execute' to Gennaro, the next victim, jumping at a thunder crash. Nedry's reflection stresses another inscribed screen between a character and his desired object as he waits for the airlock to open into cryogenic tanks, implausibly lit from within like the Ark in *Raiders of the Lost Ark* or stolen isotopes in *Kiss Me Deadly* (1955). (A photograph of Oppenheimer tacked beside Nedry's computer emphasises the force he unleashes.) As Nedry races to his rendezvous, his wheels splash mud onto the camera, obscuring vision and implying contempt for the spectator or anyone else. Tim, intercut, wearing night-vision goggles, contrasts with Nedry frantically wiping his glasses before losing the road, blinded by rain before dropping them and finally being literally blinded by the dilophosaurus. Nedry's fatal blindness, like Gennaro's, is failure to see dinosaurs as more than commodities. Tim embodies the direct vision retained by Hammond, Sattler, Grant and Spielberg's implied spectator. Tim, indeed, is first to notice the approaching tyrannosaur. A human seismic monitor, as opposed to the computerised contraption Grant resented, he instinctively visualises its presence (signified by ripples in … a pair of glasses!). Gennaro's fear registers in a close-up of his eyes in the mirror fitted otherwise illogically in the driverless Jeep, another internal widescreen frame to reflect audience apprehension.

Security screens

Tim dons the goggles again. The goat is gone. Active spectatorship, then, remembering the tattered harness after the raptors devoured the cow, aligns with Tim's knowledge and vision rather than Gennaro's. A severed limb thrown at the windshield answers

Lex's and our question: 'Where's the goat?' Smeared blood recalls the chicken smashed against the car window, the transparent yet protective screen, in *Empire of the Sun*. Lightning flickers like early film. The T-Rex eyes the camera, affronting the Hollywood convention that affirms mastery by ensuring the gaze remains voyeuristic; a convention broken only rarely, when secondary identification is sufficient that the threatening Other's returned gaze subordinates the potential threat to realism, as with traffic cops in *Psycho* and *Thelma and Louise* (1991) or Hannibal Lecter in *The Silence of the Lambs* (1991). Undermining realism works reciprocally in this instance, as in comedy: a knowing glance between text and adult spectator, recognising artifice and playfulness, just as the villain's best lines in *Hook* address adults even while calculated to frighten children.

Hereafter threat scenes repeatedly toy with penetrating the cinema screen. The T-Rex's first move is to breach the disabled electric fence separating exhibits from spectators. Through Malcolm and Grant's windshield, it resembles the *Jurassic Park* logo. The veil of rain distinctly demarcates inside and out, safety and danger, the screen plane. Lex directs a searchlight to see better, succeeding only in attracting the creature's attention. Concentric circles of light projected onto its close-up dilating eye again imply reciprocal vision. It pushes in the bubble roof of the children's Jeep, violating spectatorial space; even then the screen that brings their nightmare within breathing distance doubles as a shield, while Malcolm wipes condensation off his own windshield to see. Grant's conviction that the T-Rex senses only movement forces Malcolm and Grant into immobility, epitomising Metz's powerless spectator. Later, injuries incurred while following Grant in distracting the creature literally disable Malcolm, reduced to pure spectatorship like James Stewart in *Rear Window*. Gennaro's death features the animal from his perspective, bursting into his refuge.

Light and vision increasingly accrue conventional connotations. Light saves the children when Grant and Malcolm attract the tyrannosaur with flares, Gennaro, having abandoned them, perishes after hiding in darkness. Muldoon and Sattler bring enormous torchlights, casting beams directly into the camera, to redeem a desperate situation. When Hammond shuts down the system (because Nedry, who disabled the computers, has died with the password), the screens turn off and the lights extinguish. Without Muldoon's torchlight, the cinema screen itself would be black. No light: no *Jurassic Park*. Let There Be Light. 'Hold onto your butts!' repeats Arnold. In a chaotic criss-crossing of beams, the final act begins, all but eliminating the voyeuristic gap.

Classical crosscutting follows as events in different locations mutually impinge, unknown to the participants but in overall view of the powerless spectator. During the T-Rex attack on the gallimimus herd – strangely the outdoor scenes *are* in broad daylight – Grant, Lex and Tim observe from a secure vantage. They have entered the dinosaurs' space: their witnessing of the singing brachiosaurs, restful aesthetic contemplation and communion, ended with Lex sneezed on by one of the giants, while the gallimimus stampede placed them amid the action. 'Look how much blood…' says Tim, an inscribed child spectator, voicing what the movie in fact does not show but audiences willingly perceive.

Sun shafts through trees as Muldoon watches for raptors – respected and admired by the game hunter, although he first declared they should be killed – while Sattler searches for Arnold, still missing after going to reset the circuit breakers. Grant, unaware, alarms and amuses both the children and the audience by feigning electrocution on the fence – a performance within a performance – then actually suggests they slow down while climbing it even as Sattler approaches the switches. The camera tracks and tilts through the fence as they straddle it, an unusual and unmotivated movement except that it suggests transgression from spectatorial to exhibition space. In parallel, Sattler's delight at reinstating the current (and, emphatically, lights, re-ignited individually) is controverted: Tim is electrocuted, Arnold is discovered, dismembered, a velociraptor attacks from the darkness as through a series of screens (a grid of pipes, then chain-link panels), and two more kill Muldoon as he pursues them along a spotlight beam Sattler has restored.

Repeated screen penetrations towards the camera bring these fictional dinosaurs ever closer to the extradiegetic world, culminating in the final shots showing pelicans, their descendants, winging from the island along a trail of reflections into the sunset. In the Visitor Centre a raptor's shadow (its projection) overlays a mural of itself, collapsing different degrees of iconic-indexical representation. When a raptor eyes humans through a porthole its breath clouds the glass, again emphasising the screen as both barrier and access, the shape of which recalls an iris shot, commonly used in early cinema to concentrate vision. A rectangular frame traps Lex in the kitchen – a metal cabinet, figuring her narrative and diegetic situation – as raptors unwittingly attack not her but her reflection, an image on a flat surface they cannot pierce. In cinema's topsy-turveydom instigated in Gennaro's first shot, inverted on the water, she is saved because the dinosaurs, made real, attack her virtual Other. While raptors invade the control room's physical space, she navigates the Park's virtual space on a computer as effortlessly as the creatures move between areas, until she finds the correct site – picked out by a shaft of light – and the system locks the doors. While the humans escape, a

Jurassic Park – screen penetration

raptor jumps onto a workstation indistinguishable from the one that produced it and has its computerised genetic code projected onto it. During the cliffhanging climax as humans manoeuvre along ventilation shafts, Lex falls through a ceiling hatch into the raptor's space. It jumps up full to camera, through the frame, snapping, into our space, all barriers finally removed insofar as identification disavows the cinema screen. The T-Rex skeleton – historically the original form of reconstruction – which resembles the logo, indexical of a subsequent industry of depictions, collapses under the weight of escapees taking refuge on it, abnegating any containment of these monsters by means of mastery inherent in representation. The rib cage both traps and protects Tim, as did the overturned Jeep, metaphors for the security and risk cinema offers the regressed spectator. Climactically the raptor bursts through semi-opaque, backlit, white, plastic sheeting – the blank shot momentarily foregrounds the *actual* screen, as pure white light illuminates it rather than projects a representation onto it – seemingly into the auditorium. The tyrannosaur's entrance saves the day, permitting escape through the sunburst doors to Hammond outside in his Jeep.

Computer animation and digital imagery

Jurassic Park constantly plays with the dichotomy of virtual and real: a self-reflexivity aligned with popular and theoretical discourses surrounding computer-generated images. The mid-production switch from stop-motion to computer animation, except where dinosaurs interact physically with humans, is well documented (for example, see Baxter 1996: 379), fuelling interest in whether the 'joins' were visible.

Celebration of special-effects technology accompanied the information age's triumphant arrival, culmination of billions of dollars' worth of research and development, as computers made highly visible incursions into homes and work places. This links, Constance Balides suggests, with the film's 'hypervisible' display of its commercial motivation and potential: 'the lustre of capital itself', as much as dinosaurs, 'is an attraction in a post-Fordist economy.' Such display is apparent everywhere in the film and its merchandise, certainly not in need of theorised reading against the grain to expose its workings (2000: 160).

Resulting contradictions, between on one hand the film and its merchandising's allure and on the other potential awareness (especially for adults) of interpellation as consumers, mutually reinforce contradictions within the regime of verisimilitude. Spectators, conscious of artifice, nevertheless succumb, Robert Baird claims, to 'neurologically *hard-wired*' responses, physiological and psychological schemata (1998: 91). While biological essentialism risks short-circuiting analysis of signifying practices, it does appear that, as in *E.T.*, pre-conscious cognition stimulates pre-cultural reflexes. Less important than palaeontological accuracy is that the animations, based on existing animals, correspond to schemata which convince beyond rational perception (ibid.). This, Robert Baird argues, provides universal human recognition that prompted word-of-mouth support for promotional claims, and made theatrical attendance an event relatively unaffected by cultural difference (1998: 90). (Anthropomorphism too probably affected responses, as animators studied performance, dance, movement and mask work to internalise the motions and motivations of the creatures they strove to replicate (Magid 1993): the velociraptor coming through a door uncannily resembles Jack Nicholson in *The Shining* (1980).) Other computerised techniques reinforce the creatures' 'reality': wildlife documentary conventions – telephoto lenses, aerial perspective, intermingled species grazing unaware of the camera (Baird 1998: 92) – and imposed motion blur and artificial film grain to match flawless simulations seamlessly with technically 'inferior' live action. These increase credibility by presenting dinosaurs not as they existed in reality but because they replicate how dinosaurs would look *if we were able to see them on film.*

Further reasons, unconnected with computers, that the dinosaurs appear realistic, are considered later. However, as already discussed, 'the science fiction film can be seen as a genre focused precisely upon advocating and valorising its effects'; in doing this, nevertheless, 'science fiction film intensifies the fantastic bent of cinema in general' (Landon 1992: 89). Arnold's repeated phrase, 'Hold on to your butts!' operates analogously to a line in John Carpenter's *The Thing* (1982) that, Steve Neale argues, has 'twofold status':

> It is on the one hand a narrative event: a fictional remark made by a fictional character about a specific, fictional entity … On the other hand, it is what one might call both a 'textual' and an 'institutional' event: a remark addressed to the spectator by the film, and by the cinematic apparatus, about the nature of its special effects. (1990: 160)

Neale argues that the remark conveys undisguised self-consciousness concerning the impressiveness of the film's cinematic fabrications and of spectatorial awareness of watching special effects and of knowing now that the film knows too. It is pure showmanship, foregrounding – like the comment, 'This is reality, stupid!' in *E.T.* – the pervasive doubly-oriented discourse. As Geoff King puts it,

> We can let ourselves go, surrender to the 'wonders' of convincingly-rendered dinosaurs … but at the same time retain an element of distance and control through our awareness that we are *allowing* ourselves to delight in an illusion; and, further, that we are delighting in it precisely because of its quality *as* illusion. (2000: 56)

Concurrently, however,

> the special effects have had an effect … the effect and the awareness are interdependent. Indeed one of the keys to understanding the attraction, the pleasure – the lure – of science fiction lies precisely in the intricate intercalation of different forms, kinds and layers of knowledge, belief and judgement. (Neale 1990: 161)

As well as celebrating cutting-edge digital images, then, *Jurassic Park* presents itself and is feted as a supreme example of a 'dinosaur' entertainment mode: cinematic spectacle. As Paul Coates stresses in relation to *King Kong*, 'monster' – many science fiction movies' attraction – derives from *monstrum*, something *shown* (as in 'de*monstra*te') (1991: 80). Repeated screen 'penetrations' in *Jurassic Park*, going beyond the 1990s action-movie tendency to throw objects towards the camera (King 2000: 94–101), seemingly eliminate the boundary between diegetic space and the viewers' auditorium and, specifically, are a cinematic effect much diminished on video or computer monitor. Product placement, moreover, reinforces the effect not simply by referring to objects the spectator already knows but by creating new, 'fictional' commodities the spectator can *actually* possess (without transformation, like most toys or miniature models, into secondary imitations). This is realism so convincing it surpasses even 3D illusions, allowing you, at extra cost, to hold part of the diegesis in your hand.

Warren Buckland believes *Jurassic Park* and *The Lost World: Jurassic Park* surpass spectacle 'by employing special effects to articulate a possible world' different from fiction in being based on real-world circumstances (1999: 178). I question this distinction in that any fiction not rooted in perceptions of the real world, as Roland Barthes' (1974) proairetic code emphasises, would be incomprehensible, and because – as Michael Stern maintains – *all* cinema is a special effect that happens to be naturalised in opposition to shots specifically declaring themselves effects (1990: 69). While Buckland, like Geoff King (2000), refutes common criticism that contemporary Hollywood spectacle stifles narrative, his case relies on separating articulations of possible worlds from 'pure fantasy, imagination or fiction' (1999: 181). This distinction is spurious, akin to opposing fact and fiction, insofar as it bypasses the notion that the realist effect derives from these modes sharing intertextual discourses of representation. Buckland relies on positing a 'reference world' that is neither the actual world nor a 'purely imaginary world' but a 'possible world' (1999: 183), as though signification (elicitation of signified from signifier) requires a referent.

Buckland privileges digital effects as uniquely capable of actualising the possible world, and dismisses live-action models as 'profilmic' effects shared with theme parks and therefore not 'specifically filmic' (ibid., n. 23). This is mystification. Mise-en-scène and editing create 'effects', which by definition are an effect *on* something, in this case spectatorial belief. Realistic models and digital creations are in fact equally *causes*, not *effects*, and as such operate identically if the spectator cannot distinguish between them. Buckland points usefully to the industrial distinction between invisible and visible effects: the former being the norm, such as removal of vapour trails from skies or creation of sets too difficult or costly to produce profilmically; the latter demanding notice. However, he asserts that visible effects 'simulate events that are impossible in the actual world' (1999: 184), overlooking the explosions, meteor showers, collapsing buildings and tidal waves that constitute much contemporary big-budget spectacle. Buckland also states that the digital dinosaurs, 'while clearly visible … attempt to hide behind an iconic appearance; that is, they are visible special effects masquerading as invisible effects' (1999: 184–5). Actually they are less stable than this. When the spectator accepts the dinosaurs' diegetic existence they switch from visible to invisible effects; alternatively, they might initially be accepted, wonderment occurring subsequently. Rather than total commitment to realism as a function of suture, the spectator alternates pleasurably between Imaginary and Symbolic relations with textual effects. It is unclear why Buckland treats digital images differently from pro-filmic models, which after all are *representations* of non-existent objects – as indeed are acting, most sets and camera positions.

The verisimilitude of Spielberg's dinosaurs depends not on ontology, as Buckland claims in a valorisation of digital images derived from Bazin's championing of deep-focus sequence shots (CGI puts the dinosaurs in the frame alongside human characters). Rather it derives from convincing 'specifically filmic' techniques of direction and editing, irrespective of what technical means produce them. Realism in the tyrannosaur attack on the children's jeep is not solely dependent on CGI. Both digital and live-action modelling are of sufficient quality not to undermine the creature's credibility, hitherto established metonymically. It already possesses substance, mass and proximity (discernible in water ripples, the vibrating mirror and rustling vegetation), voraciousness (the goat) and tangibility (by association with the breathing, blinking, heavily textured live-action triceratops encountered earlier alongside its mound of excrement). The banality of rain drumming on vehicle roofs further naturalises the tyrannosaur, rather than dramatic music (in a Spielberg movie with a Williams score), while intercutting characters' reactions in conventional shot/reverse-shots accentuates audience responses. Realism requires spectatorial synthesis of these devices, not a particular ontology. As most mainstream fare shares standard editing structures and inference of off-screen space, deviations would more likely detract from realism because of unfamiliarity than inaugurate a new regime of verisimilitude.

Intertextuality

Conscious intertextuality potentially reduplicates Symbolic/Imaginary alternations prompted by *Jurassic Park*'s special effects. Further instances include *The Birds* (Wollen 1993: 9), of which the dinosaurs are genetic precursors and generic descendants. The gallimimus herd imitates stampeding veldt animals in *King Solomon's Mines* (1937), Spielberg's touchstone when briefing animators (Magid 1993: 58); an example, possibly among many, that few would recognise. Douglas Brode notes that the kitchen where Lex and Tim hide resembles Steve McQueen's sanctuary in *The Blob* (1958), and that the collapsing dinosaur skeleton in the finale echoes the end of *Bringing Up Baby* (1938) (1995: 224–5); a similar gag occurs in *On the Town* (1949). A notable quotation is the ripples heralding the T-Rex. This emphasises Spielberg's audience-involving indirectness and understatement, derived from his admiration for British cinema, an influence generally eclipsed by his blockbuster effects. The second occurrence, involving water in a footprint, confirms this is in part a homage to Jack Cardiff, whose *Sons and Lovers* (1960) employed a trembling puddle to signify a mine collapse. Cardiff also, apparently, directed the first film to posit dinosaur cloning, *The Mutations* (1974) (Freer 2001: 209). Auto-citations include the truck plummeting toward Tim and Grant in the tree (with a 'roar', writes Baird (1998: 98): like Keys' jeep in *E.T.*), and the close-up of the pursuing tyrannosaur in a side mirror; both echo *Duel*. (The mirror shot, later parodied in *Toy Story 2* (1999), is a double auto-citation, resembling also an aeroplane in a car mirror in *The Last Crusade*.) Together with the words 'OBJECTS MAY BE CLOSER THAN THEY APPEAR', etched on the mirror in the dinosaur shot – realist detail that nevertheless, if perceived, switches modality from horror-adventure to comedy – such recognition and awareness of authorship serve reciprocally to enhance spectatorial self-awareness. If, as Buckland insists, *Jurassic Park* has a reference world, it is surely 'the movies', shifting, unstable, existing variously for different interpretive communities.

Psychoanalysis

While self-reflexivity and intertextuality offer detached, conscious pleasures (interpellation as an experienced, intelligent, alert moviegoer), *Jurassic Park*'s deep structure follows Spielberg's typical Oedipal trajectory. A young boy, incongruously present at Grant's dig, denies that raptors were 'scary'. Grant delves deep into the front pocket of his jeans – phallic authority, after all, is at stake – producing a fossilised raptor claw. Sadistically describing its eviscerating function, he draws this across the boy's abdomen, then genital area, while Sattler winces. Following the boy's cowed deference, Grant expresses dislike of children, amazed that Sattler desires parenthood. The castrating, sickle-shaped claw, together with his attitudes – underlined when he tries to avoid sharing Lex and Tim's jeep – confirms him as another Hook.

The narrative constructs Lex and Tim, however, visiting while their parents divorce, as needing paternal care. Their grandfather dispatches them, with strangers, as guinea pigs on an untested tour into a jungle full of giant carnivores. Gennaro, official custodian of patriarchy ('the Law'), abandons them and is killed. Of the surviving men, one admits constantly seeking 'the next ex-Mrs Malcolm', marking him unsuitable to provide security, and undergoes symbolic castration when the tyrannosaur immobilises him with an injured leg. This leaves only Grant. The children sleep against his shoulders, while Sattler observes beatifically, as the helicopter whisks them to safety. This 'family' formation begins when Grant rescues the children from the tyrannosaur, and continues during their trek back to the Centre. Nursery music accompanies their resting together for the night, after Grant again rescues Tim (from the falling jeep). They share the spectacle of, and communion with, grazing brachiosaurs, and bond by exchanging jokes. During this idyll, significantly, Grant discards the claw, answering Lex's question, 'What are you and Ellie going to do if you don't have to pick up dinosaurs' bones anymore?' with, 'I guess we'll have to evolve too.' As Constance Balides notes, 'evolution' from childless professionals to family is inexorably naturalised by Grant and the children 'nesting' in a tree (resonant with the premise of dinosaurs evolving into birds) and subsequent discovery of hatched eggs despite scientific assurance of exclusively female cloning, to prevent reproduction (2000: 155).

Grant jettisoning the claw completes displacement of the castration threat onto the carnivores. In particular, the raptors, although female, represent the bad father (Wollen 1993: 8; hence the appropriateness of the similarity to Jack Nicholson in *The Shining*) contrasted with Grant. Grant's recuperation, Balides suggests, functions ideologically to mask ethical implications of Hammond's project, to co-opt the movie's (unusually prominent) feminist discourse, and to ignore the environmental catastrophe global commercialisation wreaks on a third-world island (2000: 156). G. Thomas Goodnight similarly relates this supposedly escapist entertainment's success to the Bush-Clinton ethos, marked by 'desperate recovery of the personal sphere as survival strategy for escaping the predatory competition of institutional life and the resulting debris of the social world' (1995: 281).

Goodnight quips that Grant and Sattler, reconciled over procreation, are a 'post-doc Adam and Eve', returned to the Creation by Hammond's enterprise (1995: 277–8). A close-up on a snake after Muldoon's death confirms the Edenic sub-text, reinforced by the initials of their first names, Alan and Ellie. One might further assert that their names paranomastically suggest 'A Land Grant' and 'Early Settler'. This would temper Balides' and Goodnight's readings by replacing family emphasis with the perennial myth of the New World as Eden. The movie, aligned with a dominant American cultural tradition (Smith 1950; Marx 1964), indicts rather than ignores the virgin land's despoilation and corruption of the American Dream it inspired. King supports such an interpretation, noting that the palaeontologists, introduced in the Montana Badlands, wear frontier dress, engage in hands-on work, and as hero and heroine their 'credentials are established … through direct engagement with the earth and through a distrust of technology' (2000: 59). The lost Imaginary, then, equates with the pioneering experience; as King observes, Grant's excursion into the beautiful yet dangerous wilderness, where the family is formed, is contingent upon electronic failure caused by a bloated, corrupt technocrat, 'entirely unsuited to any kind of practical or survival skills', who perishes (2000: 62). Contrasting the proxy family against Nedry, embodiment of consumerist, junk-food values and greed associated with Hollywood by its critics, the movie betrays profound ambivalence about its status while naturalising and ennobling family ideals.

Marek Kohn considers *Jurassic Park*'s 'extraordinary achievement' is its 'vision of reincarnation around a prime cultural symbol of extinction' (1993: 13). Kohn, of course, means dinosaurs. Yet his words apply to the family, with which Spielberg's films over a quarter century play a *fort-da* game analogous to the intermittent presence of Hammond's behemoths. It stands less for curtailment of Grant's masculine freedom (Goodnight 1995) than nostalgic desire to restore and perpetuate frontier community and optimism, represented in America as the antithesis of cultural decadence.

Carnivore carnivalesque

Similarities between humans and dinosaurs in *Jurassic Park* go well beyond anthropomorphism – even if warm-blooded, heavy-footed raptors, intrusively opening doors and demanding food, are nightmare projections of Grant's parenthood phobia. Hammond breeds carnivores and 'veggiesaurs', corresponding to human gender attributes (Wollen 1993: 8); Lex is vegetarian, and while Ellie, the only other female character, does not voice dietary preferences, she stares in revulsion at her gourmet lunch. The entire movie, Georgia Brown observes, 'alternates between the mealtimes of humans and beasts', culminating in a kitchen showdown (1993: 53). Constant and careless eating emphasises Nedry's greed. Hammond's epicurism suggests enjoyment and sharing, rather than accumulating. Hammond and Sattler comfort themselves with ice cream when all appears lost. Arnold's chain smoking implies oral fixation:

a rational, controlling man in thrall to his craving. Lex and Tim devour jelly out of animal hunger after returning to the centre.

Muldoon lives to hunt. Malcolm appears cold-blooded, saurian (Mars-Jones 1993: 16): when not spouting theory his primary aim is competition with the dominant male, to mate and move on. Social Darwinism determines Grant's emergence as patriarch, paralleled with the dinosaurs' evolution (Brode 1995: 219). Grant's claw presages the seemingly impatient raptor's, tapping in the kitchen as it stalks the children; Lex's forefinger, curved over the computer mouse, saves the remaining humans by rebooting the control program. Corporeal emphases and dissolving hierarchal distinctions again evoke carnival (literally, a period of gorging on meat). Nedry personifies social concerns and everyday frustrations associated with the Information Technology revolution consolidated in the 1990s. Pleasure accompanies his punishment – excessive yet, by the simple logic of fantasy, just – as a grotesque creature he helped produce consumes his grotesque body. Similarly Gennaro becomes victim to the anthropomorphised animal whose fierceness he intended to package for profitable consumption.

Bodily imperatives accompany humiliation as Gennaro, having abrogated the law's abstract moral authority for selfish gratification, succumbs to animal reflexes and runs to the toilet, where the tyrannosaur attacks. Grant simulates evisceration on the boy whose incipient obesity relates his cynicism to Nedry's. Ellie delves enthusiastically into the heap of dino-do. A sneezing brachiosaur coats Lex in snot. Gross-out humour for child audiences, these nevertheless reinforce materiality in a world generated both extra- and intra-diegetically by computers. The virtual becomes, and threatens to incorporate, the real. The narrative celebrates computer effects yet distrusts the technology that makes them, and itself, possible. Animals change sex. Child-haters become loving fathers. Men, unusually in a horror film, are the primary victims. A vegetarian girl and woman overcome a greedy meat-eating man's machinations to escape from both intransigent technology and voracious animals.

In carnival, shared laughter permits temporary social cohesion and levelling. The movie functions analogously, through mechanisms that encourage audience sharing of characters' awe or terror. Likewise, overt intertextuality puts director and audience equally 'in the know', reversing the situation whereby 'the viewer … lacks knowledge which those on the screen possess and impart' (Fiske 1987a: 242) – even if visceral effects a moment later demand identification achieved through processes involving subjection. The very uncertainty surrounding the dinosaurs' ontology, and blurring of *Jurassic Park* (movie) with Jurassic Park (island), conform to Bakhtin's location of carnival on 'the borderline between art and life' (1984: 7).

Carnivorous dinosaurs may ultimately embody regressive desires: thirst for violence or a primordial need to assert human superiority. Feminist tendencies are nevertheless simultaneously in play. 'In play', literally, as in carnivalesque: reversed power relations dialogise competing discourses. This may be progressive in voicing such utterances, yet recuperative in that they are presented knowingly and, arguably, subordinated to narrative closure. Lex and Sattler's strong gender-reversal, underlined several times through dialogue, is not connected, for example, with feminist critique of the family (Balides 2000: 156).

Crosscutting, employed during climactic sequences, repeatedly withdraws the object of fascination at the moment the spectator becomes intensely involved (Brode 1995: 222). Mastery, of observing several scenes, as if simultaneously, from a distance, together with promised closure, implicates its opposite: subjection to narration and encouragement to identify. The *fort-da* oscillation between involvement and separation, presence and lack, replicates on a macro level shiftings between Imaginary and Symbolic that constitute suture.

'There is a precise fit ... between the emotions felt by the characters when they first see a dinosaur, and the sense of awe felt by the audience', argues Matthew Bouch (1996: 37). This corroborates Buckland's observation that the first brachiosaur sighting positions Sattler and Grant within the shot – not a cutaway to their point-of-view but an external focalisation (1999: 187). This positions the spectator *with* them, as fellow observers, rather than encouraging secondary identification *as* them. King points out the pleasure in observing their response even before the cut from close-ups reveals the creature's splendour, because prior knowledge from the narrative image creates a 'sense of superiority established by our ability to smile knowingly' at them, even as the spectacle itself is momentarily further delayed (2000: 43). Sufficient separation occurs, I suggest, to permit extra-diegetic marvelling at the special effect as they marvel, intra-diegetically, at what is for them a real dinosaur.

Spectator positioning through formal devices interacts with various subjectivities brought to the viewing experience, permitting a spectrum of negotiated readings. As Balides states, the potential for multiple viewings and the plethora of epitexts on *Jurassic Park*'s production and special effects position spectators as knowledgeable in diverse ways: for example, as dinosaur aficionados, science fiction buffs or computer enthusiasts. The densely intertextual reception context also makes it less likely that spectators would be innocent of the terms that constitute the experience's fabricated nature (2000: 17).

Jurassic Park inflects knowledge, always present in spectatorship, that what is experienced is not real – though the experience is real and what is experienced may be realistic – by heightened awareness of the stimuli's synthetic nature. If cinema employs various effects, some noticed, others invisible, significantly the industry produces *Making of ...* books and documentaries to render the invisible visible and thereby profit from enhancing the mastery of those prepared to pay extra to sustain possibilities of *dis*belief. While the 'immersion-effect' remains, the '*Jurassic*-literate consumer ... knows that the fake is a fake' (Balides 2000: 148); spectatorial credibility becomes divided (Neale 1990). The image, Metz's Imaginary signifier, evokes something non-existent – an absence, a lack, avowed by the film's projection yet disavowed in spectatorship. Behind-the-scenes materials standing in for, anticipating or revisiting the cinematic experience, provide further substitutions that intensify the fetishistic dimension of the primary relationship with the text. They flaunt the fact that special effects involve deceit and concealment even as they celebrate something which, as Metz says, intrinsically 'flaunts itself' (1977: 665). In other words, not only does the text provide various pleasures for different interpretive communities, these also involve different modalities generated by a range of discursive formations, many produced by the vertical intertextuality of promotion and publicity: 'For many young people, knowledge of special effects techniques now offers a kind of lure of stardom and power within the industry previously available only to screenwriters, stars, producers and directors' (La Valley 1985: 141).

Baird claims that 'a viewer can remain consciously aware of film artifice even as spatial intelligence operates naively' because of 'extraconscious' survival reflexes operating as the mind monitors its visual environment (1998: 83). If true, the implication is that the duality of distanced and involved spectatorship (wrongly supposed 'active' versus 'passive' or 'critical' versus 'escapist') is inherent in viewing even the most conventionally realist texts. This supposition remains congruent with the distinction between Symbolic and Imaginary and my thesis that alternation as well as irreconcilable contradiction between the two is a significant component in pleasure that Spielberg's practices powerfully exploit.

It follows that movies do not totally subjugate the interpellated subject and that identification created by formal structures does not entail totally substituting a sense of selfhood with acceptance of a textually constructed position. This is not to say that interpellation and identification do not occur and are not conditions for optimal intelligibility within the institutional mode of representation. Nevertheless, it is futile to complain, as Goodnight does of *Jurassic Park*, that 'audiences are induced neither to investigate the limits of current situations nor to evaluate common choices, but only to enjoy tastes of "terror" and "panic" that linger on the mind less than popcorn on the palate' (1995: 270). It neither is nor has ever been a primary function of mainstream entertainment to challenge popular attitudes. To criticise a Hollywood film for not radically doing so is redundant. 'The dystopic possibilities of the natural world', Goodnight goes on to argue,

> have long provided topics revisited and deployed intermittently by artists so as to spring cohorts into arenas of larger critical activity and public concern. In postmodern reversal ... Spielberg ... absorb[s] and exploit[s] these topics by elaborating a code of cultural scepticism. (1995: 271)

Christopher Tookey notes that near-deaths by falling car, electric fence and failed computer system signal that technology is 'the real monster' (1993a: 9). Tellingly, though, Goodnight's account transmogrifies the filmmaker from popular entertainer to artist – for the sole purpose of attacking his failure as a serious artist! Such high cultural assumptions about what constitutes a successful movie ignore, in fact, that *Jurassic Park* mobilises concerns in the public domain and dramatises a Pandora's Box that it does not reseal through narrative closure. In short, critics blame the text and/or its creator for their frustration at society's failure to mobilise around the discourses it embodies.

Feminism demonstrates forcefully how reading, not textual determination, ascribes meaning. *Jurassic Park* conventionally feminises nature, and monsters are her manifestation: 'a calculating, bloody-mouthed bitch, hell-bent on obliterating man as she obliterates every lesser species' (Place 1993: 9). Place's adjective, 'calculating', ignores the narrative's predication, verbalised through Malcolm, on chaos theory. Once again, questions of subjectivity arise in relation to comprehension and pleasure, and critics propose an implied spectator and imputed effects to suit predetermined analyses. This agenda prompts Mary Evans' assertion that Muldoon, whose last words are 'Clever girl!' to the raptor that has outwitted and is about to destroy him, is 'unrepentant to the last' in infantilising women (1994: 98) – as though he is not addressing, conventionally, a female animal (not a woman) – moreover one that, as a fellow hunter, he genuinely respects.

As Buckland (1999: 192) and King (2000: 42) both discuss, and refute, many critics dismiss *Jurassic Park* as a blockbuster lacking credible characterisation and narrative motivation. John Baxter even borrows Michael J. Arlen's phrase (1979), 'the Tyranny of the Visible', with reference to the cutting that has left no reason for the triceratops' sickness, even though the sequence featuring it remains (Baxter 1996: 379). Baxter's explanation, that the model's cost assured its inclusion, not only ignores that it shows benign as well as malignant results of Hammond's project and demonstrates chaos theory in operation; it also, perversely, considers surprising or reprehensible such a movie's concern with spectacular action and that its commercial proposition is to offer something never seen before (1996: 379–80). Only a critic concerned to prove that '*Close Encounters* marked the beginning of his decline as an artist, and, some argue, of American cinema' (1996: 170), could condemn Spielberg for movies that are predominantly cinematic. If ideas and narrative coherence were all that mattered, there was already Michael Crichton's book.

'Cola v. Zola': Jurassic Park as global phenomenon

Jurassic Park's cultural and economic significance lie in its function as a global blockbuster. Blockbuster status is a marketing approach combining a simple ('high concept') story premise and visual style in the narrative image with mass promotion and simultaneous opening (Wyatt 1994: 112). The strategy maximises revenue at the box office, where attendances might quickly decline, but also in secondary markets. Television sales, as well as merchandising and home entertainment releases, depend on recognition value, which in turn advertisers buy from broadcasters (Elsaesser & Buckland 1998: 2). Successful blockbusters keep the industry buoyant.

Matsushita, after spending $6 billion on MCA/Universal, had not had a single $100 million hit – unlike Sony, who had achieved higher grosses five times since buying Columbia Tristar for $1 billion less. Spielberg too, whose image was waning after several critical or commercial disappointments, needed a certain hit – although his well-known efficiency no doubt interested Universal, whose budgets were cut by 25 per cent in 1991 (Robinson 1993).

In France, a year after Euro-Disney opened with infrastructure – including a high-speed rail link – provided by the French government, *Jurassic Park* focused concerns around cultural imperialism. Debates over whether the General Agreement on Tariffs and Trade (GATT), under negotiation between the European Union and the US, should include audio-visual industries prompted emotive protests from French filmmakers. These centred on national cinema and government subsidy for cultural production, culminating a century-long rivalry between the two countries. In this context, most French reviewers concentrated almost exclusively on merchandising and marketing. The first week there saw record ticket sales. By the end of 1993 *Jurassic Park* had achieved half the audience of *Les Visiteurs*, a 'low-cultural' French-language farce promoted through long runs and word of mouth, but twice those of *Germinal*, an epic, star-studded Zola adaptation, heavily supported by politicians, massively promoted and the most expensive film yet made in France (Jackël & Neve 1998). '*Cola versus Zola*', quipped a pithy headline in the British *Economist* (1993: 78), defining the GATT's cultural dimension as predominantly a French concern.

However, Hollywood obtained 51 per cent of box office revenues outside North America by the 1990s, suggesting market forces might reduce the exclusively US-oriented cultural content. Whereas in the 1950s movies for the US domestic market were subsequently sold abroad, undercutting local production, now, Frederick Wasser argues, 'on a per capita basis the American viewer is of no more importance than any other member of the global audience' (1995: 424). Moreover, as Wasser suggests, fears of cultural imperialism caused many countries to impose import quotas, leading Hollywood to finance local projects that helped provide infrastructure to support, for example, European art cinema. In a further twist illustrating globalisation's intricacies, the French government-owned bank Crédit Lyonnais had encouraged European producers such as Dino DeLaurentiis in financing in advance 'Hollywood' movies by preselling distribution and exhibition rights. This was happening in 1981, exactly when France's Minister of Culture, Jack Lang, made an influential speech on American imperialism, the terms of which were taken up again a decade later (Wasser 1995: 431; Jackël & Neve 1998).

MCA/Universal, part of a Japanese corporation, arguably had no particular remit to promote American values. It is noteworthy, then, that Wasser considers they and rivals Sony had not 'visibly re-oriented marketing decisions away from the [US] domestic audience'; their primary business was electronics, not programming (1991: 434). Matsushita sold MCA/Universal in 1995 to cut losses. Nevertheless, *Jurassic Park*'s worldwide marketing was enormously profitable, possibly connected with its release coinciding with VHS video reaching saturation in prosperous markets. Just as 1950s Hollywood produced widescreen spectacle to challenge television, so *Jurassic Park*'s digital wonders as a media event provided an incentive to visit a movie theatre rather than await the video. At the same time, awareness of what became the world's most profitable movie guaranteed future videocassette and subsequent DVD sales, video takings having supplanted the box office for most titles (Wasko 2003: 125).

'*Jurassic Park* can be viewed as a global rather than a specifically American film', argue Anne Jackël and Brian Neve (1998: 3). In terms of British reception, they cite Linda Colley's observation that, whereas for modern France America provides the defining other – language, republicanism and post-War reconstruction have seen to this – Britain defines its nationality in relation to European Catholicism, especially France. (She points to the Great Exhibition of 1851 as a response to British fears concerning French industrial design (1994: 17–18, 25; 1995); coincidentally, this was the first theme park outing of dinosaurs.) Certainly the British Establishment warmly embraced *Jurassic Park*: it received a Royal première, followed by a Natural History Museum reception and esteemed figures such as William Rees-Mogg, former *Times* editor, were trotted out in newspaper features to recall their childhood fears (O'Kelly 1993). The conservative *Sunday Express* reviewed it as Spielberg's 'most important film' for using a blockbuster to raise serious issues around scientific ethics (Morley 1993). Such cultural legitimacy fostered a flurry of serious media interest in palaeontology, cloning and computer imaging.

Meanwhile, classification debates provided acres of free publicity. *Variety* reported that when the film opened, UIP, its British distributor, had amassed twelve scrapbooks of clippings following $1.9 million expenditure on promotion. This started seven months earlier with posters, featuring just the logo and the release date, and an enigmatic trailer, concluding: 'Spielberg – Jurassic Park – Next Summer.' A trickling to the press of production stills, then a second trailer and pasteboard cut-outs in theatres, followed by branded product launches and nationally circulated Film Education study packs on adaptations and the science of DNA, gradually focused the marketing from a general towards a youth audience. Three months before release, title awareness was 49 per cent and definite interest 25 per cent, a target normally attempted for the opening. A month later, awareness stood at 55 per cent with definite interest 33 per cent, more than three times the norm at that stage (Brady 1993: 64). The marketing, 'a spectacle in its own right' (Balides 2000: 150), focused more free publicity as the movie became a top UK news event for June, the month before its release (Brady 1993: 68). In fact, 91 per cent of Britons had heard of it two weeks before release, with 55 per cent expressing definite interest – unprecedented figures, achieved remarkably cheaply as advertising paid for by merchandise licensees had promoted the title at a cost many times greater than Universal's direct marketing (Baird 1998: 89). Unsurprisingly, *Jurassic Park* achieved a British three-day opening record. Similar results occurred worldwide. It became, for example, India and Pakistan's most successful Western film ever (Baird 1998: 88-9).

Following a 2,842-screen US opening, *Jurassic Park* broke first-weekend records. A year after release, 98 per cent of US adults had encountered the title 25.2 times. On a $56 million budget, expanded to $65 million as special effects developed, and $20 million initial P&A, the movie grossed $916 million worldwide before *The Lost World*'s release, with $1 billion additionally from official merchandising of 5,000 products (Baxter 1996: 376; Balides 2000: 139, 149). Spielberg reportedly earned $250 million from a profits share – 'the largest sum any individual has ever made from one movie' (Perry 1998: 82). As a comparison, the *E.T.* logo appeared originally on 50 licensed products, while marketing *Jaws* had depended on begging companies to use the logo, with little of the merchandising profits returning to the studio (Baxter 1996: 163).

Despite criticism for allegedly elevating effects over characterisation, for some the movie confirmed Spielberg's status as 'an undoubted auteur' (Wollen 1993: 9). Kim Newman neatly delineated its continuity with Spielberg's previous work:

> The paring-down of a monster best-seller into a suspense machine (*Jaws*); the tackling of a popular-science childhood sense of wonder perennial with state-of-the-art effects that re-imagine 1950s B-science fiction (*Close Encounters of the Third Kind*); the all-action jungle adventure littered with incredible perils

and gruesome deaths (*Raiders of the Lost Ark*); and big-eyed creatures who range from beatifically benevolent to toothily murderous (*Gremlins, E. T.*). (Quoted in Baxter 1996: 373)

Manipulative craftsman or cinematic artist, *Jurassic Park* restored Spielberg's prof-essional reputation ready for *Schindler's List*, filmed during *Jurassic Park*'s post-production.

CHAPTER SIXTEEN

Schindler's List: darkness visible

During the ghetto liquidation scene in *Schindler's List*, violence increases and intensifies beyond virtually anything previously imagined in mainstream cinema. A storm trooper plays piano in a darkened room. Fellow officers appear. 'Bach?' inquires one. 'Mozart', insists his companion. The narrative halts to ponder coexistence of destructive evil with sublime creativity in the same culture – or species, depending on your position.

To some, this is the film's intellectual and moral core, cinematic realisation of problems theorists such as George Steiner had been examining for half a century. Others consider it banal. As will become apparent, this was among many issues that polarised responses. What commentators overlooked, however, is that the slightly jangling piano begins simultaneously with stroboscopic flashes from off-screen machine-gun fire. In parts the sequence, which echoes a Cossack attack in Eisenstein's *Strike* (1925) (Louvish 1994: 14), flickers like a silent movie. Even in Spielberg's most earnest, starkly realist mode, self-reflexivity and intertextuality remain overt. This observation – which might appear inappropriately formalist, given the events portrayed – is crucial in understanding *Schindler's List*, widely perceived as a break with the director's previous work, and the furore it prompted.

Biographical agenda setting

Critics and 'writers, activists, and politicians who usually don't take films seriously' (Hansen 1997: 77), set their agenda well in advance. Before release, the film 'attracted more press comment than any other in memory' (Anon. 1994a: 24). Reception consequently amplified discourses pre-existing what was on-screen. If any film demonstrates that audiences construct meaning within their own discursive formations, *Schindler's List* does. But the subject matter's enormity and the film's status as event raised the stakes. *Schindler's List* was Hollywood's first direct visualisation of the Holocaust *and* the latest offering from the maker of *Jurassic Park*, the biggest-grossing film in history following a massive campaign. Coinciding with the Holocaust's fiftieth anniversary, *Schindler's List* catalysed arguments surrounding the new Holocaust Memorial Museum in Washington D.C., resurgent neo-fascism and attempted genocide around the world, and the impetus such events gave to recording a dwindling number of survivors' testimony.

Schindler's List was significant as Holocaust remembrance if only because, as a Spielberg movie, it had international reach. Yet, because it drew responses from political and religious leaders and intellectuals from outside both academic film studies and popular reviewing, the argument is frequently prejudiced and impressionistic, ignoring cinematic specificity.

Spielberg partly established the context, and tone, for many of the attacks – as much against him as the film. Imperiously declaring, 'If it takes my name to get people to [see *Schindler's List*], so be it' (quoted in Schleier 1994: 13), he suggested the project might not have been viable without him and implied higher aspirations than 'mere' entertainment. Certainly a black-and-white film, over three hours long and without major stars, seemed unlikely to appeal to youthful blockbuster audiences, 60 per cent of whom were unaware of the Holocaust (Baxter 1996: 385). Publicity portrayed Spielberg, who – it was understood at the time – waived his profits until the movie broke even, as pursuing a mission. Unsurprisingly, the second wealthiest show business personality – Oprah Winfrey earned more (Baxter 1996: 406–7) – was likened to Oskar Schindler, the playboy who abandoned profiteering for a good cause. Both possess what Schindler (Liam Neeson) in the movie calls flair for 'presentation'. If Spielberg the showman was audacious enough to make a film that, Amblin's promotion asserted, sought to save lives, his awareness of his power mirrored Schindler's. Spielberg himself made the comparison that 'Schindler played Krakow ... Berlin, the way agents play Hollywood' ('*Schindler's List* and the Holocaust' video).

Schindler's redemption paralleled Spielberg's transformation from shallow crowd-pleaser to serious Jewish artist. Promotion and interviews stressed his return to ethnic roots and newfound faith. As well as identification with Schindler, Spielberg repeatedly spoke of his own anti-Semitic experiences, thereby identifying himself, a descendant of German Jews, with Holocaust victims (Anon. 1993a: B1; 1993b: 2–3).

Conflation of text and author is important for my present argument because it posited biographical interpretation before anyone had seen the film. (Not for the first time: much was made of links between *Close Encounters*, *E.T.* and Spielberg's suburban upbringing.) This pre-empted auteur-structuralist reading, which, I contend, indicates continuity with Spielberg's earlier work.

Premiere was typical in describing *Schindler's List* as 'different from anything Spielberg has done before, as far from the "movie" movie universe of *Jaws* as it could possibly be' (Anon. 1994b: 66). Equating seriousness, solemnity and quality, industry names finally recognised Spielberg, bestowing Academy Awards 'at the precise moment that [media] discourse ... was dissociating him from the practices of Hollywood' (Zelizer 1997: 26).

Spielberg's new identities – serious filmmaker, practising Jew, victims' spokesperson (also father, as he spoke repeatedly of maturity gained through parenthood) – exposed him and the film as hostages to fortune. Aware of his reputation as a lightweight sentimentalist, the director, usually reticent in personal dealings with the media, worked hard to establish credentials before and after the movie's production. Largely he succeeded: 'what is hard to fathom, even to believe, is how the maker of such popular and entertaining movies has been transmogrified into the director of such a profound, intelligent and moving film' (Anon. 1994c: 23). Taking the offensive, though, he enabled the film to be pre-judged, prompting doubts about his appropriateness and also Hollywood's to deal with its subject. Partly because of a protocol error when Amblin sought permission to film at Auschwitz from the Polish government instead of Jewish leaders and museum authorities, the World Jewish Congress made a well-publicised complaint to Poland's ambassador to the US about a prospective 'Disney' Shoah and the camp becoming 'a Hollywood backlot'. Access was denied, although six features and several documentaries had been made there (Baxter 1996: 386).

Biographical auteurism tempered many responses. Spielberg was at best interested in film for film's sake, or more cynically courting respectability by changing his image. (David Thomson (1994) suggests the real Schindler drafted his list for no more noble reason than to curry Allied favour once Germany's defeat became inevitable, and insinuates *Schindler's List* was Spielberg's similar bid for Academy Awards after *Jurassic Park*.) Many compared Spielberg with French journalist Claude Lanzmann, whose nine-hour documentary *Shoah* (1985), comprising mainly interviews and refusing both dramatisation and archive material, they lauded as driven purely by pursuit of truth. Lanzmann made negative comments on *Schindler's List* that are considered in due course; others repeated these, particularly in Israel where 'vitriolic' and 'aggressive' reactions appeared, containing 'argumentation totally unrelated to the film', often before their authors had seen it (Bresheeth 1997: 200). Competitiveness between Israel and the US over Holocaust 'ownership' partly motivated this. Others, ironically, expressed Zionist mistrust of Diaspora Jews; historian and journalist Tom Segev attacked Spielberg as the American who 'stole our Shoah' (quoted in Loshitzky 1997: 8). In Germany, where largely favourable reactions provided one focus for the reunified nation to confront its past as the fiftieth anniversary of Victory in Europe approached, considerable resentment, couched as opposition to cultural imperialism, attached to an American telling the story. This was compensated for by almost obsessive dwelling upon his Jewishness, which never featured in media responses to Spielberg's earlier work, and constantly referred to his pride in an identity hitherto disowned. Arguably this answered to newfound confidence in German identity after longstanding shame, and desires to demonstrate rapprochement with Jewishness and repudiate neo-Nazism (see Weissberg 1994: 184).

Others refused to acknowledge any change and used Spielberg's former image to disparage *Schindler's List*. One academic baldly stated her premise: 'Unfortunately Spielberg is not a great thinker' (Jacobowitz 1994: 7). Thomson described *Schindler's*

List as 'the most moving film I have ever seen – I cried more than I ever did at *The Courage of Lassie, The Glenn Miller Story, The Miracle Worker* or *Field of Dreams*', aligning it with old-fashioned sentimental or trivial tear-jerkers (1994: 45). A recurrent strategy was to stress the choice of an *exceptional* story, which deflects attention from the catastrophe in favour of 'a feel-good Holocaust film' (Horowitz 1997: 135). *Jurassic Park* inevitably prompted cracks such as Segev dubbing *Schindler's List* 'Spielberg's Holocaust Park' (see Corliss 1994: 110). Doubts existed about *any* Hollywood involvement, with its pleasurable emphases on glamour, spectacle, individualism and narrative closure, although not always expressed as forcefully as Segev's:

> In a TV interview, Spielberg came up with the following: 'This movie is my second Bar Mitzvah!' Happy birthday to you Spielberg; you did not invest 24 million dollars in your Bar Mitzvah. You invested this money in order to make a profit, as in *E.T.* and *Jurassic Park*, and that's legitimate. Just spare us the bullshit! (Quoted in Bresheeth 1997: 201)

To which one might reply – while sharing the last sentiment – if profitability were paramount surely a film about the Holocaust would be the last project to pursue. (For the record, the film was remarkably profitable and Spielberg, unwilling to keep 'blood money', started the Righteous Persons Foundation with his share (Dubner 1999: 17).)

As always, those moved to write about *Schindler's List* possess personal or political biases, although in this instance discourses around identity and loss enmeshed many commentaries, making them literally a matter of life and death. Retaining that thought, issues raised by Lanzmann's objection deserve consideration.

Representing the unrepresentable

Two crucial questions, particularly among Jewish critics, are whether the Holocaust *should* be represented and whether it *can* be. The first originates in the Second Commandment, prohibiting graven images (Exodus 20.4), but has become snarled onto the second thanks to Theodor Adorno's comment (1973) that poetry is impossible since Auschwitz, which some interpret literally as proscribing any artistic attempt to render the experience of the camps. As Haim Bresheeth points out, the Commandment's strict interpretation has led to under-emphasis on visual representation in Jewish tradition, leaving 'the Word as the main artistic and expressive domain' (1997: 199). Moreover, Israel withheld pictorial records of the Holocaust for longer than written documents and oral accounts; visual images were deemed inherently more shocking. Absence of visual heritage, together with Adorno's political championing of high art over what he saw as debased and misleading popular culture, hardly constituted a receptive climate for Spielberg's film.

Silence was a preferred aesthetic response. Documentary was permissible because naïve mimetic realism denied it constituted 'representation'. Lanzmann rightly challenged this, recognising that any image entails selection grounded in the filmmaker's subjectivity and any sequence unavoidably constructs a discourse. Furthermore,

Lanzmann refused to utilise historical footage as, far from neutral evidence, it always incorporated a viewpoint, whether anti-Semitic or of Jews' victimisation against which the Allies appear heroic saviours. Even amateur footage by German soldiers, rather than official propaganda, would unacceptably inscribe ideology. Instead, Lanzmann recorded long, probing, often painful, interviews with survivors, guards, officials and witnesses, insisting authentic discourse existed only in first-hand memories. Truth lay in gestures and expressions that inflected the primacy of the Word; cutaways to deserted railway tracks and empty buildings encouraged reflection upon the testimony.

How mainstream realism could, pragmatically, represent conditions of the camps authentically is difficult to imagine, notwithstanding ethics, taste and the dominant ideology of visual pleasure. As John Slavin states, 'The Holocaust defies imaginative comprehension' yet possesses 'monumentality' that 'demands ... we take account of it but which by its nihilistic nature and comprehensiveness immediately transforms all artistic representations, relying as they do on non-contextual elements of aesthetic association, into kitsch' (1994: 5). Objections that *Schindler's List*'s prisoners looked healthy and well-fed (Kurzweil 1994: 202; White 1994: 5) – insurmountable if mimetic realism is required, as actors appear naked – need setting against the impossibility of filming anything adequate to Primo Levi's description of his liberation from Auschwitz: 'Ragged, decrepit, skeleton-like patients at all able to move dragged themselves everywhere on the frozen soil, like an invasion of worms' (1987: 164). Survivors have likened their experience to being on another planet (Louvish 1994: 15).

But Auschwitz was *not* another planet. If descriptions such as Levi's define 'the limits of representation' (see Friedlander 1992), that does not imply meaning should not be sought in events and circumstances that created them, perpetrated upon and by human beings like ourselves. As one writer responded to Lanzmann, if atrocities are incommunicable there nevertheless remains a duty to communicate them, 'if one day we want to put together an adequate fresco of the terrible past, in order to draw a lesson from it for the future' (Memmi 1994: 7). Art explores meaning and seeks understanding differently from assembling facts. Furthermore, the feature film/documentary dichotomy is false because, as Lanzmann would concede, his film *constructs* representations – as must any expression of memory. Conventions bind, however Lanzmann tries to subvert or escape them: in selecting interviewees; composing, lighting and filming them; their choice of words; asking questions; refusing to cut away at emotional moments; selecting and sequencing; and so on. No absolute reason precludes attempting to mould mainstream cinematic conventions to voice discourses of real-life horror, provided facts are respected.

Barbie Zelizer has mooted that mistrusting popular mediations inadvertently encourages Holocaust denial. Acceding to demands for texts that efface their constructedness, that present themselves as documentary evidence, without which deniers can claim events never happened, 'we have let the possibility that there could – and should – be more than one mode of historical retelling fade into the background' (1997: 23). The crux is, the majority who praised *Schindler's List*, as well as detractors, judged it as truth, not representation, fact, not narrative.

If Lanzmann and others insisted 'any [dramatised] film true to the subject would be unwatchable' (Anon. 1994a: 24), most critics, sometimes grudgingly, praised

Spielberg's achievement. Ongoing debates hinge upon realism. 'Missing from the film', argues Sara R. Horowitz, 'is a sense of the daily attrition of hunger, disease, the numbing omnipresence of death, the "filthy louse" that even Adam Czerniakow, eldest in the Warsaw ghetto, complained of finding on his shirt' – details that inform other cinematic versions (1997: 122). This demands different emphasis from Spielberg's. But representation necessitates selection. Against Horowitz's complaints consider Janina Bauman, who has published her Warsaw ghetto memoirs and sought to correct the impression of community polarisation between

> starving and homeless people on the streets, and very rich Jews who made fortunes by all kinds of transactions with Germans and Poles ... There was a very big class of people who neither starved nor got rich, but who, like myself, just lived their daily life ... It was a hard life, it was vegetation, not life. But for the first twenty months in the ghetto we were not dying. (1994: 38)

This does not deny Horowitz's description, yet illustrates how any account is partial. Faced with the concept and mind-numbing statistics of the Final Solution – eleven million dead, over six million Jewish – alternatives are to accept silence as the proper response, or tell stories that, however inadequately, convey the material experience of events.

Silence presents a problem: at what figure do statistics become sufficiently obscene to invoke the taboo? Are there smaller numbers of deaths that are acceptable to dramatise? My question is obscene, like Nazi logic, reducing suffering to arithmetic. Yet if the story is told, whose version? (This crops up repeatedly in relation to *Schindler's List*, which foregrounds survivors, not gas chamber victims, and a good German's deeds.) As for the 'dirty louse', this again involves perspective. *Empire of the Sun* portrayed bad food, sickness, demoralisation and death, and in one sequence in *Schindler's List*, Schindler's accountant, Itzhak Stern (Ben Kingsley), approaches him with his hand on his head to warn guards he carries lice. Spielberg understands the conditions of the camps. Not detailing them was a creative decision, not ignorance. More importantly, they are the everyday reality of millions during any historical period, not unique to the Holocaust. What, after all, is a louse epidemic compared to systematic genocide? Lice, although real, stand for degradation – hence Horowitz's allusion. *Schindler's List* embraces bigger issues. Some critics deem Spielberg wise not to linger on pain and suffering, and suggest, now he has broken the taboo, the way is open for others to catalogue atrocities. 'If the anger at *Schindler's List* is as intense as it was, one can only imagine what storm would be created by a similar attempt at representing that level of human misery which he avoided touching directly' (Bresheeth 1997: 210).

Nevertheless, numerous objectors did perceive Hollywood vulgarisation. This almost invariably linked to Spielberg's reputation. Complaints concern supposed lack of ambiguity (which seem to overlook entirely uncertainty over Schindler's motivation as well as criteria for inclusion on Stern's initial list); also the ending, which allegedly elevates self-preservation above other values in a particularly American way (even though the Jews are passive recipients – another criticised aspect – of Schindler's efforts, putting himself at risk, on their behalf). Ultimately, 'the message of "water not gas" is the film's ironic and sentimental point of closure: "He who saves one life, saves the world entire"' (Cheyette 1997: 233). To regard that Talmudic verse as either ironic or sentimental, I suggest, again reduces suffering to abstraction; if it does not matter that Schindler saved 1,100 lives the absurd corollary is it matters not that millions died, for by such logic individual lives lack value. To save one life is an achievement; how much more remarkable, then, to save 1,100. So determined are some critics to attack Spielberg, rhetoric allows free and easy play with statistics which, after all, if representation is at stake, themselves represent actual lives and deaths. The article calling *Schindler's List* 'a feel-good Holocaust film' continues, 'and not because Schindler ultimately saves the lives of 1,500 Jews' (Horowitz 1997: 135). What makes this offensive, in blithely writing off 400 obscenely cruel killings to score a debating point – and it's not an isolated example: Yosefa Loshitzky derogates Schindler's 'rescue of a handful of Jews' (1997: 6), an expression used also by Omer Bartov (1997: 42) – is failure to recognise the film's effort to acknowledge how easily lives become statistics. Shortly after 10,000 bodies are exhumed and incinerated (as the caption informs), Stern – unaware of Schindler's intentions – tells him his list has reached '850, give or take.' 'Give or take *what?*' snaps Schindler. 'Stern, count them! *How many?*'

Yet the numbers game works oppositely, also against Spielberg, who allegedly sacrifices individual human truth for the values of the historical epic:

> ... more Jews, more shoes, more trains, more Holocaust. The memories get mixed into a large impersonal dough of the universal Jew with a million faces and names but not a single biography ... a single diary of one Anne Frank is more shocking as a human document than 1,100 names without embodiment. The many zeroes carefully collected throughout the film turn – with no one intending this – into human zeroes, faceless entities. (Idan Lando, quoted in Bresheeth 1997: 203)

Arguments about scale are finally the same as whether focusing on an anomaly falsifies history. 'They miss the fundamental fact that the movie interprets the mass experience of Jewish oppression. It's not a story of individual suffering' (White 1994: 56). The final caption, superimposed over the pavement made from Jewish gravestones, dedicates the film to 'the more than six million Jews murdered'. Nor is it exclusively 'about' the Holocaust. Its interest is Schindler and whether his actions teach anything, whether hope is recoverable from the edge of darkness.

Concentrating on Schindler, however, does not whitewash other Nazis, as some claim (Schemo 1994: 6E), because he is *not* committed to the Reich – he ostentatiously kisses Jews, he intentionally supplies faulty shells – and because, as the film stresses in his scene with a fellow manufacturer, others who could have followed his example did not. Yet 'the attempt of a mass-audience movie to illustrate the full panorama of genocide in all its bureaucratic horror obviously takes the film beyond the narrower character-based focus of Keneally's novel' and answers charges that Spielberg has offered a Holocaust theme park (Cheyette 1997: 229). Wide-angle, hand-held cameras place the spectator amid chaotic crowds, permitting involvement with confusion and panic. Interspersed high-angle shots, such as Schindler's viewing the liquidation, or other expansive long shots multiply, then further multiply, individual fear and helplessness and include random brutality away from centre frame, at the edge of spectatorial consciousness. Far from functioning as spectacle, inducing mastery, epic shots challenge unbelief, create distance for reflection, and emphasise the events' unimaginable scale.

Hollywood Holocaust

Spielberg's Hollywood sensibility, for detractors his weakness, is precisely what enables *Schindler's List* to balance the individual and the mass. As Armond White explains,

> A single mother separated from a child is usual ... But 200 mothers running after their abducted children belongs to a most powerful artistic vision ... Spielberg has successfully reimagined the terror of the Holocaust in an original way. In that scene, the literal rush of emotion kills you without the nicety of taste and 'truth'. It is passion made essential, kinetic, made into cinema. (1994: 55)

Thomas Elsaesser too argues that 'the list' personalises the Jews – repeatedly naming some enables recognition, giving 'each the dignity of an individual fate' – and renders their experience collective (1996: 163). Also, he suggests, Spielberg uses Hollywood suspense and melodrama to elicit authentic understanding. In Auschwitz – showing what, in actuality, happened when three hundred women and children given showers thought they were being gassed – the film elicits horror by obliging the spectator 'to infer what cannot be shown' (1996: 162). It nevertheless acknowledges what the women themselves know, that their case *was* exceptional, in point-of-view shots showing columns of people tramping into bunkers intercut with a chimney belching smoke.

Similarly, relief when Schindler prevents Stern's transportation is exploited to dramatic and didactic effect through pure Hollywood principles, creating something similar to what Robin Wood (discussing *Strangers on a Train*) terms 'the Hitchcock spectator trap' (1989: 94). The official with whom Schindler altercates clutches a list; Stern is one of many. Stern escapes fortuitously, similarly to how Leo Pfefferberg later survives only because Amon Goeth (Ralph Fiennes), the commandant, recognises his mechanic lined up for extermination. The film highlights such arbitrariness by following with momentary comedy the suspense of Stern's last-minute rescue, increased by exasperation at uncooperative bureaucrats. Schindler asks Stern: 'What if I got here five minutes later? Then where would I be?' This light tone, given the train's destination, exemplifies what perturbs the film's opponents, although it progresses Schindler's characterisation. By contrast, the situation's enormity strikes home in the next shot, which tracks past mounds of property from suitcases Jews have been deceived into leaving. Spielberg follows the Hollywood rule of three, whereby important information is suggested subtly, then confirmed for the average audience member, and finally repeated. Here the convention works cumulatively, as the spectator realises the huge piles' meaning, sees countless framed photographs to impart a human dimension to the abstract metonym, and finally confronts a box of teeth with fillings emptied before a jeweller. Those who claim Stern's escape typifies determination to make a happy movie at the expense of Hitler's victims are inattentive or wilfully obtuse.

Despite alleged differences, Spielberg acknowledges Lanzmann in visual counterparts for verbal descriptions in *Shoah*, and by incorporating cinematic allusions that confirm what the earlier film's champions often deny – that it consists in material discourse. When Mila Pfefferberg (Adi Nitzan) sees, from the cattle wagon, a child making a cutthroat gesture – an image that becomes generalised, removed from her enunciation as a subjective shot, by slow-motion repetition from a different angle outside the train – this echoes an old Pole in *Shoah* who describes making the same sign to convey to Jews their fate. Several critics point out how *Schindler's List*'s opening, which dwells on empty chairs after the praying family disappear, evokes when a *Shoah* interviewee, distressed by recollections, clambers out of shot and Lanzmann continues filming. (Not inconceivably, given Spielberg's intertextual practice elsewhere, this is double allusion: in *High Noon* (1952), an analogous account of an individual stand against oppression, Gary Cooper's sheriff hears the Judge, folding away an American flag, liken Frank Miller's reign of terror to an ancient Athenian tyranny, and the camera tracks in on a chair, a metonym for the returning outlaw.) Bryan Cheyette notes that the end of *Schindler's List*, when real *Schindlerjuden* appear alongside their cinematic embodiments – now actors in contemporary dress – opens a gap between the past and its representation that underscores the same concerns as *Shoah*; and that

> Other artistic techniques, taken wholesale from *Shoah*, include the repeated references to the everyday machinery of genocide – typewriters, lists, tables, chairs, endless queues – which are eventually filled with dread, not unlike the constant shots of railway lines in *Shoah*. (1997: 231)

In the final analysis there can be no reconciliation between people, all too conscious of the Holocaust, for whom representation is taboo and those for whom, like Spielberg, there is moral imperative to spread knowledge in accessible form among audiences who have never heard of *Shoah*, would not sit through nine hours of talking heads if they had, and may well be unaware of the Holocaust itself. Primo Levi feared screen versions were replacing personal memories, overwriting 'the scar of remembrance' (quoted in Young 1994: 185), and undoubtedly from this perspective Spielberg's appropriation of *Shoah*'s images, however well intentioned, is a travesty. Spielberg's choice of monochrome and, in key sequences, newsreel-style cinematography, intended to make the film look like an authentic image of the 1940s, raises the danger that for popular audiences, worldwide reach will render its Holocaust definitive. Jean-François Lyotard argues, 'Whenever one represents, one inscribes in memory and this might seem a good defence against forgetting. It is, I believe, just the opposite. Only that which has been inscribed can, in the current sense of the term, be forgotten, because it has been effaced' (1990: 26). Imposing onto memory shape (such as narrative) and objective form (such as images in the public domain), representation exorcises, subsuming personal immediacy that guarantees authenticity. The problem, of course, is what happens to memory not recorded. It dies with its possessor.

Thomas Elsaesser explains how Spielberg's and the 'European' versions of the Holocaust inhabit different 'master-narratives':

> Spielberg ... gives a surprisingly literal reading to 'whoever saves one life saves mankind' for he has dared to 'count' and 'reckon' the Schindler Jews not against those who perished, but by the number of their descendants (at the end, Stern comforts Schindler, who has broken down because he feels he could have done more, by insisting that because of him 'there will be generations') ... Spielberg accepts the principle that the one can represent the many, that the part can stand for the whole. *Shoah* is based, explicitly and emphatically, on the exactly opposite premise: that no one can stand in for anyone else, no one can speak for anyone else. (1996: 178)

Historiography

Schindler's List partakes in bigger historiographical debates, epitomised in conflicting terminology: Holocaust ('Sacrifice'), Shoah ('Great Catastrophe'), Chuban ('Destruction'), Final Solution (the Nazi euphemism). The film is well researched, with a Jewish tradition consultant who experienced Auschwitz and employing Pfefferberg (the survivor who introduced Thomas Keneally to Schindler's story) as special consultant, and was produced by a survivor of the camps. Its mise-en-scène replicates historical images (such as famous photographs: an orthodox Jew shorn of his locks in the street, a prisoner with a sign around his neck, kneeling, hands aloft), defensible as visually accurate. More importantly, though, *Schindler's List* coincided with a transition from personal to 'collective, manufactured' memory as remaining survivors succumbed to age (Loshitzky 1997: 3). Whose memories would be recorded, how, and by whom, before disappearing forever? *Shoah* was one principled intervention. As a record of first-hand accounts, it tends to be placed above *Schindler's List* in a hierarchy from academic historiography, down through print journalism, documentary film and television, then novels, to popular entertainment. As a result, the reality against which critics frequently judge *Schindler's List* conflates with 'official' academic history. This too is a construct, its authority dependent on informed consensus, and so contestable. History mediates the present as much as the past. Contemporary struggles overdetermine Holocaust writing, many of which inform debates around *Schindler's List*, even if most filmgoers are oblivious to them (see Loshitzky 1997). Attempts to maintain separation between 'serious' history and 'mere' entertainment, on grounds that one is inherently more reliable, are prejudiced. They perpetuate ideological distinction between work (in this instance, 'real' history) and leisure to invoke that familiar chimera, the passive cinemagoer. Nevertheless, although many who criticise *Schindler's List*'s history are not them-selves film specialists, there is nothing passive about their engagement.

Because most filmgoers know little about the Holocaust and are unlikely to turn to professional historians after seeing the film, it does matter whether Spielberg gets it right. But if *Schindler's List* becomes definitive for the foreseeable future, it is as important to judge its utility as its minute accuracy. Bartov argues:

We cannot blame it for not showing people actually being gassed, but only for showing them *not* being gassed; we cannot blame it for not showing the emaciated bodies of concentration camp inmates, but only for showing us the attractive, healthy naked bodies of young actresses whose shorn hair strangely resembles current fashions. (1997: 50)

Although disingenuous (not all the actresses *are* young), the point is valid. But if *Schindler's List* is to have the effect its makers intend – 'you go to this movie to be informed and to be changed, I hope', wrote Spielberg in an educational guide – emotional realism is as important as literal verisimilitude (and no less harrowing for audiences with Hollywood expectations). Making virtue of necessity, one could argue that the Jews' 'normal' appearance in *Schindler's List* not only retains some human dignity – the real degradation might cause audiences to recoil or leave the theatre – but also encourages identification to give meaning to the enormity of what happened, compared with the distancing effect of seeing the victims as abject, pitiable, Other.

Any historical account embodies a point-of-view. Even museums or preserved sites, where artefacts 'speak for themselves' and visitors move freely, impose 'a more or less coherent and didactic narrative … by means of their organisation, selection, captions, and so forth', the more insidious for seeming invisible (Bartov 1997: 57). Lanzmann's 'pure' filmmaking, apart from inevitable processes of mediation, is less dispassionate than supporters claim:

It seems that he sought witnesses who were both strong enough to testify at some length and coherence, and weak enough to finally break down in front of the camera under the incessant pressure of his questions, thereby providing his viewers with the personal touch he derides in Spielberg's film. (Bartov 1997: 55)

Temporal and spatial constraints render any representation partial. Lanzmann's version, five times longer than the average feature, gets no closer to the full story of the millions dead than *Schindler's List*, which also articulates survivors' experience. Anti-commercial rhetoric, resulting in a film only researchers or a coterie of festival delegates will see, silences the discourse more than a different choice of medium might have done, such as a conventional-length film, television series or book.

From a different position, akin to feminist historiography, exclusion from Keneally's novel and Spielberg's movie of Emilie Schindler's efforts has attracted criticism. This demonstrates again the impossibility of narrating entire truth: 'Spielberg made a film about the Holocaust, not about a marriage' (Rabinovitch 1994: 14). Nevertheless, Spielberg's film created interest in Emilie, prompting her autobiography. History develops, in dialogue with what is already inscribed, filling absences, modifying perceived biases, always open to contestation – never a stable, finite, self-evident body of facts prior to 'truthful' or 'distorted' presentation. Seemingly deadlocked, irreconcilable opposition between *Schindler's List* and those who assert representational impossibility is productive, maintaining space for discourse around events themselves and memorialisation.

If contention centres partly on unease about fictionalisation as opposed to raw 'truth', and connected concerns about single events, perhaps untypical, standing for larger tendencies, ideally representation would avoid selection and interpretation altogether. It would be decentred from character, conventional structure, preferred subject position, and other contingencies of limited space and time. That is effectively what Spielberg, 'with little public fanfare', has attempted in creating a multimedia archive of testimonies, the Survivors of the Shoah Visual History Foundation, part-funded by $6 million from his profits (Usborne 1996: 15). Video-recorded interviews with over 50,000 Holocaust survivors and other Jewish victims of persecution are being created alongside text, images and graphics such as maps, to be accessed on CD-ROM and, if tamper prevention can be perfected, on-line. 'Visitors' can navigate their own journeys, create authentic but possibly unique narratives, for example by requesting information about a certain day in a specific camp or the fate of a particular town's citizens, which the system customises accordingly. The project has attracted resentment and animosity from scholars and archivists, concerned that Spielberg's financial clout has led to him monopolising Holocaust memory with concomitant risk of distorting history into voyeuristic entertainment. They fear trivialisation as users surf, clicking from survivor to survivor without understanding the context (Shatz & Quart 1996).

We need master narratives, then, to avoid atomising experience. Individual testimonies require preservation as primary information about events and their impact on lives, a lesson for future generations, a humanitarian gesture towards the witnesses, and evidence against deniers. Yet, cumulatively, similar sufferings narrated repeatedly do not, of themselves, increase understanding, but do confirm and emphasise the scale of the abomination.

Whose stereotypes?

Insoluble arguments over representation foreground questions of history's 'owner-ship'. Nowhere is this more apparent than in totally contradictory, and deeply prejudiced, responses to representation of Jews in *Schindler's List*.

Bartov refers to the process discussed in relation to *Raiders of the Lost Ark*, whereby Hollywood typically 'enhance[s] ... the hero's image by a diminution of all other characters, apart, of course, from the villain' (1997: 48). That is fair comment, identifying one convention by which Spielberg's version is allegedly compromised. However, it does not follow that *Schindler's List* represents the Holocaust through German eyes, reducing Jews to offensive stereotypes (a common claim, mainly from Jewish critics: see Jacobowitz 1994; Kuspit 1994; Rosenzweig 1994). Although narrative agency rests conventionally with Schindler and Goeth as hero and villain, in representational terms that is not unreasonable as they embody where power to control events actually lay. The difficulty, it appears, is with enunciation and distribution of subjectivity.

The film constructs four main subject positions through interwoven narratives and stylistic pastiche. These are, first, 'dominant specularity' (MacCabe 1981: 221) – illusory mastery created by the narrative structure, promising closure – together with elements of the spectator's discursive formation such as prior knowledge of the outcome of the war and, from the narrative image, the outline of Schindler's deeds. 'Documentary' aspects reinforce this, particularly written captions, which imply objectivity, distance, everything already known and over, the present absence of 'the imaginary signifier'. In tension with these is secondary identification with characters, structured through cinematography, editing and narrative. This alternates mainly between various Jewish characters and Schindler. A further position, offered strategically and very briefly, upon which some critics focus disproportionately, is Goeth's. Specifically, the spectator comes close to sharing Goeth's vision as a telephoto lens pans jerkily across the camp when he shoots prisoners with a rifle. However, the position is not identical, as the view through his telescopic sight is not replicated with the usual iris shot containing calibrated cross hairs (as in marksmen's points-of-view in *The Sugarland Express*, Jones' inspection through the theodolite in *Raiders of the Lost Ark* and subsequent alignment with snipers in *Saving Private Ryan*). The effect is to show Goeth's view of death – random, distant, impersonal, a matter of sport – and to emphasise his power, rather than solicit identification with his pleasure, from which a subtle but crucial separation is maintained. Consequently, repulsion at his evil is redoubled. The partial identification prevents the crude Manicheanism with which the film has been charged (Cheyette 1997: 236). By coming close to Goeth, the comforting option of regarding Nazis as essentially different, mysteriously other, is troubled in a Hitchcockian manner. The scene, alluding to Peter Bogdanovich's *Targets* (1968), exploits American fears of arbitrary killing (Farrar 1994: 39). It also resonates withTerrence Malick's *Badlands* (1973) when Goeth places the rifle behind his neck, crucifix-style. This image releases the partial identification, by stressing the film's textuality and relating Goeth to familiar cinematic psychopaths, and ironises the Nazis' self-image as a superior Christian culture, a point overlooked by critics who complain that Schindler's blessing and prayer at the Armistice represent containment of Judaism by a Messianic saviour (Horowitz 1997: 125). *Schindler's List* does *not* trade in Manichean certainties.

Howard Jacobson wishes 'the Jews weren't all so comely of countenance, so uniformly dove-eyed ' (1994: 19), and Thomson finds them, 'without exception, decent, noble, generous, saintly, and very beautiful' (1994: 46). Strange, then, that to Bartov they appear 'a mass of physically small, emotionally confused, frantic, almost featureless Jews', although he describes the shower scene as 'a mass of attractive, frightened, naked women' (1997: 49), thereby remarkably considering a featureless mass attractive. Like others, he argues the Jews contrast with Schindler and Goeth, 'tall, handsome Aryans'; even though Schindler is notably taller than Goeth in two-shots, the cast comprises numerous tall Jews, and low angles in Schindler's scenes with Stern cause the latter to dominate alternate framings. Cheyette concludes: 'Much potential crassness is eschewed by the welcome lack of individualisation of the mass of Jews' (1994: 18). Conversely, Horowitz concentrates on the investors Schindler meets as – typically of how she thinks the film represents Jews –

straight out of a Nazi propaganda poster on eugenics and racial science. One appears apelike, with a large jaw covered in stubble. Dishevelled, large-nosed and unkempt, the Jews contrast negatively with Schindler's clean good looks, as the short stature of the Jews contrasts negatively with Schindler's towering height. (1997: 126)

Horowitz overlooks that these characters reappear in Schindler's factory, often in crowds embracing various physical types. She notes that, as the spectator shares Schindler's gaze, they 'mutter in Yiddish, the "secret" language ... a trope for the otherness of the Jew' (ibid.). This demonstrates fanatical hypersensitivity. In what language would she expect Eastern European businessmen to discuss, before the person who made it, a suspicious proposal, at a time when Jews were banned from transactions? (Moreover, the SS speak German without subtitles during the liquidation.) What kind of comments regarding authenticity would appear if the film overlooked Schindler's unusual height? (Incidentally, at least two promotional interviews mentioned Liam Neeson's enormous nose (Mansfield 1994: 122; Naughton 1994: 52, 55).)

Judith E. Doneson too objects to Jewish black marketeers in the Cathedral and to these businessmen as perpetuating Nazi stereotypes (1997: 144), as if oblivious of laws, passed immediately after *Kristallnacht*, preventing Jews from trading legitimately:

From January 1, 1939, Jews are forbidden to operate retail stores, mail-order houses, or sales agencies, or to carry on a trade [craft] independently.

They are further forbidden, from the same day on, to offer for sale goods or services, to advertise these, or to accept orders of all sorts, fairs or exhibitions. Jewish trade enterprises (Third Regulation to the Reich Citizenship Law of June 14, 1938 – *Reichsgesetzblatt*, 1, p.267), which violate this decree, will be closed by police.

(From *The Regulation for the Elimination of the Jews from the Economic Life of Germany*, November 12, 1938.)

For Horowitz the Cathedral scenes evoke 'the anti-Semitic canard of Jews desecrating sacred Christian ritual and space' and Christ's injunction (Matthew 21: 12–13, Mark 11: 15–17, Luke 19: 45–6) to banish Jewish moneychangers (1997: 12). Hence Jewish critics censure as negative representation what one might deem determined resistance or evidence of admirable adaptation. Doneson similarly condemns imputation of Jews' passivity and compliance in their fate, citing 'the female engineer who supervises building construction at Plaszów [and] takes her work for the Nazis so seriously that she loses her life' (1997: 144). This sideswipe overlooks the engineer's responsibility for the camp in which she and her community expect to live, and that the Jews' fate, now supposedly unrepresentable, was for themselves hardly predictable.

Abandonment of traditions, together with assimilation, both hastened by the Holocaust, threaten Jewish identity. It appears, though, that some reviewers look for offence. Of Schindler's view of the liquidation, one writes:

Spielberg decides to colour the cape of a little girl red so that, in the eyes of Schindler, she becomes a Little Red Riding Hood of horror ... This is nothing less than pornography ... It is also a well-known advertising trick: Emphasise the merchandising over and above the object itself by drawing attention to its wrapping (the miserable little cape) to the detriment of the body within (a little Jewish girl). (Lefort 1994: 4)

With such emphasis on 'the miserable little cape', it matters that she actually wears a substantial woollen overcoat. Moreover, the trope comes from *Battleship Potemkin*, another famous fictionalisation of history that has accrued documentary status, in which the Communist flag hoisted up the mainmast was tinted red. Consequently *Schindler's List* acknowledges its problematic representational status. Ken Jacobs hit the mark by observing, 'I don't think there is any point during this movie when you are not aware of watching a movie' (1994: 25), even if he meant this negatively. The red coat is also metonymic, so, with Schindler, the audience recognises the disinterred body an hour later. This is the film's attempt to represent and, as it must, personalise abstract horror. One could say that if the mass does not perceptibly comprise individuals, humanitarian response is almost impossible and we risk replicating the Nazi denial of Jews' individual humanity.

Despite this, the 'impersonal Jews argument' – 'they end up as extras in their own tragedy' – recurs in denunciations of the film (Bresheeth 1997: 202). Jews become '*Der Sturmer* caricatures' (Spiegelman 1994: 26), 'generic' (Rich 1994: 9), 'a backdrop of "dwarfed" (literally and narratively) Jewish slaves' (Rich in Loshitzky 1997: 114). That non-Jewish critics made few such comments underlines how a film is as much social artefact, open to multiple interpretations, as it is text. Behind apparent touchiness lies the problem of Zionism that – although it informs *Schindler's List*'s ending, as an edit transports liberated Jews from 1945 Plaszów to contemporary Jerusalem – still divides Jews worldwide. In 1937, Chaim Weizmann – later Israel's first president – dismissed European Jews who, he considered, chose not to fight for their Promised Land, as 'dust, economic and moral dust in a cruel world', destined for destruction: 'They have to accept it', the price of what Zionists saw as their passivity (Address to the 20th Zionist Congress, quoted in Bresheeth 1997: 211). Thus the ghetto Jew became an idea, Zionism's stereotyped other, ahead of Israel's establishment. In contradistinction to the dominant view in the contemporary diaspora (especially the US), which emphasises continuity and relatedness, this hardened after the Holocaust, particularly when over 6,000 Israelis, including camp survivors, died in the 1948 independence struggle. Bresheeth explains: 'Behind the question: "Why did they [ghetto Jews] not fight?" which every Israeli child was taught to pose not as a query but as a historical judgement, was the corollary of that query: "We, the new Jews, will NOT go like lambs to the slaughter"' (1997: 196).

Hence sensitivity among Jewish commentators, related to survivors or victims, to perceived negative representations. (In fact the film pre-empts the passivity argument near the start by dramatising vociferous protests to the *Judenrat*, particularly by one woman who proposes to remove her star, only to be told, 'They will shoot you.') Nevertheless, this prejudice encourages simplistic responses. Jason Epstein attributed the film's 'aesthetic and moral failure' to 'misplaced emphasis' on a singular exception to widespread acceptance and toleration of Nazism in occupied Europe. It evades 'terrible questions about the quality of our species' prompted by the Holocaust, 'questions that Stephen [sic] Spielberg, for all his good intentions and craftsmanship, did not ask, perhaps because they did not occur to him' (quoted in Shandler 1997: 160). Epstein overlooks what others have objected to: that Jews are presented, like any other examples of 'our species', as often uncooperative with each other and in certain cases exploitative. This, evidently, offends against clear-cut notions of victimhood, in which the world divides neatly into Nazis and innocent Jews. The film has the maturity to show Marcel Goldberg, the Jewish police officer, accepting Schindler's bribes, and a Jewish child in police uniform assisting at the liquidation, who spares Mrs Dresner only because he knows her daughter. A neighbour's refusal to allow Mrs Dresner refuge moments earlier is echoed when another boy, escaping consignment to Auschwitz, is repeatedly turned away by fellow Jewish children until, eventually hiding in a latrine, he is told, 'Get out! This is our place.' The inhumanity of the Nazis, whose ideology permitted 'no room' for Jews, becomes chillingly universalised. I cannot therefore agree that 'the violence of collaboration' – not Spielberg's central concern anyway – 'is barely evident' (Rose 1998: 244–5). Nevertheless, Gillian Rose is surely right to reject the unrepresentability argument on the grounds that its effect 'is *to mystify something we dare not understand*, because we fear that it may be all too understandable, all too continuous with what we are – human, all too human' (1998: 244).

A problem with condemning stereotypes is that they are unavoidable and neces-sary – we comprehend the world by defining experiences, including perceptions of other people (real or represented), under existing categories. Another is that they lack objective status: to recognise a stereotype means it already exists in the mind within a social discourse and therefore contributes to the meaning projected onto a represen-tation, rather than being integral to the representation itself. Identifying stereotypes to condemn them in relation to more 'truthful' reality is a strategy abandoned by media analysts long ago, with widespread acceptance of semiotics. Assumptions that a prefer-able alternative exists to an intrinsically false representation concentrate unduly on the paradigmatic dimension of Saussure's model of signification, whereas signs activate meaning only within a syntagm, with other signs. There is always danger of somebody else's negative stereotypes (for they inevitably implicate power relations) becoming internalised into how one views one's own group, perpetuating stereotypes even while objecting to them. Thus, in the present case, representing a cross-section of a com-munity thwarts desire for reassuringly pure images of victimhood. Both Nazi and Zionist stereotypes of ghetto Jews exist for those sensitive to such matters, reductively excluding other representations and nuances of characterisation, narrative and con-text, even if for most audiences such stereotypes (which at any rate change over time, are never fixed) have no currency. When Schindler meets the wealthy businessmen, they appear in his rear-view car mirror, aligning his gaze with ours. If the spectator sees anti-Semitic stereotypes, then so, presumably, does Schindler, which makes his transformation the more remarkable, and the stereotyping is dramatically justified; if the spectator does not see any stereotype, it is simply not an issue.

So subjective are these matters that one critic, far from perceiving Spielberg's Jews as passive, believes the director 'almost leaves himself open to the query that Schindler's apparent humaneness was in fact a Jewish conspiracy with Stern selecting workers, Stern selecting who should be bribed and so on', in an 'attempt to "control" the central character' (Slavin 1994: 11). Certainly when Stern organises birthday presents for

SS officers' families he issues instructions as if Schindler is his employee. The film overlooks one difficulty, established in Keneally's novel: the original Goldberg, one of several characters condensed into Spielberg's Stern, received handsome payment for including relatives and friends of names already on Schindler's list. The same critic argues, 'all reference to bad Jews, Jews who collaborated in the destruction of their own people [has] been expunged in the name of dramatic and cinematic clarity; the outcome is to foreground Jewishness as the essential goodness and not Oskar's ambiguous conversion' (ibid.).

In terms of narrative agency, most critics overlook what Miriam Bratu Hansen points out: 'Stern is the only character who gets to authorise a flashback' (1997: 86)– in which Goeth kills 25 Jewish workers to punish one escape – in response to Schindler light-heartedly calling the commandant 'a wonderful crook'. The same sequence contains a flash-forward, following Schindler's annoyed 'What do you want me to do about it?' which begins his attempts to save lives. As Hansen suggests, although 'Stern is deprived of his ability, his right to act, that is, to produce a future ... he can narrate the past and pass on testimony, hoping to produce action in the listener/viewer' (ibid.).

Ownership of history

Faced with the inexplicable, the unbearable, the unthinkable, one response is to assert control. Whoever attempted to represent the Holocaust for a mass audience, by whatever means, would draw passionate criticisms similar to those levelled against Spielberg. These reveal as much about critics' concerns as about the film, and really boil down to the unanswerable question, 'Who owns history?'

Schindler's List, product of an industry that for years targeted teenagers, relocates Holocaust consciousness from a generation that lived through World War Two, transforming it from personal memory into popular history. It introduces the Holocaust to an American audience, many of whom had not been aware of it. The film, emphasising rescue and continuity, 'epitomises ... "colonisation" of the Holocaust by American culture', in that the five million American Jews, some argue, constantly celebrate their survival in contrast to loss felt by those in the Old World (Loshitzky 1997: 4). Far from representing Christ and expropriating Jewish tradition, Schindler prompts Goeth to ask, 'Who are you – Moses?' when he demands, 'I want my people.' He leads them from Nazism's Egypt to modern Israel's Promised Land, which parallels the founding rhetoric of America as salvation (Elsaesser 1996: 178). The typically American narrative of a selfish individualist moving from indifference to protecting those weaker than himself has not gone unnoticed (see, for example, Lehrer 1997): *Casablanca,* alluded to visually in scenes portraying Schindler's high life with the Germans, is a prototype. Displacement of Holocaust memory from a European to an American sensibility has frequently embroiled discussion in resentment of cultural imperialism, indissoluble from the film's moral implications.

A 'victim contest' in the US compounds confusion (Loshitzky 1997: 7). Activism strategically asserts repressed history in constructing ethnic, post-ethnic and other identities, such as sexuality, gender or disability, opposed to white, heterosexual, bourgeois, male norms. Partly behind Spielberg's subsequent film *Amistad* was anti-Semitism from some African-Americans, particularly the Nation of Islam, who contrasted Holocaust survivors' economic status (above average for the Jewish community, the most prosperous US ethnic minority) with continuing black disadvantage – a legacy of slavery, which was newly foregrounded as a bigger Holocaust than the Jewish one, though it received less attention.

Religious Jews have resented Schindler, as hostilities end, making the sign of the cross over those he has saved. This allegedly asserts, insultingly, that Christian superiority has redeemed them spiritually as well as physically (Horowitz 1997: 132). Considerable mental gymnastics are required to substantiate this. The questionable premise is that the opening scene with Sabbath candles 'signals to viewers that *Schindler's List* will be a film about religion, or a religious film, specifically about Judaism' (1997: 124), which is about as sensible as arguing that *E.T.*'s opening heralds a film about astronomy. What the ritual shows is these people are Jews, and a community, while the expiring candle and the cut from its smoke to that of a steam locomotive confirm the setting is the genocide. That 'ritual acts and objects of sanctification are not given any depth or Jewish meaning', or that the 'Jewish spiritual crisis is not articulated' (ibid.) is irrelevant, for these are neither the film's concern nor its importance. To argue that Schindler, moving from promiscuity, through increasingly chaste kissing, to promising fidelity to his wife 'thus ... proves his manhood through the enactment of Christian virtue' (1997: 132) conveniently ignores the end caption announcing the couple's later separation. 'In the factory', allegedly, Schindler 'berates the rabbi for transgressing the Sabbath' (1997: 132–3), though his tone is actually benignly paternalistic irony. Furthermore, 'The (kosher?) wine Schindler unaccountably provides for the sanctification of the *Kiddush* masks the historical instances of blood accusations in Europe, where Jews were massacred on false charges of substituting Christian blood for sacramental wine' (1997: 133) – an extraordinary associative leap given the film establishes his ability to procure virtually anything, including shells during wartime and 1,100 bottles of vodka. Rekindling candles at this point supposedly asserts continuity with the start and effaces any sense of loss. This neatly disregards the Russian cavalryman who makes clear persecution will continue. Such oversights and falsifications are necessary, however, to argue that 'restoration of Jewish faith through the vehicle of the believing Christian occludes the long history of Christian anti-Semitism in Europe ... which facilitated the enactment of Hitler's Final Solution' – a history, it is insinuated though not stated, the film perpetuates (ibid.). So much for Schindler's story being exceptional (a complaint from other quarters) and his actions embodying an alternative others could have taken.

Horowitz furthermore insists American Jews and audiences generally undergo positioning alongside the Aryan Schindler *against* both European and Israeli Jews by what she reads as a Zionist ending. This over-emphasises the fact – not merely a narrative device – of Schindler's burial in Jerusalem. Her argument is supported by the observation that Jews in the film have Israeli accents, 'thus further conflating the old Jew with the Israeli' (1997: 135). Horowitz overlooks that few Polish Jews remain (although many actors were survivors' children (Cheyette 1997: 229)) and that, anyway, they would hardly have spoken English.

Faced with such extreme and divisive views, it is worth quoting Elsaesser on the ownership of history:

> At a time when history has returned to Central and Eastern Europe, to Africa and elsewhere, while the legacy of Fascism as well as Stalinism has to be confronted by the whole of Europe, the crimes named by Nazism and the Holocaust cannot possibly be 'our' history, just as it need not only be 'our' testimony or mourning work. (1996: 179)

Or, in the words of an American interrogator, son of Auschwitz victims, who empathised with the confusion of war criminals he helped condemn, and with their attraction to explanatory ideologies: 'If it weren't for the good fortune of being a Jew, I might have become a Nazi' (quoted by his daughter on *Loose Ends*, BBC Radio 4, 25 July 1998).

Schindler's List as a Spielberg text

I began by referring to self-reflexivity within a seemingly authentic and serious representation of historical atrocity. To the allusions mentioned might be added references to American television and European cinema responses to the Holocaust, such as *Heimat* (1984) and films by Rainer Werner Fassbinder (Elsaesser 1996: 163). Despite a dramatic shift in mood and subject matter, *Schindler's List* retains similarities to Spielberg's other work, particularly in relation to realism and textuality.

Like virtually all Spielberg films, *Schindler's List* separates and reunites families. The final farewell between Schindler and Stern, surrounded by a weeping audience (on-screen and off) re-runs *E.T.*, and Spielberg's recurrent communication motif emerges when segregated male and female prisoners whistle to each other, recalling the extra-terrestrial contact in *Close Encounters* and Shug's reunion with her father, through music, in *The Color Purple*. The allegedly Zionist conclusion, transporting Schindler's Jews, apparently passively, to the Promised Land, echoes Spielberg's narrative structures elsewhere: Neary's transcendence in *Close Encounters*, the pervasive sisterhood that ends *The Color Purple*, the fortuitous escape, figuring family creation, in *Jurassic Park*, or the return to Africa in *Amistad*. Yet *Schindler's List* takes risks – not simply in using monochrome and lasting three-and-a-half hours, but incorporating colour sequences, using colour-tinted effects, and mismatching film stocks and styles: constant assertions of textuality. The formal realism of hand-held, naturally-lit camerawork, jerky, grainy, occasionally unfocused, evokes wartime newsreels, the integrity of subsequent *cinéma vérité*, and old war movies (such as Andrzej Wajda's *A Generation* (1955), also set in occupied Poland). This opposes the red coat's artificiality and glossy, high-contrast images, wreathed in cigarette smoke, that glamorise Schindler's world. The coloured ending, both connecting with and distancing from the diegetic past, refuses spurious distinctions between fictional and documentary modes as purveyors of truth, and challenges audiences, in the presence of those whose stories have just been told, to deny whether what has been witnessed is 'at least a kind of consensus of fact' (Strick 1994: 47).

Heteroglossia, interweaving discourses in dialogue with each other, characterises *Schindler's List*. That auteurism would attribute this quality to the director does not, in itself, justify closing down the film's productivity, monologising it into supposedly predictable Hollywood values, as many hostile critics contend. While the Spielberg touch is demonstrably present – despite attempts to deny it, such as a *Newsweek* interview in which Spielberg claimed, 'not until *Schindler* was I really able to *not* reference other filmmakers' (Brode 1995: 236) – it constitutes one among many discourses shaping the experience.

Even favourable criticism has responded selectively to the cinematography, praising its documentary look while ignoring artificial expressive elements; these include, as when Schindler 'buys' his 'children' back from Auschwitz, film noir lighting for his shady deals, suggesting increasing danger on his journey from self-interest to confrontation with evil. As in all Spielberg films, conversely, light rays, metonymically inscribing the projector, signify desire. Bright beams connect Stern and Schindler when they finally drink together. Lamp rays bisect the scene as Schindler dictates his list, explicitly linked, via Stern's insistence that 'the list is life', with the candles at beginning and end. Grotesque, theatrical lighting distorts Schindler as he boasts to Emilie (Caroline Goodall) about his self-image as a great moneymaker, and light shafts later penetrate the Cathedral during their reconciliation. The boy trapped in the latrine looks up towards light. And Schindler realises both what imprisonment and the obscenity of anti-Semitism mean when locked in a cell, light streaming through its window. At Auschwitz, light emphasises the eyes of those inside wagons, in darkness, who thought, like the spectator, Schindler had saved them; a searchlight probes directly into the camera, causing a white-out, apparently reversing the end of *Close Encounters* – a hopeless situation redeemed when overhead light symbolically accompanies water from the showers.

Again spectatorship is potentially foregrounded. The opening prayer is focalised through a small boy. The child and his family disappear, creating loss. Vision remains, with no consistent point of identification other than, possibly, knowledge of history, as Hitler's list and a succession of unfamiliar faces fill the screen as the registration process begins. Soon, however, the leading character stands in for the spectator (and director, provided one accepts biographical parallels).

Close-ups on his hands encourage secondary identification with Schindler while he dresses – before he pins on his Nazi badge. As in *E.T.*'s initial empathy with an alien, cinematic technique achieves suture before commonsense knowledge would preclude identification. The camera follows Schindler, who drives the narrative, into a restaurant. He sits, distant, watching critically and attentively. Lighting and framing repeatedly emphasise his eyes; he is explicitly voyeuristic. Over-the-shoulder shots at beautiful women inscribe the familiar male gaze; we partly share Schindler's position of mastery – yet because he remains in shot but blurred, within the camera's own voyeuristic vision, he is also the narrative enigma. Spielberg has referred to Schindler's mysterious motivation as 'the Rosebud question' (Loshitzky 1997: 15), evoking *Citizen Kane*, another film that mixes styles self-consciously and invites speculation on conflicting truth claims of different modes of narration. A woman returns Schindler's gaze, curiously rather than coquettishly, establishing momentary identification with *her*, confirming desire to know more about him. Lit from behind, a surrogate spectator, wraithed with smoke, the hand holding his cigarette obscuring his face except the eyes, he is mysterious, slightly threatening. The camera pans from his position, enacting his surveillance, rhyming with reverse-shots arcing in a tentative dance around him. Focus racks, drawing attention to the object of his gaze in the background. Although focalisation is through him, he remains, unconventionally, central – not off-screen during reverse-shots as an absence the spectator projects into. This ambiguous subjective/objective relationship continues subsequently. Spielberg's avoidance of (melo)dramatising Schindler's motivations (Brode 1995: 230) is a prime cause of conflicting attitudes towards the film.

After he sends drinks to Nazi officers, they approach him to establish his identity, demonstrating the seductive allure of his 'presentation' as he effectively directs the entire scene. During the show Schindler intently watches the Nazis, not the performers, while we in turn are more interested in him. The cabaret similarly remains peripheral to us, though we receive privileged shots of dancers' legs outside any diegetic viewpoint, for he attracts the gaze to the background. His intriguing extravagance and detachment subvert the convention of woman as spectacle.

Schindler increasingly produces and directs events, spending fortunes to resolve narratives to his satisfaction. Thomson detects parallels with Alexander Korda's wheeling and dealing before he acquired capital or influence in Hollywood: 'Stay at the best hotels, be seen with the most beautiful women, entertain in grand style, charge everything, but tip lavishly. Then wait for offers' (1994: 44); the film noir scene in which Schindler bribes an officer reminds Thomson of David Selznick, whose father carried loose diamonds 'to impress people' (1994: 48). Schindler has, after all, 'Direktor' painted outside his office, which looks through a huge window, like a movie screen, onto the factory, and it is through a blurred chain-link fence, another surrogate screen, he first sees Jews being entrained. We view his transaction with the Jewish businessmen partly from his viewpoint, in the car mirror, and partly voyeuristically, from outside, when the rain-splashed window again inscribes a separating screen. The establishment of his hardware company resembles a film's pre-production, as when he 'auditions' secretaries in a *Citizen Kane*-like montage during the set's construction around him. He merely claps hands from his dominant vantage point and the production machinery whirrs into action. A young Jewish woman, Elsa Perlman, has difficulty getting past the front desk, but succeeds in seeing him when she returns dressed glamorously. 'Herr Direktor, don't let things fall apart: I work too hard', implores Stern who, a Jewish accountant, is the archetypal Hollywood producer pleading with an intractable director. 'Just pretend, for Christ's sake!' insists Schindler to Stern when the latter refuses to drink with him, like a director losing patience with a Method actor seeking motivation. (Interestingly, Spielberg, who has no truck with the Method (Baxter 1996: 103, 219), cast the main roles from the British stage tradition.) 'I look at you, I watch you … control is power', Goeth tells Schindler, a statement that summarises film spectatorship's illusory positioning and the actual condition of a successful director. The roles coalesce in an image of the Mirror Phase when Schindler's reflection appears on the 'screen' that is the window onto his factory, his desire, when Elsa tells him, 'They say you are good', precipitating a crisis of conscience.

Fascination with power combines with mystery surrounding Schindler's true nature in many borrowings from *Citizen Kane*, including sound bridges and other disjunctions between image and soundtrack, which produce 'irony and even counterpoint' and consequent self-consciousness in the narration (Hansen 1997: 86). The silent cinema connotations of the liquidation relate to this. Schindler observes from a safe God-like perspective – virtually the film spectator's, in psychoanalytic accounts – from which he can see everything but remain untouched, yet emotionally involved.

Like a Hitchcock film, which it resembles by doubling Schindler with Goeth, *Schindler's List* avoids facilely dividing characters into good and evil. It shows Jews implicated in oppressing their people, and the child's rejection by fellow escapees in the latrine chillingly asserts innate capacity for inhumanity as a foil for Schindler's conversion. Set against this are the bestial Goeth's contradictions. Evil incarnate, he stands back from a Jewish prisoner to avoid passing on his cold within minutes of ordering the engineer's summary execution. Later he not only recognises fellow humanity in the same prisoner (Helen, his maid) – despite his Nazi conditioning, which eventually wins – but sometimes treats her considerately and respectfully (repeatedly thanking her as she serves him) and even offers to write her a reference after the war. Those who think the film, when Goeth threatens and humiliates her, 'titillates the viewer with the suggestion that Helen Hirsch, already marked for death, will be sexually violated as well before the genocide is completed' (Horowitz 1997: 127), are themselves, if not inventing grounds for finding fault, identifying in a troubling and unwarranted manner. The assertion ignores the contradiction between Goeth's loathing of what he desires and his insane and obscene rationalisation, denying her humanity. The issue here parallels Freud's 'A Child Is Being Beaten', in which patients fantasised themselves into different roles within and outside the scenario, and in this case seems independent of textual structures or context.

Spielberg's typical scenario of two father figures explicitly parallels Goeth with Schindler, through crosscutting, as when both are shaving or looking down on their domains, or when Schindler is in the club with the cabaret singer and Goeth is on the verge of kissing Helen (Embeth Davidtz). Both scenes intercut, non-chronologically, with the Jewish wedding, the crushing of the light bulb paralleling Goeth, enraged, pushing shelves of bottles over on to Helen. Character similarities are carefully stressed, as are differences (Goeth and Schindler, frequently mirrored in earlier shots, are separated within a split screen, created by a window frame, when Schindler demands from him 'my people'), to question what makes one choose evil and the other good in relation to enduring communal values represented by the Jews. Goeth too is a spectator, desiring control from afar, choosing a rifle whereas Schindler uses bribes.

Accusations of Hollywood values overlook the perfunctory manner of the film's violence. Gunfire's hollow crack followed by the cartridge rattling on the pavement is unlike anything previously emanating from Hollywood. This device places the spectator close to the action, underlining both its coldness and that of the camera's gaze. It disturbs precisely because the violence appears not conventionally orchestrated and narratively justified but random, often peripheral to the focus of the action or composition, not highlighted or particularly individualised – just, horrifyingly, there. As Iain Johnstone points out,

Schindler's List – doubly-inscribed spectatorship: the watcher watched

when a director shows an act of horror or compassion, the grammar is to emphasise the emotion in a reaction-shot of an observer. But Spielberg never employs the
technique here. When we see cold-blooded shootings, there is never a cutaway to
a grieving widow biting a rag. It is we, the audience, who must deal with our own
emotional reaction instead of having it lived out for us by somebody else. (1994: 7)

Denying denial

I wish to conclude by using these observations to refute Geoffrey H. Hartman's
assertion that *Schindler's List* fails both because it is insufficiently realistic, trapped
in Hollywood conventions, and because it is excessively cruel, sensational and – a
view shared by many (for example, Loshitzky 1997: 110) – 'seemingly unconscious
of itself': 'A self-conscious commentary intruded into such a movie is no solution:
it would merely have weakened its grip as docudrama, or postmodernised the film'
(Hartman 1997: 64).

In fact continuous postmodern commentary is one of the film's distinguishing features, not least when Schindler asks Stern, 'Do I have to invent a whole new
language?' after the latter winces at his promise to secure him 'special treatment' at
Auschwitz, unaware of the Nazi euphemism; here the script addresses Adorno's prohi-
bition head-on. In particular, the shower scene, contrary to many critics' assumption,
does not share the SS guards' voyeuristic gaze, as it has no inscribed spectator (in a
film containing many). Voyeurism, exclusively ours, is exploited purposefully. While
the camera does initially look through the equivalent of a peephole (the shower room
door's circular window), it tracks forward inexorably to place us *in* the shower with
the women. There are, typically of Spielberg's practice, echoes even here of *Psycho*
– in which the shower murder begins with a peeping tom viewpoint and also uses
violin music – though to different effect. The allusion is anything but frivolous. This
critical moment – the closest film has come, could conceivably come, to representing

the unrepresentable – is treated self-reflexively. The doors shut, the lights extinguish, as at a screening. Light beams traverse the darkness. The spectator, crucially, experiences dread. If multiplying mother and child separation two hundred times was cinematic audacity, so is doing the same with Hitchcock's set piece. Audiences knew in advance about Hitchcock's notorious murder, but did not know when it would come. In *Schindler's List* the gas chamber had to be confronted sooner or later, or the film would be accused of evasion. When the moment arrives, self-reflexivity proclaims its cinematic fabrication, thereby pre-empting revulsion without compromising belief, even as it *alludes to* what typically occurred in actual so-called showers.

Spectatorial foreboding as the women huddle, trembling, derives from previous knowledge about Auschwitz and fulfils the prediction in their earlier conversation. Our fears parallel theirs. This is the ultimate horror movie moment – based on known fact within living memory, not fantasy – set at the threshold of what can be imagined only too well, and appears to be treated – as it had to be – with absolute authenticity. That the showers emit water rather than poison, far from evading the truth, is the only condition whereby truth *could* be represented. It is on record this occurred, even though exceptionally, so documentary requirements are satisfied. The shower scene's achievement is that it confirms emotionally what audiences already know intellectually about the Holocaust, or have learnt from the film. The women reach upwards to light and life, a reversal of *Psycho's* descent into darkness, sparing the audience the final obscenity while respecting the core of the representational taboo. That is, the scene *tests* the audience's belief that gassings normally took place, and could not succeed dramatically without that belief. In other words, *Schindler's List* 'is a memorable work because it puts the spectator's memory to the test, in the footsteps of what was intended to be a historic obliteration: that of the Jews by the Nazis' – ironically, a quotation appropriated from an account of *Shoah* that asserts 'Spielberg has done the opposite' (Niney 1994: 27). Subsequent point-of-view shots, as the women view other Jews crowding into bunkers, and the tilt up to crematorium smoke, completing the process that began with the tilt down on locomotive smoke at the start, are effective because audiences know, along with the women, that what they have just seen is exceptional, and that witnesses exist to confirm the usual process.

That is the answer to critics who claim the scene plays into the hands of Holocaust deniers. (Indeed the film incorporates the denialist argument specifically to refute it: one woman has argued earlier, to comfort herself and her fellows, 'If they [the women who told of the showers] were there, they would have been gassed.') By bringing on witnesses at the end, connecting past with present and cinematic representation with documented memory, Spielberg underlines the film's most useful fact: transformation of incomprehensible statistics into a human story to engage emotions and remind audiences what it means to tolerate repression today.

Schindler's List takes the Holocaust and ongoing rights violations as given. It uses identifications with different characters – ordinary onlookers often, observing others – whose actions, however individually dramatic, remain marginal historically. Georg Lukács (1950) advocated this mode for the realist novel, as representative of typical positions within events. It challenges audiences to consider their reactions had they been personally implicated.

Those who insist the film aligns with Goeth's vision eschew close analysis and lack theoretical perspective. As Hansen demonstrates, image/sound disjunctions during Goeth's 'Today is history' speech, in which Jewish life is seen to continue and the characters presented all survive, undercut and historicise his words. Events which, his prediction asserts, will officially have 'never happened', the six hundred years of Jewish residency in Kraków, live on because Schindler enabled inheritors of that history to live. The metadiscourse of world history, recognising the Final Solution's failure and Nazism's defeat, and authenticated by captions giving verifiable statistics concerning Jews remaining in Poland compared with the number of *Schindlerjuden* descendants, thus ironises and contains Goeth's discourse, positioning the spectator outside it. In a classic Spielberg representation of looking, Stern puts on his glasses in close-up before the camera shows the preparations for the liquidation from his point-of-view. This, analogously to the doffing of hats by Elliott's friends near the end of *E. T.* or removal of dark glasses by palaeontologists seeing a dinosaur in *Jurassic Park*, cues expectation of sights as yet unrevealed. 'Structuring of vision on the level of enunciation establishes Stern as a *witness* for the narration, for the viewer, for posterity' (Hansen 1997: 93), like Jim in *Empire of the Sun*, or the translator in *Saving Private Ryan*, aligning the narrative with the dominant history its project it is to confirm.

Yet even as astute and sensitive a critic as Hansen fears tainting by Spielberg's reputation. She distances herself from 'defending *Schindler's List* on aesthetic grounds', and concludes, somewhat self-defeatingly, that 'close attention to the film's textual work … can only provide a weak answer to the film's intellectual opponents' who are locked into 'an impasse … epitomised in the binary opposition of *Schindler's List* and *Shoah*' (1997: 94). In fact, the film incorporates that opposition, among inconsistencies, contradictions and tonal uncertainties inherent in the struggle to 'represent the unrepresentable' and in Schindler's ambiguity. Armond White contends it 'might have been an even stronger movie if it had clarified itself as a *version* of history rather than a documentary of the real thing' (1994: 56). That is exactly what its self-reflexivity implies.

CHAPTER SEVENTEEN

The Lost World: Jurassic Park: more digital manipulation

Critics committed to a biographical agenda wondered why, following the recognition and commercial success of *Schindler's List* as an adult movie, Spielberg returned after a three-year break with *The Lost World: Jurassic Park* (Freer 2001; Perry 1998). Although technically and formally highly accomplished, it appeared something of a pot-boiler: a child-oriented regression to the science fiction/action-adventure mould. The novelty of digital effects and the topicality of cloning were by now diminished. However, even Spielberg's freedom to select projects depends on delivering hits. He had a five-production deal with Universal. A blockbuster, presumably, was Universal's price for risking *Schindler's List*. Spielberg's name added value to the *Jurassic Park* franchise. Reciprocally, after the disappointing *Jaws* sequels, Spielberg's team may have decided his reputation would be better served if he stayed involved with a brand already synonymous with his name.

Pre-publicity for *The Lost World* coincided with Universal's Burbank theme park opening its *Jurassic Park* ride – which cost $110 million, twice the original film's budget. *The Lost World*'s release a year on refreshed interest in the attraction in time for the summer and similar rides at Universal's other parks.

A digital revolution

Other imperatives behind the sequel were advances in graphics software and robotic special effects. The 'supervening social necessity', in Brian Winston's phrase (1998:

6), included competition to develop techniques that, once showcased, could profitably be exploited in further movies, games and rides, and licensed to other users. James Cameron's Digital Domain – a rival offshoot from Lucas's Industrial Light and Magic (with whom Spielberg consistently worked) – had produced *True Lies* (1994) and was now developing *Titanic* for Fox. Columbia Tristar was putting together *Godzilla* (1998) which *The Lost World* pre-empted in its structurally redundant final act by changing the end from Michael Crichton's novel and freeing a tyrannosaur in San Diego. Most important, Spielberg's new studio, DreamWorks SKG, co-founded with former Disney production head Jeffrey Katzenberg and music mogul David Geffen, was preparing to challenge Disney. Katzenberg, no doubt vengeful after his ignominious 'invitation' to resign, was conversant with Disney's plans for computer-animated releases from another ILM progeny, PIXAR, whose *Toy Story* (1995) was the first fully digital feature. He was actively headhunting his former employers' talent.

This, specifically, is the import of Microsoft's Paul Allen investing $500 million for just 18 per cent of DreamWorks' $900 million enterprise and his co-founder Bill Gates providing half the $60 million capital for a short-lived software subsidiary, DreamWorks Interactive. Apart from DreamWork's investment of $100 million between them – 'reinventing arithmetic' as they retained two-thirds ownership (Perry 1998: 92), hence two-thirds of profits, as well as 100 per cent voting rights (Serwer 1995: 71) – the rest came from Korean company One World Media, part of Samsung (Baxter 1996: 404). However, these developments, and the previous two decades of Spielberg and Lucas's careers, occurred amid a far-reaching political and economic context insufficiently acknowledged in auteurist or aesthetic criticism or reviews concerned with movies primarily as diversion.

Entertainment is America's second-largest net exporter after aerospace (Wasko 2003: 174). DreamWorks, Hollywood's first new studio in seventy years, gave Los Angeles a major boost. Once established, it intended to employ 14,000 people at the former Hughes Aircraft plant. The site neatly epitomised a decade-long trend that had replaced 135,000 aerospace and electronics jobs with 144,000 in entertainment. Digital convergence, impelled by military applications, spawned 'Siliwood', a hybrid economy of Silicon Valley technology and Hollywood artistry (Hozic 1999: 290, 306).

Hollywood was traditionally conservative towards technology. Following introduction of sound, for example, few major developments occurred until Dolby Stereo, half a century later. Producers would innovate in response to perceived threats, but distributors were reluctant to implement anything outside their control (Hozic 1999: 291). Sound, to pursue the example, suffered because producers could not trust exhibition conditions. It improved only after loud, immersive rock concerts and penetration of domestic hi-fi, competitors for moviegoers' spending, exposed theatre equipment and practices as inadequate (Sergi 2002: 108–9).

However, Aida A. Hozic explains, dramatic technological change usually results from 'social, political or economic impasse' rather than prosperity (1999: 293). Accordingly, the digital entertainment revolution occurred amid US military budget cuts following the end of the Cold War, while economists speculated about Japanese pre-eminence in advanced electronics.

In discussing *Twilight Zone: The Movie* I noted how studio executives, rather than creative talent, make major decisions and profit from copyright and franchise royalties. *The Lost World* exemplifies a 'buyer-driven' commodity chain, whereby major companies (as in other industries) coordinate, rather than directly engage in, production, concentrating instead on market research, distribution, advertising and promotion. These contrast with 'producer-driven' commodity chains, such as the old studio system, which attempt to shape demand to their output (Hozic 1999: 308). Agents package talent – personnel functioning as brand names within the industry, as well as, in the case of stars (and some directors and producers), to the public – to serve franchises such as *The Lost World*. Emphasis on named individuals encourages enormous fees, afforded by hiring non-union labour where possible, exporting production when locations, studios and staff are obtainable more cheaply (one reason Spielberg works in Britain when exchange rates permit), and manipulating below-the-line costs, the one flexible part of the budget under producers' control.

Independent producers – outside the studios – have difficulty signing famous talent. This is significant in that Hozic argues maverick 1970s' directors and producers, starting with Lucas and Spielberg, succeeded because of two tendencies. Their turn to science fiction – disregarded by dominant studios at the time, which had closed special effects departments (1999: 308) – emphasised relatively inexpensive spectacle rather than stars as the attraction, thereby improving investment value. Second, asserting their rights motivated the filmmakers consciously to experiment with technology to lower costs further and also to manage merchandising and licensing in-house. Public recognition followed for both the individuals and their companies (Spielberg: Amblin; Lucas: ILM/THX/Lucasfilm).

DreamWorks intended cheapening digital technology to widen accessibility and resurrect high-quantity production, as in the studio era, while returning emphasis to products and producers rather than merchants. In contrast to the Motion Picture Association of America (representing major studio/distributors), DreamWorks recognises authors' rights by not altering work for future release without permission, awards animators percentage shares of gross profit, and has allied with craft guilds and unions in negotiating new broadcast standards. Technology, then, 'the instrument of battle between producers and merchants' for the industry's future, has prompted massive research and development investment (Hozic 1999: 294–5).

Initially, digital systems, enormously expensive and labour intensive, only slowly improved efficiency or quality. However, demand created a swing towards the entertainment industry of companies previously dependent on Pentagon spending. Military simulation technology resembles commercial computers, interactive games and CGI effects. Naval software that originally detected submarines by comparing surface patterns against computer-generated probabilities visualised the sea in *Titanic*. Theme parks and shopping malls have long housed flight simulators. Computer games employ feedback mechanisms designed for virtual rocketry and ballistics trials.

The Clinton presidency introduced incentives to advance simulation technology despite defence cutbacks. Dual-use projects involved commercial exploitation alongside more cost-effective military 'research and development' sponsorship and conversion of military applications to profitable civilian use. In short, American military and economic domination were predicated on combining warfare control and simulation systems, telecommunications, domestic and workplace computing and entertainment. This would check economically debilitating over-concentration on purely military research, while state support, despite free-market rhetoric, sought to enhance competitiveness and restore America's global position (Hozic 1999: 297–8).

Constance Balides notes of *Jurassic Park* that 'potential for multiple viewings and the plethora of subsidiary texts on … production and special effects position spectators as knowledgeable in various ways: for example, as dinosaur [aficionados], science fiction buffs and computer enthusiasts' (2000: 147). *The Lost World*'s promotion and publicity extended these points of access and forms of knowledge by promising dinosaur species unseen in the first film and unprecedented effects, while media awareness generally of developments and rivalries in digital filmmaking prompted desire to encounter and compare. The new logo – a cracked, degraded version of the original, replacing its bright corporate sheen – promised both similarity and difference, reflected in Janusz Kaminski's harsher cinematography, casting a duller, more sombre mood than Dean Cundey's colourful precursor. Both quality guarantee and enigma, the logo dated the earlier movie and its merchandise, prompting consumption by proffering the lure of novelty. Expected to gross $1.25 billion in licensed sales, over 800 products carried the logo, following a style manual which alone cost $500,000 (Anon 1996: 5). With typically 40 per cent of merchandise purchased before a film's release (Wasko 2003: 165), the products not only raised awareness but covered production costs in advance. Although aimed at family audiences, *The Lost World* again appealed to carefully differentiated age groups and tastes. Tie-in promotions included Mercedes-Benz cars which feature in the narrative. Hardly within the grasp of teenagers then believed to comprise Hollywood's prime audience, nor most families', the cars gave the movie the cachet of international quality, while themselves benefiting from association with billion-dollar global success and advanced technology. Protagonists use hand-held video and SLR cameras, product placement that associates domestic brand names, also used on professional equipment, with state-of-the-art spectacle. Chocolate bars in close-up and a computer game mentioned in the dialogue would have attracted generous payment from companies targeting children (Wasko *et al.* 1993).

For this movie, as most, 'accurate and consistent production figures beyond the rumour mill, as reported in *Variety* or other trade publications', are unobtainable outside legal challenges (Wasko 2003: 12). However, Universal quickly announced unprecedented opening weekend grosses; it earned as much as $24 million over its $73 million budget (different amounts are cited: Perry 1998: 95; Freer 2001: 247; Gomery 2003: 79). Its eventual worldwide gross, $611 million, two-thirds from overseas, was 1997's highest. These figures, excluding non-cinematic income, again proved the commercial advantages of the blockbuster approach.

A family movie

Given this background, unsurprisingly many reviewers expressed cynicism, par-ticularly about what they considered a weak plot and wooden performances. Nevertheless, despite the final San Diego section degenerating into *1941*-style slapstick, the direction and editing are anything but perfunctory.

Snarls and roars arouse expectations during 25 seconds of blackness at the start. Whether displaced dinosaur noises or from crashing waves subsequently revealed, they disturb like the indefinable sounds accompanying the track forward that opens *Jaws*. The initial shot, similarly advancing (over rather than under the sea), also links directly to *Jurassic Park*'s final shot of flying pelicans, immediately involving alert spectators by raising erroneous expectations of dinosaur migration when a caption announces the location as 87 miles from the earlier island. A tilt down from a mountain, ominous music and broadly familiar typography recall the opening of *Raiders of the Lost Ark*, establishing a dark mood. The shot continues for almost a minute, narrating with extreme economy. First it pans rightwards across stormy waves, pausing to frame an anchored cruiser before racking focus and tracking left to follow a steward across the beach, bearing champagne. It continues tracking and refocuses onto a second bottle carried into shot in close-up; pauses while a glass is poured and the bottle deposited in an ice bucket; resumes as the drink is carried to a man in a luxurious deck-chair. Further refocusing and a rightward pan reveal a third crew-member further back, serving a young girl a sandwich. Finally a track and pan left follow her past her mother, who supervises two more seamen laying a formal meal. Although there are two deckchairs, two champagne flutes and the table is set for the family, the parents do not appear simultaneously in the shot, suggesting unease between them, confirmed by subsequent dialogue. On first viewing it seems they are drinking separately. The mother, who does not know her daughter's food preferences, and tries unsuccessfully to control her – a matter of contention with the father – three shots later reaches to pour a drink after worrying about snakes, then stops herself and calls a steward. Apart from rewarding connoisseurship of its formal qualities, the shot brings humans close to dangerous nature (the turbulent maritime backdrop); introduces central themes of parenthood and responsibility (drinkers are uniformly untrustworthy); represents the rich, who provide the villains, as decadent and dysfunctional; establishes relationships through mise-en-scène and off-screen space; asserts the diegesis as pro-filmic reality (continuous in space and time); and trains the spectator to seek narrative information from anywhere (with several planes of action within the shot and penetrations of the frame from various sides), even while its presentation is highly controlled.

In respect of parenting, clearly relevant to many in the targeted audience, the father's imprecation to the mother, 'Just let her enjoy herself for once', self-reflexively alludes to hundreds of thousands of real-life arguments over the film's suitability for children. Malcolm's (Jeff Goldblum) daughter, Kelly (Vanessa Lee Chester), complains about being left with a sitter when he sets off to join his girlfriend, Sarah (Julianne Moore), to see the dinosaurs. After accusing him of negligence, she stows away and joins the adventure. The San Diego sequence completes this scenario: when a boy rouses his parents after seeing a dinosaur in the garden they immediately assume he has had a nightmare and start disputing the cause, but ultimately are terrified whereas the son excitedly takes photographs. The penultimate scene offers a droll view of the movie's awareness of its eventual use and status. The tyrannosaurs' heavily guarded return to the island – fulfilling Hammond's dream of his creatures establishing a harmonious eco-system, undisturbed by humans – provide dramatic resolution; rather than direct representation, this appears on television in the re-united Malcolm household. Popcorn suggests the family have been watching a film – in front of which both Malcolm and Sarah are snoozing.

Parenting, and social organisation generally, are explicitly addressed. 'Do you see any family resemblance here?' Nick (Vince Vaughn) asks when Kelly, played by a black actress, appears on the island. To the film's credit her progeniture is never again raised. Dinosaurs are presented as having a right to exist, manifestations of Nature that, to paraphrase *Jurassic Park*, 'always finds a way'. Unattached male humans, characterised by Ludlow's (Arliss Howard) greed and Dieter's (Peter Stomare) cruelty, constitute the greatest threat to both prehistoric and contemporary life. Hunters stake down an infant tyrannosaur to attract the buck so they can kill it. Dinosaurs, in line with Sarah's thesis, instinctively protect – and, less convincingly, avenge – their offspring. Humans, higher evolved, make choices about relationships and, as the survival alliance between the two teams demonstrates, can cooperate to mutual advantage. Whereas Sarah is at one with nature, Dieter inflicts pain on animals, becomes drunk during his watch, and loses control over the camp: 'That's the last time I leave you in charge', Tembo the hunter (Pete Postlethwaite) tells him, as if admonishing an irresponsible babysitter. Dieter and Nick edge around each other and start brawling, utterly inappropriately in view of the common danger, emphasising how little behaviour has evolved. Sarah's escape when pursuing raptors turn away to attack each other parallels this moment. Nick nevertheless possesses nurturing instincts, contrary to his initial cynicism and mercenary motives. He risks himself to protect nature, and helps Sarah heal the infant tyrannosaur. Kelly is attuned to nature too, immediately intuiting, on heeding the infant's cries, that 'The other animals are gonna hear this!' Compsognathi seemingly play 'What's the time, Mr Wolf?' with Dieter before despatching him, their anthropomorphism offering satisfying identification for child viewers, enhanced by rapidly tracking, low-level, point-of-view shots as they advance. The nature/nurture debate remains open. Survival of the fittest recognises no morality: Eddie's death, despite saving his team, balances Dieter's punishment. Nevertheless, respect is a given, and Tembo, who came to kill a tyrannosaur, has the hunter's supposed empathy for the quarry and eventually deserts Ludlow in disgust. He also compassionately entrusts Sarah to ensure Kelly remains unaware of what happened to Dieter. Some atavistic, pre-conscious pecking order instinctively bestows authority. When Ludlow cannot motivate the party to move, Nick has only to rise and say, 'Come on, guys.' Eventually human parental attributes are naturalised when a tyrannosaur, having reclaimed its infant, attacks Ludlow, but then steps back to let junior finish the job.

Intertextuality

Spielberg faced the problem that *Jurassic Park* set the standard for awe-inspiring. Given technological effects' centrality to *Lost World*'s commercial logic, it is knowingly ironic that many convincing scenes involve anticipation: dinosaurs, off-screen or hidden, are inferred from crackling vegetation or other indications established in *Jurassic Park*, such as the clear signal that ripples in a puddle betoken an imminent attack.

Continuing the first scene the girl meets, in a movie promising tyrannosaurs, a tiny bird-like compsognathus, heralded initially by rustling in the trees. As Warren Buckland notes, cutting on action as the creature jumps towards her and enters the next shot from out of frame, reinforces the notion that this digital illusion is a 'pre-existing entity' (2003a; 2003b: 92). The girl feeds the seemingly friendly animal – in a typically tight framing for this film (composed for Academy ratio) which isolates its snake-like head and neck, thus underlining the theme of a lapsed Eden – and excitedly calls her parents. Her expression, looking off-screen, abruptly transforms the mood. Recalling *The Birds*, the creature has gathered a flock of others while the camera concentrated on the human. As in *Jaws*, a beach idyll becomes a feeding frenzy. Compsognathus squeals merge with the girl's screams, motivating a cutaway to the parents' reaction, keeping the violence off-screen. *Psycho*-style screeches in the score, evocative of birds and hence a link to Grant's scientific premise in *Jurassic Park*, reinforce their panic. The climax is the mother's scream as she looks past the camera in horror. Its sound bridges a cut to *Jurassic Park*'s Malcolm, seemingly also screaming, framed against a tropical sky and palm tree, his hair blowing back as if, in Spielberg's established code, buffeted by currents from an intense vision. Malcolm's mouth closes; the scream continues, revealed to be squealing brakes as he steps away from a poster towards an arriving subway train. Spielberg utilises and extends a famous edit from *The 39 Steps*, while lightening the tone, again foregrounding narration, and jokily demonstrating visual deception without banks of computers.

The subway journey exists to introduce Malcolm. Should viewers need help, a passenger buttonholes him as 'the scientist, the guy on TV', and mockingly makes a scary dinosaur impression – self-reflexive celebrity intertextuality (conceivably this happens to Jeff Goldblum) – and he names himself on arrival, 'summoned' to Hammond's mansion. This scene is a compendium of allusions to a landmark of cinematographic, sound, acting and special effects innovation, *Citizen Kane*. Even during pedestrian exposition – filling the gaps since the first film, explaining the opening, starting the new plot – Spielberg provides embellishments that are nevertheless not gratuitous. In addition to narrative functions of indirect commentary and thematic development, these are authorial inscriptions: amusing himself and fellow cineastes; demonstrating that he is neither in thrall to effects nor divorced from cinematic tradition; and, like any classical painter or poet, flexing himself by displaying mastery of, and homage to, his predecessors.

The scene's initial shot uses a low angle that evokes Mrs Kane opening a window, as the butler, reminiscent of the discreet formal servants lurking in Xanadu, opens a heavily-latticed door. Like successive barriers falling away at the start of Welles' film, this is both metaphor, conveying imprisonment by wealth of an eccentric millionaire, and inscription of the screen plane, penetration of which takes the viewer no closer to understanding his ambiguous motivation. The suggestions are overt, from the echoing, shiny marble surfaces to the large bed on which Hammond, like the dying Kane, reclines, although he soon makes a sprightly recovery. A 74-second wide-angle shot, in which low camera positioning includes ceilings, utilises deep-focus to recreate the composition and analogous character dynamics of Welles' boarding-house scene. Ludlow, Hammond's grasping corporate lawyer nephew, whose appearance

The Lost World: Jurassic Park – Wellesian deep focus: an extended shot transposes the compositional dynamics of Mrs Kane's Boarding House to Xanadu's mise-en-scène

and manner resemble Thatcher from *Kane*, signs documents in the foreground as he speaks, effectively determining the fate of Malcolm, dwarfed in the background. Overlapping dialogue, which Welles pioneered, refers to *The Enquirer*, one of Kane's newspapers.

To punctuate a dramatic revelation – Ludlow's control of Hammond's company, Ingen – a cut flouts classical continuity, 'crossing the line' to an emplacement unmotivated by any character's position. Spielberg makes his film, the entire purpose of which is predicated upon at least intermittent credibility, blatantly artificial. Extensive bricolage is one among many playful foils to the effects' realism. (I recall feeling irritation, on first viewing, at the implausibility of Malcolm, in the final section, driving through warehouse walls, while I did not question the sedated infant tyrannosaur Sarah earlier carries struggling in her arms.) Countless cinematic references occur throughout. A stegosaur using its tail as a weapon may not be accurate palaeontology (Ball 1997), but alludes to *King Kong*, which this movie resembles even more than did *Jurassic Park*. Malcolm and Sarah's simultaneous fast talk recalls Howard Hawks's *His Girl Friday* (1940), in line with the enterprise's essentially comedic nature, while the big game hunting scenes self-consciously challenge the same director's *Hatari!* (1962). They also, with the close-ups on rods and lines and specialised guns, rerun the chase in *Jaws*. Dieter's death when responding to a call of nature parallels Genarro's demise in *Jurassic Park*. The T-Rex chase from the camp to the waterfall uses high-pitched isolated chords in the score to underline visual resemblance to an attack on schoolchildren in *The Birds*. Hunters are filmed side-on as unseen raptors kill them in long grass, apparently pulling them 'under' like Chrissie in *Jaws*. Mayhem like that in *The Sugarland Express* recurs in San Diego as a fleet of police cars arrive, accompanying a somewhat inadequate dog warden van.

Less specifically intertextual, but equally self-conscious, narration occurs throughout. A non-synchronous edit creates an overlapping sound bridge from Malcolm's confrontation with Ludlow to his interview with Hammond. Perhaps because narrative causality is an excuse here for special effects, but also because uncertainty can enhance realism, not least by concealing contrivance, indirect narration frequently occurs: 'Where's the fire?' Eddie asks rhetorically when Nick suddenly runs off in the forest, intercut with a scientific argument between Malcolm and Sarah; and then cries of 'Fire! Dr Malcolm! Fire at base camp!' motivate the unexpected discovery of Kelly preparing a meal. Malcolm's uselessness as a hero whenever technology is involved becomes a running gag, while Sarah's 'lucky' rucksack is an unashamed device to extricate her from successive perils. Particularly memorable are the raptors' metonymic introduction, in which their presence is inferred from wakes in the grass from an extreme high-angle shot as they close in on their human prey; and Ludlow's close-up, after the tyrannosaur invades San Diego, when Malcolm's face intrudes into the top corner of the frame, resembling shots in which dinosaurs attack, to deliver his chilling verdict: 'Now you're John Hammond!'

Self-reflexivity

As in *Jurassic Park*, parallels between the movie and its making, if perceived, contribute to the multiple-discourse address. Together with conscious intertextuality, and the fact that all but the youngest viewers would much of the time consciously judge special effects, these make spectators unlikely to succumb uninterruptedly to Imaginary involvement or consistently to maintain realist expectations or responses. The movie is consequently a ritual, a game, a celebration inviting participation, rather than a statement about life.

Malcolm, as Ludlow reminds him, has signed a 'non-disclosure agreement', reflecting secrecy around Spielberg productions. Hammond's transformation from 'capitalist to naturalist in just four years', provoking Malcolm's incredulity, parallels Spielberg's philanthropy. Hammond's expedition undergoes preparation in a warehouse indistinguishable from the movie's art department, as technicians customise location vehicles while drawing boards display the designs in offices upstairs. These vehicles, including an articulated Winnebago with luxurious accommodation and computers resembling an editing suite, are near identical to those used by cast and crew off-screen. On the Ingen team, financier Ludlow and hunter Tembo struggle over control of their expedition, like a studio executive and star director. 'Those are some major-league toys', comments Nick on seeing Ingen's rig, miniatures of which were in children's stores in Hollywood's 'biggest promotional programme ever' (Anon. 1996: 5). When Malcolm excludes Kelly from adult conversation, she complains, 'It's like a height restriction in an amusement park!' During the San Diego sequence, that sits like the cynically commercial excrescence that it is, the monster devours an 'unlucky bastard' (according to the credits) played by the screenwriter. At the end, Hammond, minus Scottish accent, speaks on TV in reverential tones, using florid gestures, about his vision: a mischievous impression of broadcaster-naturalist David Attenborough – brother of Richard, who plays Hammond.

Although formal and intertextual density is not sustained consistently, as action-adventure and digital spectacle inevitably dominate, familiar inscription of the cinematic apparatus remains. Routine for Spielberg, and here less philosophically intriguing than elsewhere, it nevertheless enhances the attractiveness and credibility of the special effects.

Nick is a wildlife and combat documentary filmmaker. He and Sarah spend the early scenes on the island filming and photographing. This confirms both its spectacularity and its visible co-presence for them within the diegesis. 'These images are incredible, legendary', Nick insists. 'Guys shoot their whole life, never get anything half as good ... You can give me the prize right now.' He means the Pulitzer, but read Special Effects Academy Award.

'This is magnificent', Eddie declares, awestruck by his first dinosaur, and later, 'Wow! Is this even possible?' Spectators, hearing their reactions vocalised and validated, share characters' experiences. For returning viewers (had any not seen *Jurassic Park*?) Malcolm's unimpressed reply, 'Ooh! Ah! That's how it always starts, but later there's running and screaming', nevertheless offers the pleasure of knowing more than these naïve characters, of shared mastery in dominant specularity. Rather than unproblematically enhancing realism, however, this reminder of the previous film, hence of the viewing situation, effects the frisson between Imaginary involvement and Symbolic awareness central to Spielberg's commercial successes. Hammond's team, like Neary and Jillian at the *Close Encounters* site, observe the Ingen safari and video conference preparations from a vantage point in the overlooking hills. Implied voyeurism validates fetishisation of the feared object. Dinosaurs' dismembering capacity, as *Jurassic Park*'s Grant made clear, evokes castration; one reason little boys, fascinated by them, seek mastery by memorising their complex names. (The joke is that Tembo, big daddy of all hunters, could not care less and refers to a file of laminated sheets to identify his quarry.) Transforming them into spectacle functions similarly; Symbolic awareness disavows unconscious danger. By extension, fear that digital imagery threatens by tricking the self into accepting an illusory defining Other in the screen mirror is mastered by consuming it as overt and 'impossible' spectacle. (Banality, such as scuffs on uneven paintwork with wood grain showing through on a door in *Toy Story*, is far more uncanny.)

On Isla Sorna, Nick, Eddie and Malcolm stand, backlit, looking upwards and off-screen, initially seeking Sarah. Their projected desires prompt spectatorial anticipation as they precede in the relay of the look. When a stegosaurus enters, the reverse-shot establishes a mise-en-abyme: we watch them watching, while sharing their vision from a distance. Logs in their foreground separate them from the spectacle. Then another dinosaur lumbers past, between us and them, immersing our textual surrogates in the centre of the action and repositioning us a stage closer, as if to their previous position. The sun flashes between the second creature's dorsal plates, into camera. The effect confirms diegetic solidity and depth while inscribing a metaphorical projector beam – linking it to light shafts penetrating the forest all around – and asserts the creature's virtual illusoriness as occupying the same pro-filmic reality as the cast, the set and the light that enables them to be filmed. Light, as ever in Spielberg, signifies projected desire. One example among many is the shaft illuminating the tyrannosaur nest where Tembo and Ajay await the parents' return.

Projectors require screens. Kelly, after arguing with her father in their first scene, remains behind a chain-link barrier – separating family security from dangerous adventure, although in this instance father and stepmother are part of the expedition – watching as he prepares to depart. As she enters the workshop area, unnoticed, magical music fades in while welding torches spray sparks, as when Jim encounters beloved aircraft in *Empire of the Sun*. A beam projects from behind her, into camera, as she enters the trailer – fitted, like a movie theatre, with illuminated floor strips and decorated in dark, muted colours – as she exclaims aloud, 'This is *so* cool!' An identification figure, particularly for younger filmgoers, almost silhouetted, a flat shadow, she looks up at an illuminated chart of the island and surrounding ocean. As the camera closes in on it, a direct cut to an aerial shot of the expedition boat functions not merely as temporal ellipsis but transition 'through' the screen into the Imaginary of movie fantasy.

Sarah, who has survived unthreatened until the expedition's arrival, is spontaneous and impulsive, associated – in shots when men observe her – with water, sunshine and vibrant life. Embodiment of Nature, easily co-existing and interacting with dinosaurs (despite her scientific creed being observation without intervention), and mother figure within the central human family, she represents the Imaginary as opposed to Malcolm's dark (literally: he wears black), justifiably cynical, rationality or Eddie's and the hunters' enormous guns, signifying patriarchal control. Light emanating behind Malcolm, Nick and Eddie, as if acknowledging her idealisation as their projection, evidences that this positioning of her is part of the Symbolic order. 'She's too close', they worry as she approaches an infant stegosaurus, and 'Look, she has to touch it. She can't not touch what she sees.' In a typical Spielberg mirroring, she merges in rapture at the creature until her camera motor – technology (culture, not nature) – scares it and causes conflict with its parents. The special effects similarly promise the spectator involvement in the action; not because they are more convincing than *Jurassic Park* at rendering dinosaurs, but because digital advances in plotting a three-dimensional environment allow characters and virtual creatures to occupy the same, apparently pre-existent, space. A motorcyclist in a fast-forward tracking shot, for example, rides through the legs of a galloping brontosaurus.

In San Diego, the exclusive Ingen reception to meet the T-Rex and its infant – another *King Kong* allusion – resembles a movie premiere, as celebrities arrive in stretch limousines. Radar screens represent the ship's approach – digitally, but abstractly. Viewers share characters' knowledge and foreboding while indirect narration keeps the danger, and its explanation, physically off-screen until it ploughs full steam ahead into the diegesis through the length of the pier. Like the train in the Lumières' first screening, the ship hurtles towards the spectator.

When the stegosaurs attack, one uses its tail spur to penetrate a hollow log inside which Sarah has hidden; light shafts through into the protective darkness. Compounded with sexual connotations, this damsel-in-distress scenario inaugurates a characteristic Spielberg threat, penetration of the surface between spectator and object, negative counterpart to blissful merging. Spielberg has spoken of seeing *The Greatest Show on Earth* (1952) as a child: 'My father said: "It's going to be bigger than you, but that's all right. The people in it are going to be up on a screen and they can't get out at you." But there they were up on that screen *and they were getting out at me* ' (quoted in Mott & Saunders 1986: 12). (Adapting a recurrent motif from the film, the *Jurassic Park* DVD (2000) menu features a raptor smashing through the logo towards the audience.) In *The Lost World* captured dinosaurs, their breath visible in the back-lighting, snort through bars that separate them from Sarah and Nick, who are freeing them; moments later, as Ludlow smugly announces the San Diego entertainment that will safely contain the creatures, a triceratops tears through the back of the tent. Later, a tyrannosaur, its shadow literally back-projected onto the canvas under which Sarah and Kelly are sleeping, changes from the present-absence of a two-dimensional image to a three-dimensional presence as it inserts its head through the flaps and looms over them.

As with other cinematic metaphors, this penetration motif recurs so often that enumeration would be tedious. It is naturalised almost neutrally into style. One instance worth examining, however, because of its originality and success in building suspense, occurs when the parent tyrannosaurs attack the articulated camper to recover their injured baby. Inside, Nick, Sarah and Malcolm look off-screen over the camera, as if into the auditorium. A bright reflection between them inscribes a projector to centre their searching gaze, which intensifies as focus changes while Malcolm advances into close-up. The suggestion is that the dangerous exterior within their diegesis is bounded by the screen; the diegetic/extradiegetic opposition threatens to collapse. Unexpectedly, focus changes as a T-Rex head, in the same profile as the logo, appears outside, framed in the window behind them. An exterior shot reveals the other parent at the far side, sandwiching the protagonists, with the injured baby, between them. Protective bars and rain on the glass inscribe the windows, metaphorical screens, as both aperture and protection as the tyrannosaurs look in, roaring. The creatures, after having had the baby safely returned, shove the vehicle so that the trailer hangs over a cliff. Sarah, filmed from below, falls onto a plate glass divider, previously unseen, which serves no practical function in the trailer but places a fragile barrier between her and death on the rocks far below. Her weight slowly fractures the glass. The cracks inscribe, and threaten to rupture, the movie screen itself – the only guarantee, when disbelief is suspended, of security in the *fort-da* game whereby spectators master their fears. Awareness of the screen, of the projected fantasy as Symbolic, here functions not as reassuring alternative to Imaginary immersion, but as metonym for the dreaded Real.

CHAPTER EIGHTEEN

Amistad: black and white in colour

In 1839 fifty Africans on the schooner *Amistad*, bound for slavery, rebelled, killing some of their captors. Their trial for piracy and murder, first in Connecticut, later appealed to the US Supreme Court, established that colour was not a barrier to human rights. Their actions arguably led to the establishment of the Civil Rights Movement after the American Civil War, culminating eventually in the Voting Rights Act, 1965. Self-defence overrode both the criminal charges and numerous competing property claims that complicated the case together with domestic political expediency and international diplomacy.

Spielberg necessarily simplifies. John Quincy Adams' (Anthony Hopkins) five-minute speech to the Supreme Court – protracted in cinematic terms and enough for some reviewers to pan the movie as long-winded courtroom drama – summarises a peroration in reality lasting eight hours over two days, during which a judge died. Despite such inherent difficulties in filming it, the case's symbolic importance was one reason African-American co-producer Debbie Allen initiated the project. Over three hundred other maritime slave revolts occurred (Gold & Wall 1998: 15), and such evidence of resistance is crucial to African-American historical consciousness. However, none of those changed the institutional status of slavery or race relations.

The *Amistad* insurrection ultimately achieved the captives' freedom, and whites' cooperation and support, voluntarily given despite personal risk. (Death threats against defence attorney Baldwin (Matthew McConaughey) in Spielberg's *Amistad* only hint at the dangers abolitionists risked; in a previous case a $100,000 contract had been taken out on the lives of the Tappan brothers (amalgamated into one abolitionist in the film) and a slave's ear mailed to them (Jones 1997: 38).)

The film ends relatively upbeat. But the reality since Emancipation is that equality, guaranteed in the 14th Amendment, Supreme Court decisions and civil rights legislation, remains unachieved. Highlighting the captives' success thus dramatises and leaves open the dilemma expressed by Spike Lee in *Do the Right Thing* (1989) between gradual, legal progress and Malcolm X's 'by any means necessary'. The *Amistad* affair was resolvable, though to the captives' detriment, as a property dispute. Instead abolitionists utilised it to publicise the slave trade's miseries and arbitrary injustice. The movie is analogously didactic in reviving awareness of racism's historical roots and past anti-racist struggles, asserting the power of dialogue within the ideals of the Declaration of Independence. Both the lawyers involved in the original case and later civil rights activists knew that to change the law required debate at the highest level (Jones 1997: 13).

Although some commentators feel *Amistad* lacks contemporary resonance (Breen 1999: 6), shots of President Van Buren (Nigel Hawthorne) kissing babies and sitting for a photograph during his re-election campaign underline that the original affair was a concerted media event, countered accordingly by Van Buren's team. Tappan in the film even opines cynically that martyrdom might assist the cause better than the rebels' liberation. Yet, despite objections that Spielberg too presents a white version, rendering the captives passive at their own trial (Webster 1998: 102), the film punctures the official discourse to lay bare slavery's horrors. A graphic account of the Middle Passage, answering criticisms that *Schindler's List*'s gas-chamber scene was evasive, portrays fifty chained captives deliberately drowned to conserve supplies. While Howard Jones' history mentions no such incident, its presentation emphasises commodification of human beings and generalises the case as representative of the ethos of racism. *Amistad* indicates slavery's degradations by unflinchingly showing masses of naked, chained Africans, even if film cannot easily convey the sickness, darkness, heat, stench, claustrophobia, fear, despair, anger, repugnance, pain or duration of the Atlantic crossing. As over a third died and those unable to eat suffered lashings and vinegar poured on their wounds (Jones 1997: 15), drowning – cinematic shorthand for cumulative, continuous, deliberate cruelty and the attitudes of those who inflicted it – might reasonably be preferred to survival. An earlier shot of a woman with a baby jettisoning herself overboard implies that desperate logic – an image directly echoing Beecher Stowe's *Uncle Tom's Cabin* (1993: 144) and the choice motivating Toni Morrison's *Beloved* (1987).

Such moments obtain contemporary relevance from the Rodney King beating and consequent disturbances in 1992, a seminal instance in media history when amateur video cut through postmodern babble about simulacra and virtual reality to reconnect the signifier to the referent of violence contingent upon hatred, inequality and official indifference (Ferguson 1998: 4). Other high-profile events – in addition to ongoing fallout over *The Color Purple* and *Schindler's List* (including demands by Minister Farrakhan for recognition of 'the Holocaust to black people' (Loshitzky 1997: 16n))

– were South Africa's first free elections, the Million Man March on Washington, and O. J. Simpson's televised murder trial and acquittal. These highlighted racial tensions, signalling for many Americans, black and white, civil rights' failure. Indeed the film's standoff between armed guards and the *Amistad* blacks, furious about the appeal against the first court decision and a captive's death, poignantly recalls clashes between officers and demonstrators in both 1960s America and apartheid South Africa.

Whether *Amistad* succeeds, whether – as will be considered – its factual distortions are justified, and whether a white man is qualified to purvey black narrative, it remains a remarkable intervention by Hollywood into a painful and politically incendiary area.

Allen deliberately sought Spielberg, impressed by his determination to make *Schindler's List*. She claims credit for the black abolitionist character, Joadson, who does not represent anyone in the actual trial but rather what she calls the 'many successful, free and wealthy black people' engaged in supporting abolitionists: 'I also had a woman in there, but I lost that battle. Can't get everything!' (quoted in Hemblade 1998: 78). Nevertheless she lobbied successfully for Africans, rather than black Americans, to play the captives.

Allen's comments empirically support theoretical claims that contemporary discourses, rather than self-evident lessons drawn from the past, determine historical dramatisations (Tribe 1977/8; Sorlin 1980). As the movie is apparently based on a novelisation (Owens 1997), without even the privilege *Schindler's List* occasioned to question individuals involved, it raises ethical questions about fictionalising history. These are addressed in this chapter's final section.

Saidiya V. Hartman (1997) believes filmmaking's capital-intensive and collaborative nature creates particular difficulties for black directors seeking a 'voice' commercially, unlike writers such as Toni Morrison or Alice Walker (cited by Webster 1998: 102). Effectively economic censorship, such limitations deny mainstream audiences, as well as minorities, access to films that do not articulate obviously popular sentiments. Yet the independent film *Sankofa* (1993), which dealt with North American slavery, repeatedly sold out and achieved extended runs in the US despite lacking commercial distribution. Its makers rented theatres privately and drummed up support through black community groups (Webster 1998: 106).

Under these circumstances, Allen's involving Spielberg is understandable. 'I just wept and I went through all kinds of emotions,' she recalled about William A. Owens' book. 'I felt empowered and excited that this had actually happened, yet I also felt robbed and cheated that I had never been taught about it in school. I knew it was a true story – a pivotal moment in time – that should be told to the world' (quoted in Palmer 1998: 53). The only way this could happen would be through a storyteller of Spielberg's stature.

For DreamWorks' third feature and first prestige production, Spielberg commanded a budget between $40 million (Pizzello 1998: 28) and $75 million (O'Brien 1999: 153). That it grossed $31 million in the first five weeks, barely covering the advertising (ibid.), and was judged a 'commercial failure' after taking $44.3 million domestically (Bell 1998: 10), allowed Spielberg to extol his commercial independence. 'If you're a filmmaker you don't think about the money or the profit, you just make the films you want to make,' he said, dedicating *Amistad* to his two African-American children (quoted in Norman 1998: 40).

That it was made in association with cable distributor HBO and supported by extensive educational materials suggests *Amistad* was envisaged for extended shelf life rather than instant profitability, and targeted other than regular moviegoers. While African-Americans constitute a disproportionately large theatrical audience share (Dyer 1997: 65), slavery has never been good box office, possibly because of 'resistance to films not perceived to be "entertaining"' (Muyumba 1999: 7). In contrast, the final episode of *Roots* (1977), benefiting from gradual build-up, accrued the then largest television audience ever. Sarcastic comments such as 'Spielberg has made another public service movie' and 'performs the civic good deed of giving the Hollywood imprimatur to this tale' are ironically close to the mark. Their tone originates, as so often, in preconceptions about the kind of filmmaker Spielberg is. Indeed that reviewer's next sentence paradoxically praises the movie's intent (Shulgasser 1997: B1).

Amistad as a Spielberg movie

Despite searing content and worthy social concerns, *Amistad*, like *Schindler's List*, evinces continuities with Spielberg's lighter entertainments. Overt intertextuality and self-reflexivity are especially evident. Potentially intervening between historical realist conventions and the audience, these alter modality in ways that could affect spectatorial positioning in relation to actual events. This bears crucially on the didactic intent and some critics' allegations of manipulation and falsification. I shall therefore demonstrate the pervasiveness of these discourses before relating them to questions of enunciation and representation.

Whether or not the filmmakers drew upon it, as seems likely, Jones' book opens with an image that is pure Spielberg: 'The sun beat down in the late afternoon, sending across his glass a sharp glint of light that made it difficult to see. Lieutenant Richard W. Meade adjusted his sights again, trying to bring form to the moving objects on the beach, over a mile away' (1997: 3). The problem of vision; focalisation through a character's perspective; light as simultaneously spectacle, illumination and mystery; desire; enigma; physical separation and projective involvement; voyeurism: all are strikingly familiar. Later, for Cinqué, the mutineers' leader, the sun represented Africa, the desired home (1997: 26). His cinematic counterpart (Djimon Hounsou) says of the insurrection: 'Any man would do the same to get back to his family.' As in Spielberg's work, light symbolises a quest object and quasi-spiritual transcendence. Notably in the Supreme Court, that not only freed the captives but altered inter-racial history, 'the room's only windows ... were behind the raised bench, which meant that the attorneys and spectators had to strain to see the justice's faces because of the light beaming in behind them' (1997: 171).

Characteristically, Spielberg uses similar lighting. When a surviving Spanish slaver shouts 'To Africa!', acknowledging Cinqué's order to redirect the ship, a fanfare fills the soundtrack as Cinqué, bathed in a golden glow, points his sword, token of justice and nobility, sunwards. In the next shot, from behind Cinqué, light flares across the lens as the ship's steering gear emanates a distinctly projector-like whirring, mixed much louder than other ambient sounds such as the sea or flapping sails, its rhythm synchronised with a flickering flare from the lower right of the screen.

When Cinqué, resisting arrest, plunges overboard and is filmed underwater, apparently drowning, he suddenly recovers and swims upwards through light rays penetrating the surface, similar to when Pete's ghost saves Dorinda in *Always*. Light here connotes not merely life, however. Retrospectively, after the flashback to the woman's suicide with her baby and the underwater shot of the enchained drowning captives, weighted down from the redeeming light, it becomes clear Cinqué had decided to give up the fight before changing his mind.

Light shafts permeate the abolitionist newspaper office where Joadson (Morgan Freeman) and Tappan (Stellan Skarsgård), the captives' first hopes, are introduced. A light shaft accompanies Baldwin initially entering the District Court, even though his interest here is mercenary. The effect implies controlling destiny. (I shall return to this.) Light shafts in the tavern when the abolitionists revisit Baldwin, having failed to hire Adams, exclusively favour Tappan to emphasise his idealisation of 'the battlefield of righteousness' in comparison to Baldwin's commercial pragmatism. Later, in the gloomy prison, Cinqué, like *Close Encounters*' Neary, disappears down light beams into an illuminated rectangular space, to show Baldwin how far he has travelled. Baldwin – an inscribed spectator – and the audience project speculatively into Cinqué's Imaginary.

Joadson, edging among chains in the *Amistad*'s hold, intuits despair. Close-ups reveal bloodstains, scratches and worn grooves on the timbers; a tuft of hair. Not having yet shown captives in transit, Spielberg here acknowledges – and rejects – Alain Resnais' metonymic technique in *Night and Fog* (*Nuit et brouillard*, 1955) for representing Auschwitz. Critics raised this while dismissing Spielberg's handling of the gas chamber in *Schindler's List* as pornographic and suspenseful:

> Aware of the magnitude of horror and sheer human misery of the place, Resnais' narrator momentarily pauses. 'You have to know to look,' he says quietly, before explaining what the camera reveals: fingernail marks left on the gas-chamber ceiling by the death-struggles of its victims. (Horowitz 1997: 128)

With so much at stake, I hesitate to quibble over aesthetic questions that might reduce merely to differences between high and low culture, art movie and Hollywood preferences. However, Sara R. Horowitz argues that Spielberg's representation is obscene: it 'uses the historical memory of mass murder to manipulate' and, she avers, 'titillate' (ibid.). To say, 'You have to know to look,' though, implies the camera's *inability* to represent. Resnais' resort to verbal explanation renders the visual redundant. Also, as I argued concerning *Schindler's List*, 'you have to know' before 'historical memory' intervenes, confirming the gassings without needing to show them. Spielberg, moreover, contrary to many critics' assumptions, *does* narrate indirectly or peripherally, rewarding spectators who, like his protagonists, actively look.

Examples include allusions (such as this one to Resnais) that are frequently not just gratuitous. Subtle gags recur: *Jurassic Park*'s realistically motivated inscription on a vehicle mirror, concerning closeness of reflected objects during a tyrannosaur chase, amuses only if the mirror's 'screen' surface is observed as well as the virtual image 'within' it. Metonymy includes Indiana Jones' and his father's economically implied arrival at a destination in *The Last Crusade* by showing their parked motorcycle combination, cueing the viewer to seek them out within the scene. Among *Amistad*'s intricate details, the captives' various tribal costumes and shots in which Muslims among them are praying, neither foregrounded nor framed centrally, indicate different cultures. Adams, in long shot, conversing while descending a staircase in the House of Representatives, stops to flick away with his cane a dropped coin, indicating precision, sportsmanship and a sense of order. The bloom of evaporating sweat and condensation on the witness stand's polished wood suggests both the testifier's tension and the heightened reality, veering into unreality, of Cinqué's perceptions, which the camera conveys.

Unlike Resnais, Spielberg believes cinema *can* reveal truth. Light shafts illuminate the shackles, rendering their meaning as Joadson's projection. Himself an escaped slave, he panics, drops his lantern and, screaming for light, becomes entangled in manacles. To audiences familiar with the slave trade, the purpose is self-evident, but 'you have to know' to see it. Because the film is didactic, however, aimed at those who *don't* know, or need reminding, its strategy later is to attempt a convincing representation of slavery.

Baldwin, also investigating the ship, finds a packet that Ruiz, the 'slaves'' alleged owner, has been trying to recover. Overlapping dialogue and a match cut to Baldwin's hands unwrapping the same papers create a bridge to the courtroom illuminated by a light shaft as he demonstrates that this is the Tecora's manifest – proving the captives' illegal importation. Outside an unknown assailant has attacked him, and now evening sunlight heroically tinges his face in a low-angle shot as the explanation comes: 'You took the case, Mr Baldwin.'

Amistad – 'You have to know to look': Joadson among the slave ship's manacles

Adams, approached again by Joadson, asks about the Africans: 'What's their story?' This sounds like a producer demanding a high-concept pitch. His argument, illustrated with a capsule summary of Joadson's life, is simple: to convince a court, a situation has to be reduced to bare essentials. So does a two-and-a-half-hour film covering three years of complex disputation.

When Cinqué tells Joadson his story, light shafts behind Covey, the Mende translator, suggest cinema itself is an interpreter. This conceit, *Close Encounters*' informing principle, with its casting of Truffaut and Balaban as his translator, re-emerged with E.T.'s language acquisition and Elliott's newfound empathy, and in *Empire of the Sun* with Jim's subjective understanding of the war – while *Schindler's List*, I argued, problematises it. In *Amistad*, Baldwin in close-up, the spectator's stand-in, looks up at this narration, until light shafts illuminating the communication themselves give way to flashback, cinematic retranslation of Cinqué's verbal account (and, it transpires, of the defence argument in court). Inscription of projecting rays continues into the flashback – a 'film' within the film – as light shafts, conventionally symbolising denied freedom, penetrate the Tecora's hold. Directly after the flashback, these link to rays behind Coughlan, the District Court judge, sitting to deliver his verdict that the captives are legally free.

After this judgement a beam flickers on Baldwin, emotionally staring at Cinqué, who returns the gaze before breaking down. Such moments confirm the light motif as metaphorical rather than decorative. They emphasise seeing and understanding, and implicate projection of spectatorial desire. Such processes are integral to the film's didacticism.

An earlier, surreal, cross-cultural exchange of the look occurs during an explicit foregrounding of textuality when the apparent musical score becomes diegetic in an encounter between the captured *Amistad* and a ship on which a quartet plays for an elegant banquet. Soon after, a cut from Cinqué's black, masculine figure to a white, female doll, immediately interposed by eyes reflected in a dinner knife, inscribes a narcissistic gaze personifying interests associated with Isabella II of Spain. Harsh lighting and brittle, exaggerated noises of the huge room in which she dines, alone, allude to the end of *2001: A Space Odyssey*, emphasising her remote, alien qualities in relation to the more mellow New England ambiance.

Selective subtitling of Mende (unlike Spanish, which undergoes more or less consistent translation) creates comedy when America appears strangely other from the outsiders' perspective. 'Looks like they're going to be sick,' 'They're entertainers,' and 'It's the miserable ones again,' opine Africans confronted with Christians praying and singing hymns for their salvation. As when Elliott explains a suburban child's view of existence to E.T., American culture is anthropologised, decentring norms against which otherness is assumed.

Covey, the interpreter, enters into a cacophony of Christian hymns and African chanting during a captive's funeral. Thereafter overt communication and eventual harmony between cultural representatives becomes possible. Typically, Spielberg renders this in those cultures' imagery in terms of mystical light. A warm glow shines on a captive's illustrated Bible, itself containing images of spiritual illumination. Everywhere he goes Jesus is 'followed by the sun', observes Cinqué's companion. Africans recognise affinities between themselves and this figure, and believe they are going to the same place as He after death. Moreover, their dialogue intercuts with Coughlan praying for guidance before his judgement, again creating dominant specularity from which religious faith appears a common bond. The spectator then aligns with the believing African as, through a shot/reverse-shot, he and we simultaneously, primed by a plate showing Golgotha in his Bible, perceive a ship's three masts as crucifixes. Focalisation minimises otherness. During early scenes following the rebellion, absence of subtitles rendered Mende dialogue threatening in contrast to reassurance and identification permitted by subtitling Spanish. Now Mende conversations behind bars become frustrating and appeal to voyeurism, as the spectator desires to know what the narration could relate but withholds.

Baldwin, scratching a map on the floor, shows Cinqué 'where I'm from', and the latter indicates his origins are much further away: a clear parallel with E.T. and the children learning about each other – Elliott using an atlas and globe, E.T. modelling clay to fashion a solar system – in another story about getting home. This juxtaposition of communication with mapmaking also recalls *Close Encounters*, in which Loughlan, Lacombe's interpreter, is a cartographer. Mutual acceptance, trust and reconciliation arise between beings formerly alien to each other. An early courtroom scene involves Baldwin proving the captives' African, rather than Cuban, provenance through their ignorance of Spanish. One small, slender, hairless African faithfully, if uncomprehendingly, mirrors Baldwin's smile and gestures, an image that – before this court of false claims – recalls other acts of true communication across radical divides: Lacombe face-to-face with an alien, Elliott and E.T., Celie with Shug, Jim with the Japanese and, temporarily and more ambiguously, Schindler confronting Goeth. Subsequent subtitles, granting the spectator dominant specularity, imply deep empathy beyond mutual respect, as Cinqué and Baldwin express frustration at their inability to understand each other even as, unwittingly, they echo each other's statements.

Amistad in fact replicates many *E.T.* motifs. Not only does Adams, through Anthony Hopkins' casting and Spielberg's make-up artists, have E.T.'s eyes and forehead; he is even a fellow horticulturalist, similarly carrying a heavy pot plant from room to room. When first encountered he takes a plant cutting on Capitol Hill. This implication of natural wisdom and understanding, together with his nurturing and protection of the fragile growth and dissemination of human rights, follows through when shared appreciation of an African violet, that he has kept alive in the hostile New World climate, shows Cinqué to be his spiritual brother. They gently touch the plant simultaneously, each using E.T.'s two-finger gesture. The close-up on their symbolic handshake, crossing the cultural and ethnic divide, clearly recalls the poster for *E.T.*

This is also, as the *E.T.* allusions suggest, another Spielberg movie infused with paternal symbolism. Baldwin is much younger than the 47-year-old original (Jones 1997: 37) so that Adams, Joadson, Coughlan and Cinqué can all become the Africans' protective fathers while Baldwin mounts an Oedipal challenge against injustice. Van Buren, who in reality lacked strong feelings about slavery but did not want it to hamper his re-election (Jones 1997: 57), plays the obscene father, prepared to compromise Constitutional principles and sacrifice innocent lives for his career, as does Tappan in the film's characterisation. Phallic connotations of the nail and sword – tokens of the slavers' power over Africans – juxtaposed in successive shots in the flashback, make Cinqué's rebellion also an Oedipal narrative. That this paradigm does not necessarily apply to African societies certainly supports accusations that Eurocentric discourse appropriates Cinqué's story. However, for Western audiences it symbolises his emergence as the captives' leader and helps generalise his achievement as a milestone in recognition of universal rights. For when Adams claims he won the case by using Cinqué's own words, he refers to when the African said he would consult his ancestors and that his presence was the reason for their existence. A shot foregrounds Adams' bald forehead against the Capitol dome, visual equivalence asserting an analogous identity. The real Adams – son of the second President, whose bust glows in a light shaft during Joadson's visit – took pride in descent from Saer de Quincy, whose signature and seal he saw as a young man on the Magna Carta in London, although the impact of his responsibilities to liberty did not strike him until the *Amistad* case (Jones 1997: 248). Baldwin, moreover, was grandson to a signatory to the Declaration of Independence and the xx ok?Tappanses descendants of Benjamin Franklin (1997: 37, 38). That the film lacks time to assert these specific connections neither detracts from Adams' appeal to the judges to recall the ideals of the fathers of the revolution (George Washington's portrait graces the wall behind him), nor from the Eisensteinian montage of the cut between the judge's gavel and removal of Cinqué's manacles. Far from Capraesque cliché, the historical Adams actually did point to the Declaration of Independence and insisted on 'the law of Nature and of Nature's God on which our fathers placed our national existence' (Jones 1997: 176). If, as suggested earlier, light bathing Baldwin on first entering the District Court implies destiny, it is a teleology based on the struggle to create, and have courage to defend, universal principles. These principles Cinqué and companions embrace instinctively. They do not represent, as might superficially appear, a 'Great Men' or specifically American view of history.

Enunciation and representation

Amistad's opening, when Cinqué unshackles himself and instigates butchery, renders him enigmatic and savage. Like the tyrannosaur at the start of *Jurassic Park*, he is mysterious – glimpsed momentarily in fragments – awesome, terrifying; striking instinctively, seemingly uncomprehendingly, against his captors. The comparison, however offensive, is apt. His initial depiction is truly monstrous by means of similar cinematography. Kaminski 'flashed' unexposed film to enhance graininess and contrast (Pizzello 1998: 32); Cinqué's skin consequently appears densely black, a glistening textured surface, relating him to surrounding darkness relieved only by lightning – replete with cultural connotations of evil, the unknown and unbridled natural power. Initially, big close-ups on one eye de-individualise and dehumanise him. Yet, as in *Jurassic Park*, the eye suggests knowledge and control. His superhuman effort to extract a spike from the timbers elicits inarticulate cries that make him appear, like the tyrannosaur, dangerously non-human. While a storm really did cover the event portrayed (Jones 1997: 24), darkness between lightning flashes renders the rebellion, which of course *was* horrific, particularly disturbing because of what cannot be seen.

Although, historically, the violence was justifiable, blackness appears here synonymous with revulsion and fear.

These associations accord with Southern orientation towards 'the Negro' when justifying slavery and with contemporary racist perception of otherness. The film underlines the very image of Africans contested in the *Amistad* affair and during ensuing divisions leading to the Civil War and beyond. It thus reawakens questions concerning enunciation and representation of black masculinity raised by *The Color Purple*.

The racism is not attributable to the filmmakers, however, nor is it valid evidence of white representation silencing black experience. Apart from desperate distress conveyed by Cinqué's rapid breathing, dripping sweat and bleeding fingertips, which encourage sympathy, subjective close-ups establish focalisation partly through his consciousness. Unlike scenes from the Middle Passage that represent documented horrors as explicitly as mainstream taste and decency allow, the opening is artificial and melodramatic – a partial and, when external, false representation, corrected over the ensuing film as the legal process, tending towards universal principles of justice, accords Cinqué a voice.

Those principles do not, however, emerge unproblematically. Cinqué's handshake as Baldwin becomes his attorney accompanies a defiant dare. The eye that suggests radical otherness becomes the eye that sees, a witnessing discourse to contest and supplant those informing the opening. Juttson's sidelong glances and framing of him as one small man against a mass stress his fear of the captives, the film consciously articulating white attitudes as an object language forming part of its dramatic conflict. These constitute neither the dominant discourse nor a hidden agenda discovered by hostile critics. By the time silence and slow-motion during the British officer's testimony convey the unreality for Cinqué of proceedings he cannot understand, *his* point-of-view, *his* enunciation, dominates.

Cinqué's transformation from threatening Other to respected prince can be criticised for perpetuating imagery of the noble savage, even though this was central to the Christian evangelist Tappan's moral stereotyping (Jones 1997: 39, 42). Yet before dismissing this regressive discourse out of hand, it is worth recalling its origins in eighteenth-century debates between an optimistic anthropology that supported revolution and a pessimistic one favouring the status quo, which included slavery (Ferguson 1998: 79). By retaining the characterisation of Cinqué popularised in William Cullen Bryant's poem, published as the trial opened, the film can at least claim fidelity to contemporary descriptions:

> Chained in a foreign land he stood,
> A man of giant frame,
> Amid the gathering multitude
> That shrunk to hear his name —
> All stern of look and strong of limb,
> His dark eye on the ground —
> And silently they gazed on him
> As on a *lion* bound.
> Vainly, but well, that chief had fought —

He was a captive now;
Yet pride, that fortune humbles not,
  Was written on his brow.
The scars his dark broad bosom wore
  Showed warrior true and brave;
A prince among his tribe before,
  He could not be a slave.
(*The Emancipator*, 19 September 1839; quoted in Jones 1997: 66)

However, Cinqué's romanticisation also forms part of the film's didactic project, invalidating, as necessary, possible perceptions by some white audiences and offering a role model to blacks in place of abject victimhood.

Bryant's scenario of Cinqué as object of a fearful, voyeuristic gaze, directed across a gulf, accords with the film's concerns. Nothing in the narrative suggests Cinqué and his companions change significantly. Indeed prayers and peaceful, joyful singing by the former captives, many now in purple robes, follow close upon the uprising. 'Hold your head up,' Cinqué exhorts one as they approach the court, and the captives all rise for the judge, accepting the process of law. Baldwin, by contrast, their inscribed audience, undergoes education from seeing the Africans cynically, as property disputed for personal gain, to becoming a 'committed abolitionist' (Hadden 1998: 63).

The melodramatic opening accords with 'official' views of the rebellion at the time, questioned only by abolitionists, and with twentieth-century plantation mov-ies and bodice-ripper fiction. Self-reflexivity underlines the cliché: stroboscopic lightning, in which rain makes the light itself visible, recalls a flickering movie. Spielberg purposefully adopts horror conventions. Bloody swords at one point penetrate the blank 'screen' of a sail, threatening the spectator's security: a trope repeated from earlier showmanship involving sharks and velociraptors, and from *Hook*. White enunciation of black history *is* established – then supplanted, not by exclusively black discourse but a universal consensus assumed by liberal idealism.

Selective syuzhet and style set up otherness solely for deconstruction. Cinqué's later version, showing him aghast at his situation, revises the 'white movie' version of a massacre by blacks – Tappan had to reiterate in the actual trial they were *not* cannibals (Jones 1997: 41, 149). Cinqué's inarticulate cries, far from a primitive's grunts, become shocked, horrified sobs. The appalling tableau as Cinqué impales an officer to the deck makes the rebel terrifying, partly owing to a low angle in grotesquely distorting close-up, near the 'victim's' perspective. Yet the image is ambiguous, balanced by a reverse-shot, from Cinqué's vision, of the officer. The low angle confers stature, while rain and light from above form a shaft that even without Spielberg's specific lighting code would symbolise freedom, given established connotations of water regarding spiritual cleansing and rebirth, and of illumination as divine favour. It may be no coincidence that Cinqué remains bare to the waist like the instigating mutineer in *Battleship Potemkin*, who appears a chosen one thanks to mise-en-scène modelled on Russian Orthodox icons, suggestive of shafts of light.

Straining to remove the sword, Cinqué – at least on subsequent viewing – is already the hero. In the process, though, his story is appropriated into Western myths.

The sword becomes a phallus, won in Oedipal battle against the authority purporting to own him. The effort of its extraction parallels his removing the spike, token of his initial subjection. Excesses of cinematography, performance, soundtrack and Djimon Hounsou's physique combine to accord the moment epic stature, recalling Arthur with Excalibur. In the calm following the insurrection, extreme low angles assert Cinqué's greatness. Inclusion of Spielberg's favourite starry sky is compositionally motivated to show that Cinqué understands the surviving Spaniards are changing course, but ethereal music additionally implies destiny. Crucially, the spectator makes the realisation simultaneously with Cinqué, encouraging identification.

Subtitles for Spanish, but not yet when Africans speak, emphasise their otherness. (It is appropriate, though, that the narrative filters through the whites' experience; they effectively enunciate, as at this point they held control. Later, when the situation becomes dangerous after an African's death, withholding subtitles again increases tension and uncertainty.) So too, the close encounter with elegant diners polarises savagery against civilisation, although the movie overall questions which culture is depraved, given institutionalised slavery. Attacks by deranged white prisoners and brutal guards, contrasted with the dignity of a passively staring African woman and child, elicit sympathy for the captives and disallow any assumption of white superiority. Such relativisation continues when the recaptured defendants, processing to court, spot a black carriage driver who, because of his elevated position, Western clothing and apparent power over horses and the parting crowd, they identify as a chief and address as 'Brother'. They attribute failure to respond to his being 'a white man', indicating the cultural, rather than biological, significance of difference.

The film goes to some lengths to stress this. In prison, tribal conflict flares over the placement of Baldwin's table, as different groups defend their territories. Subtitles here reveal the various peoples' inability to understand each other (hardly raised in the source text (1987)). Although the subtitles confer dominant specularity – a privileged overview unavailable to anyone in the diegesis – they disallow homogenisation of Africans as generalised Other. Moreover, an African's description of Baldwin as a 'dung-scraper' simultaneously stresses his mercenary motives and wins audience sympathy by voicing 1990s cynicism about lawyers, but also emphasises divisions on the same side in the case.

Contrast with the nightmarish blackness and intermittent light of the start could hardly be greater when eventually the freed captives return to their continent, bathed in warm light, sailing into the solar wind, accompanied by soaring African music. A rear view of Cinqué sailing into the sun accentuates fulfilment of his original desire. The sun is the film's last image, again equating narrative closure with the Imaginary, signified as light and the cinema screen. Cinqué's discourse, finally indistinguishable from Spielberg's, prevails.

The transition occurs at the flashback. Cinqué's enunciation, rendered as metaphorical cinematic projection, takes over the film to reveal truths about slavery unavailable without this interpretive apparatus. Notably, through visualisation of naked bodies sardined below deck – a well-known fact abstractly but not previously dramatised explicitly, nor featured largely by Jones (1997: 123) – Cinqué speaks for *all* slaves, rather in the manner of the ghost in Morrison's *Beloved*. The flashback is virtually a self-contained drama-documentary. After its unflinching representations, shots repeated from the opening are perceived very differently.

When subsequently the captives uniformly wear white, quasi-religious lighting renders them angelic. Knowledge of suffering and oppression reverses perceptions of blackness encouraged by the opening. That this may appear manipulative ('sentimental rubbish', wrote one reviewer ('RW' 1998: 9)) is not entirely Spielberg's fault: it could well be a ploy abolitionists used. At any rate, close-ups increasingly individualise the captives, an effect reinforced as they henceforth wear Western clothes, minimising difference. Consequently Cinqué burns his Western clothing when angered by legal obfuscation. Cursing Baldwin in Mende, he reasserts his identity, refusing objectification in other people's causes and fantasies, and again his silhouette against the flames evokes deep-rooted racial imagery.

Cinqué wears elegantly tailored clothes for his Supreme Court appearance. African and American narratives converge when he addresses his ancestors, paralleling Adams and his father, prompting the ex-President's invocation of the Founding Fathers. 'What words did you use then?' asks Cinqué of Adams' speech. The reply: 'Yours.' Baldwin proffers an African handshake and addresses Cinqué as Sengbe, his original Mende name, in their final encounter, recognising and validating his African identity, and Cinqué is last seen in a toga – based on portraits of the time (see Jones 1997: 154) – both African and evocative of classical nobility. While the last word sung on the soundtrack is 'Africa', and the film reconstructs 'The Liberation of Lomboko Slave Fortress', narrative closure is provisional. Cinqué returns home to civil war, following shots of the American Civil War precipitated partly by the *Amistad* decision.

Nevertheless the film tempers inevitable orientation towards white mainstream audiences by foregrounding specifically black issues. African drumming accompanies Joadson's discovery of a lion's tooth on the *Amistad*, which he returns to Cinqué who had obtained it by killing a lion threatening his village. It reinforces that Cinqué's heroism was not simply a function of his role in a dispute between whites. Drawn in fact from Bryant's poem (the story does not feature in Jones), it recurs as a motif for Joadson's African-American heritage as a former slave now prospering and assimilated into New England. Bestowing of the tooth as a totem ('phallus' too strongly suggests a Western paradigm) coincides with Cinqué's ability to tell his story. In finally presenting the tooth to Joadson, Cinqué affirms racial pride, history and identity.

A major difficulty when discussing enunciation and representation is that, in an image-saturated culture, intertextuality can cause aberrant decoding (Eco 1972). Subcultures constituting any mass audience make their own meanings; resultant problems can be exacerbated, however positive the originator's intention, when communication crosses racial and cultural boundaries. One damning criticism of *Amistad* is that 'the film's greatest banality ... is its idiotic presentation of the Africans, as vulgarly stereotyped as Robert Mapplethorpe's studies of black men' ('RW' 1998: 9). Stereotyping is one issue, discussed elsewhere in this book. But to cite controversial photographer Mapplethorpe – whose eroticised nudes involved 'aesthetic objectification that reduced ... black men to purely abstract visual "things", silenced in their own right as subjects and serving mainly as aesthetic trophies to enhance Mapplethorpe's privileged position as a white gay male artist' (Mercer 1993: 164) – raises serious questions akin to alleged 'pornography' in *Schindler's List*. Does *Amistad*'s implicitly white camera, albeit inadvertently, (homo)eroticise and objectify black characters it seeks consciously to render heroic and admirable, in the way feminist cultural theory argues the implicitly male camera does with the similarly idealised female form? Is this the threatening Other's fetishisation and containment in a colonial fantasy? Certainly the Africans' enforced passivity through much of the narrative – unavoidable historical fact – and position as mysterious objects of voyeuristic fascination, could accord with Mapplethorpe's work. 'Whereas [Mapplethorpe's] white gay male sadomasochistic pictures portray a subcultural sexuality that consists of "doing" something, the black men are defined and confined to "being" purely sexual and nothing but sexual – hence hypersexual' (Mercer 1993: 165). Moreover, the stark, shiny monochrome of Mapplethorpe's prints 'becomes almost consubstantial with the shiny, sexy texture of black skin', enhancing fetishisation (ibid.); in the same way flashing the film stock at the start intentionally heightens Cinqué's body surfaces, presented in unindividualised close-ups (Pizzello 1998: 32).

The opening, contradictorily, might attempt a positive representation for blacks from a white, liberal apologist standpoint, even while positing Cinqué as terrifying Other. The passage may release a discourse of what Mercer calls 'negrophilia', the repressed Other of 'darkness, dirt and danger ... manifest in the psychic representations of "negrophobia"' (Mercer 1993: 166). Nevertheless, the opening establishes meanings *in order* to reverse them when Cinqué attains enunciation. Dangers of asserting ownership of history and of responding to images or passages in isolation become apparent. So too does the impossibility of separating representation from interpretive context. Kobena Mercer himself decides finally that Mapplethorpe's pictures are progressive, in incorporating the black body into the fine art tradition of the nude from which it was hitherto excluded (1993: 170). A similar argument could be made about the increasing centrality of Cinqué's discourse in *Amistad*.

Some objections focus on 'the casting of the tall, physically intimidating Djimon Hounsou ... when the real African rebel was not as imposing a figure' (Breen 1999: 5). Aside from the fact that casting alone has little bearing on screen stature, as the diminutive Alan Ladd in *Shane* (1953) famously demonstrates, the real Cinqué was indeed 'strong and agile, taller than most of his fellow tribesmen' and, according to Tappan, 'like another Othello', of 'fine proportions' (Jones 1997: 15, 42). It is true also that, as the Havana sequence shows, importers encouraged slaves to exercise and provided oil to make their bodies glisten (Jones 1997: 17). If the animalistic, majestic black man is 'a recurring erotic fantasy of some white males' (Ferguson 1998: 227), that is no reason the classical physique should not be available to filmmakers to indicate black heroism. It is, after all, only to treat black heroes according to conventions of white male stardom.

Historiography versus didacticism (revisited)

Van Buren in *Amistad* asks: 'There are three million negroes in this country. Why should I concern myself with these 44?' The spectator also might ponder this in relation to the film. Why, some critics wonder, does Spielberg not concentrate on the estimated forty million who did not escape slavery or, alternatively, on a successful mutiny such as on the *Creole* during the *Amistad* trial?

One answer is that the *Amistad* case raises matters of duty and responsibility and provides opportunities to challenge polarised attitudes. Slavery, abhorrent and immoral, lends itself easily to divisions between clear-cut (and racialised) heroes and villains, in which the fortitude of slaves who remained and suffered or escaped and triumphed does little to change the institution or those involved. The *Creole* mutiny, in which captives on an American ship escaped to the Bahamas and freedom under Britain's Emancipation Act, raises none of the legal niceties and consequent learning opportunities of the *Amistad*, as there was no question the cargo were legally slaves. The *Amistad* forced different cultures, including three white nations with divergent laws and attitudes, into close communication – and changed history.

The contestation over ownership of the Africans, according to which Spanish and American trading remained acceptable while international trading was illegal, was as absurd and spurious as disputes over ownership of history – which is not to deny such disputes are valuable in seeking to understand conflict and contradiction in nationhood, culture, ethnicity and identity. For example, in the film the district attorney, Holabird (Pete Postlethwaite), raises the awkward matter of African complicity in slavery. This immediately complicates knee-jerk black-good/white-bad assumptions. Though Cinqué's narrative shows the practice was exploited in arms trading for tribal warfare, Jones' book describes African slave traders uncompromisingly as 'businessmen' (1997: 14).

Adams' assertion, 'Who we are, is who we were', is as true also of Africans then as of African-Americans today, and of everybody else. This is not essentialism but a declaration of the burden of history and a plea for enlightenment. Whether one believes history should be written off or that apologies are due, progress is impossible without consensus and understanding. Those are achievable only through debate, which films such as *Amistad* stimulate.

Lawrence Blum, building on past struggles, advocates moral education that stresses the importance of 'white allies' of people of colour to encourage interracial cooperation. In a cynical climate, he argues, racial justice ideals suffer diminishment by distrust among people of colour that whites will support them, and a tendency among young whites to assume only three models of racial identity are available to them: supremacism; denial that colour exacerbates injustice; or debilitating guilt (1999: 133). Accepting that inequality is structural, therefore alterable only by communal will, allows whites and people of colour to identify as the same community. Participation in projects to support not only fellow students but also other people of colour, the theory goes, promotes this aim. However, such education requires tact, to recognise that people of colour have fought their own battles and do not require white organisation and leadership (1999: 134).

Spielberg, in this conciliatory spirit, is an exemplary white ally for providing resources, talent and influence to get *Amistad* made. Blum, however, considers the film seriously flawed in its representation of abolitionists. Confidence imbued by multiculturalism has inadvertently increased suspicion of white people among other racial and ethnic communities, and students from all backgrounds question the motives of whites who supported earlier struggles (1999: 133). The film's fun poked at Christian abolitionists and Tappan's inaccurate, self-righteous and near-fanatical caricature marginalise or devalue the historical white allies of the *Amistad* captives and black American slaves (1999: 134) – an ironic variation on how Hollywood traditionally has treated non-whites.

Conversely, Cinqué's dramatic intonation, 'Give us, us free!', when exasperated by apparent lack of white support, is also gross historical distortion. He and others from the *Amistad* actually learned to read and write in English and corresponded with Baldwin and had letters published in *The Emancipator* (Jones 1997: 158, 203). One answer to Blum's legitimate objection – other than that the film separates inter-racial accord from many abolitionists' exclusively Christian agenda, which did not necessarily embrace equality – is that a film made to promote a particular model of moral education, however desirable, would come dangerously close to propaganda. It might anyway be so out of tune with prevailing discourses as to risk rejection. Here the free-market argument that Hollywood entertainments supply what audiences want explains some contradictions in Spielberg's version, along with the basic need to simplify characters and motivation to narrate efficiently.

Amistad may not be good history. Sally Hadden (1998) lists inaccuracies in detail. Elmer and Joanne Martin (1998) furiously attack the film from an essentialist black position, identifying very different distortions from Hadden's. Historians, this confirms, have no monopoly on truth; nor, given that history embodies present-day discourses, is there unanimity concerning what facts mean.

Factual distortions have to be considered against the film's ideological tendency as an assertion of black pride and white education within a broadly faithful scenario, trusting to the audience's intelligence in reading through the marketing slogans: 'A Steven Spielberg Film' and 'Based on a True Story'. That 'Spielberg inserts a historically inaccurate but morally satisfying encounter between Adams and Cinqué', while it masks abolitionists' true role and reduces 'historical forces, social movements and morally significant collectivities to single individuals' (Blum 1999: 134, 135), is typical of Hollywood practice. It does, nevertheless, assert common human values and the possibility of transcending divisions.

Anyone moved by the film to look closer is free to find more nuanced versions in published histories. Hadden remains pessimistic, complaining that 'the average American has not read or is not interested in reading history crafted by professional historians, but will devour' fictionalised versions (1998: 67). *Amistad* is, however, a new phenomenon:

> a multi-media package, not a closed text but one that points endlessly beyond itself. Alongside the movie is page after teeming web page of state-of-the-art Internet data – everything from detailed discussion of the legal issues involved, information about the law of salvage and the law of slavery in the US in 1841, through to regularly updated accounts of the plagiarism case involving Spielberg's Dreamworks [sic] and writer Barbara Chase-Riboud, who claims Spielberg stole wholesale from her novel. (Jeffries & Hattenstone 1998: 3)

Historians, in fact, objected less to the film than the accompanying study guide distributed to schools, which, by asking students to debate positions advanced by fictional characters such as Joadson, blurs fabrication with fact. Yet, as Michael Wood observes, art does not concern itself with factual accuracy, and 'smaller inaccuracies can serve larger truths' (quoted in Jeffries & Hattenstone 1998: 3). Facts do not speak for themselves. They always require interpretation.

Blum believes antiracist cooperation leads potentially beyond the white ally relationship to moral co-equality. 'Shared moral identity' can arise out of people, positioned differently in relation to an injustice, combating the same cause (1999: 136). Blum considers *Amistad* an illustration, in Joadson and Tappan's relationship before the latter's deficiencies emerge. Whereas the ally model highlights racial *difference* between partners, moral co-equality stresses *identity*. Although Blum does not make the connection, Cinqué and Adams, Cinqué and Joadson, and, implicitly, Baldwin and Joadson provide examples. Nevertheless – important, given some criticisms of the film (for example, Amarger 1998) – moral co-equality seeks neither to deny nor eliminate difference.

In reality British observers and Mende translators, moral co-equals, persuaded Juttson the captives were African – not Cinqué's later testimony (Hadden 1998: 66). So much for complaints about whites enunciating black history in this film, which in fact distorts in favour of black discourse. Barbara Shulgasser, for example, complains that 'Spielbergian cutesiness is rampant, as when he attributes sweet little misinterpretations to the Africans trying to figure out what everyone is babbling about in English', and cites their mistaking sour-faced Christians for entertainers (1997: 3). Preconceptions about Spielberg here obscure a serious comment about perception. How wrong, similarly, might slave-owners, abolitionists and (white-written) history be about the prisoners?

Spielberg dialogises. But criticism scoring points against Spielberg's popularity misunderstands the issue and perpetuates divisions the film attacks. Ryan Gilbey, for example, describes Cinqué as 'mute and symbolic' and wonders why Spielberg cannot 'show a black struggle from a black perspective, rather than filtering it through white experiences' (1998: 8). Noting the music, he comments: 'By the end, Adams' signature theme has engulfed Cinqué's; though the slaves have won their freedom, the white characters remain victorious in the battle for soundtrack' (ibid.). Despite admirable attention to the medium's specificity, this distorts by overlooking the last *word* sung on the soundtrack: 'Africa'. If the film ends on a white note the blacks have the last word, in a nice balancing of discourses. Similarly, when the jettisoned captives are drowning, African drums combine with a heavenly choir to assert integration, a shared emotional and moral response, on the level of the music – a contemporary comment on past events.

In short, the real-life abolitionists' strategy was 'all-out effort to demonstrate the humanity of the *Amistad* captives' (Jones 1997: 81); 170 years later, the film's project was broadly similar in asserting shared identity across racial boundaries. That some white liberals and black radicals find this unacceptably patronising is understandable, but needs to be measured against its utility in a continuously racist and mutually hostile culture.

Following Ferguson's example (1998: 116), one might ask of *Amistad* a few 'What if?' questions:

- *What if* a black man or woman directed it? In terms of high production values this was simply unlikely in the racist social and economic climate that produced it.

- *What if* Cinqué was not (fictitiously) shown going to the Supreme Court? The alternative would make him a pawn in whites' power struggles and beneficiary of primarily white efforts. This would fit a dominant abolitionist definition the film incorporates, through the captive who accepts conversion, precisely so Cinqué can eschew it:

> Abolitionism ... was not the same as victory over racism. The abolition of slavery was not the same as black emancipation. Abolitionism produced new stereotypes of blacks – the movement humanised the image of blacks but also popularised the image of blacks as victims ... The central icon of abolitionism, the figure of a black kneeling, hands folded and eyes cast upward, clearly carried a message. It made emancipation conditional – on condition of conversion, on condition of docility and meekness, on condition of being on one's knees. (Pieterse 1992: 60)

- *What if* Adams had been involved early on, as in reality (Jones 1997: 81–3)? There would be less sense of the difficulties of achieving justice if influential individuals – whose involvement, in fact, did much to attract publicity – were seen waiting for opportunities to test the law. Adams, as the film shows, did not regard himself as an abolitionist, but opposed slavery constitutionally. He had little interest initially in the individual *Amistad* prisoners. To acknowledge this would relegate them to passivity.

- *What if* the film dealt with complex legal arguments on both sides of the case? Impossible, of course. A partial account that constructs a particular case strategically is more tendentious but *no less accurate* than one that claims neutrality by making a different selection for the purpose of summary.

- *What if* the full text of Adams' speech were included? Goodbye budget. Goodbye distribution. Goodbye audience.

- *What if* the film did not individualise abstract and collective positions? In theory social forces might be representable cinematically, but in practice this would be unachievable granted realist constraints Spielberg had to accept if *Amistad* stood any chance of reaching its audience. Conversely, *Amistad* arguably belongs to a novelistic realist mode advocated by Lukács (1950), which explores social tendencies through representative characters.

- *What if* Cinqué and companions were more vocal in English? This might have made them more eloquent in arguing their specific cause but less representative of slavery, in which incomprehension and helplessness would have been usual. Linguistic barriers, furthermore, confirmed prejudices about inferiority used to justify the institution. Moreover, in the film Cinqué sends legal questions and suggestions to Adams via Covey, the Mende translator found by Joadson (in reality by the linguistics professor who was anything but the buffoon the film portrays): an African and an African-American thus actively control crucial points of the plot.

- *What if* the film more accurately presented Baldwin as already an abolitionist? There would be no identification figure to ease white audiences through an educational process.

- *What if* the film did not concentrate on Cinqué? It would depart further from its source materials (press coverage did single out Cinqué) and would be guilty of double standards in adopting different conventions for black and white characters.

- *What if* the film had been without didactic intent? There would be little point in telling this story as opposed to other inherently more dramatic, less convoluted tales. Where *Amistad* particularly succeeds is in concentrating less on slavery's horrors, nevertheless acknowledged, than the contemporary lesson that noble institutions can be manipulated to support factional interests:

> The film never shows the bared teeth of outright racism, simply restricting itself to the dogma that white superiority over black is part of the natural order of things. Skilled and semi-logical arguments are wheeled out repeatedly, and this aspect of the film makes the whole issue more chilling than any depiction of blind hatred ever could. (Brett 1998: 17)

Robert Ferguson points out, 'many films which combine politics, history and adventure [are] open to cheap shots', as often from liberal critics as revolutionaries or conservatives. This is especially true of those dealing with race relations through individual characters. However, *Amistad* uses individuals to demonstrate wider issues and attitudes, in sometimes complex and subtle ways, and condemn racism from a liberal perspective. Ferguson argues, having reached a similar conclusion about *Cry Freedom* (1987), 'The issue then becomes ideological. If one opposes *liberal* condemnation, it behoves one to offer alternative positions' (1998: 111).

CHAPTER NINETEEN

Saving Private Ryan: Hollywood on war

Spielberg and his star, Tom Hanks, accepted minimum payment for *Saving Private Ryan* in return for twenty per cent each of the gross. This indicates low hopes of early profitability at Paramount, for whom Amblin made it rather than DreamWorks, but shrewd negotiation by the main players' agents. World War Two movies had not been a 1990s trend; this one was unlikely to attract financing without Spielberg's name. Spielberg declared willingness to 'risk not entertaining anyone or not having anyone attend' (quoted in Magid 1998: 56). Yet it earned $440 million worldwide (Freer 2001: 272) and became *Variety*'s sixteenth-highest grosser of the decade, taking $216 million in the US after opening on 2,463 screens – $30.6 million in the first weekend (Balio 2002: 167; O'Brien 1999:157). It garnered five Academy Awards, including Best Director, consolidated Spielberg's reinvention as an adult filmmaker and, some claimed, redefined the war genre.

The success of a film widely considered unprecedentedly brutal and realistic in portraying conflict raises questions, as often with Spielberg, about marketing and relationships between representation, pleasure and ideology. That bigger receipts came from abroad makes it a global phenomenon. This problematises American criticism that *Saving Private Ryan* appeals, by glorifying militarism, to assuage post-Vietnam trauma and post-Cold War anxieties (Auster 2002; Kodat 2000). This chapter considers such accusations alongside realism, structural patterns of meaning, self-reflexivity and attendant ambiguity.

The *Guardian* stated, 'the first 30 minutes are considered the most realistic recreation of war in movie history' (Ellison 1999). To this is widely attributed its 'remarkable critical and box office success' (Landon 1998: 58). Marketing centred on realism which, in a brilliant move by DreamWorks, dominated discussion, providing endless publicity. Before the UK release, for example, Britain's Independent Television *News at Ten* reported on the American reception, asking in the opening headline: 'Has Spielberg gone too far this time?' (4 September 1998). The story featured extracts (described as 'artificially aged'), wartime newsreels, a reporter in a Normandy graveyard, an account of the Sullivan family whose experience partly inspired the film, and a British D-Day veteran who, like American interviewees in clips presumably provided by DreamWorks, attested to its realism. Which aspect extended 'too far' remained unexplored, but the agenda was established. The film's trailer occupied the commercial break, a prime slot in the schedule.

Promotion – purportedly 'low key ... "out of respect" for the subject matter' but carefully controlled (Gumbel 1998: 16) – involved parading veterans before journalists to recount psychologically damaging horrors and endorse Spielberg's reconstruction (McMahon 1998). Families bereft of several siblings reportedly 'c[a]me forward' (Helmore 1998: 8). Coverage spotlighted a helpline for US Veterans disturbed by the screen version (Gumbel 1998). Implicitly veterans, whom publicists bussed in anyway, *needed* counselling; this 'proved' the representation authentic. Realism equated with truthfulness, and both with horror.

This film, like *Schindler's List* and *Amistad*, bore witness. Looking away was cowardly, disrespectful. Spielberg, frequently accused of childish lighter entertainment and sentimental and evasive serious offerings, confirmed this in press statements pre-empting populist objections: 'It would have been irresponsible for me to undercut the truth of what that war was like', he averred. 'I think audiences today have been desensitised to violence, not only because of motion pictures but also because of video games. My hope ... is somehow to resensitise audiences to how bad it was for the men who survived, as well as for those who perished.' Distancing himself from slash-and-spatter tendencies exciting controversy around Hollywood, Spielberg proclaimed a moral purpose: 'to honour [the soldiers] with the truth and hopefully to teach something. Audiences today are often thrilled by violence. This is intended to show the other side, what that violence does to human beings.' (Reed 1998: 14)

As astute critics noted, 'promotion and media reception' – not the movie, I argue later – 'played upon public amnesia of the combat film's generic history' (Hodsdon 1999: 42), suggesting 'every previous war-flick had been a jingoistic cheese-fest starring John Wayne' (Carson 1999: 70). The BBC also followed DreamWorks' agenda and took British Normandy veterans to a screening. Responses varied, but all considered the cemetery sequences showing the elderly Ryan breaking down 'by far the most powerful and affecting' (Crace 1998: 16). Similar endorsements, asserting psychological as well as sensual realism, prompted the Motion Picture Association of America's 'R' rating (allowing accompanied under-17s) as opposed to the commercially disastrous 'NC17' (no under-17s) that would have alienated older audiences from a product with little inherent youth appeal (Reed 1998: 14). The MPAA's deliberations evoked controversies sparked by *Temple of Doom* and *Jurassic Park*, fuelling additional publicity. Their warning of 'intense, prolonged and realistically graphic' violence fed neatly into DreamWorks' strategy.

Referential realism – comparison against documented facts or direct experience – also features extensively in condemnation. Several critics quote Omaha Beach (and *1941*) veteran and D-Day war movie director Sam Fuller: 'The only way' to replicate war 'is to fire live ammo over the heads of the people in the movie theatre' (quoted in Basinger 1998: 44). The final battle, brilliantly executed – 'Each brand of machine gun has its characteristic noise, each German tank, roaring, whirring and grinding, shakes the cinema to its foundations' – 'devalues' the D-Day sequence because it is fictional (Shephard 1998). This relates to internal consistency. Because of truth claims based on corroborated details of the beach landing, a seemingly authentic sequence admits artifice and supposedly undermines veracity.

Lawrence Blum objects that, although US combatants were segregated, Spielberg ignores African-Americans and other 'culturally indicated' minorities (1999: 133): effectively a symbolic annihilation (although, it must be said, many commentators characterise Miller's squad as ethnically mixed, a war movie cliché). In Britain the exclusive concentration on American experience prompted undercurrents of resentment. Some American critics, too, denounced Spielberg for US triumphalism, contrasted unfavourably with *The Longest Day* (1962), which acknowledged other Allied efforts (Auster 2000: 102). Historians noted 'substantial and serious divergences from D-Day reality, such as the absence of naval gunfire … which helped suppress the German positions' (Cohen 1998/99: 84).

These are questions of selection – inevitable in mediation – as much as of Spielberg's treatment of highlighted events. The first major movie in a generation to return to the World War Two combat genre carries a heavy burden of representation. Selection relates to focalisation in that mainstream cinema dramatises individuals' experience. Focalisation in turn facilitates suture in a sequence constructed to maximise involvement. The landing is narrated impressionistically, largely from Miller's (Tom Hanks) perspective, a position quickly established through Hanks' star persona. Wider strategy, political implications and historical context – hardly within Miller's purview – albeit structured absences, are dramatically irrelevant in a film conveying impressions, rather than causes or justifications, of war.

Realism and authenticity

Criticism of *Saving Private Ryan*, influenced by DreamWorks' claims, widely confuses 'authenticity', implying genuineness, reliability and trustworthiness, with 'realism', involving representational conventions. The distinction informs a veteran's comment, which, objecting to Miller's squad marching in the wrong formation and too closely, concluded pragmatically: 'Of course, otherwise, they would not be able to show them having a conversation' (Ditmann 1998: 66).

Realism, although a loose, commonsense concept used freely, often as a value judgement, is controversial. John Ellis deems it 'complex because the word itself …

describes a whole series of principles of artistic construction and of audience expectation alike' (1992: 6). John Hartley defines realism as 'use of representational devices (signs, conventions, narrative strategies, and so on) to depict or portray a physical, social or moral universe which is held to exist objectively beyond its representation by such means, and which is thus the arbiter of the truth of the representation' (Hartley in O'Sullivan *et al* 1994: 257). The relationship between signified and referent ('objective' universe) is crucial; representation is tested against reality. Accordingly, many naively see realism as a function of the camera's ability to reproduce appearances. This mimetic approach assumes cinema imitates reality. As promotional materials stressed, the fact a retired Marine captain not only advised Spielberg but also put actors through military training supposedly enhances on-screen authenticity. By contrast, Ellis (and Hartley, elaborating the definition) emphasises the text (signifier) and audience expectations rather than direct relationship to profilmic reality. Conventions, such as those defining genres, create verisimilitude.

Realism does not occupy any one aspect of representation. It is a relationship between text, audience, filmmakers' intentions, and – when material is drawn from actuality – the empirical world. No text is intrinsically realistic independently of audiences reading; it has to be realistic *to someone*. Furthermore, filmmakers' intentions can be inferred only from such reading, unless declared in advance (which then confirms meaning is not inherent). More problematically, reference to the empirical world assumes reality is objective (universally agreed upon: clearly not so). This conception also, bypassing discourse, assumes the possibility of material existing either separately from reality (as if fiction bore no relation to experience) or, alternatively, that material is appropriable directly from reality without mediation transforming it.

Given these multiple relationships, easily some two-dozen conceptions of realism, each with distinct suppositions concerning effects and implications, surround *Saving Private Ryan*. 'It's meaningless for critics to write of "realism" in war movies', John Wrathall argues; most people 'have no idea what war really looks like' (1998: 34) – as though verisimilitude were divorced from architextuality and hypertextuality. Phoney distinctions separate authenticity (*Saving Private Ryan*) from imaginative works (*The Thin Red Line* (1998), released soon after) to the latter's benefit; reflective, poetic explorations are assumed inherently more truthful, more politically, psychologically and philosophically insightful, than superficial recreation that 'takes the path of formal rigour and ideological ease' (Wisniewski 2002: 3). This advocates a different realism, associated with writings by Georg Lukács and Bertolt Brecht, which look beyond naturalism to political and social structures.

Saving Private Ryan's realism is no less constructed, no less self-conscious, and not necessarily more simplistic, than avowedly artistic or expressionistic representations. There are few establishing shots, but captions place the flashback – spare, documentary-style superimpositions: 'June 6, 1944'/'Dog Green Sector, Omaha Beach'. These are doubly discoursed. As *histoire*, they identify time and place seemingly neutrally, yet are redundant within apparently subjective enunciation (the soldiers know the time and location). As *discours* they speak the metanarrative of subsequent victory: date and location have entered folklore, but the name is military code, not found on any normal map. The film, purportedly transporting us there, positions spectators as outsiders, less knowledgeable than itself, which consequently gains authority. Nevertheless this rhetorical detachment, contradicting cinematic sensory immersion, reinforces psycho-logical realism in that infantrymen had little sense of precise location and few residues of diurnal reality against which to gauge adrenaline-pumped fear and horror.

John Corner delineates in the landing 'potentially diverse types of realist illusion': *physical* realism of injuries, 'a technical achievement surpassing previous accounts' (this being the first major war movie utilising CGI); *documentary* realism, simulating news-reel; and *subjective* realism intermittently evoking horror and disorientation (1998: 72). The last involves 'three recurring motifs' for Miller's response: 'elimination of sound (cinematic), a shaking hand (performance) and a resistance to explaining his pre-war background (narrative)' (Basinger 1998: 43). Several hand-held cameras shot the landing in 'real' time, with Spielberg directing on monitors (O'Brien 1999: 156), without storyboards according to the Press Pack (although Laurent Ditmann states otherwise (1998: 66)). Blood spattering on the lens, on one interpretation signifying immediacy and involvement, was supposedly unplanned (Freer 2001: 267). A stand-ard aspect ratio, rather than widescreen, further distances *Saving Private Ryan* from 'glory mongering World War Two spectacles of the 1950s and 1960s' (Doherty 1998: 70). Technicians desaturated colour by sixty per cent (O'Brien 1999: 156). Even when the film was set, cinematographers realised that shaky monochrome equated with authenticity in war footage (Winston 1995: 162). Nevertheless, it is salutary to recall that soldiers experience battle in full colour (Bremner 1998: 50).

Some critics claim that, 'technical realism is mistaken for historical accuracy' (Kodat 2000: 95). The movie's imitation of *Life* magazine D-Day photographs dem-onstrates that technical realism is inseparable from convention. Their blurred and bleached appearance resulted from accidental melting as Robert Capa's assistant dried the negatives. Only eight of 106 pictures survived, but their streaky, grainy appearance matches urgency and chaos in verbal accounts and impressionistically realises vivid yet indistinct memory. They immediately became iconic. Spielberg's cinematographer

Saving Private Ryan – note the cinematographer standing right of frame

Janusz Kaminski stripped lens coatings to produce similar haziness, de-synchronised shutters to cause streaking, pre-flashed the film as in *Amistad*, and devised an eccentrically mounted drill attachment to replicate the impact of nearby explosions and heavy artillery. Special shutter angles reduced motion blur, so that these technical codes suggested unusually harsh, sobering clarity to enhance the sense of immediacy.

The 'indexical bond': documentary versus fiction

Bill Nichols believes *Saving Private Ryan* claims authenticity from its factual basis that asserts superiority to more conventional genre pieces. Documentary style, supporting this, nevertheless 'forsakes a documentary ethics', for 'No G. I. cameraman could possibly accompany this mobile, omniscient camera eye.' Result: adherence to 'Hollywood's psychological realism' (2000: 10). This, Nichols contends, emphasises spectacle and suspense – even if it induces what Thomas Doherty calls 'a kind of combat fatigue' (1999: 305) – rather than a critical position in relation to events. True, the film never ventures 'into the strategic or operational aspects of Omaha' (Bremner 1998: 51), predicted to be difficult, and managed incompetently (Baldwin 1999: 61). Nichols locates the violence within a wider Hollywood propensity to stylise B-genre tendencies (here body horror) into technical displays of spectacle according to blockbuster production values.

But Hollywood's business *is* spectacle. The issue is, to what ends spectacle is harnessed. Richard Combs suggests the soundtrack's precision, omnipresence, uncontainability and unpredictability – 'more like a Total Environment, more grim carnival than documentary' (1999: 50) – constitutes a new realism. Various materials, including beef carcasses dressed in uniforms, were shot using German ammunition. Combs argues: 'There's a level of specificity here that we're not used to in war films – the different sounds that bullets, for instance, make when slicing through water, bouncing off metal or smacking into flesh' (ibid.). *Saving Private Ryan*'s constructed soundscape effects the screen penetration figured visually in *Hook, Jurassic Park* and *Amistad*, as diegesis and theatrical auditorium coincide.

Nichols considers these effects bogus: unwieldy equipment rendered synchronous recording impossible in 1944 (2000: 10). This objection implies that because *Saving Private Ryan* appropriates the look of wartime footage the soundtrack should replicate those of the period. THX sound, together with CGI and other effects, offers an account of war distinct from documentary, however, with its own artistic truth claims (this, after all, being why some critics preferred *The Thin Red Line*). Nichols forgets that *Saving Private Ryan* never claims to be anything but fiction about characters in a real-life event – this lapse testifies, perhaps, to its effectiveness.

Immersion *is* a mode of taking sides, simulating the soldiers' view – rather than more detached documentary perspective – and digital sound has the opposite effect to eerie distanciation produced by silence. Barrett Hodsdon complains that *Saving Private Ryan* 'spares nothing in order to ensure a rapid and meek audience surrender to the sensory battering of spectacle' (1999: 48); yet such apparent surplus realism and audiovisual excess enact cannon fodder's helplessness and vulnerability, rather than, in themselves, produce ideologically reprehensible positioning that objections to manipulation generally presuppose. Fictional demonstration that war is hell, the raw premise for *Saving Private Ryan*'s meanings, however much contested, generates Nichols' favoured 'discourse of sobriety' (1991: 3–4) – compromised anyway in that factual war footage, in newsreels or television, typically has commentary or music.

Nichols is right that 'documentaries like *The Battle of San Pietro* (1945) show the incredible carnage of war' (though he neglects to mention John Huston staged much of that combat (Maslowski 1998: 74)); 'Works like *Night and Fog* compel us to recognise the bestial lengths to which men will go to dehumanise and destroy' (2000: 10). But dramatisation is different from, not essentially inferior to, analysis or reflection on consequences. Nichols' argument replicates the *Schindler's List* versus *Shoah* dichotomy – productive rhetorical provocation when it does not preclude debate.

The *in medias res* opening of the flashback temporarily suspends assurance of dominant specularity. Nevertheless the camera's omnipresence and mobility create the impression of chaos from what in fact is highly choreographed. The incidental nature of much of the overlapping dialogue underpins this. Unlike horror movies, which suggest dread by withholding the threat before releasing tension in its spectacular presentation, *Saving Private Ryan* portrays butchery obliquely and fleetingly – at the edge of the frame, in rapid jerky pans, immediately before a cut. Rather than fetishised it is simply, almost incidentally, there. This relates to Bazinian realism: as Geoff King observes, 'Impact effects based on cutting are generally eschewed in favour of camera movement, thus maintaining a greater sense of the substance of the pro-filmic event' (King 2000: 121). Audiovisual overload prevents mastery. Peripheral and impressionistic visual details anchor and support the sound's solid presence.

Soldiers vomiting – historically motivated by rough seas as well as indexical of fear – illustrates realism of content. Challenging noble representations, it breaks taboos of decorum, as do dismemberment, evisceration, decapitation and explosion of living bodies. Contrast the surreal beauty of bullets decelerating and blood blooming from wounds underwater. Aestheticised by relative silence, and seemingly slow-motion in comparison with jerky images above surface, these offer hyper-real momentary contemplation. There is no refuge amid this unprecedented experience, even though in reality unmediated vision would never be so clear, water would destroy the camera or drown any witness, weighed down by kit. The contrast intensifies briefly displaced noise and action.

The red tide, and dead fish washing up amid corpses – surprising yet, in retrospect, obvious – similarly defamiliarise. Dead cows providing cover, and soldiers patrolling among grazing sheep, appear surreal because previous war movies neglected such banality. The inhabited house, its side blown away yet interior intact, and the wall that collapses to reveal Germans relaxing over cards, recall Jim's quirky visions in *Empire of the Sun*. These blend with black comedy. The *wrong* (and deafened) Private Ryan learns his brothers are dead. Many soldiers die in a glider because of the weight of armour installed literally to cover a General's backside. Enemies throw helmets at each other when their guns simultaneously jam. Such details exceed generic convention; yet their particularity renders them anecdotal, almost beyond invention, testimony to a 'FUBAR' ('Fucked-Up Beyond All Recognition') situation. Near-mutiny over a German prisoner emphasises the precariousness of command, while Ryan's fortuitous discovery stresses arbitrary causality despite military planning. A gratuitous comment that British Field Marshall Montgomery is 'over-rated' invites controversy and detaches the movie from received historic or generic opinion, as do deliberate killing of surrendered German soldiers and morphine used as euthanasia. Miller's D-Day experience renders strange routine events such as shaving, pouring coffee and chewing sandwiches. Limning battle's *reverberation*, contrary to what Catherine Gunther Kodat rejects as 'panegyrics on the wonders of desaturated colour and hand-held camera' (2000: 78), is the film's achievement. As Maria DiBattista notes, 'terror is caught not in explosive bombardments, but in the isolated image of a trembling hand' (2000: 224).

Michael Herr's Vietnam journal repeatedly suggests how cultural, and specifically cinematic, myth preconditions perceptions, as when describing men 'sitting around with Cinemascope eyes' (2002: 12). He and others refer to the war as a 'movie' (2002: 192, 222, 235). As he recounts combat as an amalgam of action movies and television news, second-person *discours* anticipates *Saving Private Ryan*'s address:

> your vision blurring, images jumping and falling as though they were being received by a dropped camera, hearing a hundred horrible sounds at once – screams, sobs, hysterical shouting, a throbbing inside your head that threatened to take over, quavering voices trying to get the orders out, the dulls and sharps of weapons going off (Lore: When they're near they whistle, when they're really near they crack). (2002: 213)

Similar second-person narration, interestingly, features in Tim O'Brien's *If I Die In a Combat Zone* (1973). Relatively unfamiliar in literature, it approximates the unreality of shock – paralleling Miller's detached moments, signified by slow-motion and muted sound – but also spectatorship's double positioning. Moreover, 'Seeing warfare as theatre provides a psychic escape for the participant: with a sufficient sense of theatre, he can perform his duties without implicating his real self and without impairing his innermost conviction that the world is still a rational place' (Fussell 1975: 192). Michael Hammond relates this quotation to a 'performative impulse' whereby soldiers bear up, pretending actions and experiences are unreal (2002: 68): a reciprocal response, reported also by Peter Maslowski in relation to World War Two (1998: 69–70), that attempts mastery over unbelievable yet threatening situations through disavowal. Although immeasurably intensified by the Real's proximity, it parallels spectatorial psychic mechanisms, detached yet intensely observing. Indeed, Hammond considers the 'gap' between audience and on-screen events 'the subject' of *Saving Private Ryan*, as I repeatedly argue is the case with other Spielberg movies; the film's strategy encourages empathy '*with* the soldiers ... by not allowing the audience to turn from the screen, creating a kind of "cinema of unpleasure"' (2002: 71).

Routine critical posturing in relation to Spielberg's image clouds and possibly instigates these debates. Wheeler Winston Dixon, writing one of those laments on the Lost Golden Age of Cinema that periodically resurface in American criticism (this time entitled 'Twenty-Five Reasons Why It's All Over'), insists, 'We need to acknowledge the malign influence of Steven Spielberg and George Lucas', before citing *Saving*

Private Ryan as 'emblematic' of 'visuals over content, excess before restraint, spectacle rather than insight' (2001: 361).

In actuality, war films since the genre's beginning frequently proclaim unprecedented realism, unsanitised revision (Doherty 1999: 303). Spielberg's, according to a military strategist and historian, 'captured battle with as much fidelity as one can outside of pure documentary, and in some ways rather better' (Cohen 1998/99: 85). It did so, however, by departing from many Hollywood conventions, delineated by Maslowski. For example: 'Focusing on mini-units distorts warfare's size and scale and makes combat seem so personal that the audience exudes genuine emotion when a soldier/actor gets killed or wounded. War is not only vast but also numbingly impersonal and random' (1998: 71). That is how, though withholding for half an hour a wide shot revealing the operation's magnitude, *Saving Private Ryan*'s opening presents it. 'If an actor has a line to deliver, the audience can always hear it, even if whispered in a raspy voice by a dying man as furious combat rages all round' (ibid.); definitely not so in *Saving Private Ryan*. 'To heighten the tension or stir other emotions – as if life-and-death struggles are not enough – dramatic or beautiful music from symphonies, orchestras, choirs, and choruses dignifies the Hollywood battlefield' (ibid.); no music features during battle scenes in the film. 'And they downplay the truly obscene things that modern weapons do to the human body' (1998: 74). Whatever charges can be brought against Spielberg's film, this is not one.

Symbolism and psychoanalysis

Realism and pleasure in dominant cinema relate as much to structures that naturalise ideological norms as to surface conventions. *Saving Private Ryan* embodies discourses that in complex, variously connected and sometimes contradictory ways represent brotherhood, Jewishness, psychosexual fantasies, nationality and femininity.

War was traditionally a defining masculine experience. This myth provided a core onto which other values coalesce. According to Emerson's idealistic lecture, 'War' (1838), quoted by Corporal Upham ((Jeremy Davies) who is writing a book about the brotherhood of soldiering, membership of which he enjoys but briefly after Miller replaces his 'effeminate' typewriter with a phallic stubby pencil): 'War educates the senses, calls into action the will. Perfects the physical constitution, brings men into such swift and close collision in critical moments, so man measures man.' But, as Neal Ascherson states, 'men are no longer sustained by imagining that other men somehow know what battle is like. It's plain now that most don't and instead share attitudes once dismissed as "civilian" or "womanish" – that war is senseless, immoral and incomprehensible' (1998: 7).

War films, Steve Neale argues, stage a masculine crisis through fantasies revealing 'markedly Oedipal tensions and conflicts' (1991: 35). These concern inequalities in knowledge and power, characteristic of all narratives but coalesced in this genre by rank. Many portray top brass as an impersonal, remote force whose ineptitude unites soldiers in victimhood, thereby establishing a binary opposition against military authority and constructing an 'anti-war' ideology (1991: 40). *Saving Private Ryan*, by contrast, while glossing over responsibility for the beach slaughter, explicitly accords privileged access to why General Marshall, Army Chief of Staff, standing before a US flag, instigates Miller's search for Ryan (Matt Damon). Although G.I.s themselves are unaware and debate the issue, the narrative, showing first the War Department's (feminised) compassion through concerned stenographers, then Mrs Ryan's grief-stricken swoon, pre-confirms the cause's rightness by means of pathos, yet repeatedly questions its statistical logic. Hence the mission to save Ryan, while motivating dramatic conflict, unites ethnically and regionally diverse soldiers in brotherhood, but also with generals and civilians alike back home. All conjoin around family values endorsed by no less than Abraham Lincoln (Marshall quotes the famous Bixby letter). These contrast implicitly with Nazi barbarism and, Kodat submits, link *Saving Private Ryan* (and *Amistad*) to the Civil War, 'the righteously glorious ... other "good war" to free an oppressed people' (2000: 80). (Ironically, the compassion is not the feminised impulse it seems, but patriarchal rationalisation. Historically, A. Susan Owen, in a footnote, explains, 'primary motivation for "saving" the remaining son was preservation of the family's paternal name' (2002: 276).)

The final battle's last stand is named 'the Alamo': Spielberg's gendered narrative and rite of passage into a dying generation's unspoken knowledge occupies frontier teleology. This, moreover, Kodat shows, links to wider history. Adams in *Amistad* frees captives in the Name of the Founding Fathers, while downplaying slavery's centrality in 'American freedom through capitalism' (2000: 88); and *Saving Private Ryan* coincided with the fiftieth anniversary not of D-Day but Marshall's Plan for restoring Europe's economy, a bastion against communism and extension of America's markets. The Bixby letter, sacrosanct in 1940s home front propaganda despite questionable authenticity, links both movies, through Lincoln and Southern Reconstruction, to the reunification of America.

Miller's 'adopting' Ryan and Upham, in the service of an apparently caring Marshall, and the context of Spielberg's professed intention to 'honour' his father's generation, can hardly be read other than as Oedipal reconciliation with a patriarch. This figure is identified by Peter Ehrenhaus (2001) with right-wing presidents Nixon, Reagan and Bush Senior, and the import of the symbolic reunification is taken by several critics to be assuagement of what Bush called 'the Vietnam syndrome' (Young 2003: 253). Accordingly, Owen proposes, 'Spielberg reunifies white, masculine identity. He (re)imagines a time before the social dislocations of mid-century movements for gender and racial equality' (2002: 259). African-Americans are bracketed out; Allied nations marginalised; and women feature primarily as abstractions in sexual anecdotes to disavow homosexual implications of bonding under extreme pressure – Ryan's tale as he dries his tears after learning of his brothers' deaths, for example – or as reminders of 'Why We Fight'.

Although the film's portrayal of warfare is ostensibly material – other texts having ironised 'patriotic fervour, simple moral clarities, and broad cultural stereotypes' beyond possibility – it nevertheless embodies the 'grand moral landscape' of the Holocaust (Ehrenhaus 2001: 324). 'It flickers less as a motion picture than as a ceremonial flame for Americans, on the cusp of the millennium, to look back at the linchpin event of the twentieth century and to meditate upon the cost paid by the men who won the Good War' (Doherty 1998: 68). Through Mellish (Adam Goldberg), an assimilated Jew, the

Holocaust – which soldiers in 1944 were not consciously avenging – is expropriated as a specifically American cause. Mellish weeps after jokingly accepting a Hitler Youth dagger looted from a German corpse. Crosscutting highlights compatriots' respect for this moment. Otherwise his Jewishness is ignored except when he asserts it, in defiance of a sniper and again triumphantly to German prisoners.

Before the final battle Mellish removes Upham's helmet and places around his shoulders a bullet belt, conferring upon him adult responsibility (subsequently unfulfilled) as a combatant. Concurrently, entering the masculine bond as well as the squad, Upham learns the mysteries of 'FUBAR'. (Apart from this spoken code, the freemasonry of soldiering communicates through silent looks: discreetly averted when Mellish breaks down or the squad ignore Miller's shaking hand; mutually exchanged between Ryan and his near namesake Reiben (Edward Burns) – homophony underlining brotherhood – during the last battle after Ryan declares the company his brothers and the mission irreversibly has changed.) Resemblance between the bullet belt and, in the way Mellish places it, a Jewish prayer shawl emphasises the ritual dimension. 'Whoever saves one life, saves the world entire': the Talmudic verse from *Schindler's List*, echoed in this movie's title, relates both to American values, epitomised in Marshall's decision and confirmed by showing generations that follow, and to Upham's cringing impotence. 'Ryan is not just being saved for his family. This is an iconic restitution in the name of Family, Nation and History' (Combs 1999: 53).

The Hitler Youth dagger penetrates Mellish in explicitly sexualised close combat in a bedroom, against a Nazi whose insignia, Ehrenhaus notes, belong to the SS, the corps entrusted with the Final Solution (2001: 328). 'Woven into the fabric of this scene' (envisaged by screenwriter Robert Rodat as a loose allegory for the Holocaust (Khoury 1998: 6)), 'viewers encounter one of the most compelling reasons for the Americanisation of the Holocaust – guilt for not having acted, for not having acted sooner, for not having done enough' (Ehrenhaus 2001: 328). This plays as a primal scene for Upham, cowering impotently on the stairs but able to understand the German's tenderly intimate language (not subtitled): 'Don't struggle. I don't want this to hurt. Relax', and so on. Afterwards, the German passes him with barely a glance, adjusting his clothing as he goes, and Upham regresses, crying, into a foetal position.

Hence the lack of operational explanation for Omaha Beach. Its cause is the American 'secular covenant' – hinted at in knowingly averted eyes after Mellish accepted the dagger – 'the source of national unification and common commitment as a people' (Ehrenhaus 2001: 332) that underpins Manifest Destiny. Miller's squad represent not just diversity, tolerance and the melting pot, argues Albert Auster, but 'the very essence of American civilisation and its values' (2002: 102). Nichols, similarly but less sympathetically, considers Miller a Messiah, third in a trilogy (Schindler 'Saving the Jews', Adams 'Saving the Slaves'), whose (white, male) empathy and altruism put them, hence American values and the 'patriotic banality' they embody, insidiously beyond criticism (2000: 9).

'Messiah' may be questionable, prejudiced hyperbole. Miller nevertheless figures as good father – emphatically so, against the Nazi obscene father, in relation to the boyish Upham, but also to Ryan. For Ryan's absent father Miller's dying words substitute an elder's wisdom. To the rest of the squad he fairly and responsibly embodies the patriarchal institution of the military – insisting, for example, that griping goes up the chain of command, never down, and suppressing mutiny with self-disclosure that reveals sensitive understanding. Camera angles reinforce this reading. So do homoerotic structures of the gaze (spectacularised, as in the lightning/shell flash on Miller as Upham watches him in the near dark). Miller's quiet authority, deft practicality, anxiety for his soldiers and opportunities he creates for conversation about mothers elicit confessional imagery (candles, chiaroscuro, metal mess cans as Eucharist) when the squad bivouac in a church, occasion for personal revelations. (Spielberg's historical consultant, Stephen Ambrose, notes that, in one case that inspired the film, a lone chaplain recovered the remaining sibling (1993).) Significantly, on D-Day Miller does not order soldiers to inevitable death, as must have occurred repeatedly over the long assault (Gabbard 2000: 178).

Ehrenhaus recalls opposition to Vietnam as 'genocide' while the word 'Holocaust' (a 1959 *New York Times* coinage) was gaining currency: *Saving Private Ryan*'s 'Holocaust memory ... re-ennobles American national identity' (2001: 333). This follows emergence as sole superpower, after the Cold War and US-led incursions into the Gulf and the Balkans: victories that nevertheless, diplomatically or because the conflicts wanted proper resolution, lacked triumphalist closure (Auster 2002).

Yet, Ehrenhaus recognises, Spielberg's movie does not effect such an ideological shift comfortably or without contradiction. Upham, the WASP liberal who romanticised war and insisted on protocols, fails Mellish and Miller, but also attempts to regain manhood in a fit of bitter frustration, not through self control or rational moral choice. To adapt Antony Easthope's reading of *The Deer Hunter*, Upham's soft, pale complexion, dark hair, slight figure, talkative manner and delicate movements represent, conventionally, the feminine side. Incapable of countering the threat of castration, he remains infantilised and the narrative forgets him. Ryan, the tanned, stocky, towheaded farm boy, quietly efficient, takes the risk. He inherits the father's position, literally, by accepting Miller's dying challenge. 'The pain of war makes him an adult and a hero', and he 'achieves self-identity, wins the girl' (Easthope 1990: 62–3), and starts and ends the film surrounded by younger Ryans. Upham's final act is not redeeming heroism; moreover, it makes war personal, not waged for a larger, justifying, cause. For Ryan, by contrast, Miller's last words concern the need to *redeem* the fact his war has become personal.

The Omaha Beach scene 'runs on a castration anxiety inspired by close-ups of all those bloody stumps and mutilated torsos' (Taubin 1998: 113). It denies narcissistic pleasure, that in most war movies bolsters the ego by affirming bodily unity against the abjected, dismembered other (Easthope 1990: 65). Fetishisation of realism is a precondition for this pleasure. As Jon Dovey notes in a different context, 'The psychic charge of [the camera] reproduces simultaneously the desire for possession as well as the marking of difference. "Look at that! Thank goodness that's not me!" Desire for the real is bound up with a repulsion from what is not "normal" or safe' (2000: 70).

Mastery without identification is difficult, and absence, on first viewing, of consistent perspective renders suture unlikely. Men, literally trying to hold themselves together in confrontation with the Real, nevertheless forced by obligations imposed in the Symbolic, die crying for their mothers. The medic Wade, although at the centre of a fraternal laying on of hands, dies sobbing, 'Mama, Mama, I want to go home' – explicit confirmation of the Lacanian search that motivates all narratives but seems particularly pervasive in Spielberg's structures and imagery, including this one concerned precisely to reunite James Ryan with his mother.

Against the carnage, the Ryans' Iowa farm recalls Andrew Wyeth's painting *Christina's World*, 'this century's most celebrated depiction of the US rural idyll' (French 1998: 8), but also a feminisation of that cultural space. In contrast to other Spielberg women, Mrs Ryan receives neither a facial close-up nor dialogue; she represents *all* mothers, the archetypal lost mother, the projected female Other of masculine self-definition. The cemetery coda restores equilibrium and plenitude on a linear, formalist level for Ryan's loss of his brothers, destruction of Miller's quasi-family, and the threat to masculine integrity in fearing he has not 'earned' salvation, by surrounding him with descendants. It also, after a nearly three-hour movie, includes the only female speech.

Yet, despite staging masculine angst, 'the movie's ultra-violence', one reviewer noted, 'is almost totally devoid of machismo' (Wolcott 1998: 44). It follows, Owen explains, a 'postmodern narrative premise of "both/and" … a "mix-and-match" of gender nostalgia and post-feminism, constituted through John Miller and his relations with his men' (2002: 266). Miller expresses 1990s new male sensibility, partially assimilating feminist assumptions and post-Vietnam scepticism, which enables identification for contemporary audiences. He nonetheless exemplifies traditional virtues, recuperating these for the audience, enables identification for an older generation not habituated to cinema going, and reconciles 'the Greatest Generation', previously aspersed for their racial and gender discourses, with 'Baby Boomers'. Like most heroes, Miller crosses binary divides. To summarise Owen, his shaking hand acknowledges post-Vietnam trauma concerning warfare, but this combines with 'post-post-Vietnam' ethical understanding (2002: 266). Although frightened and exhausted, he leads professionally. Courageous and dutiful, he rejects romanticisation of war. Aware of shortcomings in command structures, he resolutely operates within them. Clearly seeing Americans violating conventions, he keeps his counsel. Under pressure, he proceeds ethically. Happily married, he permits hetero- and homoerotic innuendo. Both an English teacher and a man of decisive action, he speaks his men's language yet maintains a reputation for discretion and quiet moderation. 'Perhaps most important, when threatened with mutiny … Miller relies upon conventionally masculine leadership *and* feminised conversational style to thwart a rebellion *and* perform honourable conduct' (2002: 267). In short, he personifies discursive conflict – an aspect to which I shall return.

Neale, following Susan Jeffords (1988) and others, considers such negotiations of masculinity generic, but concludes there is no set pattern (1991: 56). Miller restores the child to the lost mother and, in a reversed Oedipal scenario, renders Marshall's patriarchy benign. The question is whether it is true 'the film reassures us that war is in fact a test of manhood and courage and that a warrior aristocracy will naturally emerge, even if Captain Miller has to take a moment to sob in private' (Gabbard 2001: 136). Actually no fewer than six times the camera dwells on soldiers weeping. Yet each time a character follows a 'feminine' impulse, punishment follows in the form of lingering death, different in representational terms from arbitrary casual slaughter in the large-scale battles. Caparzo's (Vin Diesel) blood mingles with rain as his helpless compatriots shelter from a sniper after he defies orders, trying to rescue a little girl. Wade, whose function as medic places him in a physically intimate, succouring role, dies reciprocally in receipt of the squad's cradling comfort. Upham's punctilious concern for Wade's killer results in the same Nazi returning to despatch, and symbolically rape, Mellish. Sergeant Horvath (Tom Sizemore) and Miller both die after non-judgementally caring for Upham (the former drags him to safety, even though injured himself), as if to exacerbate Upham's guilt.

Self-reflexivity and intertextuality

The alleged ideological import would be more troubling if *Saving Private Ryan* were less self-consciously narrated. Ascherson notes how, 'as soon as any director makes either a "war movie" or a film about war, someone staggers to his feet in the back row of the preview to say that war is incommunicable ... [this] may be true, but it's no reason not to make a film about it' (1998: 7). The film grasps that nettle, attempting what serious art aims at: to surpass the familiar and merely pleasurable and explore difficult experiences, ideas and emotions. To some extent it succeeds. Veterans and historians judged it 'as close as anyone will get to the real thing' (McMahon 1998: 8; see also Landon 1998: 58): praise that accepts nothing can replicate first-hand experience. Taubin's criticism that it is 'two magisterial action sequences ... and lots of standard issue in between' (1998: 113) sees as a failing what in fact is a major strength. A soldier-historian similarly described the film as '25 minutes of virtual D-Day and the invasion of Europe followed by a conventional special-unit story, a war movie made out of war movies with only high-tech spectacles at the beginning and end to distinguish it' (Hynes 1999: 42). This, I suggest, makes it an essay in metatextuality, again testing limitations of representation.

As John Hodgkins notes, reviewers likened the D-Day landing to the best reportage or Capa's photographs, not the illusion of being there. This, Hodgkins concludes, is a 'decision' by critics following the hyper-real spectacle of Gulf War television coverage (2002: 76) – not, as I would argue, because viewers are anyway conscious of the simulated nature of even the most convincing realism. If the middle section is, as Taubin claims, 'merely a banal war movie with a forced premise and clichéd characters' (1998: 113), then that accords with the 'clichés and melodrama' of 'such confections as *Sands of Iwo Jima*' (1949) and *The Longest Day*' (1962) (Fussell 1998: 3). *Saving Private Ryan* clearly references the title credits and publicity stills for the latter in a shot of Miller's upturned helmet (Landon 1998: 60). Spielberg's movie acknowledges its tradition, at the risk of seeming 'conventional and predictable' (Gabbard 2000: 177); a familiar trope couches the platoon as microcosmic America: strangers bond through testing, internal dissent, challenges to authority, but ultimate pursuit of common goals. Conversely, it appropriates brutal horror from Vietnam movies and applies it to the World War Two movie, moribund after spy thrillers replaced its action elements and entrenched disillusion and humiliation over Vietnam rendered unambiguous heroics impossible in serious representations. By the 1990s, however, as Ben Shephard notes,

Vietnam vets, speaking back with published testimonies, transmogrified from baby-killers to victims, and front-line experience again possessed authoritative mystique (1998: 1).

Saving Private Ryan comprises three films: alternative and consecutive modes of cinematic remembrance filtered through a 1990s sensibility, technology and aesthetic of violence (its contemporary vision signified epitextually in the poster's lower-case typography). The Omaha landing conveys confusion, terror and senselessness from a 1944 perspective, melding subjective memory with public newsreel depiction. The second version utilises a contrasting style, broken only during intermittent combat. Shaking camerawork cedes to a smooth tilt and forward dolly as Miller raises his canteen once the beach is taken, echoing the jerky close-up on his trembling hand in the shot that introduced him. A smooth track in onto his eyes parallels the transition to the flashback and a slow, stately crane over the beach follows, ending on the body of 'Ryan, S.', whose death inaugurates Miller's quest. The Washington sequence and Miller receiving his new mission comprise long takes, embracing detailed mise-en-scène and slow, elegant tracking choreographed to the action.

This middle stage pastiches the 'post-war buddy film': Shephard (1998: 1) and Landon (1998: 59) cite *G.I. Joe* and *A Walk in the Sun* (both 1945). Ryan is a McGuffin, permitting picaresque examination of men interacting under pressure. It also, though, Hammond perceives, resembles 'a Vietnam platoon film the mission of which does not make sense to those involved on the ground' (2002: 70), and in which the enemy is less palpably threatening than absurdities underlying the horrors encountered, as a result of the command structure's impersonal remoteness.

The third movie, the battle uniting Miller's men with Ryan's unit to defend a bridge, revisits spectacular epics of doomed heroism directed by Spielberg's masters and mentors: David Lean's *The Bridge on the River Kwai* (1957) and, culmination and finale of the initial World War Two cycle, Richard Attenborough's *A Bridge Too Far* (1977). It also, Landon notes (1998: 62), recalls closely Bernhard Wicki's *Die Brucke* (1959). All three stress dark, obsessively driven, rather than glorious professional soldiering. Evidently – as a tissue of conscious intertextuality – *Saving Private Ryan* eschews claims to referential realism celebrated by its supporters and denigrated by opponents. It permits the spectator to interrogate its representation(s) of combat, no less than does an avowedly radical art movie approach to historiography such as Milcho Manchevski's *Before the Rain* (1994), against which it has been explicitly contrasted (Tängerstad 2000).

Nichols is right to distinguish *Saving Private Ryan* from historical documentary constraints. Nobody squinting through a viewfinder could have lasted thirty seconds on Omaha Beach, and synchronised sound was impossible. (Capa, using still cameras – much lighter – shot from behind a tank and thereafter sporadically as he approached the sea wall.) Reconstruction is the only mode of naturalistically portraying events where cameras could not be present. It is many documentaries' precondition. Celebrated examples include *Night Mail* (1936)(John Grierson approved staging the travelling post office), *The Thin Blue Line* (1988) (in which Errol Morris reflexively problematises the need to fill the screen with images of a contested and unavailable past), controversial re-enactments and prophecies (*Culloden* (1964), *The War Game*

(1965)), and many other documentary dramas and drama documentaries (*Cathy Come Home* (1966), *Death of a Princess* (1980), *Hostages* (1988)). There is no reason any of these would seek to restrict its style to what contemporary reportage permitted.

I cannot agree with Hodsdon that 'the opening and closing battle scenes ... as knockout punches ... tend to cancel out the subtleties of narrative modulation' and that 'shock realism ... leaves little space for narrative contemplation or reflexivity' (1999: 47–8). Modulation comes through contrasts between sequences. The prologue and coda in the cemetery and the stylised narration invite contemplation and imply reflexivity. Self-reflexivity has its price, however, although it enriches the film by linking it to concerns of Spielberg's other output. According to Mark Steyn, 'A film cannot really be "authentic" if all you notice is the authenticity' (1998: 14). Geoff King argues, 'its very commitment to authenticity is all the more likely to be experienced as spectacle: the hyper-realistic spectacle-of-authenticity rather than authenticity itself' (2000: 136). If you think, in line with publicity, 'this realism surpasses any I've seen', you are consciously watching a movie. Moreover war, as Spielberg's obsession with it suggests, and Michael Herr's account confirms, is inherently cinematic. James Wolcott justifiably proclaims *Saving Private Ryan* 'an overture of pure cinema' (1998: 44), while Doherty recalls Godard's dictum that screen warfare invariably exhilarates (1999: 263).

The spectacle nevertheless is experienced from a subject position and involves complex perspectival interplay. While some (Murray 1998; Taubin 1998) condemn it for cheating, in that the initial flashback suggests the man in the cemetery is Miller – not, as it transpires, Ryan, who was not at Omaha Beach – much of the action after the landing is focalised through the greenhorn Upham. Upham is Spielberg's recurrent figure, an interpreter: inscribed mediator. Mostly outside the brotherhood, he integrates only during a peaceful respite, by translating Edith Piaf for his compatriots. He is also, like Lacombe's interpreter in *Close Encounters*, a cartographer. This might suggest, in juxtaposition with Miller's shaking hand, observed by his platoon as he attempts a compass reading, a metaphor for morality. 'Upham's never been under fire, never seen the panic and chaos of battle first hand', says Spielberg in the press pack, ' ... so I think he represents the audience.'

Upham also, however, especially when viewing the taking of the radar through a telescopic sight – focusing, framing, projectively involved yet spectating from a distance – figures as a surrogate filmmaker. Observing from behind a cow carcass, as Neary in *Close Encounters* observed from behind a rock, his magnified view is shared, but in the rectangular film frame, not a circular iris: explicitly cinematic vision. More concerned with communication than direct participation, Upham writes the questions as Miller shouts at the deafened first Private Ryan and it is he who instructs the wounded medic: 'Tell us what to do!' 'He was me in the movie. That's how I would have been in war', Spielberg has said (quoted in Schickel 1998: 59).

Mellish's death, then, implies devastating comment on media ineffectuality, despite Upham being the mission's conscience. It is also, since *Empire of the Sun*, Spielberg's plainest recognition of voyeurism's sexual dimension. Additionally, however, the noble, manly myth of war has seduced Upham, as it has Spielberg's generation nurtured on Hollywood glorifications – Upham quotes *Henry V* and even appears, in the church encampment, to project that role onto Miller as anxious, compassionate leader

– shattered when, like the audience already, he confronts bullets shredding living flesh to ribbons. His telescope's detachment from its rifle wryly accentuates voyeuristic impotence (Morgan 2000: 184).

Ways of seeing

The beach sequence, lacking much context and offering but fleeting identification, attaches only retrospectively to a character's perspective. (Who, without conscious will, remembers during the sensory assault the cemetery prologue and the flashback apparently motivated by individual memory?) At the outset a medic is ordered to jettison a typewriter on the sand, suggesting mediation's inadequacy and pre-empting Upham's literary project as his is ditched by Miller seconds after they meet.

Later, rain plopping heavily onto luxuriant plants is narratively excessive, part of Barthes' *effet du réel* (1968); when the sound merges imperceptibly into gunfire, it becomes also self-flaunting narration. Moreover, this constitutes almost certainly a double allusion: to Robert J. Flaherty's *Louisiana Story* (1948), a classic documentary not without its own artifice, especially licence in respect of sound; and to Powell and Pressburger's *Black Narcissus*, a previous special effects triumph. (The latter is suggested also by Kathleen Byron's casting; she appeared previously in *The Silver Fleet* (1943), *A Matter of Life and Death* (1946) (prototype for *Always*) and *The Small Back Room* (1949) (all by Powell and Pressburger), as well as *One of Our Dinosaurs is Missing* (1975), one of Disney's direst efforts, which nevertheless links a Powell and Pressburger title involving Aircraft with two other Spielberg preoccupations).The German captive's attempted ingratiation through reference to *Steamboat Willie* (1928) and Betty Boop points up contrasts between the first marriage of animation with synchronised sound and the digital effects of the beach battle.

The climax echoes the skies filling 'miraculously' with American air power at the end of *Objective, Burma!* (1945) and, as Neale notes in relation to that film, rather than offering neat closure, emphasises the preceding story's arbitrariness (1991: 44). It also nonetheless is a generic convention (recalling, for example, Jim's movie-fuelled *Empire of the Sun* vision, a 'Cadillac of the skies'). *Saving Private Ryan* is a further Spielberg engagement with seeing, returning to the unrepresentability problem, this time a self-conscious search for means adequate to articulate combat. Ryan's son, an inscribed viewer unable fully to comprehend the old man's experience, initially takes photographs in the cemetery. Immediately, in the apparent flashback's opening seconds, the film predicates and problematises a relationship between visual representation and memory: the landing craft's ramp-control wheel spins in close-up like a movie reel the exact moment machine guns start cutting down soldiers at the front. Afterwards, a camera operator features in the epic tracking shot during which Miller explains the new orders to his sergeant. Reflexive in itself, this also alludes to a self-reflexive moment following another beach invasion in *Apocalypse Now.*

Otherwise the camera, throughout, 'reveals infantrymen preoccupied, not with context or horizon, but with the few hundred yards in front of them' (*Anon.* 1998: 70). In this sense, Isabel Hilton is right to call *Saving Private Ryan* a film about battle, rather than war (1998: 38). The only wider perspective, other than collective understanding of World War Two, is the interlude when Marshall orders Ryan's salvation, and this is anomalous. It offers one idealised, patriotic discourse – dialogically challenged in Miller's explicit denunciation of it as a 'PR exercise' – to set against the others, including 'FUBAR'. In this sense Spielberg's film is a modernist throwback, multifaceted, cubist, despite surface conventionality and critics' attempts to impose unity and conformity. When Miller's squad sift through hundreds of tags for Ryan's name, battle-weary paratroopers stare blankly at their insensitivity as it appears they are playing some casual game. Like piles of expropriated possessions in *Schindler's List*, these tags metonymically signify the enormity of off-screen suffering. They are however, arbitrary, abstract signifiers, as is Ryan's name at this point except as a focus for the squad's frustration and doubts. As in *Empire of the Sun*, different wars coexist in close proximity.

The clarity and lack of stylisation of battle sounds links all these subjective visions in the context of the Real. Gore on the lens (reminiscent of the chicken splattered on Jamie's car window) reinforces horror and involvement (the replicated Real seems so close that the content impinges on the apparatus itself) yet serves to inscribe the apparatus (we are *not* there, it's a movie). Moreover, as Herr insists – an idea sustained in *Empire of the Sun* – war is a movie to hyper stimulated participants, as horror simultaneously elicits repulsion and attraction: 'You want to look and you don't want to look', writes Herr amid verbal descriptions analogous to details Spielberg's camera glimpses (2002: 18). 'Don't look at it!' – Indiana Jones' advice in *Raiders of the Lost Ark* – is one of few discernible lines of dialogue on the beach. The danger of looking, concomitant with the gaze's illusory power, figures forcibly when later a German sniper, whose point-of-view we share, is penetrated through the eye in what is literally the reverse shot from the position of Miller's sniper. (The moment recalls the Nazi cinematographer's fate at the Lost Ark's opening.)

Irrespective of whether *Saving Private Ryan* advances realism, it reinflects a tradition of representing warfare, the 'harvest of death' – figured since the American Civil War in photography, dioramas, tableaux, film and television (Klingsporn 2000) – that evidently expresses ambivalent simultaneity of sombre remembrance and voyeuristic fascination. Underwater bullets and clouds flowering from gunshot wounds aestheticise violence, similarly to Peckinpah's slow-motion balletic gunfights. But they defamiliarise warfare, encouraging spectators to feel and think afresh, as does more straightforwardly gruesome and frenetic horror above the waterline. Miller's feminised self-revelation defuses the second Mexican standoff – recalling the impasse of masculinity in Quentin Tarantino's *Reservoir Dogs* (1992), another touchstone in American movie violence. The radar scanner before which this dramatic averted mutiny occurs resembles nothing so much as the frame of a drive-in movie screen.

Densely allusive images belie Nichols' claim that the aesthetic is documentary. The red tide brings home full realisation of an authenticated phenomenon (eponymously represented in Samuel Fuller's *The Big Red One* (1980)) while taking aback the spectator, humbling audiences into recognising how little they know or can imagine from conventional representation. So too do surreal or seemingly arbitrary, contingent touches, such as the discord when Caparzo, shot, falls on a piano keyboard. A soldier, hearing Miller screaming Ryan's name in grim mirth and frustration, knows another who fits the description. After false starts, Ryan is unexpectedly met (after saving the squad despatched to save him).

Saving Private Ryan puts imagination and narrative central in making sense and willing survival: 'Close your eyes and think of these', is an erotic story's refrain that sustains masculinity in relation to the female Other. Miller play-acts with an empty espresso machine in an abandoned café: normality has become fantasy, a point already established with the estrangement of banality when the spectator looked with Miller at officers who had not landed under bombardment, nonchalantly pursuing everyday activities. This is Herr's 'Life-as-movie, war-as-(war-)movie, war-as-life' (2002: 61). The theme is emphatically reiterated. The Piaf song explicitly concerns loss and compensatory projection: 'You left me and I've been desperate ever since./I see you all over the sky, all over the earth.' Rapport occurs between Miller, the English teacher, and Ryan, who has previously exasperated him, only after the younger starts visualising – projecting – under Miller's guidance, memories of his brothers. Ryan could not recall their appearance – Jim's plight in relation to his mother in *Empire of the Sun*. Suggestively, Miller taught at Thomas Alva Edison High School, named after the inventor of electric light and moving pictures. Miller too endures by visualising his wife pruning roses, although he reserves this private movie for himself. A double impulse posits narrative as 'escapism', relief from the unbearable present, and as recognition of uncomfortable reality. The Piaf song ends with lines that recall *Empire of the Sun*, but also pre-echo the stilling of Miller's shaking hand (of which Upham becomes aware during this scene) and the words of Mellish's killer: 'And you speak softly in my ear/And you say things that make my eyes close/And I find this marvellous.' Inscribed audiences, surrounding Miller and the wrong Ryan for the black comedy (not shared by the characters) of the latter's grief at learning erroneously of his brothers' deaths, figure again when the actual Ryan receives the news and makes his speech about loyalty to the only brothers left; and when, older, he seeks confirmation that his life has been worthwhile.

One reason the second battle feels more conventional is that it is a vehicle for interpersonal drama between characters audiences know and with whom they can empathise, rather than a raw, relatively 'unmediated' immersion into confusion for which they lack preparation. Nowhere after the rescue mission starts does focalisation occur outside a soldier's experience. For example, the German sniper's optical point-of-view does not encourage identification with his position, but confirms and intensifies the squad's sense of being within his sights. Although Upham overhears German dialogue it is not translated or subtitled during Mellish's death, which is therefore – except perhaps for German speakers – not totally focalised through Upham, nor through Mellish, who presumably does not understand what is said. This distances the spectator from Upham, increasing his outsider status (and, as a corollary, intensifying empathy with the squad). Yet, paradoxically and perversely, empathy with him increases as no one else (apart from the German) knows the guilty secret of his paralysis, which precisely duplicates that of the effectively omniscient but primally emasculated spectator. It is a remarkably sophisticated, powerful and provocative effect, forcing each viewer to confront his or her attitude towards warfare.

Marshall's idealised representation, likened by several critics to a Rockwell painting, is explicitly that. From a cool, calm, spotless typing pool that contrasts dramatically with the Goyaesque carnage, a stenographer takes Mrs Ryan's three letters to officers observed from outside their glass partitions through blind – inscribed screens. A spectator rises in the foreground, establishing a voyeuristic relay of the look between the camera and the unfolding hermeneutic. Blinding 'God Light' inscribes the apparatus, foregrounding this as cinematic representation. Mrs Ryan looks through her kitchen window and a net curtain, further inscribed screens, rendering her observer and observed, a knowledgeable spectator as she senses instantly the approaching car's import without being told. The conceit follows through to the sniper's hand signals from the belfry at the Alamo (shades of Lacombe's 'pure' communication in *Close Encounters*), and the precise camera positioning whereby sunlight from behind the tower seemingly projects intelligence to Miller. Miller's subjectivised shots within this battle, silenced, distanced, as at the start, separate him momentarily from the diegesis that continues to unreel in Metz's elsewhere.

Caparzo's suicidal attempt to save a little girl is a mise-en-abyme inviting audience reflection. A humanitarian impulse, it is as irrelevant to the squad's mission as the search for Ryan is to the Allied campaign. 'There is a contradiction, then, within the film', King notes, 'that can be read to some extent as questioning its own narrative structure, its own complicity in a deeply sentimental project' (2000: 123). It also relates to the bigger causality of unintended outcomes. If Miller had not pursued Ryan, his ingenuity and expertise would not have been available to defend the bridge and secure the Allied advance; nor, Doherty observes, would the planes that save the day (too late for Miller) have arrived if Miller had not widened the mission, to destroy the radar, resulting in Wade's death and the near-mutiny (1998: 70). The effect of the dying Miller seemingly destroying a tank with his pistol, reminiscent of Jamie's misperceptions, compresses a causal narrative chain. This then suggests an interpretive frame for Miller's arithmetic (comparable to the theme of *Schindler's List*) and the multiple deaths on Omaha Beach. Miller has a bright light behind his head as, while Upham watches, he recounts having lost 94 under his command although this might have saved the lives of ten or twenty times that number. Meanwhile, another soldier transcribes Wade's bloodstained letter out of compassion for its recipients, by the aid of a flashlight. Inscribed projectors invite reflection on meanings and depictions.

Human details imply, Ian Freer suggests, that 'real heroics were … keeping your sanity, goodness and humanity intact – not only that acts of decency are possible in combat but that war can also *produce* moments of compassion and tenderness' (2001: 274). Maybe so, but not in the idealised manner Emerson claimed. It rings hollow after what is witnessed, and inappropriately egotistic from Upham ('I think this is all good for me, sir'), who has yet to engage in messy killing.

'Evil' warmongering?

Although it is hard to disagree with many of the sometimes-brilliant ideological readings of *Saving Private Ryan*, their range positions the film as a nexus of American cultural contradictions. Analysis necessitates a tightrope walk, poised between DreamWorks' agenda and hostility from critics for whom Spielberg's screen is a *tabula rasa* on which to etch scorn for popular culture and what, for some, it represents.

Some assume the filmmaker's intentions, then marshal received prejudice to condemn ideological conformity. Hodgkins sees a 1990s resurgence of movies connected overtly or indirectly with World War Two as evincing parallels with the 1991 Gulf War:

> While a few of these films (and filmmakers) ... scrutinise (and even criticise) America's traditional and self-proclaimed reputation of righteous militarism, other directors saw the chance to vanquish once and for all those doubts and fears that had been festering since Vietnam and return the US soldier to his rightful place as heroic icon. (2002: 76)

This assesses not the movie but the contextual recurrence of militaristic discourses, as well as an imputed set of personal traits, a judgement presumably influenced by Spielberg's declared aim to honour his father's wartime experience. However, to make a film about events that had become eclipsed and tarnished by subsequent policies is not necessarily to be pro-war. 'The US soldier' is an ahistorical, essentialist category, whereas Spielberg made a film about Normandy G.I.s whose represented behaviour and attitudes are wide-ranging. According to Hodgkins, *Saving Private Ryan* contains 'distinct reverberations of George Bush's wartime ideology but also echoes of the US media's and military's much heralded Gulf War "triumph of technology"' (2002: 76). The second part of this accusation is odd, given that the beach victory appears to result from overwhelming force of numbers, involving huge sacrifice, rather than superior technology; while the final defence of the bridge, until air power arrives to complete Miller's work, succeeds because of extremely low-tech improvisation of bombs.

Influential *New York Times* critic Vincent Canby scorned: 'with *Saving Private Ryan* war is good again' (1998: 1). Normandy arguably – as references to Omaha, Utah and 'the Alamo' suggest – figures as a frontier for (all-)American expansionism. More widely, Frank Tomasulo contends, Spielberg's 'oeuvre stands as one of the chief cinematic purveyors of American exceptionalism and triumphalism in contemporary filmdom' (2001: 115).

The World War Two movie originated in wartime propaganda. (1930s World War One movies such as *All Quiet on the Western Front* (1930), *Journey's End* (1930) and *La Grande Illusion* (1937) shared a very different vision, did not highlight American experience and, as individual prestige dramas issuing from different production contexts, did not constitute a recognised genre.) Blum, among Spielberg admirers, employs the rhetoric of 'the Good War, one of the most prominent US symbols of an unquestioningly heroic and admirable national endeavour' (1999: 132). In this context, *Saving Private Ryan*, 'seen as an escape from post-Vietnam trauma whilst placating our consciences over the cost of war from a suitable historical distance' (Hodsdon 1999: 45), perpetuates militarist sentiment by association with imputed 1940s values. Kodat goes further: Ryan's rescue 'provid[es] emotional closure to the nationally wounding memory of the Civil War' (2000: 88) – and, through Marshall's prominence, justifies American neo-imperialism (the Marshall Plan) by aligning it with Southern Reconstruction.

The American Legion rewarded Spielberg with a 'Spirit of Normandy Award' and the US Army with the highest civilian decoration, both of which he accepted (Cohen

1998/99: 82). Gabbard notes how the author on whose work *Saving Private Ryan* draws, Stephen Ambrose, a staunch opponent of antiwar protest during Vietnam, 'consistently glorifies … individual behaviour'. He cites as examples details incorporated into the film: Miller's use of chewing gum to fasten a mirror to a bayonet to improvise a periscope, and anti-tank 'sticky bombs' manufactured from socks and grease (2001: 132). How this constitutes glorification, rather than accounting for how the protagonists survived when others were killed, is unclear, but demonstrates determination to ascribe to Spielberg a pro-war agenda – in this case by association, as Ambrose had published hagiographic books about Presidents Eisenhower and Nixon. In contrast, Gabbard cites Paul Fussell's 'less credulous' writing, which 'dispels myths of heroic behaviour' by recalling that 'men who rushed enemy machine guns acted as much from desperation, panic, and/or fear of shame as from what is usually called courage' (2001: 134) – as if the Beach sequence did not make this apparent.

Saving Private Ryan also allegedly constitutes 'a surrogate for American triumph in the Cold War and subsequent victories', reversing previous displacement of Vietnam into Korea (*M*A*S*H* (1970)) and the American West (*The Wild Bunch* (1969)), a 'glorification' of '*fin de siecle* American triumphalism' (Auster 2002: 100, 99). Hodgkins argues that the film redresses one of the most scandalous elements of Vietnam, abandonment of American personnel (2002: 77). He points out also that American officials code-named the 1991 Iraq invasion 'G-Day' (2002: 76), evidently to summon the D-Day spirit in the context of political, military and journalistic rhetoric that cast Saddam as Hitler. From this, by asserting that Spielberg is 'retrogressively conventional, and philosophically conservative' (although, dangerously, 'unquestionably … dramatically skilful'), Hodgkins concludes that *Saving Private Ryan* advances 'America's traditional self-proclaimed reputation of righteous militarism' (ibid.).

Tomasulo uses *Saving Private Ryan*'s concentration on American troops rather than the collective Allied effort to advance the same point (2001: 118). The absence of black soldiers too confirms for many an overall right-wing agenda that craves escapism from affirmative action, civil rights, feminism (Gabbard 2000; Owen 2002: 259) – even drugs and homelessness (Hodgkins 2002: 77). Kodat believes the morph from Ryan's young to his old self effaces over fifty years of race relations; that this issue (justified historically in that the army then was segregated (Blum 1999: 133)) was not one of the film's concerns 'simply begs the question of why Spielberg chose to construct his vision of the war as he did' (2000: 90). A *Sight and Sound* correspondent further claimed: 'the film … condones war crimes (the killing of prisoners of war). This is its clear moral, and this is why it's an evil film' (Ouran 1999: 64). 'As an apparatus of the state', Gabbard concludes, writing before 9/11 and the Afghanistan and Iraq invasions, 'it re-creates a fascination and reverence for war so that, someday in the not too distant future, the state can put this fascination and reverence to use' (2001: 138), an argument Tomasulo echoes (2001: 127). Kodat repeatedly assigns agency in her choice of verbs in contending that both *Saving Private Ryan* and *Amistad* 'attempt to recruit American history to the tasks of constructing renewed credibility for (and shoring up ideological justification of) continued American global dominance' (2000: 79).

In finding such 'ideological ramifications' in 'Spielberg's "antiwar" film' (Tomasulo 2001: 127), critics conflate subject matter with meaning. They judge it not as a movie but as a representation of a specific war laden with cultural significance. Louis Menland contends that for most people World War Two countered 'an evil there is no reason to colour in shades of grey, however one might wish to portray individual enemy soldiers who fought in it, and the Americans who died in it deserve our piety' (1998: 8). By not seeking to question that received wisdom Spielberg is not necessarily a warmonger. Yet by emphasising horrific carnage, he is not necessarily a pacifist.

Recall that Iraqi civilian deaths in 1991 were officially termed 'collateral damage'. 'Humanitarian' NATO attacks on Serbia in 1999 killed hundreds of civilians when, a government leak revealed, only 2 per cent of high explosive 1,000-pound bombs and forty per cent of RAF bombs overall struck their targets, and *The Sun* of 20 March 1993 proclaimed the invasion of Iraq 'The first "clean war"' (Keeble 2003). *Saving Private Ryan,* by contrast, reminds audiences what flag-draped coffins contain.

If, as Michael Ryan and Douglas Kellner aver, 'liberal vision takes for granted the necessity of an institution like the military' (2002: 292), Spielberg's film distances itself from contemporary conflicts. Nevertheless, the 'Harvest of Death' trope links the film to a history of realist representations stretching back to Gettysburg. Although Auster considers Spielberg's version more anti-death than anti-war (2002: 101) (but without explaining how allegedly glorious victories can be achieved without death), this image has generally been accepted as pacifist in intent, hence by definition related to current and potential warfare. Certainly conservative Americans accused Spielberg of deliberately ignoring causes of World War Two so that his film condemns war in general. (Russell Jenkins (1998: 44) cites John Podhoretz and Richard Grenier). It also, however, proposes greater realism than other representations, from its content rather than the mode of mimesis, as though warfare intrinsically is more real than other experiences. As a result, it contributes to the tendency whereby warfare dominates representations of history (Klingsporn 2000), perpetuating war's privileged status and unchallenged commonsense acceptance of its inevitability, as Ryan and Kellner claim. By seeking 'more to document the reality of war than to explore the true nature of war' (Wisniewski 2002) it shows rather than explains. Yet this criticism, like many, targets what the film does *not* attempt, not its achievement.

Hollywood incorporated Vietnam, Ryan and Kellner state, 'not as a defeat from which lessons can be learned, but as a springboard for male military heroism' (2002: 287). For many critics, *Saving Private Ryan* continues that project. *Platoon* (1986) sought to restore pride to Vietnam veterans by demonstrating what most, traumatised, alienated and ostracised, were incapable of communicating. This included 'fragging' (deliberately killing officers). In *Saving Private Ryan,* a World War Two genre movie filtered through the revisionist Vietnam cycle, this threat remains in the rebellion against Miller. Miller commands 'a militarily and ethically questionable mission' (Blum 1999: 132), after other conventional expectations of military engagement have been overturned. These include execution of surrendering prisoners – spontaneously in the heat of battle near the start, but calculatedly when the squad plot revenge for Wade's killing before Upham intervenes. Moreover, seasoned reviewers confessed to finding the first executions almost justified after what, vicariously, they had just endured (French 1998; Williams 1998). Spielberg's film allows audiences, in Oliver Stone's words, to 'take stock of what a war really means', even if some young men, 'attracted like moths to light', remain heedless (quoted in Mitchell 2002: 308). Upham's cowardice frustrates audiences, who in generic terms expect him to pull himself together and save the day, but his protracted inaction forces each to ask what we might do in similar circumstances. Focalisation through an ineffectual bystander, a liability even, rather than conventional heroes, makes heroism less uncomplicated, less taken-for-granted.

Not an edifying spectacle

Subjective discourse explicitly frames *Saving Private Ryan*'s realism. The film, in Hammond's formulation, combines memory and memorial – a double positioning. 'Spielberg confronts the ideological function of traditional war memorials by exposing the carnage, confusion and tragedy of combat, normally subsumed under the iconography of remembrance and sacrifice' (Hammond 2002: 69). This extends and confirms its genre.

Geoff Dyer considers the much-touted assertion that the film does not glorify war 'a rather weak boast' after the 1914–18 War Poets (and, one might add, Vietnam):

> At this late stage in the century it would take a filmmaker possessed of genius and perversity in equal measure to make a film that *did* glorify war. It is a mistake, in other words, to overstate [*Saving*] *Private Ryan* radically overturns the earlier presentations of the Second World War. It is better seen as the culmination of that tradition. (1998: 6)

Mellish's death paradoxically involves compassion, not the displaced rape that it appears, as the killer offers a comparatively quick death: 'Let's just end it all' (Jaehne 1999: 39). To read different critics confirms confusion whether Mellish's killer is 'Steamboat Willie' and, if not, which of the two Upham slays. More important is why this matters. Is battlefield conduct finally justified by personal motives (making short shrift of ethical and military niceties debated so assiduously within the film, though the momentary narrative satisfaction immediately turns sour)? Or are enemies ethically and strategically interchangeable (as their representation, without subtitles, despite Upham's knowledge of their language and culture, implies)? Or does this logistical consideration apply only when a Jew has been, apparently cold-bloodedly (though Upham knows otherwise), murdered? These are odd questions to pose of a 'Good War' in which, Karen Jaehne contends, 'In 1944, Americans were by definition still innocent' (1999: 40).

Spielberg's portrayal of warfare in a past era allegedly yearns for the security of supposed moral certainties (Wolcott 1998: 41). According to Nichols, 'Spielberg wraps himself in an amorphous cloak of patriotic banality' akin to 'simplistic ad slogans, gushing campaign rhetoric and facile Hollywood dream works' (2000: 11). The inglorious and questioning nature of much of the action and dialogue problematises such a reading. Rather than patriotic sentiment it is perhaps the truth claims – encouraged by DreamWorks – accruing to realistic images of combat death that prompt Nichols' unease that *Saving Private Ryan* inoculates itself against criticism. The movie may well pay homage to Spielberg's father's generation, whose experiences ingrained emotional reticence silenced, Hollywood jingoism falsified and Vietnam besmirched. For an imaginative work to evoke a period ethos, even nostalgically, in attempting to honour and understand those who lived through it, is not, however, intrinsically to perpetuate its values.

Critics who do not see their ideals reflected ascribe to the film views they oppose. President Reagan was militaristic. At the fortieth D-Day anniversary Reagan predictably declared what a leader of any electable political hue would have: 'Every man who set foot on Omaha Beach that day was a hero' (cited in Auster 2002: 101). These sentiments he voiced, obviously with patriotic intent, as Americans continued suffering the aftermath of Vietnam. Spielberg a decade and a half later made a film set around D-Day. *Ergo*, many imply, he glorifies war. When Hodgkins argues, 'If the Gulf War was a military and political attempt to atone for the conflict in Vietnam, then *Saving Private Ryan* is a filmic one' (2002: 77), it must be said, given diminishing oil reserves and the Arab-Israeli conflict, that ifs rarely come much bigger. When, immediately after 9/11, George W. Bush compared the attacks to Pearl Harbor and described the terrorists as 'fascist, totalitarian, a spoke in the axis of evil' (cited in Young 2003: 254), accusations that Spielberg's film arose from a regressive militaristic mentality appeared to be confirmed. It is true, as Hodgkins and others prove, that *Saving Private Ryan* can serve sectional interests, but only by accepting partial interpretations of a highly complex text.

The portrayed brutality compromises any notion of nobility or heroism. 'Earn this' neither glorifies battle nor justifies contemporary US expansionism. Men weeping in the audience when I first saw the film were sobbing neither out of love for Uncle Sam (the cinema was in South Wales) nor uplifted by fervour. The German imitating Steamboat Willie (Mickey Mouse), declaring 'I like American' before reeling off transatlantic popular cultural references while digging his own grave at gunpoint is not an edifying spectacle.

Upham's paralysis during Mellish's death alludes to the Holocaust and hence the view that World War Two was just. The movie thereby honours the 'Greatest Generation' whose sacrifices and suffering Vietnam sullied, to say nothing of the unfashionability of their attitudes in the more sceptical and freethinking era Vietnam protests fomented. It does not, however, celebrate or advocate what they did, as the mournful musical score, silent during the fighting, underlines. According to Spielberg, the film aims 'to honour them with the truth and hopefully to teach something' rather than merely entertain (Reed 1998: 14). As commentators point out, 'full graphic detail does not necessarily teach us about war, just as hard-core pornography does not teach us about sex' (Ascherson 1998: 7; Gumbel 1998: 16). Perhaps not, but much depends on what was already believed, what representations were available. That cinematic battles, the more immersive they become, easily turn into exciting spectacle (Wolcott 1998: 44) nevertheless highlights one aspect of warfare. This does not justify war, any more than horror movies justify murder; certainly Fussell felt 'the first half-hour of this film should stifle forever all the unfeeling cant about the Good War' (1998: 3). Upham summarily executing the German does *not* redeem him as Gabbard contends (2001: 136) and his immediate release of remaining prisoners constitutes dereliction of duty. Hodgkins' assertion that Upham 'achieves a kind of self-actualisation … a type of dignity or manhood ... through killing' (2002: 78) recycles the generic expectation the narrative overturns, ironically given the explicit, and highly unusual, emphasis on contextualisation, verbalised in Miller's conversation with Ryan. Hodgkins maintains that *Saving Private Ryan* shows Americans 'fighting (and winning) for the honour of mothers and family reunification', to reinforce 'Operation Desert Comfort', a domestic public relations counterpart to Desert Storm that sought to unite the nation and its troops (2002: 79). The film I am analysing unmistakably portrays Americans committing atrocities, experiencing absurdities and dying horribly. 'Earn it!' can be read, more easily than as a call to arms, as exhortation to prevent carnage and suffering being repeated, or at least to understand what it was for and ask whether it was warranted. Gruesome statistics whereby Miller calculates the pay-off in relation to his soldiers' deaths reverse the aphorism at the heart of *Schindler's List*: 'Whoever saves one life saves the entire world.' Holocaust allusion in Mellish's demise offers one answer (Ehrenhaus 2001). Nevertheless, together with survivors like Ryan, the rest of us are left to our own understanding.

Unlike 'humanised military films' Ryan and Kellner cite (2002: 293) – *Private Benjamin* (1980), *Stripes* (1981), *An Officer and a Gentleman* (1982) – *Saving Private Ryan* does not endorse American values by equating personal achievement with military success. Quite the opposite. Although sparing Upham's subsequent presumed guilt, shame and self-loathing, it shows the elderly Ryan wracked by insecurity. The movie interrogates life's value as much as it is about war. The Möbius strip (as opposed to loop) temporal structure, far from 'a stupid and transparent gimmick' that 'cheapens the whole enterprise' (Murray 1998: 44) – 'cunning but almost sentimental and schematic' (Hodsdon 1999: 46); 'meretricious', 'lazy', 'manipulative', even 'immoral' (Taubin 1998: 113) – operates productively. Whereas personal remembrance motivates the flashback, implying the old man is Miller, focalisation shifts increasingly onto another character (Upham), before the subjectivity emerges as Ryan's, absent during the first three-quarters. Experience is collectivised and generalised, interdependence highlighted and individualism downplayed, as audiences, through Ryan's focalisation, identify with Miller identifying with Ryan's own younger self, as well as with Upham and Miller's views of each other. The force of imaginative empathy is demonstrated without claim to first-hand authenticity, and audiences encouraged to review and consider what they see – and, if point-of-view matters, to contemplate why.

Ambiguity

In short, *Saving Private Ryan* constitutes what Ellis (2002) calls 'working through', not specifically of 'national trauma and of movement toward "coming home"' as Owen avers (2002: 250) but of unresolved issues surrounding warfare and representation. The movie ultimately corroborates Emerson's dictum, but Upham's self-knowledge is neither what he hoped nor expected. Spielberg, Hodsdon contends, 'wants to shock audiences and mollify them at the same time', offering an 'each way bet' in 'a contemporary public climate of dualism between simultaneous repulsion for and memorialisation of war' (1999: 46). As big-budget filmmaking, aimed at the largest audience, such ambivalence makes commercial sense. Yet, as the film aspires to canonical status within its genre, it dialogises movie warfare to challenge assumptions. Gung-ho masculinity of John Wayne movies, 'anti-bourgeois and anti-authoritarian dropout values' of 'the Vietnam generation' and 'patriotism, nationalism and militarism' of the 1980s (Ryan & Kellner 2002: 293) all constitute the discursive formation mediating warfare, and veterans' experiences, in the 1990s.

Thus the Southern sharpshooter's prayers are not, as Owen suggests, evidence that Spielberg subscribes to right-wing, Christian fundamentalist views of the war as an American-waged crusade. They have referential origins (Herr documents extreme religious convictions and superstition in Vietnam (2002: 54, 153–4)), and are part of the discursive tensions staged. Spielberg's Private Jackson closely resembles Howard Hawks' *Sergeant York* (1941), played by Gary Cooper, but reinterpreted unsympathetically, 'haunted, slightly demented ... praying aloud as he methodically kills his prey' (Landon 1998: 61), yet able to sleep like a baby.

The flag filling the opening and closing frames recalls *Patton* (1970), which urged Americans to fight for their beliefs, but is faded, bleached out – more 'Old' than 'Glory'. The closing voice-over, Marshall reading the Bixby letter, reiterates beliefs once accepted unquestioningly. Its context nevertheless is Miller's suspicion (voiced, despite his characteristic professional detachment) that his mission is a publicity stunt. The Pentagon scene, Shephard contends, 'veer[s] uncertainly between satire and veneration': precisely the point, not evidence of a typically 'badly botched' 'job' (1998). Combs notes that at this juncture the lighting 'moves out of any realistic register as it increasingly floods the scene with burning, white light' (1999: 53). This, I suggest, is Spielberg's self-reflexivity shifting modality to declare a purely cinematic moment in the transition to the farmhouse Americana. A further lapse in realism, a cornfield erroneously golden in early June (Ouran 1999), supports this reading. However, seconds later, self-conscious narration visually parallels, in absolute sincerity, Mrs Ryan's white picket fence with crosses in the cemetery (Combs 1999: 53).

Miller's soldiers achieve strategic successes *despite* their distracting official mission, yet fight out of duty and self-preservation rather than any explicitly stated cause (certainly not desire for glory). The letter, quoted twice, is prefaced by the horror of the opening and closing battles. Furthermore, it seems unlikely that the film's writers and historical advisors were unaware of its disputed authenticity. Though Lincoln's supposed sentiments that young Americans have been sacrificed on 'the altar of freedom' are not, as Doherty states, ironic (1999: 310), freedom never constitutes part of the soldiers' vocabulary.

Doherty is wrong to assert so strongly, however, that the last image 'is not the flag that unfurls in *Born on the Fourth of July* (1989) or *Rambo* [sic], a stained prop of fake glory and scoundrel patriotism, but the real item, the star-spangled banner yet waving' (1999: 310). It *is* both of those, and *Patton*'s, and the huge, screen-filling backdrop to the lyric, 'You may say I ain't free/But it don't worry me' at *Nashville*'s (1975) cynical, post-Vietnam, bicentennial conclusion, and the cloth burnt onstage by late-1960s rock stars, and latterly the lapel pin adopted by Bush's cabinet during their 'War on Terror'. The flapping sound at its first appearance renders it material, a manufactured signifier, part of the Symbolic order, rather than a direct evocation of an Imaginary ideal. It is, Spielberg says, borrowed from Capra's *Why We Fight* Number 7, in an interview during which he explains that American World War Two films propagate distortions because their sources were propagandist (Cousins 1998). Unlike the wartime release *The Fighting Sullivans* (1944), in which the (historically documented) loss of five sons was supposedly inspiring, Marshall's appropriation of Lincoln's sentiments is meant to sound hollow (Landon 1998: 61; Steyn 1998: 14). Nevertheless, as Jeanine Basinger insists, wartime propaganda, though providing the answer, functioned to address the citizenry's question, 'Why are we doing this?' (1998: 46). *Saving Private Ryan* leaves that question open. Ultimately, the movie's realism produces contradictions that render it unanswerable. As Owen summarises: 'The full measure of sacrifice requires a full measure of horror. The full measure of horror destabilises ideological claims to "just war"' (2002: 274).

Saving Private Ryan is neither pro- nor anti-war. It represents war in concrete terms. Cowardice matches heroism and stoicism, and if they occur it is because the grunts transcend public relations. Nobility is matched with weakness, tragedy with senselessness, heightened experience with mundanity, strong silent masculinity with endless talking and sensitivity (even Mellish's killer joins in), and compassionate impulses are sometimes contingently necessary, sometimes futile or worse. Critics, right, left, jingoist or pacifist, condemn the film for not endorsing their convictions and, rather than on-screen evidence, use personal prejudices against Spielberg, allegedly liberal or conservative, as their basis (One noted, 'If Mr Spielberg wants to say something big about war, his virtuosity would be better spent on the far grimmer stories of Srebrenica or Rwanda', thereby carrying grudging praise to new heights (Anon. 1998: 70). Most offensive, as much for the critic's attitude to the audience as its tedious recycling of jibes aimed at *Close Encounters*, is the title of the article, 'And the Leni Riefenstahl Award for Rabid Nationalism Goes to: *Saving Private Ryan*' (Carson 1999)). To note these oppositions is not to champion a middle way or adopt woolly relativism, but to recall how Hemingway, seventy years earlier, rejected abstractions in a novel replete with vivid dismemberment and death. 'I was always embarrassed by the words sacred, glorious, and sacrifice and the expression in vain', states the wounded narrator, Lieutenant Henry:

> There were many words that you could not stand to hear and finally only the names of places had dignity ... Abstract words such as glory, honour, courage, or hallow were obscene beside the concrete names of villages, the numbers of roads, the names of rivers, the numbers of regiments and the dates. (1935: 143–4)

So too, as Tom Shone comments on Spielberg's soldiers' philosophising (even while underestimating the contribution of synchronised sound): 'They are just speeches, when so much of the film shimmers with the wordless power of silent cinema' (1998: 4). Todd McCarthy similarly likened *Saving Private Ryan* to 'a great silent film, in which the words are basically superfluous' (1998: 6).

Spielberg's film is characterised by *ambiguity*, which 'opposed to "clarity" would be considered a fault', but which in twentieth-century critical theory became valued in serious imaginative literature, where 'what is required of scientific language (e.g.

lucidity) is not necessarily demanded' (Fowler 1973: 7). This distinction is analogous to that between fiction and documentary. The latter, Nichols explains, creates 'less a *story* and its imaginary world than an *argument* about the historical world' (1991: 111). Where boundaries blur, as when fictional representation of actual events pastiches documentary technique, problems for Nichols and others emerge. As Nichols forcibly emphasises, 'The world is where, at the extreme, issues of life and death are always at hand. History kills … *Material practices occur that are not entirely or totally discursive, even if their meanings and social value are*' (1991: 109). Such material practices include war. *Saving Private Ryan* is precisely concerned with war's meanings and social values, which for many people are highly ambiguous, without losing sight of the human cost. While one commentator complained that the film 'pushes the limits of cinematic semiosis so far that … they finally circumscribe everything and its opposite' (Ditmann 1998: 65) – a tendency that would be praised in an art movie without low-cultural associations – most of the critical attacks disambiguate, that is monologise, its discourses. This is perhaps unsurprising, in light of Doherty's description of *Saving Private Ryan* as 'so commercially successful, critically esteemed, commemorative in spirit, and grand in ambition that it just begs to be trashed' (1998: 68). As Owen notes, Spielberg 'privileges vision over utterance', allows us to witness 'the *un*speakable carnage of war' – a trope literalised in the silence of the subjectivised shots when Miller is stunned (2002: 262, 263). Spielberg's supporters and detractors rush in to fill that verbal void.

Of course, as Fussell insists, Hollywood remains the dream factory, 'and if it really projected the whole truth about anything, it would go bankrupt speedily'; also, 'its purpose is profit, and it has learnt that violence sells' (1998: 3). Within those limitations, *Saving Private Ryan*, unusually, invites reflection. For a movie that topped the US charts for a month to do this – and to reach so many people it could hardly attempt deep subversion – is creditable. Even if 'it's an anti-war-film film' more than an anti-war film (Steyn 1998: 14), its intertextuality stages a debate, self-reflexively raises tough questions about America's ideals and militarist legacy, and challenges audiences to 'earn' the right to judge. That judgement does not come supplied.

CHAPTER TWENTY

A.I. Artificial Intelligence: eyes wide open

A.I. Artificial Intelligence was keenly anticipated, partly because of mysterious Internet marketing (Vulliamy 2001: 20; see www.cloudmakers.org), and partly curiosity. Would it be 'the ultimate meeting of two of cinema's most inventive minds' or – Spielberg's image obtruding again – 'sentimental travesty of Kubrick's intentions' (Gumbel 2001: 11)? Although Kubrick, having co-written a ninety-page treatment, asked Spielberg to direct in 1994, Spielberg penned his own screenplay from Kubrick's notes and drawings after Kubrick died – his first since *Poltergeist*, and the first of his own he had directed since *Close Encounters*.

Accordingly, authorship dominated debate. *A.I.* polarised but fascinated critics. Its title inevitably provoked variants on Roger Ebert's observation that *A.I.*'s 'facile and sentimental' conclusion 'mastered the artificial but not the intelligence' (2001: 6). Implicitly the former was Spielberg's, Kubrick's the latter. Kubrick directed surgically indifferent meditations on passivity before powerful, often humanly created, forces; Spielberg 'benevolent science fiction as seen through the sensibilities of a child' (Lyman 2001: 5). In fact only two Spielberg films fitted that description, which ignores misanthropic early work. *A.I.* continues the darker, more adult tendencies of his 1990s 'history' films. Unclear initially, moreover, was that in this 'unlikely collision of Kubrick's hardcore dystopianism and Spielberg's gushing emotional overload' (Roux 2001: 4), this 'heartfelt mishmash of *Pinocchio* and *Oedipus*' (Hoberman 2001: 16), the *Pinocchio* elements came not from *Close Encounters*' director but Kubrick.

Adjectives like 'frustrating' repeatedly conveyed inconsistencies and contradictions (Brodesser 2001: 41). Pundits declared *A.I.* unmarketable. Spielberg, characteristically, had withheld key images and plot points, but the resultant enigma was whether it resembled *E.T.* or *Saving Private Ryan*. Some thought the movie should have been more family-friendly to attract a broader audience than its American PG-13 rating allowed. Others felt promotion over-emphasised its child star, misleading cinemagoers to expect something more comforting. Executives, including several among DreamWorks' competitors, praised the campaign's tenor as corresponding to the movie's adult themes and perceived subtleties and complexities. This view corroborated a late switch to a 25-and-over arthouse-oriented market (DiOrio 2001: 9).

The hype vaguely predicted '*Titanic*-like figures' for *A.I.*, which Spielberg finished early, saving a third of the $120 million budget (Wolf 2001: 19). It grossed $29.4 million during its opening weekend, accumulating $42.7 million over the first six days, including Independence Day. While impressive, given the niche audience, this was less than *Saving Private Ryan* earned in a comparable period three years previously (DiOrio 2001), and unremarkable against the $75.1 million *Pearl Harbor* (2001), *A.I.*'s critically derided competitor, garnered during a four-day opening. This was hardly disastrous: studios banked on theatrical revenue supplying 23 per cent of domestic income (Branston 2000: 57). Nevertheless, *A.I.*'s relative failure compounded trade press reports of 'violent antipathy' from audiences, which dropped 50 per cent then 63 per cent in the second and third weeks – making it, J. Hoberman avers, not Spielberg's first perceived dud but the first to fare better critically than commercially (2001: 16).

In fact, Farah Mendlesohn states, the profits of *Star Wars*, *Close Encounters*, *E.T.* and *The Matrix* are aberrant for science fiction – explicable, she claims, by their fairy tale qualities – whereas much good science fiction flops (*2001* initially, for example): typically concerned with thought rather than action, it 'doesn't play well on the screen' (2001: 20). Spielberg, conversely, centres 'human identity … in emotional receptivity' (Arthur 2001: 25): *E.T.* 'feels' Elliott's feelings. Tim Kreider (2002) believes this explains division over *A.I.* – variously the year's best film, or plain ludicrous. As a child protagonist's wish-fulfilment fantasy, it is embarrassingly mawkish. As simultaneous commentary on the hollowness of such comforts, foregrounded by having a robot, built to replicate human attachments, pursue them beyond any life-span, it is darkly cerebral. Anthony Quinn, in educing, according to preconceptions, that 'Spielberg seems to believe he's offering something profound and uplifting', not 'bleak and hopeless' (2001: 10), like many ascribes this schism to misguided direction rather than a (conscious or otherwise) structuring opposition.

Authorship

'An Amblin/Stanley Kubrick Production': *A.I.* credits itself, albeit posthumously, as collaborative. Spielberg spoke animatedly of a fax line linking the directors' homes. The movie specifically alludes to both filmmakers' output, considered later, and evinces thematic and stylistic continuities. A machine espousing emotions while humans behave impersonally, as if programmed, is characteristically Kubrick's idea. A lost child is typical Spielberg. Yet qualities Paul Arthur identifies with Spielberg appear equally in *2001*: 'the mystic light show as harbinger of the Beyond (*Raiders of the Lost Ark*, *Close Encounters of the Third Kind*, *Always*), the magical resurrection or second coming that smacks of New Testament theology (start with *Jaws* ...)' (2001: 25). Moreover *Schindler's List*'s industrial genocide was inexorable as any of Kubrick's machine-like institutions or conditioned characters, while *Saving Private Ryan*'s beach landing shows infantrymen obeying automatic instincts (one retrieves his own severed arm).

Kubrick spent 17 years on *A.I.* with five writers, inarguably making Brian Aldiss's story, 'Supertoys Last All Summer Long', his own, having incorporated *Pinocchio* against Aldiss's judgement (Argent 2001: 53). Kubrick had apparently started *A.I.* inspired by *E.T.*'s success (Hoberman 2001: 17). *Jurassic Park* convinced Kubrick of Spielberg's technical ability to bring to the screen something previously unrealisable, and more quickly than he could. Having rejected building an automaton for the lead role, Kubrick acknowledged that his painstaking methods meant a boy actor would age during production. Spielberg, recognised for directing children, and a long-standing admirer and friend, was an obvious choice: especially as, unlike 'Supertoys', Kubrick envisaged *Pinocchio* – as writer Sara Maitland insists he called the project – as 'sentimental, dreamlike' (Argent 2001: 51).

Self-reflexivity

The dissolve from the initial contextualising shot of high waves to the silhouetted Cybertronics Corp. statue outside a rain-streaked window immediately inscribes a screen, separating the spectator from an enigmatic figure that later becomes David's (Haley Joel Osment) object of desire. The metaphor consolidates as the camera pulls back to frame Professor Hobby (William Hurt) in close-up, against darkness; it redoubles as a track along the back of a lecture theatre follows him, inscribed spectators silhouetted in the foreground. Pillars and railings constitute internal frames. A beam reflected behind Hobby shines directly into camera as intra- and extra-diegetic audiences concentrate on his vision.

Dichotomised realism ('authenticity') and illusion – that polarisation between Spielberg's critics, traceable to the Lumières and Méliès – returns in the guise of artificial intelligence versus humanity. When Hobby stabs the hand of a robot, played – like the equally fictitious human characters – by a human performer, she screams as if real, but when he asks what he did to her feelings she insists he hurt her hand. As in film acting, the manifestation is superficial, emotion inferred. With light projecting from behind her head in Spielberg's signature image of desire, she defines love as replicable 'sensuality simulations'. Hobby directs her, ordering her to undress, then stopping her – here exploiting spectatorial voyeurism and pruriently testing suspension of disbelief (surely a human body will emerge from this shapely figure?). Fetishisation of the female and of CGI effects that foreground cinematic artifice coincide as he pauses to expose the inner workings of her head. She sheds a tear, implying conscious humiliation behind her programmed complicity; equally – a fundamental ambiguity – that such symptoms are merely physiological. *A.I.* concludes after an analogous, book-ending shot of David crying over his resurrected surrogate mother (Koresky

2003); at that point in a Spielberg movie when the scene apparently solicits empathy (for many it failed), whether David's emotion is authentic is crucial. Responses depend on how convincingly the text portrays feelings viewers can share. 'The mecha quest for an impossible authenticity [that] becomes the movie's driving mechanism' (Hoberman 2001: 17) culminates in David achieving 'idealised emotional harmony we humans unconsciously crave but can never fully realise in our adult lives' (Arthur 2001: 22). This is the Imaginary, narrative's 'lost' object, substituted also in primary identification with a film.

Hobby's project for 'a perfect child caught in a freeze-frame' renders cinematic parallels explicit. David, facsimile of a real deceased boy, eventually lives on, fixed, unchanging, constituting documentary evidence for future 'super-mechas'. Recall the Lumières' review that predicted cinematography would summon deceased loved ones, or debates around *Schindler's List* as 'witnessing'. David's survival into an ice age literalises 'freeze-frame', trapping him, latent, static, as if sealed in a can awaiting projection. The toppled Ferris wheel enclosing his suspended quest aptly visualises 'the final reel'.

Sheila, Hobby's demonstration robot, applies make-up literally to repair her face before a fade to black. After a caption, '20 MONTHS LATER', Monica (Frances O'Connor) and Henry (Sam Robards), the couple who adopt David, are driving to the facility where their incurably ill son is frozen. Correspondence between Martin's (Jake Thomas) suspended animation and David's future parallels humans with robots – 'orgas' with 'mechas', as characters term themselves – implying both are human variants. So does the first shot of Monica, also applying cosmetics using a compact mirror. Self-presentation and appearance anticipate the common human need for recognition underlying David's obsession with reciprocity of his filial love.

Implied narcissism raises awkward issues in relation to Hobby replicating his dead son and Monica adopting, then abandoning, David. Do children exist, like servile robots, merely to satisfy parents (Hoberman 2001)? The mirrors furthermore inaugurate an image system of reflections, central to David's determination to escape Symbolic positioning as a mecha and merge into Imaginary unity with Monica. This involves cinematic metaphors as light flashes down on the car, reflections in its glass inscribing a screen between us and the occupants. In the clinic shafts illuminate their object of desire, the pod containing Martin.

On David's arrival home, the door opens on the overexposed exterior as on to a blank screen from which he enters, elongated by an unfocused lens. Like the *Close Encounters* aliens, he appears – as a film character is – born of light. The image recalls that David is Spielberg's progeny and recollects his diegetic 'father' as it resembles the Cybertronics statue. It also anticipates the super-mechas, evolved avatars of his artificial human intelligence. Henry has orchestrated the moment to normalise domesticity in the absence of 'digested' grief, as a doctor says, because Martin is not dead but 'pending'. Henry thereby reclaims paternity. His possible selfishness, or at least renewed identity, figures in his reflection in an illuminated-surround mirror, watching the scene.

Monica initially rejects David, partly for being too real. His reflections appear in family photos and finally on Martin's portrait. Focalisation through Monica and

Henry, staring from behind a doorjamb, suggests unease about replacing their son, rather than that these signify David's Mirror Phase; he remains an expressionless puppet until activated to love. Fractured reflections in multiple mirrors express parental uncertainties as Henry explains the irrevocable imprinting procedure. A tinkling chrome mobile reflects David; it portrays two children and a mother with a space where her heart should be. At bedtime David follows Monica towards a ribbed glass door – through it his image splits, as if on a screen that reveals, yet imposes a barrier to, her potential object of desire. Distressed, she looks from the shadows, curious, as Henry dresses David, whose image partially resolves as he advances, meets her gaze, and smiles.

Cut to the following morning: Monica is reflected in a shiny lid, one of many circles framing her and later David with her. As David, a curious toddler with a ten-year-old's body and vocabulary, intently watches her pour coffee, the top of his face comically reflects in the table surface, rendering him for the spectator as a four-eyed alien, underlining radical otherness. Birdsong and piano melodies, resolving from discordant music-box tinkles, increasingly suggest calm and normality – despite Monica's awkwardness, the clinical décor, the predominantly cold, blue hues, David's unsettling tendency to materialise unexpectedly, and his unblinking stare. (As in *Empire of the Sun*, the piano repeatedly signifies maternal bliss.) Monica, making the bed, lifts a sheet; David is there when it falls, as if projected on the blank plane. Monica's overalls resemble the utilitarian suit David arrived in, implying affinity, a Mirror Phase in which proto-mother and -son are yet to recognise mutual definition. When, rattled by his presence, she puts him in a glass-door cupboard, the light dims as he freezes, as though projection stops.

Psychoanalysis appears perversely redundant in a movie in which the boy opens the toilet door on Monica as she sits, underwear around her ankles, reading *Freud on Women*. Nevertheless, overlaying David's knowingly Oedipal narrative is less emphatic re-inscription of spectator/text relations as understood in Lacanian terms. In this scene, for example, as David stares at Monica, the camera frames her in the doorway, subjected to our gaze also. At dinner, David, aspiring to his programmed familial role but unable as a mecha to eat, imitates the adults, using empty utensils. He thus sees them as mirroring his incipient identity but seeks also to join them, to occupy the space suggested by the empty chair in the foreground.

Reciprocally, when David laughs at spaghetti hanging from Monica's lip, his manic outburst startles both parents, and viewers; relieved, they (and we) relax and share his mirth – empathy with a mechanical projection, substitute for a real human relationship (in effect ourselves taking the unused seat) – until awkwardness encroaches as David laughs too long, then halts abruptly. Far from unalloyed manipulation constantly charged against Spielberg, this supremely self-reflexive moment, Kreider observes, demonstrates, 'with a directorial flourish, how easily our emotions are coached', leaving us 'just imitating the expressions in front of us, laughing and crying at nothing, going through the motions' (2003: 33). Following its chilling account of 'sensuality simulations', the movie is as aware of, and interested in, the artificiality of its intelligence and emotions as the most disapproving Frankfurt theorist. From Hobby's seeming cruelty to the Holocaust imagery of dumped mecha parts, from Joe's chivalry towards an abused woman to Martin's mobility by means of techno-trousers, repeatedly it juxtaposes, and blurs boundaries between, humans and automata, within a reflexively cinematic metadiscourse. David's artificial imprinting and subsequent rejection motivate him with the unattainable desire for a lost object that impels the movie's audience into the cinema. As Kreider notes,

> Every character in the film seems as pre-programmed as David, obsessed with the image of a lost loved one, and tries to replace that person with a technological simulacrum. Dr Hobby designed David as an exact duplicate of his own dead child ...; Monica used him as a substitute for her comatose son; and, completing the sad cycle two thousand years later, David comforts himself with a cloned copy of Monica. (2003: 34)

The oval canopy of Martin's bed in which David simulates sleep, shot from end on, resembles a self-enclosed orb containing David and Monica, visually correlating to his Imaginary. Its blue illumination institutes David's obsession with the Blue Fairy, his quest object. Cutaways to Martin, similarly bathed in cold light and haloed in his cryogenic capsule, are Monica's subjective visions before she decides to imprint David with undying love. Taking the code from a warm red folder, she reaches out to hold him and speak the requisite words as both appear in a two-shot against radiating intense white light. This moment, in which David's relaxation seemingly transforms him into a human and is marked by transition from calling her 'Monica' to 'Mummy', explicitly equates cinematic projection with the Imaginary.

After a fade to black, David's point-of-view shot resembles a TV commercial as Henry and Monica in evening dress prepare for an outing. It frames Monica doubly within the mise-en scène; receding doorways reinforce its voyeuristic nature, emphasising David's desire as the parents argue good-naturedly over whether he is a child or toy. After she implicitly forgives him for wasting rare perfume, David, with light behind him as if projecting his concerns, asks fearfully when she will die. While a mirror shows her reactions – she is learning identification with her new role, but the circular frame also relates it to David's Imaginary – the camera cranes to look down her cleavage, as if acknowledging sexual undercurrents Martin's imminent recovery will activate.

The rape of the lock

David's perfection highlights Martin's flawed humanity. He refuses to break toys, despite Martin's urging, and helps mummy in the kitchen to prepare Martin's medication. Warm colours now suffuse the household, the characters and décor carefully coordinated. Martin chooses *Pinocchio* for Monica to read them, maliciously proclaiming 'David is going to *love* it' – the story of a puppet that yearns to become real. David listens enraptured in the corner at bedtime, silhouetted like a film spectator against a rosy glow, craning forward while Monica and Martin occupy the blue oval enclosure. The Blue Fairy (described in the book as 'my kind mother' (Collodi 1988: 140)) appears in Pinocchio's dream, kissing him after he undertakes chores on her behalf. As David stares, in calm, unspoken longing, an aquarium behind him foreshadows his fate, just as concentric shapes enclosing the bed pre-echo the whale's belly in the Pinocchio fairground ride.

Sibling rivalry climaxes when David, emulating Martin, clogs his circuits with spinach. Martin glowers at Monica, reflected, holding David's hand during the remedial operation. A sound bridge links this to Martin setting a 'special mission' he claims will make mummy love David. A 'projection beam' behind Martin unbalances a symmetrical two-shot in which the boys mirror each other in front of a mother-and-child picture: each envies the other's ego-ideal status. Castration symbolism permeates Martin's plan for David to 'sneak into mummy's bedroom' and shear a lock of hair, as well as Oedipal challenge to Henry – as the father later confirms, responding to Monica's reasoned reaction by calling David's scissors 'a knife'. On Martin's birthday, although David brings a present and Martin even defends him against bigger boys, phallic rivalry precipitates the crisis prompting David's banishment. Unable to discern difference between David and themselves, the boys ask whether he can pee. This 'lack' – robots do not pee – marks the difference between orga and mecha and their unequal treatment in the Symbolic order: exactly analogous to the Real of sexual difference.

When Martin's friend stabs David to test him – echoing Hobby's treatment of Sheila – David panics and clings to his orga brother, accidentally dragging him into the pool. After David's density sinks them, he remains, limbs outstretched in an empty embrace following Martin's rescue. This prefiguring of his future includes an optical point-of-view of mother, family, humanity: distanced, unreachable, beyond the meniscus before an overhead shot retreats to frame him in a blue, screen-shaped rectangle.

The next scene rhymes by presenting Monica, against a blue background, overlaid by reflections in a glass screen: separated from the son she chose to love when she returned to hold his hand after initial revulsion at his artificiality. A blue, circular window frames her, but excludes David; when it frames him, she remains outside it. David's crayoned letters to her express contrary feelings; his controlled demeanour belies desperation to define their relationship in words pleasing to her. His multi-coloured, if mechanical, writing is a visual residue of their short relationship; everything again now appears cold and superficial. One letter parallels orga binary logic in fantasising a Symbolic order whereby Mummy, Martin and David are real, but Teddy – Martin's mecha toy, given to David before Martin's remission – is not. Tearful and conflicted, repeatedly looking back at Henry but avoiding eye contact with David, Monica betrays him by lying: 'Tomorrow's gonna be just for us.' Continuing from David in the pool, this scene further shifts focalisation towards David as Monica now behaves artificially.

As in the previous drive in the country, the car's bubble is a reflexive screen, repeatedly whiting out as David seeks reconciliation with Monica, whose tears confirm discomfort about editing him from her movie. Robotic in determination, Monica nevertheless bypasses the Cybertronics plant where she is supposedly taking David for destruction. Instead she drives into a dazzling light shaft, a projector beam for David's Imaginary and her fantasy of giving him a chance. Abandoning him in the woods, she last sees him diminishing in a wing mirror, another oval framing, as he cries after her, centred in a cone of flickering beams.

Similar imagery links this scene of childhood innocence to the following urban scenario. Although Monica's last words are, 'I'm sorry I didn't tell you about the world', ensuing conflicts differ only in degree, not nature or motivation, from David's domestic experiences. During the transitional fade to black, a voice articulates what David is feeling: 'I'm afraid.' It is a woman's, whose bruises indicate an abusive orga partner; she is seeking solace from lover mecha Gigolo Joe (Jude Law), much as David briefly satisfied Monica's maternal needs. A surrogate for real, but flawed, human relationships, Joe personifies the diversionary aspects of popular entertainment. He embodies cinematic history, melting hearts with songs from 1930s musicals and dancing in puddles (specifically a reference to *Singin' in the Rain*, but also Kubrick's *A Clockwork Orange* (1971), which, we shall see, informs many of *A.I.*'s deepest concerns). His first song, 'I Only Have Eyes For You', immediately alludes to scopic desire and power at the heart of *A.I.* Moreover, he incarnates the cinematic apparatus. Changing appearance to suit his next client's fantasy, like a film star, he checks himself – both projecting and assuming his introjected role – in a mirror (metaphorical screen), built into his hand which doubles simultaneously as a lamp. Later, to tempt teenage boys to drive him and David to Rouge City, he projects a hologram.

An orga frames Joe for murder. David also is scapegoated for orga dissatisfaction and jealousies. While Joe seeks to escape the Symbolic by excising his operating licence, his identity, a sound bridge to David in the woods, telling Teddy, 'If I am a real boy I can go back and she'll love me', highlights the parallel. Self-reflexivity again underlines vision as David experiences unforeseen dangers. A refuse truck arrives, preceded by spotlight beams. One shot isolates David's eyes behind dumped objects in close-up before damaged redundant mechas emerge from the dazzling background to pick over body parts like a cannibal zombie horror movie. Yet they demonstrate – unlike humans – unqualified mutual cooperation in repairing themselves. One replaces an eyeball. This powerfully draws attention to his look, as indirect narration relays the spectator's scopic drive through further characters' reactions to an unseen stimulus. Another stares off-screen, upwards towards illumination, hollering, 'Moon on the rise!' as the camera tracks in on his face. Then David looks over his shoulder, before a cut to an impossibly enormous full moon. A further shot of a welder raising his mask further emphasises the spectacle (against realist logic: robot welders hardly need eye protection), then a female mecha looking up: no fewer than six inscribed looks, as Joe, on the margin of the scene, observes the brightening sky.

The moon, however, is a gigantic balloon that compounds nature and technology, beauty and danger, spectacle and observer. From the basket, sprouting cameras, movie spotlights project beams that return the characters' and the spectator's searching gaze. As Christian Metz puts it, 'the spectator is the searchlight … duplicating the projector, which itself duplicates the camera, and he [sic] is also the sensitive surface duplicating the screen, which itself duplicates the film strip' (1975: 53). The basket seats an inscribed director, surrounded by screens, using a megaphone to control capturing of replicated human forms for entertainment. The Flesh Fair he supplies parodies Hollywood, not least DreamWorks' recent success, *Gladiator* (2000). It is crowd-pleasing, American (US flags abound), spectacular. Rock 'n' roll, circus, mechanical destruction, violence, big screens and light shafts exploit and express social fears – here, of artificiality, as he invites people, 'Expel your mechas,' while the compère asserts, 'We are alive and this is a celebration of life.'

Motorcyclists pursue the mechas, effectively capturing them in their headlights. Foreground objects in parallel tracking shots impose a flickering reminiscent of silent film chases, the original action movies. A mecha, who in darkness looks normal, but has no head behind her face – two-dimensional, like a projection – stands before shafts of light reciprocal to David's searching gaze as she offers to nanny him. Light plays over David as if from a screen as he asks whether she knows the Blue Fairy. Before she can answer, the entire opposite wall collapses, leaving a bright rectangle penetrated by ferocious-looking pursuers: the recurrent Spielberg nightmare of the screen, plane of the Symbolic, as permeable barrier against the horror of the Real, counterpart to the fantasy of the screen as access to a desired Imaginary.

Another metaphorical screen incarcerates the Flesh Fair mechas, providing protection as well as vision. Orgas discharge a mecha from a cannon. His flaming, severed head, still animated, flies towards the mechas (and us) before jamming between, and sliding down, cage bars. The huge propeller through which he is fired imposes a projector sound, and blasts the unwilling captive audience with a solar wind. The control room, full of screens, where the showman's daughter takes Teddy after he claims David is human, resembles an editing suite. David, frightened and confused, as a child watching A.I. at this point might be, clasps Joe's hand. (Importantly, the images are less horrific for adults because the mechas destroyed are evidently machines.) The cage, dividing mechas from orgas, inscribes a metaphorical surface between David and his desire to join the humans; the parallel with spectatorial identification compounds when the girl, looking at David, recognises humanity in his eyes. David's escape from the arena with Joe traverses a rectangle of white light.

Rouge City too is a commercial fantasy, resembling cinema. David and Joe ascend an escalator, as in a multiplex, before passing through a whiteout to emerge among holograms and projection beams. The neon church of Our Lady of the Immaculate Heart, contrasting with the mobile that signifies Monica's heartlessness, explicitly equates the Blue Fairy to the Virgin, appropriately for this boy of no woman born. Such idealisation of motherhood resonates with the lost Imaginary and desire for identification exploited by cinematic suture, both paralleled by David's quest. The 'Dr Know' attraction, a kind of super search-engine, furthermore elevates cinema's claims to truth as it comprises a mini projection theatre in which curtains open upon a screen; its entrance is a dark blue passage with illuminated sprocket holes or screens, typical multiplex décor. Cinema once more is apotheosised, as David, in another *Persona* re-run, tries to grasp a Blue Fairy hologram and, failing, attempts to enter the screen. Finally, though, as David asserts his conviction that fairy tales are real – a self-reflexive statement permitting speculation on *A.I.*'s own pretension to serious art – the answer to his enquiry, about how the Blue Fairy could make a robot real, scrolls up the screen. (Based on Yeats's poem, 'The Stolen Child', it confirms the movie's high-cultural aspirations.) This projection – drawn lines radiate from the text – points David to 'where dreams are born'. Although, diegetically, the conundrum refers to Manhattan,

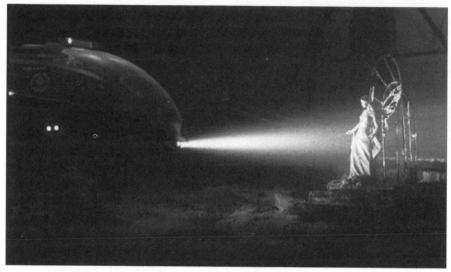

A.I. Artificial Intelligence – the inscribed apparatus: David's endless quest for the lost mother

such a description applies equally to Hollywood. By a tenuous metonymic chain, the Coney Island funfair where David finds the Blue Fairy reflects the one at Santa Monica (Hollywood's nearest resort, where the Ferris wheel rolls into the sea in *1941*), a name neatly compounding 'Our Lady' and David's 'mummy'.

On the windscreen of the amphibicopter in which David, Joe and Teddy depart, a computer graphic of Manhattan, visible both inside and out, projects their desire until the real thing coincides exactly. Droplets on the screen and dazzling white cascades create a spectacular light show, superimposed over their enthralled expressions, as they near their destination, a skyscraper entered through a whited-out rectangular aperture. Light shafts lure them through semi-translucent doors. Nursery chimes play and light radiates from behind David as he penetrates the Imaginary of his lost origins, the primal scene of Professor Hobby's office. The ensuing Mirror Phase, however, instead of regressing him to merge with his like, confronts him with the horror of the Real. 'Is this the place they make you real?' he asks, enchanted. A chair revolves, in a shot modelled on Mother's revelation as mummy in *Psycho*, only this time it is another self he meets, this robot who thinks he is unique. 'This is the place they make you *read*', his Other responds, shattering David's identity with a minuscule arbitrary difference in the Symbolic register. After innocently enquiring, 'Are you me?' David reacts, in this over-exposed theatre of light, by insisting, 'She's mine! And I'm the only one!' and smashes and decapitates his counterpart with a lamp, proclaiming uniqueness at the moment he demonstrates humanity's tragic failing. The scene shocks in direct ratio to the extent one accepts him and his emotions as real.

After Hobby intervenes, appropriating for himself the Blue Fairy role, and David repudiates him, David becomes Hobby's object of desire: lost surrogate for his deceased son. Bright lights in the dark background link Hobby's projective gaze to David across the frame. Hobby departs to summon his team, the camera positioned behind doors that slide open to convert yet another vertical plane into an aperture. David sits gazing into it like a spectator. Inquisitive, he follows lights, like Elliott encountering *E.T.*, into the space, indeed, of his conception: past a flat monitor displaying the Cybertronics logo – mise-en-abyme of the movie's second shot – and photographs of the original David. He encounters multiple copies of himself, like sequential images on film, awaiting animation; a trope literalised when one of the packaged goods, apparently backlit in their boxes, moves. His moment of clarity juxtaposes an optician's chart and instruments before the window and statue. The camera tracks towards a seated figure facing the metaphorical screen showing the symbol of David's true origins. Horror figures again, the shot repeating *Psycho*'s revelation that mother is 'not quite herself'. Instead of personality and affirmation, it presents inanimate matter in the guise of life, radically undermining identity. David looks through the eye sockets of his own death mask. Hobby, cloning mechas to deny his son's death, equates to Norman stuffing birds and keeping Mother's preserved corpse alive in fantasy. The tears at the start and end of *A.I.* recall the single tear shed in *Psycho*, when Marion is bereft of identity by another's projective vision.

David's red collar and his flesh tones now provide the only warmth among dull greys in a supposedly human environment. Wind currents but no accompanying light (Spielberg's metaphor for hope or desire) buffet David, perched alongside the statue, a Phoenix-like vision when he drew it for Martin, now a vainglorious shell. His last word, 'Mummy', is a lament rather than an appeal. With no reason to live (created solely to love), he throws himself into the sea, his plummet, reflected in the amphibicopter windscreen, superimposed over Joe's face. Here one of the movie's few moments of compassion reveals itself in a robot, just as mechas provided comfort and deactivated each others' pain receptors at the Flesh Fair. Immersed now in intense blue – metonym for motherhood – a dazzling beam appears behind David, projecting onto something off-screen, towards which, reanimated, he stretches: a recurrence of *Persona*'s keynote image. The moment he reaches to embrace the chimera, subsequently revealed as a fairground effigy, of the Blue Fairy, a real – yet appropriately artificial and mechanical – embrace clasps him: a grappling device operated by Joe, who rescues him.

Hyper-excited, like Jim seeing the American fighter at the structurally parallel point in *Empire of the Sun*, David completes his quest alone following Joe's arrest. Beams from the amphibicopter penetrate the depths, inscribing his gaze. As he approaches Gepetto's workshop, through a rectangular gateway, a reverse-shot from behind the scene of Pinocchio's manufacture presents illusory animation in the moving light. Similarly, seaweed waving in the current appears to animate the Blue Fairy's hair, her idealisation emphasised by consequent resemblance to Botticelli's Venus. (Long-standing associations link motherhood with the sea – both, analogously, sources of life; compare such disparate texts that combine childhood wonder and horror as Kingsley's *The Water-Babies* and Powell's *Peeping Tom* (1960) (Morris 1990).) Overlapping edits slow and intensify David's fetishised vision, which appears superimposed, reflected in the amphibicopter's bubble. The static image fixes eternally in his gaze. Yet, enclosed in the framework of a bower, it evokes also the archetypal spider woman, the *femme fatale*, projection of male anxieties, reciprocally trapping him. Illuminated panels behind his head echo the headlamps, suggesting a projection room. The projector, Metz writes, is 'an apparatus the spectator has behind him [sic], *at the back of his head,* that is, precisely where fantasy locates the "focus" of all vision' (1975: 52; a footnote translates 'derrière la tête' as 'at the back of one's mind' as well as 'behind one's head'). Her reflection merges with David, the long-awaited regression to the Mirror Phase, to effect Imaginary reunion.

Anything but triumphant cinematic vision, however, this moment, towards which Spielberg's entire career converges, poignantly underlines that the Imaginary is, by definition, unattainable. What could have been an intellectually satisfying, if down-beat, ending leaves David in an almost diagrammatic image of spectatorship, seated in darkness, gazing along a cone of light in primary identification with an unreachable illuminated figure, behind a screen that is both access and barrier. 'Sunk in the electri-cal narcotics of the cinemas', like popular audiences, according to Dziga Vertov (1926: 23), sustained by a false vision that distracts from effectual activity, David is fated to futile repetition – 'Blue Fairy, please, please, please make me into a real live boy' – until his batteries expire and the oceans freeze.

Two millennia later, a hand wipes a blank surface, brushing away frost to reveal David beyond. Shadows play over his face as though from a movie screen, before a benediction gesture – cinema as religion – reanimates him with a light burst. Entering now the diegesis of his vision as was never possible in *Persona*, David finally touches the Blue Fairy only to see her shatter and collapse. However, the super-mechas who restart David's freeze-frame within the inscribed reel personify cinema, as did Joe, and reassert Spielberg's faith by realising David's Imaginary. They read his discursive formation, expressed as images on their faces which become screens, while David's eyes close at last, his search over. His blue eyes reopen in close-up on a white screen, an amalgam of cinema's fundamental elements: he is back at Monica's, announcing, 'We're home!' the piano again playing. The exterior is blue, however, not green, as he runs through the house with abandon, like Jim in *Empire of the Sun*, calling 'Where *are* you?' and oversaturated colours and grainy stock emphasise this reconstruction's cinematic artificiality. A female voice allures him: the Blue Fairy, not Monica – a metonymic consolation for the lost object. 'You've been searching for me, haven't you?' she asks. He replies, 'For my whole life.' This scenario then recedes, as an exter-nalised camera position confirms it to be a movie watched by super-mecha spectators. Their circular screen exactly matches an earlier shot, seconds before news of Martin's recovery excludes David, of Monica reflected in a shiny glass hob, cooking. Light shines behind David's head now as the super-mechas communicate via the Blue Fairy, confirming how important to them his 'uniqueness' is, which he always craved.

Assuring David, 'Your wish is my command', the Blue Fairy, after David has wept that Monica cannot return, restores her for one day from the lock of hair kept by Teddy. The chrome mobile reappears. David, playing with a toy amphibicopter, remembers Joe: rather than regression to an earlier state, this is imaginary projection, anticipation grounded in current knowledge and desire. A knock at the door heralds not Mummy, but a super-mecha, in a recurrent Spielberg identification device that deceives or surprises the spectator and protagonist together. Clunking expository dia-logue finally leads to the exterior becoming natural and David walking through blind-ing light and a ribbed glass screen to where Monica is awakening alone in the marital bed. The screen whites out to that imageless purity, purgation of the Symbolic, which

Neary enters in *Close Encounters*, as David strokes her hair: a healing repetition of the traumatic instant of castration when Henry leapt out of bed, removed the scissors, and afterwards engineered David's banishment.

David fulfils his desire to please, making Monica coffee in the dazzlingly back-lit kitchen. Having once promised him 'tomorrow', she is unaware what day it is; 'Today', David tells her, film always unreeling in a perpetual present. Multiple mirrors now redouble rather than fracture the image as Monica dries and combs David's hair, a further white-out accompanying the voice-over narration that 'there was no Henry … no Martin … no grief' – that is, no patriarchy to constrain the utterly artificial 'TV-commercial-like perfection' (Robnik 2002: 7). A light shaft flares as Monica declares her love and David sheds a further tear as she returns to bed. Eventually he closes his eyes voluntarily for the first time – a real boy, he believes – and the camera tracks discreetly back, leaving him sleeping with Mummy where, the voice-over explains, 'dreams are born'. This emollient phrase, however, disguises the origins of both nocturnal and silver screen dreams in unresolved tensions and traumas. Kreider recalls that the happy incidents in David's day with Monica, causally connected, each rewrite a disaster (2002: 38): the hide-and-seek game compensates for her incarcerating and abandoning him, the haircut for his chopping off her lock, and the birthday party for the afternoon he almost drowned Martin.

Realism and fantasy

Realism is an issue both in *A.I.* and its reception. Hoberman ridicules the 'hilarious morass of Ed Wood gibberish' (2001: 17); Mendlesohn criticises the 'scientific gobbledygook' the movie resorts to in explaining its premises because it is unsure of its audience, as well as implausibilities such as David having an oesophagus, the unlikelihood of a psychologist recommending a robot 'replacement' to bereaved parents, and ignorance of the destruction ice wreaks on trapped structures (2001: 20). For Hoberman, however, 'The movie's appeal is not to reason. Its psychological terrain is far closer to the magical realms of Hans Christian Andersen or E.T.A. Hoffman than to sci-fi as we know it' (2001: 17). Certainly this 'bastard son of Sigmund Freud and Walt Disney' (Charity 2001: 85), as well as Kubrick and Spielberg, is easily reducible to formulaic structures: David as ego, Martin the id, and Teddy the super-ego.

A.I. declares itself not merely a film but a DreamWorks product, apparently acknowledging Freudian implications of the company's brand name. A plaque featuring the studio's crescent moon logo identifies the Cryogenics ward where Martin slumbers amid fairy tale murals. The figure recurs: in a rug and a light that haloes David in the nursery with its clouds wallpaper that also recalls the logo; in a light behind David during the first dinner scene; as well as in the perspective framing of a round window before which Monica rejects David and, ultimately, a super-mecha animates his dream. The clouds reappear in a shadowy, Hitchcockian vein, as headlight patterns on the wall when David cuts Monica's hair. Furthermore the roar of giant waves, signifying global warming, accompanies the opening logo instead of the familiar, reassuring guitar and orchestra. The director with the clout to authorise this change asserts a bleak realism, reinforced in the understated white-on-black credits.

David's 'monomaniacal obsession that renders him oblivious to the ugly realities around him' (Kreider 2003: 36) parallels what commonsense accounts of entertainment call escapism. Orgas attend flesh fairs or sleep with robots while the ice caps melt. David's final happiness ignores human extinction, no less, just as some critics argue *Schindler's List* provides an upbeat substitute for confronting the Holocaust. Conversely, Drehli Robnik (2002) argues, David's memory keeps the human race from oblivion. Preserved and narrated by a super-mecha voiced by Ben Kingsley – whose *Schindler's List* character was witness and enabler – it reasserts Spielberg's faith in popular cinema as cultural memory: 'Whoever saves one life, saves the world entire.' Equally, in seeking to recreate human 'spirit' in further striving for the Imaginary, the super-mechas are absolutely misguided. 'Surely human beings must be the key to understanding the meaning of existence', states the narrator, citing art, poetry and mathematics. However, Kreider sardonically observes, all 'human beings do in this film is fuck and destroy robots, and each other' (2002: 38).

Yet the Flesh Fair, whose audience is exhorted 'purge yourself of artificiality', as well as an ironically self-reflexive view of Spielberg's cinema – he, 'no less than these rabid rednecks', Hoberman implies, loves his special effects – 'might equally represent Spielberg's view of his critics. (Rather than the fantasy of *Schindler's List*, these anti-mechas are demanding the documentary *Shoah*.)' (2001: 18) Then again, *A.I.* anticipates and articulates such objections. David, proposing he could emulate Pinocchio, insists, as Monica abandons him in a fairy tale forest, 'Stories are what happens'; she, heartbroken and unable to destroy what she knows is a simulacrum, responds, 'Stories are not real.' *A.I.*, exceeding monological discourses that divide critics, stages ambiguities and contradictions, and embraces heteroglossia. David's unprecedented realism, after all, offends Lord Johnson-Johnson, who, with his religious rhetoric, echoes the effects lobby, while precisely the same quality moves the crowd to David's defence.

Intertextuality

Metatextuality again transcends postmodern pastiche by alluding to other pertinent themes and contexts. In a film explicitly concerned with story-telling, illusions, psychological needs and their relation to the Real, it furthermore, arguably, increases audience self-awareness, potentially encouraging reflection on textual strategies and associated pleasures and frustrations. The thunder rumbling outside Hobby's lecture theatre, which resembles a Victorian anatomy room with its slab-like tables, is a horror cliché signifying 'mad scientist', especially with the ominous high-pitched synthesised score as he removes Sheila's processor. Yet the Frankenstein connotations – Hobby likens himself to God creating Adam – exceed generic convention. Just as Mary Shelley's novel voiced anxieties around scientific progress and social change, Spielberg's choice of a black woman to raise the 'conundrum' of mechas programmed to love – 'Can you get a human to love them back?' – places this evolution in a procession, including abolitionism and feminism, of comparable moral problems for patriarchal hegemony. A white, middle-aged, entrepreneurial, male technocrat's single-mindedness in his multinational corporate headquarters bodes ill against the backdrop of global warming.

References across periods and genres invoke cinema as a reservoir of the uncon-scious, rendering the fantasy dreamlike yet already known: alternately strange, half-recognised and welcomely familiar. Without curbing his usual broad intertextuality, including numerous auto-citations, Spielberg emphatically emulates the look of a Kubrick movie, as epitextual cues invite audiences to note. Framing David through a doughnut-shaped ceiling light at dinner both haloes him, emphasising his nar-rative status as Chosen One, and ominously recalls *Dr Strangelove*'s War Room as domesticity becomes a battleground for technologically unleashed forces confronting humanity with its self-destructive imperfections. Brittle cutlery sounds recall typically awkward mealtimes in Kubrick. Martin's cryogenic pod evokes Disney's *The Sleeping Beauty* (1959), but also hibernation capsules in *2001*. When Martin asks if David does 'power stuff like walk on the ceiling or walls, or anti-gravity stuff', perceptive viewers might recall Fred Astaire – Joe's precursor – performing such stunts in *Royal Wedding* (1951), replicated for artificial gravity effects in *2001*. As Kreider states, the scene with Sheila recalls 'the grotesque piece of theatre in *A Clockwork Orange* in which prison officers and politicians applaud as Alex is debased and bullied ... It is the audience, not the subject, whose emotional responses are tested' (2002: 34) – and one might conclude both films' audiences are meant to find the diegetic audi-ences' lacking. Hobby's office, outside which the amphibicopter docks in a bay mod-elled from *2001*, recalls how in that film an ape evolves paradoxically into a weapon yielder: like HAL, the artificial intelligence that marks the peak of further evolution in *2001*, David is a killer. The smashed mecha and subsequently discovered copies, confirming both are mass-produced commodities, further the paradox: David, who previously refused to break toys, is only a murderer if he and it are human. David's creepy qualities – his unsettling stare, the closed loop of his programmed obsession – retain a non-human quality that prevents him from becoming entirely sympathetic and are at the heart of the film's ambivalent reception. Otherness prevails even when an unequivocally sentimental film would have portrayed him as closer to a 'real boy.'. At the end of his 'only child' sojourn with Monica, David eerily relays a telephone message in the caller's voice. This recalls not only Spielberg's recurrent theme of translation linking protagonists at the interface between levels of diegesis, but also, ominously, the boy's apparent possession in *The Shining* – referenced already in the shot following the Swinton's three-wheeled car that recalls his tricycle. The 'murder' scene echoes a 'massacre' of fashion mannequins in *Killer's Kiss* (1955), while reveal-ing, as in a Kubrick narrative, David's destiny to be contained within a bigger, unex-pected plan.

Tonal discords accompany David's confrontation with himself, similarly to Bowman observing his older self in *2001*. David, though, neither ages nor grows. As he floats, immersed in light, after attempting suicide, resemblance to Kubrick's starchild is ironically, chillingly hollow. Obsessive solipsism, a humanly implanted replication of human selfishness, rather than a cosmic breakthrough, predicates David's survival. While the rapid flight over ice fields recalls Bowman's stargate journey and the camera passes through a future craft composed of *2001*-style monoliths, the sequence in the reconstituted house where David, like Bowman, finds himself at a dining table, is an end in itself, not a way station. Finally David, although believing as some audience members may (especially those who find the movie saccharine) that he is closing his eyes to drift away into maternal bliss, forgets he is a defunct machine trapped in a frozen waste. Worse, the super-mechas, by downloading his synthetic desire in order to reconnect themselves to the humans who spawned them yet departed, retain enough flawed humanity themselves to enter the futile loop by vicariously participating and pursuing their own Imaginary. They join David – whom Kreider likens to Jack in *The Shining*, trapped in a photograph, 'happy and fulfilled, finally home, frozen forever in Hell' (2002: 39).

Subject positioning

A.I. progresses schematically, richly allusively, conscious intertextuality challenging monological readings. Intriguingly cerebral, it fails as mainstream entertainment. It undermines its apparent premises and ironises the pleasures, whether associated with realism or fantasy, ordinarily contracted with blockbuster audiences. At no point does this movie (which with typical Kubrick mischief names the psychiatrist who catalyses the entire plot 'Dr Frasier' after an inept sitcom character) approach the authenticity or sustained Imaginary involvement it appears knowingly to reflect upon as part of David's yearning. Its contradictions self-cancel. David, unlike Collodi's original, does not develop in his quest. The tragedy, a word applicable here only as a conventional term, is that his emotion, while real – he is programmed, like a human, to feel it – means nothing. Consequently, neither does the emotion the movie ostensibly appears to strain after.

Initial focalisation with Monica stresses David's otherness. A shift occurs, with awareness of David's jealousy upon Martin's entrance. Neither overtly expressed nor performed, however, this is spectatorial projection. Facilitated by Martin's initial half-machine appearance, such empathy is the nub of the film. Roger Ebert argues that David 'only seems to love. We are expert at projecting human emotions into non-human subjects, from animals to clouds to computer games, but the emotions reside only in our minds' (2001: 6), a view that chimes with Anne Friedberg's theorised account of identification with non-human characters (1990). From this, Ebert concludes the answer to the Cybertronics seminar question – 'What responsibility does a human have to a robot that genuinely loves?' – is 'none' (2001: 6). However this is less simple. If pre-programming means David's capacity to love is not real, where does that leave human parental or filial love, evolutionarily and psychosexually programmed? Henry's logic, meanwhile, is flawed, machine-like and incompassionate as that of any HAL, his Oedipal rationalisation predicated on a non sequitur: 'If [David] was created to love it's reasonable to assume he knows how to hate.' Monica realises again David is a machine when, during his operation, he assures her, 'It's OK, Mummy, it doesn't hurt.' The film fails whenever the audience forgets he is a mecha, as the synthetic emotion appears sentimental and false as human drama, whereas this is precisely the point the movie addresses through focalisation via David – a robot programmed, remember, to feel as a ten-year-old. His reaching for Joe's hand at the Flesh Fair is the key moment of *human* sympathy that links with *E.T.*, *Always*, *Schindler's List* and *Amistad* and divides those films' critics; it occurs as the diegetic audience, who think they are celebrating authenticity by disposing of artifice, confront mortality by watching its symbolic enactment, rendered painless, by technological substitutes.

It is a short step to the mecha conversation at the Flesh Fair about how 'history repeats itself' as orgas strive to 'maintain numerical superiority' by apparently perpetrating atrocities to reassert difference. Yet when the Flesh Fair proprietor calls, 'You! Boy!' it is doubtful many spectators question David's acceptance of the interpellation. Focalisation aligns us with David and against – as at the start of E.T. – our fellow orgas. Difference, then, on which the narrative is predicated, is severely problematised, leaving in place more questions than are answered.

CHAPTER TWENTY-ONE

Minority Report: through a glass, darkly

Following critical and box office disappointment that soon caused *A.I.* to 'fade into obscurity' (Gomery 2003: 79), damage limitation appears to have extended to playing down Spielberg's involvement in *Minority Report*. Marketability depended on promoting Tom Cruise in an action thriller, rather than Spielberg directing science fiction, despite his long-standing association with the genre and the two movies' similar setting and visual style. Indeed Spielberg's name was absent from billboard advertisements. Yet *Minority Report* embodies and extends the director's most interesting and typical concerns.

Seeking clarity

The ostensible narrative begins with a rapid montage portraying a murder. Bleached-out hazy shapes rack focus: a couple making love; scissors; a man climbing stairs, optically distorted to suggest mental derangement but incidentally emphasising the film plane; discontinuous dialogue. Tantalising glimpses of lust, violence and melodramatic emotion, accompanied by disturbingly percussive, echoing sound, recall a movie trailer. Close-ups on eyes – The murderer's? The victim's? An onlooker's? – culminating in an extreme close-up on an iris, underline the enigma. Similarity to key shots in *Psycho* and *2001* evokes both Hitchcock's thrillers and Kubrick's science fiction. Pointed scissors penetrating an eye in a cardboard cut-out – patently a reference to *Un Chien Andalou* (1929) and, especially pertinently, Dali's dream sequence for Hitchcock's *Spellbound* (1945) – allude to visceral and psychological horror, specifically associated with the vulnerability of eyes and the guilt of voyeurism. *Minority Report* consciously aligns with modernism and the art-house tradition.

In a sense this sequence *is* a trailer. Establishing the tone, generic expectations and enigmas according to which the film, which elaborates the same narrative, is understood (a science fiction mystery thriller concerned with the theme of vision and containing some Bergmanesque mise-en-scène and metaphysical explorations) it also briefly previews, like a trailer, a forthcoming event. That this foreshadows a definite narrative occurrence, were the warning not heeded, parallels in mise-en-abyme the function of the movie itself and its defining genre in predicting a preventable future. Like any trailer it also stimulates desire by presenting a trace of a film not yet seen, redoubling the notion of present absence, an Imaginary signifier.

Agatha's (Samantha Morton) large eyes and shaven head, together with her blank white background, locate the Pre-Cog, whose vision this is, in a line of mystical Others in Spielberg's science fiction. She is, furthermore, another personification of cinema. Not only a star within the diegesis, attracting tons of fan mail, she also receives visions and projects them onto a screen in the so-called Temple she and her two fellows inhabit. Its dark, quilted walls and geometrically interspersed spotlights would pass for a movie theatre. The rectangular window looked through by Anderton (Tom Cruise), the active surrogate directed according to her visions, flanked by speakers amplifying his voice, in this analogy inscribes a screen. So, reciprocally, does the surface of the 'photon milk' suspending her (light as nurture!), which she breaches whenever engaged in the action, sinking back when less involved in her unfolding dreams. Amniotic associations compound the analogy with cinema as maternal Imaginary.

The opening prophecy, interspersed with, on first viewing, incongruous violent splashes, instating an image system of water, retrospectively positions the spectator with Agatha. The peritext of the Twentieth Century-Fox and DreamWorks logos and the titles confirm this apparent identification: all, oddly for a colour movie, are monochrome and ruffled by surface ripples that link directly to emergence of the seeming epitext of the 'trailer'. The water contains the diegesis (*Minority Report*'s dystopia) and non-diegetic paratexts (inscription of institutions behind its funding, production and distribution), rather like the dissolve from the Paramount logo that opens *Raiders of the Lost Ark*. So too do product placements that, paradoxically, substantiate the nightmarish foretelling. Penetration along the z-axis of the water/screen surface by Agatha as spectator (reverse of *Jurassic Park*'s velociraptor threat) is, spatially, a similar liminal crossing.

The far-reaching implication: *all* of *Minority Report* is Agatha's (or our) dream. Cold, blue colour links most of its narrative to Agatha's initial vision, not unlike the green tinting of *The Matrix*, implying that it too unfolds in an alternate reality projected from the mind of the participant-spectator/protagonist, immobilised yet incorporated in the action. (For confirmation, compare *Ghost in the Shell* (1995), a Japanese *anime* that clearly influenced mise-en-scène and thematic concerns in *The Matrix*, *A.I.* and *Minority Report*. DreamWorks distributes its sequel.)

Once the plot mechanism comes into play, literally realised in the 'lottery ball' contraption the Pre-Cogs trigger, self-reflexivity imbues the action. Its pervasiveness and centrality advance this aspect of Spielberg's practice beyond anything since *Close Encounters*. Anderton, ahead of the camera, enters through a sliding glass door. Lettering on the door moves laterally off-screen like a caption, succeeded by extra-diegetic captions that anchor setting and period: the Department of Pre-Crime, layer upon layer of transparent screens, between which suspended walkways echo the chute for the wooden balls. The Pre-Cogs' circular bath, viewed overhead, is both a movie reel and a lens. Video screen witnesses to Anderton's investigations and fellow officers, to whom the film cuts at crucial moments, are inscribed spectators: 'Oh, I love this part', says Anderton's sidekick, like a voluble moviegoer, as one investigation starts. Classical music provides intra-diegetic accompaniment and the lights dim as for a movie; we look back through a screen of moving images while Anderton voyeuristically spectates, seeking mastery over the fragments, and indeed edits before our eyes the clips we are about to see from shots already seen. Numbers at the edges of Anderton's screen suggest the writing on filmstrips and the time code burned into footage for editing. Virtual knobs he turns to freeze, advance and reverse frames are futuristic shuttle controls.

Whether the coherent suburban images relate Anderton's subjective perception of the precognition, or constitute narrative crosscutting within the present tense, remains unclear. Either way, his seeking clues in the mediation, which when the image fills our screen is crammed with disorientingly rich mise-en-scène, not yet dissected according to continuity principles, recalls other self-reflexive movies such as *Blow-Up* (1966) and *The Conversation* (1974) while enacting the spectator's unfolding comprehension. This positions viewers externally: as spectators – our view presumably matches the witnesses'– yet also projectively involved in the crime fighter's work. He, in further twists, shortly fulfils the impossible desire of spectatorship by intervening in the narrative his comprehension constructs.

Minority Report – conducting an investigation in the editing suite

Inchoate fragments from the Pre-Cogs coalesce into the same form and diegesis as the framing movie, as Anderton seemingly imposes conventional editing. 'Howard Marks, where are you?' he asks, followed by a cut to a woman's voice, 'Howard', as a man leaves a house, this name having initially appeared in close-up on the wooden ball: the Hollywood rule of three. A lawn sprinkler emits a projector sound (there is no music in the remediated diegesis): one of many circular motions that gradually cede to what appears to be linear narrative. Repeated close-ups on scissors, the predicted murder weapon, metonymically inscribe Anderton's cutting-room activity, while the eye penetration, repeated, cements the relationship between this and the previous vision. Here the face is recognisably Abraham Lincoln and the child with scissors recites from the Gettysburg address: a first hint about Constitutional repercussions of the Pre-Crime programme we immediately hear about as Federal Agent Witwer's (Colin Farrell) arrival motivates overt narration. Spielberg's characteristic backlighting, realistically justified by a large, white conservatory, presents Marks's fragile family ideals as a dazzling projection from which, in a Bergman-like composition, the darker adjoining kitchen separates him. The vision foregrounds the husband's voyeurism as his wife's lover enters the house, the sprinkler sound again resembling a projector while also rhythmically heightening tension.

Anderton verbalises minute observations for forensic purposes but also, as *discours* in effect, inviting equally close spectatorial scrutiny. Multiple frames slide across Anderton's screen, stroboscopically shifting as on a Zoetrope. The merry-go-round that explains the puzzle of a small boy oscillating between frames, with Anderton's image superimposed, reinforces this metonym visually.

Mirrors and edgy, hand-held camerawork intensify the action, further underlining reflexive structures. The lovers are doubled. Howard, intensely backlit, raises the scissors. A mirrored door closes, bringing him, in darkness, into the same diegetic space as the brightly-lit adulterers, like a continuity cut. Flash pans inscribe in point-of-view shots Anderton's actively searching gaze, duplicating the spectator's, more explicitly than would glance/object editing. 'The cinema depends on a series of mirror-effects organised in a chain,' argues Metz (1975: 53); here rendered apparent. 'Which house?' Anderton asks, articulating the hermeneutic. The merry-go-round strobes his image, enhancing scopic stimulation in a manner similar to Spielberg's solar wind, disclosing and threatening to remove the ego-ideal: an intensified *fort-da* game that transforms banal narcissistic identification into something closer to *jouissance*.

Witwer, designated official 'observer', superimposed over the Pre-Cogs or looking through a widescreen window at the departing officers, watches the watchers. He embodies an enclosing discourse, a further relay of the look that permits troubling conscious awareness in the shifting focalisation. In short, without causing alienation these structures refuse comfortable identification with the protagonist one might expect in a mainstream movie. Witwer appears to enable a metanarrative against which to gauge the present-tense green, grainy diegetic 'reality' and the Pre-Cogs' enclosed blue, grainy vision, while the murder plays out, backlit, against a huge and highly improbable rectangular window, an inscribed wide screen.

Knowledge and vision thus initially equate, and an ocular leitmotif advances as when Marks, ready to kill his wife and her lover, repeats a conversation heard in the kitchen: 'I came for my glasses. You know how blind I am without my glasses.' The spectacle appears literally through one of the spectacles. Rapid montage ensues, in which Marks holds his glasses and the scissors in the same hand, emblematic of *Psycho*'s equation of vision with aggression. Anderton rushes upstairs, occluded by banister rails that impose a stroboscopic effect. Officers abseil through a 'widescreen' skylight, penetrating the apparent projection surface, and Marks's hand holding the scissors smashes through a window. 'Look at me', Anderton orders Marks, projecting a beam into his eye for optic identification: harnessing his vision and interpellating him firmly into the Symbolic as he arrests him, then immobilises him, for a potential crime. Meanwhile the Pre-Cogs, observed by Witwer, are increasingly agitated, intensely engaged spectators of the scene they themselves project while mouthing the dialogue. Wally (Daniel London), their carer, ordered to 'erase the incoming', in effect switches them off as they settle into peace and their screen fades. They are, literally and metaphorically, human projectors.

A Government commercial extols Pre-Crime; a retrospective explanation, like *Jurassic Park*'s Visitor Centre presentation. A cut then dissimulates this as not *discours* addressed to the spectator, but rather a projection onto walls in the squalid inner city where Anderton is jogging, an indication of audiovisual advertising and propaganda's extensive reach. The commercial introduces the programme's head, Lamar Burgess (Max von Sydow). His name (apart from partially coinciding with Ing*mar Berg*man, for whom the actor playing him starred many times) alludes to the author of *A Clockwork Orange*, a novel concerned with free will and ethical limits of crime prevention (Vest 2002: 108). The tribute is later emphasised by eyelid clamps that incapacitate Anderton during surgery (performed by a character played by another of Bergman's company), similar to those in Kubrick's adaptation that force Alex to watch violent footage. The commercial includes the phrase 'and the pursuit of Happiness': an inalienable Right, along with Life and Liberty, from the Declaration of Independence, compromised by Pre-Crime.

A blind drug dealer recognises Anderton before the latter, seeking to buy 'clarity', sees him. Visual evidence – the premise on which both detective movies and Pre-Crime operate – is thus questioned. In a Grand Guignol moment that exploits voyeuristic fascination and its disturbing consequences, the dealer removes his shades to reveal sockets, proclaiming, 'In the land of the blind, the one-eyed man is king.' Only an eyeless individual, operating outside the political economy regulated by optic surveillance, enjoys freedom in the Land of the Free.

Clippings by Anderton's bedside of reports of returned missing children register deep personal trauma, affirmed by his apartment's untidiness, 'neuroin' inhalers scattered everywhere. Together with an excess of family portraits, they signal Spielberg's recurring theme of parent/child separation. This obsession, related to psychoanalytic ramifications of narrative cinema as quest for lost object, thus affirms 'the film's ongoing subthemes – addiction, grief and addiction to grief ... with addiction to images as the primary metaphor' (James 2002: 13). Although first we view Anderton through a screen as he eats from a cereal packet decorated with noisy animated cartoons, the camera arcs through the 180-degree line and aligns with him as spectator as the whole wall becomes a movie screen. Bulbs flicker in close-up, evoking archaic cinema technology despite the futuristic setting. Anderton's distant reflection with a beam overhead explicitly likens his home, as much as his workplace, to a movie theatre as the camera pulls back to reveal him in the foreground with another beam apparently projecting from his eye. His son Sean's hologram steps out of the scene along the light beam – literally, leaving a shadow hole in the background, like Peter Pan, another boy never to grow up. Absence becomes present for Anderton, who actively projects himself into his projected memory, speaking in unison with his recorded voice, identifying totally with his scopic Other. Like the Pre-Cogs he is a participant spectator, except he views the past, they the future: a parallel emphasised when screen reflections of water shimmer over his face. Streaks flowing out behind Sean's image along Anderton's eye-line afford the most explicit confirmation yet of Spielberg's equation of his solar wind with projective vision. 'A sort of stream called the look ... has to be pumped into the world', in Metz's analogy, 'so that objects can come back up this stream ... arriving at last at our perception' (1975: 53). *Minority Report* joins numerous recent art movies that, Emma Wilson shows, self-reflexively interrogate cinema, often incorporating 'home movie' footage, as commemoration of and response to loss, particularly of children (2003: 13).

Inhaling 'clarity' before viewing his wife's spectral image, Anderton relives her urging him to 'put the camera down'. This completes inscription of the cinematic apparatus ('I am the camera, pointed yet recording', says Metz (1975: 53)). Resemblance to a scenario in *Peeping Tom* (already referenced in the name Marks, shared by the earlier self-reflexive film's screenwriter and protagonist, and later when officers pursue Anderton to Powell Street) potentially communicates a psychopathological aspect to Anderton's cinephilia. A side view renders the hologram flat and insubstantial (as if on a screen) despite its presence for him. As the camera crosses behind it, it regains pseudo-perspective, maintaining real-life proportions for him just as a movie spectator, sliding into the Imaginary, disavows the projection's unnatural size and two-dimensionality. Traversing the plane, we voyeuristically observe the couple's intimacy yet are addressed directly (to camera) as what would normally be part of a shot/reverse-shot is superimposed to place Anderton and Lara's (Kathryn Morris) image into a two-shot. Like him, we become simultaneously involved and detached – invited to identify, yet distanced by formalism – poised, or alternating, between Imaginary and Symbolic. Pathetic fallacy – rain-streaked windows – brings the scene to a conventionally sentimental close, yet Anderton's narcotic dependence and disturbed personality reinforce the complex effects of multiple focalisation, discouraging easy identification. He apparently has ambiguous depths like a Hitchcock protagonist and, while focalisation often aligns us with his experience, is no simple hero. When, later, the Pre-Cogs identify him as a killer, we are no more confident than he, who believes in Pre-Crime, of his innocence.

'*Can – you – see ...?*'

Minority Report seemingly unfolds from subjectively inflected claustrophobic drama to exploit spectacular science fiction and action-adventure effects. Anderton speeds along elevated freeways in a *Metropolis* (1927) cityscape. Lens flare, artificially contrived, as this is clearly a computer-generated shot, enhances realism, facilitating Imaginary involvement. It also flaunts textuality by potentially drawing attention to the (non-existent!) camera, craft technique and Spielberg's typical inscription of projections. These, together with allusion to generic precursors, encourage Symbolic awareness. That the ribbons of roadway resemble loops of film hardly seems fanciful in this context. They evoke the television system in *Things to Come* (1936) that consists of transparent strips suspended between buildings, on which frame grabs flow like the clear sheets on which images in *Minority Report* are stored and viewed.

Walkways in the Pre-Crime headquarters, divided like film strips into frames, infinitely multiplied in surrounding glass surfaces, confirm this similarity. To enter is to become entangled in cinematic imagery. Entry requires furthermore an optic scan from a device that resembles an eyeball, figuring reciprocity of vision on which social surveillance, like the ideological apparatus of cinema, depends – after all, the personalised commercials Anderton encounters on the street are *literal* interpellations. Viewing Burgess and Anderton behind layered screens and railings is voyeuristically intriguing and places them, indeed imprisons them, within a textually inscribed cinematic diegesis. When Anderton, silhouetted, looks up admiringly to Burgess as a superior figure as if on a screen, or when, later, at Burgess's house, blinding shafts backlight him from Anderton's perspective, the Oedipal implication, as with Jim's view of Basie or Upham's of Miller, compounds metaphors of psychic and cinematic projection.

When Witwer states Pre-Crime's 'fundamental paradox' – 'It's not the future if you stop it' – his words equally apply to dystopian satires and, more intriguingly, to what I shall eventually argue is the movie's outcome. Anderton's response, after rolling a ball that Witwer catches – 'The fact that you prevented it from happening doesn't change the fact that it was going to happen' – echoes a movie plot's inevitability, predetermined by scripting and filming, always already finished except for the spectator, endlessly repeating like a Zoetrope, yet seeming from within the experience to unfold linearly:

> a little rolled up perforated strip which 'contains' vast landscapes, fixed battles, the melting of the ice on the River Neva, and whole life-times, and yet can be enclosed in the familiar round metal tin, of modest dimensions, clear proof that it does not 'really' contain all that. (Metz 1975: 47)

And yet, the film hints by using Schubert's Unfinished Symphony in the 'editing' scenes, completion and closure are not always achieved.

Pre-Crime officials and Pre-Cogs keep 'strict separation', like the voyeur and the object of desire, a point underlined when Wally insists, 'I can't touch you!' after the dividing screen is ordered open. Like stars – whose glamour occupies a different order of existence from ordinary moviegoers, and who provide space within narratives for fantasy precisely because their *being* rather than *performing* feels as if it is caught unawares, offering voyeuristic satisfaction (Ellis 1992: 99) – 'It's better if you don't think of [Pre-Cogs] as human.' 'No, they're much more than that', muses Witwer as the camera tilts to display the glittering firmament inside the Temple: 'Science has stolen most of our miracles. In a way they give us hope – hope of the existence of the

Divine.' Yet their serotonin is monitored so they neither sleep too deeply nor are too awake. ('It is easier to fall asleep in a film than is often admitted', Ellis insists (1992: 40).). Participants in Metz's 'cinematic fiction as a semi-oneiric instance [and] mirror identification' (1975: 18), they reciprocally register the returning current. Between Witwer breaching 'the segregation of spaces that characterises a cinema performance' (Metz 1975: 64) and the ensuing disastrous events there is implicit correlation if not direct causality. If Anderton did not find himself inside the Temple, Agatha could not communicate directly her minority report, he would not commence his independent investigation, and Burgess would not require his removal.

Whatever the narrative motivation, the movie continues as a heady cornucopia of quotation and allusion, to specific movies and cinema generally, too rich to detail – with, I argue later, anything but frivolous implications. Although it might seem irrelevant to liken Agatha's unexpected warning to Anderton to the protagonist's gaining of burdensome responsibility in *The Man Who Knew too Much* (1934/1956), or the way she slips back underwater staring at her hand to the *2001* Starchild, the next scene should dispel any doubt: the Department of Containment. In this vast, literal panopticon, immobilised convicts' thoughts play before their eyes on imprisoning glass cylinders, which project beams above them reminiscent of the Twentieth-Century Fox logo at the start. Gideon, their jailer, plays an organ to 'relax' them. Underlining his Bible Belt religiosity, this equally shifting from extra-diegetic to diegetic status, again blurring screen boundaries – evokes a cinema Wurlitzer, its organ pipes replaced by stacked tubes rising impressively from the bottomless pit, and is perhaps also an auto-citation (*Close Encounters*). While narrative focuses on significant action unfolding on a high-tech screen centred in the composition, a child's revolving lampshade from the 1950s occupies a third of the frame in the foreground. Cowboys and Indians chase endlessly around an illuminated parchment contrasting in colour with everything else. This proto-cinematic novelty peripherally acknowledges generic origins of the chase movie *Minority Report* becomes, while the shot overall – the screen in front, light projected over Anderton's shoulder, the organ in the background – concurrently inscribes cinematic history and spatial arrangement.

Extraordinary technique fetishises cinematic practice for its own sake. In one 13-second shot the red ball spirals in oscillating close-up down its transparent tube; focus racks onto Anderton's assistant in the background, then shifts again as he advances before a hand in big close-up grasps the ball; a tilt up pulls focus on the assistant's face and the camera pans right to the ball in Anderton's hand; focus adjusts once more so his name on it becomes legible. Such painstakingly brilliant yet easily readable filmmaking is at once invisible narration and bravura display, eliciting a response from form as much as content, unsettling spectatorial positioning at whatever level of consciousness it is registered.

On my first viewing it was not until, in a subsequent escape, Anderton kicked out the window of a car travelling vertically several hundred metres up the side of a building and started jumping between vehicles – a futuristic variant on silent-movie chases along railroad cars – that incredulity intruded. I had accepted every preposterous premise. At this point, when Anderton breaks through the screen to face the world alone, like Jim in *Empire of the Sun*, 'reality' most resembles a Hollywood adventure.

Anderton's existence is movie-saturated, mediated. Commercials, not merely glanced at or ignored, constitute a virtual environment. Anderton's picture emerging on constantly updated *USA Today* covers as he sits nervously trapped on a train ratchets up a suspense device from *The 39 Steps*. Fight sequences when he escapes arrest – first in The Sprawl, utilising rocket backpacks and flaming explosions as well as 'sick sticks' that elicit a haptic, visceral audience response; later in the novel setting of the automated car factory – mount a serious challenge to Bond films. Windows and floors are repeatedly penetrated, while a father sits passively watching television amid Spielberg's most extravagantly spectacular action; fantasy and mundane reality meet, light-heartedly and amusingly, as jetpack exhausts ignite hamburgers broiling on a stove. In the assembly plant, dazzling lights into camera underline this set piece as *cinematic*. Nevertheless *Saving Private Ryan*'s fast shutter-speed recurs, stroboscopically inscribing artificiality yet evoking the cold clarity of immediacy and presence. This hyperrealist device renders spectatorship both involved and detached.

'KEEP OUT – NO TRESPASSING' signs, as at the start of *Citizen Kane*, guard Iris Hineman's (Lois Smith) lush, overgrown garden. Anderton scales walls topped – significantly, as will become apparent – with broken glass to enter this flawed Eden, with its Medusa-like genetically-modified phallic creepers: a shattered Imaginary (Hineman jokingly describes herself as 'the Mother of Pre-Crime'), a lesser Jurassic Park, where he seeks answers. Hineman potters in a huge greenhouse, the safe place of light and life hitherto encountered in *E. T.*, *Empire of the Sun* and *Amistad* (her manner and vocal delivery recall Quincy Adams). Yet she is a darkly ambiguous nurturing mother, embodying what Barbara Creed (1989) calls 'the Monstrous Feminine' – a well-intentioned scientist whose experiments to treat children of neuroin addicts created Pre-Cogs as a side-effect, many of whom died in the refinement of the programme she accepts is imperfect. She lovingly tends her plants and brews herbal tea to cure Anderton's poisoned wounds, yet is coldly detached concerning Pre-Cognition. She evidences unsettling sado-masochism when demonstrating a point by almost crushing the life out of a seemingly sentient plant but not flinching at the vicious cut it inflicts. She wears a dark, halo-like brim as Anderton asks, disbelievingly, 'Are you saying I've haloed innocent people?' and she kisses him, sexually, on the lips after imparting the desired information about minority reports. Her characterisation is not entirely misogynistic, despite her point about females being always the most gifted, as the decadence of Burgess, her former associate, hinted at in the profusion of flowers bedecking his home, counterbalances it. Nevertheless it makes clear there is, for Anderton, no going back, no return to comforting Imaginary innocence.

In this lapsed utopia science produces dangerous addictive drugs and excuses for imprisoning the innocent, sacrifices children for progress, but has not cured the common cold. Anderton sniffs, Witwer coughs, and Burgess drinks herbal tea and honey. The gross-out eye transplant that grants Anderton anonymity, but also conveys the idea of new vision, starts with the back street surgeon dragging a string of mucus from his nose. The grotesque body, emphasised in the hideously made-up nurse and the dismemberment intimated in excavated eyeballs, combines with inversion of authority and sanitary procedures, together with abandonment of decorum, in the context of a festival of film allusions. Carnivalesque undermines monological realism, twisting generic expectations to encourage playful and flexible responses. From Spielberg's point-of-view, perhaps, the colourised versions of old movies playing unregarded, audiovisual wallpaper interspersed with commercials, summarise this culture's obscenity. That Anderton once had the surgeon convicted for sadistic procedures he filmed as 'performance pieces,' as the dialogue recounts against the video-projected background of brutal killings, problematises our pleasure: we don't *have* to watch. Simultaneously it inscribes a history of crime movies and romantic heroism (*The Mark of Zorro* (1940)) that then raises the likelihood of spotting allusions to *Blade Runner* (1982) (a plastic bag containing eyes) and *Farewell My Lovely* (1944) (the detective vulnerable with eyes bandaged).

Blinded, Anderton relives his separation from Sean. The swimming pool recalls the Pre-Cog tank, and crucially, establishes Anderton's capacity for immersion. A richer, although still artificial, colour spectrum makes this the film's most vivid scene. Rapidly panning point-of-view shots as Anderton panics, looking for his lost child in an indifferent holiday crowd, clearly cite *Jaws*.

The business with the rancid milk and sandwiches exemplifies spectatorial duality. It facilitates focalisation through Anderton on a visceral level, necessary in that visual identification with blindness is difficult to achieve if, as here, the audience needs to see more than the character (his face appears twice on television as a wanted man), rendering our relationship with him explicitly voyeuristic. It also confirms that voyeurism is sadistic (Metz 1975: 63).

Voyeurism and detachment from Anderton continue as former colleagues send 'spyders' into the apartment block where he hides, and overhead camera movements track their progress, from a dominant position of surveillance as if through the ceilings, while private activities lovemaking, a domestic quarrel, defecation – cease momentarily for the State to check citizens' identities. The camera then descends through a roof fan, replicating a celebrated effect from *Citizen Kane*, to realign with Anderton and show how his new eyes fool the authorities' system.

Having changed his 'look' in another sense with a facial deformer provided by the surgeon – a trace, presumably, of a sub-plot excised in the final cut – Anderton liberates Agatha from Pre-Crime and, in a further imbrication of self-reflexivity, takes her to a virtual reality palace where punters pay to have fantasies simulated. As the proprietor, awed by Agatha, attempts to download her minority report, Anderton asks, 'Are you recording this?' and he is not – a studio floor error, plausibly, with which Spielberg is familiar. She projects instead Ann Lively's murder, shown on our screen as well as intra-diegetically, in reverse, once again accentuating textuality. Following this, she protects Anderton from Pre-Crime pursuers by anticipating every action. This confirms her powers as genuine, suggesting Anderton *will* murder; yet her intervention *causes* events, paradoxically creating destiny according to the predictions – self-fulfilling prophesy, as his previous agenda traps him.

The reception desk in the hotel, where Agatha predicted Crow's (Mike Binder) murder, looks like a cinema box office. In a shot modelled from *Persona*, as Anderton and Agatha form a Janus-faced image, suggestive of merging of identity or personalities, she reminds him he is free to depart. Yet desire for knowledge drives him to determine, in the room with a wall-mounted widescreen flat television and 'widescreen' windows, that his previously unknown intended victim murdered Sean. He decides he is not being set up, as this is the one discovery he believes could drive him to kill. Furiously he smashes Crow against the mirror. Agatha, screaming in empathy as an inscribed spectator, reminds him again, desperately, about free choice. Unlike every haloed suspect he, uniquely, aware of the minority report, possesses an alternative. There is no telling his response as zero approaches. The composition of him holding the gun is the obverse of its prediction; we looked through the screen then, or perhaps the scenario, or our relation to it, has subtly changed. He does not shoot. As the alarm sounds and the deadline passes, he arrests Crow and reads him his rights. A light behind Agatha creates the impression she is projecting the conversation as Crow reveals Anderton was indeed being manipulated towards killing him, before he grabs the gun and pulls the trigger, the shot propelling him through the plate glass window.

Light beams link the screen to Burgess's face as he watches the television report of this apparent homicide. Shortly after, he kills Witwer, who has used projections to show discrepancies between Agatha's and the other Pre-Cogs' visions of Lively's murder. Somewhat inconsistently, Agatha, taking refuge with Anderton and Lara at the latter's house, projects verbally the future Sean would have had, in a scene imbued with 'God Light', even though she seemed unaware of Burgess killing Witwer. Again she demonstrates pre-cognition, sensing Pre-Crime too late, as they apprehend and halo Anderton.

The big sleep

The final twenty minutes ostensibly vindicate Spielberg's sternest critics. *Minority Report*'s dystopian themes, retro-noir style and frustrated Oedipal challenge point to it being a downbeat adult movie in which the flawed hero becomes the fall guy – standard fare from *The Postman Always Rings Twice* (1946/1981) to *The Man Who Wasn't There* (2001) – yet Spielberg cannot let matters rest. Refusing this satisfactory, if dark, closure, he cranks the plot for another turn, as in *A.I.*, resulting in a lengthy movie in which the final act gratuitously reverses all that precedes.

After Anderton's incarceration, his estranged wife, transformed by Agatha's projection of family contentment, visits Burgess. The old man's dual nature, hitherto concealed, becomes apparent as we see him alongside his reflection. Nervousness reveals itself when he pricks his finger at Lara's inquiry about Lively's murder, and carelessly discloses knowledge of the method, arousing Lara's suspicions.

Lara frees Anderton, using his eyeballs to gain entry and threatening Gideon with her husband's gun. Incongruously perfunctory after all the previous complexities, this is also logically inconsistent. If Agatha is back in the Temple – reconfirmed when she later predicts Anderton's murder – she would anticipate Gideon's death, were Lara seriously prepared to use the gun. Without this warning, Gideon would know he was safe and would not cooperate. This is explicitly demonstrated, earlier, when Witwer deals calmly with a threat from Anderton – 'Put the gun down, John; I don't hear a red ball' – becoming anxious only after the klaxon sounds.

There is a smack of adolescent self-righteousness in Burgess's hubris being punished for betraying Anderton's and the public's trust and killing Agatha's mother and

Witwer. Changing from benign patriarch to obscene father – von Sydow's perform-ance recalls John Huston's monstrous villain in *Chinatown* (1974), and the actor had formerly starred as a kindly grandfather exposed as a former SS perpetrator of genocide in *Father* (1990) – Burgess suffers humiliation and disgrace at a reception to celebrate his career. He is last to see Anderton's screening of the murder. He shoots himself using the ornamented weapon presented at his retirement, an official recognition of his phallic potency – acknowledging his error and seeking Anderton's forgiveness.

The screened murder evidences the deceit which predicated and now discredits Pre-Crime. Witwer's paradox works through before the Jefferson Memorial, restoring American Justice. Witwer, who personified a younger Oedipal threat to Anderton's authority, yet as agent of a more powerful department embodied the castrating power of the Father, is avenged, retrospectively, as a filial equal. Psychoanalytic convolu-tions – Witwer's ambition derived from his policeman father's murder when he was fifteen, while Anderton torments himself for having failed as a father, having lost his son – achieve instant resolution. 'You see the dilemma?' Anderton asks Burgess, while Agatha vicariously lives through the drama. 'If you don't kill me the Pre-Cogs were wrong and Pre-Crime is over. If you do kill me you go away. But it proves your system works. The Pre-Cogs were right.'

Burgess's suicide exercises the free will his *Clockwork Orange*-like programme has denied others, and everything comes right in the kind of sickly sentimental Hollywood ending Spielberg's detractors consider his stock in trade (Wilson 2003: 4; Felperin 2002; McDonald 2003). Anderton's voice narrates Pre-Crime's closure. He and Lara, pregnant, appear together, intimating the all-American family reconstituted, lit with rain shadows from the window to recall Anderton's home-movie viewing and illus-trate how wishes expressed then now become fulfilled. The Pre-Cogs, long-haired Romantics in hand-knitted sweaters and a golden glow, pass their days devouring books before an open fire. The camera cranes back to show them enclosed in a pastoral idyll in a quaint cottage on an otherwise deserted island, bathed in a beautiful sunset. Released during the aftermath of 9/11, when officials urged Americans to anticipate and prevent terrorist crime (James 2002: 15; Vest 2002: 108), the movie played its ideological role in asserting faith in the humane values of ordinary folks and distrust-ing shadowy state organisations, even while suspects were held in contravention of US civil law and international human rights agreements at Guantánamo Bay.

Yet all is not so simple. Following the clues that the '6' outside where Anderton was supposed to murder Crow turned out to be a '9' and the third man was an external billboard image, there is an alternative ending, a minority report so to speak, as befits a film that renders appearances deceptive, encourages close scrutiny and questions visual evidence. Just as *Jurassic Park* ends with pterodactyl-like pelicans approaching the mainland, intimating the story's continuance and making room for a sequel, as the sun hits the lens and Spielberg's credit appears, so *Minority Report* ends with a long – tenaciously long – shot of the tranquil scene, also a final inscription of the cinematic apparatus as the credits, starting with Spielberg's, roll. This movie, comprising allu-sions to other movies, ends self-reflexively. As Jason Vest intriguingly suggests, the mise-en-scène of the last shot of the Pre-Cogs, 'sitting in a loose circle … surrounded by water … reminds the thoughtful viewer of the circular water tank' they inhabited

(2002: 109). Vest's point is that their difference leaves them detached from society. But a starker possibility remains: the tank is where they stay, while we see a fanciful sublimation of their true state. This is consistent with Vest's conjecture that the last part of the film occurs within Anderton's haloed head. Following Anderton's wrongful arrest for murdering Crow and Witwer, necessary for Burgess's cover-up, we see Agatha returned to the Temple; Gideon tells Anderton's comatose figure: 'It's actually a kind of rush. They say you have visions. That your life flashes before your eyes. That all your dreams come true.' The remainder of the film plays on Anderton's mindscreen as he descends into darkness with a projector light above his head. The halo glows as a cut introduces Burgess declaring to Lara, 'It's all my fault!'

This movie that coalesced out of a shimmering primal scene finishes with Anderton, another Spielberg solipsist, positioned like Metz's spectator in profound solitude (1975: 64). In relation to the spectator's ego, Metz observes:

> the question arises precisely of *where it is* during the projection of the film (the true primary identification, that of the mirror, forms the ego, but all other identifications presuppose, on the contrary, that it has been formed and can be 'exchanged' for the object or the fellow subject). Thus when I 'recognise' my like on the screen, and even more when I do not recognise it, where am I? Where is that someone who is capable of self-recognition when need be? (1975: 50)

Anderton in suspended animation, submitted to the Name of the Father, is Metz's spectator: regressed prior to knowledge of loss, immersed and immobilised, subjected to reflections of his hopes and fears, desires and fantasies, reduced to illusory all-seeingness and mastery that substitute for the emptiness of the position hollowed out for the self. Such fantasies can seem enormously realistic; witness the fine detail of an aircraft light sliding across the sky, maintaining continuity between shots, during the showdown between the symbolic Father and Son. Repeated penetrations of windows figure in a movie in which 'reality' is mediated on glass screens. Anderton, stacked in a jar, kicks the glass canopy out of a car he imagines himself trapped in and later outruns the Law in another that is entertainingly, if improbably, constructed around him, fully enclosing him. Underwater fantasies swirl around his unlikely evacuation of the Pre-Cog tank with Agatha. Images of blindness and eyelessness, one involving surgical apparatus that clamps the head like a Pre-Crime halo, return obsessively. But slips and logical inconsistencies, give the game away. Anderton's capacity to remain immersed, associated with the moment of family destruction, is never utilised narratively in that when he hides from the 'spyders' in bath water he *does* reveal himself by exhaling. He is *not* blinded, as we are led to fear, when they shine beams in his eye. Sean's tricycle, shiny-new, remains casually overturned in Lara's yard – *six years* after his disappearance. Similarities between both Crow's and Burgess's killings, both, remarkably, suicides – although Anderton seemingly holds the gun both times – evince compulsive repetition, while another coincidence is the identical numbers on Crow's hotel room and Anderton's incarceration flask. Anderton's apparent reunion with Lara could be memory rather than a jump forward in a film that repeatedly undercuts its own veracity.

In the final shot, the sun moves ninety degrees. As CGI begins with coordinates, the light source being fundamental, this appears unlikely to be technical error. Because the shot starts and ends, however, with the sun shining into camera – Spielberg's equation of light with projective desire – and the movie questions and undermines subject positions, this is equally explicable as flawed, inconsistent, decentred narration, such as a dream. The imaginary lost object motivating Anderton's narrative is no less than his life, a closed loop like a drawing of a clown somersaulting in a Zoetrope: following *A.I.*, a second feel-good ending that crumbles under scrutiny.

CHAPTER TWENTY-TWO

Catch Me If You Can: captured on celluloid

Purportedly factual, *Catch Me If You Can* again raises questions of veracity and interpretation – if not as serious as those concerning *Schindler's List, Amistad* or *Saving Private Ryan*, at least commensurate with its biopic status, which is how critics categorised it (French 2003, Norman 2005). Its autobiographical source, however – reissued with the movie's strap-line, 'The true story of a real fake' – follows a remarkable disclaimer: 'To protect the rights of those whose paths have crossed the author's, all of the characters and some of the events have been altered, and all names, dates and places have been changed' (Abagnale 2001). How 'true,' then, remains anything, even discounting the need to approach cautiously a conman's autobiography?

Spielberg's version toys with these problems, interpreting the book loosely and light-heartedly as a caper movie. It overlays contemporary style and sensibility on attitudes and fantasies prevalent in mainstream entertainment from its 1960s setting, an era rippled with sophistication and innocence, manifested in both Frank Jr (Leonardo di Caprio) and his dupes. Self-consciously arty credits, accompanied by John Williams' cool, Mancini-inspired score, set the tone. Flat animated graphics, characteristic of the period, recall *The Pink Panther* (1963), the Bond series, *The Charge of the Light Brigade* (1968) and sequences by Saul Bass (particularly *Anatomy of a Murder* (1959)). They are straight, affectionate pastiche, not parody. Spielberg's trademark shooting stars accompany the director's credit, harnessing these old-fashioned elements to his vision.

Heteroglossia imbues a fairly straightforward tale with ambivalence and ambiguity. The credits give way to the proclamation, 'Inspired by a true story'. Superimposed on TV screen static, this dissolves to a game show in an on-screen frame as the accompanying hiss resolves into applause. Maze-like title lettering, 'To Tell the Truth', echoes the programme's set design, the blue, white and yellow of which match the movie's promotional graphics. While these details alone suggest a highly mediated story, the show's format introduces logical complications.

Three identically dressed individuals claim to be Frank, 'the most outrageous impostor that we've ever come across on this show', before cross-examination. The contestant who is not an impostor will thereby reveal himself – as a professional impostor. Four voices repeat, 'My name is Frank William Abagnale.' Recognition of Leonardo DiCaprio and the fact he plays 'Frank' throughout does not authenticate the narrative. From the flashback when DiCaprio's character names his captor as Carl Hanratty (Tom Hanks) – a central character who hardly features in the book, and under a different name – this might not be Frank's story but another contestant's concoction, based partially on known events. As in the show, we decide.

Such convolution accords with confidence tricks perpetrated in both book and film, some identical, others different, by Frank – pronunciation of whose surname the film makes an issue, implying uncertainties at every level. The film in some respects shows more restraint than the book, in which Frank pilots an airliner, medically examines a newborn baby, and runs a Rolls-Royce. Frank's father (Christopher Walken), whose relationship with the film's protagonist is central and whose death is a dramatic turning point, does not die in the book; he is, however, unlike the film's father, Frank's first victim. Abagnale's company website, in addition to phonetically spelling his name, insists the book's ghost writer dramatised and exaggerated for profit, and that Spielberg made 'just a movie ... not a biographical documentary' (Abagnale 2002).

This helps explain the movie's success. It grossed $351.1 million worldwide – excluding home entertainment, nowadays 'far more lucrative' (Wasko 2003: 125) – on a $52 million budget with marketing estimated at $35 million. It became one of only two biopics in the top hundred moneymakers. While biographical movies have always been prestigious, their impetus comes from filmmakers, fascinated by an exceptional individual, rather than studios, which distribute them but leave financing to independents. Audiences seldom share fascination for the individual portrayed; hence the life has to be romanticised or sensationalised to tell an interesting story, a compromise the filmmaker may resist. The process in turn alienates those with existing interest, whose criticisms may harm the film commercially. The residual core of Frank W. Abagnale's exploits; their preposterousness; the verve of their narration; the apparent authority of an autobiographical source; that his was hardly a household name, while facts immediately available in the public domain did not contest the movie's apparent claims: all retain the sense that he achieved something stranger than fiction. Moreover, the narrative's self-containment – Frank turns to crime, enjoys glamour and success, suffers capture, pays his dues and achieves redemption during little more than a decade, subsequently garnering even greater riches legitimately – makes for satisfying completeness, easily adaptable, irrespective of factual liberties. Most biopics simplify, selecting episodes to represent a lifetime in two or three hours, to say nothing of inferring motivation or implying judgement. As Barry Norman (2005) suggests, these leave non-expert audiences wondering 'What happened next?' and specialists dissatisfied by arbitrary choices.

Spielberg's uncharacteristically complex and fragmented flashbacks facilitate and motivate tonal and mood shifts. These are inherently intriguing and stimulating as well as accordant with Frank's ambiguities and audience pleasure in his deceptions. A grim prison succeeds the light-hearted opening, yet already framed within reassurance of survival and rehabilitation. Frank's induction into fakery, posing as his father's chauffeur to impress bank officials, plays as comedy when the inexperienced driver, although warned not to, hits the kerb but avoids the usual slapstick cliché, collision with a hydrant. Inverted power relations are carnivalesque throughout, finally redeeming Spielberg as a comedy director more than two decades after *1941*. Frank humiliates bullies by masquerading as a no-nonsense substitute teacher. Beginning his career, he gains from an airline official vital knowledge and documents by posing as a student writing a project. Following arrest, his suggestion that better hotel rooms are available elicits: 'It's the best the FBI can afford.'

Flexible focalisation – including scenes begun with direct-to-camera shots of others addressing Frank, which reinforce identification yet by departing from classical conventions emphasise slight unreality – ensures Frank's motivation remains obscure and his actions frequently surprising. That 'No little people are involved and no one is put in danger', as Philip French points out (2003: 7), precludes serious moral condemnation. Frank bears nobody malice; while the Principal interviews his parents over his imposture, he shows a fellow student how to pass forged notes convincingly. Frank and his father giggle together over his first scam, begun as self-defence.

Rows of cheques on the floor, embossed with transfers soaked from a bath full of model aeroplanes, visually render Frank's audacity absurd by grounding it unexpectedly in the mundane. So too, narratively, do serendipitous events such as a hotel manager telling him airports cash cheques, as verbally does airline jargon ('Are you dead heading?') and the fear he instils in a junior doctor by asking, 'Do you concur?', parroted from *Dr Kildare* (1961–1966). In the spirit of this humour is how he follows airhostesses through a hotel lobby, subjecting them to his appraising gaze, as would a Cary Grant character or Connery's James Bond. Realistic logic evaporates as chance shapes his destiny. Repeated opportunities for trickery result from others' ingenuousness and self-centredness, paralleling his, in an inward-looking, image-conscious, alienated culture. Once only, and then inadvertently, does he merely exploit greed: wearing a Bond suit (having successfully impersonated a real secret agent), he fleeces a high-class prostitute *and* sleeps with her. Circumstances become increasingly surreal. In Brenda's wealthy parents' Irish Lutheran home, invited to say Grace he charms the mother by repeating his father's homily about two little mice. Having apparently passed the Louisiana Bar exam after two weeks' study, he bemuses a solitary judge in closed session by appealing dramatically about a non-existent defendant to a non-existent jury. Later when his father, thinking he is a pilot, asks whether he knows a good lawyer, he answers honestly, 'Well, I sort of am a lawyer now.' At their engagement party, when Frank produces suitcases full of banknotes and confesses to Brenda, before escaping arrest, that he is 17, not 28, and has several aliases, she responds, incredulously, 'You're not a Lutheran!' Meanwhile, outside, in an exchange of rapid dialogue reminiscent of 1930s comedy, her mother addresses Carl as 'Ratty'.

The comedy is bittersweet, however. Frank's departure leaves Brenda clutching banknotes, not a bouquet. A lace curtain blows over the lovers, flickering shadows over Brenda's confused expression while Frank outlines his romantic project for their elopement; the moment recalls female-centred melodrama in *Rebecca* (1940) or *Suspicion* (1941). Mood changes occur as Frank plans his escape: from paranoia or possibly justified anxiety as he sees agents everywhere at the airport to an exhilarating montage as he 'recruits' trainee stewardesses to augment his pilot disguise and ease his way past officers. Whether Brenda has been pursued to their rendezvous or is a witting snare remains uncertain; when Frank sighs, 'Oh, Brenda!' this could express betrayal or sympathy. As his US career closes, a plane, soaring skywards while Carl is humiliatingly decoyed, with great visual economy confirms Frank as a supreme trickster – Bugs Bunny outsmarting Elmer Fudd.

Earlier, ominous music suggests a thriller as Carl enters Frank's Los Angeles motel room. The standoff, though, as Frank brazenly impersonates a secret agent becomes more realistically tense following Carl's evident unfamiliarity with unholstering his gun. When Carl arrests Frank in a French printing press, the showdown's industrial setting, chiaroscuro lighting, tilted angles and police aggression suggest the hostile world of film noir, contrasting with the candlelit Christmas mass across the square. Yet, between moments of pathos and what appears initially to be Spielbergian sentimentality, as Frank learns of his father's death and subsequently looks in, as a stranger, on his mother's new household, he daringly escapes from an airliner. Controlled focalisation makes this disappearance magically impressive, akin to young Indiana Jones' vanishing trick on the train, followed comically by Carl's undignified attempt to follow him headfirst down the toilet.

'You really got me'

Apart from a Kinks song, Frank Sr's pretence to Carl that Frank is in Vietnam, and a Bond clip, there is little – despite precisely rendered period detail – to suggest the turmoil of the 1960s. Kennedy's assassination, the Cold War, Vietnam protests, Civil Rights receive no mention. Instead of historical specificity the film offers a nostalgic Imaginary of superficial innocence and unsought opportunity. This represents Frank's consciousness, a further addition to Spielberg's gallery of solipsism. The film does not accept uncritically, let alone endorse, his vision.

Catch Me If You Can shares a quality Tim Kreider identifies in *A.I.*, of telling two stories simultaneously. One is a 'fairy tale' – literally in *A.I.*'s voice-over narration and *Pinocchio* references; similar properties obtain in the unstated moral significance and magic-realist wonder of Frank's charmed life as a trickster, and the Horatio Alger myth implied in the closing titles that summarise his later career. He continues an American tradition embracing Brer Rabbit (Bugs Bunny's precursor), Huck Finn and, more darkly, Herman Melville's *The Confidence-Man*. 'Calming anxieties, explaining away apparent ambiguities, glossing over gaps and contradictions in the story, and falling conspicuously silent at moments of cruelty and horror', this discourse in *A.I.*, Kreider argues, accompanies a 'story for adults, presented visually … very different. It's a story about human attachments and our bottomless capacity for self-delusion' (2002: 33). In common with duplicity in much American literary narration, rather than the simplistic Hollywood values critics habitually ascribe to Spielberg, *Catch Me If You Can* is as slippery as its protagonist.

French prison officers momentarily leave Frank unguarded to wash lice off their hands. Appalling conditions contrast with the rosy glow and stars and stripes flag of the subsequent scene, a flashback to Frank Sr's elevation to the Rotary Club roll of honour. Initially this might seem an assertion of American values, verging on xenophobia. But America's portrayal is not so positive. Is Frank Sr, given his financial difficulties (he faces prison for tax fraud) and repeated assertion of appearance over reality, for all his determined optimism and folksy homilies, quite what he seems? Or indeed, given that his friend Jack Barnes (James Brolin), who welcomes him onto the platform, is sleeping with Frank Sr's wife, who later divorces to marry him, is *anything* what it seems, except in the eyes of 14-year-old Frank, who leads a standing ovation?

Having lied about his father's funeral, bribed and flattered to obtain a suit so Frank can pose as his chauffeur, Frank Sr, seeking a bank loan, appeals to patriotic justice. 'This is America, right?' he whinges, citing his war record and lifetime Rotary membership, before revealing his colours: 'It's the biggest bank in the world. Where's the fu–? Where's the risk?' In the Land of the Free, he considers himself hounded by one Federal institution, the Internal Revenue Service, and becomes a lowly employee with another, the Post Office. Frank Jr too merges into grey, faceless bureaucracy in the final tracking shot through FBI headquarters. Design and lighting here emphasise uniformity and dull conformity. After Frank Jr's glamorous adventures (not to mention elision of five years in jail, for which the judge recommended solitary) one can hardly argue, as *Sight and Sound* did, that 'It's perverse (but perhaps predictable)' – the standard critical response – 'of Spielberg to try to turn his defeat into a happy ending' (Macnab 2003: 40). That reading uncritically accepts light comedic aspects while ignoring darker elements, which the film acknowledges without foregrounding them.

Mrs Abagnale, determined to maintain appearances, wears fur when she drives Frank to his new school, despite the family's straitened circumstances. A sad, elderly substitute teacher who has struggled to reach the school loses out when Frank usurps her role – first of many female victims. Frank is alone at home, making pancakes on his sixteenth birthday, while his mother is supposedly seeking work, although ensuing events suggest she may be with Jack. Authorities are untrustworthy: Frank, despite amassing his fortune deceitfully, ironically becomes upset when Carl, having promised in Paris he could call his father on landing in America, tells him he has died.

As Frank's activities warn, take nothing at face value. Transactions ultimately rely on confidence. He writes to his father that he flies for 'Pan Am, the most trusted name in the skies' – an airline now long gone, its fate sealed by mistrust after Lockerbie although, if the film is reliable, security lapses were not restricted to that company. Cheque-encoding machines were, after all, obtainable at auction. The movie's sexual politics, too, refer to, rather than utilise innocently, 1960s values. 'The Girl from Ipanema' plays as bathing beauties disport themselves at the Hollywood motel Frank resides in; theirs is a merely decorative, at best scene-setting function, signifying the good life in contrast to Carl's hardworking existence, as the camera tracks away from them to the narrative action. Epitomising this conformist society, bikini-clad sunbathers turn over together as a timer rings by the pool of Frank's luxury Atlanta apartment. Like his fondue set and crates of champagne, women are props, associated with the swimming pools that link Frank's career to a *Goldfinger* (1964) extract. Women's supposed availability reflects newfound, pre-feminist 1960s freedom. But also Brenda's (Amy Adams) initiatory sexual passion feeds into adolescent male fantasies about nymphomaniac nurses – made real by Frank's deceiving charms, acquired glamour and endless money supply. Nevertheless, he restores vulnerable, shy Brenda's confidence, reconciling her with her parents. A veil draws over her life after he leaves.

Frankie goes to Hollywood

It would be surprising if Spielberg did not identify with Frank, who like him enjoys elevation at a young age to dizzying jet-setting glamour. Making films entails possessing and inspiring confidence and – as Korda and Selznick, discussed in relation to *Schindler's List*, demonstrate – like other businesses, may involve confidence trickery. Spielberg's age is a thorny issue, biographers point out, since he signed with Universal at twenty, a claim that suited his and the studio's publicity, although legally he would have been a minor. Conversely, when the financier of his first 35mm project, *Amblin'* (1968), tried to make Spielberg honour an agreement to direct for him again within ten years, Spielberg claimed to have been underage at the time, thereby invalidating that deal. The dispute led to a $33 million suit (Baxter 1996: 51, 54, 168, 406). Spielberg momentarily becomes cagey in the BBC *Film '98* interview when Barry Norman ingenuously congratulates him on his recent fiftieth birthday. Less contentiously, the Spielberg legend includes establishment at Universal by wearing a suit and carrying an empty briefcase past security, occupying an empty office, and ejection from Hitchcock's set.

A showman after Méliès, Spielberg relishes magic and cannot resist narrative deceits. Frank's disappearances from the sick bay and the plane toilet, albeit astonishing, depend on simply pointing the camera elsewhere. Spielberg repeatedly establishes involvement with protagonists through formal structures that dramatise subjective misreadings of situations, a device Hitchcock perfected when Scotty 'sees' Madeleine in Ernie's restaurant in *Vertigo*. An example involves Frank discovering a man's jacket in the apartment when the context, suggested by a previous scene, momentarily suggests a visiting divorce lawyer is his mother's lover (thereby compromising her, without assertion or denial). Less portentously, a gag entails Frank imitating his father by distracting a bank teller with a necklace, before a pan reveals that a male manager has replaced her. Later, after another teller counts out cash for Frank, now in pilot's uniform, the same manager intervenes, causing momentary tension, only to shake hands thankfully for his custom. An almost gratuitous example occurs near the end when narrative logic dictates that running feet herald Frank's late arrival at an FBI meeting and instead another agent enters. As well, cinematic style and confidence echo and underline Frank's élan. Consider the closing shot, a technically brilliant yet unobtrusive camera movement which emulates another movie magician's self-reflexive work in the boarding house scene in *Citizen Kane*.

Abagnale's own metaphors suggest the project's attraction to Spielberg. As a forger, he describes himself as 'an independent actor, writing, producing, and directing my own scripts' (2001: 99) and acknowledges being 'a con man of Academy Award calibre' (2001: 11). Interestingly, if one takes *Minority Report* as Anderton's disembodied fantasies, Abagnale explains how he survived prison by channelling creativity, recalling past exploits and dreaming up new impostures, including 'A movie director, making an Oscar-winning epic' (2001: 174). When, contrary to the film, he offers assistance to the FBI, he is working as a projectionist (2001: 210). This account involves the entire apparatus. Similarly cinematic imagery pervades the movie, as all of Spielberg's.

Frank is director of his remarkable life, and spectator as well as character, on an exhilarating trajectory, identifying with roles he creates or finds himself cast into. Postmodern knowingness is explicit in the *Goldfinger* clip, edited seamlessly into continuity, after Frank discovers newspapers liken him to Bond. This intercuts with a bravura flying crane reverse-shot along the projector beam, over the cinema audience, to Frank in the middle of a row, enthralled. There he mirrors the spectator, for whom he is the ideal ego, just as Bond on the diegetic screen, indistinguishable from our screen, is his.

From constantly shifting frame size and shape in the credits, typically Spielbergian self-conscious narration dominates. Convoluted flashbacks together with extensive captions continually emphasise narration. Film and fantasy together equate in Frank's escape from the dilemma of which parent to stay with; intercut flash-forwards of him running away recall Truffaut's *Les quatre cents coups* (*The 400 Blows*, 1959) as the lawyer pressures him to decide. Ostentatious effects, always subsumed to narrative, include slow-motion, to indicate a fetishised moment as Frank observes pilots and stewardesses stepping out of cabs, ingeniously combined with normal-speed surrounding action within the same shot. Another is a track back and 135-degree pan inside an airliner cockpit (revived from *The Sugarland Express*) before light shines onto Frank's agitated face during his first flight. Cineaste details embrace ironic allusion to *It's a Wonderful Life* as Frank throws out his arms and yells 'Merry Christmas!' while cheques flutter around him and lights outside festoon Montrichard town square, and auto-citations such as squad car convoys with flashing lights arriving both times Carl arrests Frank, in Montrichard and Long Island.

The cinematic trope features numerous inscribed frames. Neither a shot through Frank's cell peephole, of Carl and a French warder approaching, nor a further shot of Carl through a 'widescreen' grille, the reverse of his view of Frank, involves optical point-of-view. Rather they enunciate the metaphor of Frank's life as movie. At his engagement, abandoning the only illusion of security he has created after leaving home, Frank looks down through a rectangular frame into the hall as Carl arrives intending to arrest him – spectating from outside into his own (already other) life. His French arrest is filmed from interior darkness through a police car windshield. An airliner window frames New York before a lateral track inscribes several near-identical frames, like a strip of film, before resting on Frank and Carl. A 'widescreen' window in his American cell leaves his outline just perceptible. A complex pan and track follows Carl through numerous glass screens as he enters the prison visiting room, tightly framing Frank behind a rectangular surface.

Inscribed spectators redouble the audience's look. The Rotary awards resemble an Oscar ceremony as diners applaud. Minor characters, from autograph-seeking children to ogling FBI agents, who treat pilots and their cabin crews like film stars, represent the cinema-going public. Frank Sr becomes both audience and co-enunciator as Frank's voice-overs solidify into direct audiovisual representations of what the father reads in Frank's letters. Frank watches *Dr Kildare* and *Perry Mason* (1957–66) for medical and legal tips, sitting up close in the dark, projecting his desiring gaze rather than the casual glance associated with television. Flickering light fills the airliner as Carl asks what also intrigues spectators: how Frank passed his bar exam. Frank twice looks out at freedom and security through patrol car windows while being driven away.

These inscribed screens associate with others such as the chain-link mesh through which prisoners spectate in Perpignan. At school, Frank's shadow graces a 'widescreen' blackboard as he spontaneously projects his new identity as teacher. Glass framing a forged diploma in Frank's apartment reflects Carl and his agents as they pursue their suspect. The lace curtain at Frank and Brenda's farewell becomes a screen that accesses vision yet separates them. Before his final impersonation, Frank, tempted, looks up at a mannequin in pilot's uniform, his reflection superimposed in a costume rental store window.

Frank is programmed, like *A.I.*'s mechas, to perform. Indefatigable, he must run, even when escape is impossible, to the extent of having a gun held to his head. Performance, the basis of fictional film and dramatic credibility, is foregrounded. Carl believes Frank's hacking cough is feigned; then, genuinely concerned, he demands a doctor. Frank continues coughing and collapses as he escapes from the sick bay, yet makes a remarkably swift and complete recovery. A later flashback compounds the ambiguity, as he simulates the same cough in attempting to cash a forgery.

Inscribed projector beams render these performances evidently cinematic. In Perpignan, Frank, cheered on during his abortive escape by spectating prisoners, runs towards camera along backlit reflections. A light on the wall at the award dinner redoubles spotlight beams onto the stage, while the Rotary International logo overlooking the event compounds two Spielbergian motifs: a movie reel and a sun. These recur in a close-up on a slide carousel as an actual projector features in Carl's FBI presentation – an expositional device as in *Jurassic Park*. On Frank's first morning at his new school the sun shines directly into camera, then casts a flashing 'projector beam' in the lobby before bullies dash Frank's optimism. This trope returns at key moments: at the station while buying his ticket with a cheque after running away; in the hotel lobby, where previously a 'projected' pilot signed an autograph, as Frank now writes a personal cheque and learns that payroll cheques are worth more; accompanying his voice-over when Frank Sr reads his letter – 'I have decided to become an airline pilot', his dream for his son; along with a sun ray wall clock as the hospital administrator casts 'Dr Frank Conners' into his movie; and again when Brenda's father installs him as Assistant Prosecutor, having had the sun shining over his shoulder while projecting onto Frank the role of a fellow romantic. Projection – moving shadows from car headlamps – metonymically heralds Carl's closing in as Frank isolates himself from his engagement party. Looking over his shoulder, the proverbial guilty man, he projects back knowledge of potential imminent arrest. Like Elliott encountering E.T., Carl follows a series of lights (and fluttering banknotes) to where Frank should be.

As 'director', Frank 'casts' bank tellers, picking them carefully for both sexual gratification and inside information. Like Schindler choosing secretaries, Frank auditions his bogus cabin crew – one even sings for him. Their selection is like an awards ceremony, with piano accompaniment and applause.

The scene with the judge, sitting before a large rectangular window through which white light pours, combines these aspects of the apparatus. Light beams and cast shadows, projection and reflection, defy optical logic. A similar concatenation of cinematic metaphors occurs at Frank's mother's house. He looks in to the rosy interior and taps gently at the window, its surface, both barrier and access, inscribed by frost. Here occurs another Spielbergian reflection, with a little girl – Frank's half-sister – embodying the life he could be leading, for which he yearns, and from which he finally acknowledges exclusion, as she trustingly imitates him – privileged communication that parallels spectatorial identification. Raising his hands in surrender to the authorities, he waves to her with E.T.'s two-finger gesture. There follows a complex shot: Frank intently gazing, framed in the 'widescreen' rear-view mirror, emergency lights flashing on the dashboard and reflected in the windscreen, twinkling like Christmas tree bulbs between fairy lights that decorate the house and vignette the idealised family now grouped at the open door with a bright projector-like light above them. They become unfocused and partially obscured as the car reverses and snow smears the windscreen, relegating his sustaining vision into memory.

'Put the blame on Mame, boys'

The flashbacks require spectatorial activity to establish chronology, causality and motivation. The task, analogous to Carl's detection, also resembles psychoanalysis. Even more than most Hollywood movies, in which expected conventional closure underlines that the narrative is already written, already over, though it unfurls in present tense, *Catch Me If You Can* – especially as its narrative image includes autobiography – implies a sense of working through. (Appropriately, then, as an in-joke the real Frank W. Abagnale, freed from the neuroses that impelled his cheating, plays the officer arresting his younger self.) The opening titles double as a prologue preceding the panel game and then Frank's extradition from languishing in prison, ensuring that the broad plot is already known. Interest focuses therefore on *how* events occurred and their meaning.

Structure and style inaugurate further image systems that suggest inevitability and narrative unity. During the first overt deception – Frank Sr bribing a store assistant – the camera positions father and son together behind bars as the shop door's security gate is closed. Implied criminality therefore links to earlier complicity while leaving the school. Frank's ticket purchase is shot through the booking office bars and cuts immediately to him shackled in Paris. The next scene, a flashback to eviction from a cheap hotel after rent cheques have bounced, also plays from behind the cashier's bars, as too when Frank cashes his first forged payroll cheque, seen from over the teller's shoulder. Ultimately, Venetian blinds in office cubicles imply he remains imprisoned while on parole with the FBI.

Recaptured in the French prison, Frank tells Carl, 'Let's go home.' More than the USA, 'home' refers to his family, whose break-up precipitated his escape into crime. Desire to repair it motivates him. Flashback to the warmth of the Rotary dinner, his father's finest hour, opposes the prison scene's cold blue cast. This colour dualism – domesticity versus exclusion – continues, starting with the exterior of the Abagnales' large comfortable house, wintry afternoon light contrasting with the Nativity scene on the lawn and the glow indoors. Inside, Frank Sr displays his award, a Christmas tree twinkles, and Frank dances with his mother. These memories, the earliest in the case, constitute its Imaginary. Frank, delightedly repeating phrases and filling gaps, identifies with his father re-telling the parents' meeting. Both males idealise the mother, calling her 'a blonde bombshell' although her hair is brown. Oedipal tensions surface as Frank Sr, now dancing proprietorially with his wife, returns Frank's gaze as he watches through the doorway from the cold blue hall. Frank has fetched a towel to mop up red wine she has spilt, a detail that returns with hallucinatory intensity in close-up as the parents' dancing feet tread the stain into the pale rug. He returns with a glass of milk, a maternal symbol in the context of his mother's insinuated carelessness – a troubling flaw, replete with sexual implications, in an otherwise pristine scene. Like the duplicitous brunette Judy in *Vertigo*, whose image Scotty shapes into a lost blonde ideal, scapegoating her for masculine insecurities she nevertheless exacerbates, she is dressed all in green.

Aircraft on Frank's bedroom wallpaper link later impersonations to the childhood home. Frank Sr's petty frauds and self-deluding insistence that appearance is everything, despite inability to satisfy his wife or manage his business, combine buoyancy with denial of reality. Frank inherits these traits, together with specialised knowledge of stationery, and applies them in attempting to emulate and surpass his father in making everything right. The jobs he fakes – teacher, pilot, doctor, lawyer – are professions any parents seeking respectability would be proud for a child to pursue.

In the downsized family apartment, a horizontal light beam in the rectangular frame demarcating the kitchen suggests the trope of an absent Imaginary, a blank screen, which Mrs Abagnale then comfortingly occupies while Barnes dissimulates after Frank nearly catches them *in flagrante*. A temporal jump to Paris during his extradition sees Frank asking to call his father. Back at the start of his career, he impersonates a pilot and his father re-enters the movie, reading a letter from Frank that ends in denial: 'How's Mum? Have you called her lately?' A subsequent letter promises to recover all 'Daddy's' money. When father and son reunite, Frank attempts to give him a Cadillac to compensate for the car traded in when his business collapsed and suggests they 'drive over to Mum'. A snippet of dialogue discloses shared but repressed understanding that, as previously hinted, Barnes may not have been her only lover – indeed, she may have been a gold-digger using Frank Sr to leave France. When Frank asks whether she knows the store is closed down, his father replies, among bitter incoherencies, 'Your mother. I've been fightin' for her ever since ... since the day we met.' Frank replies: 'Daddy. Out of all those men – you were the one that took her home. Remember that.' The marriage, in Frank's focalisation, partial memory focused on

Catch Me if You Can – remembering Mum

one cherished Christmas, masks elaborate pretence. Tellingly, though, Mum's version is never put. Frank Sr, almost breaking down, again recounts their first meeting, just as, moments earlier, he has re-told the tale of the mice. Stories twist reality, re-shape memory and influence conduct.

His stoically proud father remains Frank's role model, even while he seeks his approval by taking him to fancy restaurants. Complex undercurrents of identity formation further figure when Frank Sr, relishing successful fatherhood, projects fantasies onto Frank. He legitimises Frank's Mirror Phase, as it were, telling him, 'You see these people staring at you … ' – which Frank denies, though it confirms the recognition he craves over and above financial gain.

Frank Sr, a pathetic failure in his own terms despite earlier good humour and later dogged independence, is too close to Frank and too ineffectual to threaten. Both embrace ideals that lack confirmation. Frank Sr assumes Carl, at their one meeting, is childless: 'If you were a father you'd know I would *never* give up my son,' he twice asserts. Crosscut to Brenda crying: *her* parents banished and disowned her after forcing her into an abortion. Frank immediately proposes, to provide the respectability of engagement to a doctor. While Frank otherwise repeatedly exploits women – their sexuality in particular – as both the means to and reward for his hustles, other male authority figures also ease his way. They are variously too trusting, kind but distracted, careless, romantic – a hotel manager, an airline official, a hospital administrator, Brenda's father – facets of Frank Sr's own weaknesses. Carl, possessing none of these qualities, reinforces patriarchal Law. Much of the comedy, epitomised by Carl in the launderette, his shirts dyed pink, intercut with Frank in 007 guise easily outwitting a would-be sophisticated seductress in a five-star hotel, depends on his humiliations as Frank's nemesis. Carl, apart from Brenda – whose loss, along with the security her family offers, represents the cost of Frank's livelihood – is the only fully characterised victim of Frank's otherwise almost abstract deceptions. Universalisation of Frank's criminality into Oedipal conflict effaces questions of immediate morality, thus easing identification with his unreality and exhilaration, and permitting the comic tone.

In an uncertain world where, as he should know, trust guarantees nothing, Frank places confidence in Carl. They share characteristics. Frank's deceptions, like Carl's detections, demand observation and understanding of human behaviour. On the other hand, Carl mirrors Frank Sr. During their two-minute encounter Frank notices Carl's ring. It transpires Carl has a daughter, fixed in memory as four years old; Frank discovers a four-year-old half-sister who, in his fantasies, should have been Frank Sr's daughter. Carl works for the bureaucratic government Frank Sr compulsively evades. Like Frank Sr, Carl is a divorced loner living humbly. The diminutive FBI Christmas tree dismally echoes Frank's childhood memory and the lamp on Carl's desk figures him as a projection of Frank's need. Carl fails to realise, even while crowing that Frank has nobody else to call at Christmas, that at the location Frank offers for a meeting Carl could easily detain him.

One night Frank observes wistfully, again voyeuristically through a doorway, Brenda's parents dancing together while washing dishes to the song his parents played that special Christmas. While his biological father, obsessed with worries, becomes a fantasist, Brenda's father initially is the obscene father. His justified suspicions – Brenda has landed a doctor *and* a lawyer! – and forensic probing, intensified by the coincidence of having qualified at an institution Frank claims to have attended, together with his distant, quietly menacing, patrician manner and dry humour, match Frank's ingenuity. Once Frank wins his confidence, however, he becomes a confidant, so trusting as to reject Frank's truthful confession.

Following Frank Sr's revelation, as he and Frank sit silhouetted against a glass-block 'screen' under a Christmas wreath, of mum's remarriage – a shock that ends Frank's regressive plans (he has invited them together to his wedding) – Frank vows, 'It's over.' He pleads with his father to ask him to stop. Frank Sr, however, regards him as an anti-Government co-conspirator. As Frank rises to leave in a two-shot, light flickers from behind Frank Sr's head as he encourages Frank to continue his esca-pades, and projects his own desired narrative, his own need for belief: 'Frank, where you goin' tonight? Some place exotic? Tahiti? Hawaii?' Frank reacts by phoning Carl – who awaits the call in his office, the tree in the background – from a bar festooned with Christmas lights, insisting he wants to end his spree and requesting a truce. The following scene, the engagement party that ends Frank's American career, begins with him customarily peeling the label from a bottle. His idiosyncrasy underlines how identities rely on naming. The product's name: Dad's. (At the start, Frank removed a wine label as his father's name joined the Roll of Honour.) Frank Jr and Sr alike, in common with many Spielberg protagonists, are far from being 'the psychologically noncomplex, comic-book characters' who 'all know who they are', as John Belton claims (2005: 364), routinely lumping Spielberg with Lucas.

Another Christmas Eve, when Carl catches Frank in Montrichard, Frank accuses Carl of lying about the police outside. Carl insists he would never lie to Frank, at which the latter points out his wedding ring. Carl explains he told Frank he 'had' a family, but no longer. Carl swears on his daughter that police will shoot Frank if he attempts escape. His confidence won, Frank applies the handcuffs himself only to believe Carl has outwitted him when the gendarmes are slow to arrive. Carl repeatedly entreats Frank not to worry as French police take him into custody – a new stage in their relationship, as Carl is now protecting him. Eventually, on the plane, during yet another Christmas, Carl sympathetically discloses Frank Sr's death. Frank's grief accompanies hypersensitivity that Carl lied by withholding this. As Frank regards his reflection in the toilet mirror a flashback to his parents dancing – now, possibly, recognised as a performance and certainly the origin of his career in lying to others – re-emphasises that moment's primacy in his subject formation. His clandestine visit to his mother's house, when he sees her with Barnes and encounters his half-sister, while remaining literally out in the cold, at last dissolves his motivation. Life has advanced. Accepting reality, he completes his transference to Carl as father figure, welcomes arrest and subsequently subsumes himself, under Carl's mentorship, into the FBI's surrogate family, the Symbolic, the Law – and, as the closing titles explain, family life, Midwestern respectability and millionairehood: the American Dream.

The means, nevertheless, opposes Frank Sr's anti-Government, pro-small business populism and, as suggested, the rows of grey steel and brown Formica connote imprisonment. The movie's retro setting, despite nostalgic appeal, does not figure Frank's attitude to his history. It emphatically does not – as Belton claims postmodern works do – contrast 'the incoherence of the present to the coherence of the past'; nor does its ambiguous closure assert an ideological image of past individual unity and wholeness against contemporary alienation (2005: 359–60).

CHAPTER TWENTY-THREE

The Terminal: all that jazz

'Give me your tired, your poor,
Your huddled masses yearning to breathe free,
The wretched refuse of your teeming shore,
Send these, the homeless, tempest-tossed to me,
I lift my lamp beside the golden door!'
          – Emma Lazarus (1849–87), plinth of Statue of Liberty

Just off the plane

The Terminal opens with the camera craning over a departures board. Rapidly flipping letters spell multitudinous destinations, connoting escape and opportunity, glamour, romance, apprehension, adventure. For Viktor Navorski (Tom Hanks) this screen surface, clicking and whirring like a film projector – not an arbitrary association: the board displays the movie's titles – will reiterate denial rather than access. Viktor soon inhabits the terminal: metaphorically the spectator/screen border, an interstice separating everyday normality from desires, aspirations or emotional confrontations.

    The airport, like Hollywood movies, is a selective microcosm of, and insight into, the USA, with which it is contiguous and whose values and institutions it embodies and represents, without being identical to. (Security supervisor Frank Dixon's (Stanley Tucci) framed picture of a US flag, for example, replicates an actual flag outside his window.) In the fifth shot a security ribbon spans the screen, excluding the camera and, retrospectively, Viktor from the flag-bedecked concourse. 'Welcome to the United States – almost,' Dixon says, having made Viktor 'a free man ... within the confines of the international transit lounge.' A glass door, emblazoned 'Department of Homeland Security' with the Great Seal of the United States, shuts onto the camera. Like the screen, it lets us peer into the Imaginary, the 'homeland' embraced maternally by Liberty. As the Symbolic sign of the Law, the stern, paternal profile of the sharp-eyed Bald Eagle seals us out, also like the screen.

As Siliwood's denizens undoubtedly know, soldiers at the US Army National Training Center in Fort Irwin, California, fight a simulated enemy, modelled on a former Soviet republic, called 'Krasnovia' (Der Derian 1994). *The Terminal*, increasingly focalised through Viktor, from the closely homophonous Krakhozia, reverses the conceit. America becomes the virtual goal and antagonist. Comparison with *The Truman Show* (1998), scripted by *The Terminal*'s co-writer and executive producer, Andrew Niccol, is apt – both feature an individual trapped in a seemingly flawless controlled environment that, in textbook Baudrillardian fashion, effaces the equally constructed reality it serves.

Viktor enters the transit lounge through a 'screen' (rectangular double doors) along a 'projector beam'. It seemingly signifies what he desires ('Where do I buy the Nike shoes?') but his indeterminate status precludes him reaching. It resembles those shopping malls that house multiplexes – within which *The Terminal* found most of its theatrical audience. Its New York Kennedy prototype is, like the movie's extraordinarily detailed set, a simulacrum.

The first scene introduces Viktor as spectator, watching officials chase untrustworthy travellers, and that is how he last appears before leaving the airport – gazing as Amelia (Catherine Zeta-Jones) disappears with her lover; observing, with a crowd of others, Gupta's (Kumar Pallana) civil disobedience, through glass panels, repeated rectangular frames, which overlook the airport apron. Viktor's enforced passivity, subject to imposed events, reflects the spectator, subject to narration. During his several months' sojourn, Viktor uses his skills to craft panelling and an elaborate fountain. Neither project seeks financial gain or social recognition. Rather self-expression compels him to impress meaning on existence and leave a mark on his environment. Like *Close Encounters*' Neary and Jillian, he pursues a vision. Nevertheless, success gains him employment. Mounted contractors' lights, a stepladder, and plasterers' and carpenters' materials conflate the dark, empty diegetic space with its profilmic origin – a studio (more precisely, a simulated airport functioning as a studio simulating an airport that simulates America). Viktor, seizing opportunities to create significance within external constraints and to shape his idea accordingly, is both director and set designer/constructor. He creates the mise-en-scène of his living quarters and co-produces and directs a scene, involving Gupta as a juggler – pure entertainment – in a fabricated restaurant.

Screens and frames within screens and frames recall *Minority Report*, which *The Terminal*, with emphasis on surveillance, state security, dystopian alienation, ambivalently pervasive commercialisation and cinematic metaphors, comically counterpoints. Borders bookshop, a suspended structure of transparent screens, punning on the adjacent Customs and Border Protection, figures as another screen interface peddling fiction, history and guides to real places. The large terminal windows constantly reinscribe a screen, the nearest Viktor can reach to the outside world but still an inward-looking, circumscribed view as 'America is closed'. For him, the US is no more accessible than Krakhozia. Yet when Viktor truthfully tells flight attendant Amelia, 'I go from one building to another,' she interprets this as sympathetically mirroring her experience (having just completed four round-world trips). Reality, mediated, is a state of mind.

A physical screen, sliding glass doors, excludes Viktor from a private lounge with a widescreen TV on which the Krakhozian turmoil unfolds (one of the less plausible details; US news does not pay such attention to political events in obscure countries unless America is involved); he cries, like the spectator of a sentimental film. Viktor collides with plate glass as he exits a shop while seeking work. Snow emphasises the terminal's glass cladding as a dividing screen that provides spectacle yet protects, transforming external life into image. Viktor celebrates Krakhozia's liberation in the 'New York Grill' bar – still in the airport. Thanks to the common humanity of Dixon's underling, who originally detained him, Viktor finally penetrates the barrier into the life-affirming reality of snow, accompanied by an upwash of John Williams' music; the *It's a Wonderful Life* moment encompasses Manhattan panoramically reflected in the building's exterior. Shots of his taxis to and from the city feature windscreen wipers and smeared snow on the glass, reaffirming his vision as mediated.

'Projector beams' and intense backlighting as usual bind together these cinematic tropes. An audience of construction workers, before a light shining directly into camera, watch Viktor, unaware of observation, before he lands his job. Spotlights from a taxiing plane whiteout his lair, externalising his fears, prompting raised hands: 'Don't shoot!' That he shouts in English suggests the airport is less comforting than it appears. Extreme backlighting also corresponds with Dixon's desire as Dixon briefs his team prior to an official inspection. A headlight on Viktor's construction helmet as he translates *Fodor's* Guide in order to learn English, reading about the TV show *Friends* (1994–2004) (the world's dominant access to New York's exhibited lifestyle), emphasises vision as projective. Dazzling light on Viktor's face heralds Enrique's arrival on a cart, bringing food. Backlighting for the catering/baggage- handling area stresses its sense of community and belonging.

1930s-style star lighting on Amelia, Viktor's object of desire, is a further self-reflexive trope. Her name, recalling pioneer aviator Amelia Earhart, who disappeared on a trans-Oceanic flight, hints at her being a female embodiment of America – she would be his one reason for staying – but confirms the idea, motivated by her complicated existing relationships, of a lost, unattainable Imaginary. The screen whitens with 'God Light' when Viktor kisses Amelia before the fountain – revealed like a screen from behind a curtain under spotlights, with cinema-style seats arranged before it. In its dazzling central reflection, the characters become silhouettes. Water casts cinematic flickers on the walls and ceiling as the camera tracks back. On the blank white screen that covers a cut, Viktor's friends, backlit, loom into shot to inform him of another fulfilled desire: 'The war is over.'

Enclosing these cinematic metaphors is a metadiscourse of internal surveillance and external mediation through TV. Much narration occurs on actual inscribed screens.

The Terminal – on-screen narration: Reality TV?

Analogously to Anderton in *Minority Report*, Dixon asserts panoptical control and anticipates crimes from a bank of monitors, their flat large screens reduplicating the ubiquitous glass that partitions federal and commercial areas alike. A complex relay of looks and representations shows officials spectating at Viktor electronically, through dividers, and between the plastic curtains screening his hideaway from the terminal beyond. An enforced outsider, Viktor looks through glass at the US, both its direct representation on our screen and as mediated intra-diegetically. Viktor learns from TV about the Krakhozian conflict and the later liberation. Dixon, watching with his officers, joins audiences closely observing Viktor intra- and extra-diegetically as he earns a living from returned trolley deposits. The authorities, remotely operating cameras to follow Viktor, resemble filmmakers or Reality TV producers – staging situations such as opportunities for him to escape – and spectators as they voyeuristically observe from their eagle's nest above the concourse. Viktor refuses direction, however, and insists on controlling his own movie.

Product placement

Philip French (2004: 9) laments *The Terminal*'s 'relentless product placement'. International brand names dominate the airport concessions. As Janet Wasko explains, this is a significant source of Hollywood income, with agencies representing labels as well as players, while decisions now involve '"above-the-line" talent, in other words, writers, directors, and the stars' (2003: 158). Commentators frequently cite *E.T.* in connection with this trend: the sweets Elliott uses to lure E.T. are Reece's Pieces; although hardly apparent in the movie, holograms on two million packets established this in American minds. Studios gain direct payment from commodifying their movie's narrative image, but also increased awareness among potential audiences.

Product placement suits marketers for many reasons. Brands acquire kudos from Hollywood glamour. Filmgoers constitute fairly precisely targeted and captive audiences. Removal from an overtly advertising context naturalises the product's presence, sometimes rendering awareness almost subliminal, and thereby circumvents resistance to a harder sell. If the product concerned did not feature, a rival commodity or an anonymous substitute would fulfill its narrative function anyhow. Moreover, in return for initial outlay, the product's promotion continues indefinitely with return visits or home viewing and the impracticability of editing it from broadcast versions. Consequently product placement is a multi-million dollar enterprise.

But its effectiveness depends on narrative context – normally beyond brand owners' control. Not all publicity is good. Intended adverts may inadvertently 'subvert'. Product placement has risen alongside postmodern irony and consciousness of advertising's cynicism. Yet these are recuperable, despite the risk. Filmmakers have it both ways, as in *Wayne's World* (1992), which parodies placement while still endorsing products through association with hip knowingness. Overt recognition by text and audience implies openness and honesty that reflect well on advertisers, equating the products with goodwill and cleverness; the audience, 'superior' to marketers' stratagems, are not dupes, thus defusing sinister motivations critics might ascribe. Flattery, in other words, sanctions consumer sovereignty.

Any realistic portrayal of a modern airport could hardly avoid foregrounding storefront names. Moreover, in *The Terminal*, as in *Minority Report*, they constitute part of a critique of US politics and culture, explicitly presented as class-stratified. The global capitalism of fast-food multinationals, designer labels and executive lounges depends on embittered State-employed security managers paid less than moonlighting builders; on minimum-wage catering employees; and on an army (only three feature, but three more than in most mainstream films) of cleaners, baggage handlers and warehouse personnel with a separate behind-the-scenes existence in barren, concrete limbo. Many are immigrants, and bolster incomes by scavenging. 'As long as I keep my floor clean, my head down, they have no reason to notice me,' states Gupta, whose presence is tolerated, though he faces charges for stabbing a policeman in India, because he provides reliable cheap labour. That Viktor's eventual friends suspect him initially of CIA affiliation indicates profound tension. Greeted in the Promised Land with vouchers for free food and telephone calls, and advised 'There's only one thing you can do here – shop,' Viktor experiences the limitations of the myth of the self-made man. The authorities' intervention quickly compromises it, despite framed posters extolling 'Success' and 'Opportunity' on Dixon's wall: he creates an official trolley collector to curb Viktor's free enterprise and kick him back down the ladder.

Meals indicate economic status as Viktor forages crackers and sauce sachets, having worked up from a burger to a laden tray, while staff bin untouched food. (Dixon is frequently eating and drinking.) The Land of the Free, haven for huddling masses – New York, specifically, Kennedy Airport, seems hardly an accidental choice – deems an honest, talented, kindly, hardworking, self-reliant and enterprising individual repeatedly 'unacceptable'. Meanwhile CNN interviews a formerly bankrupt British ex-royal, welcomed and feted as a celebrity. Viktor soon adapts the system's trappings to his utilitarian needs, for example storing food in a refrigerated vending machine.

Viktor's official role is to remain radically other, alongside crazed loners with knives, drug smugglers and anonymous hordes of Eastern infiltrators against which America protects and defines itself. His humanity poses a problem for such neat binaries. During the 'situation' with the desperate Russian, Dixon traverses the glass doors to fetch Viktor, who, filmed through screens and dark frames, serves as translator, a recurrent Spielberg trope. Enrique (Diego Luna) yearns for Officer Dolores through glass. Viktor as go-between facilitates their marriage, which transcends several divides: American official versus (according to Dixon) 'undesirable' immigrant, Black versus Hispanic, 'Trekkie' versus 'alien' – a pointed allusion: *Star Trek* (1966–69*)*, a popular cultural product confronting its era's prejudices, included the first interracial kiss on American television.

As Ryan Gilbey states, Viktor, although 'unacceptable', nevertheless 'teaches his hosts about hard work and fair play; he promotes American ideals more diligently than any American' (2004: 87). Ordinary people – store clerks, hamburger flippers, service staff, even, eventually, lower-ranking immigration officers – rally behind him. The ensuing cult, with its iconic standard (Viktor's photocopied hands), is a spontaneous, grass-roots, dialogic alternative to the multi-million dollar Presidential contest fought during the movie's production and release, involving xenophobia, image manipulation and enforced imposition of democracy overseas. Fear of immigrants, in the airport's epitome of a nation composed of them, extends even among first-generation arrivals: 'Stay off my mop, my job,' Gupta admonishes Viktor early on. Viktor neither embraces nor seeks entry into the American Dream, which he refuses not ideologically but ignores as irrelevant. Without money, Viktor has no function, no identity. Apart from refused entry, his misunderstanding makes a pun on 'US Customs' – he shakes an official's outstretched hand, for example, instead of surrendering his passport. Like much comedy, his presence carnivalises Symbolic logic. Viktor escapes interpellation by following different priorities. Eventually Times Square represents New York as a city of light, the ultimate capitalist spectacle. Yet a snowy New York Christmas, that commoditised emblem of movie sentimentality and shopping-break tourism, is not Viktor's object. From the start Viktor clutches a can – the plot's McGuffin – mysteriously described as 'a promise' and enigmatically explained to his airport friends as 'jazz'. He sits and contemplates it in his darkened corner while lights flicker beyond the plastic covering the windows. Like the magic can in *The Twilight Zone* or the can in which *Saving Private Ryan*'s sergeant collects gritty samples of reality, it suggests a further filmic metaphor for Viktor's subjective agenda. While his motivation for staying in the airport remains unstated, the reason is plain enough. Without passport and ticket, confiscated on arrival, he cannot return home. Only arrogant ethnocentricity assumes he intends illegal immigration.

Sharing much with Chaplin's comedy (not least *The Immigrant* (1917)), *The Terminal* employs humour, sentimentality and pathos to unite audiences with the dispossessed little man: slapstick, as when quarters hit penniless Viktor in the face from a deposit-return machine; physical comedy in his tramp-like attempts to sleep on bench seats with separating armrests; and admirable resourcefulness in his removing electrical fuses to restore darkness and quiet from *The Terminal*'s 24-hour nightmare. His signature theme, Eastern European light orchestral dance style, renders Viktor essentially old-fashioned and harmless, while outrageous puns resulting from his attempts to master English emphasise his non-assimilation but equally his alternative perspective, which increasingly the spectator shares. Pathos occurs when he sees Amelia waving, he assumes at him, as also do we thanks to a familiar Spielbergian point-of-view deployment, before her lover rushes past, knocking Viktor's cracker meal flying.

Cumulatively, again like Chaplin, the movie subtly and perhaps surprisingly critiques the state and consumerism. Gupta's catchphrase, 'Do you have an appointment?' parodies soulless bureaucracy, and is absurd in Viktor's situation, where time is meaningless outside his daily Entry application (rejection of which, incidentally, counts further against each subsequent one). Gupta, sitting with his soda, laughing at repeated pratfalls as passers-by slip on his polished floor despite carefully placed warning signs (indicative of his social invisibility), parallels the spectator but equally parodies Dixon.

In the Land of the Free, official procedures are reversed and their hollowness exposed. Opportunity depends on who you know. Dixon exploits asylum loopholes and creates deliberate security lapses to make Viktor somebody else's problem. Viktor's job is part of a tolerated black economy. Amelia's 'friend' procures Viktor a one-day visa; how is never explained. Dixon's personal vindictiveness prevents Viktor from using it. Lower-ranking officials in turn subvert Dixon.

Intertextually, of course, Viktor's doomed love for Amelia, whose heart belongs to another man, resonates with *Casablanca*. That also, with Rick's American Café set on the edge of an airport and cloaked in prison imagery, deals with itinerants attempting to dupe the authorities. Viktor's useless phrase book, which confirms his comic role as a latter-day Hyman Kaplan and accords with verbal howlers ('Eat shit' for 'He cheats') also recalls *Casablanca*'s humour from refugees practising English. (Spielberg moreover alludes to *The Usual Suspects* (1995), titled from *Casablanca*, when Dixon drops his coffee as he realises Gupta has evaded security and walked onto the apron to defy him.) '*Casablanca*', as is well known, translates as 'White House', and consequently is readable as political allegory concerning US entry into World War Two. *The Terminal*, through such allusions, may equally signal amenability to political interpretation. Viktor's true objective to complete his father's autographs is, although 'highly flattering to US culture' (French 2004: 9) – arguably: jazz originated in oppression – *not* the American Dream, but personal, filial. Horatio Alger is evoked only to be sidelined.

Dixon, with his shaven head, aquiline nose and sharp observation, personifies the American Bald Eagle featured in a photograph in his office. As Gilbey (2004) notes, when Dixon assures Viktor 'You will not set one foot in the United States of America', he points like Uncle Sam in the recruiting poster. His stars and stripes lapel badge relates him to the politicians of George W. Bush's administration. 'Dixon' puns on 'Dick's son' and rhymes with 'Nixon', hinting possibly at the values of 'Tricky Dicky's' earlier Republican era. The name underlines parallels with Vice President Dick Cheney, also bald and bespectacled. (Another second-in-command, who formerly worked for Donald Rumsfeld under Nixon, and as Defense Secretary waged the first Gulf War, Cheney during the 'War on Terror' has operated largely behind the scenes. Dixon, then, as well as the director in *The Truman Show* (1998), more darkly resembles the brass-hat tactician battling with real lives on remote monitors in *Black Hawk Down* (2001).) Dixon's violent outburst when Viktor outwits him over the Russian, during which he expresses incomprehension, frustration and rage at how foreigners from the East behave, and explicitly threatens 'war', hardly seems innocent. Photocopied hand-prints from Dixon holding Viktor forcibly over the accidentally activated machine suggest biometric security procedures, anticipated in *Minority Report*, that US airports planned to introduce during autumn 2004, within the diegetic timescale (after the movie's production and concurrent with release). Dixon is a hypocritical neoconserva-tive: confident and aggressive in pursuing his cause, nevertheless expediency drives him, not principles or morality. Despite overseeing one huge fast-food outlet that provides the array of choice corporate capitalism can offer, he prefers a packed lunch. He adopts at best laissez-faire attitudes towards the poor, and treats foreigners with indifference (he fails to find Viktor a translator) or hostility. Psychoanalytically Dixon is the obscene father: contrasted with Gupta, whose courage inspires Viktor; other officials, who treat Viktor decently; Viktor's deceased biological father, whose project Viktor completes; and ultimately Spielberg, the text's progenitor who constructs the ideological facet of focalisation (Rimmon-Kenan 1983: 71) against Dixon.

A mainstream film with US law enforcement authorities as the villains against an Eastern European protagonist (and in which the American heroine badly lets him down) is, to say the least, interesting in the context of New York as a melting pot and especially the political climate precipitated by the 11 September attacks on that city. 'Compassion for the people – that's the foundation of this country', the Field Commissioner, Dixon's retiring boss, reminds him before potential regime change within the Customs and Border Protection microcosm – a coded election-year warn-ing from a friend of Bill Clinton and Tony Blair?

A backlit 'projector beam' in the jazz club, Viktor's long-awaited destination, extends the cinematic metaphor by presenting saxophonist Benny Golson as filmic spectacle, the right-hand side of the screen becoming pure white as Viktor watches him playing. In many respects, *The Terminal* continues the solipsistic and self-referen-tial tendencies Christopher Wicking detected, while overcoming their limitations:

> Spielberg may well have proved himself to be Hitchcock's heir (it is worth remem-bering in view of his flop, *1941*, that Hitchcock too had trouble with comedy). Though their concerns may be different, their approach to the medium is almost exactly the same, a stylistic dialogue with the audience which insists that the only reality is the reality on the screen. (Wicking in Pirie 1981: 231)

Spielberg's self-conscious authorial touches are evident, as when Amelia and Viktor jettison their pagers (*Hook*) to end intrusions from reality (for the former at least) that repeatedly force them apart, or arrival of the Sugarland Express carrying a SWAT team who aim at Gupta in a subjective shot (*Jaws*). Indeed, the act of literally inscribing Spielberg's signature occurs three times in the end credits, alongside those of other above-the-line talent. Their significance, though, extends beyond the text and is, I sug-gest, confirmed in Spielberg's 1995 acceptance speech for an honorary Cèsar, France's

Oscar, during cinema's centenary. He acknowledged indebtedness to thirty French filmmakers, starting with Godard, 'whose influence', John Baxter claims, 'not even the most alert critic had noted' (1996: 407) – the present book then being at an early stage. As in Godard/Gorin's *Tout Va Bien* (1972), which commences with signing cheques to key production personnel and stars, signatures necessary to get the film made ('in the can') are highlighted, and may conceivably be, in *The Terminal*'s case, political endorsements. Spielberg's airport as microcosm parallels Godard/Gorin's obviously Brechtian cutaway factory set, advertising studio and supermarket. Liberal rather than revolutionary, and realist rather than modernist, despite its self-reflexive overtones and allegorical dimension, *The Terminal* is more tendentious, in the non-derogatory sense, than most mainstream product and potentially more challenging than critical prejudice acknowledges. Viktor's long-delayed green stamp (he needs a signature for his visa) represents the 'green light' for getting the film made. 'Business or pleasure?' officials ask arrivals at the terminal. The question applies equally to the double facet of film, whether considered in relation to Spielberg's motivation (he can command blockbuster budgets and production values for relatively light and idiosyncratic movies like *The Terminal*) or in terms of political economy versus spectator-oriented critical approaches. Neither alternative embraces Viktor's reason for being there, which is duty.

Spielberg too, who made this film during political turmoil (Gilbey wonders 'which bigwig at US Customs and Border Protection will get their knuckles rapped for co-operating with the production' (2004: 87)), just as Viktor is compelled to construct his artefacts, deserves recognition for choosing to do so. It was not an immediate hit, eliciting a 'disappointing $18.7 million weekend box office take for a Hanks-Spielberg movie' (Ayres 2004: 18) but showed, in David Thomson's words, the director 'still thinking, still growing, still challenging himself' (2004: 1B).

CHAPTER TWENTY-FOUR

War of the Worlds: rays in the mirror

If *Hook* entered 'a minefield of psychosexual obsessions' (Baxter 1996: 364), and *A.I.* was 'a seething psychological bonanza' (Hoberman 2001: 16), these are understatements compared to *War of the Worlds* (2005). It retreads familiar Spielberg concerns, combining large-scale disaster-movie spectacle, science fiction fantasy involving alien contact, technological trauma, technical virtuosity, cinematic self-reflexivity and auto-citation, with family psychodrama. *Close Encounters'* and *E.T.'s* negative, it resurrects a darker, misanthropic Spielberg glimpsed intermittently over three decades. Its blockbuster treatment of America threatened by an unstoppable alien force is *Jaws* writ large. Also evident, infinitely multiplied, is masculine testing against a 'projected' mechanical double as seen in *Duel*, which, I suggested, alludes to earlier versions of *War of the Worlds*. Most remarkable is these discourses' inextricable interweaving.

The family of man

H. G. Wells' *The War of the Worlds* retains mythical status for establishing key science fiction iconography and presciently describing mechanised warfare against civilians. Published amid fears of Germany's developing power, as it recognises (1946: 39), it especially resonates during heightened international tension. Orson Welles' 1938 radio broadcast fed anxieties concerning Hitler's designs on America, the 1953 movie joined a cycle of Cold War creature features, and Spielberg's version, released just a week before the worst bomb attacks on London since World War Two, is replete with imagery from recent humanly-perpetuated cataclysms. The New York skyline following the credits, collapsing buildings, dazed dust-covered crowds, roadside displays of hand-made posters seeking missing loved ones, and a crashed airliner recall 9/11 and associated outrages. Massed bodies floating downstream universalise inhumanity beyond the West's immediate concerns by evoking Rwandan genocide.

Colin MacCabe likens the movie to 'Operation Shock and Awe from the point-of-view of an Iraqi' (2005: 9). This makes sense in shots of heavily-armed troops looking down indifferently from passing trucks at the helpless protagonist before launching a conflagration, struggling to maintain order among panicking refugees, or standing by as, eventually, a war machine topples ignominiously like Saddam's statue. 'Shock and awe' also describes expectations of a state-of-the-art science fiction horror movie. As the allusions to real-life conflict suggest, the alien invasion projects human attributes onto an imaginary Other. The return of the repressed, always informing these genres, reveals worst fears about human capabilities and the destructive power members of our species possess.

The central family, however, is not merely a point of access for focalisation but appears to originate the cataclysmic events. These, in a personal mise-en-abyme of the wide-scale socio-political allegory, represent the protagonist's relationships and inner turmoil in an unusually literal realisation of projection metaphors and doubling. 'Projection', psychoanalytically, embraces 'qualities, feelings, wishes, objects, which the subject refuses to recognise or rejects in himself [sic] [and which] are expelled from the self and located in another person or thing' (Laplanche & Pontalis 1973: 349). Ray (Tom Cruise), then, up in his crane at the start, reflects the alien that slips, dying, out of the fallen tripod at the end. From his vantage point of dominant specularity, Ray looks down, 'cool and unsympathetic ... with envious eyes' on human affairs, along with 'intellects vast' – the imminent invaders, to whom these words in the narration actually refer and whose point of view a montage of aerial shots suggests. Ray jokes with his children about his imaginary brother – between them they 'know everything', the brother having the answers to questions that defeat Ray. His surname, Ferrier, encapsulates this duality: he 'ferries' his daughter to safety and mirrors the 'ferrous' invaders. Like Elliott's counterpart, E.T., but different in that they are isolated rather than telempathically connected, the alien realises Ray's unconscious desires by venting his frustrations against the human race with its Heat-*Rays* – as Wells' novel (with a very dissimilar and anonymous protagonist) names them.

This superior vantage point evokes the power of the all-seeing Father that Ray would like to be – embodied in Morgan Freeman's Wellesian Voice-of-God framing narration. Cocky at work, but a responsible teamster who follows union rules rather than a maverick, Ray fails in familial roles. 'What are you – your mother or mine?' he asks his precociously wise daughter, confirming his gender-role confusion. Mocking his ex-wife's partner's car as 'one safe-looking new vehicle', he drives a souped-up sports car, unsuitable for family use, yet still arrives late to take custody of his children. Later, fleeing with them in the one operational vehicle following the attack, he drives a smaller, cheaper, older version of Tim's people carrier. He is unprepared for the children's stay and has no food (not that he knows what they eat). Class difference, between his clapboard house under the freeway, and Mary Ann's (Miranda Otto) luxurious villa and his former in-laws' Boston townhouse, corresponds with his masculine inferiority. He fails to quell his surly rebellious teenage son (Justin Chatwin), whose name, Robbie, hints at a castration threat that drives the entire narrative.

Playing baseball catch in the yard, that archetypal US father/son bonding ritual, but wearing different teams' caps, Robbie and Ray appear more like squabbling brothers. They trade insults until Ray, hurling the ball forcibly, brings the sexual undercurrents to the surface by accusing Robbie of being 'such a dick'. Robbie misses the catch and the ball smashes a window – the first significant disruption to normality and the first damage to property, correlating with escalating destruction that will approach apocalyptic proportions. This physical manifestation of Ray's failure breaches domesticity, social values and security before any attack commences.

1960s horror effected a shift, from community and domesticity threatened by external threats to danger latent within the family (Wood 1986). *War of the Worlds* unites the two, paralleling Ray's domestic dysfunction, in a street bedecked with patriotic flags, with a journey to the seat of the American Revolution. A Minuteman statue, pointedly encrusted with invasive weed, recalls the origin of a (masculine) gun culture that according to the film exacerbates conflict and leads to murder. Ray's guns – his pistol which, relinquished, almost immediately kills another refugee in a crisis where no official leadership is evident, and Ogilvy's (Tim Robbins) rifle, over which he and Ray wrestle – are no match against ray guns. That the war machines have been long buried, awaiting their moment, clearly relates to former paranoia concerning Reds under the bed and contemporary fears of terrorist sleeper cells, but suggests also civilisation's deep-rooted potential to undermine itself from within.

The broken window precipitates the invasion in the way Jim in *Empire of the Sun* more consciously believes he has prompted war with Japan. Once the assault begins, Ray has to take responsibility. A mirror shot figures his acceptance of the Symbolic. He delivers Rachel (Dakota Fanning) (his 'Ray-child') safely to Mary Ann ('Take care of our kids', she has charged him), and has to release Robbie to his manly destiny. He regains patriarchal respect on both counts from Robbie, who, having survived, greets him with an embrace, and from Mary Ann and her parents. The ending seems bathetic, however, as this successful pursuit of the Lost Mother is a hollow victory, an illusory Imaginary; the marriage is long over and Mary Ann pregnant by another man, while the alien defeat results from harmless bacteria rather than the combined military forces of history's greatest superpower. Irrespective of intercultural and interpersonal conflicts, life, as in *Jurassic Park*, 'finds a way', symbolised by Mary Ann's bulging figure and the green bud on the desiccated branch in the final shot, while Ray remains, as he started: alone.

Self-reflexivity

'Every film is a veritable drama of vision', Stephen Heath, citing *Jaws*, insists (1986: 397). *War of the Worlds* is no exception to Spielberg's self-reflexive highlighting of this. As a representation of social and cultural insecurities (for of course, the protagonist, being a textual construct has no unconscious), the movie implicates its own mechanisms in the fantasy. The preceding Paramount logo materialises out of falling stars, Spielberg's signature motif but here also narratively motivated as (the novel explains) the aliens' descent. Sinister music accompanies the DreamWorks logo, consisting of clouds and a moon that return during the first scenes, the brand name practically screaming for psychoanalytic reading of the projected nightmare. The opening shots blend metaphorically and metonymically like dream condensations. DNA strands, anticipating the strings of invasive alien weed, control bugs within a water droplet that morphs into the Earth, which dissolves into Mars, which in turn becomes a red traffic light, part of a montage of crowded cities, before the entire screen becomes blank as the sun shines into camera, mirroring the projector beam.

Inscribed screens, literal and metaphorical, frame much of the action. TV news reports, largely ignored by the characters, narrate the imminent threat and place the US invasion within a global attack. Passers-by record the brewing storm on pocket cameras and the first human massacre appears on a vaporised victim's camcorder viewfinder. Sunlight shines in a focused beam through the rose window of a church as its façade breaks away. Ray later discovers, along with the viewer, the secret of the lightning via a freeze-framed video in an outside broadcast van. 'You ain't seen nothing yet!' a CBS journalist misquotes *The Jazz Singer* (1927) to Ray: doubly oriented address promising the audience technological marvels of wonder and realism. Screen doors, car windows, a kitchen window with a peanut butter slice adhering to it, and cobwebs frequently come between the camera and protagonists looking off-screen. These inscribe the fourth wall, the movie's screen, allowing its rupture to figure in reverse point-of-view shots. Among these, a mob smashes the car windshield, an off-screen plane crash causes it to explode with flames and a shock wave before the auditorium plunges into darkness, and an alien, the first seen in close-up, pushes through

War of the Worlds – nowhere to hide: the screen explodes

net curtains. Rachel, carried from one horror to another, wide-eyed and alternating between hysteria and catatonia, particularly represents spectatorship. A rectangular patch of light illuminates one eye as she witnesses her father in life-and-death struggle with an older patriarch over a phallic gun; the outcome is so traumatic Ray blindfolds her and the ensuing act occurs behind a closed door. Widescreen-shaped windows in dark cellars, often with light beams flickering through, provide views onto the unfolding catastrophe (notably contrasting with a 'triangular hole' and 'vertical slit' in the novel (Wells 1946: 130)).

As ever, the fantasy is explicitly cinematic and its intertextuality, including allusions most obviously to the film's literary, radio and cinematic precursors, and to Hitchcock's *The Birds*, involves numerous auto-citations. These range across Spielberg's career, and include an alien's fascination with a bicycle, the wheel playing no part in their technology according to Wells, which is also a nod to *E.T.* in the midst of a tense threat scene. Humour plays its part elsewhere, as in the prominent 'No Littering' sign while the first tripod lays waste to the neighbourhood. Particularly noteworthy, however, in a movie that foregrounds special effects, are examples of technique, rendered 'invisible' by comparison – presumably CGI-processed – that in any other context would be breathtaking. The first shot of Ray on the crane arcs seamlessly from an aerial extreme long shot to close in on him, safely encased in glass in the cab. Hand-held camerawork in Ray's house jumps edgily between close-ups on significant details in extended takes, narrating visually without apparent edits. As the family's requisitioned car careens at speed through stalled freeway traffic the camera captures their conversation in a two-minute-and- 23-seconds shot which arcs more than 720 degrees around them, passing through both side rear windows, moving back and forth, up and down, between long shots and medium close-ups, eventually pulling out from the front, craning up and panning around as the car accelerates away. Typically, numerous points of access and levels of address and appreciation exist, with respite from continual psychological assault and opportunities for reflexive and identificatory readings or the *jouissance* of repositioning between them. This is neither mindless bombardment nor unilateral manipulation.

Wells' book, published in serial form in 1897, coincided with early demonstrations of the cinematograph. This new technology, far more than a couple of motor cars and oblique references to experiments with flight, informs Wells' nightmarish vision of twentieth-century scientific-technical rationality. Surveillance, whether 'across the gulf of space', from where humans appear no more than 'infusoria under the microscope' (1946: 9) or atop a war machine is central to the invaders' power. Wells' narrator explicitly uses the word 'camera' in describing the machines (1946: 69, 119), while the imagery surrounding them evokes the flickering of early cinema:

> And this thing I saw! How can I describe it? A monstrous tripod ... A flash, and it came out vividly, heeling over one way with two feet in the air, to vanish and reappear almost instantly as it seemed, with the next flash ... [A] great body of machinery on a tripod stand ... So much I saw then, all vaguely for the flickering of the lightning, in blinding highlights and dense black shadows. (1946: 51)

Fitted like a camera with a pan-and-tilt mounting, 'the brazen hood that surmounted it moved to and fro with the inevitable suggestion of a head looking about it' (ibid.). Recalling that the Lumières' cinematograph doubled as camera and projector, this is strikingly similar to Metz's image of vision as simultaneously projective and introjective, particularly as 'a light-ray, like the beam of a … searchlight' (1946: 40) precedes the Heat-Ray the aliens 'project' (1946: 32).

Aghast spectators complete the inscribed apparatus, their scopophilia, like that of the audience at a horror movie, taking the form of irresistible morbid desire. 'I did not dare to go back towards the pit, but I felt a passionate longing to peer into it' (1946: 27), reports Wells' narrator, while so powerful is Robbie's compulsion to look that he risks his life for the spectacle of the military counter-attack. Loss of self, engulfment by fascination with the object of the gaze, adds the spectator's projective and introjective gaze, voyeuristic in the sense of wanting to maintain mastery by seeing without being seen, to commingle with the opposing currents of the aliens' look. The initial spectacle of the storm conforms to Spielberg's trademark 'solar wind' – a character even attributes it to a solar flare – as washing lines flap and leaves swirl. However, as Ray points out, the current flows unusually towards the eye of the storm, reinforcing the trope that it emanates from the frightened citizens, and rather than project onto their faces it seems to suck light from the bleached cinematography.

The mother of all wars

Part of the tripods' dreamlike monstrosity is their dizzyingly intangible suggestive-ness. On the one hand they are emphatically phallic assertions of voyeurism's simultaneous sadism and masochism. As giant cameras, they have blades in their tripods to impale the spectator-victims whose reflections they are, like that of the protagonist in *Peeping Tom*. One of the most intensely threatening images involves penetration into the cellar of a cobra-like tentacle equipped with a lens and spotlights, recalling a body-penetrating endoscope, which visualises the intrusive, dangerous, sexual power invested in the gaze, the castrating threat implied in reducing its object to just that. (Spectatorship and horror imbricate with sexual difference when Rachel, reflected light flickering over her face, confronts the floating corpses after withdrawing from her father's sight to gain privacy to pee.) Hanging beneath each machine's body at the top of its legs are two testicular baskets, containing its live human food store. These giant, devouring, obscene fathers require emasculation for Ray to secure his place in the Symbolic. In fact, Robbie has earlier argued that if they 'had the balls' they would fight the aliens.

Conversely, before Rachel and Ray's incorporation into the machine its dazz-ling light shaft transfixes them. Medusa-like, with hanging tentacles, the machine exemplifies Barbara Creed's (1989) conception of the monstrous-feminine. Possessing, as MacCabe put it, 'what looks like the largest and most aggressive vagina in the history of the planet' (2005: 8), she is the voracious archaic mother. The vagina dentata links also with menstrual imagery as Ogilvy, the man in the basement, associates the machines' red discharge with reproduction ('fertiliser' he calls it, believing it relates to the red weed). The aliens thus equate with Ray's aggression towards Mary Ann, whose advanced pregnancy highlights motherhood. Having already hacked the end off the one-eyed snake with an axe, he now shows he 'has the balls' when he enters the vagina and withdraws, leaving two hand grenades inside, thereby effecting the only human defeat of a machine. Ray's figured rebirth, as a 'real' man, parallels an alien's on-screen death, continuing the uterine imagery: the machine's waters break and the creature, essentially a smaller version of the body containing it, emerges head first, and dies. From this stew of sexual anger in the midst of Spielberg's darkest fiction, it is a small step to seeing this as representing the wished-for stillbirth of Mary Ann's baby, disavowing Ray's irrevocable exclusion from 'his' family.

Ray's protection of Rachel again illustrates the Talmudic verse from *Schindler's List* – 'Whoever saves one life, saves the world entire' – borne out in the framing discourse that 'neither do men live nor die in vain', part of a holistic environmental message that puts faith in the planet's natural selection to defend itself. Yet this is a bleak outlook when extended beyond evolution of resistance to organisms such as the common cold and applied to human relationships. In saving Rachel, Ray murders in cold blood – the act itself literally *ob*-scene, out of the scene – Ogilvy, another obscene father in Ray's eyes (the act juxtaposed against his castration of the tentacle), who creepily promises to look after Rachel. Ogilvy appears to have no narrative function other than to undergo death by the hero. Ray's actions cancel the value of the *Schindlerjuden*'s survival because 'there will be generations', Cinqué and Adams' appeals to their ancestors in *Amistad*, and Ryan's 'earning' of Miller's death. Plumbing the depths, his ambiguous heroism achieves nothing beyond perpetuating his genes and a futile attempt at protecting Imaginary childhood innocence against power struggles in the Symbolic and the horrors of the Real. He advances out of the sun's low projected rays to deliver Rachel to her family. They don't even invite him in.

CHAPTER TWENTY-FIVE

Munich: bitter fruit on the olive branch

Avner's List

Days after *War of the Worlds'* successful opening a terse statement quietly announced Spielberg had started a film based on the massacre of 11 Israeli athletes during the 1972 Olympics. It opened in the USA less than six months later, after low-key, almost minimal marketing – a review, background feature and exclusive interview with the director in *Time* magazine to support pre-release advertising, but no test, press or industry screenings – and elsewhere fairly quietly in ensuing weeks.

The tenor and positioning of *Time's* materials evoked an old-fashioned documentary 'discourse of sobriety' (Nichols 1991: 3–4). The cover featured the director, solemn in a black polo neck, minus baseball cap, and the headline 'Spielberg's Secret Masterpiece'. This implied a revelatory dimension underlined by the production's surrounding secrecy (itself hardly unusual in Spielberg's career) and claimed high-cultural auteur status. Spielberg declared profit was not his object. Using commercial power again to follow a blockbuster with a personal venture (albeit on widescreen for $70 million or more), he presented *Munich* as his 'prayer for peace' (Schickel 2005a: 66; 2005b: 70). The cover flagged 'Spielberg on why his movies have changed', as if oblivious to the possibility of *Jurassic Park IV* and *Indiana Jones IV* (both confirmed shortly after as projects he intended to direct, even though he had passed *Jurassic Park III* (2001) on to Joe Johnston).

The initial announcement of the forthcoming production of Munich provoked controversy that persisted without DreamWorks' input. *Munich*'s long-contested source book, George Jonas's *Vengeance* (1984), reappeared with a foreword by its protagonist 'Avner', purportedly a Mossad assassin. (The filmmakers reportedly spoke to Avner 'at great length' while shielding his identity (Schickel 2005a: 66); others dismissed him as a fantasist.) Aaron J. Klein, a *Time* journalist who also happens to be an Israeli intelligence officer, published simultaneously with the film's release a book, puffed heavily in the *Time* feature, claiming access to secret documents and interviews with Mossad agents and high-ranking officials. He also appeared in at least two television documentaries timed with *Munich*. Klein offered a different account from Jonas's (in terms of Mossad's motivation and strategy, although not at the level of physical details of the killings), thereby reviving questions about Avner. Yossi Melman and Steven Hartov claimed to have evidence that Avner 'never served in Mossad, or any Israeli intelligence organisation' (2006: 26), but did not share it. Given the premise of *Vengeance* and *Munich* that Avner officially does not exist, and the journalists' unlikely credentials – specialising in 'intelligence affairs' and editing *Special Operations Report* – it hardly takes a conspiracy theorist to sense a smoke screen. 'Leaked' reports that Spielberg, afraid of condoning or condemning Israel's action (Harris 2005), had consulted former President Bill Clinton over the script, and enlisted some of his top aides to influence Jewish-American and Israeli opinion over the movie's reception, reinforced the cachet of a significant cultural and political event. When Jonas lambasted Spielberg's 'humanising' of Palestinian 'demons' more publicity followed (Anthony 2006: 4), not only surrounding the movie but also the book. (Few publishers, after all, would counsel an author merely to provide non-newsworthy endorsement in these circumstances.)

Munich's release coincided with political crisis instigated by the serious illness of Prime Minister and former Major-General Ariel Sharon, under whose leadership *ex talionis* ('an eye for an eye, a tooth for a tooth') had 'become a guiding principle and tool of the Israeli army' (Avner in George Jonas 2006: xiv). Simultaneously militant Islamists won the Palestinian Authority election without a majority. Meanwhile hullabaloo raged over 'extraordinary renditions' abroad of American-held prisoners for torture. This again questioned what 'civilised' conduct is (2006: xiv, 24), just as Golda Meir (Lynn Cohen) in the film argues: 'Every civilisation finds it necessary to negotiate compromises with its own values.' The violence of Middle East politics was prominent as ever, making the film, with its parallels with more recent American policy, a timely intervention.

Pundits who had not seen it again pre-determined a Spielberg film's reception. A Jewish pressure group demanded a boycott well in advance (Corn 2005). Whereas DreamWorks solicitously screened it to relatives of the murdered athletes, who praised its treatment and intent, extreme right-wing pro-Israelis initiated viral opposition predicated less on historical accuracy than political presuppositions. One email, evoking a familiar spectre, urged readers to shun 'this Nazi propaganda movie made by Steven Spielberg in support of Arab murderers', even though in a rare interview Spielberg insisted 'this film was not in any way, shape or form going to be an attack on Israel' (both cited in Freedland 2006: 5). *New York Post* columnist Andrea Peyser predicted either:

(i)   Steven Spielberg is too dumb, too left and too Hollywood (or is that redundant?) to tackle such complex and polarising themes as Islamic fundamentalism and Jewish survival.

(ii)   Spielberg is a decent enough filmmaker to persuade some people that Israel has outlived its usefulness and should – as enemies in Iran maintain – be wiped off the face of the earth. (cited in Corn 2005)

And this is the filmmaker vilified by some for Zionist leanings in *Schindler's List*. Conversely, Abu-Daoud, who admitted masterminding the Palestinian terrorists' operation at Munich, objected to Spielberg's showings for Israeli widows while neglecting Palestinian victims' families (Ascherson 2006: 13). Conflicting opinions gained coverage partly to fill a vacuum created by Spielberg's reticence.

It is evident why the project attracted Spielberg. Aside from its Jewish theme, the moral issue of forceful pre-emption echoes *Minority Report*. The arithmetic of retribution evokes qualms over quantifying and trading lives familiar from *Schindler's List*, *Saving Private Ryan* and, once more, *Minority Report*, in which Burgess intends Lively's murder to safeguard Pre-Crime to prevent further murders. Like *Saving Private Ryan*, *Munich* dramatises a mission that turns personal. Narrative and moral ambiguities inherent in a real-life manhunt in which identities are inevitably changed and events officially never happened or are deliberately obfuscated suggest a darker version of *Catch Me If You Can*, again showing Spielberg's misanthropy: few characters or positions emerge unscathed. Whereas *Catch Me If You Can* is 'Inspired by a true story', *Munich* proclaims itself 'Inspired by real events'. This asserts higher modality yet denies documentary claims. It simultaneously allows for Avner's account to Jonas being as false as critics claim, although no less worth recounting.

Avner's relationship with father figures elaborates a recurrent theme. Carl, the secret agent from *Catch Me If You Can*, returns as Carl the burly Mossad agent similarly seen in phone booths wearing a porkpie hat, distinctive glasses and tightly buttoned suits. Avner's actual father, prominent in the book, remains an unseen presence in the movie. The grotesque 'Papa' (Michael Lonsdale), an international Godfather selling names, services and weaponry to the highest bidder in the name of anarchy but clearly for gain, becomes his surrogate. Other symbolic fathers, such as Mossad and several assassination targets, involve Avner in Oedipal conflicts in which good father and obscene father become indistinguishable, while Avner's doubts grow with his emergence into paternity and eventual need to protect his family from forces he has served.

Munich equally foregrounds motherhood. Avner's wife's pregnancy, mothers and grandmothers on both sides watching the Munich atrocity on television, and the centrality of Meir, as Avner's dispatcher, and of his mother, whose convictions contrast with his nightmares, evoke an Imaginary, associated with the nation and family he initially reveres, that looms close to the Monstrous Feminine.

Moreover, the book presents Avner as movie-obsessed, like Jim in *Empire of the Sun*: 'America had become his whole inner life, his fantasy' (Jonas 2006: 12). Aged 12, Avner moved with his parents from Tel Aviv to Frankfurt – 'more real ... more intense than John Wayne' (2006: 15) – where 'they'd go to see a Hitchcock movie or

Munich – terrorism as media event: Avner and his wife watch the Munich atrocity unfold

sometimes a western. Always an American picture; they were Father's favourites too. It was heaven!' (2006: 18). As a teenager, in a kibbutz, Avner fantasises being Wayne, 'hero and protector of his people, the fastest gun in the Middle East' (2006: 22) an imaginary alter-ego maintained during his Mossad years (2006: 34, 50, 300).

Genre

Munich is adapted from a third-party account based initially (like *Schindler's Ark*) on a meeting with 'a man who had an interesting story to tell' (Jonas 2006: xvii). Unlike *Schindler's List*, however, precise facts cannot be corroborated. Jonas openly concedes his method's limitations, and provides lengthy notes recognising discrepancies between his and other versions. His preface acknowledges inability to match historians' 'rigorous standards':

> Inescapably, for some of my information I was relying upon a single source whom I could not name. Certain details of his story were incapable of verification. I could satisfy myself on other details but would have to alter some of them to protect my informant or my other sources. When basing a story on confidential information, the ideal journalistic practice is to have two sources independently verifying each other: a requirement which in this book I could not always meet. (2006: xvii)

Jonas observes also, however, that this confirms merely that two people say something is true, not that it is true (2006: 363).

Covert operations are by definition unverifiable. Intelligence organisations play convoluted 'games of deception' (2006: 332), to which responses to the book and film, I suggest, further contribute. That reportedly internecine executions within Arab factions might actually have been Mossad missions complicates *Munich*'s story, while Mossad was prepared to take credit for assassinations performed by others (Klein

2006: 134, 246–7). Given this treacherous milieu, it is noteworthy that Klein's book, promoted on its jacket as 'the first full account', informs readers: 'In some cases, for dramatic effect, minor details of certain instances have been changed, in keeping with the known habits and demeanour of participants' (2006: 254). Similarly the documentary, *Munich: Mossad's Revenge*, broadcast the night before *Munich*'s UK release, contains supposed interviews with agents whose 'appearance has been changed and their words spoken by actors'.

Munich's creators called it 'historical fiction' to recognise that as, producer Kathleen Kennedy says, it 'is clearly a thriller from a movie-making standpoint' (Schickel 2005a: 67). The Academy Award-winning documentary, *One Day in September* (1999), had already pieced together and extended known facts about the massacre. Spielberg concentrated on its human and ethical cost, using thriller conventions to reach a mainstream audience. Most reviewers recognised this, ambivalently. 'Whereas *Schindler's List* was a meticulous work of art, *Munich* is much more of a dramatic genre film', writes Andrew Anthony, as much value judgement as description; but he defines it too as 'an action thriller that is also something of a morality tale' (2006: 4). Weaving 'ethical drama into a jet-setting spy thriller', *Munich*, Michelle Goldberg notes, explores how 'vengeance and violence – even necessary, justified violence – corrupt both their victims and their perpetrators' (2006).

French dismisses 'agonising dialogue' about 'rightness', 'guilt' and 'the way they're being morally corrupted by the incessant killing' as 'pure Hollywood' (2006: 14). Yet the film faithfully reproduces this from Jonas – which does not preclude, of course, movies having influenced Avner's account. Given that in the heat of the Beirut machine-gunning, executioners shine torches onto photographs to verify victims' identities, it is inconceivable none experienced misgivings. Accepting that *Munich* is 'avowedly fictionalised', Peter Bradshaw questions the movie's 'attempts to insulate Avner's men from the mucky business of doing business with ideologues and political agencies by having them get all their information from an apolitical French mafia capo: a deeply unlikely invention which is frankly an insult to the intelligence' (Bradshaw 2006: 7). But Jonas plausibly accounts for Papa's organisation, described in the film as 'ideologically promiscuous'. Amid proliferating militancy, Papa promotes a free market in terror, reasoning that most causes are ultimately just and that if factions are going to kill each other anyway they might as well get on with it, thereby destabilising governments – which Papa mistrusts – and providing him with rich pickings (Jonas 2006: 137–41). This, after all, if Papa is fictitious, is not unlike the amorality of international arms trading, legitimate or otherwise.

Munich then, as Richard Schickel insists, 'is, morally speaking, infinitely more complex than the action films it superficially resembles' (2005a: 65). With little agreement over the Israeli-Palestinian conflict, nor the considerably more trivial question of the film's status or genre, *Munich* is another productively ambiguous offering. As a thriller it keys with Jonas's use of focalisation to construct split subjectivity:

> I decided to tell the agent's story looking over his shoulder as it were – hanging it on the double threads of his point-of-view and my own. I used the same method with many of the other individuals in the book. Unlike a first-person narrative,

it enabled me to see events through the eyes of my sources – at times my only evidence – without forcing me to be uncritical of their vision. (2006: xviii)

This dual focalisation disquiets those expecting certainty through unproblematic identification, comforting fiction, undisputed evidence or overt ideological statement. It features in an oddly 'subjective' shot in the first sex scene, which begins with Avner's wife looking desirously towards the camera, even though he has entered her, heavily pregnant, from behind. (Possibly a Hollywood first, this deviation from mainstream notions of the sexualised female body both advances realism claims and draws attention to itself.) After the prologue the status of the Munich reconstructions becomes ambiguous. Are they subjective flashbacks, as the editing suggests – except Avner was not there – or 'objective' drama-documentary to reinforce metonymically the modality of the fiction?

While *Munich* deals with the Mossad myth, deserved or not, that no antagonist was safe from reach, Melman and Hartov considered disturbing

that it is substantially a fiction – which, given Hollywood's influence, may soon be regarded as a definitive account. The troubling question emerging from the film is whether there should be an obligation to historical accuracy in a work of art that portrays real-life figures such as Golda Meir and uses documentary footage to support its thesis. We believe the answer is yes. (2006: 26)

Here they evoke the gullible spectator, unable to distinguish Hollywood thriller from documentary. They claim events are 'more than 30 years' past – not so according to Klein, who recounts assassinations into the 1990s – and claim preposterously that Spielberg could have phoned former Mossad and Black September heads for a definitive account. Neal Ascherson, by contrast, insists 'The Israeli authorities remain unwilling to discuss the operation, still less the men and women who took part' (2006: 12) – who, Klein notes, 'led secret lives even within the Mossad' (2006: 133).

Inaccuracy claims, and fears over confusion, recall recurrent furore surrounding the television hybrids drama-documentary and documentary-drama (Paget 1998: 1), sometimes known as 'faction', of which *Munich* in many respects is a high-budget variant. In television, Andrew Goodwin and Paul Kerr incisively observe, '"drama-documentary" is not a programme category, it is a debate' (1983: 1). Derek Paget argues that 'dramadoc', the predominantly British form, is essentially documentary-based, while docudrama, its American counterpart, is entertainment-driven, although this is not a value judgement.

Debates around *Munich*, and those focusing on Spielberg, concern the individual film less than pre-existing discourses about contentious issues: Middle East politics and, as often with what is frequently termed 'docudrama' for convenience, dramatising factual material. A key moment is Avner's conversation with Ali, the gunman killed when guarding the team's next victim, about Palestinian aspirations. Critics considered this contrived, although again Jonas recounts, albeit less sensationally than the initial standoff in the movie, that Avner's team found themselves sharing a safe house with Palestine Liberation Organisation members. 'Without that exchange, I would have been making a Charles Bronson movie – good guys vs. bad guys and Jews killing Arabs without any context', Spielberg argued (in Schickel 2005a: 67). And this is the heart of the issue. To some the discussion treats both sides as morally equivalent, which does not fit their politics. To some, that it never really happened compromises whatever truth the movie might claim. Docudrama itself is 'problematical', Paget explains, because like *Munich*'s initial caption, 'it openly proclaims both a documentary and a dramatic provenance. This "both/and" claim is often met with a critical refusal, an "either/or" counter-claim' that ends up treating it as 'bad documentary, bad drama, or both' (1998: 1, 3).

As a thriller, *Munich* is not diametrically opposed to documentary. *Munich: Mossad's Revenge* contains along with interviews with named sources and strident voice-over narration, thriller-style reconstructions, documentary and news clips and stills, and dramatic music, structured sensationally with climaxes around commercial breaks. *Munich* similarly includes documentary elements in the form of library footage. This nevertheless undergoes overt mediation. Rather than edited seamlessly into the film's address, it appears on-screens within the diegesis, or in close-up so that television scanning lines are prominent. Despite this, actual documentary material, a typical feature of docudrama, provides exposition and authenticates the narrative without disrupting its flow, anchors action in time and place 'and connects it visibly to its documentary claims' (Paget 1998: 69). Close-ups of poor-quality documentary footage, Paget argues, 'suture' the framing narrative into reality (1998: 74). *Munich* not only includes broadcast television images within its mise-en-scène, sometimes almost as a backdrop to interactions, but reconstructs the reporters' stakeouts to camera that produced them.

Munich does not claim to follow the so-called 'Woodhead doctrine' that treats the form as factual 'journalism, not dramatic art', and insists everything on-screen must have documentation: 'No invented characters, no invented names, no dramatic devices owing more to … creative imagination than to the implacable record of what actually happened' (David Boulton, quoted in Goodwin & Kerr 1983: 29). Nevertheless, referring to another controversial dramatic treatment of Middle East events, the television film *Hostages*, Paget argues: 'The dramadoc form had been used to tell this particular story because, at the inception of the project, it was believed that there was "no other way to tell it"', a phrase from producer Leslie Woodhead. Formulated 25 years before *Munich*, it justifies, Paget continues,

> journalism of the 'last resort', whereby public interest considerations de-manded that a story enter the public domain by this means or not at all. Because there were no cameras present when the historical events represented in the film took place, the extra dimension of dramatic presentation (and, necessarily, speculation) was used to enable the story to be told. The ultimate aspiration … is to make a difference in the historical and political world … by going to places that are originally denied to the camera. (1998: 10)

While describing a different aesthetic and claim to truth, this parallels Spielberg's 'prayer for peace'. One recurrent problem with dramadoc/docudrama, to which *Munich* is subject, is that personalisation of issues, inherent in naturalistic drama, militates against objectivity and detachment in relation to moral and ethical predicaments. *Munich* deals, however, with human implications of policies and prejudices, rather than questioning the rightness of positions. As popular, mainstream experience, Paget argues, there is political potential in engagement and involvement: 'viewers may not even need to be convinced that a film shows exactly how it was, but if they are drawn to [it] at all, and even partially convinced by a "new light" claim, then they will be drawn into ongoing public debate' (1998: 197).

Whereas classical narrative cinema sutures the spectator through identification and produces catharsis, documentary addresses a distant and dispassionate observer (1998: 16). Contradictorily mixing forms enhances the double interpellation – common enough in Spielberg – in *Munich* occasioning either suspicion and rejection or productive tension. Paget hypothesises docudrama's 'ideal spectator', 'seeking to ratify emotionally what he or she already knows intellectually' (a position akin to that which I argued *Schindler's List* offers). The process, Paget suggests, is reversible, with the possibility of an ideal spectator drawn in by voyeuristic pleasure who 'accepts at a fundamental level both the possibility and the provisionality of the form (it might have looked and sounded like this – or it might not)' (1998: 204). Crucially, the partly detached spectator can wonder whether *Munich*'s meaning would differ if the documented (and speculated) events did not look and sound precisely like their screen enactments.

Julia Hallam discerns a 'critically contentious trend', epitomised by *Saving Private Ryan*, whereby Hollywood movies exploring political and social concerns utilise stylistic intertextuality to advance truth claims; this courts accusations of confusing 'fact and fiction, official history and popular memory' (2000: 119). She identifies three variants, each discernible in *Munich*, different from the ironic and consumerist aesthetic of postmodern entertainment. *Locations* that are (or, in *Munich*, artfully appear to be) where events actually occurred provide an ontological referential link between text, public memory and actuality. *Period referencing* appropriates an era's stylistic techniques: *Munich* frequently adopts a 1970s style uncharacteristic of Spielberg, utilising zooms in conjunction with pans, tilts and racking focus, and panning and tracking to link parts of a location. Intertextuality once again is double-edged. Inherent to discourse, it is inevitably central to the effect of the real; yet to the extent it is recognisable it declares textuality. This is particularly apparent in *intertextual referencing*, incorporating other films as 'reference points'. *Munich*'s television footage – much of it recognised from *One Day in September* and, for older spectators, from first-hand memory – affords Spielberg's reconstruction an authenticating iconography. It furthermore intensifies, through the present absence of the cinematic apparatus, the 'photo effect', Barthes' concept described by John Ellis as sometimes 'an almost intolerable nostalgia' and 'an appalling sense of loss and separation' integral to the severance created by the recording technology (1992: 59). This is especially apparent in *Munich*'s moments of double separation: when optimism expressed on diegetic television-screens filters through the irony of knowing the outcome or when a roll call of dead athletes accompanies their living, smiling images in flickering monochrome on an oblique screen, intercut with Mossad's assembling of photographs of its intended targets.

Intertextual referencing also operates consciously and specifically, producing, as always in Spielberg, differential address that itself contributes to ambiguity and hence controversy. As Paget observes, 'the more texts you know, the more likely will diverse texts "show through" the particular text with which you are dealing at the time. This is useful because it … articulates a way of viewing the world through texts' (1998: 134). Thus subtle allusion to a recurring Spielberg reference point – *Dr Strangelove*, a satire on Mutually Assured Destruction, evoked by the Mossad war room with its suspended strip lights – may for some underline *Munich*'s implicit questioning of the utility and morality of retribution. The milk blending with blood and wine after the first assassination recalls Frankenheimer's *The Manchurian Candidate* (1962) – another paranoid thriller concerning shady governmental operations and the power of a monstrous mother. The final sex scene, intercut with the Munich slayings, makes sense intellectually even if it fails dramatically when recognised as a homage to Coppola's *The Godfather*, in which a christening alternates with a killing spree: the life force inextricably linked with violence in a self-perpetuating cycle of corruption. The closing of Coppola's *The Conversation*, when espionage ultimately rebounds on its perpetrators, is recalled when Avner's activities return to haunt him – an eye for an eye – and he slashes apart his mattress and frantically dismantles his phone and television in search of explosives. These allusions overlap with period referencing, as do thematic, structural and stylistic parallels with *Dirty Harry* (1971) and *Death Wish* (1974), the latter explicitly recalled when Ephraim tells Avner, 'You're not … Charles Bronson', a far more problematic comparison than his John Wayne image in *Vengeance*. French (2006) compares Spielberg's Mossad with its representation in the thriller *Les Patriotes* (1994) and notes that Yvan Attal, who starred as a French Jew enlisted by Israel, also plays in *Munich*. As if to remind alert spectators they are watching a film, several auto-citations occur, such as the severed forearm hanging from a fan after the hotel bombing, graphically similar to a horrific moment in *Jurassic Park* but modally very different.

Casting of well-known public stories, Paget notes, entails 'look-alike' performers enhanced by make-up and costume. Whereas in *Munich* the protagonists' identities are unknown, Meir and several Mossad targets 'resemble their real historical counterparts sufficiently for an audience to accept the simulated identity with no significant interruption to the suspension of disbelief necessary to enjoy realist drama' (1998: 76). The casting nevertheless may involve celebrity intertextuality to articulate ways of viewing. Daniel Craig (Steve), announced as the next James Bond, appropriately for a spy thriller, also brings high cultural and political connotations from *Our Friends in the North* (1996), the BBC's most expensive drama serial, and art-house fodder such as *Sylvia* (2003); both dramatised real events. Mathieu Kassovitz (Robert) directed the searing social realist work *La Haine* (1995) and is known from French films with international appeal such as *Amelie* (2001). Ciarán Hinds (Carl) has been long associated with docudrama (notably he starred in *Hostages*). Hans Zischler, a German, and Australians Eric Bana and Geoffrey Rush (best known for *Shine* (1996), another factual dramatisation) complete the ensemble, stressing the international composition of Israeli Jewry and increasing the movie's appeal in various national markets.

'With drama-documentary', a television executive told Paget, '"there's always somebody who doesn't want it made"' (1998: 40). As Klein confirms a CIA and PLO link alleged in the film, efforts to undermine *Munich*'s credibility are unsurprising (2006: 217). A contemporaneous release, *Walk the Line* (2005), which presumably claims to be more than 'inspired by real events', did not provoke debates about accuracy, nor did *The New World* (2005), the events in which have less obvious direct impact on current affairs. Authenticity is questioned only when texts challenge comfortable assumptions.

Self-reflexivity

Self-reflexivity underscores *Munich*'s dialogic relationship with history and fiction. A Jean-Paul Belmondo poster appears prominently during Louis and Avner's negotiations. 'They're movie stars', one of Avner's team complains when the freed Munich terrorists appear on television. Exposition of the kidnapping and several later events, such as the Lufthansa hijacking and a letter bomb campaign against Israeli embassies, occurs on television screens in Israeli and Palestinian homes and cafes, on monitors in an outside broadcast control room and viewfinders of news teams' massed cameras. The Munich outrage, the defining moment of modern-day terrorism, was deliberately a media event to spotlight Palestine (Klein 2006: 34). Over 900 million watched, including the captors themselves who became aware of police approaching from live coverage of the intended rescue. Spielberg memorably reinforces the point by juxtaposing within a single shot the iconic image of a ski-masked terrorist stepping onto the balcony on a monochrome television with his identical action, seen from indoors, reconstructed simultaneously in colour within the movie diegesis.

As suggested already, this dimension is apparent in the book, and may have contributed to Spielberg's interest in adapting it. Ephraim's response to Avner and Steve for breaching their rules of engagement to execute Carl's assumed killer, a *femme fatale* worthy of any thriller, is 'Maybe in the movies' (Jonas 2006: 301). The complex funding, logistics, location scouting, playacting, choreography, procurement, and direction of assassinations – even their necessary secrecy – recounted in some detail by Jonas, recall filmmaking (2006: 110, 128–9). A central aspect of *Munich*'s visual style parallels how, during the agents' training described in the book, 'They were being taught how to use all reflecting surfaces – store windows, car doors – as mirrors so as to be constantly aware of what was going on around them' (2006: 44).

Such image systems and metaphors, present throughout Spielberg's work, again transcend formalism and problematise the spectator's position in relation to the movie and events portrayed. The squad's first hit, the poet Zwaiter, gives a talk on the relationship of narrative to survival. At the risk of trivialising terrible real events, one could argue that their obsession with revenge, or even more that of their paymasters, manifests desire to master loss through repetition of trauma, an extreme parallel with the process of cinematic pleasure. Sexualisation of their violence pathologises the Mossad killers. It remains unclear whether they are sadistic as a result of previous trauma (associated with shared experience of Jewish history) or become warped by their actions. The Dutch woman's horrible death, in the manner of Mickey Spillane, indicates their depravity in concurrence with Robert's declining the unauthorised mission on grounds of wanting to remain righteous. Their actions degrade them as much as their victims, to whose level retribution sinks them. Hans, drunk, laments, 'I wish I had let you close up her housecoat.' Ascherson considers this execution 'humiliating for the watcher' (2006: 12), while for Quinn it is 'indefensible as anything you'll see in an Asian gangster movie' (2006: 6). But killers in those movies rarely express remorse. The scene arguably constitutes further self-reflexivity: Spielberg did not have to show the disturbing frontal view of the dead woman for audiences to realise what the killers have done. But without it their behaviour would be less problematised and less compromised, along with the tricky issue of turning such events into morbidly fascinating narrative spectacle, which any audiovisual coverage, from the original television broadcasts from Munich onwards, can hardly avoid.

Munich contains Spielberg's usual inscriptions of the apparatus. Robert's toy Ferris wheel (recall the full-size versions in *1941* and *A.I.*) resembles a movie reel. As in *Peeping Tom*, there is a close-up on it, accompanied by projector-like whirring, immediately before his life ends violently, if inadvertently, by his own hand. Prime Minister Meir in her cabinet room sits in a projected beam, as does Papa during his last phone call to Avner. A flashback to Munich materialises on a DreamWorks cloudscape, Avner's projection on the rectangular surface of the airliner porthole as he flies to his mission in Geneva. The horrors that materialise seem very immediate in comparison with the news coverage shown, although Avner was not there. Diegetic sounds fade to silence at key moments, as in *Saving Private Ryan*, enhancing psychological realism and emphasising textuality. Papa's household, traversed by light shafts when Avner encounters him, is followed by Avner looking back through the car window at an unattainable Imaginary after he, who was himself sent to a kibbutz, is 'excluded' by Papa: 'We'll do business. But you aren't family.' Steve's image, refracted through a ribbed glass door after Robert's death, is an expressionist projection of Avner's anxieties and disintegration. Avner's reflection in a kitchen showroom window, representing the Imaginary comfort and domesticity he craves, is joined by a hallucination of Robert, quickly replaced by Louis, returning him to the Real and subjection to Symbolic obligations.

Artistically motivated flourishes either enhance classical continuity or impede its flow if noticed, such as Mossad's accountant blowing dust off his files bridging a cut to drifting rubbish as Avner and Ephraim walk by the sea. The first scene showing Avner in bed with his wife ends as he pulls the sheet over his head – blanking out the image – prior to his official disappearance as he signs away his rights and identity. Hyperrealism – spurting blood and smoking bullet wounds – fascinates and repels, occasioning the contradiction, or *jouissance*, of simultaneous, or uncertainly alternating, Imaginary and Symbolic relations.

Paget maintains that combining fictional form with dramatised real events challenges suspension of disbelief and interpellates the spectator as both thinking and feeling, moving in and out of the Imaginary (1998: 201–4). As I have suggested, throughout this book, this is fundamental to the pleasure of Spielberg's films. It is a subject position that allows contradictions, unlike that of the Classic Realist Text. Docudrama often exists precisely to re-open unresolved issues and hence does not rule out progressive potential. *Munich*'s final shot, for example, showing the World Trade Center, evokes the photo effect; it therefore declares artifice and with it confronts the spectator, leaving unanswered questions about the point of including it.

Spielberg's archetypes – the Imaginary, restoration of the family, Oedipal conflict – reappear curiously. Avner having been 'abandoned' in a kibbutz, his wife suggests: 'Now you think Israel is your mother.' Meir, a wise, sensitive matriarch, tough and determined yet small and vulnerable, knows Avner's mother, emphasising Israel's closeness and symbolic status as 'motherland'. His mother in turn personifies Zionism when she tells Avner proudly he is what she and other Holocaust survivors 'prayed for'. Future Israeli Prime Minister Ehud Barak's participation wearing drag during the Beirut killings (a well-documented fact) bizarrely convolutes the state/mother conflation.

'Family matters', Meir ambiguously says when explaining her non-attendance at the athletes' funerals because of her sister's death. Is she asserting 'family is important' or acknowledging 'family obligations'? Either way, 'family', far from idealised, is complicated. At the outset, when American athletes help the Black September gang over the compound gates, instinctive 'universal' human cooperation prevails, contrary to loyalties, alliances and divisions that drive the narrative. The act ironically demonstrates the law of unintended consequences that colours subsequent events.

Like *Schindler's List*, *Munich* does not treat Jews as a homogenous community. Relationships between family, nation, state, ethnicity, politics and identity are problematised when, as in *Vengeance*, Avner is described not simply as an Israeli but a *Yekke*, of assimilated Western European roots – an 'outsider' – as opposed to Galicianers originally from Eastern European ghettoes (Jonas 2006: 23–5). The multinationalism of Avner's team – German, Belgian, South African and Ukrainian, which permits them to operate discreetly in Europe – underlines the point.

The only families seen, other than distraught relatives of both the Israeli athletes and the Black September terrorists, are those Avner destroys (the second target with his wife and daughter in Paris; those, including a wife who is killed, with the targets in Beirut); subsequently Avner with his, although he misses most of his daughter's infancy; and Papa's extended household. That Avner moves his family, and eventually himself, from Israel to New York sits uneasily with Zionism's agenda of establishing and defending a homeland. Ephraim, an older, paternal authority, eventually refusing to accept Avner's traditional Jewish offer of hospitality, repudiates Avner and his qualms. Meanwhile, Avner's Imaginary alternative to his horrific mission – he has told his wife in the maternity room: 'You're the only home I have' – represented in the kitchen showroom he returns to gaze into, is quashed when she says of their New York apartment: 'The kitchen's too big.'

Avner cooking gourmet meals at the head of his team, a virtual family, clearly parallels Papa. Papa's self-delusion allows him to claim, noticing Avner's 'butcher's hands', like his own, that these signify 'gentle souls', an affinity between them. Family and home equate with closeness to the land. 'Papa was a rolling stone', sings Steve nervously before one bombing, 'Wherever he went there was his home' – a throwaway detail like the radio request in *E.T.* that underscores absent fatherhood, but here also recalls Jewish statelessness before Israel. Avner in New York at the end is raking a vegetable patch when Ephraim calls. Ali's declaration, 'We want to be nations – home is everything', follows Avner asking whether he misses his father's olive trees. Papa's garden full of fruit, flowers and sunshine parallels the good life, the Promised Land, for which Avner is fighting. Like Israel, guards patrol it. It is a corruption, an abomination. To do business, Avner negotiates compromise with his principles, preparing offal for Papa (which presumably he also eats), contravening kosher dietary regulations. If ethnicity rooted in religion is the basis of Israel's fiercely contested nationhood, strategic abandonment of its principles is no light matter. Meir's speech about negotiating compromise either renders her sinister – prepared to compromise sacred values – or indeed compromised, hence essentially good, as soft focus on her suggests. However, a photograph of her with a laughing Richard Nixon emphasises her political status but associates her with another leader whose compromising of the highest values was his downfall.

Papa, like Avner's mother, was traumatised by family deaths in World War Two. He echoes Meir's greeting to Avner, 'How is your father? How is your family? Are they well?' An obscene father, attentive yet deadly, he embodies the super-ego's repressed dark side, in other words Avner's doubts, and contrasts with the Mossad chief, General Zamir, who on first meeting Avner declares: 'I don't remember you. Of course, I know your father.' Oedipal implications of Avner's activities – exterminating those who would symbolically castrate Israel – are apparent in that Zwaiter and the second target Mahmoud Hamshari, in reality in their thirties, are cast as middle aged. The Oedipal imbroglio further complicates uncertainty over whether Louis deliberately double-books the Athens safe house to PLO operatives out of rivalry with Avner for his apparent place in Papa's affections, or on Papa's orders as punishment for working for a government in the Beirut raid, using information his organisation supplied. The ultimate patriarch, Papa seems omnipotent and omniscient. He knows Avner's name and ambiguously promises, 'No harm will come to you from me' (which does not rule out Louis or another client).

Politics

Munich's postmodernism consists not in superficial pastiche overlaying internally consistent realism; rather self-deconstruction through heteroglossia. It offers not an 'anything goes' of emptied signifiers, nor propaganda for a fixed position, but a post-9/11 engagement with real uncertainties. Objections to the film's politics express made-up minds. They monologically impose fixed agendas. As *Munich* enters 'perhaps the most intensely-disputed conflict in the world' (Freedland 2006: 5), this is unremarkable. Nevertheless, some of those views require consideration to demonstrate how *Munich* parleys them.

Schindler's List ended with allegedly pro-Zionist sentiment; it stressed continuity between surviving Jews and contemporary Israel to the tune of 'Jerusalem the Golden'. *Munich* seriously questions Israel's policies. Spielberg was criticised, amid expectations of excessively pro-Israeli tendencies, for recognising that some Mossad victims were, as he put it, even if living double lives, 'reasonable and civilised too' (quoted in Schickel 2005a: 66). Conversely, Joseph Massad, a professor of Arab politics, unequivocally labels Avner's team a 'terrorist cell' and protests that Spielberg 'humanise[s]' them

(2006: 15). The movie's core is indeed the dawning recognition of the ambiguity of 'counter-terrorism'. The phrase equally implies *action against* terrorism and an opposing force that *uses* terrorism, even if Jonas insists these 'inhabit two different moral worlds' (2006: 345). As Klein comes close to suggesting, counter-terrorism shares terrorism's goals: propaganda and fear (2006: 18, 108). In Spielberg's movie the post-Munich retaliation is, one general says, 'not just a publicity stunt'; it is clearly stated Israel wants everyone to know it will protect itself.

The world would be simpler, with fewer moral qualms, if terrorists were not human, just as it would be nice to think Nazis were a different species. But the accusation that Spielberg 'humanises' any 'demon' (Jonas's allegation) misses the point in a film – and arguably an oeuvre – so misanthropic that humans are irredeemably flawed. And whatever one thinks of Mossad's executions, to deny humanity in those who perpetrate them and those targeted would diminish the enormity of events portrayed. Klein's unsentimental inside account humanises Mossad's targets – the first described is eliminated while planning to 'surprise his wife, Dima, and their three children with [a] new car' (2006: 6) – yet represents the agency as coldly efficient, concerned 'to fulfil the task, not analyse it' (2006: 118). Some operatives are doggedly persistent for personal reasons (2006: 10). Their mission combines prevention, deterrence and revenge, but Klein accepts that revenge was central (2006: 12–13, 2006: 107). In *Munich* the defence chiefs' first meeting makes clear that already sixty Arabs have died in retaliatory attacks.

Munich strives to maintain detachment, challenging the spectator to reach a conclusion. Inappropriate expectations of Hollywood heroism and villainy, or of authoritative documentary exposition, cause critics to detect unacceptable bias. Arabic dialogue subtitled into English in Munich makes Black September seem foreign – but then so is Hebrew, spoken in Mossad headquarters, during the same sequence. Avner's conversation with an imminent target on a hotel balcony emphasises common humanity and the possibility of dialogue. This actually occurs in the safe house when Ali states the PLO position – 'We want to be nations. Home is everything' – and in the compromise over music on the radio.

From a pro-Israeli position, Jonas distinguishes the mission's 'rightness' from its 'usefulness' and the utility of counter-terrorism generally (2006: 335, 339). The debate surrounding morality in the film was already waged in its source book 22 years previously, as was the question of the narrative's veracity (2006: 341–56). Klein too proclaims 'utility' while ducking the issue of 'justness' as 'well beyond the scope' of his account (2006: 247). Yet these are precisely issues that the film, combining intellectual and emotional affect and alternating Symbolic and Imaginary involvement, raises without offering answers.

Klein has no doubt about Mossad's effectiveness in preventing attacks (2006: 173). The real Mossad in his account, however, is more ruthless and less cautious than *Munich*'s fictionalisation suggests (2006: 137, 167, 168, 220), and he does not shy from calling their methods murder (2006: 109). Klein stresses the emphasis on protecting innocents in attacks (2006: 107), but implies public relations drove this as much as moral scruples (2006: 108).

When Spielberg shows Avner in a low-angle telephoto shot on the hotel balcony the composition unmistakably recalls the famous Associated Press photograph of a hooded Munich terrorist. This does not *assert* moral equivalence but, as in mirroring structures in *War of the Worlds*, invites consideration of the possibility. Similarly, Israeli commandos changing clothes after landing in the Lebanon raid parallel the Munich terrorists after traversing the gates at the start. Jonas emphatically does not liken the assassins to terrorists, although they become equally fanatical (2006: 268), and he reports them debating the distinction, with some of them indifferent to it (2006: 244). This pre-empts certain highly placed Israelis and friends of Israel who accused *Munich* of 'incorrect moral equation', such as Leon Wieseltier trenchantly insisting: 'it is worth pointing out that the death of innocents was an Israeli mistake but a Palestinian objective' (quoted in Freedland 2006: 5). The film takes pains to make this clear by stressing the team's efforts to protect innocents, such as Hamshari's daughter, and its downplaying of a mistaken assassination by another squad in Lillehammer. (Contrary to some accusations of pro-Israeli bias, the movie does not overlook Lillehammer completely, for those who know about it: the name appears among the cities from which 'Munich' emerges in the title graphics, a design replicated in the print advertising.)

Debates about distortion and bias could continue endlessly, missing the points that no representation is neutral and that *Munich* is not concerned with supporting one side or the other but with exposing an endless cycle of violence. Ascherson objects that, although some Palestinians are presented sympathetically and given a voice, albeit briefly, before being executed, 'apart from some shots of families watching television as the Munich tragedy unfolds, the Palestinians we see are almost exclusively terrorists' (2006: 13). But other than Avner's wife and child and the Munich victims, almost every Israeli shown is either an assassin or a supporter of the policy. In fact Spielberg presents Zwaiter's 'public persona' that Mossad 'did not buy into' (Klein 2006: 119) – gentle, civilised, reasonable, polite, amusing – but does not go as far as Klein who unequivocally states, 'Looking back, his assassination was a mistake' (2006: 123). Hamshari and his French wife passionately put the PLO case to Robert, posing as a journalist, and cite recent (post-Munich) bloodshed at the hands of Israel. Klein shows Israel in arguably a far worse light than Spielberg, whose film is about 11 lives for 11 lives, in observing of the two-day attack on south Lebanon after Munich, that 'None of those killed [45 alleged terrorists] or captured [16 Palestinians] had any covert or operational affiliation with Black September' (2006: 95). Revenge was less discriminating than the film suggests: 'Anyone vaguely connected to a terrorist organisation or act was immediately placed on the top of a slippery slope; assassination waited below', depending on accessibility (2006: 111), the aim being 'to create a sense of permanent threat in the minds of Palestinian operatives and potential inductees' (2006: 116).

Steve's conclusion, 'The only blood that counts for me is Jewish blood' – a hard-line position uncomfortably mirroring that which spawned the Holocaust – is one position in a debate, not that of all Israelis and not the film's. 'By revealing Israel's internal dissent', Jonathan Freedland argues, pro-Israeli artists, such as Spielberg, show the nation 'in its best light' (2006: 5). Israel has never officially accepted responsibility for assassinating PLO members blamed for Munich. While times may have changed, or not, reflection on past deeds and current policies must be a prerequisite for progress.

Klein argues that Israel considered the assassinations effective in reducing attacks on Israeli targets abroad (2006: 208), although others attribute this to Palestine gaining recognition (2006: 210). Ephraim unsurprisingly puts the Israeli case when he tells Avner: 'If these guys live, Israelis die. Whatever doubts you have.' He argues, 'Why cut my fingernails? They'll grow back' – a verbal refutation of a visual image of Ali Hassan Salameh, split into multiple reflections like a hydra, during Avner and Steve's abortive attempt at shooting him.

In *Munich: Mossad's Revenge*, Barak, who led the Beirut raid, states that some younger officers had voiced doubts. Ankie Spitzer, a Munich victim's widow, expresses her lack of sympathy with the killings and poses the question Avner asks, why the alleged perpetrators could not be captured and tried. The contradictions *Munich* embodies are less to do with the representation itself, inevitably attacked, and more to do with the paradox it dramatises, nowhere more apparent than in Meir's speech to a special gathering of the Israeli parliament one week after the atrocity:

> From the blood-drenched history of the Jewish nation, we learn that violence which begins with the murder of Jews, ends with the spread of violence and danger to all people, in all nations ... We have no choice but to strike at terrorist organisations wherever we can reach them. That is our obligation to ourselves and to peace. (cited in Klein 2006: 100–1)

Munich turned the spotlight on events Israeli leaders would rather keep quiet. Klein acknowledges that Zwaiter's death provoked an announcement that 'Fatah [the Palestinian militant force] stresses again that the pursuit and assassination of our fighters will only increase its determination to carry on with its struggle and revolution' (2006: 124). In *Munich*, Avner's team discuss Carlos the Jackal and the rise of new, more ruthless forms of terrorism. Avner concludes, 'There's no peace at the end of this.'

The myth of Mossad's effectiveness and tenacity equally suits Israel and Palestinian organisations involved in in-fighting (Klein 2006: 243). Truth is unlikely ever to emerge or criticism concerning the film's authenticity to be definitively contestable. Whether Avner really existed is spurious. Events outside his direct experience are already in the public domain. Divergences from competing accounts are minimal (whether a bomb was inside a telephone or the table underneath) and alternative versions provide no higher degree of certainty. *Munich* acknowledges arguments and facts on both sides and on examination confirms a striking attempt at balance. Without proposing an alternative – that is not the role of art – or seriously questioning the necessity of Avner's team's actions (although certainly their effectiveness), *Munich* nevertheless highlights the human and moral cost of such operations carried out, not only by Israel, in the name of freedom and civilisation. It is important that the horror of both sides' activities is brought home in the aftermath of the hotel bombing, machine-gun executions in Beirut and spurting bullet holes in the Dutch assassin's naked body, as well as in the Munich atrocity. Avner's mother, who has stated earlier, 'I look at you and I know everything you do', does not want to discuss his activities, declaring herself just thankful for 'a place on earth'. She and Papa represent every comfortable, 'apolitical' individual who inhabits an economy heavily reliant on arms dealing or who would rather not know what violence governments perpetrate in the name of freedom.

CHAPTER TWENTY-SIX

Audiences, subjectivity and pleasure

Reading Spielberg

Mainstream cinematic pleasure depends on *active* subject positioning, determined by interaction between specific textual strategies and discourses always already in play. Barthes' assertion that 'writable' texts 'make the reader no longer a consumer, but a producer of the text' (1974: 3) now extends to all textual encounters: 'works are made to mean through the process of reading' (Allen 1987: 75). Accepted wisdom concerning passive spectatorship, assuming classical narration to be 'invisible', has ceded to cognitivist notions of mental schemata cued by narrational devices. These processes are unconscious insofar as narratives obey extrinsic (such as generic) norms, already internalised by the spectator, and intrinsic norms based on the primacy effect in that classical narration is typically consistent (Bordwell *et al.* 1985: 37).

That preferred readings invite acceptance of positions as a function of intelligibility replaces belief that positioning results directly from interpellation, which unhelpfully conflated spectator as audience member with a textual effect. Examples include Spielberg's direct address to cinephiles, through self-reflexivity and overt intertextuality, which occurs without explicit marks of enunciation, yet dramatically inflects the films' status and meaning. Nevertheless other readings are possible (indeed more prevalent). These range from wide acceptance of the films as uncomplicated entertainment, through negotiated readings (for example, Walker's identification of E.T. as 'a

Being of Colour' (Jaehne 1986: 60)), to oppositional readings that deem them symptomatic of cultural malaise. Moreover, *all* readings are variously preferred, negotiated and oppositional, in differing combinations at different points, rather than monologically one of these, and with varying degrees of consciousness. Theory increasingly 'distinguishes between the subject positions proposed by texts and the "social subject" who may or may not take up that position' (Bennett & Woollacott 1987: 229).

Despite abandonment of crude interpellation to explain positioning, Louis Althusser's insights remain valuable. The human individual is no longer the prior constituting subject, the unitary consciousness that creates or stores knowledge of the world, society, history, the self (and texts). Rather, interaction between contesting psychosexual processes and social discourses constructs the subject. Colin MacCabe's classic realist text is questionable precisely because it posits fixed and limited inherent meanings passively accepted by readers within the subject position offered. Stephen Heath argued that constructing and placing the subject in social and ideological formations is one and the same interminable process, each social encounter offering another imaginary mirror (1986). Any single interaction (as with a text, if reading is reducible to anything as simple as a 'single interaction') will not therefore automatically have significant lasting effect – hardly the belief out of which models of interpellation grew.

Textual negotiations position subjects, comprising multiple discourses in process, in 'unstable, provisional and dynamic' ways (Morley 1980: 166), the negotiating subject being the residual sum of a lifetime's countless other positions. Otherwise every spectator would read identically and critical debate would be redundant. A further complication is intertextuality: texts too consist of interwoven discourses each offering its own position. Reading becomes a matter of 'consistency-building' through which subjectivity in process assigns meaning to the text's sequential stimuli (Allen 1987: 81).

This implies each reading is unique, creating its own meaning. Nevertheless, certain discourses dominate in social interaction and construction of subjectivity, allowing for broad congruence of meaning without which attempts at communication would be futile. Attitudes, knowledge and competencies constitute 'members' resources' of the various discursive communities individuals inhabit (Fairclough 1989). David Morley points out that any individual is the site of 'articulation of different, contradictory subject positions or interpellations', such as the worker who 'can be interpellated as "national subject" by the television discourses of the dominant news media, but as "class/sectional" subject by the discourses of his/her trade union organisation or co-workers' (1980: 165, 166). Further examples include conventions whereby texts cue readers to perform acts of interpretation, and, more specifically, the 'cine-literacy' that self-reflexive readings of Spielberg demand. Because no two readers have the same discursive history, a 'preferred reading' is no more than an ideal construct, albeit one over which there is reasonable agreement.

'Preferred meaning' itself requires problematisation, as it is often treated as a textual effect. In practice, as my questioning of dominant readings of Spielberg implies, preferred meanings are almost invariably defined paratextually, in marketing, publicity and reviewing, as well as in more general discourses around the subject matter. *Jurassic Park*, for example, was as much a *constituent* of popular understandings of genetic engineering as a *reflection* of such debates (as if these somehow occurred elsewhere in a 'real world' untainted by the 'escapism' of entertainment).

Identification

Members' resources determine marketing, production and reception of films. Specified audiences are routinely targeted, products tailored to their tastes and interests. Desire to see a film begins with acceptance of interpellation – recognition of one's image as potential audience in promotion and publicity – together with creation of a narrative image. The latter synthesises experience of previous examples from the same star, genre or director and from other discourses around the subject matter (primarily encountered in different media similarly targeted towards one's socio-economic, age and interest groups). Spielberg's blockbusters, contrary to much contemporary Hollywood practice, cater for a wide audience, offering different pleasures to children (for the last decade much less so), teenagers, parents, 'serious' adult filmgoers and knowledgeable fans, which partly explains their profitability. Furthermore, blanket promotion, comparatively cheap per capita, exploits this potential and supports more specialised marketing to targeted sub-groups, and creates a media 'event'.

Cinema-going entails *social* identification – cultural construction of the self as Tom Cruise fan, as boyfriend who remains cool during horror films, as *Gone With the Wind* fan who has seen it 27 times and knows the dialogue by heart, as art-house patron who eschews the dubious pleasures of mainstream fodder. *Spectatorial* identification, a major component of pleasure, is highly complex, multiple and fractured, constituting different spectators differently as subjects through the same film. Metz's primary and secondary identification (with the apparatus, and thereby with on-screen characters) have since the 1990s fragmented into much more subtle, provisional and fluid relationships, delineated in terms such as point-of-view versus viewpoint, involvement, engagement, investment, structure of sympathy, alignment, allegiance, keying (Branston 2000: 144–5) and focalisation. Whatever the refinements, identification with fictional protagonists involves conventions such as shot/reverse-shot structures, characters' centrality in narratives, narration of more or less information than characters possess, and coded behaviour and appearance. Such formal features are themselves interpreted within extra-textual reading formations, as controversies over alleged stereotyping in *The Color Purple* and *Schindler's List* confirm. My best example occurred when watching *Full Metal Jacket* (1987) in a provincial cinema with a Friday night audience comprising mostly adolescent males. A character who obviously (to me) existed as a negative critique of the *Rambo* image – a macho Sylvester Stallone look-alike, complete with bandana and bullet belts, whose bigoted aggression and individualism repeatedly jeopardised his platoon – was accepted wholeheartedly as the hero by a vociferous part of the audience, who cheered his every action. They were not going to allow such trivialities as narrative logic or the foregrounded presence of a sensitive, angst-ridden protagonist to interfere with peer group definition of appropriate reaction to a war movie. This demonstrates the difficulty of ascribing preferred meanings to the text, and illustrates the problems when director and audience have few members' resources in common other than genre conventions.

Fantasy's imbrication with wish fulfilment offers the spectator as subject of the enunciation a position in the imaginary scene as protagonist, 'a sense of seeing the constituent parts of the spectator's own psyche paraded' (Ellis 1992: 43). According to Rosemary Jackson, in fantasies 'subjects are unable to separate ideas from perceptions, or to distinguish differences between self and world' (1981: 50): symptoms familiar from Spielberg's protagonists, whether in films that fit the fantasy genre or that feature protagonists who fantasise to escape suffering and sustain desire. Jackson continues by discussing fantasies about 'doubles or multiple selves' (that recurrent Spielberg theme) in which 'the *idea* of multiplicity' – interpellation into different discursive formations and the desire to regress through the Mirror Phase – 'is no longer a metaphor, but is literally realised, self transforms into selves' (ibid.).

Identification with main characters relates fulfilment of their desires to partial fulfilment of the spectator's own. The recurrent theme of 'an ordinary man [sic] in extraordinary circumstances', Michael Pye and Lynda Myles suggest, 'may be why certain Spielberg films have so extraordinarily wide an appeal' (1979: 226). More specifically, Spielberg's favouring of subjective shots, aligning spectatorial vision with protagonists', facilitates identification and may be an important factor in the films' emotional power. Identification with seeing itself precedes identification with characters. Emotional impact resulting from Spielberg's conflation of the spectator's look with the protagonists' is, moreover, squared through reaction-shots of inscribed audiences that cue, or at least legitimise, responses to crucial re-enactments of the Mirror Phase. Within this standard Hollywood practice, Spielberg devotes almost as much attention to reaction-shots as to the objects of the 'audience's' gaze (be they Neary's disappearance into the mothership during Jilly and Barry's re-union, Elliott's farewell to E.T., Celie's reunion with her sister and children or Jim's with his parents, Schindler's departure or Ray's final embrace with Robby).

Robert B. Zajonc (1960) reported that other people's mere presence produces heightened physiological arousal in crowd members (confirmed by Schapiro & Leiderman 1967). 'Heightened arousal,' however, 'is not the same as an emotional state. An emotional state needs some *content*, euphoria, anger or whatever' (Gahagan 1975: 132). I suggest the films' fantasy elements provoke emotion, while identification with the inscribed audience releases the spectator's sense of identification with the actual surrounding audience, otherwise disavowed by the voyeuristic situation – darkness, immobility, comparative silence. (This presupposes, in absence of empirical evidence, both that a represented crowd elicits similar physiological responses to membership of a real crowd, and that such presence has the same effects on individuals in the viewing situation as elsewhere.)

The spectator is inescapably involved in regressive mechanisms, denied a position outside the relay of looks. (Refusal to participate pre-empts spectatorship.) These identifications are precisely how classic realism supposedly aligns the imputed reader in ideology. Yet at such moments Spielberg's films evidence artificiality, foreground the apparatus, which they always invoke in relation to perception and desire, and narrate self-consciously. One might speculate that the disavowal thus invited is why critics so easily accuse Spielberg of sentimentality – for of course *they* are not 'taken in', without realising that no one else is. Yet, in fact, they really are: such a dismissive term (why 'sentimentality' rather than 'emotion'?) asserts a distancing from their own response and thus superiority to the film and its popular reception.

Analysis and reflection reveal ways in which emotional empathy is elicited. These are primordial yet at times astoundingly sophisticated in execution. For example, empathy channelled through inscribed audiences may have much to do with 'postural echo' (a technique consciously used in counselling on the basis of body-language research): their situation, grouped together yet apart from the focus of attention, looking raptly upwards into the 'solar wind', echoes the spectator's. In *E.T.*, Elliott's mutual empathy with the alien ('He feels his feelings') echoes the spectator's empathy with the screen image, explicitly when Elliott enacts telepathically the scene E.T. watches from *The Quiet Man* (1952). When Elliott cuts his finger and E.T.'s finger glows empathetically, the alien's pupils dilate as he heals the wound. Part of the uncanny realism of the puppetry (no actor could perform so convincingly), this shows how Spielberg deliberately exploits unconscious responses to non-verbal communication – as have Disney animators for decades. This involves nothing inherently sinister or manipulative: the device is clearly visible, and demonstrates care taken to deliver the experience promised.

The gap between Imaginary identification and simultaneous awareness of the text as Symbolic enhances emotion by establishing conflict between credulous and incredulous positionings of the spectator, who is moved, astonished that he or she is moved, enthralled by excessive spectacle, and in awe at the power of the apparatus to produce such an effect. Just as laughter originates in contradiction, the impossibility of the wish fulfilments in Spielberg provokes confusion, resulting in tears and joy – or accusations of manipulation from intellectuals terrified by momentary loss of self-control, which makes them no different from the rest of the audience whose interests they otherwise profess to represent.

Self-reflexivity and spectatorship

'Laying bare the device' relates to connoisseurship encouraged by references to other films, in that only a minority might perceive it (see Bordwell *et al.* 1985: 22). Roger Corman, under whose mentoring several of Spielberg's 'Movie Brat' peers began, encouraged 'two-tiered' films including 'special grace notes for insiders ... for the cognoscenti, and soaring, action charged melody for the rest' (Carroll 1982: 74). Spielberg's auto-citations range from a brief but overt moment when Elliott plays with a *Jaws* toy in *E.T.* to *Empire of the Sun*'s subtle location shot when a bomber tail plane compositionally echoes a shark's fin. Umberto Eco proposes the term 'metacult' to explain when E.T. is mistakenly attracted to a child dressed as an alien from *The Empire Strikes Back*:

> Nobody can enjoy the scene if he [sic] does not share, at least, the following elements of intertextual competence:
> (i) He must know where the second character comes from (Spielberg citing Lucas),
> (ii) He must know something about the links between the two directors,
> (iii) He must know that both monsters have been designed by Rambaldi and

that, consequently, they are linked by some form of brotherhood.

The required expertise is not only intercinematic, it is intermedia, in the sense that the addressee must know not only other movies but all the mass media gossip about movies. This ... presupposes ... cult has become the normal way of enjoying movies. (1987: 210)

The films reward 'being in the know' – again, paradoxically, re-inscribe the spectator as subject of the enunciation at moments of disengagement from the Imaginary. The spectator feels part of a special (extratextual) community, whereas in fact hundreds of thousands of others enjoy similar identification; what is thus celebrated *en masse* is (individual, secretive, voyeuristic) knowledge of spectatorship.

Annette Kuhn notes that 'pastiche as enunciation proposes for the spectator a position of stability and mastery' (1990: 179). This postmodern effect sounds remark-ably like the classic realist text thesis. An important difference, however, is that classic realism allegedly 'places' the spectator in that position, whereas postmodern spectators *approach* the text with pre-existing knowledge and confidence. As Graeme Turner observes, the 12 to 24 age group comprising the majority of moviegoers 'seems to be a group for whom knowledge of the latest movies may well be of some social or subcultural importance' (1988: 95). Add to that, emergence of 'boomer audiences', 'the strong new audience segment, approximately 32 per cent of American society, 43 to 56 years old, empty-nesters with time and money and strong appetites for interest-ing films' (Filmprofit 2005) – the 1970s audience grown up – and sophistication, experience and involvement balance the jeremiads about childishness and spectacle over narrative.

A.I., Minority Report and, to an extent, *The Terminal*, like *The Sugarland Express*, *Close Encounters, Poltergeist* (scripted by Spielberg), *Empire of the Sun* and *Always* before them, dramatise interaction and confusion between the diegetic and an alternate, subjective or artificial 'reality,' just as the *Jurassic Park* movies toy with the digitally imaginable becoming real. Increasingly films such as *Total Recall* (1990), *Pulp Fiction* (1992), *Strange Days* (1995), *The Usual Suspects, The Truman Show, eXistenZ* (1999), *The Matrix* (1999), *The Limey* (1999), *Being John Malkovich* (1999), *Memento* (2000), *Adaptation* (2002), *Irreversible* (2002) and *Eternal Sunshine of the Spotless Mind* (2004) attract attention for formally or metaphorically self-reflexive narratives. No less deserv-ing of interest, but frequently dismissed because of seeming conventionality, because they do not flaunt modernism but ironise their themes and premises, Spielberg's films are overlooked as manipulatively commercial. The sense of being able to read cultishly is clearly good for business, especially as those enjoying the pleasure are, by definition, more attentive, perceptive and regular cinemagoers: consequently likely opinion lead-ers. Alongside critics who consider Spielberg too conservative are many film fans who, as a cursory glance at reviews on the Internet Movie Database shows, reject him for being mainstream. Thus, by virtue of having bothered to write and post such reviews, these filmgoers utilise Spielberg's films, as do many professional critics and academics, in their own self-definition.

Those who are able to see beyond Spielberg's standard blockbuster appeal are, ironically, 'low-cultural' variants of those avant-garde audiences for whom Noël Burch

(1969) speaks: 'And why shouldn't the *eye* exercise itself? Why should filmmakers not address themselves to an elite, just as composers have always done at different periods? We define "elite" as those people willing to see and resee films (many films) ... ' (quoted in Bordwell (1986: 283), who notes the passage's omission from the English translation). 'Ironically', because research shows frequent cinemagoing during Spielberg's rise to fame to have been an increasingly elitist activity (Jowett & Linton 1980: 81–2), while part of 'a new generation' has 'time and spending money and a penchant for ... repeated viewings of their favourite films' (Schatz 1993: 19), and because Burch has bemoaned elsewhere that mainstream practice has 'co-opted' self-reflexivity's 'distancing' effect (1982: 32). Nevertheless, such moments in Spielberg's work are excess; they exclude nobody who misses them from the standard cinematic pleasures on offer.

Audiences respond differently to the same signs. ('Popular culture' can be elevated into 'art' or deconstructed, as well as consumed). Discourse constitutes as much as describes its object, be it experiencing a film or anything else. As Antonia Quirke suggests in relation to Spielberg's cinematic solipsism, '*They grew up watching movies* is the squat complaint often levelled at the post-*Cahiers* generations. It's never levelled at poets. *That Ted Hughes, he just grew up reading poetry*' (2002: 62). Meaning depends on the subject's reading formation; reception of art and entertainment are tightly bound to social positioning. Much art cinema (and high-budget pseudo-art cinema such as *The English Patient* (1996)) flatters viewers into feeling superior: if the film is not easily understandable or enjoyable, it must be 'profound' (must therefore possess qualities of 'great' art and literature); the intelligentsia, to the entertainment industry's commercial advantage, recuperates a formerly despised medium. Popular cinema conversely is taken to have no aspirations to artistic status; therefore no claim on serious attention except insofar as demonstrating ideological processes. (The exception is auteurism, 'redeemer' of certain mainstream practitioners, theoretically unfashionable for years despite continued classification and everyday discussion of films in terms of directors both in academia – 'where it is nominally barred' (Lapsley & Westlake 1988: 127) – and in much popular discourse.) Rigidified false divisions, lack of close analysis, superficial generalisation and categorisation, and differential watching according to films' perceived status vitiate both theory and popular culture.

Consider, for example, the following definition, entirely compatible with readings offered here of Spielberg:

> What is peculiar to these films is the fact that in them to one degree or another the cinematic signifier abandons the status of a neutral and transparent vehicle at the direct behest of a manifest signified which alone is important (= the script), and that on the contrary it tends to inscribe its own action in them, to take over a more and more important part of the overall signification of the film...

That is Metz defining avant-garde cinema (1975: 40). Compare Mark Nash on art cinema, whose description again applies with little difficulty to Spielberg's work:

> As textual system, art cinema can be distinguished from the traditional Hollywood product by a number of features: an engagement of the individual,

rather than the impersonal point-of-view; an interiorisation of dramatic conflict with an emphasis on character ... and most strikingly, the foregrounding of an authorial voice. (1981: 7–8)

Another critic writes:

> Fellini once declared that the act of memory was like watching 'a dozen films simultaneously' ... There is always doubt about whether Guido [in *8½*] is directing 'real' or 'imaginary' scenes, or a mixture of the two. He appears to retreat from the real ... into a more private world in which he shapes, and to some extent controls, his life by framing it within cinematic images ... Fellini finds the magic and illusion which a film has to try to recapture within childhood itself. (Sales 1988: 120–1)

Clearly 'the mode of reading ... determines the construction of art cinema as a genre' (Willemen 1978: 62). Spielberg's output repeatedly explores precisely the same concerns – arguably more accessibly and coherently.

Spielberg and his 'Movie Brat' contemporaries are well versed in avant-garde, experimental and art, as well as mainstream, cinema but rarely share the same critical discourse (see Pye & Myles 1979: 57). Scorsese, many of whose films, significantly, engage with 'serious' issues combined with a generous measure of Catholic guilt, is the exception proving the rule. Thus, as Nick James points out, 'one of the problems of writing about Spielberg is that his films are littered with so much resonating movie stuff – both objects and concepts – yet he's never given the credit of being a film buff that goes to his contemporary Martin Scorsese' (2002: 15). (No one, to my knowledge, has attempted to relate *E.T.*'s, cinematography, with its emphases on characters' feet, to Bresson's *Lancelot du Lac* (1974), yet critics frequently invoke that director's work in connection with *Taxi Driver*.) Subjectivity and meaning are mutually defining. The subject becomes exposed to a text, chooses it and accepts its interpellation, from prior discursive positioning. To be addressed is to posit an addresser:

> The text chooses me, by a whole disposition of invisible screens, selective baffles: vocabulary, references, readability, etc.; and, lost in the midst of a text (not *behind* it, like a *deus ex machina*) there is always the other, the author.
>
> In the text, in a way, *I desire* the author: I need his [sic] figure (which is neither his representation nor his projection), as he needs mine... (Barthes 1975b: 4)

The mode of production makes it easier to accept individual authorship in avant-garde and art cinema, conveniently maintaining traditional values of creativity against the anonymity of most mainstream product that institutionally defines the individual spectator as part of a mass. Furthermore, 'the author's name characterises a particular manner of existence of discourse. Discourse that possesses an author's name is not to be immediately consumed and forgotten ... Rather, its status and its manner of reception are regulated by the culture in which it circulates' (Foucault 1977 in Caughie 1981:

284). The signature 'Oshima' or 'Tarkovsky' attracts not only a particular audience but a reading mode and type of criticism. Most popular cinema lacks such a signature, although criticism ascribes authorship to certain directors, re-appropriating how their films are discussed.

Spielberg is known partly because he was feted as an auteur during his early career, but chiefly because to be phenomenally successful in show business is to become famous – a point not overlooked in marketing his films. Serious criticism has difficulty placing Spielberg, so tends to ignore his work as anything other than exemplary of mass culture's imputed effects. It is partly that materialist theory necessarily professes anti-individualism. Perhaps his films also threaten critics' self-definition who prefer to trace influences and allusions for themselves, rather than have them displayed. Professional credibility at stake, they maintain separateness from popular taste by championing novelty or difference. Another, more populist and extremely important, strand of cultural studies achieved self-definition by concentrating on pleasures of the most critically despised entertainments, namely soap opera and violent American blue-collar movies, with emphasis on understanding the audience rather than examining the text.

Fantasy films furthermore are not only traditionally marginalised as childish or adolescent escapism, but also 'provide the ground for certain forms of cinephilia' (Neale 1980: 44), characterised by using Spielberg's films as happy hunting grounds for intertextual references to fill fan magazines. This facilitates self-recognition in relation to Spielberg, the (equally cine-fetishistic) idealised Other – 'A Legend', a 'Master', 'King of the World', discussed in terms of 'beards' and 'jumpers of extraordinary hue' (Anon. 2001b: 10, 64, 3). According to Terry Lovell, 'discerning of aesthetic form itself must be seen as a major source of pleasure in the text – the identification of the "rules of the game"' (1983: 95). Identifying references contributes to this illusory mastery.

So does possession of film-related merchandise, making present and real the absent Imaginary signifier in anticipation or recollection of spectatorship, reducing the gap which voyeurism necessitates. Marketing of *Jaws*, *Close Encounters*, *E.T.*, *Jurassic Park* and *The Lost World* especially exploited this phenomenon. Press releases made much of secrecy surrounding the first three productions. Promotional images for *Close Encounters* showed only mysterious lighting. *E.T.*'s posters and trailers focused on his hand. *Jurassic Park*, dependent on its dinosaurs' astonishing realism, made a fortune from plastic models yet its logo featured, enigmatically, a silhouetted skeleton. Before *The Lost World*'s release we had 700 tea bags in our kitchen so my sons could enjoy proud ownership of mugs and coins advertising the film, which they were too young to see. The desired object's unavailability is the ultimate condition for voyeuristic fetishisation: for my children, merchandising literally substituted for the film. For most potential spectators, the title *The Lost World: Jurassic Park* both anticipated and began the narrative of recovered absence; the subtitle traded on memory, and a recycled version of the original logo, 'calcified and distressed' (Romney 1997: 45), promised difference. Merchandise consumption also, of course, renders audience-community membership visible – important for the fashion-conscious, given media coverage of 'event' movies in return for press packs and interviews.

These subject formations, identifications, projections and splits interact during screening in spaces the text offers for the subject of enunciation, which as point of unity is subjectivity in process, not position. 'Invisible' continuity causes classical narration to be experienced as performance rather than as text. To acknowledge this implies, however, someone – an other – performing. This becomes undeniable when, as in Spielberg, enunciation shifts from *histoire* to *discours* and transparent 'realism' becomes spectacle, consciously textual. Even to recognise enunciation shifting to *discours*, as in my analyses, presupposes the auteur's presence. Without comparison with other films, it would be hard to argue that what is taken here to be inscription of the cinematic apparatus is, in any single instance, anything more than dramatic lighting – which is all it is in most of the now countless imitations of 'God lighting' and 'solar wind'. In-joke reminders of watching a Spielberg movie would mean nothing if we were unaware we were watching a Spielberg movie.

Excess

'Classical cinema does not efface the signs of production, it contains them,' argues Heath (1986: 402). Containment implies regulation of excess. Nevertheless genre functions precisely to *display* cinema's spectacular possibilities: 'Hence ... the science fiction film, where ... the narrative functions largely to motivate the production of special effects' (Neale 1980: 31). Excess pulls the spectator out of the imaginary to invite marvelling at technology and talent. Dislodgement from the position of enunciation does not threaten pleasure, for it is accompanied by confirmation of self in relation to the author constructed to fill that space. 'The attempt to move beyond *auteurism* has to recognise the ... fascination of the figure of the *auteur*, and the way he is used in the cinephile's pleasure' (Caughie 1981a: 15).

Shifting is as much part of classical narrative's pleasure as of disruption to identification in 'Brechtian' texts. Metz characterises the immobile, hyper-perceptive spectator as

alienated and happy, acrobatically attached to himself [sic] by the invisible wire of sight, a viewer who only retrieves himself as subject at the last moment, by a paradoxical identification with his own self, stretched to the limit in the pure act of watching. (1981: 230)

This performance metaphor recalls cinema's circus origins – identification and spectacle for their own sake – as much as in fiction, visual art and the stage. (It is to the circus Guido regresses in *8½*, while of course Spielberg references *The Greatest Show on Earth* in *Close Encounters*, and *Dumbo* in both *The Sugarland Express* and *The Last Crusade*.) As Thomas Elsaesser observes, 'the primary material of the cinema is ... the viewing situation itself' (1981: 272). The subject is spectator and performer, subject of the enunciation and the enounced, voluntarily relinquishing selfhood to risk disequilibrium and conflict in the sure knowledge of the safety net of narrative closure.

A hierarchy of discourses, assumed in the classic realist text, exists in Spielberg's work. However it does not smooth out contradiction by overlaying a dominant discourse against which to judge everything else. Discourses surface at different points and supplement, distract from or clash with each other rather than impose a univocal reading. Overt intertextuality; the *Gone With the Wind* poster that 'comments on' Jim's situation; Celie's naïve African visions (giraffes galloping majestically before a huge sun); Frank's misreading of his parents' relationship; parallels in *War of the Worlds* with real-life conflict: all address a position simultaneous with yet contradictory to identification. Expository titles in *Close Encounters, The Color Purple, Empire of the Sun* and elsewhere, far from 'break[ing] the spell of complete absorption' as an early theorist complained (Krows 1930: 109), demonstrate that 'complete' absorption is a critical fiction.

Bravura cinema exploits simultaneous absorption and disavowal, as well as violent shifts between Imaginary and Symbolic, as aspects of pleasure. Audiences enjoy trickery or surprise, jolting out of Imaginary identification, as indicated by laughter following the unexpected shark attack on the diver's cage in *Jaws* and similarly start-ling moments in *Psycho*. Yet such a return to self-consciousness and the Symbolic is partial, as demonstrated by both films' trick of releasing suspense through false alarms to relax the spectator before a bigger shock.

Spectatorship, interactive, plays 'upon introjective identification' (the sense of 'absorbing' and mastering) 'while at the same time providing the illusion of projective identification' (Friedberg 1990: 39). It offers knowledge, intelligibility and truth as final equilibrium, but withholds these for the pleasures of constant repositioning. Pastiche and spectacle help work that repositioning and defer closure. So too do narrational devices that flagrantly exploit presence/absence to establish enigma, such as off-screen sightings of UFOs in *Close Encounters* or withholding shots of the shark in *Jaws* or dinosaurs in *Jurassic Park*. *E.T.*'s opening follows a mystery film convention, which 'makes its narration quite overt: a shot of a shadowy figure or an anonymous hand makes the viewer quite aware of a self-conscious, omniscient, and suppressive narration' (Bordwell *et al.* 1985: 40). Such presence of absence underscores the present absence of the signifier itself, intensifying the distance and desire for mastery that constitute voyeurism. Spielberg's showmanship and address increase what was always already there in continuity editing for, as Burch notes, the shot/reverse-shot puts 'the absence/presence of the spectator at the very centre of the diegetic process' (1982: 22).

'Showmanship' in both narration and spectacle is a form of exhibitionism, the necessary corollary that engages the scopic drive, the desire to look and know. 'Cinema depends on voyeurism, and voyeurism is inseparable from exhibitionism. Both must always exist together, and to precisely the same degree' (Neale 1980: 34). As with partly-hidden jokes in *Close Encounters*, Spielberg's New Hollywood sound recording and performance styles often submerge or skate quickly over dialogue, rendering part of the film absent – withdrawing, obscuring, or interrupting before the spectator can 'possess' it, before it signifies. The effect, assuming engaged spectatorship, is keener concentration and involvement. This again counteracts distancing tendencies of self-reflexivity, contributing to confusion already suggested as partially explaining the emotional effect.

Spectatorial belief division is not clear-cut. Imaginary and Symbolic are not either/ or but a mutually defined, fluid, shifting relationship, cutting across discourses and positions in play. This dynamic conception marks an important advance on monolithic models of subject-positioning, such as Adorno's understanding of audiences for popular culture, who 'force their eyes shut, and voice approval, in a kind of self-loathing, for what is *meted* out to them, knowing fully the purpose for which it is manufactured' (1989b: 57). For Adorno, a powerful influence in ideological criticism, there are fixed, incompatible subject positions. A false consciousness that seduces people away from politically liberating but intellectually challenging works (read: 'high culture') opposes a self-aware, essential, instinctive grasp of the truth that forever allows itself cravenly to be led astray by easy pleasures, thereby guiltily subjecting itself to the hegemony of corporate capitalism, of which the entertainment industry is the propaganda division.

Whatever the merits of Adorno's case, oversimplification of mechanisms involved compromises his broader argument. For most spectators, impossibilities such as the flying scene in *E.T.* mark the experience as fantasy, and enjoying the film requires accepting the premise of that impossibility. It is unlikely any but the youngest child is unaware of the disavowal involved, and equally unlikely that any but the most puritanical zealot feels even a twinge of discomfort (although, as seen in the Introduction, puritanical zealots appear to be the spectators most likely to publish their reactions). Likewise, it is true that the escape from bland suburbia in *Close Encounters*, while uplifting, neither analyses what is wrong with suburban values nor offers help to disaffected suburbanites who wish to change their lives. But no normal cinemagoer expects it to. Audiences are hardly duped in these instances, nor are they deluding themselves. As Metz argues:

> If the most extravagant spectacles and sounds or their most improbable assembly, the one most remote from all real experience, do not prevent the constitution of meaning (and to begin with do not *astonish* the spectator ...) – that is because he [sic] knows he is at the cinema. (1975: 51)

When texts fully engage the scopic drive part of the psyche always remains detached.

Similarity and difference, genre's structuring principle, is central to classical narration. Familiarity with conventions, sometimes foregrounded as 'rhetorical flourishes' (Bordwell *et al.* 1985: 29), offers security and establishes expectations that are not simply fulfilled but delayed and subverted. Again, this would not be pleasurable if the spectator were not aware to some degree of the process. In fantasy, the stranger or more implausible the content, the more conventional narration has to be to maintain credibility. As Steve Neale suggests, and *Uncle Josh* showed a century ago, 'wonder' – solicited by Spielberg's science fiction and explored in *The Color Purple* and *Empire of the Sun* – requires 'a division of belief so strong that it often requires the imaginary attribution of two spectators, one of whom is completely duped while the other "knows better" and is not taken in at all' (1980: 39; see also Metz 1975: 70). Hence

Spielberg's pigeonholing as a 'children's director', despite contrary evidence, and the virulence of ideological criticism attacking the power his films allegedly exercise on *others*. Both strategies attempt to recuperate the myth of the unitary self by expelling and projecting elsewhere the credulous, regressive parts of the psyche.

The spectator as subject of the enunciation experiences satisfaction as 'the totalising [agent] of whatever appears before their eyes', a transcendent subject able to effect resolution, despite full awareness that such power is denied in reality (Andrew 1984: 113). To this extent the spectator resembles Theodor Adorno's 'old woman who weeps at the wedding services of others, blissfully aware of the wretchedness of her own life' (1989a: 80). Spielberg's inscribed audiences as identificatory doubles heighten awareness of spectatorship and its relation to the sense of self. The emotion of the climaxes, hardly *simply* 'escapist', derives from multiple conflicts; these are irresolvable rationally during the screening as romantic music and the 'solar wind' – putting hair, clothing and background foliage in constant movement, exciting the scopic drive – create audio-visual overload in which cinematic spectacle releases inhibition, legitimising fantasy fulfilment.

Adorno condemns such a process as 'only the scant liberation that occurs with the realisation that at least one need not deny oneself the happiness of knowing that one is unhappy and that one could be happy' (1989a: 80). His severity presupposes constant misery among entertainment-seekers and that the only legitimate function of popular culture is to pave the road to happiness by promoting social and political change. While this is understandable, given Adorno's experience of Nazi Germany and then Depression and World War Two America, it is questionable whether unqualified unhappiness is what draws young, relatively wealthy and educated audiences to films today.

Revolutionary texts are not notably successful in attracting audiences, let alone changing mass consciousness, although they garner approval from intellectuals whose self-image they bolster. Politically effective popular cinema would have to recognise and learn from classical narration's appeal, through identification and psychic regression, to mobilise the challenge fantasies offer to the conservative myth of unified character. (In the present context, Adorno was unwittingly close to the mark in observing, 'Emotional music has become the image of the mother who says, "Come and weep, my child"' (1989a: 80).) It would need to remember also that distanciation is neither the unique privilege of Brechtian cinema nor inherently unpleasurable.

Textual pleasures relate closely to public and social pleasures, 'shared and socially defined aspirations and hopes ... a sense of identity and community', all as important as their re-working of the subject's first positioning in language (Lovell 1983: 95). These lock spectatorial pleasure into ideology: while alignment of self to social attitudes is comforting, it also permits individuals to subsume themselves to hegemony. History, Adorno knew too well, shows the consequences of unquestioning identification with the mass and with one's prescribed position in oppressive formations. This does not mean, though, that entertainment appealing to a huge audience because it mobilises widespread psychic and social conflicts is of itself oppressive.

Andrew Britton would disagree: 'To respond *inappropriately* is to find oneself excluded from the human community, for it is essential to the entertainment emotion that one should find that others are responding appropriately elsewhere' (1986: 7). This may be valid, but is hardly surprising given story-telling's bardic function since time immemorial. (Fiske & Hartley (1978) appropriated the term 'bardic' to conceptualise television's central role in recirculating myths and conventions that reinforce communal self-representation and sense of cohesion.) Marxist intellectuals, by definition, always 'respond inappropriately'. Substitute 'dominant social values' for Britton's rhetorical 'human community' and what remains is a truism.

There is a facile tendency to argue thus: Hollywood offers spectacle, emotional music and appeal to deep-rooted desires. Spielberg exemplifies these qualities, thereby reaching enormous audiences. Hitler mobilised the masses through spectacle, emotional music and appeal to deep-rooted desires. *Ergo*: Spielberg's cinema is fascistic. (Lest this seem grotesque parody, consider these titles: 'Close Encounters of the Authoritarian Kind' (Williams 1983); 'Close Encounters with the Third Reich' (Entman & Seymour 1978).) It may be that characters' passivity, together with conflict resolution by outside agency – extra-terrestrials in *Close Encounters* and *E.T.*; Shug in *The Color Purple*; pure chance in *Empire of the Sun*; Schindler's puzzling magnanimity in protecting 'his' Jews; natural selection in *War of the Worlds* – reveals desire to have problems solved by putting faith in a superior power. It may well be that widespread abdication of personal responsibility fuelled Hitler's rise. To make too much of this, however, is to ignore that Spielberg in the first two offers fantasy (quite possibly a universal fantasy, considering the tenacity of religion) that is explicitly portrayed as fantasy and received as fantasy, in the second two presents characters who are fantasists, in the fifth offers unresolved enigma and in the last retains the source text's scientific logic.

Other hostile critics have condemned Spielberg's intertextuality (hermetically 'separate' entertainment world) as evasion or refusal of the real. To equate popular pleasure indiscriminately with Nazism – especially when the overt message of Spielberg's films is 'Be good', learn to see things afresh, trust children and women rather than men in authority – is nothing short of obscene given the huge success concurrently with his career of films starring muscle-bound supermen. The best to be said of such crude ideological criticism is that it exemplifies the cynical logic of professional advancement: 'careers are best made by adopting a deviant way of reading' (Stern 1990: 60).

As Valerie Walkerdine insists, 'we should look to the desire for forms of mastery that are present in our own subjectification as cultural analysts before rushing to "save" "the masses" from the pleasures of imaginary wish-fulfilment' (1986: 341). Too often political criticism in the name of equality serves instead to reinscribe the commentator's own superiority, and frequently seizes upon textual parallels with real life to assert some kind of unexplained causality. The result is mystification rather than political enlightenment. Spielberg, as the ultimate embodiment of Hollywood success, particularly comes in for this kind of attack. Consider the following condemnation of *E.T.* and, by implication, its audiences, through insinuation via analogies, and ask what general point readers of the otherwise excellent textbook in which it appears are supposed to take from it:

> Reagan promised to bring America back to life, much as he himself had
> bounced back after John Hinckley's unsuccessful attempt to assassinate him

in 1981. Reagan's own recovery served as a symbolic enactment of things to come; his presidency would make the light go back on, much as it does near the end of *E. T.: The Extra-Terrestrial*, when the sympathetic alien miraculously recovers from apparent death. (Belton 2005: 378)

Reproduction of ideology is not a problem with individual texts, which, to fulfil their entertainment function, are hardly likely to challenge current ideological norms; there is simply no incentive for them to do so. Yet popular cinematic representations do change over time (if only superficially) in response to other discourses. Given the expense, which militates against risk-taking, and time that film production involves, popular cinema probably lags behind other media as a site for contesting hegemony. Other factors (such as press and broadcasting institutional attitudes and practices, the family and schooling) are more crucial. The range of discursive positions, the cultural capital, available to an individual, together with social context, determine the political influence of texts (acceptance or otherwise of preferred readings) and to a large extent which texts are encountered in the first place.

Cinema is easily dismissible as a mass opiate: 'No independent thinking must be expected from the audience: the product prescribes every reaction: not by its natural structure (which collapses under reflection), but by signals. *Any* logical connection calling for mental effort is painstakingly avoided' (Adorno & Horkheimer 1977: 361). My textual analyses of Spielberg's films question whether highly popular cinema *necessarily* invites passive reading: I quote Adorno and Horkheimer here because by subsuming historical spectator and positioned subject under 'audience', anticipating influential 'Screen Theory', they perpetuate a self-fulfilling prophecy: any spectator approaching a text with such attitudes will find them unchallenged. To redefine the spectator as a theoretical *construct* 'produced and activated by the cinematic apparatus' (Flitterman-Lewis 1987: 182), a space anyone can occupy, is to accept that the subject who enjoys a film is not the historical subject who holds beliefs and attitudes outside that experience. However, those prior positionings will affect its meaning, and may be modified or reinforced by it. Even the subject position inscribed by the classic realist text is no more than 'a condition for its intelligibility'. As David Morley explains, 'it does not follow that because the reader has "taken the position" most fully inscribed in the text, sufficient for the text to be intelligible, he/she will, for that reason alone, subscribe to the ideological problematic of that text' (1980: 167). *Rambo*, for example, is unacceptable to many spectators because it offers a subject position so alien to beliefs and attitudes they bring to the film that, although it does not explicitly inscribe marks of enunciation, it is received as *discours*, precluding Imaginary identification; to those whose historical subjectivity is broadly congruent with the textual position offered, the film presumably functions as untroubling *histoire*.

Spectatorship's social context is an often-underemphasised determinant of read-ing. If the Lumières' first audience really *did* run from the theatre at the sight of an approaching train (despite the camera being 30 degrees from the tracks), logically this should have recurred at subsequent performances. That it did not is a reminder that even at the basic level of realism, let alone its ideological ramifications, making mean-ing is extremely more complicated than either a simple 'hypodermic' or positioning process. In taking account of real viewers' complex meaning-making, to go beyond imputed reactions – whether or not based in textual analysis – and helpful but somewhat limiting uses-and-gratifications approaches, a theorised critical position remains essential. While respecting respondents and their responses, commonsense acceptance is insufficient: postmodernism's emergence and the rise in audience studies in the 1980s, with emphasis on 'choice' of meanings, chime with Reaganite/Thatcherite discourses of consumer hegemony. A few years ago I heard a conference paper on empirical audience research in relation to *Braveheart* (1995). The presenter reported a young man's comment that he had laughed when the English king threw a character out of a window, although he did not really find it funny but felt he should laugh because everyone else did. This was purportedly significant, evidence – as it undoubtedly was – of the influence of others on a response. (It also, incidentally, confirms spectatorial self-awareness.) Textual analysis, however, might have related the response to something more significant, or at least worth investigating. In a film that equates nationalism with masculinity, the defenestration occurs during a homophobic Oedipal struggle, in which the king – the narrative's obscene father – suppresses a challenge from his overtly effeminate son whose 'advisor', equally coded as gay, he despatches. To overlook this is inadvertently to ignore a potentially substantial component of the phenomenon under investigation. While textual analysis and interpretation offer only possible meanings, to record 'real viewers' responses without critical mediation is merely to increase the evidential base, not to overcome subjective, impressionistic or overly abstract biases. The challenge remains to effect a synthesis of approaches.

Cultural imperialism

Much criticism of Hollywood focuses not just on its ideological reproduction within the US but also on cultural imperialism. Peter Wollen states, and contextualises, the argument succinctly:

> The problem with the American dominance of global cinema ... is not that it prevents Britain (and other countries) from developing cultural identities for themselves but ... it also threatens to deprive America itself of views of America from the outside. American dominance simply reinforces America's own powerful, yet provincial cinematic myths about itself ... structured around terrifying misrecognitions and appallingly narcissistic fantasies ... harmful not simply to everyone else in the global market but also, above all, to America itself. (1998: 134)

Yet, Janet Wasko notes, 'Hollywood films are more than ever these days deliberately created for international markets' (2003: 177). She also argues that, through market research and the mechanisms of the marketplace, 'audiences are said to influence the films that are produced and distributed, [although] such influence is mainly a matter of choosing between the films that are actually made available' (2003: 224). It would seem, though, to make commercial sense for Hollywood not to make for export films that are overtly pro-American at a time when America's activities as a superpower are at least controversial, where not widely resented, or to rely heavily on specifically American cultural references. *War of the Worlds*, for example, which opened simultaneously in 78 countries, presents a Bakhtinian inversion of American hegemony, with its citizens dysfunctional in personal relationships, a leaderless and disorganised violent mob, and the armed forces ineffectual; Americans, as representative of the human race, survive by evolutionary accident, no action of their own. Myths propagate themselves subtly, however. The brutally realist *Maria Full of Grace* (2004), rightly praised for dramatising sympathetically depredations, degradations and impossible conflicts undergone by a drugs mule, concludes with a relatively feel-good individualist ending as Maria finds her salvation by escaping from South America to the US. Most critics ignore Viktor's indifference to American values in *The Terminal* – far more adventurous ideologically. Moreover, Brian Winston's view of satellite broadcasting and cultural imperialism seems equally applicable to movie exports: 'The long-term ideological significance of the importation of foreign television signals … remains something of a mystery. It is by no means the case that such importation reproduces the ideology of the imported programmes' (1998: 303). Indeed, Armand Mattelart argues, 'The messages of mass culture can be neutralised by the dominated class who can produce their own antidotes' (1980: 20). Who, among the critics who alleged *Saving Private Ryan*'s complicity in resurrecting militaristic discourses, could have foreseen, or anticipated the discursive conflations involved in, numerous ABC network stations' cancellation of its Veterans' Day broadcast, introduced by a war veteran Republican senator, exactly one week after George W. Bush's re-election? The reason: its language. This occurred amid increasing censorship following Janet Jackson's breast exposure during the Superbowl final the previous year. The Federal Communications Commission had tightened regulations, backed by heavy fines, following a judgement on pop star Bono saying 'fuck' on television. This confusion of moral outrages, voiced by pressure group the Parents' Television Council, did not allude to the fact that at the same time American troops were storming Fallujah, 18 months after hostilities in Iraq officially had ceased.

No escape

As Jacqueline Bobo's empirical research on black women's responses to *The Color Purple* shows (1988; 1995), as well as less considered but impassioned responses to the same film,   cinema is a social institution, despite spectators' intimate and intense relationship with the screen in the darkness. Cinemagoers seek entertainment, escape from the house, an excuse for an evening out with friends. That Spielberg has 'an intuitive grasp of cultural archetypes' (Ontario 1989: 74) makes the experience peculiarly satisfying and involving – for those it does not alienate – but is not the whole picture.

> People go to the movies for the various ways they express the experiences of our lives, and as a means of avoiding and postponing the pressures we feel. This latter function of art – generally referred to disparagingly as escapism – may also be considered as refreshment, and in terms of big city life and small town

boredom, it may be a big factor in keeping us sane. (Kael, quoted in Ontario 1989: 73; see also Dyer 1977).

This commonsense account needs to be problematised and developed. 'Keeping us sane' might equate to 'making us conform to accept oppression'. Some ideological criticism condemns popular entertainment for declaring 'otherness' from life, and so down-playing the 'content' of its wish-fulfilment (e.g. Britton 1986). If, however, fantasy's appeal originates in fundamental psychic needs, 'content' is not an issue unless dangerous in itself. (*Field of Dreams*, in the guise of charming light entertainment, sought to obliterate a troubling stain in American history at a time when mainstream political rhetoric also appealed to nostalgia and a return to older (reactionary) values. It was not desire for the Imaginary, to escape conflict, which was reprehensible, for that is precisely what 'escapism' is for; disturbing was how it mobilised fantasy to recuperate a powerful national myth already appropriated by other, repressive discourses.) Entertainment is too easily attacked not for what it is, but for what it is not, in attempting mastery by ranking texts qualitatively according to external criteria; the touchstone is something that consciously sets out to question society and its values, or that (like 'great' auteur movies) can be thus recuperated. By the same puritanical argument, sleep is reprehensible as escape from ideological conflict.

If anything, Spielberg's characteristic theme of the ordinary person escaping the sterility of suburbia or other frustration underscores life's dissatisfactions and keeps alive the dream of escape. 'Utopian' popular culture gains commercial success by simultaneously resisting and conforming to dominant values (Branston 2000: 20). Certainly the dream needs to be alive, desire for change in place, for the film to satisfy. 'Film at its most devastating is not escape from reality,' writes Emma Wilson, 'but an encounter with the real we seek to leave behind in the movie-theatre' (2003: 10). There is no justification for blaming films (comparatively minor events in most lives) if other discourses that do *not* claim to offer 'escape' – news and current affairs, the press, family and peer group values, education – perpetuate conflicts from which escape is desired and have not produced radically critical cinemagoers. Narrative's function is not in itself to explain the world, but to symbolise and help individuals come to terms with contradictions and to share inwardness with others. Disruption of equilibrium institutes lack, giving rise to desire, fulfilled by the concluding equilibrium's Imaginary wholeness in a manner unparalleled in everyday life. Texts cannot contain contradictions. That is why audiences return for more.

BIBLIOGRAPHY

Abagnale, Frank W. (2002) 'About Frank' and 'Comments'. On-line. Available at http://www.abagnale.com/aboutfrank.htm and http://www.abagnale.com/comments.htm (8 April 2005).

Abagnale, Frank W. with Stan Redding (2001) [1980] *Catch Me If You Can*. Edinburgh and London: Mainstream Publishing.

Adair, Gilbert (1982/83) 'E.T. cetera', *Sight and Sound* 52, 1 (Winter), 63.

Adorno, Theodor (1973) [1966] *Negative Dialectics* (trans. E. B. Ashton). London: Routledge and Kegan Paul.

_____ (1989a) [1941] 'On Popular Music', in Bob Ashley (ed.) *The Study of Popular Fiction: A Source Book*. London: Pinter, 73–81.

_____ (1989b) [1967] 'Culture Industry Reconsidered', in Bob Ashley (ed.) *The Study of Popular Fiction: A Source Book*. London: Pinter, 52–9.

Adorno, Theodor and Max Horkheimer (1977) [1973] 'The Culture Industry: Enlightenment as Mass Deception', in James Curran, Michael Gurevitch and Janet Woollacott (eds) *Mass Communication and Society*. London: Edward Arnold/Open University, 349–83.

Aldiss, Brian (2001) [1969] 'Supertoys Last All Summer Long', in *'Supertoys Last All Summer Long' and Other Stories of Future Time*. London: Orbit.

Allen, Graham (2000) *Intertextuality*. London and New York: Routledge.

Allen, Robert C. (1987) 'Reader-Oriented Criticism and Television', in Robert C. Allen (ed.) *Channels of Discourse: Television and Contemporary Criticism*. London:

Routledge, 74–112.

Althusser, Louis (1973) *Lenin and Philosophy and Other Essays*. London: New Left Books.

Altman, Rick (1999) *Film/Genre*. London: British Film Institute.

Amarger, Michel (1998) 'America Absolves the Slave Trade', *Ecrans D'Afrique/African Screen* 23, alternate pages 114–24.

Ambrose, Stephen (1993) *Band of Brothers. E Company, 506th Regiment, 101st Airborne from Normandy to Hitler's Eagles Nest*. New York and London: Simon and Schuster.

Andrew, Dudley (1984) *Concepts in Film Theory*. Oxford and New York: Oxford University Press.

Andrew, Geoff (1984) 'Boys Own Brat', *Time Out* 721 (14–20 June), 16–17.

_____ (1989) *The Film Handbook*. Harlow: Longman.

Anon. (1982) Article on *E.T. The Extra-Terrestrial, Hollywood Reporter*, 274, 17 (9 November), 1.

_____ (1988a) Article on *E.T. The Extra-Terrestrial, Hollywood Reporter*, 304, 11 (16 September), 1, 38.

_____ (1988b) Article on *E.T. The Extra-Terrestrial, Hollywood Reporter*, 304, 43 (28 October), 3, 49.

_____ (1989) Review of *Always, Variety* (20 December), 22.

_____ (1993a) 'Cola v Zola' (on French release of *Jurassic Park*), *Economist* (UK) 329, 7883 (16 October), 78–9.

_____ (1993b) *Washington Post* (15 December), B1.

_____ (1993c) *Guardian* (16 December), 2–3.

_____ (1994a) Review of *Schindler's List, Premiere* 1,12 (January), 66.

_____ (1994b) 'Racism on Screen and in Raw Life', *Guardian* (19 February), 24.

_____ (1994c) 'Profile: Steven Spielberg – From Lost Ark to a New Covenant', *Observer* (20 March), 23.

_____ (1996) *Evening Standard* (25 June), 5.

_____ (1998) 'Literalism on the Littoral' (*Saving Private Ryan* review), *Economist* 348 (8 August), 70.

_____ (2001a) 'This Week's Hottest US Release' (*A.I.*), *Times* (14–20 July) *Play*, 6.

_____ (2001b) *Empire: The Directors Collection: Steven Spielberg: The Life. The Films. The Amazing Stories*. London.

Anthony, Andrew (2006) 'Steven Spielberg: the Interview' (on *Munich*), *Observer* (22 January), *Review*, 4.

Argent, Daniel (2001) 'Steven Spielberg as Writer: From *Close Encounters of the Third Kind* to *A.I.*', *Creative Screenwriting* 8, 3 (May/June), 49–53.

Arlen, Michael J. (1979) 'The Air: The Tyranny of the Visible', *New Yorker* 55 (23 April), 125ff.

Arthur, Paul (2001) 'Movie of the Moment: *A.I. Artificial Intelligence*', *Film Comment* 37, 4 (July/August), 22–5.

Ascherson, Neal (1998) 'Missing in Action' (on *Saving Private Ryan*), *Observer* (6 September), *Review*, 7.

_____ (2006) 'A Master and the Myths of Munich', *Observer* (15 January), *Review*,

12–13.

Askari, Brent (1996) '*Jaws*: Beyond Action', *Creative Screenwriting*, 3, 1 (Summer), 31–6.

Aufderheide, Pat (1986) 'The Color Lavender', *In These Times* (22–26 January), 15.

Auster, Albert (2002) '*Saving Private Ryan* and American Triumphalism', *Journal of Popular Film and Television*, 30, 2 (Summer), 99–104.

Auty, Chris (1982) 'The Complete Spielberg?', *Sight and Sound*, 51, 4 (Autumn), 275–9.

Ayres, Chris (2004) 'Flight Delayed' (on *The Terminal*), *Times* (22 June) T2, 18.

Baird, Robert (1998) 'Animalizing *Jurassic Park*'s Dinosaurs: Blockbuster Schemata and Cross-Cultural Cognition in the Threat Scene', *Cinema Journal*, 37, 4 (Summer), 82–103.

Bakhtin, Mikhail (1973) *Problems of Dostoyevsky's Poetics* (trans. R. W. Rotsel). Ann Arbor: Ardis.

_____ (1981) *The Dialogic Imagination* (ed. Michael Holquist, trans. Caryl Emerson and Michael Holquist). Austin: University of Texas Press.

_____ (1984) *Rabelais and His World* (trans. Helene Iswolsky). Bloomington and Indianapolis: Indiana University Press.

Balaban, Bob (1978) *Close Encounters of the Third Kind Diary*. Paradise Press.

Baldwin, Frank (1999) 'Saving Face' (letter on *Saving Private Ryan*), *History Today* 41, 2 (February), 61.

Balides, Constance (2000) 'Jurassic Post-Fordism: Tall Tales of Economics in the Theme Park', *Screen* 41, 2 (Summer), 139–60.

Balio, Tino (2002) 'Hollywood Production Trends in the Era of Globalisation, 1990–99', in Steve Neale (ed.) *Genre and Contemporary Hollywood*. London: British Film Institute, 165–84.

Ball, Alex (1997) 'The Science behind *The Lost World:Jurassic Park*', *Waterhouse Times* (staff magazine of The Natural History Museum, London) 12 (August), 6–7.

Ballard, J. G. (1985) *Empire of the Sun*. London: Panther.

Barker, Martin with Thomas Austin (2000) *From Antz to Titanic*. London: Pluto Press.

Barkley, Richard (1984) 'Better than a Ride on the Ghost Train', *Sunday Express* (17 June), 22.

Barrie, J. M. (1993) [1911] *Peter Pan*. Bristol: Parragon.

Barthes, Roland (1968), 'L'effet du reel', *Communications* 11, 87–112.

_____ (1974) *S/Z* (trans. Richard Miller). London: Jonathan Cape.

_____ (1975a) [1966] 'Introduction to the Structural Analysis of Narratives', in *Image-Music-Text* (ed. and trans. Stephen Heath). London: Fontana, 79–124.

_____ (1975b) [1968] 'The Death of the Author', in *Image-Music-Text* (ed. and trans. Stephen Heath). London: Fontana, 142-8.

_____ (1975c) [1973] *The Pleasure of the Text* (trans. Richard Miller). New York: Hill and Wang.

Bartov, Omer (1997) 'Spielberg's Oskar: Hollywood Tries Evil', in Yosefa Loshitzky (ed.) (1997) *Spielberg's Holocaust: Critical Perspectives on Schindler's List*. Bloomington and Indianapolis: Indiana University Press, 41–60.

Basinger, Jeanine (1998) 'Translating War: The Combat Film Genre and *Saving Private Ryan*', *Perspectives: American Historical Association Newsletter* 36, 7 (October), 1, 43–7.

Baudry, Jean-Louis (1974/75) 'Ideological Effects of the Basic Cinematographic Apparatus', *Film Quarterly* 28, 2, 39–47.

Bauman, Zygmunt and Janina Bauman (1994) 'On *Schindler's List* and *The Holocaust for Beginners*' (interviewed by Max Farrar), *Red Pepper* 2 (July), 38–9.

Baxter, John (1996) *Steven Spielberg: The Unauthorized Biography*. London: Harper Collins.

Baxter, Peter (1975) 'On the History and Ideology of Film Lighting', *Screen* 16, 3 (Autumn), 83–106.

Bazin, André (1967) *What is Cinema?* Vol. 1. (selection and trans. Hugh Gray). Berkeley, Los Angeles, and London: University of California Press.

Beecher Stowe, Harriet (1993) [1852] *Uncle Tom's Cabin* (ed. Christopher Bigsby) reprinted with Frederick Douglass, *Narrative of the Life of Frederick Douglass, an American Slave*. London: Everyman.

Bell, Emily (1998) 'A Dream Works Out for Spielberg at Last', *Observer* (8 November), 10.

Belton, John (2005) *American Cinema/American Culture*. New York: McGraw-Hill.

Benchley, Peter (1974) *Jaws*. London: Pan.

Bennett, Tony and Janet Woollacott (1987) *Bond and Beyond: The Political Career of a Popular Hero*. London: Macmillan.

Bennett, Ray (1993) 'Theme Parks Fix on F/X from Pix', *Variety* (14 June), 10.

Benson, Peter (1989) Letter on psychoanalysis and criticism, *Movie*, 33 (Winter), 63–4.

Benvenuto, Bice and Roger Kennedy (1986) *The Works of Jacques Lacan: An Introduction*. London: Free Association Books.

Berger, John (1972) *Ways of Seeing*. London and Harmondsworth: British Broadcasting Corporation and Pelican.

Beyer, Lisa (2005) 'The Myths and Reality of Munich', *Time* (12 December), 68–9.

Biskind, Peter (1975) 'Between the Teeth' (essay on *Jaws*), *Jump Cut* 9 (October–December), 1, 26.

Black, Larry (1993) 'Extinction Threatens Hollywood Dinosaurs' (on *Jurassic Park*), *The Independent on Sunday* (4 July), *Business on Sunday*, 8.

Blum, Lawrence (1999) 'Race, Community and Moral Education: Kohlberg and Spielberg as Civic Educators', *Journal of Moral Education* 28, 2, 125–43.

Bobo, Jacqueline (1988a) '*The Color Purple*: Black Women's Responses', *Jump Cut*, 33 (February), 43–52.

_____ (1988b) '*The Color Purple*: Black Women as Cultural Readers', in E. Diedre Pribram (ed.) *Female Spectators: Looking at Film and Television*. London: Verso, 90–109.

_____ (1995) *Black Women as Cultural Readers*. New York: Columbia University Press.

Bordwell, David (1986) *Narration in the Fiction Film*. London: Routledge/University Paperbacks.

Bordwell, David, Kristin Thompson and Janet Staiger (1985) *The Classical Hollywood*

Cinema: Film Style and Mode of Production to 1960. London: Routledge.

Bouch, Matthew (1996) 'Towards an Understanding of Steven Spielberg', unpublished MA dissertation, British Film Institute and Birkbeck College, University of London.

Bowles, Stephen E. (1976) '*The Exorcist* and *Jaws*', *Literature/Film Quarterly* 4, 3 (Summer), 196–214.

Bradbury, Malcolm (1987) *Mensonge.* London: Arena.

Bradshaw, Peter (2006) 'Road to Nowhere' (*Munich* review), *Guardian* (27 January), *Film & Music* section, 7.

Brady, Mary (1993) 'Steering Dinomania in UK', *Variety* (27 December), 64, 68.

Branigan, Edward (1992) *Narrative Comprehension and Film.* London and New York: Routledge.

Branston, Gill (2000) *Cinema and Cultural Modernity.* Buckingham and Philadelphia: Open University.

Breen, Jennifer (1999) '*Amistad* Colloquium Raises Questions of Critical Dialogue', *Black Camera* 14, 1 (Spring/Summer), 5–6.

Bremner, Ian (1998) *Saving Private Ryan* review, *History Today* 48, 11 (November), 50–1.

Bresheeth, Haim (1997) 'The Great Taboo Broken: Reflections on the Israeli Reception of *Schindler's List*', in Yosefa Loshitzky (ed.) (1997) *Spielberg's Holocaust: Critical Perspectives on Schindler's List.* Bloomington and Indianapolis: Indiana University Press, 193–212.

Brett, Anwar (1998) *Amistad* review, *Film Review* (17 March), 17.

Brewster, Ben (1982) 'A Scene at the Movies', *Screen* 23, 2 (July–August), 4–15.

Britton, Andrew (1986) 'Blissing Out: The Politics of Reaganite Entertainment', *Movie* 31/32 (Winter), 1–42.

Brode, Douglas (1995) *The Films of Steven Spielberg.* New York: Citadel Press.

Brodesser, Claude (2001) 'Crix Deliver Fascinating Mix' (on *A.I.*), *Variety* (9–15 July), 41.

Brontë, Emily (1965) [1847] *Wuthering Heights.* Harmondsworth: Penguin.

Brooks, Richard (1991) 'Hollywood Hangs Hopes on *Hook*', *Observer* (12 August), 22.

Brown, Georgia (1993) 'Prospero Cooks' (*Jurassic Park* review), *Village Voice* (26 June), 53.

Brown, Liz (1978) '*Some Women of Marrakesh*', *Screen* 19, 2 (Summer), 85–118.

Brown, Tony (1986) 'Blacks Need to Love One Another', *Carolina Peacemaker* (4 January), in Alice Walker (1996) *The Same River Twice: Honoring the Difficult. A Meditation of Life, Spirit, Art, and the Making of the Film 'The Color Purple'.* London: The Women's Press, 223–5.

Buckland, Warren (1999) 'Between Science Fact and Science Fiction: Spielberg's Digital Dinosaurs, Possible Worlds, and the New Aesthetic Realism', *Screen* 40, 2 (Summer), 177–92.

____(2003a) 'The Artistry of Spielberg's Long Takes', 'The Question Spielberg: A Symposium', *Senses of Cinema.* On-line. Available at http://www.sensesofcinema.com/contents/03/27/spielberg_symposium_films_and_moments.html#filmo (9 November 2004).

_____ (2003b) 'The Role of the Auteur in the Age of the Blockbuster: Steven Spielberg and DreamWorks', in Julian Stringer (ed.) *Movie Blockbusters*. London and New York: Routledge, 84–98.

Burch, Noël (1969) *Praxis du Cinema*. Paris: Gallimard.

_____ (1982) 'Narrative/Diegesis – Thresholds, Limits', *Screen* 23, 2 (July–August), 16–33.

Burgess, Anthony (1962) *A Clockwork Orange*. London: Heinemann.

Burgess, Sonia (1983) 'Science Fiction and Film Education: A Study in Science Fiction with Special Reference to the Film *E.T.*', unpublished MA dissertation, University of London Institute of Education.

Buscombe, Ed (1980) 'Close Militarist Encounters', *Tribune* (2 May 1980), British Film Institute microfiche.

Butler, Cheryl B. (1991) '*The Color Purple* Controversy: Black Women Spectatorship', *Wide Angle* 13, 3/4 (July/October), 62–9.

Campbell, Christopher P. (1995) *Race, Myth and the News*. London: Sage.

Campbell, Joseph (1988) [1949] *The Hero With a Thousand Faces*. London: Paladin.

Canby, Vincent (1998) 'War Movies: The Horror and the Honor of a Good War' (*Saving Private Ryan* review), *New York Times* (10 August), Late Edition – Final, Section E, 1.

Carroll, Lewis [Charles Lutwidge Dodgson] (2005) [1871] *Alice Through the Looking Glass*. London: Walker Books.

_____ (1996) [1876] *The Hunting of the Snark: An Agony in Eight Fits*. London: Penguin.

Carroll, Noël (1982) 'The Future of Allusion', *October* 20, 51–78.

_____ (1991) 'Notes on the Sight Gag', in Andrew S. Horton (ed.) *Comedy/ Cinema/ Theory*. Berkeley, Los Angeles and Oxford: University of California Press, 25–42.

Carson, Tom (1999) 'And the Leni Riefenstahl Award for Rabid Nationalism Goes to: *Saving Private Ryan*', *Esquire* 131, 3 (March), 70–5.

Caughie, John (ed.) (1981a) *Theories of Authorship*. London: Routledge/British Film Institute.

_____ (1981b) 'Rhetoric, Pleasure and Art Television', *Screen* 22, 4, 9–31.

Charity, Tom (2001) *A.I.* review, *Time Out* (19–26 September), 85.

Chase-Riboud, Barbara (1989) *Echo of Lions*. New York: Morrow, Williams & Co.

Chatman, Seymour (1978) *Story and Discourse: Narrative Structure in Fiction and Film*. Ithaca, NY, and London: Cornell University Press.

Cheyette, Bryan (1994) 'The Holocaust in the Picture-House', *Times Literary Supplement* (18 February), 18–19.

_____ (1997) 'The Uncertain Certainty of *Schindler's List*', in Yosefa Loshitzky (ed.) (1997) *Spielberg's Holocaust: Critical Perspectives on Schindler's List*. Bloomington and Indianapolis: Indiana University Press, 226–38.

Chion, Michel (1992) 'Wasted Words', in Rick Altman (ed.) *Sound Theory/Sound Practice*. New York and London: Routledge/American Film Institute, 104–10.

Christie, Ian (1994) *The Last Machine: Early Cinema and the Birth of the Modern World*. London: British Film Institute/BBC Education.

Coates, Paul (1991) *The Gorgon's Gaze: German Cinema, Expressionism, and the Image of Horror*. Cambridge: Cambridge University Press.

Cohen, Eliot (1998/99) 'What Combat Does to Man: *Private Ryan* and its Critics', *The National Interest* 54 (Winter), 82–8.

Colley, Linda (1994) *Britons: Forging the Nation 1707–1837*. London: Pimlico.

_____ (1995) 'How British is British?', *The Daily Telegraph* (8 July), *Arts and Books*, 1.

Collins, Jim (1993) 'Genericity in the Nineties: Eclectic Irony and the New Sincerity', in Jim Collins, Hilary Radner and Ava Preacher Collins (eds) *Film Theory Goes to the Movies*. New York and London: Routledge/American Film Institute, 242–63.

Collodi, Carlo (1988) [1882] *The Adventures of Pinocchio* (trans. E. Harden). London: Jonathan Cape.

Combs, Richard (1978) *Close Encounters of the Third Kind* review, *Monthly Film Bulletin* 45, no. 531 (April), 63–4.

_____ (1981) *Raiders of the Lost Ark* review, *Monthly Film Bulletin* 48, no. 571 (August), 159–60.

_____ (1983) *Twilight Zone: The Movie* review, *Monthly Film Bulletin* 50, no. 597, 281–2.

_____ (1988a) 'Master Steven's Search for the Sun', *The Listener*, 119, 3050 (18 February), 29.

_____ (1988b) *Empire of the Sun* review, *Monthly Film Bulletin* 55, no. 657 (April), 95–7.

_____ (1993) 'Plastic People with Sex Appeal' (on *Jurassic Park*), *Guardian* (5 August), Section 2, 6.

_____ (1999) 'Saviour Cinema: *Saving Private Ryan*', *Metro* 119, 50–7.

Cook, Pam (1982) 'Masculinity in Crisis?' *Screen* 23, 3–4 (September–October), 39–46.

Corliss, Richard (1994) 'Schindler Comes Home', *Time* 143, 11 (14 March), 110.

Corn, David (2005) 'A Post-9/11 Cautionary Tale?' (on *Munich*), *The Nation*. On-line. Available at http://www.thenation.com/blogs/capitalgames?pid=42787 (15 December 2005).

Corner, John (1998) 'Seeing Is Not Feeling' (letter concerning *Saving Private Ryan*), *Sight and Sound* 8, 12 (December), 72.

Corrigan, Timothy (1992) *A Cinema Without Walls*. London: Routledge.

Cousins, Mark (1998) '"War Stories": Mark Cousins Talks to Steven Spielberg' (television interview tx 13 September), BBC2 (UK).

Crace, John (1998) 'This Film [*Saving Private Ryan*] Will Make Sure No One Will Forget', *Evening Standard* (10 September), 16.

Crawley, Tony (1983a) *The Steven Spielberg Story*. London: Zomba Books.

_____ (1983b) Interview with George Miller, *Starburst*, 57, 34–9.

Creed, Barbara (1989) 'Horror and the Monstrous-Feminine: An Imaginary Abjection', in James Donald (ed.) *Fantasy and the Cinema*. London: British Film Institute, 63–89.

Cribben, Mik (1975) 'On Location with *Jaws*', *American Cinematographer* 56, 3 (March), 274–7, 320, 330–1, 350–1.

Crichton, Michael (1991) *Jurassic Park*. London: Arrow Books.

_____ (1995) *The Lost World*. London: Century.

Daily Telegraph (1991) 'Time to Grow Up' (leader on *Hook*) (10 December), 16.

Daly, David (1980) *A Comparison of Exhibition and Distribution Patterns in Three Recent Feature Motion Pictures*. New York: Arno Press.

Der Derian, James (1994) 'Cyber-Deterrence', *Wired* 2.09. On-line. Available at http://www.umass.edu/polsci725/cyberdeter.html (23 February 2005).

Diawara, Manthia (1988) 'Black Spectatorship: Problems of Identification and Resistance', *Screen* 29, 4 (Autumn), 66–76.

DiBattista, Maria (2000) 'Saving Private Ryan', *Rethinking History* 4, 2, 223–8.

Digby, Joan (1993) 'From Walker to Spielberg: Transformations of *The Color Purple*', in Peter Reynolds (ed.) *Novel Images: Literature in Performance*. London: Routledge, 166–8.

DiOrio, Carl (2001) '*A.I.* Stirs Ad Men's Angst: Even Crix Scuffle over Spielberg Soufflé', *Variety* (9–15 July), 9, 41.

Ditmann, Laurent (1998) 'Made You Look: Towards a Critical Evaluation of Steven Spielberg's *Saving Private Ryan*', *Film and History* 28, 3–4, 64–9.

Dix, Carl (1986) 'Thoughts on *The Color Purple*, *Revolutionary Worker* (3 March) in Alice Walker (1996) *The Same River Twice: Honoring the Difficult. A Meditation of Life, Spirit, Art, and the Making of the Film 'The Color Purple'*. London: The Women's Press, 191–8.

Dixon, Wheeler Winston (2001) 'Twenty-Five Reasons Why It's All Over', in Jon Lewis (ed.) *The End of Cinema As We Know It: American Film in the Nineties*. New York: New York University Press, 356–66.

Doane, Mary Ann (1982) 'Film and the Masquerade: Theorizing the Female Spectator', *Screen* 23, 3/4, 74–87.

Doherty, Thomas (1998) *Saving Private Ryan* review, *Cineaste* 24, 1, 68–71.

_____ (1999) *Projections of War: Hollywood, American Culture, and World War II*. New York: Columbia University Press.

Dole, Carol M. (1996) 'The Return of the Father in Spielberg's *The Color Purple*', *Literature/Film Quarterly* 24, 1, 12–16.

Donald, James, Anne Friedberg and Laura Marcus (eds) (1998) *Close Up 1927–1933: Cinema and Modernism*. London: Cassell.

Doneson, Judith E. (1997) 'The Image Lingers: The Feminization of the Jew in *Schindler's List*', in Yosefa Loshitzky (ed.) (1997) *Spielberg's Holocaust: Critical Perspectives on Schindler's List*. Bloomington and Indianapolis: Indiana University Press, 140–52.

Douglass, Frederick (1993) [1845] *Narrative of the Life of Frederick Douglass, an American Slave* (ed. Christopher Bigsby) reprinted with Harriet Beecher Stowe. *Uncle Tom's Cabin*. London: Everyman.

Dovey, Jon (2000) *Freakshow: First Person Media and Factual Television*. London and Sterling, VA: Pluto Press.

Dubner, Stephen J. (1999) 'Inside the Dream Factory', *Observer* (21 March), *Magazine*, 12–18.

Dworkin, Susan (1985) 'The Strange and Wonderful Story of the Making of *The Color Purple*', *Ms.* (December), reprinted in Alice Walker (1996) *The Same River*

Twice: Honoring the Difficult. A Meditation of Life, Spirit, Art, and the Making of the Film 'The Color Purple'. London: The Women's Press, 174–82.

Dyer, Geoff (1998) 'On With the War' (on *Saving Private Ryan*), *Guardian* (20 August) Section 2, 6–7.

Dyer, Richard (1977) 'Entertainment and Utopia', *Movie* 24 (Spring), 2–13.

_____ (1979) *Stars*. London: British Film Institute.

_____ (1997) *White*. London and New York: Routledge.

Eagleton, Terry (1983) *Literary Theory: An Introduction*. Oxford: Basil Blackwell.

_____ (1991) *Ideology: An Introduction*. London and New York: Verso.

Easthope, Antony (1990) *What a Man's Gotta Do*. London and New York: Routledge.

Ebert, Roger (2001) *A.I.* review, *Chicago Sun Times* (29 June), no page reference; quoted in 'This Week's Hottest US Release', *Times* (14–20 July), *Play*, 6.

Eco, Umberto (1972) [1965] 'Towards a Semiotic Inquiry into the TV Message', in *Working Papers in Cultural Studies* 3, Birmingham: University of Birmingham, 103–21.

_____ (1987) [1984] '*Casablanca*: Cult Movies and Intertextual Collage', *Travels in Hyperreality*. London: Picador 197–211.

Ehrenhaus, Peter (2001) 'Why We Fought: Holocaust Memory in Spielberg's *Saving Private Ryan*', *Critical Studies in Media Communication* 18, 3 (September), 321–37.

Ellis, John (1982) 'The Literary Adaptation: An Introduction', *Screen* 23, 1 (May–June) 3–5.

_____ (1992) *Visible Fictions: Cinema, Television, Video*. London: Routledge.

_____ (2002) *Seeing Things: Television in the Age of Uncertainty*. London and New York: I. B. Tauris.

Ellison, Michael (1999) 'Pentagon Award for *Private Ryan*', *Guardian* (12 August), British Film Institute microfiche.

Elsaesser, Thomas (1975) 'The Pathos of Failure: American Films in the 70s: Notes on the Unmotivated Hero', *Monogram*, 6, 13–19.

_____ (1981) [1969] 'Narrative Cinema and Audience-Oriented Aesthetics', in Tony Bennett, Susan Boyd-Bowman, Colin Mercer and Janet Woollacott (eds) *Popular Television and Film*. London: British Film Institute/Open University, 270–82.

_____ (1996) 'Subject Positions, Speaking Positions', in Vivian Sobchack (ed.) *The Persistence of History: Cinema, Television and the Modern Event*. New York and London: Routledge/American Film Institute, 145–83.

Elsaesser, Thomas and Warren Buckland (1998) 'The Ontology of the Digital Image: Hollywood Cinema in the Post-Photographic Age', paper delivered at *Hollywood and Its Spectators* conference, University College London (14 February).

Elsaesser, Thomas and Warren Buckland (2002) *Studying Contemporary American Film*. London: Arnold.

Empire (2001) *Empire: The Directors Collection: Steven Spielberg: The Life. The Films. The Amazing Stories*. London.

Entman, Robert and Francis Seymour (1978) 'Close Encounters with the Third Reich', *Jump Cut* 18, (August), 3–6.

Evans, Mary (1994) 'Fairy Tales of Our Time', *Women: A Cultural Review* 5, 1, 96–9.

Evening Standard (1996) 'Jurassic Sequel's Monster Sales' (25 June), 5.

Fairclough, Norman (1989) *Language and Power*. London and New York: Longman.

Falk, Quentin (1981) 'Movies in Production' in David Pirie (ed.) *Anatomy of the Movies*. London: Windward, 160–89.

Farber, Stephen and Marc Green (1988) *Outrageous Conduct: Art, Ego and the* Twilight Zone *Case*. New York: Arbor House.

Farrar, M. (1994) 'Zygmunt and Janina Bauman on *Schindler's List* and *The Holocaust for Beginners*', *Red Pepper* 2 (July), 38–9.

Felperin, Leslie (2002) *Minority Report* review, *Sight and Sound* 12, 8 (August), 44.

Ferguson, Robert (1984) 'Black *Blue Peter*', in Len Masterman (ed.) *Television Mythologies: Stars, Shows and Signs*. London: Comedia.

_____ (1998) *Representing 'Race': Ideology, Identity and the Media*. London: Arnold and New York: Oxford University Press.

Filmprofit (2005) 'Filmprofit: The Business of Successful Films'. On-line. Available HTTP: http://www.filmprofit.com (16 July 2005).

Fiske, John (1987a) *Television Culture*. London: Routledge.

_____ (1987b) 'British Cultural Studies', in Robert C. Allen (ed.) *Channels of Discourse: Television and Contemporary Criticism*. London: Routledge, 254–89.

_____ (1994) *Media Matters: Everyday Culture and Political Change*. London: University of Minnesota Press.

Fiske, John and John Hartley (1978) *Reading Television*. London and New York: Methuen.

Fitzgerald, F. Scott (1941) *The Last Tycoon*. New York: Scribners.

Flitterman Lewis, Sandy (1987) 'Psychoanalysis, Film, and Television', in Robert C. Allen (ed.) *Channels of Discourse: Television and Contemporary Criticism*. London: Routledge, 172–210.

Foucault, Michel (1977) [1969] *Language, Counter-Memory, Practice*. Oxford: Basil Blackwell.

Fowler, Rebecca (1998) 'Faithful Witness', *Sunday Times* (20 February), Section 9, 7.

Fowler, Roger (ed.)(1973) *A Dictionary of Modern Critical Terms*. London: Routledge Kegan Paul.

_____ (1986) *Linguistic Criticism*. Oxford: Oxford University Press.

Fraker, William A. (1979) 'Photographing *1941*', *American Cinematographer*, 60 (December), 1208–11, 1246, 1248–9, 1277–9.

Franklin, B. J. (1981) 'Promotion and Release', in David Pirie (ed.) *Anatomy of the Movies*. London: Windward, 94–102.

Freedland, Jonathan (2006) 'Blood Breeds Blood' (on *Munich*), *Guardian* (13 January), 5.

Freer, Ian (1998) 'The Feat of Steven: *Empire*'s Tribute to Steven Spielberg', *Empire* 105 (March), 96–112.

_____ (2001) *The Complete Spielberg*. London: Virgin.

French, Philip (1984) 'The Crack of Doom' (*Indiana Jones and the Temple of Doom* review), *Observer* (17 June), *Review*, 21.

_____ (1998) 'Ryan's Slaughter', *Observer* (13 September), *Review*, 8.

_____ (2003) 'Con Brio' (*Catch Me If You Can* review), *Observer* (2 February), *Review*, 7.

_____ (2004) 'Hanks at the Point of No Return' (*The Terminal* review), *Observer* (5 September), *Review*, 9.

_____ (2006) 'Pitfalls on the Road to Revenge' (*Munich* review), *Observer* (29 January), *Review*, 14.

Frentz, Thomas S. and Janice Hocker Rushing (1993) 'Integrating Ideology and Archetype in Rhetorical Criticism, Part II: A Case Study of *Jaws*', *Quarterly Journal of Speech* 79, 1 (February), 61–81.

Freud, Sigmund and Josef Breuer (1972) [1893] 'A Child Is Being Beaten: A Contribution to the Origin of Sexual Perversions', in *Sexuality and the Psychology of Love*. New York: Collier, 107–32.

Friedberg, Anne (1990) 'A Denial of Difference: Theories of Cinematic Identification', in E. Ann Kaplan (ed.) *Psychoanalysis and Cinema*. New York and London: Routledge/American Film Institute, 36–45.

Friedlander, Saul (ed.) (1992) *Probing the Limits of Representation: Nazism and the 'Final Solution.'* Cambridge, Massachusetts and London: Harvard University Press.

Fussell, Paul (1975) *The Great War and Modern Memory*. New York: Oxford University Press.

_____ (1998) 'Hell and High Water' (on *Saving Private Ryan*), *Observer* (2 August) *Review*, 3.

Gabbard, Krin (2000) '*Saving Private Ryan*'s Surplus Repression', *The International Journal of Psychoanalysis* 81, 1 (11 February), 177–93.

_____ (2001) 'Saving Private Ryan Too Late', in Jon Lewis (ed.) *The End of Cinema as We Know It: American Film in the Nineties*. New York: New York University Press, 131–8.

Gahagan, Judy (1975) *Interpersonal and Group Behaviour*. London: Methuen.

Genette, Gerard (1980) *Narrative Discourse: An Essay in Method*. Ithaca, NY: Cornell University Press.

_____ (1997) *Paratexts: Thresholds of Interpretation* (trans. Jane E. Lewis). Cambridge: Cambridge University Press.

Gilbey, Ryan (1997) *The Lost World: Jurassic Park* review, *The Independent* (25 July), *The Eye*, 8.

_____ (1998) 'Spielberg Chained to Mediocrity', *The Independent* (27 February), *Eye on Friday*, 8.

_____ (2004) *The Terminal* review, *Sight and Sound* 14, 9 (September), 86–8.

Glaister, Dan (1998) 'How to Perfect the Art of Making Invisible Profits', *Guardian* (5 March), British Film Institute microfiche.

Gledhill, Christine and Linda Williams (eds) (2000) *Reinventing Film Studies*. London: Arnold and New York: Oxford University Press.

Gold, Claudia and Ian Wall (1998) *Amistad*. London: Film Education.

Goldberg, Michelle (2005) 'The War on *Munich*', *Spiegel Online* (20 December). On-

line. Available HTTP: http://www.spiegel.de/international/0,1518,391525,00.
html (6 February 2006).

Gomery, Douglas (1996) 'Hollywood Corporate Business Practice and Periodizing Contemporary Film History', in Steve Neale and Murray Smith (eds) *Contemporary Hollywood Cinema*. London: Routledge.

_____ (2003) 'The Hollywood Blockbuster: Industrial Analysis and Practice', in Julian Stringer (ed.) *Movie Blockbusters*. London and New York: Routledge, 72–83.

Goodnight, G. Thomas (1995) 'The Firm, the Park and the University: Fear and Trembling on the Postmodern Trail', *The Quarterly Journal of Speech* 81, 3 (August), 267–90.

Goodwin, Andrew and Paul Kerr (1983) *BFI Dossier 19: Drama-documentary*. London: British Film Institute.

Gordon, Andrew (1980) '*Close Encounters*: The Gospel According to Steven Spielberg', *Literature/Film Quarterly* 8, 3, 156–64.

_____ (1991a) '*Raiders of the Lost Ark*: Totem and Taboo', *Extrapolation: A Journal of Science Fiction and Fantasy* 32, 3 (Fall), 256–67.

_____ (1991b) 'Steven Spielberg's *Empire of the Sun*: A Boy's Dream of War', *Literature/Film Quarterly* 19, 4, 210–21.

Gottlieb, Carl (2001) *The Jaws Log: 25th Anniversary Edition*. London: Faber and Faber.

Greenberg, Harvey Roy (1991) 'Raiders of the Lost Text: Remaking as Contested Homage in *Always*', *Journal of Popular Film and Television* 18, 4 (Winter), 164–71.

Grenier, Richard (1991) *Capturing the Culture: Film, Art and Politics*. Washington, DC: Ethics and Public Policy Center.

Griffin, Nancy (1999) 'Death Fish', *Neon* (February), 200–5.

Guerrero, Ed (1988) 'The Slavery Motif in Recent Popular Cinema: *The Color Purple* and *Brother from Another Planet*', *Jump Cut* 33 (February), 52–9.

Gumbel, Andrew (1998) 'How Spielberg's D-Day Hit Movie Was Secretly Hyped', *Independent on Sunday* (2 August), 16.

_____ (2001) 'Kubrick's Lost Masterpiece to Top a Year of Film', *Independent* (6 January), 11.

_____ (2006) '*Munich*: Spielberg's Take on the 1972 Olympics Massacre', *Independent* (5 January). On-line. Available HTTP: http://enjoyment.independent.co.uk/film/features/article336644 (6 February 2006).

Hadden, Sally (1998) '*Amistad* (1997): An Internet Review of Merit', *Film and History* 28, 1–2, 62–8.

Hall, Sheldon (2002) 'Tall Revenue Features: The Genealogy of the Modern Blockbuster', in Steve Neale (ed.) *Genre and Contemporary Hollywood*. London: British Film Institute, 11–26.

Hall, Stuart (1977) 'Culture, Media and the Ideological Effect', in James Curran, Michael Gurevitch and Janet Wollacott (eds) *Mass Communication and Society*. London: Edward Arnold, 315–48.

Hallam, Julia with Margaret Marshment (2000) *Realism and Popular Cinema*. Manchester and New York: Manchester University Press.

Halprin, Sara (1986) 'Community of Women: *The Color Purple*', *Jump Cut* 31, 1, 28.

Hammond, Michael (2002) 'Some Smothering Dreams: The Combat Film in Contemporary Hollywood', in Steve Neale (ed.) *Genre and Contemporary Hollywood*. London: British Film Institute, 62–76.

Hansberry, Lorraine (1969) 'The Negro in American Culture' [WAB1-FM: New York, January 1961], in C. W. E. Bigsby (ed.) *The Black American Writer*. Florida: Everett/Edward, 93.

Hansen, Miriam Bratu (1997) '*Schindler's List* Is Not *Shoah*: Second Commandment, Popular Modernism, and Public Memory', in Yosefa Loshitzky (ed.) (1997) *Spielberg's Holocaust: Critical Perspectives on Schindler's List*. Bloomington and Indianapolis: Indiana University Press, 77–103.

Harris, Joel Chandler (1901) *Uncle Remus*. London: Chatto and Windus.

Harris, Paul (2005) 'Spielberg's Take on Terrorism Outrages the Critics', *Observer* (10 July), 24.

Hartman, Geoffrey. H. (1997) 'The Cinema Animal', in Yosefa Loshitzky (ed.) (1997) *Spielberg's Holocaust: Critical Perspectives on Schindler's List*. Bloomington and Indianapolis: Indiana University Press, 61–76.

Hartman, Saidiya V. (1997) *Scenes of Subjection: Terror, Slavery and Self-Making in Nineteenth-Century America*. New York and Oxford: Oxford University Press.

Harwood, Jim (1975) 'Anticipated Success Mutes Squawks on Costs, Rental Terms' (of *Jaws*), *Variety* (4 June), British Film Institute microfiche.

Harwood, Sarah (1995) 'Family Fictions in *E.T.*', *Changing English* 2, 2 (Autumn), 149–70.

_____ (1997) *Family Fictions: Representations of the Family in 1980s Hollywood Cinema*. London: Macmillan.

Haskell, Molly (1975) *Jaws* review, *Village Voice* (23 June), British Film Institute microfiche.

Hauke, Christopher (2001) '"Let's Go Back to Finding out Who We Are": Men, *Unheimlich* and returning Home in the Films of Steven Spielberg', in Christopher Hauke and Ian Alister (eds) *Jung and Film: Post-Jungian Takes on the Moving Image*. Hove: Brunner-Routledge, 151–74.

Hawthorn, Jeremy (1994) *A Concise Glossary of Contemporary Literary Theory*. London: Edward Arnold.

Heal, Sue (1992) 'Dastardly Dustin Gets Spielberg Epic off the Hook', *Today* (10 April), 21, 24.

Heath, Stephen (1976) '*Jaws*, Ideology and Film Theory', *Framework* 4 (Autumn), 25–7.

_____ (1981) *Questions of Cinema*. London: Macmillan.

_____ (1986) [1976] 'Narrative Space' in Philip Rosen (ed.) *Narrative, Apparatus, Ideology: A Film Theory Reader*. New York: Columbia University Press.

Helmore, Edward (1998) 'Saving Private Ryan ... and Private Borgstrom ... and Sergeant Niland', *Guardian* (7 July), Section 2, 8–9.

Hemblade, Christopher (1998) *Amistad* review, *Empire* (March), 76–9.

Hemingway, Ernest (1935) [1929]. *A Farewell to Arms*. Harmondsworth: Penguin.

Henderson, Brian (1980–81) '*The Searchers*: An American Dilemma', *Film Quarterly*, 34, 2 (Winter), 9–23.

Herr, Michael (2002) [1977] *Dispatches*. London: Picador.

Hess, Judith and John (1974) 'Sugar-Coated Pill' (on *The Sugarland Express*), *Jump Cut* 2 (July/August), 3.

Heung, Marina (1983) 'Why E.T. Must Go Home: The New Family in American Cinema', *The Journal of Popular Film and Television* 11, 2 (Summer), 81.

Hilton, Isabel (1998) 'Battle Fatigue' (on *Saving Private Ryan*), *New Statesman* 127, 4402 (11 September), 38.

Hitchens, Christopher (1986) 'Spielberg on the Blacks', *The Spectator* (29 March), 11–12, 14.

Hoberman, J. (1984) *Indiana Jones and the Temple of Doom* review, *The Village Voice* (5 June), cited in Postone and Traube.

_____ (1994) 'Myth, Movie, and Memory' (*Schindler's List* round table discussion), *The Village Voice* (29 March), 24–31.

_____ (2001) 'The Dreamlife of Androids' (on *A.I.*), *Sight and Sound* 11, 9 (September), 16–18.

Hodge, Robert and Gunther Kress (1988) *Social Semiotics*. Cambridge: Polity Press.

Hodge, Robert and David Tripp (1986) *Children and Television*. Cambridge: Polity Press.

Hodgkins, John (2002) 'In the Wake of Desert Storm: A Consideration of Modern World War II Films', *Journal of Popular Film and Television* (Summer), 74–84.

Hodsdon, Barrett (1999) 'Where Does War Come From? Reprising the Combat Film: *Saving Private Ryan* and *The Thin Red Line*', *Metro* 119, 40–9.

Hollywood Reporter (1982) Report on *E.T.* becoming highest-grossing domestic release ever (9 November), 1.

_____ (1988a) Report on success of *E.T.* video release (16 September), 1,38.

_____ (1988b) Further report on success of *E.T.* video release (28 October) 3, 49.

Holt, Linda (1997) 'There Was Nothing We Could Do', *Observer* (13 July), *Review*, 18.

Horowitz, Sara R. (1997) 'But Is It Good for the Jews? Spielberg's Schindler and the Aesthetics of Atrocity', in Yosefa Loshitzky (ed.) (1997) *Spielberg's Holocaust: Critical Perspectives on Schindler's List*. Bloomington and Indianapolis: Indiana University Press, 119–39.

Hozic, Aida A. (1999) 'Uncle Sam Goes to Siliwood: of Landscapes, Spielberg and Hegemony', *Review of International Political Economy* 6, 3 (Autumn), 289–312.

Hynes, Samuel (1999) '*The Thin Red Line*', *The New Statesman* (26 February), 42.

Izod, John (1988) *Hollywood and the Box Office 1895-1986*. London: Macmillan.

_____ (1993) 'Words Selling Pictures', in John Orr and Colin Nicholson (eds) *Cinema and Fiction: New Modes of Adapting, 1950-1990*. Edinburgh: Edinburgh University Press, 95–103.

Jackël, Anne and Brian Neve (1998), 'The Reception of American Film in Britain and France in the Late Twentieth Century: The Case of *Jurassic Park*', paper delivered at *Hollywood and Its Spectators* conference, University College London (14 February).

Jackson, Rosemary (1981) *Fantasy: the Literature of Subversion*. London: Methuen.

Jacobowitz, Florence (1994) 'Rethinking History through Narrative Art', *CineAction* 34 (June), 4–19.

Jacobs, Ken (1994) 'Myth, Movie, and Memory' (*Schindler's List* round table discussion), *The Village Voice* (29 March), 24–31.

Jacobson, Howard (1994) 'Jacobson's List', *The Independent* (2 February), 19.

Jaehne, Karen (1986) 'The Final Word' (*The Color Purple* article), *Cineaste* 15, 1, 60.

_____ (1999) *Saving Private Ryan* review, *Film Quarterly* 53, 1 (Fall), 39–41.

James, Nick (2002) 'An Eye for an Eye' (*Minority Report* review), *Sight and Sound* 12, 8 (August), 13–15.

Jameson, Fredric (1979) 'Reification and Utopia in Mass Culture', *Social Text* 1 (Winter) 130–48.

Jeffords, Susan (1988) 'Masculinity as Excess in Vietnam Films: The Father/Son Dynamic of American Culture', *Genre* 21, 487–515.

Jeffries, Stuart and Simon Hattenstone (1998) 'In the Light of History', *Guardian* (6 February), 2–3, 24.

Jenkins, Russell (1998) 'Spielberg's Soldiers' (on *Saving Private Ryan*), *National Review* (1 September), 48–9.

Johnstone, Iain (1994) 'Drawn into the Heart of Darkness' (*Schindler's List* review), *Sunday Times* (20 February), Section 9, 6–7.

Jonas, George (2006) [1984] *Vengeance*. London, New York, Toronto and Sydney: Harper Perennial.

Jones, Anita (1986) 'Scars of Indifference', *Carolina Peacemaker* (4 January) in Alice Walker (1996) *The Same River Twice: Honoring the Difficult. A Meditation of Life, Spirit, Art, and the Making of the Film 'The Color Purple'*. London: The Women's Press, 225–8.

Jones, Howard (1997) [1987] *Mutiny on the Amistad*. New York and Oxford: Oxford University Press.

Jowett, Garth and James M. Linton (1980) *Movies as Mass Communication*. Beverley Hills: Sage.

Joyce James (1967) [1914] 'The Dead', in *Dubliners*. London: Grafton, 199–256.

Kahn, Jack (1976) 'The Crocodile, the Whale and the Shark', *New Society* (1 April), 12–13.

Kaplan, E. Ann (1983) *Women and Film: Both Sides of the Camera*. New York and London: Methuen.

Kawin, Bruce F. (1986) 'Children of the Light', in Barry Keith Grant (ed.) *Film Genre Reader*. Austin: University of Texas, 236–57.

Keeble, Richard (2003) 'The Myth of Gulf War 2'. Inaugural Professorial Lecture, University of Lincoln (25 November).

Kelly, Richard (1999) 'Retrospective: Robert Bresson', in *The 53rd Edinburgh International Film Festival Catalogue* (15–29 August), 137–9.

Keneally, Thomas (1983) *Schindler's Ark*. London: Hodder and Stoughton.

Kennedy, Colin (2001) 'The Apotheosis of Crowd-pleasing Craft' (*Jurassic Park*), *Empire: The Directors Collection: Steven Spielberg: The Life. The Films. The Amazing Stories*. London, 94.

Kent, Nicholas (1991) *Naked Hollywood: Money and Power in the Movies Today*. London: British Broadcasting Corporation.

Khoury, George (1998) 'Private Ryan's War Journal: An Interview with Robert Rodat', *Creative Screenwriting* 5, 5 (September/October), 4–8.

Kilday, Gregg (1988) 'Landis' Final Cut' (Review of Stephen Farber and Marc Green (1988) *Outrageous Conduct: Art, Ego and the* Twilight Zone *Case*), *Film Comment* 24, 4 (July/August), 71–2, 74.

King, Geoff (2000) *Spectacular Narratives: Hollywood in the Age of the Blockbuster*. London & New York: I. B. Tauris.

Kingsley, Charles (1995) [1863] *The Water-Babies*. Oxford: Oxford University Press.

Klein, Aaron J. (2006) *Striking Back: The 1972 Munich Olympics Massacre and Israel's Deadly Response* (Mitch Ginsburg trans.) New York: Random House.

Klingsporn, Geoffrey (2000) 'Icon of Real War: *Harvest of Death* and American War Photography', *Velvet Light Trap* 45 (Spring), 4–19.

Kodat, Catherine Gunther (2000) 'Saving Private Property: Spielberg's American DreamWorks', *Representations* 71 (Summer), 77–105.

Kohn, Marek (1993) 'They're Back. And This Time It's Personal' (*Jurassic Park* review), *The Independent* (12 July), 13.

Kolker, Robert Phillip (1988) *A Cinema of Loneliness: Penn, Kubrick, Scorsese, Spielberg, Altman*, 2nd ed. New York and Oxford: Oxford University Press.

Koresky, Michael (2003) 'Twilight of the Idyll' (essay on *A.I.*), 'The Question Spielberg: A Symposium', *Senses of Cinema*. On-line. Available HTTP: http://www.sensesofcinema.com/contents/03/27/spielberg_symposium_films_and_moments.html#filmo (9 November 2004).

Kreider, Tim (2003) *A.I. Artificial Intelligence* review, *Film Quarterly* 56, 2, 32–9.

Krows, Arthur Edwin (1930) *The Talkies*. New York: Henry Holt and Company.

Kuhn, Annette (ed.) (1990) *Alien Zone: Cultural Theory and Contemporary Science Fiction Cinema*. London: Verso.

_____ (1994) *Women's Pictures: Feminism and Cinema*, 2nd ed. London: Verso.

Kurzweil, Edith (1994) *Schindler's List* Review, *Partisan Review*, 61, 2 (Spring), 201–3.

Kuspit, Donald (1994) 'Director's Guilt', *Artforum* 32 (February), 11–12.

Lacan, Jacques (1968) *The Language of the Self: The Function of Language in Psychoanalysis*. Baltimore and London: Johns Hopkins University Press.

Landon, Brooks (1992) *The Aesthetics of Ambivalence: Rethinking Science Fiction Film in the Age of Electronic (Re)production*. Westport, CT & London: Greenwood Press.

Landon, Philip (1998) 'Realism, Genre and *Saving Private Ryan*', *Film and History* 28, 3–4, 58–69.

Laplanche, Jean and Jean-Bertrand Pontalis (1973) *The Language of Psychoanalysis*. London: Hogarth Press.

Lapsley, Robert and Michael Westlake (1988) *Film Theory: An Introduction*. Manchester: Manchester University Press.

Laskos, Andrew (1981) 'The Hollywood Majors', in David Pirie (ed.) *Anatomy of the Movies*. London: Windward, 10-39.

La Valley, Albert J. (1985) 'Traditions of Trickery: The Role of Special Effects in the Science Fiction Film', in George S. Slusser and Eric S. Rabkin (eds) *Shadows of the Magic Lamp: Fantasy and Science Fiction in Film*. Carbondale and Edwardsville, IL: Southern Illinois University Press, 141–58.

Lefort, Gerard (1994) '*Les armes d'Hollywood face à l'horreur*', *Libération* (2 March), 4.

Lehrer, Natasha (1997) 'Between Obsession and Amnesia: Reflections on the French Reception of *Schindler's List*', in Yosefa Loshitzky (ed.) (1997) *Spielberg's Holocaust: Critical Perspectives on Schindler's List*. Bloomington and Indianapolis: Indiana University Press, 213–25.

Levi, Primo (1987) *If This Is a Man* and *The Truce*. London: Abacus.

_____ (1994) 'Revisiting the Camps', in James E. Young (ed.) *The Art of Memory: Holocaust Memorials in History*. Munich and New York: Prestel-Verley and the Jewish Museum, 185.

Lévi-Strauss, Claude (1955) 'The Structural Study of Myth', *Journal of American Folklore* LXXVIII, 270, 428-44.

_____ (1966) *The Savage Mind*. London: Weidenfeld and Nicolson.

Levin, Andrea (2005) 'Film Review of *Munich*: Spielberg and Kushner Smear Israel', *Camera: Committee for Accuracy in Middle East Reporting in America* (21 December). On-line. Available HTTP: http://www.camera.org/index.asp?x (6 February 2006).

Levy, Emanuel (2005) '*Munich*: Spielberg's Hot-Button Movie'. On-line. Available HTTP: http://emanuellevy.com (6 February 2006).

Lewis, Eileen (1991) 'Ideology and Representation in *Raiders of the Lost Ark*', unpublished M.A. dissertation, University of London Institute of Education.

Lightman, Herb A. (1973) 'The New Panaflex Camera Makes Its Production Debut', *American Cinematographer* 54, 5 (May), 564–67, 608–20.

Loshitzky, Yosefa (ed.) (1997) *Spielberg's Holocaust: Critical Perspectives on Schindler's List*. Bloomington and Indianapolis: Indiana University Press.

Louvish, Simon (1994) 'Witness' (essay on *Schindler's List*), *Sight and Sound* 4, 3 (March), 13–15.

Lovell, Terry (1983) *Pictures of Reality*. London: British Film Institute.

Lowentrout, Peter M. (1988) 'The Meta-Aesthetic of Popular Science Fiction Film', *Extrapolation: A Journal of Science Fiction and Fantasy* 29, 4 (Winter), 349–64.

Lukács, Georg (1950) *Studies in European Realism* (Edith Bone trans.). London: Hillway.

Lyman, Rick (2001) '*E.T.*'s Scarier Half-Brother' (article on *A.I.*), *Observer* (1 July), *Review*, 5.

Lyotard, Jean-François (1990) *Heidegger and 'the jews'* (sic) (Andreas Michel and Mark S. Roberts trans.) Minneapolis: University of Minnesota Press.

MacCabe, Colin (1981) [1974] 'Realism and the Cinema: Notes on some Brechtian Theses', in Tony Bennett, Susan Boyd-Bowman, Colin Mercer and Janet Woollacott (eds) *Popular Television and Film*. London: British Film Institute/Open University, 216–35. Originally in *Screen* 15, 2.

_____ (2005) 'Midnight in America' (*War of the Worlds* review), *The Independent* (1 July), *Arts and Books Review*, 8–9.

McArthur, Colin and Douglas Lowndes (1976), 'Fears to Shatter Complacency', *Tribune* (23 January), British Film Institute microfiche.

McCarthy, Todd (1998) 'Saving Private Ryan', *Daily Variety* (20 July), 6.

McDonald, Keith (2003) *Minority Report* review, *Scope: an On-Line Journal of Film Studies* (August). On-line. Available HTTP: http://www.nottingham.ac.uk (18 November 2004).

McGillivray, David (1981) 'Failures', in David Pirie (ed.) *Anatomy of the Movies*. London: Windward, 304-13.

McKee, Robert (1998) *Story: Substance, Structure, Style, and the Principles of Screenwriting*. London: Methuen.

McMahon, Barbara (1998) 'At Last, the True Story of the D-Day Carnage: The Way the Water Runs Red is the Way It Was' (article on *Saving Private Ryan*), *Evening Standard* (24 July), 8–9.

Macnab, Geoffrey (2003) *Catch Me If You Can* review, *Sight and Sound* 13, 3 (February), 39–40.

Magid, Ron (1993) '*Jurassic Park*: Making Effects History', *Cinefantastique* 24, 5 (December), 54–8, 60.

_____ (1998) 'Blood on the Beach', *American Cinematographer* 79, 12 (December), 56–8, 60, 62, 64, 66.

Maio, Kathi (1988) '*The Color Purple*: Fading to White', in Kathi Maio *Feminist in the Dark*. Freedom, Ca.: The Crossing Press, 35–44.

Malcolm, Derek (1998) 'Saving the Director's Bacon', *Guardian* (6 August), Section 2, 11.

Malmquist, Allen (1985) *Indiana Jones and the Temple of Doom* review, *Cinefantastique* 15, 2 (May), 40–2.

Mansfield, Stephanie (1994) 'Neeson Easy', *Empire* (February) 120–3.

Marcuse, Herbert (1955) *Eros and Civilization*. Boston: Beacon Press.

Mars-Jones, Adam (1993) 'Spare the Rod, Spoil the Child' (*Jurassic Park* review), *The Independent* (16 July), 16.

Martin, Elmer P. and Joanne M. Martin (1998) 'A Lesson in Mythmaking, Heroics and Betrayal', *Ecrans D'Afrique/African Screen* 23, 115–25.

Marx, Leo (1964) *The Machine in the Garden: Technology and the Pastoral Ideal in America*. New York: Oxford University Press.

Maslowski, Peter (1998) 'Reel War vs. Real War' (on *Saving Private Ryan*), *Military History Quarterly* (Summer), 68–75.

Massad, Joseph (2006) 'The Moral Dilemma of Fighting Fire with Fire' (*Munich* review), *Times Higher Education Supplement* (27 January), 15.

Mattelart, Armand (1980) *Mass Media, Ideologies, and the Revolutionary Movement*.

Sussex: Harvester.

Mayne, Judith (1993) *Cinema and Spectatorship*. London and New York: Routledge.

Meehan, Eileen R. (1991) 'Holy Commodity Fetish, Batman! The Political Economy of a Commercial Intertext', in Roberta E. Pearson and William Uricchio (eds) *The Many Lives of the Batman*. London and New York: British Film Institute/Routledge, 47–65.

Melman, Yossi and Steven Hartov (2006) 'Munich: Fact and Fantasy', *Guardian* (17 January), 26.

Melville, Herman (1964) [1857] *The Confidence-Man*. New York: Signet.

____ (1972) [1851] *Moby-Dick*. Harmondsworth: Penguin.

Memmi, Albert (1994) '*La Question de sens (suite)*', *Libération* (14 March), 7. Quoted in translation in Natasha Lehrer 'Between Obsession and Amnesia: Reflections on the French Reception of *Schindler's List*', in Yosefa Loshitzky (ed.) (1997) *Spielberg's Holocaust: Critical Perspectives on Schindler's List*. Bloomington and Indianapolis: Indiana University Press, 213–25.

Mendlesohn, Farah (2001) 'Adopted Feelings' (*A.I.* review), *Times Literary Supplement* (28 September), 20.

Menland, Louis (1998) 'Jerry Don't Surf' (*Saving Private Ryan* review), *New York Review of Books* 45, 14 (24 September), 7–8.

Mercer, Kobena (1993) 'Just Looking for Trouble – Robert Mapplethorpe and Fantasies of Race', in Ann Gray and Jim McGuigan (eds) *Studying Culture: An Introductory Reader*. London and New York: Edward Arnold, 161–73.

Metz, Christian (1975) 'The Imaginary Signifier', *Screen*, 16, 2 (Summer), 14–76.

____ (1977) '*Trucage* and the film', *Critical Enquiry* (Summer), 657–75.

____ (1982) *The Imaginary Signifier: Psychoanalysis and the Cinema* (trans. Celia Britton, Annwyl Williams, Ben Brewster and Alfred Guzzetti). Bloomington: Indiana University Press.

Michaels, Lloyd (1978) 'The Imaginary Signifier in Bergman's *Persona*', *Film Criticism*, 2, 2–3, 72–7.

Millar, Peter (1992) 'Robbed in Dreamworld' (*Hook* review), *Times* (14 April), 12.

Milloy, Courtland (1985) 'A Purple Rage of a Rip-Off', *Washington Post* (24 December), B3.

____ (1986) 'On Seeing *The Color Purple*', *Washington Post* (18 February), C3.

Milne, Tom (1974) *The Sugarland Express* review, *Monthly Film Bulletin* 41, no. 486 (July), 158.

Mitchell, Sean (2002) [1986] '*Platoon* Marks "End of a Cycle" for Oliver Stone', in Steven J. Ross (ed.) *Movies and American Society*. Oxford and Malden, MA: Blackwell, 305–8.

Monaco, James (1979) *American Film Now*. New York: Oxford University Press.

Morgan, Walter (2000) *Saving Private Ryan* review, *International Journal of Psychotherapy* 5, 2 (1 July), 182–4.

Morley, David (1980) 'Texts, Readers, Subjects', in Stuart Hall, Dorothy Hobson, Andrew Lowe and Paul Willis (eds) *Culture, Media, Language: Working Papers in Cultural Studies 1972–79*. London: Hutchinson, 163–73.

Morley, Sheridan (1993) *Jurassic Park* review, *Sunday Express* (18 July), 43.

Morris, N. A. (1990) 'Reflections on *Peeping Tom*', *Movie* 34/35 (Winter), 82–97.

Morrison, Toni (1988) [1987] *Beloved*. London: Picador.

_____ (1992) *Playing in the Dark: Whiteness and the Literary Imagination*. Cambridge, Massachussetts: Harvard University Press.

Mott, Donald R. and Cheryl McAllister Saunders (1986) *Steven Spielberg*. Bromley: Columbus Books.

Mulvey, Laura (1981)[1975] 'Visual Pleasure and Narrative Cinema', in Tony Bennett, Susan Boyd-Bowman, Colin Mercer and Janet Woollacott (eds) *Popular Television and Film*. London: British Film Institute/Open University, 206–15.

_____ (1990) 'Afterthoughts on "Visual Pleasure and Narrative Cinema" inspired by *Duel in the Sun*', in E. Ann Kaplan (ed.) *Psychoanalysis and Cinema*. New York and London: Routledge/American Film Institute, 24–35.

Murray, Scott (1998) *Saving Private Ryan* review, *Cinema Papers* 128 (December), 43–4.

Muyumba, Walton (1999) 'Slavery on the Big Screen', *Black Camera* 14, 1 (Spring/Summer), 6–7.

Myles, Lynda (1981) 'The Movie Brats and Beyond', in David Pirie (ed.) *Anatomy of the Movies*. London: Windward, 130–1.

Nash, Mark (1981) Editorial, *Screen* 22, 1, 7–9.

Naughton, John (1994) 'The Man Who Loves Women' (Article on Liam Neeson), *Premiere* (UK) (March), 50–5.

Neale, Steve (1980) *Genre*. London: British Film Institute.

_____ (1982) 'Hollywood Corner: *Raiders of the Lost Ark*', *Framework* 19, 37–9.

_____ (1983) 'Masculinity as Spectacle', *Screen* 24, 6 (November–December), 2–16. Reprinted in Mandy Merck (ed.) (1992) *The Sexual Subject: A Screen Reader in Sexuality*. London: Routledge, 277–87.

_____ (1990) 'You've Got to Be Fucking Kidding! Knowledge, Belief and Judgement in Science Fiction', in Annette Kuhn (ed.) *Alien Zone: Cultural Theory and Contemporary Science Fiction Cinema*. London: Verso, 160–8.

_____ (1991) 'Aspects of Ideology and narrative Form in the American War Film', *Screen* 32, 1 (Spring), 35–57.

_____ (2000) *Genre and Hollywood*. London and New York: Routledge.

Neill, Alex (1996) 'Empathy and (Film) Fiction', in David Bordwell and Noël Carroll (eds) *Post-Theory: Reconstructing Film Studies*. Madison: University of Wisconsin Press, 175–94.

Nichols, Bill (1991) *Representing Reality*. Bloomington: Indiana University Press.

_____ (2000) 'The 10 Stations of Spielberg's Passion: *Saving Private Ryan, Amistad, Schindler's List*', *Jump Cut* 43, 9–11.

Nicholls, Peter (1984) *Fantastic Cinema: An Illustrated Survey*. London: Ebury Press.

Niney, François (1994) '*Shoah* and *Schindler's List*', *Dox: Documentary Film Quarterly*, 2 (Summer), 27.

Norman, Barry (1998) 'I Don't Think About the Money. I Just Make the Films I Want to Make', *Radio Times* (21–27 February), 40–1.

_____ (2005) 'On Film Biographies', *Radio Times* (19–25 March), 55.

O'Brien, Daniel (1999) 'Dreamworks', additional chapter (Chapter 6) of Philip Taylor (1999) *Steven Spielberg*, 3rd edn. London: Batsford, 149–60.

O'Brien, Tim (1995) [1973] *If I Die in a Combat Zone*. London: Flamingo.

O'Kelly, Lisa (1993) 'Of Dinosaurs, Demons and Childhood Fears', *Observer* (20 June), 53.

O'Sullivan, Tim, John Hartley, Danny Saunders, Martin Montgomery and John Fiske (1994) *Key Concepts in Communication and Cultural Studies*. London: Routledge.

Ontario Ministry of Education (1989) *Media Literacy Resource Guide*. Toronto: Queen's Printer for Ontario.

Ouran, D. L. (1999) 'Evil *Ryan*', *Sight and Sound* 9, 3 (March), 64.

Owen, A. Susan (2002) 'Memory, War and American Identity: *Saving Private Ryan* as Cinematic Jeremiad', *Critical Studies in Communication* 19, 3 (September), 249–82.

Owens, William A. (1997) [1953] *Black Mutiny*. New York: Plume.

Paget, Derek (1998) *No Other Way to Tell It: Dramadoc/docudrama on Television*. Manchester and New York: Manchester University Press.

Palmer, Martyn (1998) '*Amistad*', *Total Film* 14 (March), 50–5.

Perry, George (1998) *Steven Spielberg: The Making of His Movies*. London: Orion.

Pfeil, Fred (1993) 'From Pillar to Postmodern: Race, Class and Gender in the Male Rampage Film', *Socialist Review* 23, 2.

Pierson, Michele (1999) 'CGI Effects in Hollywood Science-Fiction Cinema 1989–95: The Wonder Years', *Screen* 40, 2 (Summer), 158–76.

Pieterse, Jan Nederveen (1992) *White on Black: Images of Africa and Blacks in Western Popular Culture*. New Haven and London: Yale University Press.

Pirie, David (ed.) (1981) *Anatomy of the Movies*. London: Windward.

Pizzello, Stephen (1998) 'Breaking Slavery's Chains', *American Cinematographer* 79, 1 (January), 28–43.

Place, Vanessa (1993) 'Supernatural Thing', *Film Comment* 29, 5 (September/October), 8–10.

Pollock, Griselda (1976) *Jaws* review, *Spare Rib* 4 (April), 41–2.

Postone, Moishe and Elizabeth Traube (1985) 'The Return of the Repressed: *Indiana Jones and the Temple of Doom*', *Jump Cut* 30 (March), 12–14.

Propp, Vladimir (1975) *The Morphology of the Folk Tale*. Austin: University of Texas Press.

Pye, Michael and Lynda Myles (1979) *The Movie Brats: How the Film Generation Took Over Hollywood*. London: Faber and Faber.

Pym, John (1978) 'The Middle American Sky', *Sight and Sound* 47, 2 (Spring), 99–100, 128.

Quinn, Anthony (2001) *A.I.* review, *The Independent* (21 August), *Review*, 10.

_____ (2006) 'Let the Games Begin' (*Munich* review), *The Independent* (27 January), *Art and Books Review*, 6.

Quirke, Antonia (2002) *Jaws*. London: BFI.

Rabinovitch, Dina (1994) 'Portrait: Schindler's Wife', *Guardian* (5 February), *Weekend* 14.

Reed, Christopher (1998) 'Director Delivers X-rating on His Real-Life War Epic', *Guardian* (1 July), 14.

Rich, Frank (1994) 'Extras in the Shadows', *New York Times* (2 January), Late New York Edition, section 4, 9.

Rimmon-Kenan, Shlomith (1983) *Narrative Fiction: Contemporary Poetics*. London: Methuen.

Roberts, Philip (2005) Unpublished preliminary audience survey for study of American adaptations of British books. University of Lincoln.

Robinson, Cedric (1984) 'Indiana Jones, the Third World and American Foreign Policy: A Review Article', *Race and Class* 16, 2, 83–92.

Robinson, Philip (1993) 'The Dinosaurs Take On Arnie in Clash of the Film Giants', *Times* (25 June), 27.

Robnik, Drehli (2002) 'Saving One Life: Spielberg's *Artificial Intelligence* as Redemptive Memory of Things', *Jump Cut* 45. On-line. Available HTTP: http://www.ejumpcut.org (9 May 2003).

Romney, Jonathan (1997) *The Lost World:Jurassic Park* review, *Sight and Sound* 7, 7 (July), 44–6.

Rose, Gillian (1998) 'Beginnings of the Day: Fascism and Representation', in Bryan Cheyette and Laura Marcus (eds) *Modernity, Culture and 'the Jew'*. Cambridge: Polity Press, 242–56.

Rose, Jacqueline (1992). *The Case of Peter Pan, or, The Impossibility of Children's Fiction*. London: Macmillan.

Rosenbaum, Jonathan (1995) *Placing Movies: The Practice of Film Criticism*. Berkeley, Los Angeles & London: University of California Press.

Rosenzweig, Ilena *The Forward*. Quoted by Frank Rich (1994) 'Extras in the Shadows' (article on *Schindler's List*). *New York Times* (2 January), Late New York Edition, section 4, 9.

Rosten, Leo (1959) *The Return of H*Y*M*A*N K*A*P*L*A*N*. London: Pan.

Roth, Lane (1983) 'Raiders of the Lost Archetype', *Studies in the Humanities* 10, 1 (June), 13–21.

Roux, Caroline (2001) 'Planet of the Drapes' (on *A.I.*), *Guardian* (15–21 September), *The Guide*, 4–7.

Rubey, Dan (1976) 'The Jaws in the Mirror', *Jump Cut*, 10/11, 20–3.

Rushing, Janice Hocker and Thomas S. Frentz (1995) *Projecting the Shadow: The Cyborg Hero in American Film*. Chicago & London: University of Chicago Press.

'RW' (1998) 'Help! Director Overboard' (*Amistad* review), *Guardian* (27 February), *Screen* section, 9.

Ryan, Michael and Douglas Kellner (2002) [1988] 'Vietnam and the New Materialism', in Steven J. Ross (ed.) *Movies and American Society*. Oxford: Blackwell.

Saïd, Edward (1978) *Orientalism*. London: Penguin.

Sales, Roger (1988) *Tom Stoppard: Rosencrantz and Guildenstern Are Dead*. London: Penguin.

Salisbury, Mark and Ian Nathan (1996) 'The Jaws of Fear', *Fangoria* 150 (March), 83–8.

Sandhu, Sukhdev (2006) 'Spielberg's Quiet Bombshell' (*Munich* review), *The Daily*

Telegraph (27 January), 27.

Sanello, Frank (1996) *Spielberg: The Man, the Movies, the Mythology*. Dallas, Texas: Taylor Publishing Company.

Scapperotti, Dan (1985) 'Raiders of the Lost Serials', *Cinefantastique* 15, 2 (May), 43.

Schapiro, D. and P. H. Leiderman (1967) 'Arousal Correlates of Task Role and Group Setting', *Journal of Personal and Social Psychology* 5, 103–7.

Schatz, Thomas (1993) 'The New Hollywood', in Jim Collins, Hilary Radner and Ava Preacher Collins (eds) *Film Theory Goes to the Movies*. New York and London: Routledge, 8–36.

Schemo, Diana Jean (1994) 'Good Germans: Honoring the Heroes. And Hiding the Holocaust', *New York Times* (12 June), 6E.

Schickel, Richard (1998) 'Reel War' (*Saving Private Ryan* review), *Times* (10 August), 57–9.

_____ (2005a) 'Spielberg Takes on Terror' (*Munich* review), *Time* (12 December), 64–8.

_____ (2005b) 'His "Prayer for Peace"' (Interview with Steven Spielberg), *Time* (12 December), 70–1.

Schleier, Curt (1994) 'Steven Spielberg's New Direction', *Jewish Monthly* 108, 4 (January/February), 12–13.

Sergi, Gianluca (2002) [1998] 'A Cry in the Dark: The Role of the Post-Classical Film Sound', in Graeme Turner (ed.) *The Film Cultures Reader*. London and New York: Routledge.

Serwer, Andrew E. (1995) 'Analyzing the Dream', *Fortune* 131 (17 April), 71.

Shandler, Jeffrey (1997) 'Schindler's Discourse: America Discusses the Holocaust and Its Mediation, from NBC's mini-series to Spielberg's Film', in Yosefa Loshitzky (ed.) (1997) *Spielberg's Holocaust: Critical Perspectives on Schindler's List*. Bloomington and Indianapolis: Indiana University Press, 153–68.

Shatz, Adam and Alissa Quart (1996) 'Spielberg's List', *Village Voice* (9 February), 31–4.

Shay, Don and Jody Duncan (1993) *The Making of Jurassic Park*. London: Boxtree.

Sheehan, Henry (1992) 'The Panning of Steven Spielberg', *Film Comment* (May–June), 54–60 and (July–August), 66–71.

_____ (1993) 'The Fears of Children', *Sight and Sound* 3, 7 (July), 10.

Shelley, Mary (1963) [1818] *Frankenstein, or The Modern Prometheus*. London and New York: Everyman.

Shephard, Ben (1998) 'The Doughboys' D-Day' (*Saving Private Ryan* review), *Times Literary Supplement* (Friday 18 September), accessed at http://www.the_tls.co.uk.

Shone, Tom (1997) *The Lost World:Jurassic Park* review, *Sunday Times* (20 July) Section 11, 4–5.

_____ (1998) 'Interview with Steven Spielberg', *Sunday Times* (13 September), *Culture* magazine, British Film Institute microfiche.

Shulgasser, Barbara (1997) *Amistad* review, *San Francisco Examiner* (12 December), B1.

Shuv, Yael (1998) *Amistad* review, *Total Film* 14 (March), 83.

Simon, John (1986) 'Black and White in Purple', *National Review* (14 February), 56.

Sinyard, Neil (1987) *The Films of Steven Spielberg*. London: Hamlyn.

Skimpole, Harold (1990) Article on *Always*' critical reception, *Sunday Telegraph* (1 April), 9.

Slavin, John (1994) 'Witnesses to the Endtime: The Holocaust as Art', *Metro* 98 (Winter), 4–13.

Smith, Adam (2001) 'The Movie Brats', *Empire: The Directors' Collection: Steven Spielberg: The Life. The Films. The Amazing Stories*. London, 22–8.

Smith, Henry Nash (1950) *Virgin Land: The American West as Symbol and Myth*. Cambridge, Massachusetts: Harvard University Press.

Solomons, Jason (2004) 'Me and My Troll' (interview with Jeffrey Katzenberg), *Observer* (4 July), *Review*, 6–7.

Sorlin, Pierre (1980) *The Film in History: Restaging the Past*. New Jersey: Barnes and Noble.

Spiegelman, Art (1994) 'Myth, Movie and Memory' (*Schindler's List* round table discussion), *The Village Voice* (29 March), 24–31.

Spielberg, Steven (1993) 'Why I Had to Make this Film' (*Schindler's List*), *Guardian* (16 December), 2–3.

Stam, Robert (1985) *Reflexivity in Film and Literature*. New York: Columbia University Press.

_____ (2000) *Film Theory: An Introduction*. Oxford & Malden, MA: Blackwell.

Stam, Robert, Robert Burgoyne and Sandy Flitterman-Lewis (1992) *New Vocabularies in Film Semiotics: Structuralism, Post-Structuralism and Beyond*. New York and London: Routledge.

Stepto, Robert B. (1987) 'After the 1960s: The Boom in Afro-American Fiction', in Malcolm Bradbury and Sigmund Ro (eds) *Contemporary American Fiction*. London: Edward Arnold, 89–104.

Stern, Michael (1990) 'Making Culture into Nature' in Annette Kuhn (ed.) *Alien Zone: Cultural Theory and Contemporary Science Fiction Cinema*. London: Verso, 66–72.

Sternberg, Meir (1978) *Expositional Modes and Temporal Ordering in Fiction*. Baltimore: Johns Hopkins University Press.

Stevenson, Robert Louis (2001) [1883] *Treasure Island*. London: Kingfisher.

Stewart, Garrett (1978) 'Close Encounters of the Fourth Kind', *Sight and Sound*, 47, 3 (Summer), 167–74.

_____ (1998) 'The Photographic Ontology of Science Fiction Film', *Iris* 25 (Spring), 99–132.

Steyn, Mark (1998) 'Authentic but Not True' (*Saving Private Ryan* review), *Asian Age* (22 September), 14.

Stiller, Lewis (1996) '"Suo-Gan" and *Empire of the Sun*', *Literature/Film Quarterly* 24, 4, 344–7.

Strick, Philip (1994) *Schindler's List* review, *Sight and Sound* 4, 3 (March), 47–8.

Stuart, Andrea (1988) '*The Color Purple*: In Defence of Happy Endings', in Lorraine

Gamman and Margaret Marchment (eds) *The Female Gaze: Women as Viewers of Popular Culture*. London: The Women's Press, 60–75.

Sullivan, Randall (1984) 'Death in the Twilight Zone', *Rolling Stone* (21 June), 31.

Tängerstad, Erik (2000) '*Before the Rain* – After the War?', *Rethinking History* 4, 2, 175-181.

Tashiro, Charles S. (2002) 'The *Twilight Zone* of Contemporary Hollywood Production', *Cinema Journal* 41, 3 (Spring), 27–37.

Tasker, Yvonne (1993) *Spectacular Bodies: Gender, Genre and the Action Cinema*. London: Routledge/Comedia.

Taubin, Amy (1998) 'War Torn' (*Saving Private Ryan* review), *Village Voice* (28 July), 113.

Taylor, Philip M. (1992) *Steven Spielberg*. London: Batsford.

Thomson, David (1981) 'Directors and Directing', in David Pirie (ed.) *Anatomy of the Movies*. London: Windward, 120–9.

_____ (1994) 'Presenting Enamelware' (article on *Schindler's List*), *Film Comment* 30, 2 (March–April), 44–50.

_____ (2004) *The Terminal* review, *The Independent on Sunday* (4 July) ABC, 1B.

Todorov, Tzvetan (1977) *The Poetics of Prose*. Oxford: Blackwell.

Tomasulo, Frank P. (1982) 'Mr Jones Goes to Washington', *Quarterly Review of Film Studies* 7, 4 (Fall), 331–40.

_____ (2001) 'Empire of the Gun: Steven Spielberg's *Saving Private Ryan* and American Chauvinism', in Jon Lewis (ed.) *The End of Cinema As We Know It: American Film in the Nineties*. New York: New York University Press, 115–30.

Tookey, Christopher (1990) 'Hepburn Up to Her Knees in Corn', *Sunday Telegraph* (25 March), 48.

_____ (1993a) 'Dynamic Dinosaurs', *Daily Mail* (13 July), 9.

_____ (1993b) 'Spielberg Brings Fossils Back to Life', *Daily Mail* (16 July), 46.

Torry, Robert (1993) 'Therapeutic Narrative: *The Wild Bunch*, *Jaws* and Vietnam', *The Velvet Light Trap* 31 (Spring), 27–38.

Traube, Elizabeth G. (1991) *Dreaming Identities: Class, Gender and Generation in 1980s Hollywood Movies*. Boulder, Colorado and Oxford: Westview Press.

Tribe, Keith (1981) [1997/78] 'History and the Production of Memories', in Tony Bennett, Susan Boyd-Bowman, Colin Mercer and Janet Woollacott (eds) *Popular Television and Film*. London: British Film Institute/Open University, 319–26.

Truffaut, François (1978) *Hitchcock*. London: Paladin.

Tuchman, Mitch and Anne Thompson (1981) 'I'm the Boss: George Lucas Interviewed', *Film Comment* 17, 4 (July-August), 49–57.

Turner, Graeme (1993) *Film as Social Practice*. London: Routledge.

Twain, Mark [Samuel L. Clemens] (1977) [1885] *Adventures of Huckleberry Finn*. New York: Norton.

Usborne, David (1996) 'Spielberg Builds Huge Holocaust Database', *The Independent on Sunday* (7 January), 15.

Vertov, Dziga (1926) Introduction to 'Provisional Instructions to Kino-Eye Groups', quoted in Christopher Williams (1980) *Realism and the Cinema*. London:

Routledge Kegan Paul/British Film Institute, 23–8.

Vest, Jason (2002) *Minority Report* review, *Film and History* 32, 2, 108–9.

Virilio, Paul (1994) *The Vision Machine*. London: BFI and Bloomington and Indianapolis: Indiana University Press.

Vulliamy, Ed (2001) 'Spielberg Weaves Cryptic Web in Cyberspace to Promote Movie', *Observer* (6 May), 20.

Walker, Alice (1983) *The Color Purple*. London: The Women's Press.

_____ (1996) *The Same River Twice: Honoring the Difficult. A Meditation on Life, Spirit, Art, and the Making of the Film The Color Purple Ten Years Later*. New York: Scribner and London: The Women's Press.

Walkerdine, Valerie (1990) [1986] 'Video Replay: Families, Films and Fantasy', in Manuel Alvarado and John O. Thompson *The Media Reader*. London: British Film Institute, 339–57.

Wallace, Michele (1993) 'Negative Images: Towards a Black Feminist Cultural Criticism', in S. During (ed.) *The Cultural Studies Reader*. London: Routledge, 118–31.

Wasko, Janet (2003) *How Hollywood Works*. London: Sage.

Wasko, Janet, Mark Phillips and Chris Purdie (1993) 'Hollywood Mets Madison Avenue: The Commercialization of US Films', *Media, Culture and Society* 15 (2), 271–93.

Wasser, Frederick (1995) 'Is Hollywood America? The Transnationalisation of the American Film Industry', *Critical Studies in Mass Communication* 12, 423–37.

Webster, Daniel (1998) 'Slavery in American Cinema', *Ecrans D'Afrique/African Screen* 23, 101–7.

Weissberg, Lilliane (1994) 'The Tale of a Good German: Reflections on the German Reception of *Schindler's List*', in Yosefa Loshitzky (ed.) (1997) *Spielberg's Holocaust: Critical Perspectives on Schindler's List*. Bloomington and Indianapolis: Indiana University Press, 171–92.

Wells, H. G. (1946) [1897] *The War of the Worlds*. Harmondsworth: Penguin.

West, Nathaniel (1969) *'Miss Lonelyhearts' and 'The Day of the Locust'*, New York: New Directions.

White, Armond (1986) *The Color Purple* review, *Films in Review* (February), 113.

_____ (1994) 'Toward a Theory of Spielberg History', *Film Comment* 30, 2 (March–April), 51–6.

White, Les (1994) 'My Father Is a Schindler Jew', *Jump Cut* 39 (June), 3–6.

Wicking, Christopher (1981) 'Thrillers' in David Pirie (ed.) *Anatomy of the Movies*. London: Windward, 220–31.

Willemen, Paul (1978) 'Notes on Subjectivity: On Reading Edward Branigan's "Subjectivity under Seige"', *Screen* 19, 1 (Spring), 41-69.

Williams, Richard (1998) '*Saving Private Ryan*: Omaha Strikes Gold', *Guardian* (11 September), 10.

Williams, Tony (1983) 'Close Encounters of the Authoritarian Kind', *Wide Angle*, 5, 4, 22–9.

Wilson, Emma (2003) *Cinema's Missing Children*. London and New York: Wallflower

Press.

Winston, Brian (1995) *Claiming the Real: the Documentary Film Revisited*. London: British Film Institute.

_____ (1998). *Media Technology and Society: A History: From the Telegraph to the Internet*. London and New York: Routledge.

Wisniewski, Christopher 'The Spectacular War' (on *Saving Private Ryan*), PopPolitics. com. On-line. Available HTTP: http://www.alternet.org (30 September 2002).

Wolcott, James (1998) 'Tanks for the Memories' (*Saving Private Ryan* review), *Vanity Fair* 456 (August), 38–44.

Wolf, Matt (2001) Untitled article on *A.I.*, *Times* (21 June), Section 2, 19.

Wollen, Peter (1993) 'Theme Park and Variations' (essay on *Jurassic Park*), *Sight and Sound* 3, 7 (July), 7–9.

_____ (1998) 'Tinsel and Realism', in Geoffrey Nowell-Smith and Steven Ricci (eds) *Hollywood and Europe: Economics, Culture, National Identity 1945–1995*. London: British Film Institute, 129–34.

Wood, Robin (1970) [1965] *Hitchcock's Films*. New York: Paperback Library.

_____ (1979) 'An Introduction to the American Horror Film', in Robin Wood and Richard Lippe (eds) *The American Nightmare*. Toronto: Festival of Festivals, 7–28. Reprinted in Bill Nichols (ed.) (1985) *Movies and Methods*, Vol. 2. Berkeley: University of California Press, 195–219.

_____ (1985) '80s Hollywood: Dominant Tendencies', *CineAction!* (Spring), 2–5.

_____ (1986) *From Hollywood to Vietnam*. New York: Columbia University Press.

_____ (1989) *Hitchcock's Films Revisited*. London and Boston: Faber and Faber.

Wrathall, John (1998) 'On the Beach' (*Saving Private Ryan* review), *Sight and Sound* 8, 9 (September), 34–5.

Wyatt, Justin (1994) *High Concept: Movies and Marketing in Hollywood*. Austin: University of Texas Press.

Young, James E. (ed.) (1994) 'Myth, Movie and Memory' (*Schindler's List* round table discussion), *The Village Voice* (29 March), 24–31.

Young, Marilyn B. (2003), 'In the Combat Zone' (on *Saving Private Ryan* and subsequent Hollywood war films), *Radical History Review* 85 (Winter), 253–64.

Young-Breuhl, Elisabeth (ed.) (1992) *Freud on Women*. New York: Norton.

Zajonc, Robert B. (1960) *Social Psychology: An Experimental Approach*. Belmont, CA: Wadsworth.

Zanuck, Richard and Dan Brown (1975) 'Dialogue on Film', *American Film* 1, 1 (October) 37–52.

Zelizer, Barbie (1997) 'Every Once in a While: *Schindler's List* and the Shaping of History', in Yosefa Loshitzky (ed.) (1997) *Spielberg's Holocaust: Critical Perspectives on Schindler's List*. Bloomington and Indianapolis: Indiana University Press, 18–35.

Zimmermann, Patricia (1983) 'Soldiers of Fortune: Lucas, Spielberg, Indiana Jones and *Raiders of the Lost Ark*', *Wide Angle* 6, 2, 34–9.

Zizek, Slavoj (1992) *Enjoy Your Symptom! Jacques Lacan in Hollywood and Out*. London: Routledge.

INDEX

Secondary sources appear by surname and initial(s) unless cited also as individuals: Adair, G. Real people otherwise appear by surname and first name(s): Adams, John Quincy. Fictional characters appear alphabetically by whole name: Betty Boop.